Decision Making

DECISION MAKING

A Psychological Analysis of Conflict, Choice, and Commitment

IRVING L. JANIS

LEON MANN

THE FREE PRESS
A Division of Macmillan Publishing Co., Inc.
NEW YORK

Collier Macmillan Publishers
LONDON

The Free Press
A Division of Macmillan Publishing Co., Inc.
866 Third Avenue, New York, N.Y. 10022

Collier-Macmillan Canada, Ltd.

Library of Congress Catalog Card Number: 76-19643

Printed in the United States of America

printing number

1   2   3   4   5   6   7   8   9   10

Library of Congress Cataloging in Publication Data

Janis, Irving Lester
   Decision making.

   Bibliography: p.
   Includes index.
   1. Decision-making. 2. Conflict (Psychology)
3. Stress (Psychology) 4. Commitment (Psychology)
I. Mann, Leon, joint author. II. Title.
BF441.J3   153.8'3   76-19643
ISBN 0-02-916160-6

Various proprietors of copyright have granted permission to reprint material in this book. In addition to those identified in credit lines for figures and tables, thanks are due to United Feature Syndicate, Inc., and the *New Yorker*, for permission to reprint cartoons, and to Prentice-Hall, Inc., and Farrar, Straus & Giroux, Inc., for permission to quote from the following works:

   David W. Miller and Martin K. Starr, *The Structure of Human Decisions* (Englewood Cliffs, N.J.: Prentice-Hall), copyright © 1967.

   Mary McCarthy, *On the Contrary* (New York: Farrar, Straus & Giroux), copyright © 1953, 1961 by Mary McCarthy.

For Marjorie and Leah

Contents

List of Figures

xi

List of Tables

Preface

"How could I have been so stupid?" President John F. Kennedy asked after realizing how badly he had miscalculated when he approved the Bay of Pigs invasion. Every private citizen asks himself the same question each time he finds himself embroiled in a personal Bay of Pigs. Why do people so often fail to look into the available alternatives with care even when vital consequences are at stake? Under what conditions are they most likely to make a sound choice that they can live with? Under what conditions are they most likely to do such a poor job of appraising the consequences that they head straight for catastrophe?

In attempting to answer such questions, we have been mindful of Kurt Lewin's famous assertion that nothing is so practical as a good theory. When he made that statement several decades ago, psychologists and other behavioral scientists were quite skeptical. But now, after a decade of huge expenditures of money and effort on ill-fated research programs that were supposed to have instant relevance for social policy, many accept it as a piece of proverbial wisdom. We are among them.

We expect the conflict theory presented in this book to be useful not only for generating basic studies of psychological processes involved in conflict, choice, and commitment but also for developing practical means to improve the quality of decisions made by individuals and groups. As will become readily apparent, the key assumptions in our theory and the principles on which they are based have come from observations in the clinic and in field settings as well as in the laboratory. In turn, one of the major criteria we apply to establish the validity of the theory is whether the prescriptive hypotheses, in the form of practical implications for decision counseling, are supported by the acid test of improved decision making.

In this book our aim is to fill a long-existing gap in the behavioral sciences—to provide a comprehensive descriptive theory of how people actually cope with decisional conflicts. The theory pertains directly to decisions concerning choice of career, marriage and divorce, health-related activities, community welfare programs, management of small and large firms, governmental policies, and a variety of other kinds of significant choice.

Our main theoretical assumptions come from extensive research on the psychology of stress. We describe five distinctive patterns of coping with stressful decisional conflicts, which we believe everyone uses at one time or another. Our theory specifies the antecedent conditions—relating to degree of concern about losses, optimism about finding a satisfactory solution, and deadline pressures for making a final choice—that together determine which type of coping pattern a decision maker will adopt. The consequences of each coping pattern, particularly with regard to the quality and stability of the decision, are discussed in detail. We also present a subsidiary "stage sequence" schema and a "balance sheet" schema, which are used to analyze changes in the components of a person's decisional conflict from the time of the initial warning or challenge that sets the decision-making process into motion through all the successive steps up to the final acts of adherence to an irrevocable commitment.

We believe that the theoretical model presented in this book is applicable to all consequential decisions. In our account of the testable implications of the model, we attempt to integrate research findings from a wide variety of topics in psychology and related disciplines, such as the effects of warnings, information processing, social influence and attitude change, commitment, group dynamics, and organizational policy making. Given our aim to formulate a general theory of decisional conflict, we think it appropriate to be uninhibitedly eclectic in marshaling illustrative observations and substantiating evidence from all sorts of field studies, laboratory experiments, biographies of politicians, autobiographies by candid writers, case reports on community planning, and historical analyses of major foreign policy triumphs and fiascos. In this respect our approach is interdisciplinary, drawing upon concepts and findings from research psychologists, psychotherapists, sociologists, political scientists, economists, management consultants, and policy analysts. We hope that this book will find audiences among an equally wide spectrum of students in all the various disciplines of the social and behavioral sciences that deal with one or another aspect of personal or policy decision making.

With a variety of audiences in mind, we ourselves have been confronted with some thorny decisions as we have agonized over what to include in our book—how to cover all the essential points without allowing the book to become too long. We did not wish to overburden the text with details and risk losing the interest of readers with scant background in psychology and other behavioral sciences. Yet we wished to include sufficient discussion of theoretical issues and controversies to engage the interest of scholars and advanced students. To accomplish both ends, we have relegated the technical details of research and the fine points of theory, including issues involving comparisons with other theories, to a section of notes at the back of the book.

In line with some of our notions concerning the value of realistic warnings about potential risks, we conclude this preface with a few pertinent warnings for critical readers:

1. There is, of course, no way that we or any other authors can eliminate unconscious bias when selecting and summarizing case material to illustrate a theory. Accordingly, we suggest that all case studies presented in this book be regarded as part of the exposition of our theory rather than as substantiating evidence, even at the lowest level. Empirical support for our theory is to be found in the large number of field experiments and other systematic research investigations that we describe.

2. To arrive at an original solution to any perplexing research problem, one must be prepared at some point, after conscientiously piling up all the relevant observations one can get hold of, to climb to the top of the heap and make a big inferential leap into the unknown void. Leaving behind the solid ground of well-established facts and principles, one must rely on the buoyancy of imaginative thought. Each time we reach such a point in this book we shall give ample warning to prepare any unsuspecting reader for the precarious takeoff.

3. Finally, a general caveat about caveats. "If I want to hear someone's opinion," Goethe once asserted, "it must be expressed positively; I have enough ambiguity in myself." We assume that all readers have enough ambiguity in themselves that they do not need constant reminders of the tentativeness of the theoretical ideas we present and of the deficiencies of the evidence on which they are based. We shall call attention at least once to whatever shortcomings in our theory and to whatever limitations of the substantiating evidence we are aware of. But, in accord with Goethe's admonition, we have set ourselves the general objective of presenting an unambiguous and highly readable account of theory, research, and applications by expressing ourselves positively.

We hope that this book will stimulate critical and original thinking as well as systematic research on the many unsolved problems relating to how and why people fail to make full use of their personal and social resources when in the throes of decisional conflict. And we continue to follow Kurt Lewin in expecting that any theory of decision making worth its salt should provide valid guidelines for practitioners who want to avoid gross errors when making crucial choices.

Acknowledgments

We wish to thank a number of colleagues at Yale University who gave us valuable suggestions for revision of early drafts of the book—John Bassler, Elaine Blechman, Phoebe Ellsworth, Richard Hackman, Don Quinlan, and Judith Rodin. We are especially indebted to Robert P. Abelson for a detailed critique of a near-final draft, focusing especially on our interpretations of findings from social psychological research, which we used in making our final revision.

Many advanced students as well as faculty members in seminars at Yale University and at Harvard University gave us extremely helpful comments bearing on one or several chapters—including Ronald Abeles, Karl W. Deutsch, Claude Fischer, Arthur Jago, Herbert Kelman, Ellen Langer, Hillel Levine, William McGuire, James Miller, Richard Nisbett, Robert Sternberg, Shelley Taylor, Victor Vroom, Donald Warwick, and others.

While at the Center for Advanced Studies in the Behavioral Sciences at Stanford, California, during 1973–74, Irving Janis had the benefit of intensive discussions of our theoretical assumptions and major hypotheses with David Hamburg, Joshua Lederberg, James March, Robert Merton, and Ulric Neisser. Alexander George of Stanford University was also extremely helpful in providing suggestions for clarifying our theoretical model and for specifying implications for political policy decisions. We have made extensive use of Stephen Weiner's case study of a community desegregation decision, which he originally presented at a fellows' seminar at the center, and subsequently supplemented with additional observations in private discussions with both of us at Stanford University.

We are also grateful to many other leading scholars in a variety of academic fields who responded to our request for comments by raising incisive questions or by making valuable suggestions that we used in revising one or more chapters—Ellen Berscheid, Jack Brehm, Alan Elms, Shirley Feldman-Summers, Jonathan Freedman, Robert N. Hamburger,

Abraham Kaplan, Charles Kiesler, Rollo May, Judson Mills, Michael Pallak, Amos Tversky, Elaine Walster, and Daniel Wheeler.

We wish to thank Miriam Gallagher at the Center for Advanced Studies in the Behavioral Sciences for her superb editorial work on an early draft of the book, and Ginny Bales at Yale University for excellent editorial assistance on the final manuscript.

Our collaboration on the book was begun during 1967–68, while Irving Janis was holding a Senior Research Fellowship awarded by Yale University and Leon Mann was on leave from the University of Melbourne. Progress in writing the book was subsequently facilitated by concurrent fellowship awards for 1973–74 to Irving Janis from the Guggenheim Foundation and the Center for Advanced Studies in the Behavioral Sciences. Many of the recent research studies summarized in this book were supported by research grants from the National Science Foundation to Irving Janis as principal investigator.

Other research investigations reported in this book were supported by research grants to Leon Mann from the Foundations' Fund for Research in Psychiatry, the National Institute of Mental Health (U.S. Public Health Service), and the Office of Education (U.S. Department of Health, Education and Welfare). As a former faculty member of the University of Melbourne, Harvard University, and the University of Sydney, Leon Mann is grateful for the institutional support provided by these universities and acknowledges the encouragement of Flinders University of South Australia where he now teaches.

Thanks are also extended to the Western Behavioral Sciences Institute and Stanford University for making available facilities for working on the book. Acknowledgment is also made to the Australian-American Educational Foundation for a Fulbright travel award to Leon Mann for a period of study leave at Stanford University in 1975, which enabled us to meet several times while working on the final revisions.

For dependably wise counsel on the most difficult problems we encountered at every stage of the work, we are deeply grateful to Marjorie Graham Janis and Leah Mann, to whom this book is dedicated.

PART 1

Sources of Error

CHAPTER 1

Man, the Reluctant
Decision Maker

THE ACUTE AGITATION OF men and women in the throes of decisional conflict is often depicted in movies, television, magazines, and other mass
media. People are constantly being reminded of what they already know
from personal experience—that making a consequential decision is a worrisome thing, and one is liable to lose sleep over it. Yet in the extensive
writings by social scientists on decision making we find hardly any mention of this obvious aspect of human choice behavior, or any analysis of its
nonobvious implications. One of the major purposes of the present book is
to fill this gap by describing when, how, and why psychological stress
generated by decisional conflict imposes limitations on the rationality of a
person's decisions in his personal life and in his work life, whether in
essential tasks required by his job or in his role as a decision maker in the
government, in industry, or in any other type of organization.

Considering the theoretical and practical importance of descriptive research on how people arrive at decisions, we have been surprised to discover in our search of the literature that there are relatively few pertinent
contributions. Most of the work by behavioral scientists who deal with
problems of decision making consists of developing exclusively normative
models that specify how they think decisions *should* be made and that are
usually tested by asking college students to answer questions about
hypothetical choices or nonconsequential issues. In contrast, our theory
and research deals with what people of all ages *actually do* when they
make personal, organizational, or political decisions that entail serious
consequences.

3

Key Themes

For many years we have been collecting cartoons that capture something of the essence of stressful human choices and sometimes embody what we suspect are important truths that have not yet been taken into account by current theories in the behavioral sciences. To convey the key themes of this book, we begin by showing some of our favorite cartoons depicting man's imperfections and foibles as a decision maker.

The book is concerned with what the woman in our first cartoon refers to as "little" decisions—those that affect the welfare of one or another member of the family, of the family as a whole, of the community, or of an organization with which the decision maker is affiliated—and not with the mere *opinions* of people like her husband, who may enjoy talking grandiosely about "big" national and international issues but who are in no position to make such "big" policy decisions. The theory and research with which we are primarily concerned deal with important life decisions—the decision to go to medical school or to law school, to switch jobs in mid-career, to get married, to get a divorce, to buy a house, to go on a diet, to quit smoking, to undergo surgery, to participate actively in a political movement or in an election campaign, and so on. Our analyses pertain equally, however, to the genuinely big decisions made by presidents and other governmental leaders, directors of large corporations, or community leaders. All such decisions, whether made by individuals in their roles as husbands or wives, breadwinners, or policy-making executives, give rise to a proliferation or branching out of new subdecisions—a "decision tree," as it has been called—in that the decision maker is committed to a certain line of action as he faces a series of subsequent choices over a relatively long period of time (Simon, 1976). Decisions are socially committing because they require efforts at implementation if the decision maker is to fulfill his role in the community and maintain his public reputation as well as his self-image as a reasonably reliable person.

We are not particularly concerned here with the endless round of minor, routinized decisions a person faces when he looks over a menu in a restaurant, selects a movie, or chooses to take a different route home to avoid a crowded freeway. Except for abnormal personalities suffering from obsessive-compulsive neurosis, such choices are seldom, if ever, associated with conflict, commitment, or long-term, consequential rewards and punishments.

We deliberately exclude from our compass personal beliefs and opinions about political and social issues that do not have any direct bearing on people's actions. There is considerable evidence, some of which we shall review shortly, that opinions not requiring a person to take any significant course of action are readily influenced by a variety of communications and events that have little or no influence on major choices. The husband who pontificates about what the government ought to do to

"Lou makes all the <u>big</u> decisions . . . like should we have a trade agreement with China, should we set up a space station on the moon. He leaves all the <u>little</u> decisions to me . . . like where we should live, where we should send the kids to school."

solve the big issues can easily reverse himself whenever he encounters a new, persuasive argument from an authoritative TV or newspaper commentator that contradicts his previous views; there is very little cost involved in changing his verbal statements. In contrast, he or anyone else is likely to show great resistance to persuasive attempts that run counter to any of those "little" decisions that have direct consequences for himself and his family—because of the high costs of failing to live up to contracts or other commitments. In short, the psychological laws of opinion and attitude change are not necessarily the same as the psychological laws of decision making, although there may be some overlap. We believe that the principles governing consequential decision making probably are substantially different from those governing verbalized choices on nonconsequential issues.

One aspect of the husband's behavior implied in our first cartoon is of particular interest: his self-inflated notion that he is too busy with big issues to worry about the petty decisions that affect his own and his family's welfare. We shall have a great deal to say later on about the way people evade taking responsibility for decisions that can have vital consequences for them—sometimes by "passing the buck" to their spouses.

Our second cartoon speaks directly to a point that is only indirectly implied in the first one. In the last panel Linus seems to be mouthing a conventional piece of wisdom to Charlie Brown, but he ends up by standing it on its head. Linus's aphorism is a complete turnabout of the old platitude that the more important and difficult a decision is, the more dogged the effort and ingenuity required to solve it. What he actually says jolts us into acknowledging that just as much effort and ingenuity is often mobilized to *evade* important decisions. No matter how pressing the issue and no matter how ramified the consequences, he tells us, we can always find some way to *avoid* making a choice.

A decision maker under pressure to make a vital decision affecting his future welfare will typically find it painful to commit himself, because there are some expected costs and risks no matter which course of action he chooses. One way of coping with such a painful dilemma is to avoid making a decision. Our analysis of decision-making behavior assumes that in the repertoire of every person is a proclivity to procrastinate or, if that is not possible, to invent rationalizations for ignoring the worrisome doubts that make for decisional conflict. Procrastinating and rationalizing are components of the pattern of *defensive avoidance*, a means of coping with the painful stresses of decision making that can be just as detrimental as the pattern of overreacting to impending threat by taking impulsive, ill-considered action in a state of panic.

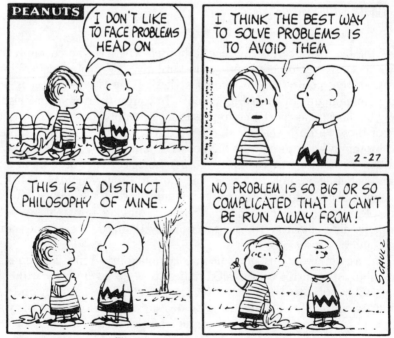

Schulz's next cartoon tells us something about the motivation that underlies all the effort and ingenuity that go into a search for a good solution—or for a good way to avoid having to find a solution. Like the head beagle sitting in his office, everyone derives a sense of self-satisfaction from making decisions that will affect his own fate and that of other people. But there is a strong deterrent to exercising such power freely—namely, the sudden, deflating realization that those decisions may be wrong. The professional decision maker has to confront his batting average for successful decisions. No one expects every decision to turn out right, but a string of 120 misses is a devastating blow to one's status and self-esteem. The head beagle has plenty to worry about; he could soon find himself kicked out of his exalted position. Fear of damaging outcomes can act as both a goad and a deterrent to decision making, as we shall indicate in chapter 3, when we examine the extensive research on psychological stress dealing with human reactions to warnings that urge people to take precautionary actions.

The change in the head beagle's mood depicted in the cartoon leads us into another major problem in the psychology of decision making. Under what conditions will a person's feelings of self-confidence and self-satisfaction about a past decision be replaced by a dejected mood of post-decisional regret? Much of the theory and research presented in later chapters deals with this problem.

"I'd know. That's who would know!"

The classic cartoon of the shipwrecked couple highlights an aspect of decision making that is generally neglected in the behavioral-science literature on the subject. We are often left with the impression that people generally choose whatever course of action will give them the most pleasure and utilitarian gains, provided there is no threat of social disapproval. But as this cartoon indicates, a proposed course of action can sometimes have everything going for it and the person will still abstain from making that choice, because of internal standards of appropriate behavior. Throughout this book, we shall pay special attention to self-reactions to alternative courses of action, including the decision maker's efforts to ward off feelings of guilt or to enhance his sense of moral worth and self-esteem. We shall see that seemingly irrational choices sometimes make good sense once we realize that a person may be willing to renounce utilitarian and social rewards in order to avoid the pain of self-disapproval

for violating internalized moral standards. Our conception of the decisional balance sheet (see chapter 6) embodies the assumption that self-
approval is an essential requirement for being satisfied with a decision.
Gaining utilitarian and social rewards is not enough; the person has to be
able to live with himself.

On the surface, our last cartoon is poking fun at people who take their
cues from the opinions of others. It can also be seen as poking fun at
attempts by social scientists to quantify the personal choices of an individual in the same way that they deal, through public opinion polls, with
large samples of the population. (This antimeasurement sentiment, incidentally, is not one we fully share, although we admit that some foolish
attempts at measurement have been publicized and that relatively little
progress has been made so far in developing valid ways of measuring a

*"I'd say I'm about forty-two per cent for Nixon, thirty-nine
per cent for Rockefeller, and nineteen per cent undecided."*

Drawing by Dana Fradon; © 1959 The New Yorker Magazine, Inc.

person's preferences for various alternatives.) At a somewhat deeper level, the cartoon speaks to the ambivalence each of us has about selecting one alternative to the exclusion of all others. When the time comes to cast our vote, we cannot remain only 42 percent in favor of our preferred candidate and 58 percent opposed or undecided. We are required to choose one of the options open to us, even though none of the alternatives is wholly satisfactory, and we are tempted to call a plague o' *all* your houses.

What seems to be the most ludicrous part of the man's statement—that he is 19 percent undecided—may nevertheless represent a state of mind familiar to many a decision maker. People are sometimes keenly aware of a low-level sense of uncertainty and concern that some crucial bits of information not yet available might make them regret whatever choice they make. During the period when the Watergate scandal was gradually building up in the press, as each fresh piece of evidence concerning the Nixon administration's criminal conduct was being made public, it was precisely this "undecided" component that was growing stronger among congressmen who continued to support Nixon, until the point was reached where their doubts became so strong they were willing to consider voting for his impeachment. Again, we cannot obtain a precise quantitative measure of the strength of such tendencies because our technology of measurement has not been sufficiently developed, but we can at least crudely assess changes in the relative attractiveness of alternative courses of action that a person is contemplating.

Quality of Decision Making

Outside the realm of single-valued decisions—that is, those intended to achieve only a single objective, such as making money or obtaining a large vote—it is very difficult for behavioral scientists to determine how well a decision has worked out. In the sphere of personal life, when we examine decisions such as those involving the choice of a husband or wife, a career, or a religious affiliation, we invariably find that in some respects the decision maker's hopes are realized and in other respects not. Similarly, the multiple objectives of most policy decisions made by a business firm or a government are attained to varying degrees; there are always some hoped-for gains that do not materialize and some undesirable losses that do. To evaluate the ultimate success of a decision one would need to take into account the negative values of the bad consequences as well as the positive values of the good consequences. But since there is no way of obtaining quantitative scores for these values, one would have to ask decision makers to give *subjective* ratings of the degree of their postdecisional satisfaction or regret. Such ratings, however, are of doubtful validity because they are subject to a variety of errors deriving from face-saving distortions and rationalizations (see Cannell and Kahn, 1968; Merton, 1936; Weick, 1968).

We are then confronted with this somewhat demoralizing question: if we have no dependable way of objectively assessing the success of a decision, how can we apply and test the implications of propositions specifying favorable and unfavorable conditions for decision-making activity? Our answer is that all such propositions—including some to be presented shortly on the effects of low and high levels of psychological stress— can be firmly anchored in observable measures by examining the *quality of the procedures* used by the decision maker in selecting a course of action. By this means, we expect to be able to predict whether a given decision is likely to lead to satisfaction or regret.

From the extensive literature on effective decision making (Etzioni, 1968; Hoffman, 1965; Janis, 1972; Katz and Kahn, 1966; Maier, 1967; Miller and Starr, 1967; Simon, 1976; Taylor, 1965; Vroom and Yetton, 1973; Wilensky, 1967; Young, 1966), we have extracted seven major criteria that can be used to determine whether decision-making procedures are of high quality. Although systematic data are not yet available, it seems plausible to assume that decisions satisfying these seven "ideal" procedural criteria have a better chance than others of attaining the decision maker's objectives and of being adhered to in the long run.

The decision maker, to the best of his ability and within his information-processing capabilities

1. thoroughly canvasses a wide range of alternative courses of action;
2. surveys the full range of objectives to be fulfilled and the values implicated by the choice;
3. carefully weighs whatever he knows about the costs and risks of negative consequences, as well as the positive consequences, that could flow from each alternative;
4. intensively searches for new information relevant to further evaluation of the alternatives;
5. correctly assimilates and takes account of any new information or expert judgment to which he is exposed, even when the information or judgment does not support the course of action he initially prefers;
6. reexamines the positive and negative consequences of all known alternatives, including those originally regarded as unacceptable, before making a final choice;
7. makes detailed provisions for implementing or executing the chosen course of action, with special attention to contingency plans that might be required if various known risks were to materialize.

Our first working assumption is that failure to meet any of these seven criteria when a person is making a fundamental decision (one with major consequences for attaining or failing to attain important values) constitutes a defect in the decision-making process. The more defects, the more likely the decision maker will undergo unanticipated setbacks and experience postdecisional regret.

When a decision maker meets all seven criteria, his orientation in arriving at a choice is characterized as *vigilant information processing*. Especially for complex choices involving multiple objectives, we expect that a moderate or high degree of vigilant information processing is a necessary, albeit insufficient, condition for arriving at a decision that will prove satisfactory to the decision maker in the long run.

A major problem for social psychological research is to determine the social conditions under which decision makers tend to use a vigilant information-processing orientation. What factors determine whether a person will operate at one extreme (vigilant to the best of his capabilities), at the opposite extreme (engaging in little search and deliberation), or somewhere in the middle of the continuum (meeting some of the criteria for vigilant information processing but not others)?

Vigilant information processing is not an all-or-nothing affair; it is manifested to varying degrees under different conditions. We can conceive of each of the seven criteria as forming a scale, with ratings varying from zero to, let us say, ten. (Thus, if a decision maker focuses exclusively on one course of action that someone recommends, spends no time at all thinking about what the alternatives might be, and asks no one in his social network to suggest alternatives, his score on the first criterion would be zero; if he devotes considerable time and effort to thinking about and seeking advice concerning a wide variety of alternatives, his activity would warrant the maximum score of ten.) When we say that a decision maker fails to display a vigilant information-processing orientation, we mean, in effect, that an objective observer who was in a position to know all the details of the person's decision-making activity would give him a very low rating (say two or below) on every one of the seven criteria.

Variations in the degree to which the criteria for vigilant information processing are met by the same person in the course of making a career decision were observed by Hilton (1962) in a study of thirty seniors at Carnegie Institute of Technology. Monthly interviews revealed that during the early months of their final year, the students resorted to decision-avoidance devices and hardly ever thought about the decision. (Thus, they would obtain low ratings on the seven criteria.) As the end of the year approached, however, many shifted in the direction of more thorough search and appraisal (meeting several of the criteria), although some still tended to postpone the decision and to avoid weighing specific alternatives.

In general, one encounters a wide range of intermediate degrees of meeting the criteria—extending from fairly high vigilance, such that the decision maker meets all the criteria except one (e.g., a man confronted with an opportunity to advance his career engages in an abbreviated information search concerning the attractive job offer, warranting a very low score on criterion no. 4, while obtaining medium or high scores on the other six criteria), to the almost total absence of vigilance (e.g., a chief executive relies on obtaining a consensus among the members of his advisory group, but with conscientious assimilation of all information brought to his attention, thus scoring high on criterion no. 5 while scoring very low on the other six criteria).

We assume that the more adequately each criterion is met, the lower the probability that the decision maker will make serious miscalculations that jeopardize his immediate objectives and long-term values. Consider what is likely to happen to the chief executive who relies on consensus in making decisions but accurately processes the information he receives, so as to fulfill criterion no. 5. As a result of his failure to meet the other criteria, the chances are quite high that he will subsequently run into a great deal of trouble (and experience much postdecisional regret) from having overlooked the negative consequences of his chosen course of action. Nevertheless, as a result of having met criterion no. 5 he is not likely to have miscalculated the degree of support he can expect to receive from those who had notified him of their opposition in advance. Had he failed to meet this criterion, by discounting their warnings, the chances are that in addition to suffering all sorts of unexpected losses from the ill-considered policy he had committed himself to, he would also undergo the shock of realizing that his policy was being criticized and sabotaged by some of the very people he had erroneously counted on to implement his decision.

We do not assume that people will always be better off in the long run if in making every one of their decisions they attain the highest possible scores on all seven criteria. Obsessional mulling over the uncertainties of a major decision and preoccupation with the search for an ideal choice often lead nowhere and may even be detrimental. The obsessed person may become so overloaded with information that he ends up failing to appreciate the most important factors that need to be taken into account. Where potential losses are not very serious—for example, whenever one is deciding to buy a household item that costs less than 1 percent of his weekly income—we certainly would not expect the person to gain a net advantage from investing time and energy in carrying out the best possible information search and doing all the other things required to satisfy all the criteria. Even when facing vital choices—where his entire future career or his personal survival or the survival of his organization is at stake—the decision maker may have learned from his prior experience in dealing with comparable problems that he is best off to be highly selective in his information search and deliberations, confining his attention to only a few viable alternatives he knows in advance are the only ones worth considering. A high degree of selectivity may often save the decision maker from unproductive confusion, unnecessary delays, and waste of his resources in a fruitless quest for an elusive, faultless alternative. Nevertheless, in some sizable proportion of instances, the highly selective decision maker runs the risk of being wrong in his initial selection of viable alternatives and of giving up the opportunity to find a much better solution. If, in the course of a selective approach, he fails to meet one or more of the seven criteria, the general assumption still applies: the chances of unanticipated losses are greater if the decision maker obtains a very low score on any of the criteria than if he attains a medium or high score. The optimal scores may vary from one type of decision to another, but will always be above zero.

Long before arriving at his final choice on any issue, every decision maker at least tacitly assesses how much of his resources of time, energy, and money he is going to invest in searching for and deliberating about information concerning the alternatives open to him. Vroom and Yetton (1973) describe the questions executives typically ask themselves when making preliminary judgments about *who* in the organization should spend *how much* of the organization's resources on a decision. Among the key questions are these. Is the decision important enough to warrant a high-quality solution? What additional information is needed, who possesses it, and how can it be collected? Do I have sufficient skill and expertise to solve the problem myself, or do I need the aid of subordinates or consultants? Is acceptance of the decision by subordinates critical to effective implementation and contingency planning? Do subordinates share the organizational goals to be attained in solving this problem?

Except for those questions specifically relevant to determining whether to delegate responsibility to subordinates, essentially the same type of determinations enter into an individual's judgments about using his own resources in arriving at personal decisions involving the choice of a job, a mate, or a self-fulfilling activity. If for any reason the person invests little time and energy in making any such choice, he is likely to attain very low scores on the criteria for vigilant information processing. The lowest scores of all, and subsequently the highest degree of postdecisional regret, are to be expected when the person makes the preliminary judgment tacitly, with little forethought about the need for search and appraisal.

Sources of Miscalculation

The major focus of this book is on the causes and consequences of patterns of decision making that interfere with vigilant information processing. When and why do decision makers fail to look into the available alternatives with care even when vital issues are at stake? How do they deal with unanticipated setbacks resulting from their lack of vigilance?

Here and there in the behavioral-sciences literature we find fragmentary, partial answers to these questions. The most explicit discussions are to be found in the writings of administrative scientists, who have long recognized dysfunctional constraints imposed by organizational traditions, bureaucratic procedures, and the rigorous demands of the executive role. All these constraints prevent decision makers in an organizational setting from applying their full resources to intensive search and deliberation on any given problem. In the next chapter we shall review the contributions of administrative scientists to our understanding of defective decision-making strategies, which form an essential part of the background for a social psychological approach to the central problems with which we are concerned.

Throughout the remaining chapters of this book we shall draw upon empirical evidence from psychological research on such diverse topics as cognitive defenses, situational anxiety, acceptance of fear-arousing warnings, obedience to authority, forced compliance, selective exposure to persuasion, determinants of self-control, bystander intervention, reliance on reference groups, delay of gratification, risk-taking behavior, and psychological preparation for future stress. We believe that many of the major research studies dealt with under these separate headings can be integrated by means of a comprehensive theoretical framework concerning the ways people cope with decisional dilemmas.

Kurt Lewin, the great pioneer who first envisaged an analysis of decision making in terms of psychological conflict, called attention to the lack of objective standards for appraising alternative courses of action, which heightens one's susceptibility to the influence of social pressures and other sources of erroneous judgments (1947). Lewin (1951) opened up research on the psychological consequences of social commitment to a decision, which he described as having a "freezing effect," inclining the decision maker to be highly resistant to subsequent social pressures attempting to induce him to change his mind. Lewin's work on commitment and related phenomena was developed further by another pioneering social psychologist, Leon Festinger, whose experiments on cognitive dissonance indicate that once a person has committed himself, there is "less emphasis on objectivity and there is more partiality and bias in the way in which the person views and evaluates the alternatives" (Festinger, 1964, p. 155).

The new conceptual model of decision making we present in this book is anchored in empirical findings on the effects of commitment and related phenomena, and is basically congruent with Kurt Lewin's original image of man's vulnerability to gross errors in arriving at a decision through superficial search and biased information processing. Like Lewin, we see man not as a cold fish but as a warm-blooded mammal, not as a rational calculator always ready to work out the best solution but as a reluctant decision maker—beset by conflict, doubts, and worry, struggling with incongruous longings, antipathies, and loyalties, and seeking relief by procrastinating, rationalizing, or denying responsibility for his own choices.

The crisis in social psychology that became manifest during the late 1960s arose partly because of the breakdown of a widely accepted theoretical assumption that purported to explain why people accept or reject new information; more and more social psychologists realized that the full range of psychological phenomena involved in attitude change and decision making could not be accounted for by any single formula in terms of reducing cognitive dissonance or striving for cognitive consistency (Abelson et al., 1968; Greenwald et al., 1968; McGuire, 1973; Smith, 1973, 1974). In the 1970s, a new trend seems to be emerging in psychological research on information processing as it relates to social behavior. This trend consists of making fewer attempts to test deductions from broad theoretical assumptions about man's proclivity toward maximizing the internal consistency of his cognitions and, instead, directing more effort toward elucidating hitherto unexplored flaws and limitations in human information processing, such as the propensity of decision makers to be distracted by irrelevant aspects of the alternatives, which leads to loose predictions about outcomes (Abelson, 1976); the tendency of decision makers to be swayed by the form in which information about risks is packaged and presented (Slovic et al., 1976); their reliance on faulty categories and stereotypes, which leads to erroneous decisions relating to social groups and ethnic minorities (Hamilton, 1976); and their illusion of control, which makes for overoptimistic estimates of outcomes that are a matter of chance or luck (Langer, 1975).

Tversky and Kahnemann (1974) describe various other illusions, some notorious and others not yet well known, that arise from intuitive assessments of probabilities that may incline all but the most statistically sophisticated of decision makers to make biased miscalculations in using evidence about the consequences of alternative courses of action. They discuss several misconceptions about how chance operates, one of which is the well-known gambler's fallacy: clear-cut information about the probability of an event is not taken into account because people believe that chance is a self-correcting process, such that a deviation in one direction will necessarily be followed by a deviation in the opposite direction (e.g., "It rained more than the average the past few months and therefore it will rain less than the average next month—so let's decide to take our vacation then").

People make another type of error, Tversky and Kahnemann have found, when they are given worthless information about the consequences of an action: when exposed to obviously irrelevant information, they tend to regard the chances of the outcome as 50:50; whereas when no such information is available they are more likely to take correct account of prior information about the baseline probability, which could be considerably greater or considerably less than 50 percent. Other sources of error in intuitive evaluations of evidence are attributable to insensitivity to sample size and to the unreliability or inaccuracy of the criteria used for making predictions. Sound evidence about the low risks of a given course of action is especially likely to be ignored if possible unfavorable outcomes are brought to the decision maker's attention, especially if it is easy to imagine the ensuing disasters. All these and several other sources of illusory judgment described by Tversky and Kahnemann pertain directly to failures to meet criterion no. 5, which deals with assimilating correctly and taking account of information to which the decision maker is exposed.

Much less is known about sources of failure to meet the other six criteria. Some useful leads can be gleaned from studies of cognitive complexity as a source of confusion and misjudgment (Bruner, Goodnow, and Austin, 1956; Carroll and Payne, 1976; Estes, 1957; Meehl, 1954; Miller, 1956; Pollack, 1962; Osgood, Suci, and Tannenbaum, 1957; Shepard, Hovland, and Jenkins, 1961; Shepard, 1964). When the degree of complexity of an issue exceeds the limits of cognitive abilities, there is a marked decrease in adequacy of information processing as a direct effect of information overload and ensuing fatigue.

Scope of the Book

Over and above the direct effects of information overload, harassed decision makers, realizing that they are confronted with tasks too complicated to manage, suffer a further decline in cognitive functioning as a result of the anxiety generated by their awareness of the stressful situation. Alexander George, a political scientist who has made detailed studies and analyses of decisional processes among governmental policy makers, calls attention to the psychological tension generated by the cognitive complexity of the issues requiring a decision. He points out that considerable stress is evoked in a decision maker merely by his trying to cope with the cognitive limits on his ability to work out a good solution to the problem at hand. He cites a vivid illustration of cognitive stress under conditions of inadequate knowledge and conflicting information, quoting what President Warren Harding said to a friend to whom he was unburdening himself:

> John, I can't make a damn thing out of this tax problem. I listen to one side and they seem right, and then God! I talk to the other side and they seem just as right, and there I am where I started. I know somewhere there is a book that would give me the truth, but hell, I couldn't read the book. I know somewhere there is an economist who knows the truth, but I don't know where to find him and haven't the sense to know him and trust him when I did find him. God, what a job [George, 1974, p. 187, quoted from Fenno, 1959].

Besides cognitive complexity, there are major sources of stress in decision making, including profound threats to the decision maker's social status and to his self-esteem, that intensify decisional conflict. Our theoretical framework, presented in part 2 of the book, chapters 3–7, focuses on how people cope with the stresses of decisional conflict. It has been developed from our earlier formulations of conflict theory (Janis, 1959; Janis and Mann, 1968), which draw upon another facet of Kurt Lewin's theory and research—viz., his description of the way people deal with various types of decisional conflicts. In particular, we have taken as our point of departure Lewin's (1935) account of the tendency of people to *withdraw* from stressful conflict situations when they become aware of the predominantly undesirable consequences to be expected from whichever choice they make.

Our present version of conflict theory differs from earlier formulations by specifying in more detail the factors that determine whether a person will deal with his decisional conflict by withdrawing, by becoming increasingly vigilant, or by adopting other coping patterns. Using the rich data base of recent research on psychological stress, we extract a set of general propositions concerning the conditions under which decision makers will fail to carry out the search and appraisal activities essential for meeting the criteria specified for vigilant information processing. These propositions generate a number of predictions that differ somewhat from those made by other current psychological theories.

After reviewing the behavioral-sciences literature on decision-making strategies in chapter 2, we present in chapter 3 the main concepts of conflict theory. In chapters 4 and 5 we summarize research bearing on some of the main predictions of the theory and show how the coping patterns specified by the theoretical model can be applied to a variety of hitherto neglected empirical problems concerning the causes of defective decision making. To specify the consequences of defective coping patterns, we introduce two additional analytic schemas in part 2 to supplement the main theoretical model—the decisional balance sheet (chapter 6) and the sequence of stages essential for arriving at a stable decision (chapter 7).

While the conflict-theory model leads to novel hypotheses about important aspects of decision making, its main use in this book is as a general theoretical framework for integrating diverse findings from psychological research on a wide variety of seemingly unrelated topics, all of which provide evidence on factors affecting the quality of decision-making procedures. Thus, in part 3 (chapters 8–12) we review and discuss the main body of psychological research bearing on the determinants of decisional conflicts and their resolution; among the main topics covered are selective exposure to information (chapter 8), the effects of uncertainty about gains and risks (chapter 9), threats to freedom of choice (chapter 10), the effects of irrevocable commitment to a chosen course of action (chapter 11), and the effects of unanticipated setbacks that generate postdecisional regret (chapter 12).

Part 4 (chapters 13 and 14) is devoted to research on effective interventions designed to prevent defective coping patterns. We discuss recent field studies designed to test prescriptive hypotheses that indicate how a counselor or consultant can help a person improve the quality of his decision-making procedures so as to increase the likelihood of his meeting the criteria for vigilant information processing. Some interventions pertain primarily to personal decisions involving the individual's career, marriage, health, and future welfare; others are more directly applicable to executives in large organizations who have the responsibility for making basic policy decisions. The evidence from field research on the prescriptive hypotheses, while pointing to practical ways that people can be helped to make decisions of better quality, also helps validate the main assumptions of the theoretical analysis presented in part 2, from which the prescriptive hypotheses are derived.

CHAPTER 2

Decision-making Strategies

WHEN PEOPLE ARE REQUIRED to choose among alternative courses of action, what types of search, deliberation, and selection procedure do they typically use—that is, what decision-making strategy do they adopt?[1] Unfortunately, this question has so far received relatively little attention in behavioral science research. Most of the pertinent observations of decision-making strategies consist of case studies, impressionistic surveys, and anecdotes reported by scholars in administrative science and related fields that deal with organizational policy making. Administrative scientists have much more to say than social psychologists, both in their descriptions and in their theory, about when and why a decision maker uses one type of strategy rather than another. Although originally formulated in terms of organizational policy making by managers or bureaucrats, the concepts of specialists in organizational behavior embody relevant universal psychological assumptions about human beings as imperfect decision makers. Accordingly, we shall examine the answers they give concerning how "administrative man" typically carries out the tasks of decision making. The answers provide essential background material that we shall draw upon in developing a conflict theory concerning the causes and consequences of defective information processing—a theory we believe to be equally applicable to personal decisions (pertaining to marriage, career, health, life style, and all sorts of personal matters) and to executive decisions in an organizational context.

Optimizing and the Perils of Suboptimizing

Specialists on organizational decision making describe the optimizing strategy as having the goal of selecting the course of action with the highest payoff. Such a strategy requires estimating the comparative value

21

of every viable alternative in terms of expected benefits and costs (see Young, 1966, pp. 138–47). But, as Herbert Simon (1976) has pointed out, human beings rarely adopt this decision-making approach: people simply do not have "the wits to maximize" (p. xxviii). Part of the problem is that determining all the potentially favorable and unfavorable consequences of all the feasible courses of action would require the decision maker to process so much information that impossible demands would be made on his resources and mental capabilities. In his attempts to obtain the degree of knowledge needed to anticipate alternative outcomes, the decision maker is likely to be overwhelmed by "information inundation, which can be quite as debilitating as information scarcity" (Miller and Starr, 1967, p. 62). Moreover, so many relevant variables may have to be taken into account that they cannot all be kept in mind at the same time. The number of crucially relevant categories usually far exceeds 7 ± 2, the limits of man's capacity for processing information in immediate memory (see Miller, 1956). Handicapped by the shortcomings of the human mind, the decision maker's attention, asserts Simon, "shifts from one value to another with consequent shifts in preference" (p. 83).

It is very costly in time, effort, and money to collect and examine the huge masses of information required when one uses an optimizing strategy to arrive at a decision. Furthermore, decision makers are often under severe pressure of time, which precludes careful search and appraisal. Managers in large companies, for example, seldom have time to engage in long-range planning because they are constantly occupied with current crises requiring emergency "fire fighting." The manager is likely to be "so busy solving immediate problems that he cannot effectively apply their solutions on a long-run recurrent basis; so busy manning the fire hose that he cannot devise a fire prevention program" (Young, p. 146).

As a result of personal limitations and various external constraints, a decision maker who does the best he can to use an optimizing strategy is still prone to such gross miscalculations that he ends up with an unsatisfactory *suboptimizing* solution, one that maximizes some of the utilities he expected to gain at the expense of losing other utilities. Miller and Starr (1967) cite the example of an executive who chooses a new job that is optimal in terms of his main professional objectives but requires so much overtime and travel that he has little time available for family life. "This may have such adverse effects that the executive will find that his optimization in terms of one objective has produced an overall result which is much less than optimal in terms of all his objectives" (p. 48).

The perils of suboptimization abound in large organizations, where different units and different types of personnel have incompatible objectives. A hospital administrator may decide to hire a sizable number of paramedical aides to relieve overburdened nurses of nonprofessional chores and to provide additional services to the patients, such as writing letters for those who are incapacitated and separated from their families.

But the additional personnel may unexpectedly overcrowd the hospital cafeteria, the rest rooms, the parking lot, and all the other employees' facilities to the point where the physicians, nurses, and orderlies become dissatisfied with the deterioration in their working conditions and demand that new facilities be built. The decisions made by policy makers in large organizations are, according to Young, "usually of a suboptimal nature, and only rarely can we assume that an ideal or unimprovable solution has been achieved" (p. 144). It needs to be emphasized, however, that a suboptimal policy is not necessarily unsatisfactory, even though it fails to attain all the policy makers' objectives; it may be a marked improvement over the former policy and constitute a step toward an optimizing solution.

Evidence from various social science disciplines indicates that, besides man's severe limitations as a processor of information, other recurrent conditions also militate against the use of an optimizing approach, even though it might often seem to be the ideal strategy for making decisions (Brim et al., 1962; Etzioni, 1968; Johnson, 1974; Katona, 1953; Miller and Starr, 1967; Simmons et al., 1973; Steinbrunner, 1974; Taylor, 1965; Vroom and Yetton, 1973).

> Contemporary developments in economics have emphasized the lack of realism of the assumption that individuals act so as to maximize their utility. There has not been an attack on the proposition that individuals should act so as to achieve a maximization of their utility. Rather, there has been sufficient evidence and supporting reasons to show that they do not act in this way. Among the reasons suggested have been the following: the inability of the individual to duplicate the rather recondite mathematics which economists have used to solve the problem of maximization of utility; the existence of other values (the higher values originally excluded by [Adam] Smith) which though not readily quantifiable, do cause divergences from the maximization of utility in the marketplace; the effect of habit; the influence of social emulation; the effect of social institutions.
>
> . . . The work of psychologists would certainly tend to confirm the assertion that human beings have a variety of diverse motivations which do not lend themselves to maximization of utility—at least so long as utility is defined in terms of the *satisfactions* resulting from marketplace phenomena. . . . Similarly, sociologists have accumulated considerable evidence to demonstrate the enormous influence of social institutions, habit, and tradition on the choices and decisions made by individuals. The effect of these psychological and sociological factors leads individuals to make decisions and to take actions without recourse to maximization of utility in the classical economic sense. Alternatively phrased, it can be said that these factors cause people to act irrationally—but it should be noted that this is simply a matter of definition, rationality having been defined as maximization of economic utility [Miller and Starr, 1967, pp. 24–25].

Even in decisions made by business firms, where the overriding value would seem to be to make the greatest amount of profit, decision makers often do not orient themselves toward finding the course of action that will maximize profits and other tangible net gains. Without careful search and appraisal, corporation executives often make judgments about a multiplicity of conflicting objectives, including "good will," "growth potential," "acceptability within the organization," and other intangible gains that are difficult to measure in any way (see Johnson, 1974).

In a study of corporate decision making, Stagner (1969) found that many policy-making business executives, rather than focusing primarily on maximizing profit, were guided by numerous values pertaining to the future welfare of the organization. To examine high-level decision-making practices, Stagner mailed a questionnaire to 500 vice-presidential-level executives belonging to 125 of America's largest and most successful corporations, as selected by *Fortune* magazine. Returns were received from about 50 percent of the executives. The data revealed that in many firms cost and marginal-profit estimates are not carefully made. In fact, a substantial number of executives (28 percent) indicated that only "rough estimates" were made of such variables; 65 percent of them reported that judgments about the company's public image often outweigh profit considerations; and 50 percent reported that considerable weight in making business decisions is attached to company tradition and past policies.[2]

Stagner points out that corporate decisions are not always made in terms of the long-range welfare of the organization, because some powerful executives are inclined to favor the objectives of their own division over those of the firm. Decisions by the manager of a unit are likely to be made with an eye toward local group loyalties and one-upmanship in the competitive struggle for power and influence among rival units, if not for personal advancement. According to numerous other observers, even when a policy maker is thinking in terms of the organization as a whole, he usually gives the devils of bureaucratic politics their due (Allison, 1971; Halperin, 1974; Lindblom, 1965; Johnson, 1974; Vroom and Yetton, 1973). Indeed, an executive risks failure if he overlooks the obligation to work out a policy that will be approved by higher executives or legal authorities within the organization and accepted by the managers who will be required to administer it. Then, too, he must try to avoid stirring up employee opposition, which could lead to disastrous slowdowns or a strike. Aside from the most obvious forms of employee resistance, there are other, subtle costs of implementing decisions that require the workers in a plant to change their work routines, to learn new operations, or to regroup into unaccustomed units: all such decisions result in some measure of lowered productivity.

Similarly, when an individual makes a vital decision bearing on his career, marriage, or health or on any other aspect of his personal welfare, he does not think only about the major utilitarian goals to be attained. He also takes account of a multiplicity of intangible considerations bearing on the probable effects of the chosen and unchosen courses of action on relatives and friends. Anticipated feelings of high or low self-esteem with regard to living up to his own personal standards of conduct also affect his preferences for one alternative rather than another (see chapter 6).

Miller and Starr (1967) emphasize that there is no sound way to combine all the considerations involved in decision making into a single, objective utility measure, even though the decision maker might be capable of giving honest ratings of the subjective utility value of every consideration that enters into his choice.

> The utility an individual gains from a commodity or a service can be measured to some degree by observable market phenomena (e.g., how much of the commodity he will buy at different prices). But there is no convenient measuring unit for the utility of an intangible such as dignity. Therefore, even if these other factors can be theoretically expressed in terms of [subjective] utility, the difficulties involved in measuring the utilities prevent the theory [of maximization of utilities] from satisfactorily explaining observed behavior and decisions [pp. 25–26].

Many behavioral scientists regard the optimizing strategy as an excellent *normative* (or *prescriptive*) model—that is, a set of standards the decision maker *should* strive to attain when making vital decisions (to avoid miscalculations, wishful thinking, and vulnerability to subsequent disillusionment). Some, however, like Miller and Starr, question whether optimizing would very often prove to be the optimal strategy in view of its high costs and the usual constraints on the decision maker's resources; they strongly oppose prescriptive recommendations that might inadvertently encourage decision makers to strive blindly for optimizing solutions, regardless of the circumstances. Even more objections have been raised against the assumption that the optimizing strategy provides an accurate *descriptive* model of how people actually *do* make decisions. The numerous critiques we have just summarized pose a major problem for the psychology of decision making: if optimizing is *not* the dominant strategy actually used by most decision makers most of the time, then what is?

Satisficing

The most influential hypothesis concerning the way administrative man arrives at a new policy has been formulated by Herbert Simon (1976). The decision maker, according to Simon, *satisfices*, rather than maximizes; that is, he looks for a course of action that is "good enough," that meets a minimal set of requirements. Businessmen, for example, often decide to invest in a new enterprise if they expect it to return a "satisfactory profit," without bothering to compare it with all the alternative investments open to them. Sometimes more than one criterion is used, but always it is a question of whether the given choice will yield a "good enough" outcome. An executive looking for a new job, for example, is likely to settle for the first one to come along that meets his minimal requirements—satisfactory pay, good chance for advancement, adequate working conditions, and location within commuting distance of his home. The satisficing strategy involves more superficial search for information and less cognitive work than maximizing. All that the person has to do is consider alternative courses of action sequentially until one that "will do" is found.

Simon argues convincingly that the satisficing approach fits the limited information-processing capabilities of human beings. The world is peopled by creatures of "bounded or limited rationality," he says, and these creatures constantly resort to gross simplifications when dealing with complex decision problems. Man's limited ability to foresee future consequences and to obtain information about the variety of available alternatives inclines him to settle for a barely "acceptable" course of action that is "better than the way things are now." He is not inclined to collect information about all the complicated factors that might affect the outcome of his choice, to estimate probabilities, or to work out preference orderings for many different alternatives. He is content to rely on "a drastically simplified model of the buzzing, blooming confusion that constitutes the real world" (Simon, 1976, p. xxix).

According to Johnson (1974), executives often feel so uncertain about the outcome of what seems to be the best choice that they forego it in order to play safe: they gravitate toward a more conventional, "second-best" choice that will cause little immediate disturbance or disapproval because it will be seen as "acceptable" by superiors and peers who will review the decision and by subordinates who will implement it. Cyert and March (1963) suggest that the more uncertainty there is about a long-term outcome, the greater the tendency to make a policy decision on the basis of its short-term acceptability within the organization.

Organizational theorists assume that individuals use a satisficing strategy in personal decisions as well as organizational decisions (Etzioni, 1968; Miller and Starr, 1967; Simon, 1976; Young, 1966). As Etzioni puts it, "Simon's important distinction between optimizing and 'satisficing' . . . is . . . independent of any socio-political system. It applies as much to a consumer in a supermarket as to the President of the United States" (p. 253). Whenever the consumer, the president, or anyone else is looking only for a choice that offers some degree of *improvement* over the present state of affairs, his survey, analysis, and evaluation are usually limited to just two alternatives—a new course of action that has been brought to his attention and the old one he has been pursuing. If neither meets his minimal requirements, he continues to look for other alternatives until he finds one that does. Consequently, the use of a satisficing strategy does not preclude contemplating a fairly large number of alternatives, but they are examined *sequentially*, with no attempt to work out a comparative balance sheet of pros and cons.

The simplest variant of the satisficing strategy takes the form of relying upon a single formula as the sole decision rule, which comes down to using only one criterion for a tolerable choice. Paradoxically, this crude approach often characterizes the decision-making behavior of people who are facing major personal decisions that will affect their future health or welfare. Men and women in serious trouble are likely to consult whichever physician or lawyer is recommended by a trusted friend and then to accept whatever course of action the adviser recommends, without spending the money and effort required to get a second opinion. The sole decision rule in such cases is often simply "Tell a qualified expert about your problem and do whatever he says—that will be good enough." Simple decision rules are also prevalent in consumer behavior. Studies of consumer purchases indicate that people in shops and supermarkets sometimes buy on impulse, without any advance planning or deliberation (Engel, Kollat, and Blackwell, 1968; Hansen, 1972). The person notices something attractive that he would like to have, and, if the price is within the range he regards as "reasonable," he immediately decides to buy it. A similar decision rule may come into play when a customer impulsively decides to appropriate an attractive piece of merchandise if he sees that no one in the store is looking.

Quasi-satisficing

Some people use a simple moral precept as the sole rule when making a decision to help someone in trouble. Schwartz (1970), in his account of the psychological basis of altruism, describes this approach as "moral decision making." Once the person realizes that someone requires aid and that there is some obvious way help can be given, he promptly takes action without deliberating about alternatives. This use of a simple decision rule is similar to a satisficing approach in all respects except one: the helper does not share the full-fledged satisficer's belief that his choice is *minimally* satisfactory. Instead of regarding his action as merely "good enough," the moral decision maker is convinced that it is the *best*, that no other course would be morally justifiable. Later on we shall examine well-documented examples of moral decision making observed when a member of the family of a patient suffering from kidney disease is asked to donate his own kidney to save the relative's life.

When a decision maker does not accept responsibility for dealing with another person's problem, he is not likely to use a moral precept as his decision rule. The more responsibility he feels, the greater the likelihood that he will follow a simple normative prescription of offering help when someone needs it. To some extent, the findings from experiments on altruism by Bickman (1971, 1972), Latané and Darley (1970), Piliavin, Rodin, and Piliavin (1969, 1975), and others illustrate this relationship between perceived responsibility and a normative approach. The evidence indicates that a person is especially likely to help a stranger if he perceives that he is the only one available to give help. Not everyone, however, adheres to a simple normative rule when he perceives himself as responsible; some people weigh carefully the costs and benefits of giving aid to a needy person. The more frequently a person has told others he is committed to the moral norm that one should selflessly give aid to others when they need it, the greater the likelihood that he will subsequently use that norm as the basis for his decision to intervene.

When a person uses a simple normative precept as his sole decision rule, he usually feels it would be immoral for him to deliberate about any other options open to him. There is a moral-imperative quality to the norm that makes him resist violating it. When this normative decision rule is used, anticipated self-disapproval and social disapproval take precedence over any utilitarian considerations that might be implicated by the decision.

It is apparent from the examples just cited that personal choices based on a quasi-satisficing strategy that relies on a simple decision rule can result in either socially desirable or socially undesirable actions. The same can be said about domestic and foreign-policy decisions made by government leaders. Alexander George (1974) calls attention to the proclivity of national policy makers to rely on a simple formula rather than to attempt to master cognitively complex problems by means of careful search and analysis and weighing of alternatives. One type of decision rule frequently resorted to in a bureaucracy consists of using a simple criterion of "consensus," which requires only the single piece of information that could, in effect, be supplied by an opinion poll of the most powerful persons in the organization; thus, any policy is good enough to be adopted if the majority of influential people want it and will support it. Other simple decision rules sometimes used by policy makers consist of relying on, as a guide for action, a general ideological principle—e.g., "No appeasement of the enemy!"—or an operational code—e.g., the best tactic for dealing with an ultimatum from an enemy is to respond promptly with a more drastic ultimatum—(see George, 1974; Leites, 1953; Lindblom, 1965).

When making a major policy decision for which well-known historical precedents immediately come to mind, many national political leaders, according to historian Ernest May (1973) and political scientist Robert Jervis (1975), follow the simple decision rule "Do what we did last time if it worked and the opposite if it didn't."

Policy-makers ordinarily use history badly. When resorting to an analogy, they tend to seize upon the first that comes to mind. They do not search more widely. Nor do they pause to analyze the case, test its fitness, or even ask in what ways it might be misleading. Seeing a trend running toward the present, they tend to assume that it will continue into the future, not stopping to consider what produced it or why a linear projection might prove to be mistaken [May 1973, p. xi].

There is always a grave danger, as George (1974) points out, that relying on a simple decision rule will lead to a premature choice that overlooks nonobvious negative consequences. Some of those consequences might be averted if the decision were delayed until more thorough deliberation and evaluation were carried out after obtaining information from available intelligence resources.

What Are the Variables?

Although it is not explicitly stated in the descriptive accounts of satisficing and quasi-satisficing by Simon, Jervis, May, George, and others, these strategies differ from optimizing in more than one important dimension. We find that at least four different variables are involved:[3]

1. *Number of requirements to be met:* One characteristic feature of the satisficing strategy is that the testing rule used to determine whether or not to adopt a new course of action specifies a *small number of requirements* that must be met, sometimes only one (e.g., that a personal choice should be acceptable to one's spouse or that a policy choice should be acceptable to the majority of a policy-making group). The decision maker ignores many other values and spheres of interest that he realizes might also be implicated by his decision. In contrast, when the decision maker is using an optimizing strategy he takes account of a large number of requirements or objectives, with the intention of selecting the course of action that achieves the greatest possible satisfaction of the entire set of requirements. This is perhaps the most obvious characteristic that distinguishes satisficing from optimizing.

2. *Number of alternatives generated.* A decision maker using a satisficing strategy sequentially tests each alternative that comes to his attention; if the first one happens to be minimally satisfactory, he terminates his search. Since he makes little effort to canvass the full range of possible courses of action by searching his memory or by seeking suggestions from advisers, the decision maker is likely to generate *relatively few alternatives*. If he uses an optimizing strategy, on the other hand, the decisior maker makes a thorough search and attempts to generate as *many* good alternatives as he can.

3. *Ordering and retesting of alternatives.* When using a satisficing strategy, the decision maker typically tests the alternatives only once and in a haphazard order, as one after another happens to come to his attention, until he finds one that meets his minimum requirements. When using an optimizing strategy, however, he selects the best alternatives and

reexamines them repeatedly, ordering them in pairs or in some other way so as to make comparative judgments.

4. *Type of testing model used.* When testing to see if an alternative meets a given requirement, the satisficing decision maker typically limits his inquiry to seeing whether it falls above or below a *minimal cutoff point.* If there is more than one requirement, he treats each cutoff point in the same way, as equally important. In contrast to this simple, unweighted threshold model, the model used in the optimizing strategy is typically a weighted additive model, which requires the decision maker to arrive at an evaluation that takes account of the *magnitudes* of all the pros and cons with due regard for the relative importance of each objective. This gives him the opportunity to consider possible "tradeoffs" from gaining very high values on some important requirements in exchange for tolerating relatively low values on less important ones.

When a person's procedures fall at the low end of the continuum on all four variables, his decision-making strategy would be unambiguously classified as satisficing; when at the upper end of the continuum on all four variables, his strategy would be unambiguously classified as optimizing. But what if a person's pattern on the four variables is not consistent? Obviously, we can expect to find instances of quasi-satisficing or mixed strategies, where satisficing tendencies predominate on one or two variables but optimizing tendencies predominate on the others.

Even when someone warrants high ratings on all four variables, he might still fail to maximize all possible values, and hence fall far short of a genuinely optimizing strategy. Moreover, an unskilled or unwary decision maker with good intentions might obtain high ratings but nevertheless make gross miscalculations through ignorance, bias, overconcern about the foreseeable immediate consequences, or rigid belief in "the too-ready assumption that actions which have in the past led to the desired outcome will continue to do so" (Merton, 1936, p. 901). High ratings on the four variables might, therefore, be regarded as necessary, but not sufficient, conditions for optimizing.

Not unexpectedly, the four variables overlap to some extent with the seven criteria for vigilant information processing (see chapter 1). Anyone who uses a relatively pure satisficing strategy, as defined by the four variables, would obtain low scores on at least four of the seven variables that define vigilant information processing: he would fail to canvass a wide range of alternatives (criterion no. 1), to take account of the full range of short-term objectives and long-term values to be fulfilled by the choice (criterion no. 2), to weigh all he knows about the costs and risks of each alternative (criterion no. 3), and to reexamine the positive and negative consequences of all known alternatives (criterion no. 6). But the use of a satisficing strategy does not preclude meeting some of the criteria for vigilant information processing. Even within the confines of a pure satisficing strategy, a decision maker can still carry out an intensive search for relevant information, conscientiously assimilate information, and make provisions for implementation along with detailed contingency plans. Furthermore, it is possible for someone to meet all seven requirements for vigilant information processing and yet not obtain a high score on one or two of the variables that enter into the optimizing strategy, so that he would be classified as using a "quasi-optimizing" strategy. Taking account of the limitations of a "pure" optimizing strategy discussed earlier, we expect that for purposes of predicting gross miscalculations in decision making and subsequent postdecisional regret, the seven variables specified as the criteria for vigilant information processing will prove to be more valuable than the set of four variables differentiating between satisficing and optimizing.

Elimination by Aspects

Instead of a single decision rule in a satisficing or quasi-satisficing strategy, a set of decision rules, involving perhaps up to half a dozen considerations, is sometimes used. Still, the decision maker does not engage in anything like the amount of cognitive work that would be required if he were to evaluate and weigh the alternatives using an optimizing strategy. One such multiple-rule variant, designated as the *"elimination-by-aspects" approach*, has been described by Tversky (1972). It consists essentially of a combination of simple decision rules, which can be applied to select rapidly from a number of salient alternatives one that meets a set of minimal requirements. Tversky illustrates this type of quasi-satisficing strategy by citing a television commercial screened in San Francisco. An announcer says:

> There are more than two dozen companies in the San Francisco area which offer training in computer programing. [*He puts some two dozen eggs and one walnut on the table to represent the alternatives.*] Let us examine the facts. How many of these schools have on-line computer facilities for training? [*He removes several eggs.*] How many of these schools have placement services that would help you find a job? [*He removes some more eggs.*] How many of these schools are approved for veterans' benefits? [*This continues until the walnut alone remains. The announcer cracks the nutshell, revealing the name of the advertised company.*] This is all you need to know, in a nutshell.

When the elimination-by-aspects approach is used, decision making becomes essentially a sequential narrowing-down process, similar to the logic employed in the popular game Twenty Questions. Starting ordinarily with the most valued requirement, all salient alternatives that do not contain the selected aspect are eliminated, and the process continues for each requirement in turn until a single expedient remains. For example, in contemplating the purchase of a new car, the first aspect selected might be a $4,500 price limit; all cars more expensive than $4,500 are then excluded from further consideration. A second aspect might be high mileage per gallon; at this stage, all cars are eliminated that do not have this feature. Yet another aspect, say power steering, is examined for the remaining alternatives, and all cars not meeting this criterion are crossed off the "mental list." The process continues until all cars but one are eliminated.

Of course, the decision maker may run out of aspects before he arrives at a single remaining expedient; he will then have to introduce another decision rule in order to narrow his choice. Or he may run out of alternatives before he exhausts his list of minimal requirements. From a normative standpoint, however, a much more serious flaw of this complex form of satisficing lies in its failure to ensure that the alternatives retained are, in fact, superior to those eliminated. For example, in the alternative arrived at in the television commercial, the use of placement services as a criterion for elimination might lead to the rejection of programs whose overall quality far exceeds that of the advertised one despite the fact that they do not offer that particular service. Similarly, in the choice of a car, the use of power steering as a criterion for elimination could lead to rejection of vehicles otherwise far superior to the vehicle purchased. Part of the problem is that minor criteria may creep in early in the sequence or may survive to determine the final choice. Perhaps this drawback could be corrected in a way that would transform the elimination-by-aspects approach into a quasi-optimizing strategy by introducing procedures that reflect the decision maker's judgments about the differential weights to be assigned to various aspects. Even without any such refinement, however, this approach appears to be one of the most sophisticated and psychologically realistic of the quasi-satisficing strategies and might result in fewer miscalculations than the simpler variants that rely exclusively on a single decision rule (Abelson, 1976).

Some social science theorists would describe reliance on a single decision rule as less "rational" than the elimination-by-aspects approach, and all variants of satisficing as less "rational" than optimizing. But terms like *less rational, nonrational,* and *irrational* carry invidious connotations ("stupid," "crazy") that often do not correspond at all to the evaluations that would be made by objective observers. Indeed it could be argued that in certain circumstances it is not rational to waste time and effort in maximizing; even when the relevant information is available, a very simple form of satisficing sometimes may be the most sensible orientation, especially for many minor issues. For example, consumer research organizations have recommended that when purchasing aspirin at a registered pharmacy, one should follow the simple rule of selecting whichever brand is cheapest (because all brands must meet rigorous U.S. government specifications and, despite advertising claims to the contrary, there are no significant differences among them). As Miller and Starr (1967, p. 51) point out, "It is always questionable whether the optimum procedure is to search for *the* optimum value." Accordingly, we avoid characterizing the satisficing strategy or any other decision-making strategy in terms of "rationality" or "irrationality." We do not intend to bypass the important issue of determining the conditions under which one or another decision-making procedure will have unfavorable consequences for the decision maker; but we shall attempt to relate specific types of conditions to specific types of unfavorable consequences without using overinclusive, misleading labels like *irrational*.

Incrementalism and Muddling Through

Organizational theorists recognize that despite its shortcomings, a satisficing strategy can result in slow progress toward an optimal course of action. Miller and Starr (1967), for example, speak about *incremental improvements* that sometimes come about as a result of a succession of satisficing policy choices, each small change presumably having been selected as "good enough" because it was seen as better than leaving the old policy unchanged. "Over time," Miller and Starr assert "both individuals and groups may be better off to move in incremental steps of reasonable size toward the perceived and bounded optimum than in giant strides based on long-range perceptions of where the ultimate optimal exists" (p. 51).

Charles E. Lindblom (1959, 1963, 1965) has given a detailed account of the incrementalist approach in an analysis of "the art of muddling through." When a problem arises requiring a change in policy, according to Lindblom, policy makers in government or large organizations generally consider a very narrow range of policy alternatives that differ to only a small degree from the existing policy. By sticking close to this familiar path of policymaking, the incrementalist shows his preference for the sin of "omission" over the sin of "confusion" (Lindblom, 1965, p. 146).

Incremental decision making is geared to alleviating concrete shortcomings in a present policy—putting out fires—rather than selecting the superior course of action. Since no effort is made to specify major goals and to find the best means for attaining them, "ends are chosen that are appropriate to available or nearly available means" (Hirschman and Lindblom, 1962, p. 215). The incremental approach allows executives to simplify the search and appraisal stages of decision making by carrying out successive comparisons with respect to policy alternatives that differ only slightly from the existing policy. Slovic (1971) postulates, on the basis of his experiments on the cognitive limitations displayed in gambling situations, that decision makers find the incremental approach attractive because it enables them to avoid difficult cognitive tasks: "Examination of business decision making and governmental policy making suggests that, whenever possible, decision makers avoid uncertainty and the necessity of weighting and combining information or trading-off conflicting values."

Often decision makers have no real awareness of trying to arrive at a new policy; rather, there is a never-ending series of attacks on each new problem as it arises. As policy makers take one small step after another to gradually change the existing policy, the satisficing criterion itself may change, depending on what is going wrong with the existing policy.[4] If there are strong objections to the policy on the part of other bureaucrats who have to implement it, the policy makers may find a satisficing solution that involves making a compromise in accord with the realities of bureaucratic politics. Incremental changes are often made primarily to keep other politically powerful groups in the hierarchy sufficiently satisfied so that they will stop complaining and will not obstruct the new trend (Halperin, 1974).

Braybrooke and Lindblom (1963) regard muddling-through incrementalism as the typical decision-making process of groups in pluralistic societies. Since the term *muddling through* evokes images of incompetence and aimlessness, it is tempting to conclude that it could be the preferred technique only of lazy or third-rate minds. But Braybrooke and Lindblom view it as the method by which societal decision-making bodies, acting as coalitions of interest groups, can effectively make cumulative decisions and arrive at workable compromises. Whenever power is distributed among a variety of influential executive leaders, political parties, legislative factions, and interest groups, one center of power can rarely impose its preferences on another and policies are likely to be the outcome of give and take among numerous partisans. The constraints of bureaucratic politics, with its shifting compromises and coalitions, constitute a major reason for the disjointed and incremental nature of the policies that gradually evolve.

Lindblom and his associates argue that incremental decisions based largely on the criterion of consensus, rather than on the actual values implicated by the issue, may avoid some of the social evils of undemocratic, centralized decision making. But other social scientists point out that incrementalism based largely on keeping fellow power holders reasonably contented cannot be expected to do very much about the vital needs of underpriviledged people and politically weak groups (see Etzioni, 1968, pp. 272–73; Dror, 1969, pp. 167–69.)[5] Moreover, there is no guarantee that in the atomic age our government leaders will always somehow muddle through successfully as they "stagger through history like a drunk putting one disjointed incremental foot after another" (Boulding, 1964, p. 931). On the one hand, incremental policy formation based on a succession of satisficing choices can have functional value for decision makers who want to avoid the risks of drastic societal changes that "may easily lead," as Popper (1963, p. 158) says, "to an intolerable increase in human suffering." But on the other hand, there is the danger that it can prove to be a zigzag passage to unanticipated disaster.

Relatively little is to be found in the social psychological literature about muddling through on personal decisions. Probably the same type of incremental change, based on a simple satisficing strategy, is adopted whenever a person is ignorant of the fundamental issues at stake or when he wishes to avoid investing a great deal of time and energy in wrestling with a problem that appears, at the time, insoluble. Important life decisions are sometimes incremental in nature, the end product of a series of small decisions that progressively commit the person to one particular course of action. A stepwise increase in commitment can end up locking the person into a career or marriage without his ever having made a definite decision about it (see chapter 11).

Many individuals do not make a deliberate occupational choice but in haphazard, trial-and-error fashion leave their job whenever something that seems somewhat better comes along. Ginzberg et al. (1951) suggest that incremental steps may determine the career choices made by a sizable number of people even in skilled occupations. A man or woman starts off getting a certain type of job training and then finds it more and more difficult to switch to another type of career. The person anticipates social disapproval for "wasting" his training, which tends to increase with each increment of training or advancement. And, of course, he is also deterred from changing by his own sense of prior investment of time, effort, and money in the direction he has already moved.

Matza (1964) indicates that the careers of lawbreakers are often arrived at in the same stepwise, drifting fashion, without any single stage at which the offenders decide they are going to pursue a life of crime. Rather, they start with minor offenses, get into more and more trouble with the police, and proceed slowly to enlarge their repertoire of criminal acts until they reach the point where they are regularly committing serious crimes. Each successive crime in the series appears to be not very much worse than the preceding one, and in this stepwise fashion the person proceeds to move from minor delinquency to major crime.

A similar stepwise process has been reported for the decision to marry. Waller (1938, p. 259) noted that during the early decades of the twentieth century the process of mating unfolded gradually, in a series of steps whereby the person became increasingly committed in his own eyes and in those of others to the decision to marry. Each step involved the use of a few simple criteria, with no effort to weigh alternatives.

These observational reports about incremental decision making on such vital personal choices as marriage and career, although not sufficiently detailed to enable us to draw definitive conclusions about decision-making processes, suggest that the succession of small decisions may often be based on a satisficing or quasi-satisficing strategy, just as in the case of the incremental policy-making decisions described by administrative scientists.

Mixed Scanning

Etzioni (1967) has outlined a conglomerate strategy called mixed scanning, which he sees as a synthesis of the stringent rationalism of optimizing and the "muddling," slipshod approach of extreme incrementalism, displayed by bureaucrats who use consensus as their only satisficing criterion. The mixed-scanning strategy has two main components: (1) some of the features of the optimizing strategy combined with essential features of the elimination-by-aspects approach are used for fundamental policy decisions that set basic directions; and (2) an incremental process (based on simple forms of satisficing) is followed for the minor or "bit" decisions that ensue after the basic policy direction is set, resulting in gradual revisions and sometimes preparing the way for a new fundamental decision. Etzioni argues that this mixture of substrategies fits the needs of democratic governments and organizations. In noncrisis periods, it is easier to obtain a consensus on "increments similar to the existing policies than to gain support for a new policy" (p. 294). But in times of serious trouble, a crisis stimulates intensive search for a better policy and serves "to build consensus for major changes of direction which are overdue (e.g., governmental guidance of economic stability, the welfare state, desegregation)" (p. 294).

Etzioni uses the term *scanning* to refer to the search, collection, processing, evaluation, and weighing of information in the process of making a choice—i.e., the main cognitive activities that enter into the orientation we call vigilant information processing. The intensiveness of scanning can vary over a wide range, from very superficial to extremely intensive, depending on how much "coverage" the decision maker strives for when he surveys the relevant fields of information, how much detail he "takes in," and how completely he "explores alternative steps." Each time he faces a dilemma that requires choosing a new course of action, he has to make a deliberate prior judgment about how much of his resources of time, energy, and money he is willing to allocate to search and appraisal activities.

Etzioni's description of the mixed-scanning strategy includes a set of rules for allocating resources to scanning whenever a policy maker faces the type of crisis that leads him to realize that earlier policy lines ought to be reviewed and perhaps changed.

> Put into a program-like language, the [mixed-scanning] strategy roughly reads:
>
> a. *On strategic occasions* . . . (i) list all relevant alternatives that come to mind, that the staff raises, and that advisers advocate (including alternatives not usually considered feasible).
>
> (ii) Examine briefly the alternatives under (i) . . . and reject those that reveal a "crippling objection." These include: (a) utilitarian objections to alternatives which require means that are not available, (b) normative objections to alternatives which violate the basic values of the decision-makers, and (c) political objections to alternatives which violate the basic values or interests of other actors whose support seems essential for making the decision and/or implementing it.
>
> (iii) For all alternatives not rejected under (ii), repeat (ii) in greater though not in full detail. . . .

(iv) For those alternatives remaining after (iii), repeat (ii) in still fuller detail. . . . Continue until only one alternative is left. . . .

b. *Before implementation* [in order to prepare for subsequent "increment-ing"] (i) when possible, fragment the implementation into several sequential steps. . . .

(ii) When possible, divide the commitment to implement into several serial steps. . . .

(iii) When possible, divide the commitment of assets into several serial steps and maintain a strategic reserve. . . .

(iv) Arrange implementation in such a way that, if possible, costly and less reversible decisions will appear later in the process than those which are more reversible and less costly.

(v) Provide a time schedule for the additional collection and processing of information. . . .

c. *Review while implementing.* (i) Scan on a semi-encompassing level after the first sub-set of increments is implemented. If they "work," continue to scan on a semi-encompassing level after longer intervals and in full, over-all review, still less frequently.

(ii) Scan more encompassingly whenever a series of increments, although each one seems a step in the right direction, results in deeper difficulties.

(iii) Be sure to scan at set intervals in full, over-all review even if every-thing seems all right. . . .

d. *Formulate a rule for the allocation of assets and time among the various levels of scanning.* . . . [pp. 286–88]

The only testing rule specified for fundamental decisions in the above program is one that would be rated as satisficing on one of the pri-mary variables that defines the satisficing strategy—namely, rejecting every alternative that has a "crippling" objection, which is tantamount to using a minimal cutoff point. But instead of a quasi-satisficing approach, a quasi-optimizing approach could be used when dealing with those alterna-tives that survive the initial rejection test: each time the surviving alterna-tives are reexamined, the testing rule might be changed in the optimizing direction by raising the minimum standard (from "crippling" objections to more minor objections) or by introducing a comparative type of testing for selecting the least objectionable alternative. Etzioni no doubt assumes that the standards are raised each time the surviving alternatives are re-tested, since if the definition of *crippling* were to remain constant there would be little point in reexamining the alternatives, except to catch and correct blatant errors made the first time. In any case, if we assume that the proposed upgrading of the testing rule is introduced into Etzioni's program for making fundamental decisions, the program would directly or indirectly embody the seven criteria we have specified for a vigilant information-processing orientation. Four of the criteria are explicitly men-tioned (no. 1—thorough canvassing of alternatives; no. 2—taking account of the full range of objectives and values to be fulfilled; no. 4—intensive search for new information; no. 7—detailed provisions for implementation, with contingency plans). Moreover, in order to carry out all the quasi-optimizing steps conscientiously, the decision maker would be required by the program to meet the other three criteria as well (no. 3—careful weighing of consequences of each alternative; no. 5—thorough assimilation of new information; no. 6—reexamination of consequences before making a final choice).

Although intended for policy makers, the same program, with minor modifications, could be applied to an individual's work-task decisions and to personal decisions involving career, marriage, health, or financial security. (Only a few slight changes in wording would be necessary—e.g., in step a (i), for personal decisions, *the staff* would be replaced by *family and friends.*)

The program for mixed scanning is presented by Etzioni primarily as a normative or prescriptive model, specifying what decision makers *should* do. The mixed-scanning strategy obviously has the virtue of adaptive flexibility at different stages of decision making, with a quasi-optimizing approach being used only while selecting the trunk of a new decision tree and a satisficing approach being used after the new fundamental policy has been chosen, as one moves out along the branches. Etzioni expects that decision makers will improve their effectiveness in attaining their actual goals if they follow his recommendations to differentiate "fundamental" from "bit" decisions and carry out the intensive scanning procedures he prescribes for the fundamental ones.

Etzioni suggests further that the mixed-scanning strategy may be an accurate descriptive model of what governmental policy makers *actually* do. He offers no systematic evidence, however, to support this hypothesis, although he mentions a few case studies that seem to fit the model. He challenges the overgeneralizations that have been drawn from the finding that the United States Congress generally makes only marginal (incremental) changes in the annual budget for federal agencies, raising or lowering the amounts allocated by just a slight percentage from the amounts allocated the preceding year (Fenno, 1966). He points out that congressmen occasionally make a fundamental decision to increase drastically the percentage of the gross national product to be devoted to the federal budget, as they did at the outbreak of the Korean War in 1950. The U.S. defense budget jumped from 5.0 percent of the GNP in 1950 to 10.3 percent in 1951; thereafter it fluctuated between 9.0 and 11.3 percent during the next decade, reflecting incremental decisions. Etzioni cites a similar jump in the budget for the national space agency in 1958, when Congress agreed to support a new program for space exploration, which was followed by incremental changes during the subsequent years. In these instances, what appears to be a series of incremental decisions turns out to be an extension of a fundamental, nonincremental policy decision. Whether the fundamental decision in each instance was made in the way described by Etzioni's program, however, requires further evidence—

which Etzioni does not examine—concerning the procedures used by the decision makers in arriving at a new policy. It remains an open, empirical question whether any sizable population or subpopulation of decision makers does, in fact, proceed along the lines specified in Etzioni's description of the mixed-scanning strategy.

The Decision Maker's Repertoire

Implicit in Etzioni's account is the assumption that every decision maker has in his repertoire all the component substrategies and orientations we have described in the preceding sections. Adopting a given strategy at one stage of the decision-making sequence does not preclude use of another strategy at a later stage, particularly if the earlier one proves ineffective in resolving the conflict. For some people, the work of making a decision involves switching from low-cost, low-energy substrategies to more costly, effortful ones as they realize they are unable to settle the decisional conflict.

We expect that when different strategies or substrategies are used, different information-processing orientations in the decision maker's repertoire come to the fore. When he is trying to optimize, as we have seen, the decision maker consistently behaves like an intelligent realist, pursuing maximum satisfaction or utility with single-minded attention. He uses his mental capacities to a remarkable degree while searching for all viable alternatives and trying to understand all their possible consequences.

When operating as a "mixed scanner," the decision maker solves the problem of his limited capacity to process information by classifying decisions as either fundamental or minor. He conserves his time and energy by scanning intensively only those choices that are the most important or most troublesome, treating all other choices much more superficially.

When satisficing, on the other hand, the decision maker deals with fundamental decisions in the same way as minor ones; he relies on one or a few rock-bottom principles that enable him to reduce a complex decisional problem into a matter of judging what will do and what won't do, which requires much less time and effort for search and appraisal. When in response to a profound challenge the decision maker functions as an incrementalist muddler, he resorts to the simplest form of satisficing, making only slight adjustments in an obsolete policy after doing little more than checking on the agreement of other interested parties. This crude form of satisficing is more likely than other strategies to lead to gross failures to meet the criteria for vigilant information processing. For vital decisions, the most damaging consequences are to be expected when the preliminary appraisal of the challenge is itself based on such a low level of vigilance that the person fails to realize the importance of the objectives and values at stake. But a muddling strategy might be adaptive in a stable environment, where few fundamental challenges to existing policies are encountered.

According to a general assumption presented in chapter 1, we expect that irrespective of the strategy adopted—i.e., whether the decision maker strives to optimize, settles for satisficing, or tries to follow a mixed strategy—the likelihood of miscalculation and postdecisional regret increases as a function of the degree to which he fails to engage in vigilant information processing (as defined by the seven criteria) during the period preceding commitment. Hence, according to this assumption, when attempting to predict the consequences of a satisficing strategy—or any other strategy—one needs to inquire into the degree to which the decision maker meets the seven criteria.

If we make the additional assumption that practically all the various strategies and substrategies we have discussed are in the repertoire of every decision maker, we find ourselves confronting a new set of research questions that need to be answered in order to develop an adequate descriptive theory of decision making. The old question, which has been addressed by many social scientists, was "Which strategy is the one most decision makers use most of the time?" The answer is still being debated, because no consistent evidence has as yet emerged. But the analysis presented in this chapter inclines us to be dubious about ever finding a general answer that will hold across all types of major and minor decisions, and in all circumstances. After all, being extremely careful to meet the criteria for vigilant information processing would be almost as inappropriate for a trivial or routine decision among substitutable alternatives as superficial satisficing would be for a major decision. In *Up the Organization*, Robert Townsend, the former chairman of the board of the Avis Corporation, gives some conventional wisdom, well known to business executives who have managed to survive at the top, about how to approach different kinds of decisions:

> There are two kinds of decisions: those that are expensive to change and those that are not.
> A decision to build the Edsel or Mustang (or locate your new factory in Orlando or Yakima) shouldn't be made hastily; nor without plenty of inputs from operating people and specialists.
> But the common or garden-variety decision—like when to have the cafeteria open for lunch or what brand of pencil to buy—should be made fast. No point in taking three weeks to make a decision that can be made in three seconds—and corrected inexpensively later if wrong. The whole organization may be out of business while you oscillate between baby-blue or buffalo-brown coffee cups [Townsend, 1970, p. 45].

We suspect that in addition to using a simple satisficing approach to relatively unimportant decisions and an optimizing approach to the most important ones, many executives use some form of mixed strategy when dealing with decisions in the intermediate range that fall between the two extremes Townsend is talking about. The important point, however, is that people cannot be expected to use the same strategy for all types of decisions.

Instead of the old question, then, about which strategy is most prevalent, a new set of questions must be confronted: Under what conditions are people most likely to adopt a nonvigilant, satisficing strategy as opposed to a more vigilant one? Under what conditions are people most motivated to devote the resources of time, energy, and money necessary to seek an optimizing solution? What intervention procedures are available to remedy careless, superficial, or impulsive approaches to decision making when vital consequences are at stake?

In the chapters that follow, we present a general theoretical framework for formulating hypotheses about major variables that are likely to enter into the answers to these questions. The framework is especially pertinent for specifying when and why people gravitate toward simple strategies that lead to miscalculation and regret. Two types of explanation, as we have seen, are offered by specialists in administrative sciences. One type, based mainly on findings from experimental cognitive psychology, takes account of the limitations of the human mind for perceiving and processing information. The second type, derived mainly from documented accounts of policy decisions in large organizations, focuses on the intrusions of bureaucratic politics, which incline policy makers to avoid instituting a major shift in policy, no matter how badly it is needed, so as to keep all the powerful persons and groups within the organization satisfied or at least so as not to provoke them to mobilize to oppose those responsible for an unwelcome change in policy. A central thesis of this book, stated in the first chapter, is that in addition to these and other well-known sources of constraint on effective decision making, there is another source to be reckoned with—psychological stress.[6]

We turn in the next chapter to a set of major hypotheses, derived from what is known about the psychology of stress, that form the basis for our theoretical framework. We shall try to show how these hypotheses can be used to explain why decision makers frequently fail to make use of the resources available to them for engaging in vigilant information processing—within the limits of their cognitive capabilities and within the limits imposed by powerful persons or groups whose wishes have to be respected—with the result that they subsequently find themselves caught up in fiascoes that they could have averted.

PART 2

Hot Cognitive Processes

CHAPTER 3

A Conflict Model
of Decision Making

THOSE BEHAVIORAL SCIENTISTS who are intrigued by the great potentialities of a rational approach to decision making sometimes give the impression that all policy makers in government and business ought to be highly detached, cool, and utterly objective when calculating the expected utility of whatever choices they make. Some writers on decision making even suggest that purely personal choices concerning one's career, marriage, health, and life style ought to be made in the same coolly calculated manner. These writers may be partly right, in the sense that people are likely to regret in leisure the impulsive decisions they make in haste while undergoing emotional turmoil. But the desirability of cool detachment as an ideal is highly questionable. A world dominated by Dr. Strangelove and like-minded cost accountants might soon become devoid of acts of affection, conscience, and humanity, as well as passion.

Even if the ideal were somehow worth striving for, the fact remains that human beings, programmed as they are with emotions and unconscious motives as well as with cognitive abilities, seldom can approximate a state of detached affectlessness when making decisions that implicate their own vital interests or those of their organization or nation. Among public officials who make major decisions affecting the fate of their country, we find a high degree of ego involvement in prior commitments, persistent longing for the gains they expect, and acute worry about the high costs and risks of intolerable losses (Janis, 1972). These considerations give a strong emotional coloring to their deliberations about policy alternatives, just as when they make personal decisions in private life. Using the terminology of Robert P. Abelson (1963), we can say that thinking about vital, affect-laden issues generally involves *hot* cognitions, in contrast to the cold cognitions of routine problem solving.

An executive may be able to control his emotions well enough to avoid

45

making decisions in the midst of the intense heat of passionate love, fear, anger, or hate. But even when he is in a relatively placid, calm state, he is still a warm-blooded mammal who cannot contemplate the goals he wants to attain and the threats he wants to avoid without some degree of emotional arousal. The theoretical concepts introduced in this chapter are intended to take account of the influence of unpleasant emotions on intellectual judgments when human beings are required to make decisions on highly ego-involving issues.[1]

Decisional Conflicts as Sources of Stress

Intense conflicts are likely to arise whenever a person has to make an important decision, such as whether to get married, take a new job, sign a business contract, or agree to a political compromise on behalf of the organization or government he represents. Such conflicts become acute as the decision maker becomes aware of the risk of suffering serious losses from whatever course of action he selects. In addition to these hot cognitions, there are others pertaining to the difficulties of reversing the decision, which also contribute to the intensity of decisional conflict. Beset with uncertainties, the decision maker is reluctant to make an irrevocable choice.

When we speak of "decisional conflicts" we are referring to simultaneous opposing tendencies within the individual to accept and reject a given course of action. The most prominent symptoms of such conflicts are hesitation, vacillation, feelings of uncertainty, and signs of acute emotional stress whenever the decision comes within the focus of attention. A major subjective characteristic of decisional conflicts is an unpleasant feeling of distress.

Theodore Sorensen (1966) reports that during the Cuban missile crisis the members of President Kennedy's Executive Committee spent sleepless nights worrying about the possibility that whatever action they decided to take might provoke Russia to start World War III. But it does not require the risks of a nuclear holocaust to evoke stress reactions in government leaders. In his autobiographical book *Six Crises*, written in the two years after his defeat by Kennedy in the 1960 presidential election, Richard Nixon talks about his own stress symptoms when he had to make major decisions. Nixon vividly describes a "crisis syndrome" that he experienced in 1948 when, as a young congressman, he suddenly found himself confronted with the problem of whether or not to initiate a congressional inquiry in order to proceed against Alger Hiss (a high-ranking State Department official who had been accused of being a Communist agent). "I was 'mean' to live with," Nixon admits, "at home and with my friends. I was quick-tempered with the members of my staff. I lost interest in eating and skipped meals without even being aware of it." Nixon also speaks of "almost unbearable tensions [that] build up [during a period of doubt], tensions that can be relieved only by taking action, one way or the other." In a later crisis—the furor over the Nixon "fund" during his 1952 vice-presidential campaign, which led to the celebrated "Checkers speech" on television—Nixon reports that he had the same nervous symptoms, all of which disappeared when he swung into action. During yet another crisis—his uncertainty about how far to go, as vice-president, in initiating government policies during the long weeks of President Eisenhower's recovery from a heart attack in 1955—he was again in a state of acute emotional tension. "Not knowing how to act or not being able to act," Nixon comments about this crisis, "is what tears your insides out. . . ."

The emotional symptoms Nixon describes, including the strong desire to take action in order to alleviate emotional tension, are typical stress reactions that have been observed in many public officials during periods when they are facing a crucial decision that could affect the future success of their political cause as well as their own careers. When deciding what to do as the Watergate coverup began to be exposed, Nixon was certainly not the only participant to display symptoms of acute stress (see Chapter 10). Many a private citizen also becomes agitated and sleepless when faced with a decisional dilemma that entails risks to important personal values.

Stress Symptoms

The symptoms of stress that are often observed at the time of making a difficult decision include feelings of apprehensiveness, a desire to escape from the distressing choice dilemma, and self-blame for having allowed oneself to get into a predicament where one is forced to choose between unsatisfactory alternatives ("Why did I let myself get into this box? Now I'm damned if I do and damned if I don't"). These stress symptoms were systematically investigated in a study by Epstein and Fenz (1965) of sports parachute jumpers who had made over 100 jumps. The investigators found that avoidance feelings do not reach a peak when the danger is greatest—when the experienced parachutists are on the plane waiting to jump or during the free fall. Rather, the point of maximal stress, as indicated by the parachutists' ratings of avoidance feelings, occurs well before they leave the ground, at the time of their *initial decision* to participate in the airplane jump scheduled for that day. While on the flight, feelings of avoidance decrease, even though objectively the parachutists are closer to the danger situation, and avoidance feelings continue to decline when the objective danger is greatest, during the free fall.

Starting with a pioneering experiment by Gerard (1967), psychologists have begun to investigate physiological concomitants of decisional conflict, observing changes in autonomic arousal that point to varying levels of stress during the decision-making process. Some of our own data on physiological reactions support the notion that decisional conflicts produce marked increases in stress when a person is required to choose between two alternatives both of which are known to have some unpleasant consequences. In an experiment by Mann, Janis, and Chaplin (1969) (discussed more fully in the next chapter), coeds at the University of Melbourne were confronted with a choice between two unpleasant forms of stimulation, either of which would enable them to fulfill their contract with the experimenter. In order to assess emotional tension during the decision sequence, each subject's heart rate was monitored (a) near the beginning of the session, (b) during the predecision period, (c) during the interval coinciding with the decision, and (d) after the experimenter's debriefing. Figure 1 presents the heart rate data at each of the four periods.

During the predecision period, heart rate increased sharply under the two experimental conditions, both when subjects expected to receive additional information about the choice alternatives and when they did not expect additional information. Heart rate reached a peak during announcement of the decision, and then dropped off rapidly during the debriefing session. These records of physiological arousal suggest that the demand to announce a decision acted as a stressor. Later, when subjects learned they would not have to go through with the decision, they manifested marked relief.

FIGURE 1.   **Changes in heart rate during a decision-making experiment.**

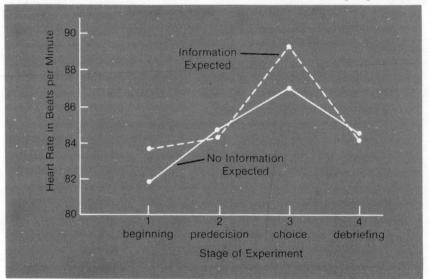

Source: L. Mann, I. L. Janis, and R. Chaplin, "Effects of Anticipation of Forthcoming Information on Predecisional Processes," *Journal of Personality and Social Psychology*, 1969, *11*, 14. Copyright 1969 by the American Psychological Association. Reprinted by permission.

Similar changes in autonomic responses have been reported in the initial experiment by Gerard (1967) and in subsequent experiments by Fleischer (1968) and Jones and Johnson (1973).[2] The striking feature in all these experiments is that regardless of the level of difficulty or importance of the decision, autonomic indicators of stress increase as subjects move toward a decision and afterwards gradually return to the level of the resting state.

In general, the intensity of physiological and psychological symptoms of stress appears to depend upon the *perceived magnitude* of the losses the decision maker anticipates from whatever choice he makes. At one time or another, everyone is likely to face a vital decision that evokes extreme symptoms. But, of course, decisions in everyday life usually involve much less serious losses and evoke correspondingly less stress than those in the examples cited from the Cuban missile crisis, Nixon's *Six Crises*, and the study of parachutists. Nevertheless, even the mild stress that arises when a decision maker anticipates slight losses or uncertain risks may have discernible effects on the quality of his search and appraisal activities.

We turn next to propositions relating decision making to the antecedents and consequences of stress, which form the core of our conflict-theory model. The model appears to be compatible with Herbert Simon's (1967) analysis of the role of motivation and emotion in controlling cognitive behavior. Drawing on concepts formulated by Hebb (1949), Neisser (1963), and Taylor (1960), Simon views man as "a basically serial information processor endowed with multiple needs [who usually] behaves adaptively and survives in an environment that presents unpredictable threats and opportunities" (p. 39). He conceptualizes the arousal of anxiety or any other unpleasant emotion as an interruption mechanism that allows the processor to respond adaptively to urgent needs, except that when emotional arousal is extremely intense and persistent, it becomes disruptive and produces nonadaptive behavior.

Our theory attempts to specify the contrasting conditions that determine whether the stress engendered by decisional conflict will facilitate or interfere with vigilant information processing. The key concepts and propositions derive from an analysis of the research literature on psychological stress, especially that bearing on the hot cognitions induced by *warnings* that require emergency decision making in the face of oncoming disaster and fear-arousing messages that urge protective action to avert health hazards or other serious threats. (See, e.g., Appley and Trumbull, 1967; Baker and Chapman, 1962; Barton, 1963; Coelho, Hamburg, and Adams, 1974; Committee on Disaster Studies, 1955; Horowitz, 1976; Hovland, Janis, and Kelley, 1953; Janis, 1951, 1958, and 1971; Janis and Leventhal, 1965; Killian, 1952; Lazarus, 1966; Leventhal, 1968 and 1973; McGuire, 1969; Radloff and Helmreich, 1968; Sarason and Spielberger, 1975; Spielberger and Sarason, 1975.)

Five Basic Assumptions

Psychological stress is used as a generic term to designate unpleasant emotional states evoked by threatening environmental events or stimuli (Janis, 1958; Janis and Mann, 1968). A "stressful" event is any change in the environment that typically induces a high degree of unpleasant emotion (such as anxiety, guilt, or shame) and affects normal patterns of information processing. The functional relationships between psychological stress and decisional conflict can be stated in five general propositions that we use as our basic assumptions.

1. *The degree of stress generated by any decisional conflict is a direct function of the goal strivings that the decision maker expects to remain unsatisfied: the more goals expected to be unfulfilled and the more important the needs to which those goals correspond, the greater the stress.*

Stress is not aroused unless the decision maker realizes that he stands to gain or lose significant goals in the sphere of utilitarian values, social approval, or self-approval. When there is no threat of loss or of failure to attain positive goals, there is no stress.

2. *When a person encounters new threats or opportunities that motivate him to consider a new course of action, the degree of decisional stress is a function of the degree to which he is committed to adhere to his present course of action.*

Whenever the decision maker is tempted to change, the losses he expects to suffer from failing to fulfill a prior contract or any less formal commitment constitute a major source of threat that discourages switching to a new course of action. The greater the commitment to a prior decision, the greater the anticipated utilitarian losses, social disapproval, and self-disapproval from failing to continue the present course of action and hence the greater the degree of stress.

3. *When decisional conflict is severe because each alternative poses a threat of serious risks, loss of hope about finding a better solution than the least objectionable one will lead to defensive avoidance of threat cues.*

Defensive avoidance is manifested by lack of vigilant search, selective inattention, selective forgetting, distortion of the meaning of warning messages, and construction of wishful rationalizations that minimize negative consequences. Among the cues that induce a decision maker to lose hope about finding a *better* solution are signs that little or no further information is available and that members of his most relevant reference group agree that one of the alternatives is preferable to all others.

4. *In a severe decisional conflict, when threat cues are salient and the decision maker anticipates having insufficient time to find an adequate means of escaping serious losses, his level of stress remains extremely high and the likelihood increases that his dominant pattern of response will be hypervigilance.*

The state of hypervigilance, which in its most extreme form is called panic, arises when time is short for escaping from oncoming threat. A person in this state experiences so much cognitive constriction and perseveration that his thought processes are disrupted. The person's immediate memory span is reduced and his thinking becomes more simplistic in that he cannot deal conceptually with as many categories as when he is in a less aroused state. Disaster studies indicate that panic is most likely to occur when people believe that the danger is great and the only available escape routes will soon be closed. Expecting that he will be helpless to avoid being victimized unless he acts quickly, the person in a state of hypervigilance fails to recognize all the alternatives open to him and fails to use whatever remaining time is available to evaluate adequately those alternatives of which he is aware. He is likely to search frantically for a solution, persevere in his thinking about a limited number of alternatives, and then latch onto a hastily contrived solution that seems to promise immediate relief, often at the cost of considerable postdecisional regret.

5. *A moderate degree of stress in response to a challenging threat induces a vigilant effort to scrutinize the alternative courses of action carefully and to work out a good solution, provided the decision maker expects to find a satisfactory way to resolve the decisional dilemma.*

When the decision maker experiences very little conflict, his level of stress will be so low that he will be unmotivated to give the decision much thought or to search for new information. In contrast, when conflict is induced by an actual setback or by a verbal warning of undesirable consequences, the decision maker becomes motivated to seek relevant information, to discuss the problem with others, and to think carefully about the alternatives in an effort to arrive at the best possible solution—provided that he is optimistic about having the resources to find a good solution and believes that there is sufficient time in which to look for it.

The five assumptions are expected to hold irrespective of the personality predispositions and habitual modes of coping that make a decision maker more or less emotionally responsive than his fellows. According to the last assumption, the decision maker becomes motivated to work out a good solution when a moderate degree of emotional stress is aroused by a decisional dilemma. A very low initial level of stress results in insufficient concern about the possibility of overlooking unfavorable consequences that might subsequently be regretted. At the other extreme, according to assumptions 3 and 4, very intense stress is likely to give rise to defensive avoidance or disruptive hypervigilance, which interferes with the cognitive processes essential for arriving at a viable solution. The optimal degree of stress would thus fall somewhere in the intermediate range between the two extremes. For convenience we use the term *moderate stress* to refer to this broad, intermediate range.

In general, we expect the best-quality decision-making performances, as assessed according to the seven criteria, under conditions where the decision maker's level of psychological stress is in the intermediate range throughout all the stages of decision making. To put it another way: extremely low stress and extremely high stress are likely to give rise to defective information processing, whereas intermediate levels of stress are more likely to be associated with vigilant information processing. These stress effects, of course, have to be evaluated against a baseline of the individual's usual level of information processing under conditions of little or no stress arousal, as when a person works on a problem just for the fun of it or makes a choice on a hypothetical issue that will have no particular consequences for him.

A Model of Emergency Decision Making

We take as our point of departure the five main assumptions just presented, which are fairly well supported by evidence from a variety of investigations on psychological stress. We shall now add a few supplementary assumptions based on field studies and experiments. These enable us to extend the analysis of decisional conflict by specifying the conditions that decrease the probability that a decision maker will meet the criteria for vigilant information processing, resulting in low-quality decision making that leads to postdecisional regret and failure to adhere to the commitment he makes. We regard the entire set of assumptions as forming a rudimentary theory of decisional conflict from which testable predictions can be made. (Evidence bearing on the predictions will be presented in later chapters.)

Five Coping Patterns

In the research cited earlier (p. 49) on human reactions to objective threats and to warnings urging protective action, we have discerned five basic patterns of coping behavior that affect the quality of decision making. One of the patterns—*vigilance*—results in thorough information search, unbiased assimilation of new information, and other characteristics of high-quality decision making as described in our account of vigilant information processing. The other four patterns are occasionally adaptive in saving time, effort, and emotional wear and tear, especially for routine or minor decisions that do not have serious consequences. But they often result in defective decision making when the decision maker is confronted with a vital choice that has serious consequences for himself, for his family, or for the organization on whose behalf he is making the decision. These four patterns are: (1) *unconflicted inertia*; (2) *unconflicted change* to a new course of action; (3) *defensive avoidance*; and (4) *hypervigilance*.

The conflict model, which is an elaboration of the five main assumptions, specifies the psychological conditions that mediate each of the five coping patterns. After describing the model, we shall discuss briefly the behavioral consequences of each of the five patterns, using illustrations drawn from research on consequential decisions. In later chapters, we shall illustrate how the model can be used to interpret data from psychological research in a way that generates fresh hypotheses concerning interacting variables that have hitherto been neglected by adherents of other theories dealing primarily with cold or lukewarm cognitive processes.

The initial data base for our model consists of research findings concerning typical reactions to emergency warnings about oncoming disasters that are matters of life or death, such as severe illness, radiation poisoning, earthquakes, tornadoes, floods, and air raids. Emergency decisions made in response to warnings about personal or community disasters have been extensively investigated by psychologists, psychiatrists, and sociologists. (For summaries of the literature see Appley and Trumbull, 1967; Baker and Chapman, 1962; Coelho, Hamburg, and Adams, 1974; Janis, 1951, 1958, 1971; Janis and Leventhal, 1965; Lazarus, 1966.)

Every disaster warning constitutes a powerful challenge to whatever business-as-usual activity the recipients of the warning are engaged in. Such a warning impels them toward a decision to take precautionary action, such as going to a medical clinic for inoculation, giving up smoking, undergoing surgery, using a basement shelter, or evacuating a threatened section of the city. Taking account of cognitive, emotional, and behavioral responses evoked by signs of serious threat, we are able to combine the five main propositions into a single model of decision making under conditions of stress. Obviously, emergency life-or-death decisions differ in many important ways from individual decisions about career, marriage, and personal welfare and from group decisions about economic or political policies, to all of which we intend to apply the model. Nevertheless, we make the working assumption that studies of the way people react to warnings of extreme danger illuminate the same fundamental processes of psychological stress that operate more subtly when decisional conflicts arise concerning consequential issues that generate milder degrees of stress. In this chapter—and throughout the rest of the book—we deal primarily with ambiguous threat situations, where the decision maker's perceptions and cognitions largely determine his actions.

Studies of personal as well as community disasters indicate that when people receive emergency warnings, they ask themselves a number of vital questions, the answers to which determine their choice of action (Arnold, 1960; Coelho, Hamburg, and Adams, 1974; Janis, 1974; Lazarus, 1966; Leventhal, 1975; Withey, 1962). As Withey points out, the cognitive appraisals of persons exposed to disaster warnings include estimates of (1) the probability that the dangerous event will materialize, (2) the severity of personal losses if it does materialize, and (3) the probable advantages and disadvantages of the alternative means available for averting or minimizing the danger. In short, people are capable of making emergency decisions on the basis of essentially the same types of cognitive judgments that they use when they make other consequential decisions.

In two main ways emergency decisions in the face of oncoming disaster differ from the usual decisions of everyday life. One is that there is much more at stake in emergency decisions—often the personal survival of the decision maker himself and of the people he values the most. A second important difference is in the amount of time available to make a choice before crucial options are lost. The time is generally much shorter for emergency decisions, sometimes only a few seconds. Because of the very high emotional arousal evoked by emergency warnings, the cognitive processes that enter into the making of emergency decisions are much hotter than those attending the more usual decisions of everyday life. Partly for this reason, we believe that we can see in extreme form in emergency decisions the ways in which psychological stress affects cognitive functioning. When cognitions are boiling hot, we can see more clearly how emotions influence judgment and action. When cognitions are not quite so hot, as in the case of ego-involving decisions that might affect a person's future career, the same types of effects can be expected to occur, although to a lesser degree.

The five coping patterns, based on the key assumptions about decisional stress, are shown in figure 2, which represents a conflict model of emergency decision making. The answers to the four basic questions given in the figure constitute the psychological conditions that mediate each of the five coping patterns. We propose to use this model of emergency decision making as the nucleus for developing a more general model applicable to the making of all consequential decisions.

A deliberate intellectual approach to the four basic questions might sometimes occur among military commanders, airline pilots, and others who are well trained to cope with anticipated disasters. But we assume that in most emergency situations the questions are not the subject of intellectual deliberation. Rather, they are frequently posed and answered on the basis of a very hasty surmise, sometimes limited to split-second perceptions of what is happening and what might happen. When a person notices danger and within a few seconds takes protective action, we assume that his apperceptions of the danger situation can be broken down into a very rapid series of cognitive responses that constitute answers to the four basic questions.

Embedded in figure 2 are the five key assumptions that constitute the core of our theoretical analysis.

1. When a person is confronted with a warning, the first basic question he puts to himself is "*Are the risks serious if I don't take protective action?*" The person's initial appraisals directed toward answering this question generally take account of the credibility of the communicator ("Does he really know what he is talking about?" "Is he telling the truth?"). If the

FIGURE 2. **A conflict-theory model showing basic patterns of emergency decision making evoked by warnings of impending danger.**

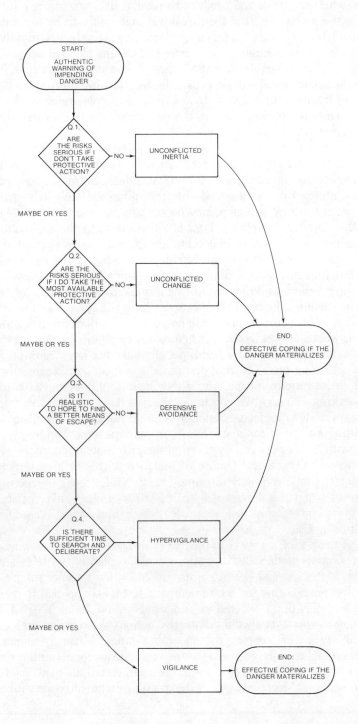

person takes the message seriously, he examines environmental signs that show whether or not the predicted threat is likely to affect him. If he judges the probability that the threat will materialize to be so small as to be negligible ("It won't happen here") or if he judges the magnitude of the danger to be low enough to be tolerated ("Nothing bad will happen to me or mine"), his answer to the first question will be *no*. In that event, little or no emotional arousal will be evoked by the warning (assumption no. 1). He will complacently decide to continue doing whatever he has been doing, ignoring the warning and the accompanying recommendations to take protective action.

Sometimes, of course, a negative appraisal is quite realistic and justified, as when people fail to take seriously the dire warnings issued by overexcited rumormongers, scare propagandists, or unscrupulous advertisers. But negative appraisals of official warnings are likely to be maladaptive, as in the case of emergency flood warnings issued by the National Weather Service, which are typically disregarded if the population has been aware of the buildup of flood waters gradually over a period of many days. Studies that compare public reactions to floods and other disasters that build up slowly with those evoked by tornadoes and other disasters that have a more rapid onset indicate a marked difference in responsiveness to warnings (Fritz and Marks, 1954; Janis, 1968). Authoritative warnings given just before a nonprecipitant disaster strikes are frequently ignored, whereas those given just before a precipitant type of disaster are not. When warned about a flood, people make the false assumption that there are no serious risks from doing nothing at present because they will have ample time to escape later if they wait until flooding starts in their neighborhood. Then, when a long-expected flood reaches their vicinity, those formerly complacent residents who do not drown are likely to end up sitting on a roof for many hours, or perhaps days, awaiting a rescue boat, with ample opportunity to regret their decision to ignore the evacuation orders. The central feature of the early stages of a nonprecipitant disaster is that the initial warnings, being somewhat ambiguous as to where or when the danger will strike, fail to arouse sufficient stress to evoke vigilant search and appraisal, which makes for a complacent, "business-as-usual" response.

2. If the person's answer to the first basic question is *yes* or *maybe*, he will become emotionally aroused, and will vigilantly begin seeking for escape routes. Arnold (1970) points out that when we encounter a situation that poses a threat, "we remember what has happened to us in the past, how this thing affected us and what we did about it" (p. 174). In addition to whatever specific protective actions are recalled, at least one feasible means of escaping the oncoming danger is usually salient, as a result of public announcements in the mass media concerning the orders issued by the authorities or informal recommendations made by friends and neighbors. Moreover, prior social training on how to cope with poten-

tial disasters, such as fire drills in schools and factories, makes it likely that specific escape routes will spontaneously come to mind when a familiar type of disaster is impending. If the impending disaster is of an unfamiliar nature, the person is likely to generate alternatives by searching his memory in an effort to remember similar threats encountered by himself or others in the past and what was done to avoid being victimized.

As soon as the person begins to think about the possibility of adopting any form of protective action, he asks himself the second basic question: *"Are the risks serious if I take this particular protective action?"* The appraisals made in answering this question concern the expected effectiveness of the protective action ("Will I still be in danger even if I do it?") and the losses and risks entailed by executing the protective action ("Will I suffer if I do it?"). If the person's answer to the second basic question is a confident *no*, his state of arousal will subside and he will promptly start to carry out the protective action in an unconflicted way.

Public health warnings to air travelers about the danger of contracting typhoid fever, typhus, or cholera in foreign countries frequently evoke this type of unconflicted action. Even when inoculations are not required by immigration authorities, many travelers choose without hesitation to obtain them if they regard them as providing adequate protection and are not concerned about the risks or costs of discomfort and untoward side effects. Similarly, clerks and customers watching a fire in a next-door office building will comply without hesitation when warned by firemen to evacuate their building because the flames might spread. The only exceptions would be those employees who had previously accepted the assigned duty of guarding the merchandise, since they would be deterred from leaving by the threat of social censure for failing to carry out their prior commitment and would therefore hesitate and remain in a state of relatively high stress (assumption, no. 2).

3. If the person's answer to the second basic question is *yes* or *maybe* for each protective action he contemplates, the person's aroused emotional state will not subside and may become more intense. He will become preoccupied with finding a better means of escape than the risky routes being advocated. In order to continue the search, the person must maintain the hope of finding a better escape route (assumption no. 3). We postulate that as soon as a person gives a *yes* answer to the first two basic questions, he asks himself the third basic question, *"Is it realistic to hope to find a better means of escape?"* The answer to this question generally depends upon the person's appraisal of external social resources (for example, "Is there anyone who can give me good advice?"). His answer may also depend on his assessment of his own internal resources (for example, "Am I smart enough to work out a good escape plan?").

If his answer to the third basic question is a definite *no*, the person will pessimistically give up searching for a better solution, despite being dissatisfied with the options open to him. Instead of vigilant search and appraisal, his dominant mode of coping with the emergency will be to avoid cues that stimulate anxiety or other painful feelings. This *defensive avoidance* pattern can take a number of different forms. One involves a defensive lack of interest in the problems posed by the emergency: the person becomes selectively inattentive to threat cues and avoids thinking about the oncoming danger by distracting himself with other activities, taking alcohol or other drugs, developing fatalistic beliefs that support a precariously optimistic outlook. This *evasive* form of defensive avoidance is likely to occur in situations of imminent threat only when no escape route is perceived as offering any better chance of survival than doing nothing at all, as in the case of infantrymen pinned down in front-line positions during prolonged periods of heavy artillery bombardment. These are the circumstances that make for the well-known adage "There are no atheists in foxholes." Extreme examples of this form of defensive avoidance have been observed among military personnel who have spent many months in combat. For example, when they lose hope of being removed from the front lines after witnessing the death of many buddies, seasoned infantrymen who are "old" in combat experience develop a set of symptoms known as the "old sergeant syndrome" (see Janis, 1971, pp. 183–84). They decide not to take cover during artillery attacks and ignore other elementary safety precautions, having become fatalistic or apathetic about the dangers of combat.

Closely related to the evasive form of defensive avoidance is buck passing, depending upon someone else to make the decision, which often occurs in response to disaster warnings when the individual is carrying out an assigned role in an organization in which responsibility for making emergency decisions can be shunted up or down the hierarchy. The person may rationalize that others know better than he how to make the right choice or that the problem is in someone else's bailiwick. When the decision involves dealing with one's own illness or other personal dangers, buck passing may take the form of relying on outside agents of dubious reputation who promise a less painful solution than the genuine experts, who insist that the person himself must take responsibility.

Another form of defensive avoidance consists of ignoring the available information about the defects of the least objectionable escape route and developing rationalizations that argue against evidence of its potentially unsafe features. This bolstering form of defensive avoidance is likely to occur only when the person is under pressure to commit himself to a course of action and has no hope of finding any better way out. Typical examples of bolstering are to be found among certain types of cancer victims (Cobb et al., 1954; Weinstein and Kahn, 1955). Many of them ask no questions and selectively misperceive what their physicians are saying about the unpleasant and potentially dangerous consequences of the recommended radiation treatment or radical surgery. They also develop rationalizations to convince themselves that after the treatment their worries will be over.

4. If the endangered person's answer to the third basic question is *yes* or *maybe*, vigilance tendencies will remain dominant over defensive avoidance tendencies. A crucial determinant of the person's coping pattern is his answer to the fourth basic question: "*Is there sufficient time to make a careful search for and evaluation of information and advice?*" If he can see that real danger is rapidly approaching, or if he has been given authoritative information that the deadline for choosing an escape route before it is too late is almost at hand, his answer will be a definitive *no*. Realizing that it is essential to find a reasonably safe escape route and expecting that a satisfactory one can be found, the endangered but hopeful person becomes more emotionally excited and more vigilant than ever as soon as he realizes that he is confronted with an imminent deadline (assumption no. 4).

Hypervigilance is typically evoked in disasters when people fear imminent entrapment because they can see that they have very little time left in which to find a safe way out. The most extreme form of hypervigilance, popularly referred to as panic, occurs, for example, when people are confronted by a rapidly approaching fire, realize that it is possible to escape, but can see that the escape routes are rapidly being closed off (Committee on Disaster Studies, 1955; Foreman, 1964; Quarantelli, 1954). Although each victim believes that a satisfactory escape route may be available (the answer to the third basic question being *yes* or *maybe*), he surmises that time is too short to make a thorough search for the safest way to avoid entrapment. He makes a quick survey of the situation and a snap judgment about the best thing to do, often being unduly influenced by what the people around him are trying to do. In an acute state of hypervigilance, he fails to use whatever time he has to try to find the safest exit, which requires taking account of many complexities, such as whether the number of people around is so large that their convergence on one exit will create a blockage. He gravitates toward simple-minded decision rules such as "Do whatever the others around you are doing." He is likely to fail to notice the obvious defects of the escape route he chooses and the detours that might lead to a much safer exit.

Evidence from disaster research indicates that when people are warned about oncoming danger that will materialize within a very short time interval, their fear mounts to such a high level and they act so inappropriately that they would be better off with no warning at all. Fritz and Mark (1954) present data from a study of community reactions to a tornado showing an association between last-minute warnings and maladaptive behavior. The data indicate that the incidence of death and severe injury was extraordinarily high in those families who were forewarned less than one minute before the tornado hit the town, as compared with families with longer forewarning time and those with no forewarning at all. Although recognizing that a number of extraneous factors might influence these correlational results, the authors tentatively conclude that "people who had only brief forewarning took action with a protective *intent*, but . . . the actions taken may have actually increased their danger or they may have been caught unprotected during the process of taking [inappropriate] protective action" (Fritz and Marks, 1954, p. 38). The people who received a forewarning less than one minute before the danger impact presumably became so hypervigilant that they exercised poor judgment and acted in an inefficient manner, which increased their chances of becoming casualties.

A certain minimum amount of time may be required for working out an effective plan of escape in the face of oncoming disaster. But if this were the main factor operating, we would expect the casualty rate among families that had a brief forewarning time to be essentially the same (if not slightly lower) than the casualty rate among those that had no forewarning at all, both groups having been deprived of sufficient time to make emergency plans. The findings show that those with brief forewarning do much worse than those with no forewarning. This result is consistent with the hypothesis that perceived lack of time for finding a safe means of escape from oncoming threat gives rise to hypervigilance, which makes for poor judgment and inefficient action. Such reactions are probably accompanied by mounting feelings of helplessness to avert catastropic losses under conditions where the threat is perceived to be both severe and imminent. Feelings of helplessness and the accompanying reactions of hypervigilance are also likely to increase when external circumstances of imminent threat impose sensory deprivation (e.g., total darkness), restriction of activity, or lack of contact with supportive persons (Janis, 1962, 1971).

Kelley and his coworkers (1965) have investigated reactions to imminent entrapment in a laboratory situation in which male and female students were confronted with the threat of painful electric shocks, which aroused clear-cut symptoms of fear. The students were told that only a very limited amount of time was available for the entire group to escape and that it was necessary to escape one at a time, by making certain specific responses (involving pushing certain "escape" buttons) which they had the opportunity to execute at whatever moment they decided was the right one for taking action. The experimenter also explained how they could judge accurately when the exit was not being used by someone else, so that each subject could choose the best time to escape without jamming the exit. In the threatened group, a relatively small percentage of the frightened subjects made an appropriate decision that enabled them to escape successfully within the time limit. The results indicate that the greater the perceived danger and the higher the level of fear in a situation of potential entrapment with a very short deadline, the smaller the percentage of persons who make full use of the available information and choose an effective course of action.

Another laboratory experiment using the threat of painful electric shock bears out the assumption that the more imminent the threat is perceived to be, the higher the level of stress (Monat, Averill, and Lazarus, 1972). Male college students were separated into four groups differing in degree of uncertainty induced as to when or whether a painful shock would occur; physiological measures of stress were obtained, along with systematic self-reports of affective arousal and cognitions. The findings indicate that

> under conditions in which the person knows exactly when the aversive event is to occur, and regardless of how certain or uncertain he is about whether it will occur, his thoughts turn increasingly toward vigilant examination of the anticipated event as it grows imminent; and this increased vigilance is accompanied by an increase in arousal. In contrast, under conditions in which the person does not know when the event is to occur, that is, temporal uncertainty, the person's thoughts tend increasingly toward avoidant-like modes of coping, and these coping strategies in turn lead to progressively lowered levels of affective arousal" [Monat et al., 1972, p. 250].

The disruptive effects of a high level of stress in circumstances requiring immediate protective activity are illustrated by the thoughtless action taken by a law enforcement agent during the race riot in Detroit in 1967, as described in the Report of the National Advisory Commission on Civil Disorders (1968, p. 98). A white National Guardsman believed that his own life was in immediate danger from snipers when he heard shots nearby after having been summoned by a nightwatchman to investigate looting. Instead of taking cover and watching to see what was going on, he promptly decided to shoot to kill when he caught sight of a black man holding a pistol. The victim turned out to be the nightwatchman, who had shot his pistol into the air to scare off the looters.

When a person is in a hypervigilant state, errors in judgment occur partly because of the marked lowering of efficiency in cognitive functioning that accompanies extremely high emotional arousal (Beier, 1951; Berkun et al., 1962; Easterbrook, 1959; Hamilton, 1975; Osler, 1954; Sarason, 1975). As Easterbrook (1959) has pointed out, high emotional arousal is most disruptive of performances on the "most demanding" cognitive tasks, those requiring the utilization of the largest number of cues. Consequently, we would expect to find that when a decision maker faces a highly conflictful dilemma involving a threat of serious losses and a very short deadline for making a choice, the quality of his thinking will be poorest of all on multivalued decisions (those that require evaluating the consequences of alternative courses of action in terms of a large set of values, not just in terms of one or two objectives). In an international crisis, which Hermann (1969) defines as an "unanticipated situation of severe threat and short decision time," national policy makers are likely to display a narrowing of time perspective along with other characteristic symptoms of cognitive constriction under high stress. Holsti's (1972) content analysis of historic policy-making documents written by major heads of state in Europe during the crisis that led to the outbreak of the first world war revealed a relatively constricted time perspective, focused almost entirely on immediate threats. Only a narrow subset of the available alternatives was considered, and little attention was given to the long-range consequences of those alternatives.

5. If the person's answer to the fourth basic question is *yes* or *maybe*, his vigilance persists in a much less excited form. Vigilance will be the dominant pattern so long as the endangered person maintains hope of being able to escape intact and continues to believe that he has sufficient time to find a safe way out (assumption no. 5). This pattern is characterized by careful search and appraisal, as specified by the seven criteria of vigilant information processing. This high-quality type of decision making is well exemplified by the way most well-trained pilots respond to an emergency warning during flight, such as a signal indicating a jammed landing gear that could cause the plane to crash on landing. The self-confident pilot, having been through repeated emergency training exercises, makes a rapid but thorough assessment of the information at hand within the aircraft, consults with technicians in the control tower of the airport, canvasses and evaluates carefully the alternative courses of action open to him, and works out a new set of contingency plans before deciding what to do. Sometimes this search and appraisal is done very rapidly, within a matter of minutes. But whether the ordeal goes on for a short or long time, the pilot's attitude is generally one of high confidence in working out a solution to the problem, as long as he maintains strong hope of finding a way to avert the threatened crash and believes that he has sufficient time to do so. It should be noted that the vigilant pilot's high confidence pertains solely to *finding a satisfactory solution*, and does not pertain to his level of confidence about whatever risky course of action he is contemplating. Relatively *low* confidence about the least objectionable alternative currently being considered combined with *high* confidence about finding a more satisfactory alternative are two of the essential conditions for vigilant information processing.

As figure 2 indicates, the conflict-theory model specifies four conditions as prerequisites for the pattern of vigilance:

1. awareness of serious threat if no protective action is taken (i.e., low confidence in the prior course of action or inaction);
2. awareness of serious risks if the most salient protective action is taken (i.e., low confidence in whatever new course of action is being considered);
3. moderate or high degree of hope that a search for information and advice will lead to a better (i.e., less risky) escape route (i.e., high confidence that a satisfactory solution exists and can be discovered);
4. belief that there is sufficient time to search and deliberate before any serious threat will materialize (i.e., high confidence that the as yet undiscovered satisfactory solution cᵃn be found within the time available).

Each of these conditions can be fostered by appropriate informational inputs and other situational variables, such as exposure to prior training in simulated emergencies similar to the current one. Whenever all four conditions are present, the person is most likely to meet the criteria for vigilant information processing.

The first two of the four conditions make for arousal of decisional conflict—the person wants to avoid expected losses by taking whatever protective action is available but at the same time does not want to take the most salient course available; he is deterred by the realization that the new course of action could result in other potential losses that he also wants to avoid. In this state of conflict, he becomes vigilant and seeks a better means of escape than the one he has just been contemplating. He will mobilize his cognitive resources, scanning his memory intensively for previously acquired information about how to cope with the threat. He will also examine and appraise any external sign or verbal communication from others that offers the promise of helping him to find a more satisfactory escape route. His vigilant state mobilizes him to initiate social contacts, seeking advice and information from anyone he regards as potentially knowledgeable. (See Festinger, 1954; Janis, 1971; Jones and Gerard, 1967; Schachter, 1959.)

The third condition takes account of observations concerning the importance of *hope* as a crucial determinant of the quality and duration of vigilant behavior (Farber, 1968; Forman, 1963; Frank, 1968; Korner, 1970; Lazarus, 1966; Stotland, 1969). In order to continue to search for a safe means of warding off or escaping the danger, the person must maintain the belief that the chances are good that a better escape route exists than the risky ones he is reluctant to adopt, and that helpful information can be obtained if he continues to seek it.

The fourth condition pertains to the decision maker's belief that there is sufficient *time* to find the safest way out. Unlike a person in a paniclike (hypervigilant) state, a person in a vigilant state does not make snap judgments about the best thing to do, or become unduly influenced by what the people around him are trying to do. Rather, he uses whatever time he has to look for and evaluate potential escape routes. He notices obvious defects in the escape routes he is examining and does not overlook more complicated detours that might lead to a much safer way out. Thus, the person in a state of vigilance does not suffer from the cognitive constriction, perseveration, and errors of judgment that occur when one becomes temporarily hypervigilant.

We do not assume that the *only* causes of hypervigilance or of defensive avoidance are the conditions described in our model. Other conditions—such as taking certain drugs, witnessing a horrifying automobile accident, or becoming aware of one's own state of high physiological arousal—can also evoke hypervigilance or defensive avoidance. An experiment by Krisher, Darley, and Darley (1973) showed that young adults were much more likely to become fearful and then to display symptoms of defensive avoidance in response to a fear-arousing warning about the need for vaccination against mumps if they were made aware of their own allegedly fast heartbeats by being given false EKG auditory feedback than if they were given the same warning without the false autonomic feedback.

Adaptive and Maladaptive Behavior

When warnings of oncoming danger come from trustworthy authorities, such as public health experts, the behavior resulting from the first four patterns of emergency decision making shown in figure 2 generally can be characterized as "defective" or "maladaptive" in the sense that the person exposes himself to unnecessary damage or does not survive because he fails to discover the best means for escaping from danger, whereas he might have had a good chance of surviving unharmed if he had engaged in more careful search and appraisal. Of course, in certain circumstances, any of the four "defective" patterns can turn out to be a quite successful way of dealing with the crisis. For example, people in Panama City, Florida, were given a hurricane warning urging them to evacuate, but it turned out to be a false alarm because the storm unpredictably changed its direction. Those who displayed the pattern of unconflicted inertia simply kept on with business as usual and ignored the warning. It turned out that they saved themselves a great deal of trouble by not evacuating in the middle of the night. Paradoxically, however, many of the people who did not leave their homes said, when interviewed a few days later, that they felt they had made a bad mistake even though the warning proved to be a false alarm. They learned from news reports that the hurricane had caused enormous destruction to a town that was in its path and came to realize the enormous damage they could have suffered if it had not unexpectedly changed its course (Killian, 1952).

In general, the pattern of unconflicted inertia is likely to have positive value only when warnings turn out to be false alarms or pertain to improbable dangers not worth the time and effort to do anything about. Similarly, unconflicted change can sometimes be adaptive but often prove to be maladaptive, especially in those emergencies where the danger is a novel one and the authorities' recommendations are vague or based on guesswork. Defensive avoidance, which results in ignoring unpleasant information about threats, may sometimes help a person to avoid becoming completely demoralized or suicidal during long periods of deprivation or illness; but it generally reduces the chances of averting serious losses at times when protective action is essential. Hypervigilance facilitates taking drastic action that a person might refuse to consider in a less aroused state, but it rarely facilitates successful escape. Most often it leads to maladaptive actions, as in the notorious panic reactions that occur during fires. A person in a burning apartment house, for example, who realizes that within a few minutes his floor will be engulfed in flames may rush frantically into an unsafe elevator when it would have taken only a fraction of a minute to discover a nearby staircase that would be a safe escape route.

The pattern of vigilance, on the other hand, generally leads to adaptive choices—though not under all circumstances. When all escape routes are extremely risky and are closing off rapidly, a person's impetuous choice in a state of hypervigilance may give him a better chance of survival than remaining in a more controlled state of vigilance, which makes for delay in taking action. In such a case, the person's expectations of finding a safer escape route in the limited time available might soon prove to be fatally wrong, and hence vigilant search for and appraisal of alternatives could be an inappropriate reaction to the danger of immediate entrapment. But in most other circumstances of impending disaster, when the danger is not immediately imminent, the pattern of vigilance is likely to lead to effective emergency action with a much better chance of a successful outcome than hypervigilance or any of the other patterns.

Rapid Answers to the Basic Questions

When a person responds to a warning of danger and takes protective action within a few seconds, we assume, as we have remarked, that his apperceptions of the danger situation can be broken down into a very rapid series of cognitive responses that constitute answers to the four basic questions. They may not necessarily occur, of course, in the sequence shown in figure 2. Some or all of the questions and answers might occur in the form of visual images, rather than in verbal form. For example, if a person suddenly sees a blazing fire in his fifth-floor apartment, he may visualize himself trapped in the elevator with the power shut off and then see himself, in a brief fantasy, emerging safely onto the sidewalk outside the door at the bottom of the staircase. The speed of these hot cognitive processes should not be surprising in the light of evidence from the psychology of perception, indicating that similar questions can be answered in the fraction of a second that it takes to arrive at a perceptual judgment about a visual signal (Garner, 1972; Neisser, 1967).

Rapid questions and answers may also occur when a person *denies* a threat despite clear and present danger signals. Consider, for example, the toxicological disaster that occurred in Atlanta in 1951 (Powell, 1953, pp. 87–103). Hundreds of lower-class blacks unknowingly poisoned themselves by drinking methyl alcohol (methanol) and developed symptoms of illness, including feelings of nausea, weakness, and impaired vision. Some of the men and women rushed to a hospital in a hypervigilant state; others ignored the symptoms even to the point where after becoming half-blind they denied that there was anything wrong with their eyesight.

In terms of the conflict model, we assume that every physical symptom a person notices in himself constitutes a warning signal. The person asks himself if the symptom (or combination of symptoms) means that he is in a dangerous condition and in need of help. In the present example, if his initial answer concerning the very first, mild symptom of nausea is *no*, he goes on with business as usual. But if his symptoms become worse, the stricken person would give a positive response to the first question and would immediately start to think about what protective action he should take—for example, phoning a doctor, going to the emergency room of a hospital, or telling a relative about the worrisome symptoms. As he contemplates such protective actions, the images conjured up in his mind might involve very grave threats, such as being subjected to frightening, painful medical procedures, being humiliated and mistreated as a black person in a southern white hospital, and other extremely high costs.

In this momentary state of conflict, the person would ask himself whether he could hope to find a better way to escape the dilemma than just waiting for the symptoms to go away. A negative response would lead to a defensive avoidance pattern, including distracting himself and developing rationalizations to explain away his unusual illness. One Atlanta woman developed acute symptoms of poisoning shortly after having been told about the poisonous whiskey, but, even while trying to help two other stricken victims in her household, she dismissed her own illness as merely a typical stomach upset and decided to take a home remedy for it. She continued to deny the danger until she became, as she put it, "blind as a bat," which suddenly made her feel "scared to death." Speaking about the period of denial, she said, "I think if I would've ever thought that it could've happened to me, I would've had a heart attack."

After a short time, a stricken person's defensive avoidance pattern might abruptly change to hypervigilance if he encounters a new, dramatic danger signal—for example, if a relative tells him that his illness could be terribly serious because others in the neighborhood are going blind from having drunk methyl alcohol and that time is running out because the victims die unless they get help from a doctor immediately. Later on, we shall present some evidence indicating that when a decision to do nothing at all about a threat is based on the pattern of defensive avoidance, the decision maker is extremely vulnerable to new signs of threat and is likely to respond in an ineffective way.

In contrast to those who displayed a pattern of defensive avoidance, others, according to Powell's account of the methanol disaster, became very frightened and displayed reactions of hypervigilance as soon as they noticed the first mild symptom in themselves, such as a headache. Of the 433 persons who came to the emergency clinic of Emory University's Grady Hospital, only 40 percent proved to be genuine casualties (Powell, 1953, p. 91). Most of the people seen at the hospital, having heard that people in their community were dying from poisonous whiskey, had misconstrued their own minor symptoms as being a highly dangerous sign of their having been poisoned. Many rushed in a paniclike state to the hospital's emergency room to get medical attention before it was too late for the doctors to save their lives. In some instances, this hypervigilant reaction had adaptive value, in that the person had indeed imbibed methyl alcohol and could be treated in time to cure him. But in many other cases, the panicky person had not imbibed poisonous alcohol. Some had drunk no alcohol at all. Nevertheless, having heard that others in the neighborhood who had similar mild symptoms soon went blind or died if they were not rushed to the hospital, these people felt—perhaps because they heard so many confused reports and rumors that they were not sure what was causing the epidemic—that if they did not get help quickly they would meet the same fate. We assume that they gave positive responses to the first three basic questions and a negative response to the fourth one, just before dashing off to the hospital. The net effect of large numbers of people reacting this way was to overload the emergency medical facilities. One of the contributing factors to the high incidence of hypervigilance in the community was social contagion: rumors become rife when people witness horrifying casualties, which demonstrate how serious the danger might be and how rapidly victims succumb.

Our discussion of the Atlanta toxicological disaster highlights the point made earlier, that the four basic questions are not conceptualized by us as necessarily involving the sort of analytical approach that we see in some meticulous people who are inclined to make their decisions in a deliberate, organized manner. On the contrary, we assume that the apperceptions and images involved in raising and answering the four basic questions can occur in a matter of seconds, mediating a rapid change from business as usual to energetic protective or defensive action in response to a sudden emergency.

Extending the Model to All Consequential Choices

The foregoing analysis of emergency decision making in terms of the decision maker's answers to four basic questions provides a basis for integrating many disparate findings from psychological studies on the effects of warnings and confrontations with danger signs. We have already described some research findings from the field of psychological stress that can be readily accounted for in terms of the model. We shall continue to draw upon other findings, particularly from studies on the effects of public health warnings, when we describe the conditions under which answers to each of the four basic questions will tend to be affirmative or negative. But, as stated earlier, we do not intend to restrict the application of this model to emergency decisions made under conditions of disaster warnings. In line with our approach to decision making in terms of stress dynamics, we propose to use essentially the same model as a *general* model to apply to the analysis of all consequential choices.

In extending the emergency decision-making model to other decisions, we must be prepared to take some huge conceptual leaps. Consider, for example, a policy-making executive, sitting on a board of directors, who is trying to decide whether to vote in favor of his company's meeting the demands of a labor union that is threatening a strike. Or consider an assistant professor of chemistry who is trying to decide whether to take advantage of an opportunity to switch his specialty to research in immunobiology by accepting a two-year postdoctoral training grant in that field, with a stipend much less than his current salary. These decision makers worry about outcomes that are very remote from the emergency, life-and-death issues on which the model is based. Nevertheless, they are likely to be deeply concerned, and they might even lose some sleep as a result of anxiety about the possibility of losing money, status, the esteem of close friends, and perhaps even their self-esteem. A conceptual leap is required when we assume that the psychological stress generated by a managerial decision or personal career choice has essentially the same consequences for decision-making processes as that generated by the threat of disasters imperiling physical survival.

A similar conceptual leap is required in applying the model to political decisions, such as domestic- and foreign-policy decisions made by government leaders, and to other types of work-task and personal decisions, such as those involving professional ethics, marriage, health, or life style. We assume that essentially the same hot cognitive processes come into play in the course of all fundamental decisions. We also assume that the same five patterns of dealing with the challenge are in the repertoire of every decision maker, that the use of one rather than another pattern is determined by the same psychological conditions, and that each pattern leads to the predicted set of behavioral consequences. In short, our main working assumption is that the model will apply to any decision maker facing uncertainty and risk.

We are prepared to push to the limit the analogy between the risks of not surviving a disaster and those present in all other types of consequential decisions, whether they entail threats to the decision maker's personal welfare or to the welfare of the organization on whose behalf a new policy is being chosen. So far as we can see in light of the data accumulated so far, it is worthwhile to do so because some accurate predictions can be made about whether the decision maker will display a vigilant approach or one or another of the four deviations from that ideal pattern that make for defective decision making. In later chapters, when we examine evidence from social psychological research, we shall show how the model has led us to test specific predictions that do not follow directly from any other theory. The model also enables us to raise provocative questions about the influence of hitherto neglected variables when we examine data from prior studies of decision making—questions that can be settled by further systematic research.

We must emphasize, however, that the model applies only to decisions that have real consequences for the decision maker and thereby generate some discernible manifestations of psychological stress. Hence, the model is not necessarily applicable to the simulated or hypothetical decisions so often investigated in the laboratory—research that may be valuable for elucidating cold cognitive processes but that seldom applies to the hot ones generated by consequential decisions. One of the implications of our assumptions is that when a person is required to make a choice entailing potentially unfavorable consequences for himself or for significant others, his information-processing behavior will change markedly from that displayed when he is required to make essentially the same judgment on a purely hypothetical basis. Recent experimental research on role playing and forced compliance, self-attributions, perceptual judgments, halo effects, and postdecisional reevaluation of alternatives has converged with regard to the importance of *consequentiality* as a determinant of the psychological reactions evoked by the judgmental tasks imposed on subjects in the laboratory. The results from all these different types of investigations show that when people are confronted with a consequential choice, they often react in an entirely different way than when they are confronted with the same cognitive problem as a purely hypothetical issue or as an intellectual exercise (Cooper, 1971; Collins and Hoyt, 1972; Deutsch, Krauss, and Rosenau, 1962; Gerard, Blevans, and Malcolm, 1964; Nel, Helmreich, and Aronson, 1969; O'Neal, 1974; Singer and Kornfield, 1973; Taylor, 1975).[3]

"Consequential" decisions include those that evoke some degree of concern or anxiety in the decision maker about the possibility that he may not gain the objectives he is seeking or that he may become saddled with costs that are higher than he can afford, either for himself personally or for a group or organization with which he is affiliated. Among the possible costs of a decision are failures to obtain gains that might otherwise be obtainable if a better course of action were chosen, which are referred to as "opportunity costs" (Miller and Starr, 1967). Also included are uncertain risks as well as known costs with regard to money, time, effort, emotional involvement, reputation, morale, or any other resource at the disposal of the decision maker or his organization. These risks or potential losses are perceived as threats to important utilitarian, social, or ethical goals within the decision maker's value system.

Reformulations

Figure 3 is a modification of figure 2, the initial chart that represents our conflict model of emergency decision making. In order to extend the model for emergency decisions to all consequential decisions, it is neces-

FIGURE 3.   **A conflict-theory model of decision making applicable to all consequential decisions.**

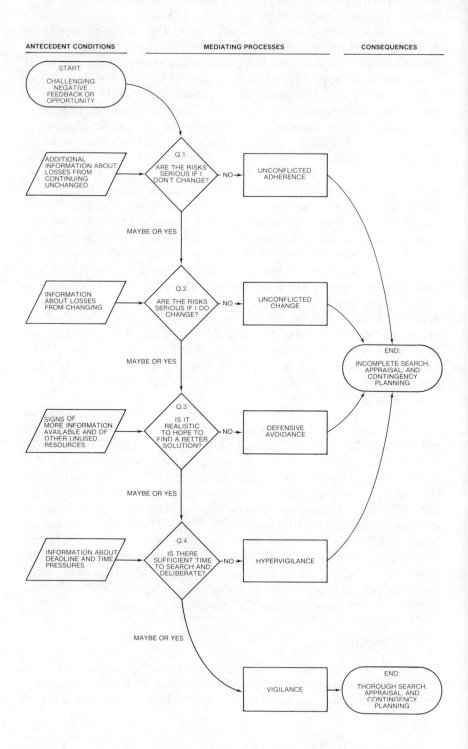

sary to replace two of the key terms that appear in the crucial questions shown in figure 2. The phrase *take protective action* in questions 1 and 2 is replaced in figure 3 by *change* (meaning "change to a new course of action"). The latter term denotes adopting any new action or policy that the person had not previously carried out, which could range from relatively simple acts (such as initiating an acquaintanceship by making a friendly telephone call) to highly formal, contractual obligations (such as getting married, accepting a high-level executive position in a large corporation, or signing an international agreement as chief executive of a national government). Humorists sometimes view taking on such awesome obligations as equivalent to being confronted with an oncoming disaster. We are obliged to go along with them in a very sober way. We assume that the decision to take protective action in the face of danger represents in extreme form a prototype of the stress situation that confronts a decision maker whenever he encounters a challenge that represents a threat to any of his values or an opportunity to attain an unfulfilled goal that requires changing to a new course of action whose outcome is uncertain.

The second key term to be replaced (in question 3 of figure 2) is *means of escape*. The equivalent of escaping from danger following a disaster warning is solving the problem of averting the risks attendant to making a decision. We use the phrase *better solution* in figure 3 to refer to a course of action that is perceived by the decision maker as having a more satisfactory outcome than the risky ones he has been considering, which holds forth the promise of enabling him to attain his main objectives.

Antecedent Conditions

The mediating processes specified by the model, which consist of the person's answers to the four basic questions, are anchored in observable antecedent conditions. The left-hand column of figure 3 shows the types of antecedent communication variables that influence those mediating processes. Communication variables are given prominence (rather than other situational or predispositional determinants) because much of our analysis of decision making focuses directly on the influence of warnings, reassurances, and other relevant information presented to the decision maker by the mass media, private counselors, representatives of reference groups, and other communicators. But it should be recognized that many other situational factors also function as antecedent conditions. For example, the likelihood of hypervigilance as a response to a sudden financial crisis is increased if the person has recently been exposed to a similar crisis in which his failure to take prompt action was followed by drastic financial losses and social humiliation. Other antecedent conditions, including personality variables and other predispositional characteristics of the decision maker, also determine sensitivity to warnings (see Elms, 1972, 1976; Janis, 1974). All of these factors are likely to affect the decision maker's readiness to give positive or negative answers to the four basic questions. But knowledge about various antecedent conditions is still very primitive. We believe that by focusing on the structures presented in figure 3, productive research on the antecedent conditions of each of the five patterns of decision-making behavior will be stimulated.

What is unique about the model is the specification of conditions relating to conflict, hope, and time pressure that mediate distinctive decisional coping patterns. Our claim is that the five coping patterns are linked dependably with the conditions we have specified, a claim that has testable implications about environmental circumstances that generate vigilance and about deliberate interventions that could counteract the beliefs and perceptions responsible for defective coping patterns.

Just as in the case of emergency decisions, the decision-making sequence shown in figure 3 starts with signs of threat indicating that serious losses (or failure to obtain desirable gains) will result if the person adheres to his present course of action or inaction. The threat (or opportunity) may be conveyed by direct verbal statements (such as being told by the boss that one will not be promoted if one doesn't become more productive) or by indirect signs or events (such as not being asked by the boss to attend an important policy-making meeting). According to the model, a person's initial response to any such challenge is to pose to himself the first basic question concerning the risks of not changing. A confident negative response might promptly come to mind if he recalls having received solid inside information that the boss is himself about to be fired for making exhorbitant demands on his underlings. In such a case, the person will be quite indifferent to the boss's threats and will not bother to contemplate any alternative to his present course of action; rather, he will complacently continue adhering to it. But if his answer to the first basic question is *maybe* or *yes*, he will think about some new course of action that strikes him as a viable way to handle the challenge—such as putting in more hours of work each day or volunteering to take on more tasks. He will then consider question 2, concerning the risks of changing to that new policy. If his answer to question 2 is a firm *no*, he will immediately decide to adopt that solution and proceed to commit himself to it without giving the matter any further thought. If his answer is *maybe* or *yes*, perhaps as a result of his realizing that extra work might be excessively fatiguing and disruptive of his family life, he will begin thinking about other alternatives, such as looking for a new job. If none of the alternatives evokes a confident negative response to the second basic question about the risks of changing, he will be in a state of high decisional conflict, wanting to change in order to avoid the serious risk of not being promoted, but at the same time not wanting to change in order to avoid the costs and risks of any new course of action.

In this context, the first general assumption about stress dynamics, discussed earlier in this chapter, is applicable. If the challenging communication or event does not generate any anticipation of loss—in the sphere of utilitarian values, social approval, or self-approval—no stress is generated and the person does not become sufficiently vigilant to contemplate changing or to inquire into the matter any further. The more important the needs that are threatened to be unfulfilled, the greater the stress and the greater the likelihood that the person will be motivated to try to find a new course of action superior to the apparently defective old one.

Unconflicted change is often the dominant pattern when an executive adopts a very crude satisficing strategy. Once an executive realizes that there is something wrong about his current policy he focuses on a salient alternative that differs only slightly from the policy to which he is committed, which he believes will patch up the defect. Seeing nothing grossly wrong with it if the other powerful persons in the organization say it is satisfactory, he promptly adopts it. Thus, the pattern of unconflicted change is likely to be the one that mediates "incrementalism." The original policy is changed slightly in response to a new threat and then, when the modified policy in turn runs into trouble, yet another modification that seems to be free of serious risks is uncritically adopted. In each instance the decision maker gives a positive response to the first basic question and a negative response to the second one. Thus he makes a series of incremental changes without ever canvassing or evaluating the full range of available alternatives.

A major deterrent to switching to a new course of action is the threat of violating prior commitments to the original course of action. According to assumption no. 2, the more committed the decision maker, the greater the stress when a challenging communication or event motivates him to search for a better course of action. Thus, the likelihood that a decision maker will give a *yes* answer to the second basic question depends partly upon the degree to which he is committed to his current course of action. The more committed he is, the greater the threat of his being subjected to social disapproval and other penalties for changing.

Once decisional conflict is generated by affirmative responses to the first two basic questions, the next question pertains to optimism or pessimism about finding a better solution than the least objectionable one at hand. A man who has become worried about being fired from his job may be unable to think of any way of satisfying his boss's demands (perhaps having already gone through a long series of unsuccessful attempts to satisfy the despot). If he knows that the current job market for a man with his qualifications is extremely poor, he feels hopeless about being able to find a satisfactory solution. Here assumption no. 3 enters into the analysis: when a person has lost hope about finding a better solution than the objectionable ones he has been contemplating, he will display the pattern of defensive avoidance. In the employment situation, this might take the form of selectively ignoring the issue by discounting the boss's complaints—for example, by rationalizing that the boss simply likes to assert his machismo but has no real intention of carrying out his blustering threats.

When defensive avoidance becomes the dominant tendency, the person tries to keep himself from being exposed to communiations that might reveal the shortcomings of the course of action he has chosen. A mother and father who had openly disapproved of their daughter's marriage, for example, are likely to find that precisely during the period of post-honeymoon disillusionment, when the distraught bride has begun to realize that her parents' dire forecasts about the unscrupulous and exploitative nature of the man she chose to marry are coming true, she has somehow become too busy to visit them or even to talk to them over the phone. If unwillingly exposed to an unfavorable comment, the disillusioned person's attention is readily distracted so that the message is not fully absorbed, and its meaning may even be grossly distorted. In any case, the person spends little time thinking about the implications of unwelcome information.

If an affirmative answer to the third basic question is accompanied by a negative answer to the fourth question, concerning whether sufficient time is available to search for a better solution, the decision maker will manifest a very high level of psychological stress. He will become frantically preoccupied with the threatened losses in store for him if he believes that a rapidly approaching deadline precludes an adequate search for a better solution, knowing that one or another set of undesirable consequences will soon materialize. The predicted pattern of hypervigilance in response to deadline pressures, when all the available alternatives pose a threat of serious loss, follows directly from assumption no. 4. A person in a hypervigilant state becomes obsessed with nightmarish fantasies about all sorts of horrible things that might happen to him, and fails to notice evidence indicating the improbability of their actual occurrence. The person is constantly aware of pressure to take prompt action to avert catastrophic losses. He superficially scans the most obvious alternatives open to him and may then resort to a crude form of satisficing, hastily choosing the first one that seems to hold the promise of escaping the worst danger. In doing so, he may overlook other serious consequences, such as drastic penalties for failing to live up to a prior commitment.

A positive response to the fourth question results in a lowering of the level of stress, because the person has confidence about finding an adequate solution. For example, when confronted with harsh demands from a boss to engage in unethical activity that would make a job intolerable, an employee would be unlikely to act impulsively if he sees signs that foster an image of somehow ameliorating the situation, either by getting the boss to withdraw his unacceptable demands or by getting himself shifted to a different unit under a new boss who would not make unacceptable demands. Such images maintain the hope of finding a better alternative so long as the person believes that there is sufficient time to look for it. Under these conditions of moderate stress, as specified by assumption no. 5, the person is likely to make a thorough information search and to weigh carefully whatever he discovers concerning the pros and cons of each alternative before making his choice.

Earlier we stated our ancillary assumption that all five coping patterns are in the repertoire of every decision maker. The pattern that is temporarily dominant depends upon external and internal cues that influence the answers a decision maker gives to the four basic questions. And again we expect marked individual differences in the readiness of decision makers to respond with vigilance rather than with defensive avoidance or one of the other patterns. Fluctuations from one pattern to another are also to be expected in any decision maker, as the determining external or internal cues alter the person's answers to the four questions. The model shown in figure 3 represents the decision maker's state of decisional conflict *at any given moment* and predicts the pattern of behavior that will be dominant *at that particular time*. So long as the answers to the basic questions remain constant, the person's coping pattern will remain constant. The model is expected to be especially useful for predicting *changes* in coping behavior that will ensue from new informational inputs that alter the person's responses to one or another of the four basic questions.

So far we have been applying the conflict model to vital decisions that could affect a person's future welfare or the attainment of his major life goals. But we propose to apply the model, as well, to the more commonplace decisions made by executives in routine meetings, in executive committees, and in the privacy of their offices. We also expect the model to apply to everyday personal decisions concerning such matters as how to handle work assignments, whether or not to carry out social obligations, and the like—provided that they evoke at least a mild degree of worry about the outcome. The subjective utility values of these everyday decisions certainly do not generate red-hot cognitions like those involved in the examples from disaster studies on which the model is based. Still, these more routine decisions are not at the other extreme of completely cold cognitions, like the hypothetical decisions posed in questionnaires given to college students. We make the working assumption that the same series of basic questions will occur, so long as the decision maker is aware of at least one mildly worrisome consequence. And the answers to the four basic questions will presumably be influenced by the same communication and situational variables that influence the answers in the case of fundamental decisions. We also expect the motivational and behavioral consequences of whatever coping pattern becomes dominant to be essentially the same as in the case of emergency decisions. The answers to the four basic questions posed by an everyday decision can be regarded as hot cognitions if each of the cognitive responses is influenced by the decision maker's state of emotional arousal and if, in turn, each response determines whether his level of emotionality will increase or decrease, with corresponding effects on his decision-making behavior.

Behavioral Consequences

Figure 3 is an incomplete presentation of our theoretical model in that it does not specify the observable behaviors that result from the mediating psychological structures. (We have omitted this information to avoid overloading a single chart.) This gap is filled by the description in table 1 of the major behavioral consequences of the five basic patterns, presented with respect to the seven criteria of high-quality decision making described earlier.

The first two patterns—unconflicted adherence and unconflicted change—fail to meet six of the seven criteria, as a result of lack of interest in the issue. The one criterion that is fulfilled when a decision maker is unconflicted is that requiring unbiased processing of whatever new bits of information bearing on the issue are brought to the focus of his attention: a person's capacity to assimilate new information efficiently and accurately is unaffected when his level of stress is very low, even though he has little interest in seeking the information.

The pattern of defensive avoidance, however, involves errors in assimilation of new information, as well as failure to meet all the other requirements. Not only does the person avoid being exposed to disturbing information, but when an unwelcome message is brought to his attention he distorts its implications by engaging in wishful thinking. The person's cognitive efficiency in processing new information is generally impaired by selective inattention in addition to selective apperception of the meaning of messages that deal with the emotionally disturbing issue.

The pattern of hypervigilance entails complete failure to fulfill five of the requirements and fluctuating performances involving partial failures on the other two. These deficiencies occur as a result of the impaired cognitive efficiency that characterizes frantic search and appraisal in a state of very high emotional arousal.

In contrast to the other four patterns, vigilance is characterized by satisfactory performance on all seven requirements. The person is sufficiently aroused and motivated to engage in all the essential cognitive tasks of decision making, but is never so highly aroused that his cognitive efficiency becomes impaired. Consequently, when a person displays the pattern of vigilance he is most likely to discover and select a successful optimizing solution to resolve the decisional conflict.

Subsidiary behavioral consequences pertaining to manifestations of conflict and related symptoms of stress are summarized in table 2 for each of the five patterns. As will be seen shortly, research evidence bearing on predictions of these subsidiary effects is relevant for testing the mediating psychological processes specified by the conflict model. The model depicted in figure 3 together with the specification of the behavioral consequences of each of the patterns in tables 1 and 2 constitute, in effect, a set of testable hypotheses that we shall examine in the light of evidence from

TABLE 1. **Predecisional behavior characteristic of the five basic patterns of decision making.**

PATTERN OF COPING WITH CHALLENGE	*Criteria for High-quality Decision Making*							
	(1) THOROUGH CANVASSING OF ALTERNATIVES	(2) THOROUGH CANVASSING OF OBJECTIVES	(3) CAREFUL EVALUATION OF CONSEQUENCES		(4) THOROUGH SEARCH FOR INFORMATION	(5) UNBIASED ASSIMILATION OF NEW INFORMATION	(6) CAREFUL RE-EVALUATION OF CONSEQUENCES	(7) THOROUGH PLANING FOR IMPLEMENTATION AND CONTINGENCIES
			a. of current policy	*b. of alternative new policies*				
Unconflicted adherence	−	−	−	−	−	+	−	−
Unconflicted change	−	−	+	−	−	+	−	−
Defensive avoidance	−	−	−	−	−	−	−	−
Hypervigilance	−	−	±	±	±	−	−	−
Vigilance	+	+	+	+	+	+	+	+

KEY: + = The decision maker meets the criterion to the best of his ability.
 − = The decision maker fails to meet the criterion.
 ± = The decision maker's performance fluctuates, sometimes meeting the criterion to the best of his ability and sometimes not.

All evaluative terms such as *thorough* and *unbiased* are to be understood as intrapersonal comparative assessments, relative to the person's highest possible level of cognitive performance.

TABLE 2. **Manifestations of conflict and related symptoms of stress for each of the five basic patterns of decision making.**

PATTERN OF COPING WITH CHALLENGE	SUBJECTIVE BELIEFS (INDICATORS OF mediating psychological conditions specified in figure 3–2)	LEVEL OF STRESS	DEGREE OF VACILLATION OF PREFERENCE FOR ALTERNATIVE COURSES OF ACTION
1. Unconflicted adherence	· No serious risk from current course of action	Low: persistently calm	No vacillation
2. Unconflicted change	· Serious risk from current course of action · No serious risk from new course of action	Low: persistently calm	No vacillation
3. Defensive avoidance	· Serious risk from current course of action · Serious risk from new course of action · No better solution can be found	Variable from low to high (predominantly pseudo-calm, with breakthrough of high emotional arousal when signs of threat become salient)	Little or no vacillation (except when signs of threat are salient)
4. Hypervigilance	· Serious risk from current course of action · Serious risk from new course of action · A better solution might be found · Insufficient time to search for and evaluate a better solution	High: persistently strong anxiety	Very high rate of vacillation, but occasionally practically none as a result of perseveration
5. Vigilance	· Serious risk from current course of action · Serious risk from new course of action · A better solution might be found · Sufficient time to search for and evaluate a better solution	Moderate: variations within intermediate range, with level depending upon exposure to threat cues or reassuring communications	Moderate to high rate of vacillation (depending on content of new information)

social psychological experiments and other investigations on consequential decisions.

Testable Predictions

We regard the five patterns delineated in figure 3 and tables 1 and 2, together with the general assumptions on which they are based, as constituting the rudiments of a theory of decisional conflict. (We are referring to the entire set of assumptions whenever we speak of our "conflict theory" of decision making.) From this set of interrelated propositions a number of testable predictions can be made concerning some of the crucial conditions that determine whether a decision maker's information search will be cursory or thorough, whether his predecisional deliberations will be biased or unbiased, and whether his adherence to a decision after he commits himself will be short-lived or persistent.

The theory is not sufficiently general in scope to make specific predictions concerning all the important aspects of decision making in all circumstances. Nevertheless, it will soon become apparent that in the limited spheres to which it does apply, the theory makes some specific predictions that are not made by other current theories.[4]

Underlying all the propositions in our conflict theory is the assumption that the same determinants that affect the decision maker's thought processes, including the degree of bias in his information-processing activities, operate *before as well as after a person makes a committing choice*. Thus we draw two major inferences that differ from expectations generated by some other theoretical analyses: (1) decision makers will be open to evaluative information and will be relatively unbiased in their processing of the information *after* as well as before they commit themselves to a choice, when the conditions that foster vigilance rather than avoidance are present; and (2) decision makers will display bolstering and other distortions in information processing *before* as well as after they commit themselves to a choice, when the conditions that foster defensive avoidance rather than vigilance are present.

Experimental evidence bearing on the first inference will be presented in the next chapter from a field study of draft resisters by Janis and Rausch (1970), which indicates that under certain conditions people will display vigilant attention to communications that attack a vital decision to which they are committed. One of the prime conditions suggested by this study is that the committed decision makers are still facing threats that create a dilemma about alternative ways of implementing their prior decision. Evidence bearing on the second inference will be presented from an experiment by Mann, Janis, and Chaplin (1969), which shows that bolstering will occur before commitment when decision makers who are still in a state of high conflict are led to believe that they have already received all the available information.

Other inferences from conflict theory generate predictions about how people react to loss of choice alternatives. These predictions will be discussed and evaluated in the light of evidence from a field experiment by Mann and Dashiell (1975), showing how young men facing the prospect of being drafted to fight in Vietnam changed their evaluations of career alternatives after receiving good or bad news about their status in the draft lottery (see chapter 10). Several other field experiments that bear on some of the implications of our theoretical analysis for effective interventions in the decision-making process (Colten and Janis, in press; Mann, 1972; Hoyt and Janis, 1975) will also be described (see chapter 6). In chapters 13 and 14 we shall discuss evidence from research on counseling procedures that counteract defensive avoidance and on other interventions that improve the quality of decision making during the predecisional period, some of which promote adherence to a difficult course of action by preventing backsliding when negative consequences are encountered after commitment. Research that bears out the predicted effects of the new types of intervention cannot be regarded as definitively confirming the theory; nevertheless, it increases the weight of evidence in support of the theory. (Certainly, if the research persistently failed to bear out such predictions we would have to revise the assumptions or even discard the theory altogether.)

We expect that as more evidence accumulates bearing on the causes and consequences of decisional stress, our theoretical framework can be developed more fully, so that a wider range of predictions can be made concerning decision-making behavior. We do not assume that conflict theory will necessarily replace all other psychological theories purporting to explain and predict decision-making behavior. On the contrary, we know from experimental evidence already available that under certain conditions, attribution theory correctly predicts how new information will be assimilated, and under certain other conditions cognitive dissonance theory predicts whether or not bolstering will occur, expectancy theory predicts changes in preferences for alternatives, and so on. Ultimately, we hope that as evidence accumulates on decision-making behavior, an integrated theory will emerge that will synthesize all the solid features of present-day theories. We believe that the propositions about decisional stress that we have singled out as basic assumptions for our conflict model have an excellent chance of becoming some of the key postulates in any such comprehensive theory. But the evidence now at hand is fragmentary, and we must await future research developments. In the meantime, our conflict theory enables us to make some specific predictions that are not made by other theories. In the chapters that follow, we shall try to highlight the distinctive features of our theoretical approach that enable us to fill in some important gaps in the study of decision-making behavior.

CHAPTER 4

Defective Search and Appraisal under High Conflict

UNDER CONDITIONS OF unrelieved high conflict, information processing can be impaired in two different ways. One type of impairment stems from *hypervigilance* and the other from *defensive avoidance*.

Anyone may temporarily succumb from time to time to a paniclike state, accompanied by a marked loss of cognitive efficiency, at moments of extraordinary crisis—such as when one's marriage, health, financial security, or future career is at stake—especially if one is confronted with a rigid and imminent deadline for making an irrevocable choice. Nevertheless, hypervigilance appears to be a relatively rare reaction, largely confined to certain limited types of decisions, such as those made by medical patients facing an immediate threat of physical suffering or death. Even in large-scale disasters, when emergency warnings are given to large numbers of people, hypervigilance and the accompanying symptoms of severe cognitive impairment have seldom been observed, despite the readiness of some influential journalists to raise the specter of mass panic (see Baker and Chapman, 1962; Committee on Disaster Studies, 1955; Quarantelli and Dynes, 1972). Perhaps the relative infrequency of hypervigilant reactions is attributable to the rarity of the prime antecedent conditions that we postulate for the appearance of this pattern—namely, awareness of imminent danger of serious loss with moderate or high hope that it can be escaped but with a very short deadline because all apparently adequate escape routes appear to be rapidly closing off.

Defensive avoidance, on the other hand, seems to pervade many different types of decisions: business decisions, career decisions, marital decisions, and even routine decisions of everyday life. Its pervasiveness may be due to the frequent occurrence of the antecedent conditions of high conflict with little hope for a satisfactory solution. In this chapter we shall deal primarily with theory and research on impairments in information processing resulting from the pattern of defensive avoidance, with only occasional reference to hypervigilance.

Bolstering the Preferred Alternative

One phenomenon involving defective search and appraisal has been intensively investigated by social psychologists—namely, cognitive bolstering of the chosen course of action. In his theory of cognitive dissonance, Leon Festinger (1957, 1964) singles out this phenomenon, which we regard as a prime manifestation of defensive avoidance, as a prototypic feature of decisional behavior. Festinger's contribution was pioneering, both in developing the concepts that elucidate the causes and consequences of bolstering and in initiating productive research on the phenomenon. We shall first present a brief summary of his analysis and indicate how certain of his formulations are incorporated into our conflict model, with some modifications that we regard as essential for conceptual clarity. (The gain in clarity comes from being able to specify more fully the conditions under which bolstering will and will not occur.)

Festinger (1957, 1964) assumes that inconsistent or dissonant cognitions motivate the individual to change his ideas or beliefs about the world. He also assumes that cognitive dissonance invariably follows every decisional choice, because the selected alternative always has some negative features and the rejected alternatives have some positive features. These considerations, which become salient after the person has made his choice, give rise to cognitive restructuring in the direction of bolstering the decision taken. Bolstering is accomplished partly by magnifying the attractiveness of the chosen alternative—the gains to be expected are played up and the potential losses are played down. Bolstering may also involve diminishing the attractiveness of alternatives that were *not* chosen, playing down their positive features and playing up negative ones. Thus, this dissonance-reducing activity results in a change in the decision maker's subjective evaluations of the chosen and unchosen alternatives: the chosen course of action comes to be regarded more highly and each unchosen alternative is regarded less highly, so that the decision maker's ratings of their attractiveness are more spread apart than they were before the decision. This manifestation of bolstering is referred to as "spreading of the alternatives."

A number of social psychological experiments and field studies indicate that after people have committed themselves to a choice they are likely to avoid dissonant information and to evaluate dissonant communications in a biased way that facilitates spreading of the alternatives (Brehm, 1956; Brehm and Cohen, 1962; Erlich, Guttman, Shonbach, and Mills, 1957; Festinger, 1957, 1964; Mann and Abeles, 1970; Knox and Inkster, 1968; Vroom, 1966). Erlich et al. (1957), for example, carried out a door-to-door survey of new-car owners and found that if the owner had purchased, say, a Ford, he was more likely to read newspaper and magazine advertisements about that make than about other makes. Such advertisements, of course, bolster the attractiveness of the chosen alternative. Presumably the purchasers were experiencing dissonance and used the advertisements to dispel their doubts. Business firms that seek to satisfy their customers recognize the need to assist the purchaser in bolstering a shaky decision by "sweetening the pie" with bonuses or by introducing congratulatory information that emphasizes the attractiveness of the chosen item.

Festinger (1964) takes the position that social commitment to a choice—by announcing the decision to one or more persons—is the one condition that is necessary and sufficient for dissonance reduction to occur in the form of spreading of the alternatives or bolstering. He argues on theoretical grounds that bolstering *never* occurs before commitment and supports his arguments with some indirect evidence from social psychological experiments, which we shall cite shortly. According to his account, people always tend to evaluate the alternatives objectively before they announce their final choice.

We have been skeptical about Festinger's assumption that bolstering occurs only after commitment because occasionally we have observed people who were trying to make an important personal decision displaying the characteristic manifestations of bolstering—oversimplifying, distorting, evading, and omitting major considerations bearing on the less acceptable alternatives—before they committed themselves. For example, some patients with hernias and other nonmalignant disorders, when told by their physicians that they ought to undergo elective surgery, tend to evade or ignore information and advice concerning the advantages of alternative medical treatments and sometimes even play up the necessity for the operation by imagining that their disorder might turn out to be cancer; they do this before they announce their decision (Janis, 1958).

Fellner and Marshall (1970), in their study of twenty kidney donors, present clinical evidence of the way in which information is avoided or distorted before commitment in order to bolster the intention of volunteering to save the life of a relative. According to their account, the medical teams took great pains to provide careful explanations of the pros and cons of what is involved in a kidney transplant operation and asked each potential donor not to decide until he had thought the matter through carefully. Yet, some of the donors told the investigators that they had silently made up their minds about the "right thing to do" as soon as they were asked to consider whether they would be willing to make the sacrifice to save the life of a member of their family. These donors reported that they were not really very curious about or interested in what the doctors were telling them. They appear to have applied a simple normative decision rule as soon as they realized what the physician was driving at: if a medical authority sounds you out about your willingness to make a sacrifice to save the life of someone in your family, you can't say no. The physicians' information about risks and dangers was ignored or distorted in a manner that served to bolster the course of action to which they were about to commit themselves. One donor remarked, "What the doctors said went in one ear and out the other. They know what they're doing." A number of prospective donors also indicated that before being asked for their final decision they had obtained social support and reassurance by talking to others who had previously donated a kidney or undergone a transplant operation. This clinical evidence is far from conclusive, of course, because the donors may have retrospectively distorted their accounts to present themselves in a favorable light; but if their reports are valid, they indicate that some of the donors bolstered their intention before commitment.

Evidence has also been reported from a study by Simmons, Klein, and Thornton (1973) in which intensive interviews and questionnaires were given to eighty persons who had donated a kidney to a relative. Only about 16 percent of the donors reported having made a deliberative type of decision involving careful search and appraisal of the costs and gains. Of the rest, 68 percent reported having made an immediate choice without deliberation. These people apparently adopted without any hesitation the normative strategy of relying on a simple moral precept as the sole decision rule. And again, there are some indications that before being asked to make up their minds, some of the donors bolstered their choice by playing up their family responsibilities or the precepts of their religion. One patient, despite being fully informed about the risks involved, asserted that the hospital staff had told him there was no risk at all, and that was what he believed.

We have encountered similar bolstering tendencies in case studies of marital and career decisions. For example, in an autobiographical essay written at the beginning of the senior author's graduate seminar on personal decision making, a young man in professional training who had just married recalled that a few weeks earlier, while he was trying to make up his mind to marry his girlfriend, all his thoughts and daydreams about the future had concentrated on the favorable consequences he was hoping for. He would list the unfavorable consequences to himself while pondering the issue, but he never permitted himself to imagine what they really might be like. Moreover, he retrospectively realized that when he had consulted married men in his professional school for information concerning financial and housing problems, the ones he sought out were those he believed to be happily married. He carefully avoided discussing the issue with his roommate, whom he suspected would oppose his getting married, even though he had been accustomed to sharing all his plans and aspirations with his roommate.

The case studies just cited suggest that bolstering tendencies can become dominant before a person has socially committed himself to a choice. We shall present some experimental evidence shortly that bears on predictions from the conflict-theory model concerning the conditions under which predecisional bolstering will and will not occur. First we shall discuss the assumptions of our version of conflict theory from which predictions can be made.

Implications of Conflict Theory

The version of conflict theory we presented in chapter 3 agrees with cognitive dissonance theory that cognitive restructuring in the direction of bolstering a decision frequently occurs after commitment. But we regard bolstering as one of the most common forms of defensive avoidance, and we assume that it is motivated primarily by a need to ward off the stress of postdecisional conflict rather than by an invariable tendency to reduce cognitive dissonance. In our view, bolstering not only satisfies a person's need to maintain cognitive consistency (which may be a weak need in many individuals) but also satisfies a powerful emotional need—to avoid anticipatory fear, shame, and guilt.[1] While emotional needs have rarely been investigated in laboratory experiments on decision making, numerous indications of their influence on search and appraisal can be discerned in case studies. We shall describe and illustrate these manifestations later in this chapter.

Our analysis of hot cognitive processes in decision making takes into consideration the various phenomena of bolstering described in Festinger's account of dissonance reduction. But since we assume a different motivation for bolstering than Festinger does, we are led to specify certain conditions as determinants of bolstering that are different from the ones implied by his analysis.

In terms of the conflict model, the essential preconditions for bolstering and other forms of defensive avoidance are summarized in figure 4. There are two essential mediating conditions: (1) the decision maker is in a state of relatively high decisional conflict resulting from two clashing types of threat that make it impossible for him to adopt any easy resolution (that is, he gives positive responses to the first two crucial questions), and (2) the decision maker has lost hope of finding a solution better than the defective ones he is considering (that is, he gives a negative response to the third crucial question).

Antecedent conditions that contribute to such loss of hope include being exposed to the following stimuli or circumstances: (1) a trustworthy expert's judgment that all the available information has already been obtained by the decision maker, (2) markedly diminishing returns from prolonged information search, indicating that the information supply has been exhausted, (3) impressive warnings about unacceptable losses from adopting any of the proposed alternatives, and (4) a consensus of pes-

FIGURE 4. A conflict-theory model of three types of defensive avoidance.

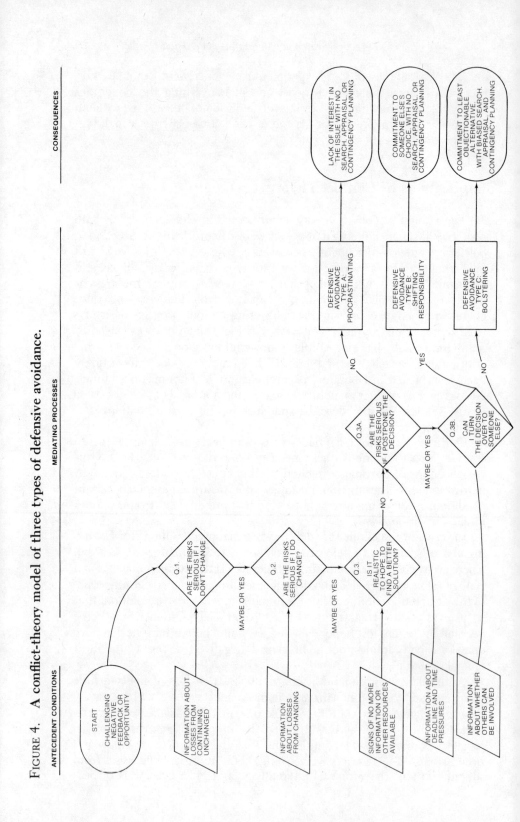

simism among those from whom the decision maker seeks advice about arriving at any promising new ways to resolve the conflict.

In figure 4, the answers to two supplementary questions ("Are the risks serious if I postpone the decision?" and "Can I turn the decision over to someone else?") are shown as determinants of the form that defensive avoidance will take. One form consists of *procrastinating*; a second involves *shifting responsibility* for making the decision onto someone else—for example, onto one's spouse if it is a personal decision or onto a colleague if it is an organizational decision. The third form consists of *bolstering* the least objectionable alternative by exagerating the positive consequences or minimizing the negative consequences. All three forms provide a way of escaping from the decisional conflict generated by the double source of threat (being damned if you do and damned if you don't). When he expects no penalty for postponing action indefinitely or for "passing the buck," the decision maker feels free to "leave the field"; he puts off the decision altogether or gives it over to others, turning his attention away from the conflict to other, less distressing matters. But when he is unable to evade the dilemma because of the pressure of a firm deadline and the insistence of others in his social network that he take responsibility, he will be motivated to accept one of the alternatives as a satisfactory course of action (despite its shortcomings) and reject all the others as substantially inferior. Under these circumstances he latches onto the least objectionable alternative and bolsters it, dismissing all the others as far less acceptable.

The form of avoidance adopted depends partly on personality predispositions, but situational variables are nevertheless among the major determinants. When the two essential conditions of defensive avoidance (high conflict and loss of hope for a better solution) are present, information or advice that induces the decision maker to expect no serious penalties for postponing his decision will encourage the tendency toward defensive procrastination: he will stop thinking about the issue, avoid discussing it with anyone who is interested in the outcome of his deliberations, and stay away from social situations where he might be put under pressure to make up his mind. But if he knows that there is a tight deadline with strong penalties for postponement, the decision maker's defensive avoidance tendencies are more likely to take the form of either shifting responsibility or bolstering. If the former, he directs his thoughts and actions toward getting others involved, rationalizing why they, not he, should make the decision and why they, not he, should take the blame if it turns out badly. If defensive avoidance takes the form of bolstering, the decision maker will continue to think and talk about the conflictful issue but will ward off stress by selective attention and distorted information processing. All three forms of defensive avoidance enable the decision maker to escape from worrying about the decision by not exposing himself to cues that evoke awareness of anticipated losses. Bolstering is the form that has been most extensively investigated, and the remainder of this chapter will be mainly devoted to evidence bearing on its causes and consequences.

Bolstering before Commitment

According to the conflict-theory model, then, if the decision maker is aware of the risk of serious loss from whatever course of action he might choose and believes he has obtained all the relevant information for making the decision—or if for any other reason he loses hope of finding a more satisfactory solution—he will tend to bolster the least objectionable alternative, unless, of course, he believes he can safely postpone the decision or foist it onto someone else. Whenever this set of conditions is present prior to commitment, we should observe a spreading of alternatives, similar to the phenomenon frequently observed in studies of postdecisional dissonance. Perhaps bolstering occurs much less often during the predecisional period than during the postdecisional; but if so, according to our analysis, it is only because the conditions that produce it are less frequently present before commitment.

In a forced-choice situation, where there is a fixed and imminent deadline, a crucial determinant should be signs that new information will or will not be available. If the decision maker is led to believe that he cannot obtain any new information, he will move toward resolution by selecting the least objectionable alternative; he will consolidate his choice by inventing rationalizations and using other defensive avoidance tactics that result in a spread of the alternatives. In contrast, when the individual is led to believe that there is a possibility of obtaining new relevant information right up to the time of announcing his decision, he will show little or no tendency to spread the alternatives before he is required to commit himself. An adequate test of this "expected information" hypothesis should, at the same time, put to the test the opposing position argued by Festinger and his collaborators (1964), that bolstering *never* occurs before commitment.

Evidence is available from an experiment designed specifically to test the hypothesis, derived from the conflict-theory model, that when a person is forced to choose between obviously imperfect alternatives he will tend to bolster the least objectionable choice before he is asked to commit himself *if he is led to believe that no additional information is forthcoming*. The experiment was carried out with women students at the University of Melbourne, Australia (Mann, Janis, and Chaplin, 1969). The women were told that the experiment had to do with the effect of unpleasant physiological stimulation on the ability to carry out intellectual tasks. They were given a choice between noxious taste and noise stimulation after being informed that each might possibly produce temporary side effects such as nausea, dizziness, headaches, and other disagreeable symptoms. In one experimental condition the subjects were led to expect more information—the experimenter said that factual reports about the percentage of people suffering side effects from the different stimulations would be provided later on. In a contrasting, "no additional information" condition, subjects were told that, regrettably, no such information would be available. Before and after these statements were made, the female experimenter obtained ratings of the subjects' feelings about the alternative forms of unpleasant stimulation. She told the subjects that they were not being asked to make their decisions. After the second predecisional rating, the experimenter announced to subjects in both experimental conditions that the meager information in her files showed that the same small number of people had suffered side effects from the two stimulations. Each subject was then asked to state her actual choice. As a final procedure, the purpose of the experiment was revealed. The subjects expressed considerable relief when they learned that they would not be required to go through with the unpleasant stimulation. (See the data on stress and relief from this experiment shown in figure 1.)

The main dependent variable was the amount of spreading of the ratings of the alternatives, which was computed by subtracting the difference between the alternatives on the first rating from the difference between the alternatives on the second ratings: $(C_2 - N_2) - (C_1 - N_1)$, where C_1 and C_2 are the initial and final ratings of the alternative to be chosen, and N_1 and N_2 are the initial and final ratings of the alternative not chosen.

The results of this experiment support the "expected information" hypothesis. When the subjects were led to believe that no additional information bearing on the decision could be expected, they tended to bolster the least objectionable alternative, thus spreading the attractiveness ratings of the two alternatives. But when the subjects were led to expect more information relevant to the decision, there was virtually no tendency to bolster. The difference between the magnitude of spreading in the two conditions was statistically significant ($p < 0.05$). Another analysis of the same data shows that 38 percent of the subjects spread the alternatives in the no-information-expected condition, whereas only 10 percent did so in the information-expected condition. This 28 percent difference, too, was statistically significant ($p = .01$).[2]

Although bolstering occurred in only a minority of the subjects, this study indicates that when all the information for making a consequential decision appears to be at hand, and a firm deadline is approaching, there is a significant increase in the tendency to bolster *prior* to making a commitment. A question still remains, however, as to what was happening to the large percentage of subjects in the no-information-expected condition who showed no evidence of bolstering. Two young women had announced that they wanted to quit the experiment (and of course they were permitted to do so) as soon as they learned about the undesirable alternatives they were being offered. Were many others perhaps contemplating refusal to permit the experimenter to inflict either form of disagreeable stimulation? If so, the appropriate measure of bolstering, which would require assessing changes in their appraisal of the attractiveness of the hidden third alternative—i.e., refusing to go on with the experiment—was not obtained from them. With hindsight we now realize that laboratory studies of this kind, in which essentially an avoidance-avoidance conflict is generated, are likely to supply only part of the story unless measures are obtained of alternatives that involve escaping from the conflict by "leaving the field."

It could be argued, of course, that the crucial turning point may occur when the decision maker spontaneously arrives at an implicit decision, which could happen some time before the experimenter requires an overt expression of choice. According to this argument, the expectation of no more information induces the decision maker to regard his predecisional preferences as equivalent to a final decision, at which point he may begin bolstering the most preferred alternative (see Aronson, 1968; Festinger, 1964, p. 4; Weick, 1965; Wicklund and Brehm, 1976, p. 245). Festinger (1964, p. 42) has cited indirect evidence that does not appear to support this conception of the turning point. This evidence led him to conclude that bolstering or spreading of alternatives occurs only after a person is socially *committed* to a decision. Our findings pertain directly to this conclusion, since our subjects were unambiguously informed that they were not committing themselves at the time of the second (predecisional) rating. Since the results do not support Festinger's conclusion that bolstering of the most attractive alternative occurs only after the person commits himself to a decision, they call into question the assumption that precommitment and postcommitment processes are dynamically different. The results of this experiment support the conflict-theory view that bolstering will occur before commitment if the situational conditions fostering that mode of defensive avoidance are present.[3]

In summary, our theory and research lead us to expect that before an overt committing decision is made there may be either bolstering activity or unbiased scanning of the alternatives, depending upon the presence or absence of certain conditions. One main determinant, as we have seen, is the amount of information about the alternatives that the decision maker still expects to obtain. Both the experimental evidence and case-study observations support the conclusion that predecisional processes do, in fact, vary as predicted:

1. When an uncertain decision maker believes that the supply of information about the alternatives is exhausted, the likelihood increases that he will bolster the least objectionable alternative, thus spreading the attractiveness of the alternatives, as he moves toward resolution.
2. When an uncertain decision maker believes that new relevant information about the alternatives will be forthcoming, the likelihood increases that he

will remain hopeful (about finding a good solution), vigilant, and open-minded; as a result, he will avoid moving toward resolution and will abstain from bolstering the most promising alternative.

These two propositions are consistent with conflict-theory assumptions about the conditions under which defensive avoidance rather than vigilance will be the dominant pattern of decision making.

Six Bolstering Tactics

In our research and observations bearing on decision making in every-day life, we have repeatedly observed the formation of cognitive defenses by which the decision maker bolsters his chosen course of action. *Bolstering* is an umbrella term that includes a number of different psychological tactics that contribute to creating and maintaining the decision maker's image of a successful outcome with high gains and tolerable losses. On the basis of a large number of interviews with persons we have followed through the successive stages of decision making—people who were, for example, choosing a career, changing jobs, refusing to be drafted into the armed forces, contemplating a divorce, giving up smoking, or going on a diet—we have discerned a common set of rationalizations or defensive beliefs that appear to be the most frequent ones used to bolster the to-be-chosen course of action.

In summarizing six main bolstering tactics, we shall indicate the typical content of the defensive beliefs or rationalizations manifested by what the decision maker says when he is presumably talking sincerely about the choice alternatives. Some of the tactics are well known, but others are less obvious and can be detected only through subtle manifestations.

1. *Exaggerating favorable consequences*. The most obvious tactic is playing up all the potentially favorable consequences so as to convince oneself that the most attractive alternative is well worth the costs and risks involved. The resulting exaggerated image of the net gains to be expected from the preferred course of action enables the decision maker to resolve a conflict that otherwise would leave him in a painful state of indecision. For example, when offered the honor of heading an important committee that will require enormous amounts of time and energy, the nominee may reduce the stress of indecision by overestimating the prestige to be gained.

2. *Minimizing unfavorable consequences*. Without necessarily playing up the good consequences, the decision maker may play down potentially bad ones that would otherwise make him feel hesitant and conflicted about the risks he is taking. He may also rely on the comforting belief that if worse comes to worst he can always manage to reverse or undo the decision before any really bad consequences materialize. Having adopted this belief, he gives little further thought to the difficulty of detecting the onset of danger, the costliness of reversing the decision, or the necessity for

working out contingency plans. Biased discounting is often directed toward playing down the good features of an alternative course of action that is being rejected, giving rise to the well-known "sour grapes" type of rationalization. A scientist in an industrial organization may acknowledge that certain good consequences like gaining more money, achieving more prestige, and having more freedom to work on self-selected projects will attend his accepting an offer to become the head of a new laboratory, but if he is strongly inclined to reject the opportunity he can discount those attractive considerations by developing rationalizations that enable him to belittle the gains he is renouncing (e.g., by conjuring up the corrupting effects of power).

3. *Denying aversive feelings.* Conflict is minimized by denying the aversive character of whatever bad consequences will follow from the preferred policy. When reality signs or social pressures prevent the decision maker from minimizing undesirable consequences, he can manage to view them as being acceptable and even desirable by selecting plausible arguments from existing ideologies and value systems that make certain types of deprivation and adversity appear to be attractive. (For example, when a man is inclined to accept an attractive job even though some of the work will be dangerous, he might tell himself, "It will give me a chance to prove myself" or "It is a fascinating challenge.") Thus, the expected bad feature is transformed into something good.

4. *Exaggerating the remoteness of the action commitment.* Another way to discount the known negative consequences of a choice is to assume that no action at all will be required in the foreseeable future, that after announcing one's choice nothing needs to be done for such a long time that one can forget about it. In Goethe's *Faust*, when the hero is tempted to sell his immortal soul in exchange for satisfying his present frustrated needs, he asks, "And what exact return am I to make?" Mephistopheles assures him, "That's so far off the thing may be dismissed." Facing more mundane decisions, any person can present to himself essentially the same Mephistophelian argument if he believes that there will be no costs or risks in the immediate future. It can, indeed, be a devilishly good argument, because this form of cognitive defense has, of course, a legitimate basis in reality. If the action required is to be postponed until the remote future—as in the case of a student committing himself to get married right after graduating several years hence—all of the person's calculations about the long-range consequences of the decision may become irrelevant because of unanticipated events (including changes in his or her own values). This realization helps to make the temporal-distancing defense effective in keeping one's mind off the disturbing risks of the chosen course of action, just as when one is convinced that he can safely postpone making the decision.

5. *Minimizing social surveillance.* A person may distort his conception of the course of action to which he is about to commit himself by

assuming that it is a private or secret affair and practically no one else will know anything about it. In extreme instances, this cognitive defense leads the decision maker to believe that it will not matter to anyone whether he lives up to his commitment or not. Thus, he may regard his verbal assent to an invitation to join a new organization or committee as merely a courteous gesture on precisely this comfortable assumption, which he may painfully discover to be entirely unwarranted soon after he has committed himself. If membership is seen as having symbolic status value, and participation in the work of the group as entirely voluntary, a person who is invited to join may set aside his reluctance to commit himself by assuming that there will be no social surveillance, so that no demands will be made on his time or energy. A similar minimization of social surveillance occurs when a man decides to leave his wife and young children in order to live like a "swinger" and assumes that this aspect of his private life will remain completely hidden from others in his community. The would-be "swinger" may convince himself that there is practically no danger of damaging his career or his social status through provoking the censure of "squares" who regard such behavior as irresponsible.

6. *Minimizing personal responsibility.* Whenever powerful external pressures are brought to bear in an attempt to influence someone to carry out a risky, unethical, or illegal action, the decision maker can seize upon these social pressures as a basis for a cognitive defense whereby he denies his own personal responsibility for making the choice. He attributes his choice to the external pressures brought to bear on him, and denies that he personally wants to do what he is agreeing to do. (See the discussion of Milgram's experiments on the "Eichmann effect" in chapter 10.) The decision maker can build up a case that he is being forced to take the action by the requirements of the organization he is serving, so that he has, in effect, no choice. This form of bolstering sometimes borders on shifting responsibility to someone else, which we have classified as a separate mode of defensive avoidance. Shifting responsibility involves deliberately arranging for others to take responsibility for a decision—for example, by assigning the decision to someone in a subordinate position or by persuading someone in a coordinate or superior position to take over a decision that should and could be made by the person himself. When a decision is bolstered by minimizing personal responsibility, however, the decision maker realizes that he is the one who has made or is going to make the decision, but he disclaims full responsibility by maintaining to himself and to intimates that he would refuse to carry out such an action if he were not required or forced to do so. Obviously, the stronger the external pressures for overt compliance and the greater their legitimacy according to the law or community norms, the easier it is for anyone to adopt this cognitive defense.

The above list is neither definitive nor exhaustive; but, from our preliminary observations of how various decision makers bolster their choices just before and just after committing themselves, we are encouraged to try to investigate more fully the conditions under which these defenses are most likely to occur. Our observations suggest that the prevalence of any given type of cognitive defense depends only partly on the predispositions of the decision maker; the choice of defense will also vary according to the type of decision and the situational context. For example, many heavy smokers we interviewed reported that after having unsuccessfully tried to quit smoking, they reluctantly decided to continue smoking two to three packs of cigarettes a day even though they openly acknowledged having aversive feelings when they thought about the health hazards of smoking so prominently emphasized in the mass media. Among these heavy smokers the most prevalent type of cognitive defense is minimization of the chances that a dangerous disease such as lung cancer will materialize in their own particular case. We have never encountered anyone who used the cognitive defense of denying aversive feelings about the threat of becoming a victim of lung cancer. On the other hand, among graduating law students we interviewed, those who had decided to take their first job in a governmental or corporation bureaucracy generally admitted that there would be unfavorable consequences, such as being required to spend much of their time on tedious, seemingly trivial tasks, but many of them denied the aversive feelings that this type of work would evoke in them (e.g., "It won't be boring or annoying because I'll welcome getting practical legal experience for my future career"). Thus, the preferred cognitive defense appears to depend partly upon the nature of the unwelcome consequences that have been brought to the decision maker's attention.

The anticipated consequences of adopting a new course of action are always a matter of estimating probabilities of future events. Whenever we have no hope of finding a better solution than the least objectionable one, we can always take advantage of the difficulties of predicting what might happen. We can bolster our decision by tampering with the probabilities in order to restore our emotional equanimity. If we use our imagination, we can always picture a beautiful outcome by toning down the losses and highlighting the gains. In general, cognitive defenses are fostered by ambiguities and uncertainties in the information available to the decision maker concerning the consequences of alternative courses of action. For example, warnings in the mass media asserting that one's chances of developing lung disease are generally increased by smoking have more ambiguous personal implications and hence are far less effective than a warning from one's own physician asserting that he has diagnosed the onset of a lung disease that cannot be arrested or cured unless one gives up smoking. The less ambiguous the information, the less the opportunity for distortion in the service of defensive avoidance.

We postulate that whenever a decision maker reaches a point when one alternative is clearly more satisfactory than the others, he puts an end to residual conflict by judging that the uncertain good consequences are more probable and the uncertain bad consequences less probable than he had initially thought. This type of bolstering can be of positive value for the decision maker only if it occurs after thorough search and appraisal, at the point when the decision maker finally has to make a choice and take action. Last-minute bolstering can help the decision maker to avoid being demoralized by a decisional dilemma, to feel less uncertain about the choice he has selected as the best solution, and to move more confidently toward commitment. But the consequences can be extremely detrimental if the decision maker resorts to bolstering tactics prior to careful search and appraisal. At one time or another probably all of us have been lulled into the illusion that we have arrived at a judicious decision when, in fact, we may have been more concerned with terminating a decisional conflict rapidly than with being vigilant in our search for a good solution.

Defensive Avoidance and Preconscious Biases

When a person is fully aware of the incentives that attract him toward or repel him away from a given course of action, his appraisal of these incentives can be readily modified by new information and impressive verbal arguments. Fresh evidence can convince him that he is overestimating or underestimating the gains or losses to be expected. Such evidence is much less likely to modify a decision maker's appraisals if the expected gains or losses are mediated by hopes or fears that are not consciously conceptualized, but rather operate at a preconscious or unconscious level. On the basis of early emotional conditioning, social modeling, and direct experiences of extreme frustration and gratification, every person acquires certain emotional biases that are not wholly mediated or controlled by verbal thought sequences and language. Such unconceptualized biases may sway a decision maker to make apparently impulsive and irrational choices. Preconscious emotional impulses triggered by fatigue, alcohol, or crowd excitement may also produce biased and subsequently regretted decisions.

Transient emotional impulses, as well as the more chronic types of emotional bias, are frequently not "unconscious" in the Freudian sense of the term, inasmuch as the person is capable of becoming at least partially aware of his feelings if someone induces him to scrutinize his thoughts and behavior. Hence they can be characterized as "preconscious," the term used by Freud to designate those "wishes" or "impulses" that the person is unaware of at the time he takes action, but is capable of becoming aware of when he introspects or is given appropriate communications by others. Preconscious incentives are thus assumed to be susceptible to change through information and persuasion. It is conceivable, for example, that an angry executive about to make an impulsive decision to undercut a competitive business firm can be deterred from doing so if one of his advisers suggests that he ought to wait a few hours and reexamine the issues when he might be in a better position to recognize the disparities between his objective appraisals of what is really at stake and his spontaneous emotional feelings. In a less excited mood, he might make a different decision that takes account of the undesirable publicity for his firm and other important consequences of such drastic action.

To illustrate how preconscious incentives enter into decisional conflict behavior, we shall briefly describe an experiment on the way people react to impressive information about the harmful effects of smoking. The study was carried out by Janis and Terwilliger (1962) with a sample of thirty-one adults, ages 18 through 55, representing a broad range of occupations and educational levels. This group contained roughly equal numbers of smokers and nonsmokers.

During an interview, each subject was exposed to a pamphlet asserting that heavy smoking causes cancer and recommending that everyone should avoid or cut down on cigarette smoking. The basic communication was made up mainly of authentic quotations from medical authorities. For half the subjects, a strong fear appeal was inserted into the basic communication: seven paragraphs vividly describing the suffering and poor prognosis of lung cancer victims. For the other half of the subjects, a mild fear appeal was inserted, which used more objective language and did not elaborate on the most threatening aspects of the disease.

The communication was presented to each subject one paragraph at a time. He was instructed to read each paragraph aloud and then express all his thoughts and feelings about it. An experimental device called an "auditory feedback suppressor," which delivers a white noise through earphones and enables the subject to speak aloud without hearing the sound of his voice, was used so that the subject's unheard verbalizations would more closely approximate his silent thoughts than if he could hear himself talk.

Tape recordings of the subject's verbalizations were transcribed and the associations were analyzed according to a systematic content-analysis procedure. The findings for strong versus mild fear appeals tended to confirm the following "defensive avoidance" hypothesis: when fear is strongly aroused by warning statements but is not fully relieved by reassurances contained in the same communication, the recipient will be left with relatively little hope of finding a satisfactory way of dealing with the threat and will become motivated to ignore, minimize, or deny its importance.

Of primary interest for our inquiry are the findings comparing smokers with nonsmokers (Janis, 1959). For the nonsmokers, the fear-arousing material stimulated some degree of anxiety about cancer, but this anxiety did not involve a decisional conflict, inasmuch as they were already abstainers. For the smokers, on the other hand, anxiety about suffering

from a horrible disease became a central component in a decisional conflict. Thus the communication introduced a powerful negative incentive,
the fear of loss of health, which challenged every smoker's current course
of action.

On a common-sense basis, one might expect the smokers to show
much more concern about the dangers of smoking, since the threat is
much more relevant to them than to the nonsmokers. A content analysis
of the verbal associations given by smokers and nonsmokers during exposure to the fear-arousing pamphlet, however, indicates that smokers displayed a defensive reaction. They made many more statements than the
nonsmokers to the effect that they were unconcerned about the possibility
of developing cancer or of suffering from the disease ($p < .05$). The smokers also showed less agreement with the points made in the antismoking
communication ($p < .05$). Follow-up interviews conducted from two to
five weeks later indicated that some subjects subsequently became aware
of their original defensive attitude toward the communication and experienced postponed anxiety. Thus the initial pattern of resistance appears to
have been at the *preconscious* level. The general picture emerging from
this experiment, then, is that minimization of threat in the service of
maintaining a comfortable sense of personal invulnerability constitutes a
dominant type of preconscious response when decisional conflict is stimulated by a challenging warning. The smokers minimized their personal
vulnerability to the threat and denied the impressiveness of the fear-
arousing information, enabling them to suppress awareness of the terrible
things that could happen to them. In this way, they managed to remain
temporarily free from conscious decisional conflict about whether to continue smoking. The pseudocalm that characterizes the coping pattern of
defensive avoidance, however, differs from the genuine lack of concern
that characterizes the pattern of unconflicted adherence.

Other studies also report more resistance among smokers than among
nonsmokers in response to fear-arousing communications concerning
lung cancer and other dangers of smoking (Cannell and MacDonald,
1956; Feather, 1962, 1963; Leventhal and Watts, 1966). The findings of
Leventhal and Watts (1966), for example, show that heavy smokers, after
being shown a dramatic movie on the dangers of smoking, were much
more likely than others to express "blanket reassurance" attitudes involving denial of personal vulnerability. Many more heavy smokers than light
smokers said they would *not* be vulnerable to lung cancer. The heavy
smokers, having much more to lose, were less likely to agree with public-
health recommendations that people should avoid smoking, in addition to
denying that they personally had anything to worry about. Similar results
were reported from a study on the effects of a warning concerning automobile accidents. Drivers minimized the threat more than nondrivers
and were less likely to accept the recommendation to use seat belts (Berkowitz and Cottingham, 1960). Further experimental studies along these

lines are obviously needed to investigate factors that promote sustained vigilance rather than defensive reactions to authentic warnings.

Defensive Avoidance and Unconscious Conflict

On the basis of psychoanalytic case studies, it seems plausible to assume that certain sources of gratification (positive incentives) and certain sources of threat (negative incentives) evoke approach or avoidance motivations that remain *unconscious* because of repression and other defense mechanisms, which protect the person from anxiety, guilt, shame, or other painful affects (A. Freud, 1936). As a consequence of disturbing socialization experiences and traumatic events in childhood, everyone is left with defensive reactions that prevent full awareness of forbidden sexual and aggressive drives. Defense mechanisms prevent the coming into consciousness of certain wishes or goals and also prevent the full use of thought sequences in mediating the choice of the most appropriate action to be taken. A prime example is the well-known self-punitive tendency of the widow who is struggling with unresolved ambivalence and guilt toward her dead husband. She cannot understand why she makes such poor investments of her insurance money that she ends up suffering severe financial losses, social disapproval, and damaged self-esteem, even though consciously she had wanted to avoid all these undesirable consequences. Insofar as the major underlying reasons for an important decision are unconscious, they remain relatively immune to self-insight and are extremely resistant to attempts at persuasive influence on the part of others.

The findings from controlled experiments are, of course, the preferred type of scientific evidence for determining the causal factors behind people's actions; but so far experimental research has failed to shed much light on the causal role of unconscious processes in decision-making behavior. For ethical as well as technical reasons, the investigator is rarely able to introduce into a laboratory setting a decisional conflict sufficiently intense to trigger deep-seated unconscious motives. If the study of unconscious motives and defense mechanisms that affect decision making is to proceed, it is necessary to take account of other types of research, including psychoanalytic observations in intensive case studies.

Many important leads concerning the ways unconscious factors influence the intensity and resolution of decisional conflicts can be obtained from detailed clinical case reports in the psychoanalytic literature. We shall briefly examine a classical case study by Sigmund Freud and a more recent one by Theodore Lidz. These two case studies show how extreme forms of psychological defenses are linked with unconscious sources of unresolved decisional conflict, interfere with information processing, and give rise to defective search and appraisal.

An Unresolved Sexual Conflict: Freud's Case Study of Dora

Unconscious motives that enter into a person's recurrent manifestations of unresolved sexual conflict were described by Freud in a number of his early papers, most notably in his famous case study describing the psychoanalysis of Dora, an 18-year-old neurotic girl (1901, translated 1971). From the case history, we are informed that Dora had a number of symptoms of hysteria that were fairly common at the time. She was subject to fits of coughing, sometimes followed by complete loss of her voice (aphonia); she suffered from excessive fatigue and often was unable to concentrate on her studies; she was depressed at times and on one occasion alarmed her parents by writing them a suicide note; and occasionally she had dramatic attacks of loss of consciousness followed by amnesia. Dora's father informed Freud that her last attack had occurred after an argument with him during which she was angry at his not breaking off relations with his close friends, Mr. and Mrs. K. Dora hated Mr. K because two years earlier he had made what she considered to be an indecent proposition. She had indignantly turned down his proposition, but a short time later had developed her most acute hysterical symptoms.

There were many indications that during the succeeding two years Dora was repeatedly in a state of postdecisional conflict about having refused the opportunity for having an illicit love affair with Mr. K. She continued to be preoccupied with thoughts about him, always maintaining consciously that she intensely disliked the man. She had vivid daydreams about encounters with him, and her free associations indicated that he was also represented in her repetitious night dreams, particularly in the context of her visit to his summer home two years earlier, when he had allegedly tried to seduce her. Thus, she continued to be preoccupied with and agitated about the entire affair—or perhaps one should say the lack of an affair.

From a variety of indications, Freud concluded that Dora was "filled with regret at having rejected the man's proposal, and with longing for his company and all the little signs of his affection." Freud added that "these feelings of tenderness and longing were combated by powerful forces." Dora mobilized her defenses "to protect herself against the feelings of love which were constantly pressing forward into consciousness," and she repeatedly tried "persuading herself" that she was finished with Mr. K.

Why so much postdecisional regret? Why, two years later, was it still necessary for Dora to resort to extreme defenses to convince herself that she was right to have rejected Mr. K?

If we assess Dora's postdecisional conflict in terms of the known incentives, we find many anticipated losses and few anticipated gains in connection with the unchosen course of action, acceptance of Mr. K's proposition. Having a sexual liaison with a married man would have obvious unfavorable consequences for herself and her family. Within her social milieu in Vienna at the turn of the century, she would be risking her reputation and her chances for a good marriage. The few relatives she told about it completely approved of her decision to reject Mr. K's proposition, and two of them (her father and her uncle) actually took steps to reprimand him. With respect to self-reactions, rejection of the proposition was apparently in accord with this young woman's moral code. And so the only positive incentives at the conscious or preconscious level would presumably be the opportunity for sexual gratification and affection, and a sense of adventurous excitement. But Dora had many opportunities to meet other suitors; and so the gains she could expect from having taken advantage of the opportunity to start an affair with Mr. K would be very small as compared with the expected losses. She ought, therefore, to have had relatively little postdecisional conflict about her refusal.

Why wasn't Dora's decisional conflict readily resolved? Why didn't she forget about the whole episode and redirect herself toward finding someone more suitable with whom she could have a satisfactory love affair or marriage?

Freud's detailed account of psychoanalytic sessions with Dora provides some clear-cut answers to these questions, all of which indicate that she was strongly overreacting to a set of positive incentives of which she was unaware—incentives that stemmed from the symbolic significance she unconsciously attached to having a sexual affair with Mr. K. In the course of the treatment it became clear that she was still longing for an intimate relationship with Mr. K because he was the first man to arouse her sexually (at age 14) and because her attachment to him, as a substitute for her father, served a defensive function in warding off forbidden Oedipal wishes. She also had unacknowledged longings for a homosexual attachment to Mrs. K, which she displaced by concentrating on the woman's husband. Thus, she remained neurotically attracted to Mr. K, unconsciously wanting intimacy with him but extremely afraid of allowing her forbidden wishes to be gratified. The unconscious positive incentives prevented her from being able to work through and resolve the postdecisional conflict in a normal fashion.

Her unresolved conflict necessitated extreme modes of defense. One of her most persistent defenses was a strong reaction formation. She expressed bitter hatred toward Mr. K, denounced him to her family, and constantly urged her father to break off relations with him. At times, her defensiveness interfered with her cognitive functioning. For example, harking back to the summer vacation when Mr. K attempted to seduce her, she vehemently accused him of having tried to take advantage of her presence in his house as a guest, citing what happened one afternoon when everyone else was away. She awoke from a nap to find that he had entered the room where she was sleeping, and she refused to believe his excuse that he had come to fetch something he needed. In condemning Mr. K for his intrusion, she ignored the fact that she had known she was alone in the house with him and had chosen to take her nap in his bedroom.

Dora's extreme defenses prevented her from realizing how she really felt about Mr. K, and largely for this reason she could not exercise sound judgment in deciding how to deal with him. Only after it was pointed out by Freud did she become aware of the fact that her aphonia and other acute hysterical symptoms usually occurred when Mr. K was out of town and that the symptoms cleared up again as soon as he returned. Reluctantly, she also acknowledged that others noticed that she became positively excited each time she saw him. In the course of her treatment with Freud, she also came to realize that Mr. K's proposal was not necessarily insulting, that what he was suggesting may well have been that they should become lovers with the prospect of getting married after he divorced his wife, and that her earlier cordiality might have led him to expect that she would be receptive to such a suggestion. She had cut him off before he could finish his proposal by slapping him in the face, assuming that all he had in mind was an indecent sexual proposition. Although still denying her own role in bringing about Mr. K's proposal, she finally recalled that a friend of hers who had observed her behavior in the presence of Mr. K at that time had told her, "Why, you're simply wild about that man!" In the very last session before she quit the treatment, Dora admitted that she might once have been in love with Mr. K, but she persisted in claiming that now and for the past two years she felt nothing but hatred.

In terms of the conflict-theory model of decision making, Dora's dominant coping pattern was defensive avoidance. Clinging to this coping pattern, she decided to quit analysis when it threatened to bring the entire conflict to the surface. Her unconscious ambivalence toward Mr. K involved not only longings for his love but also considerable anxiety and guilt over the unconscious meaning she attached to a relationship that symbolized incest and other forbidden gratifications. At the time of his proposal, she probably perceived, without being fully aware of it, that the least objectionable solution was for her to avoid anxiety and guilt by rejecting him as a lover. But because of her deep unconscious attachment to him and all the positive incentives that she was forced to renounce, she evidently had little hope of finding a satisfactory solution to the dilemma. She bolstered the least objectionable solution with an intensity that matched the intensity of her unconscious longings. Thus, she managed to escalate Mr. K's ambiguous proposal into an insultingly crude sexual advance, to express vehement hatred toward him every time his name came up, to misinterpret her own feelings in response to his presence and absence, and to commit herself to complete rejection of him by denouncing him to her relatives and demanding that her father avenge the insult to her honor.

Ordinarily, after a flurry of such bolstering activity, the decisional conflict would gradually die down over a period of several weeks. Thereafter, in the absence of any fresh external challenge, there would be so little conflict that no fresh acts of bolstering would be required. But in Dora's case, the decisional conflict flared up time and again during the two years between the time of Mr. K's proposal and the time she started treatment with Freud, and it continued to be reactivated throughout her psychoanalysis. Spontaneous reactivations were manifested in her fantasies and dreams, which contained derivatives of her unconscious longings for him to be her lover.

From Freud's case study, we infer that, some two years after rejecting Mr. K's proposal, Dora was still, at the unconscious level, giving strong affirmative answers to the first two basic questions. Consciously, she denied that there were any serious risks from continuing to rebuff Mr. K, but her unconscious answer to the first question was quite different. She regretted not having frequent contact with him, not having his warmth and affection, and not having the sexual gratifications he once offered her. To the second basic question, her conscious response would have been "There certainly would be some serious risks if I were to change my mind about rejecting his proposal." The risks she had in mind would be the usual ones faced by any young, middle-class woman in Europe during the Victorian era, as well as the social humiliation to be expected from reversing her vehement stand after having heaped so much scorn on him. At the unconscious level, her positive response to the second question would be strongly reinforced by the anxiety and guilt evoked by any step, whether in real life or merely in her private thoughts, toward entering into a taboo sexual relationship. Her conflict between wanting and not wanting to take such steps was reactivated whenever she caught a glimpse of Mr. K on the street or heard his name mentioned in her household, and, above all, whenever he made one of his frequent appearances in her free associations during the day or her dreams at night.

We surmise that Dora's answer to the third basic question was negative. Given the intensity of the anxiety and guilt generated by her unconscious longings for Mr. K, she could hope for no better solution than completely renouncing all forms of real-life contact with the man despite her fixation on him. Suffering acutely from the constant reactivation of her unconscious conflict, Dora could gain little relief from postponing thinking about the issue (procrastination), nor could she turn the decision over to someone else (though she made unsuccessful efforts to induce her father to break off his friendship with Mr. and Mrs. K). Thus, the clinical data presented by Freud seem to fit the psychological structure we have presented (in figure 4) for the bolstering type of defensive avoidance. When we take account of the unconscious determinants that probably influenced her answers to the basic questions, it becomes understandable that fresh acts of defensive bolstering were constantly required. In response to repeated internal challenges, Dora continued to muster her resources to attack Mr. K and actively resisted her analyst's efforts to call attention to evidence that contradicted her conscious attitudes.

Here we see what is likely to happen to a person's capacity to attune his or her judgments to reality when the main source of decisional conflict remains unconscious. A person is more likely to resort to extreme modes of defense when conflict-producing incentives are at the unconscious level than when they are at the preconscious or conscious level. Moreover, when a person is repressing an anticipated gratification, he or she is not so likely to undergo the type of successful inner readjustment that normally occurs following a decision that requires renouncing that source of gratification. Skilled marriage counselors, for example, learn to identify the symptoms of persistent unconscious conflict following a person's decision to obtain a divorce by observing defensive overreactions of the type Freud described in diagnosing Dora's unresolved conflict. They know that intensive psychotherapy would be required to enable the person to become at least partly aware of the unconscious incentives that are continuing to activate the conflict and to work out a solution that takes account of them. In brief forms of treatment the therapeutic odds are not very favorable, especially because the client is likely to resist probing into the conflict by breaking off treatment, just as Dora did.

From Freud's case history we learn that Dora's decision to stop seeing Freud was heavily determined by unconscious sources of anxiety and guilt that were powerful enough to outweigh all motives that favored continuing the treatment. In retrospect, Freud tried to understand why this patient, who was still suffering from acute neurotic symptoms, made an antitherapeutic decision that was not in her own best interests. It was at this point that he discovered the importance of transference reactions, inappropriately displacing intense love, bitter hate, and other emotional attitudes pertaining to a significant person in the past onto the analyst. (When Freud treated Dora at the turn of the century, he had not yet learned how to deal with such reactions.) This discovery led Freud to formulate his well-known technical rule that the analyst should give priority to analyzing negative transference reactions. Part of the rationale for the rule is that if signs of negative transference are neglected, the patient might make an impulsive decision to quit treatment on the basis of unconscious anxiety or anger directed toward the analyst. This rubric seems to imply the same general proposition mentioned earlier concerning unresolvable decisional conflicts, namely, that when an incentive contributing to a decisional conflict remains at the unconscious level, its influence is relatively unmodified by objective information and external events; whereas when such an incentive is at the preconscious or conscious level, it is much more likely to be dissipated or counteracted by corrective information.

An Unresolved Career Conflict: Lidz's Case Study of a Physician

Freud's case study provides an example of a decisional conflict constantly reactivated by internal challenges posed by fantasies or trains of thought that represent unconscious symbolic meanings. Sometimes, however, decisional conflict is reactivated by realistic frustrations, but the person clings to his old decision and continues to bolster it because of powerful unconscious needs that run counter to his conscious goals. Lidz (1976) has described such a case in his account of Dr. R, a 35-year-old physician whose unconscious need for expiation and self-denial played a major role in his choice of career and who became increasingly dissatisfied because other strong needs failed to be fulfilled.

Dr. R consulted a psychiatrist on his return from military service because he was becoming increasingly dissatisfied with his life as a physician, despite having attained considerable success both in private practice and in medical research. He resented the time-consuming demands that were made on him, which required him to forego his former interests in art and architecture, but he dismissed all opportunities for shifting to a different career on the grounds that he had too many obligations and family responsibilities to consider such a drastic change. In reviewing the steps that led him to medicine, Dr. R recalled that during his junior year in college, when he was trying to decide what vocation to pursue, the question was essentially whether he should become an artist or an architect; medicine was not considered an alternative until the very last moment. In the course of psychotherapeutic treatment, he revealed to himself and to the therapist a number of unconscious motives that had influenced his choice of medicine. Particularly revealing were his infantile fantasies stemming from memories of how close he had felt to his mother when she took care of him during a siege of rheumatic fever as a young child. One of the attractions of a medical career was the fact that a physician could receive free medical care from his colleagues. He also recalled that he had made the choice partly because he wanted to resist his parents, who expected him to make use of artistic abilities. When they praised him for displaying his artistic talents, he distorted and discounted what they said by interpreting their encouraging comments to mean that they liked him only for his achievements and did not love him "for himself."

After arriving at all these recollections Dr. R, with considerable anxiety and embarrassment, recalled something else that apparently had greatly influenced his choice of a medical career. At the age of 15, while away from home, he had become ill. Knowing that a cousin had recently died of leukemia, he worried that his illness might, like his cousin's, prove to be fatal cancer.

> His concerns mounted, and in his anxiety R. prayed and made a vow that if God would let him live for another twenty years, he would devote his life to the welfare of mankind. As usually happens, after he recovered, his pact with God

was forgotten. But during the year of decision in New York [at the age of 20] when he became anxious, depressed, and hypochondriacal, his vow returned to plague him. He doubted that the life of either artist or architect would redeem his pledge of self-sacrifice; one would be too enjoyable and the other too lucrative. . . . [He feared] that he might soon die and recalled his earnestly given pledge, which helped explain his curious decision to launch into doing what he least wanted to do. It was a means of redeeming his vow. . . . R. was further shaken when the psychiatrist pointed out to him that the twenty years of life he had sought from God had [just] been completed . . . and that now he was again uncertain about his future [Lidz, 1976, p. 378].

It appears, then, that one of the main reasons Dr. R chose to enter the medical profession was that he saw it as a form of self-sacrifice that would enable him to redeem the vow he had made at the age of 15 to lead an ascetic life, devoting himself to the welfare of mankind. Asceticism, according to Anna Freud (1936), is a defense that functions to protect a person against the internal threat of forbidden impulses, and is frequently observed in adolescents. By making an ascetic choice in selecting a career, R was seeking expiation for harboring forbidden thoughts and impulses, which, we learn from Lidz's account, included ambivalent longings for passive gratification from his parents along with a desire to rebel against them. His strong guilt feelings were evidently assuaged by choosing a vocation he did not really like. But while the choice may have satisfied his unconscious needs, it failed to satisfy other important needs, with the result that he became completely dissatisfied and constantly regretted his choice.

For Dr. R, the challenge that was generating postdecisional regret consisted of realistic frustrations arising from the marked discrepancy between his personal objectives and the demands of his profession. Dr. R's response to each of the recurrent challenges was to bolster his original decision by playing up all the difficulties that would prevent him from making a change in his career, and by continuing to repress memories that revealed the persistent guilt feelings and the self-punitive needs that had loomed so large in his choice of a medical career. In this case, postdecisional bolstering may have had some positive value in enabling the person at age 35 to come to terms with the tremendous investment he had made of many years of his life in a specialized career. Lidz indicates that Dr. R became a successful member of a medical school faculty and was able to "shift his creative urges into disciplined research" (p. 384).

In both case studies we have just reviewed, we can see that a person's extreme defenses are likely to persist when his or her decisional dilemma is constantly being reactivated because of unconscious sources of motivational conflict. Like the common, garden variety of rationalizations and other cognitive defenses that typically enter into the bolstering of everyday decisions, the most extreme defense mechanisms—such as repression, reaction formation, and denial—fail to protect the decision maker from the stresses of renewed conflict when unambiguous negative feedback is encountered. Nevertheless, the various kinds of defense serve to alleviate stress at least temporarily. The functional value of defensive avoidance tactics, as we have seen repeatedly throughout this chapter, lies in the temporary reduction of high conflict, which enables the decision maker either to continue living up to past commitments in the face of distressing challenges or to make a relatively unambivalent choice of a new course of action rather than remain demoralized and immobilized. Often, however, the price paid for these short-term advantages is defective search and appraisal, which can result in serious long-term losses.

CHAPTER 5

Defensive Avoidance among Policy Makers

EXAMPLES OF THE DETRIMENTAL consequences of defensive avoidance are certainly not limited to the psychoanalytic consulting room. Defensive avoidance in the form of procrastination, buck passing, and bolstering is a common occurrence in modern organizations, such as the military, law enforcement agencies, hospitals, and school systems. The temptation for defensive avoidance is especially strong whenever a difficult policy decision is to be made, because within a huge bureaucracy there are other groups and individuals to whom it is usually possible to shift responsibility. "The buck stops here" was printed on the plaque President Harry Truman kept prominently displayed on his desk in the Oval Office presumably to remind himself—and whoever came in to advise him—of this obvious aspect of governmental bureaucracies. When prime conditions for defensive avoidance are present and neither passing the buck nor procrastination is possible, members of a policy-making group are likely to make an ill-considered decision bolstered by shared rationalizations and a collective sense of invulnerability to threats of failure (Janis, 1972).

Instructive examples of defensive avoidance are to be found in well-authenticated accounts of what goes on inside high-level executive offices in large business and governmental organizations. In this chapter, we present illustrative case studies of defective policy-making decisions that affected the lives of large numbers of people.

Wishful Thinking in the Nixon Administration

Our position concerning the determining conditions of defensive avoidance differs from the popular view of what constitutes wishful thinking. At the beginning of the oil shortage crisis in early December 1973, for

107

example, *Time* magazine described the large number of warning signs
that had gone unheeded by the Nixon administration during the preceding years and concluded that the deepest roots of the energy crisis were
psychological, lying in "the disinclination of people to think about potential unpleasantness until it can no longer be avoided" (*Time*, December
10, 1973, pp. 39–40). According to this explanation, people are always
inclined to avoid bad news and to assume that "it can't happen here." We
agree that avoidance tendencies often interfere with adequate planning,
but we regard the explanation of such behavior in terms of a universal
tendency to avoid thinking about impending unpleasantness as superficial
and misleading. Our conflict theory postulates a strong competing tendency to become *vigilant* in response to signs of potential danger and
emphasizes the need to specify the conditions under which vigilance or
avoidance will dominate in decision makers' reactions to warnings.

In *Time's* account of the Nixon administration's failure to heed warnings of the oncoming energy crisis, we can discern numerous indications
that the essential conditions for defensive avoidance, as specified by the
conflict-theory model (figure 3), were present. For example, the article
quotes David Freeman, a former White House energy adviser, as to why
nothing came out of the high-level conferences held eighteen months
earlier, when policy makers were talking over what could be done to
prepare for the bad times ahead: "Maybe these solutions were so difficult
that the policy makers avoided moving." *Time* gives an impressive list of
the undesirable repercussions anticipated by government leaders that
would have created acute political problems for the Nixon administration,
threatening the chances of a Republican victory in national elections:
consumer resentment against rationing, higher prices for gasoline, or
higher taxes on gas-guzzling cars; opposition from the oil industry for
interfering with profits and tax benefits; adverse public opinion, especially
among businessmen, resulting from any government action that went
counter to the dominant national myth that America's economic prosper-
ity requires more production and more per capita consumption of energy.
Under these conditions, the policy makers could not be expected to harbor much hope of finding a satisfactory solution.

Evidently it was not just a matter of reasoned calculation on the part of
top administrators in the Nixon administration to avoid an unpopular
course of action. The men in the White House, according to another
adviser who was in a position to know, showed "a general lack of interest"
and "paid no attention to the problem until after the election," by which
time it was too late to head off an acute crisis. Comments like these
suggest that the administrators were displaying a characteristic pattern of
defensive avoidance, which enabled them to set aside the threats that
challenged their long-standing policy of doing nothing to prepare for the
predicted oil shortage. Neither the Congress, nor the President, nor any
member of his cabinet imposed a firm deadline on the responsible plan-

ners for the formulation of a new policy to deal with the impending energy crisis, leaving them free to procrastinate.

In figure 4, we have depicted four psychological conditions that make for a pattern of *defensive procrastination* in response to a warning that challenges a current course of action or inaction: (1) awareness of the threat of serious losses from failing to take preventive action, (2) awareness of the threat of serious losses from changing to any of the available alternative courses of action, (3) lack of hope of finding a solution that will keep the risks at a tolerable level, and (4) lack of deadline pressures for announcing a definite decision to which the decision maker will be committed. If the observations reported in *Time*'s story are accurate, it seems likely that all four essential conditions for defensive procrastination were present during the two years preceding the oil shortage crisis.

Thus, in any example like this one, where decision makers fail to respond to impressive warnings, we do not accept *Time*'s simple explanatory formula that says that people always incline toward wishful thinking. Rather, we look to see whether or not certain specific types of circumstances and behaviors were observed, corresponding to the antecedent conditions and consequences of the pattern of defensive avoidance, as delineated by the conflict-theory model. This is the way we approach the two historic policy decisions to which we devote the rest of this chapter.

Ineffectual Planning for Desegregation

We turn now to a lengthy case study of policy making in a large, heterogeneous community beset by a complex problem involving clashing interests among discordant groups, some of which collectively showed symptoms of defensive avoidance. Stephen Weiner (1975) has described the decision-making process that led to a city-wide desegregation plan for San Francisco, which was officially adopted in the summer of 1971. An organizational or community decision-making enterprise of this type differs, of course, in many important respects from personal decision making. From the standpoint of the role obligations of the individual manager or bureaucrat who participates in the decision-making process of a large organization, the long-term objectives of any chosen course of action are supposed to be primarily those that promote the welfare of the organization. Any new policy is also expected to gain consensus or agreement among all those participants who are expected to accept, implement, and live with the decision. Special analytical schemes, such as those derived from engineering systems analysis, are generally used to take account of the acknowledged policy objectives (Etzioni, 1968; Katz and Kahn, 1966; Miller and Star, 1967; Young, 1966). Nevertheless, as we have seen in the preceding three chapters, there are many unacknowledged objectives, threats, and opportunities that influence the way decision makers in policy-making groups arrive at a final choice, just as when they are making their personal decisions in private life. In this case study, we shall use the conflict-theory model for analyzing certain aspects of organizational decision making that are not dealt with by systems analysis or by other approaches used in administrative sciences—notably, the causes and consequences of defensive avoidance and other coping patterns.

The instigating event that led to desegregation planning in San Francisco was a legal suit by the NAACP arguing that the school system in San Francisco had engaged in discriminatory acts resulting in a pattern of school segregation and demanding immediate desegregation of all 102 elementary schools in that city. In September 1970 a U.S. district judge ruled in favor of the NAACP suit, warning that if the Supreme Court authorized the use of busing (in one or another of the unresolved cases then being decided), he would require the desegregation of all elementary schools by September 1971. The judge urged the Board of Education and the administrators who headed the San Francisco School District to start developing plans that could be fully implemented the following year.

The board and the top decision-making group of school administrators did little more than take token actions. They directed a few professionals within the school system to collect data and prepare memoranda; they also set up a Citizens Advisory Committee to make recommendations. This committee was intended to give tacit recognition to all the various ethnic and neighborhood groups that had been demanding a voice in community policy making during the preceding decade. As in many other large American cities during the 1960s and 1970s, the school system in San Francisco had been caught in a cross fire between militant black groups demanding compliance with the Supreme Court rulings on desegregation and equally militant white groups that were vehemently opposed to busing and were threatening to send their children to private or parochial schools rather than allow them to mingle with nonwhite classmates in public schools. Only two years earlier, thousands of parents had unexpectedly turned up at public forums to voice their opposition to cross-town busing, and at one such mass meeting there had been a violent attack by white segregationists that had resulted in severe injury to several participants. The explosiveness of the issue was heightened in San Francisco by demands from the Latin-American and Chinese-American communities that any desegregation plan not overlook their own special needs.

The story of what happened in San Francisco is of exceptional interest because none of the power holders inside the school system and few of the would-be power wielders outside the system made any substantial use of the opportunity to mold the school desegregation policy. The top bureaucrats in the school system gave the matter no attention until it was too late because the deadline for a desegregation plan was already at hand. For a variety of reasons, representatives of the black community did not bother to push for their demands. Nor did representatives of any other ethnic groups seize the opportunity to have their voices heard in the bargaining process. The only effective group of policy makers turned out to be a small subgroup of the Citizens Committee composed largely of white liberals. Most of the members were middle-class housewives who wanted to help improve ethnic relations within the community, in line with their liberal ideology. As the final deadline approached, this small group of concerned citizens had to put in such a large amount of time that they called themselves the Round-the-Clock group.

This group submitted a simple plan that met relatively little political opposition and was ultimately adopted by the Board of Education and found acceptable by the U.S. district judge. The school administrators, black community organizers, and other interested parties did little more than push for minor changes in specific details of the plan. In contrast, the professional planners within the school system produced a complicated plan, which appeared to require much longer bus rides across the city and evoked so much incredulity that it was promptly dismissed as unfeasible.

Thus it turned out that essentially the only persons who actively engaged in policy making were the members of a self-appointed group of well-educated, liberal housewives, who were sincerely interested in complying with the spirit of the Supreme Court's desegregation rulings in a way that would create a minimum of civic disturbance. The members of the Round-the-Clock group, by virtue of faithfully attending community meetings and doing their homework, ended up becoming the real wielders of power; they were the ones who made the effective decision as to what the desegregation plan would be.

Weiner's analysis points to a number of specific factors that help explain how a power gap developed and how that gap happened to be filled by a group that initially had relatively little power potential. Making use of the details supplied by Weiner's analysis, we shall examine briefly the preliminary decision made by the members of each of the contending groups as to *whether or not to participate in the planning of the desegregation policy*. We shall try to show how the coping patterns represented in our conflict-theory model help explain the way a power gap can arise despite vociferous verbal demands for power by many contending groups. At the same time, our analysis enables us to formulate more precisely the conditions under which the members of a comparatively powerless group can emerge as the dominant policy makers on a vital community issue.

Let us start with the two most powerful policy-making groups in the San Francisco school system: the seven-member Board of Education, appointed by the mayor, and the twelve top bureaucrats in the school system hierarchy (occupying the positions of superintendent, associate superintendents, and assistant superintendents). These two groups comprised the leaders with real power, who in 1971 had the responsibility for administering a school operating budget of well over 100 million dollars; they would normally be expected to be the ones who would decide upon any new policy affecting the way pupils would be assigned to the schools of their city. But they did little more than make a few token gestures to show their interest in the problem. The main action the bureaucrats took was to hire a computer consultant and allow the school system's data processing office to use its computers to collect and analyze some relevant statistics. They were eager to make use of the computer facilities, and the desegregation issue gave them an opportunity to expand those facilities.

As for substantive desegregation planning, the bureaucrats merely assigned three professional analysts to spend a little time on the problem and mainly left it up to the Citizens Advisory Committee of sixty-seven people who had been appointed by the Board of Education. Neither the members of the Board of Education nor the top bureaucrats took the trouble to give the Advisory Committee any direction or to attend its meetings. Perhaps there was some reason for abstaining—their active guidance might have been construed as undue interference—but many members expressed disappointment that they had so little contact with the top administrators. Weiner's interviews of board members and superintendents indicated that all of them were extremely busy with other matters and that none exercised any leadership or spent any substantial amount of time working on desegregation planning, even though they knew that the redistribution of some fifty thousand elementary school children in their city would have profound effects on the entire educational system.

Weiner lists a number of factors accounting for the bureaucrats' evasion of the decision, all of which appear to fit the pattern we have described as buck passing. Their policy was essentially to do nothing, to "let George (in this case, the Citizens Advisory Committee) do it." The major conditions that make for buck passing, as depicted in figure 4, are high conflict and pessimism about the prospects of finding a satisfactory solution (which are the prime determinants of all forms of defensive avoidance), combined with two additional factors—awareness of serious losses to be expected from postponement, and availability of another group to whom responsibility for the decision can be shifted. Once the judge gave his deadline to the top administrators in the school system, the first three components were present. The administrators were reluctant to introduce wholesale, sweeping changes and realized that the desegregation issue was loaded with political dynamite. They knew that, as in other cities that had tried and failed to come up with a satisfactory plan, the top administrators would be attacked by all disgruntled groups. They also knew that if they failed to meet the deadline set by the judge, their postponement would invite legal penalties as well as distressing confrontations with militant blacks and vociferous civil rights workers.

Late in April 1971, the judge announced that in view of favorable rulings by the Supreme Court, he now required a desegregation plan to be submitted by June 1971. Having seven weeks to meet this deadline, the top administrators continued to evade responsibility. They did nothing more than remind the professionals in the school system that it was up to them and the Citizens Advisory Committee to work out a plan.

From September 1970 to April 1971, it had been all too easy for the busy administrators to set the decision aside, especially when there were so many fires around that needed to be put out immediately. Weiner points out that the school administrators were "beset by a veritable nightmare of crises and other catastrophes" (p. 237). These included boycotts by teachers and parents at two predominantly black schools, a confrontation with six hundred teachers who presented themselves uninvited at a Board of Education meeting to protest the oversize classes in their schools, and a walkout by two hundred teachers protesting the Board of Education's unwillingness to give rehiring guarantees.

Because of their inclination to evade the politically explosive desegregation issue, the Board of Education and the top administrators in the school system allowed seven crucial months to pass without doing anything themselves or even looking into the planning activities of the Citizens Advisory Committee.[1] Then, even after they were given an unambiguous deadline of seven weeks to present a desegregation plan to the district judge, the bureaucrats still continued to leave the matter in the hands of a group of professionals within the school system and the Citizens Advisory Committee. None of the twelve top administrators was assigned the task of working on the plan and none spontaneously devoted any time to it. The bureaucrats made no serious effort to interview teachers and parents or to collect any relevant information other than the routine statistical data generated by their busy, heretofore underutilized computer facilities. Thus, the pattern of response on the part of the bureaucrats appeared to be essentially a form of defensive avoidance based on feelings of hopelessness about arriving at a solution that would be satisfactory to all interested parties in the community. They permitted a power gap to develop by taking no active interest in the desegregation policy planning despite mounting signs that a deadline crisis would soon be at hand.

Let us look now at the ill-starred professional staff that was assigned the task of devising a desegregation plan in seven weeks to meet the judge's deadline. The members of this group included the school system's data-processing specialists and a number of consultants from the California Department of Education. These professionals knew that their assignment was extremely difficult and fraught with the danger of exposing themselves, along with all the top bureaucrats in the school system, to a terrible barrage of public abuse. Two years earlier, a seemingly sound plan worked out for the San Francisco school system by the reputable staff of the Stanford Research Institute had met with such tumultuous protests and violent confrontations that the superintendent and the Board of Education were "chastened by the public opposition."[2] With few exceptions, the professionals within the school system were pessimistic about being able to work out a better solution. The professional planners were "hamstrung," according to Weiner, partly because of a shortage of information. They were keenly aware of the lack of crucial information about the ethnic distribution of the student population, the migration pattern of families within the city, and feasible bus routes. But they had little hope of obtaining the essential facts and figures. Facing a seemingly insoluble problem, the professionals decided to support a plan developed by the recently appointed computer consultant, who had practically no familiarity with the administrative and political problems of the school system. The computer specialist was enthusiastic about using a standard, textbook approach to rational decision making: the thing to do was to gather relevant information, formulate clear operational criteria for the "best" possible plan, examine all feasible alternatives, and choose among the alternatives according to the operational criteria. But although a set of rational procedures of this type may often be an aid to effective decision making, in this case the attempt failed badly.

In formulating the criteria of a good desegregation plan, the consultant left out some of the most crucial considerations that are given high priority by sophisticated community planners. The supposedly rational plan constructed by the computer specialist and endorsed by the professionals completely ignored the strong opposition within the community to extensive cross-town busing, which posed the threat of "white flight" from the schools and other forms of white backlash, including outbursts of interracial violence. The professionals also failed to take account of the need for gaining acceptance of the plan among key members of the community who were in a position to mobilize political support. Instead of consulting with and attempting to gain the backing of the Citizens Advisory Committee, the professionals acted on the assumption that the committee would passively acknowledge the superiority of the "rational" plan they were advocating. But the committee members were unwilling to agree with the professionals' formulation of the criteria in general terms, because they were concerned about the different implications of the criteria for each specific neighborhood. The professionals were "frustrated and angered" by the committee's lack of cooperation (Weiner, p. 242). "Until the end of the planning process," Weiner asserts, "the professionals refused to accede to the arguments raised by white members of the Round-the-Clock group that the . . . [so-called rational] plan involved unacceptable political risks" (p. 241). Ignoring clearly hoisted signals of potential political opposition to their plan, the professionals proceeded to work out the details independently of the committee, perhaps expecting the opposition to melt away. When their final plan, which entailed extensive cross-town busing, was promptly voted down by the Citizens Advisory Committee, the professionals viewed the committee as irrational and parochial; they left with feelings of "bewilderment" and "bitterness" (Weiner, p. 243).

The huge errors of omission made by the professionals in listing their criteria, their defective search for and appraisal of alternatives to extensive cross-town busing, and their failure to correct their errors after being repeatedly warned by the Citizens Advisory Committee of the need to overcome political opposition appear to fit the pattern of defensive avoidance. From the outset, as we have seen, the professionals had little hope of being able to obtain the information necessary for sound planning. Their reliance on the so-called rational approach of the computer specialist seems to have been merely a smokescreen with which they covered their pessimism about carrying out a decision-making assignment with so many clashing objectives that it seemed to them to be a hopeless mess.

To summarize: the plan endorsed by the professionals failed to meet the requirements of political feasibility because it was constructed in terms of an incomplete set of criteria. The professionals bolstered their choice by selective inattention and rationalizations. They failed to reappraise the plan when they encountered clear-cut negative feedback from the Citizens Advisory Committee. They continued to believe that their plan was the only satisfactory one, and they developed unrealistic rationalizations concerning the ignorance and pigheadedness of the people who warned that it would be unacceptable, thus dismissing the opposition as irrational. As a result of their gross failure to take account of the major political requirements of the decision, they were promptly defeated at the very first step in trying to gain acceptance for the plan they endorsed and thereafter had practically no influence on the plan that was finally accepted by the San Francisco school system.

Another important group that had been expected to exert considerable influence on the community's decision-making process but failed to do so was the coalition of black activists, who had initially taken the lead in demanding that San Francisco conform to the Supreme Court's desegregation rulings. The blacks attended the initial meetings of the Citizens Advisory Committee in large numbers, but after a short time most of them stopped coming to the meetings altogether. Interviews of those who had become inactive indicated that some were much too busy elsewhere playing a leading role in the struggle for racial equality. For these black activists, the challenge posed by the opportunity to develop a school desegregation plan was relatively weak compared with those posed by other burning issues of the day. Their pattern of response appears to have been essentially one of unconflicted inertia—taking a casual interest in the planning effort and verbally supporting it, but not personally devoting any time or energy to it. Some of the black people who had originally been on the Citizens Advisory Committee asserted that it was not necessary for them to participate because the committee "was in good [white integrationist] hands." The decision by leaders of the black community to abstain from active participation was probably also reinforced by their awareness that the NAACP was at work on planning for desegregation of the schools in San Francisco, which would represent their interests. Interviews of inactive members from other minority groups suggest essentially the same response of unconflicted inertia.

Weiner reports that his interviews with the white women who dominated the planning process, the Round-the-Clock group, indicated that they were

> motivated not only by a desire to participate in decisions that affect the future school assignment of their own children and by an ideological commitment to civil rights but also by a desire to exercise untapped organizational skills. For many of these women, participation in school district affairs became an outlet for existing personal competencies that range beyond the skills required of a homemaker and wife [pp. 249–50].
>
> Unlike the professional planners on the district staff who were immobilized by lack of data and formal criteria for a plan, the white women were able to devise zonal maps for desegregation based upon their impressionistic grasp of ethnic composition and attitudes toward busing in various San Francisco neighborhoods [p. 240].

Deeply concerned about the seemingly irreconcilable demands from the black community and from local antiintegrationists who threatened various forms of white backlash, these liberal women nevertheless maintained the hope of finding a satisfactory solution. Unlike the professionals—who were juggling a number of complicating objectives in addition to racial desegregation, such as socioeconomic integration and efficient utilization of school buildings—the liberal women were striving for a simple plan that would be politically acceptable throughout the entire city. They spoke optimistically about the "lessons" of the recent desegregation attempts in San Francisco. One such lesson was that a committee like theirs could be effective in promoting desirable changes in the school system; another was that political opposition to desegregation could be defused if a desegregation plan did not require very much cross-town busing. Thus they felt fairly confident of being able to work out a good solution and at the same time were alert to the various threats that could ruin the chances of successfully introducing any proposed plan. These are, of course, essential components of the pattern of vigilance.

The members of the Round-the-Clock group took the opportunity posed by the deadline seriously, as a rare chance to make a contribution to their community. Working intensively in a small group, they became committed to each other and developed a "sense of ownership" (p. 239). Their success in solving technical problems, as they continued to collect and weigh information concerning details about the schools in each neighborhood, contributed to their sense of mastery and deepened their commitment to produce a plan that would be acceptable to all sides. After much hard work on "their baby," involving long hours spent not only in attending meetings but also in doing extensive homework to obtain crucial data about the school population in each neighborhood throughout the city, they outlined a detailed plan, which proposed setting up seven school zones within the city. They felt that their plan could gain public acceptance because it would minimize cross-town busing and could be presented as merely enlarging the boundaries of current neighborhood school districts. Evidently their hopes were warranted, since their plan evoked no effective opposition within the community and was duly accepted.

Now we return to the question posed at the outset of this case study: how could a small group of seemingly powerless housewives come to play the major role in formulating a policy decision on a crucial community issue that had long been the subject of a power struggle among local bureaucrats, neighborhood organizations, and militant minority groups? Our analysis in terms of conflict theory specifies a number of crucial determining factors, which we believe are not given sufficient weight by other theorists. Weiner, for example, applying the concepts of organizational decision making to his case study, specifies only two major factors as supposedly determining the degree to which a potential policy maker will actively participate in formulating policy. The two he singles out are the degree of interest or concern the potential policy maker has in the issue being considered and the degree to which he or she is sufficiently free from other obligations to be able to spend large amounts of time on the given task of decision making. Weiner points out that high intensity of participation creates a "positive feedback loop": the more interest a person has and the more time he devotes to the task, the more knowledge and competence he acquires as compared with others, which, in turn, leads to increased activity. This feedback loop is most pronounced when the active policy makers become a small interacting group—as in the case of the Round-the-Clockers, who ended up with a "near monopoly position concerning the competencies required" (p. 247).

Weiner emphasizes the crucial importance of the time investment factor by postulating a "garbage ejection" model of how community decisions are evolved under conditions where there is little agreement within the community on the values and objectives to be obtained (see Cohen, March, and Olsen, 1972). Before a deadline is imposed, he asserts, a community issue such as school desegregation can be viewed as a garbage can into which people dump all sorts of other problems and solutions intended to satisfy their own group's needs. Once a deadline is imposed, however, the active participants realize that they do not have the energy or resources required to solve all the problems that have accrued to the issue, and so they start ejecting all the garbage they regard as disposable. Only those problems and objectives are retained that have a "carrier."[3] In the case of the San Francisco school desegregation issue, a number of major objectives—such as desegregating secondary schools and integrating inner-city schools with suburban schools—were ejected because none of the original advocates of those objectives remained active in working on the issues. For a given objective to enter into the final plan, someone must be willing to give more than lip service to it, by spending the necessary time and energy.

We agree with the substance of Weiner's theoretical analysis as far as it goes, but we regard it as an incomplete account of the conditions under which a potential policy maker will devote time and energy to participating in the making of an organization or community decision. Our analysis in terms of the coping patterns delineated in the conflict model has led us to look into a number of determining conditions besides the degree to which the person is interested and has time free from other obligations. We do not question Weiner's assertion that the housewives in the Round-the-Clock group wanted to participate and had a relatively large amount of free time as compared with the bureaucrats and the professionals, the black activists, and others with full-time jobs. But we do not believe that this simple fact by itself provides a satisfactory explanation of the power gap that enabled these women to become the effective policy makers.

Whenever an organization is facing a complicated decisional issue, like that posed for the San Francisco school system by the judge's desegregation deadline, the leadership typically delegates the detailed tasks of planning to members of their staff who are professional experts. But they usually continue to take a directive role in formulating the policy by briefing the professionals, participating in some of the planning sessions, having informal chats with the leading experts as to the tentative solutions being developed, preparing critiques of the staff's working papers, and subsequently participating in evaluation meetings where the final decisions are made. The bureaucrats in the San Francisco school system, however, failed to exert any influence on what the staff was doing and in effect created a power gap by abdicating their leadership function on this issue.

According to our analysis, the bureaucrats in the school system who did essentially nothing during the many months when planning could have gone on were displaying a defensive avoidance response of passing the buck. This pattern was only partly attributable to lack of time owing to other pressing obligations. When organizational leaders acknowledge that serious losses will result from ignoring a challenge, they somehow manage to carve out sufficient time from their busy schedules to participate vigilantly in planning so as to avert the threat. Consequently, we must look for other factors, as specified by our conflict-theory model (figure 3). We have seen that lack of hope was present at the outset. Subsequently, when the bureaucrats were informed by the judge that there was a firm deadline of seven weeks and the threat became loud and clear, they still refrained from becoming personally involved in shaping the desegregation plans, probably because they still had little hope of finding a satisfactory solution and because the problem could be foisted onto another group. From the standpoint of surviving intact in their high-level positions, this defensive avoidance pattern may have been adaptive for the top bureaucrats in the public school system. After all, by abstaining from active participation in the decision-making process on the politically explosive issue of school desegregation, they appreciably reduced the responsibility (and blame) that could be placed on them for redistributing the school population, a legally required change that they believed was bound to evoke anger and resentment in one or another sector of the community.

Since the top bureaucrats delegated responsibility for policy planning to members of their professional staff, why did the professional staff fail to emerge as the dominant policy makers? Not only did the professionals have the delegated power, but they also had much more expertise and better informational resources for working out a solution than any other group interested in the issue. The crux of their failure, according to our analysis, again involved a pattern of defensive avoidance, and this had little to do with lack of interest or lack of time. But for many long months they did little except collect some statistics (which we can interpret as defensive procrastination). When, at last, under the deadline pressure of the judge's order they finally did come to spend a great deal of time evaluating a plan, they relied primarily on the work of a technical consultant and their efforts were misdirected. They spent their time working out the details of a grossly inadequate solution that overlooked two major objectives—gaining general public acceptance and defusing the opposition of militant opponents—that had to be taken into account for any desegregation plan to succeed. We can interpret this failure as resulting from defensive avoidance in the form of bolstering the least objectionable alternative. The professional staff ignored what they knew about the obvious political opposition that would prevent their plan from being accepted, not because they were ignorant or taken in by misleading information but because of their own psychological need to cope with a seemingly insoluble problem that engendered high conflict and for which they had little hope of finding an adequate solution.

Our emphasis, therefore, is quite different from Weiner's, since we attribute a large part of the failure of the San Francisco school system to exercise its policy-making power to the defensive avoidance pattern displayed by the professional staff to whom the power had been delegated. Defensive avoidance also entered into the failure of the bureaucrats themselves to become active participants. Thus, our analysis highlights the decision makers' defensive efforts to ward off emotionally disturbing cognitions as a key concept in explaining the defective planning on the part of both the professional staff and the top bureaucrats in the school system. This pattern of defensive avoidance, occurring in the context of other potentially powerful groups having decided to remain inactive, allowed the vigilant participants in an advisory group with little prior power to emerge as the dominant policy makers.

Our theory does not purport to explain all aspects of the power gaps that arise when power holders delegate policy planning to others, nor does it enable one to predict when bargaining and coalitions will arise. A more complete analysis of the outcome of power struggles within an organization or community would require the use of concepts from sociological theory and systems analysis (see, for example, March, 1966; Katz and Kahn, 1966; Young, 1966). Nevertheless, our analysis in terms of conflict theory can illuminate the microprocesses that enter into the decision-making activity of members of rival groups within an organization or community who are potential wielders of power. The conflict-theory model helps to account for the degree of participation displayed by each of the contending groups. It also helps to account for the degree to which they make use of their internal and external resources in working out their policy solution and in making plans for a political struggle to gain acceptance of their solution.

Admiral Kimmel's Failure at Pearl Harbor

Our next example illustrates the bolstering form of defensive avoidance as it occurs in high-ranking policy-making groups. The leader of a large organization is typically backed by an advisory team of experts who can, among other things, act as a counterweight to balance the leader's misperceptions and oversights. But all too often an advisory group spontaneously takes on the role of a protective shield, reinforcing the leader's efforts to protect himself from having to face unpalatable facts and agonizing choices. The Pearl Harbor fiasco is an example of how leader and group mutually bolster each others' misjudgments, thereby protecting one another from the discomforts of a painful decision.[4]

In the summer of 1941, as relations between the United States and Japan were rapidly deteriorating, Admiral Kimmel, Commander in Chief of the Pacific Fleet, received many warnings concerning the imminence of war. During this period he worked out a plan in collaboration with his staff at Pearl Harbor, which gave priority to training key personnel and supplying basic equipment to U.S. outposts in the Far East. The plan took account of the possibility of a long, hard war with Japan and the difficulties of mobilizing scarce resources in manpower and material. At that time, Admiral Kimmel and his staff were keenly aware of the risks of being unprepared for war with Japan, as well as of the high costs and risks involved in preparing for war. They appear to have been relatively optimistic about being able to develop a satisfactory military plan and about having sufficient time in which to implement it. In short, all the conditions were present for vigilance, and it seems likely that this coping pattern characterized their planning activity.

But during the late fall of 1941, as the warnings became increasingly more ominous, a different pattern of coping behavior emerged. Admiral Kimmel and his staff continued to cling to the policy to which they had committed themselves, discounting each fresh warning and failing to note that more and more signs were pointing to the possibility that Pearl Harbor might be a target for a surprise air attack. They repeatedly renewed their decision to continue using the available resources primarily for training green sailors and soldiers and for supplying bases close to Japan, rather than instituting an adequate alert that would give priority to defending Pearl Harbor against enemy attack.

Knowing that their sector and the rest of the U.S. military organization were not ready for a shooting war, they clung to an unwarranted set of rationalizations. The Japanese, they thought, would not launch an attack against any American possession; and if by some remote chance they decided to do so, it certainly wouldn't be at Pearl Harbor. Admiral Kimmel and his staff acknowledged that Japan *could* launch a surprise attack in any direction, but remained convinced that it would not be launched in their direction. They saw no reason to change their course. Therefore, they continued to give peacetime weekend leave to the majority of the naval forces in Hawaii and allowed the many warships in the Pacific Fleet to remain anchored at Pearl Harbor, as sitting ducks. In the three-hour Japanese air raid on the morning of December 7, 1941, which was the worst military disaster in American naval history, nineteen vessels were sunk or badly damaged, with a loss of 2,340 lives and a large number of wounded.

Defensive Handling of the War Warnings

Superficially, Admiral Kimmel's reactions to the warning messages from Washington and elsewhere might resemble the calm inertia that characterizes unconflicted adherence to an old policy. But when we look closely into the way Kimmel handled each of the successive warnings, we can discern symptoms of considerable conflict and defensiveness.

Kimmel regularly discussed each warning with members of his staff. At times he became emotionally aroused and obtained reassurance from the members of his in-group. He shared with them a number of rationalizations that bolstered his decision to ignore the warnings. On November 27, 1941, for example, he received an explicit "war warning" from the chief of naval operations in Washington, which stirred up his concern but did not impel him to take any new protective action. This message was intended as a strong follow-up to an earlier warning, which Kimmel had received only three days earlier, stating that war with Japan was imminent and that "a surprise aggressive movement in any direction including attack on Philippines or Guam is a possibility." The new warning asserted that "an aggressive move by Japan is expected within the next few days" and instructed Kimmel to "execute appropriate defensive deployment" preparatory to carrying out the naval war plan. The threat conveyed by this warning was evidently strong enough to induce Kimmel to engage in prolonged discussion with his staff about what should be done. But their vigilance seems to have been confined to paying careful attention to the way the warning was worded. During the meeting, members of the staff pointed out to Kimmel that Hawaii was not specifically mentioned as a possible target in either of the two war warnings, whereas other places—the Philippines, Malaya, and other remote areas—were explicitly named. Kimmel went along with the interpretation that the ambiguities they had detected in the wording must have meant that Pearl Harbor was not supposed to be regarded as a likely target, even though the message seemed to be saying that it was. The defensive quality that entered into this judgment is revealed by the fact that Kimmel made no effort to use his available channels of communication to Washington to find out what really had been meant. He ended up agreeing with the members of his advisory group that "there was no chance of a surprise air attack on Hawaii at that particular time."[5]

Since he judged Pearl Harbor not to be vulnerable, Kimmel decided that the limited-alert condition that had been instituted months earlier would be sufficient. He assumed, however, that all U.S. Army units in Hawaii had gone on a full alert in response to this war warning, so that antiaircraft and radar units under army control would be fully activated. But, again, reflecting his defensive lack of interest in carrying out tasks that required acknowledging the threat, Kimmel failed to inquire of Army headquarters exactly what was being done. As a result, he did not discover until after the disaster on December 7 that the Army, too, was on only a limited alert, designed exclusively to protect military installations against local sabotage.

On December 3, 1941, Kimmel engaged in intensive discussion with two members of his staff upon receiving a fresh warning from naval headquarters in Washington stating that U.S. cryptographers had decoded a secret message from Tokyo to all diplomatic missions in the United States and other countries, ordering them to destroy their secret codes. Kimmel realized that this type of order could mean that Japan was making last-minute preparations before launching an attack against the United States. Again, he and his advisers devoted considerable attention to the exact wording of this new, worrisome warning. They made much of the fact that the dispatch said "most" of the codes but not "all." They concluded that the destruction of the codes should be interpreted as a routine precautionary measure and not as a sign that Japan was planning to attack an American possession. Again, no effort was made to find out from Washington how the intelligence units there interpreted the message. But the lengthy discussions and the close attention paid to the wording of these messages imply that they did succeed in at least temporarily inducing decisional conflict.

By December 6, 1941, the day before the attack, Kimmel was aware of a large accumulation of extremely ominous signs. In addition to receiving the official war warnings during the preceding week, he had received a private letter three days earlier from Admiral Stark in Washington stating that both President Roosevelt and Secretary of State Hull now thought that the Japanese were getting ready to launch a surprise attack. Then on December 6, Kimmel received another message from Admiral Stark containing emergency war orders pertaining to the destruction of secret and confidential documents in American bases on outlying Pacific islands. On that same day, the FBI in Hawaii informed Kimmel that the local Japanese consulate had been burning its papers for the last two days. Furthermore, Kimmel's chief naval intelligence officer had reported to him that day, as he had on the preceding days, that despite fresh efforts to pick up Japanese naval signal calls, the whereabouts of all six of Japan's aircraft carriers still remained a mystery. (U.S. Naval Combat Intelligence had lost track of the Japanese aircraft carriers in mid-November, when they started to move toward Hawaii for the planned attack on Pearl Harbor.)

Although the various warning signs, taken together, clearly indicated that Japan was getting ready to launch an attack against the United States, they remained ambiguous as to exactly where the attack was likely to be. There was also considerable "noise" mixed in with the warning signals, including intelligence reports that huge Japanese naval forces were moving toward Malaya. But, inexplicably, there was a poverty of imagination on the part of Kimmel and his staff with regard to considering the possibility that Pearl Harbor itself might be one of the targets of a Japanese attack.

The accumulated warnings, however, were sufficiently impressive to Kimmel to generate considerable concern. On the afternoon of December 6, as he was pondering alternative courses of action, he openly expressed his anxiety to two of his staff officers. He told them he was worried about the safety of the fleet at Pearl Harbor in view of all the disturbing indications that Japan was getting ready for a massive attack somewhere. One member of the staff immediately reassured him that "the Japanese could not possibly be able to proceed in force against Pearl Harbor when they had so much strength concentrated in their Asiatic operations." Another told him that the limited-alert condition he had ordered many weeks earlier would certainly be sufficient and nothing more was needed. "We finally decided," Kimmel subsequently recalled, "that what we had [already] done was still good and we would stick to it." At the end of the discussion Kimmel "put his worries aside" and went off to a dinner party.[6]

Here we see a typical sequence that occurs when the pattern of defensive avoidance is dominant: the decision maker manifests considerable worry about his old policy and also about any new one that seems capable of handling the threat that is challenging the old policy; he has no hope of finding a better solution than the old policy, even though he now knows that it entails some serious risks; finally he ends up reducing his conflict by bolstering the old policy in a way that denies the importance of the challenging warnings. In this way, through the use of bolstering tactics, the decision maker achieves a state of *pseudocalm* at the expense of effective search and appraisal. In his pseudocalm state, the decision maker fails to engage in the full set of vigilant activities that normally are expected when a person is confronted with a serious, consequential choice. The search for relevant information is extremely limited and is generally characterized by highly selective attention, excluding information about the most threatening consequences of the least objectionable course of action. New information to which the decision maker is exposed is processed in a biased way, strongly influenced by wishful thinking.

Neglected Alternatives

From his temporary manifestations of agitated worry, we surmise that Kimmel privately gave positive responses to the first two crucial questions: that is, he believed that serious losses might occur if he continued his long-standing policy and he also believed that there would be serious losses if he were to order a full alert. (With regard to the latter option, Kimmel has testified that he was keenly aware of the extremely high costs and risks involved in instituting a full alert. He would have to give up trying to meet his current objectives, because training and supply activity would have to be severely curtailed. Even more crucially, a complete air reconnaissance would rapidly use up his limited supplies of aircraft fuel and, since there were no replacements for spare parts, all aircraft in Hawaii would have to be grounded within a few weeks.) Moreover, Kimmel realized he could not shift responsibility or postpone the decision, since daily operating schedules affecting tens of thousands of men depended upon what sort of alert he ordered. Thus the essential conditions for bolstering of the least objectionable choice were present.

What Kimmel failed to consider was the compromise alternative of a partial increase in surveillance with some dispersal of warships, cancellation of weekend leaves, full alert of antiaircraft units, and other precautionary measures that could have increased the safety of the fleet at Pearl Harbor without being exorbitantly costly. Because he and his staff denied Pearl Harbor's vulnerability, they did not consider any alternatives between the two extremes of maintaining the limited-alert condition that had already prevailed for several months and instituting a very costly full alert. A stepped-up alert well short of complete air surveillance might have reduced to a tolerable level the costs and risks of responding to the threat. In agreement with many other military analysts and historians who have studied the record of decision-making events at Pearl Harbor, Samuel E. Morison, in his history of naval operations during World War

II, has concluded that a reasonable condition of readiness could have been established at Pearl Harbor without interfering with training schedules and other preparatory activities.

Another neglected alternative was to notify the Army to keep its antiaircraft batteries at full strength and to operate its radar network on a twenty-four-hour-alert basis. Because Kimmel failed to take these relatively uncostly steps, the antiaircraft guns remained undermanned and the radar network was almost totally ineffective. Since the army treated the latter mainly as a training operation and its working hours were only from 4:00 A.M. to 7:00 A.M., the radar network was of little use for detecting enemy aircraft. Nevertheless, two army privates happened by chance to be engaged in a training exercise shortly after the usual closing hour on Sunday morning, December 7, 1941, and spotted on their radarscope a massive cluster of what they realized might be Japanese aircraft flying toward them, 137 miles north of Oahu. But when they reported this to the Army's radar center, they were told to forget it. The duty officer, having heard nothing about the recent war warnings, knew that a flight of U.S. B-17s was expected that morning and assumed that that was what must have appeared on the radar screen. If Kimmel had ordered a stepped-up alert and had asked for the radar network to be used for detecting hostile aircraft, this error probably would have been avoided and almost an hour of advance warning would have been given, preventing much of the damage of the Japanese surprise attack.

Thus we see a pattern of defensive inaction despite exposure to powerful challenges that evoked decisional conflict. The decision maker's behavior in such circumstances is entirely different from the complacent type of inertia that we refer to as "unconflicted adherence to the old policy," which is based on weak challenges that do not induce expectations of any serious losses or risks. The testimony of Kimmel and his associates indicates that during the weeks of imminent war warnings, the top naval commanders at Pearl Harbor relied upon a number of flimsy rationalizations that enabled them to set aside their worries about the potential defects of their limited-alert policy.

Cognitive Defenses of Kimmel and His In-group

When we look carefully into the behavior of Kimmel, his in-group, and other naval officers at Pearl Harbor, we can discern a number of prominent cognitive defenses.

1. *Misjudging the relevance of warnings.* With the support of the other naval commanders in his advisory group, Kimmel discounted the strong war warnings received on November 24 and November 27, 1941, by assuming that the threat of a Japanese surprise attack could not possibly be applicable to Hawaii. Kimmel and his advisers shared the unwarranted belief that Japan would never risk attacking their "invulnerable" fortress at

Pearl Harbor, and assumed that the messages from Washington must refer only to the necessity to be prepared for possible acts of sabotage. Although shaken in his complacency from time to time, Kimmel was responsive to reassurances from his advisory group, which took the optimistic view that it was unnecessary to interrupt training schedules and supply operations so as to institute an alert. In agreement with the others in his group, he acknowledged the threat of a possible Japanese surprise attack, but firmly believed that the only potential targets were thousands of miles away. Admiral King, who headed a government investigation committee (which ended by court-martialing and demoting Admiral Kimmel for failing to take proper precautions), concluded that at Pearl Harbor there was an "unwarranted feeling of immunity from attack" (Morison, 1950, p. 138).

Kimmel's way of handling the war warnings shows how biased a responsible decision maker can become in evaluating fresh warnings from trustworthy sources. When the conditions making for defensive avoidance are present, a leader can mobilize the members of his advisory group, without any of them being aware of it, to look for loopholes and exceptions that will enable him to reject the warnings. Thus the leaders and his advisers fail to assimilate new information that might otherwise induce a change to a less risky course of action.

2. *Inventing new arguments to support the chosen policy.* Kimmel and his advisers bolstered their assumption that Pearl Harbor was immune from attack by inventing a number of erroneous arguments. At the time, all the faulty arguments seemed to be based on hard facts, but they could have been promptly corrected if anyone had taken the trouble to check out those alleged facts. The arguments were, in effect, rationalizations that enabled Kimmel and the members of his in-group to avoid thinking about the losses that might ensue from their unswerving policy of continuing to devote all resources to training and supply functions, without taking any special precautions to protect Hawaii from a surprise air attack. Among the rationalizations they invented were: (1) Japan would focus first on weak targets, such as the British and Dutch territories, before attacking any possession of the most powerful nation in the world; (2) in view of the great power of the U.S. Pacific Fleet, the risks of sending even one Japanese aircraft carrier close enough to attack Pearl Harbor were so great that Japan would never do so (i.e., the fleet at Pearl Harbor was seen as a deterrent, not as a possible target); (3) if the Japanese were foolish enough to send aircraft carriers, they could certainly be detected and destroyed in plenty of time, for even with only ten minutes' warning from the radar stations practically all attacking planes could be shot down; and (4) warships anchored at Pearl Harbor could not be sunk by aircraft because the only available torpedo bombs (i.e., the only ones known to the U.S. Navy at that time) required a depth of sixty feet, whereas Pearl Harbor was only thirty to forty feet deep. In view of all these considerations, there was obviously no need to waste the time of military personnel and use up

their equipment flying extensive reconnaissance missions. Nor was it necessary to deprive the fleet of its usual peacetime weekends in port, even though war with Japan could be expected to start at any time.

As it turned out, all these comfortable assumptions proved to be false. But in order to continue to feel comfortable, the decision makers had chosen, from among many possible inferences and interpretations, those conjectures that would enhance the case for their present, risky policy and help stifle their doubts about its validity.

Not all the naval officers at Pearl Harbor, incidentally, shared the rationalizations of Kimmel and his in-group. The officers aboard the *West Virginia*, for example, believed the fleet vulnerable to a surprise Japanese air attack that could occur at any moment, and they worked out effective emergency plans for their own warship (see Morison, pp. 107ff.). But the vast majority of naval officers evidently took their cue from their Commander in Chief and his close associates.

3. *Failing to explore ominous implications of ambiguous events.* During the days preceding the attack on Pearl Harbor, Kimmel became somewhat worried about the inability of Naval Combat Intelligence to locate the six Japanese aircraft carriers, and he asked his intelligence officers about the possible implications. He was informed that the carriers were probably in the Far East or possibly in home waters, as they had been on an earlier occasion when radio contact with them was temporarily lost. He did not probe any further, nor did he raise any embarrassing questions about alternative possibilities, except jokingly to suggest that the missing carriers might be proceeding toward Hawaii for a planned attack on Pearl Harbor.

Had Kimmel tried to piece together the implications of all the various warning messages and intelligence data at his disposal, he and his staff probably would have arrived at the conclusion that the Japanese carriers might well be on their way to carry out a surprise attack against Hawaii. Because this ominous inference was never considered, not a single reconnaisance plane was sent out to the north of the Hawaiian Islands, which allowed the Japanese to win the incredible gamble they were taking in attempting to send their aircraft carriers within bombing distance of Pearl Harbor without being detected.

A similar failure to entertain even tentatively an obvious interpretation that would challenge a comfortable assumption occurred on the morning of December 7. More than an hour before the Japanese attack started, a U.S. minesweeper reported to the harbor control post that its crew had tracked down and sunk a Japanese submarine near the entrance to Pearl Harbor. The watch officer, knowing that the presence of a Japanese submarine might be a prelude to an all-out attack, desperately telephoned all the relevant naval officers he could think of. But he was unable to convince anyone that this could possibly be an emergency. The higher-ranking officers he reached refused to act on the possibility that it was a

Japanese submarine and consequently did not sound an alert. Admiral Kimmel himself was informed, but, like the others, he was still waiting for confirmation that it was indeed an enemy submarine when Japanese aircraft started bombing the U.S. fleet.

These instances show how ambiguous events that could suggest to a vigilant decision maker the urgent necessity to reconsider his current policy can readily be interpreted in a reassuring way when he or she is motivated to avoid awareness of the defects of the chosen course of action. The decision maker entertains only those hypotheses that are consistent with his inclination to explain away any potentially ominous events; he fails to formulate or pursue alternative hypotheses that might represent a strong challenge to his decision.

Two other psychological devices that contribute to warding off challenging warnings—forgetting and misperceiving—may well have been displayed by Admiral Kimmel and other members of his staff, but we do not have documentation of any specific instances. There are well-authenticated instances at Pearl Harbor, however, of other high-ranking officers in the Navy exhibiting these behaviors.

4. *Forgetting information that would enable a challenging event to be interpreted correctly*. Before dawn on the morning of December 7, 1941, five hours before the Japanese started their air attack, two U.S. mine-sweepers just outside Pearl Harbor spotted an unidentified submerged submarine, which they presumed to be Japanese. But the captains failed to report the incident to their harbor control post. A naval officer at the naval command post accidentally overheard the radio conversations between the two captains, but he too failed to report the incident to anyone on Admiral Kimmel's staff. All three of the officers had evidently forgotten the explicit warning they had received from naval headquarters less than two months earlier stating that an encounter with a single Japanese sub should be regarded as a sign of extreme danger because it could imply the presence of a nearby Japanese aircraft carrier. This appears to be an example of the forgetting of previously learned information that, if remembered, would lead the person to realize the full significance of a challenging event.

5. *Misperceiving signs of the onset of actual danger*. On the morning of December 7, 1941, five minutes before the Japanese attack began, Commander Ramsey, an Operations officer at Pearl Harbor, observed an aircraft dive-bombing Ford Island, at the center of Pearl Harbor. But he misperceived it as an American plane. He assumed that the plane belonged to a hot U.S. pilot "flathatting," and he started to prepare a report to bring charges against the offender. Only when he saw and heard the explosions of the bombs did the commander finally realize that protective action was required. Belatedly, he rushed into the radio room and sent out the first official warning of the attack: "Air raid Pearl Harbor—this is no drill."

When unfavorable events begin to unfold that go counter to a person's expectations, he may shield himself from becoming aware of the challenge by misperceiving what is happening. This type of misperception, although a very flimsy mode of defense in the face of mounting calamity, enables a person temporarily to ward off psychological stress by maintaining an illusion of invulnerability, despite the onset of events that, if perceived correctly, would evoke acute awareness of impending danger.

These five modes of defensive behavior can be regarded as constituting an interrelated set of psychological processes that enter into defensive bolstering. They enable the decision maker at least temporarily to avoid taking account of disturbing information, and thereby protect his preferred policy from challenge. Often such bolstering is maladaptive, as in the examples just cited, since the decision makers ignore realistic warnings that require a prompt change in order to avert serious losses. But bolstering does not always have adverse consequences. During a disaster, when members of a military unit or civilian rescue team find themselves surrounded by danger, these same defensive devices may help the men survive by bolstering their decision to take the only available escape route, even though the odds seem overwhelmingly against them. Similarly, a cancer victim, having accepted his physician's recommendation to undergo a long and painful series of radiation treatments, may be able to avoid postdecisional regret and demoralization by ignoring the signs that the first few treatments are making him suffer more without bringing about any noticeable improvement. But the bolstering devices used by Admiral Kimmel and other top-level naval commanders preceding the Pearl Harbor disaster show how drastically search and appraisal can be affected when defensive avoidance becomes the dominant reaction to a series of challenging warnings.

Groupthink: A Collective Pattern of Defensive Avoidance

The case study of Kimmel and his in-group also illustrates how defensive avoidance tendencies on the part of the leader of an organization are encouraged when he receives social support from advisers who concur with his judgments and share in developing rationalizations that bolster the least objectionable choice. In this case, the rationalizations were apparently all the more convincing because they were shared by all members of the in-group. This is a prime example of a concurrence-seeking tendency that has been observed among highly cohesive groups. When this tendency is dominant, the members use their collective cognitive resources to develop rationalizations supporting shared illusions about the invulnerability of their organization or nation and display other symptoms of "groupthink"—a collective pattern of defensive avoidance (Janis, 1972).

Many historic fiascoes can be traced to defective policy making on the part of government leaders who receive social support from their in-group of advisers. A series of case studies of historic fiascoes by Janis (1972) suggests that the following four groups of policy advisers, like Kimmel's in-group of naval commanders, were dominated by concurrence seeking or groupthink and displayed characteristic symptoms of defensive avoidance: (1) Neville Chamberlain's inner circle, whose members supported the policy of appeasement of Hitler during 1937 and 1938, despite repeated warnings and events indicating that it would have adverse consequences; (2) President Truman's advisory group, whose members supported the decision to escalate the war in North Korea despite firm warnings by the Chinese Communist government that U.S. entry into North Korea would be met with armed resistance from the Chinese; (3) President Kennedy's inner circle, whose members supported the decision to launch the Bay of Pigs invasion of Cuba despite the availability of information indicating that it would be an unsuccessful venture and would damage U.S. relations with other countries; (4) President Johnson's close advisers, who supported the decision to escalate the war in Vietnam despite intelligence reports and other information indicating that this course of action would not defeat the Vietcong or the North Vietnamese and would entail unfavorable political consequences within the United States. All these groupthink-dominated groups were characterized by strong pressures toward uniformity, which inclined their members to avoid raising controversial issues, questioning weak arguments, or calling a halt to soft-headed thinking.[7]

Eight major symptoms characterize the groupthink or concurrence-seeking tendency as it prevailed in these historic fiascoes. Each symptom can be identified by a variety of indicators, derived from historical records, observers' accounts of conversations, and participants' memoirs. The eight symptoms of groupthink are

1. an illusion of invulnerability, shared by most or all of the members, which creates excessive optimism and encourages taking extreme risks;
2. collective efforts to rationalize in order to discount warnings which might lead the members to reconsider their assumptions before they recommit themselves to their past policy decisions;
3. an unquestioned belief in the group's inherent morality, inclining the members to ignore the ethical or moral consequences of their decisions;
4. stereotyped views of rivals and enemies as too evil to warrant genuine attempts to negotiate, or as too weak or stupid to counter whatever risky attempts are made to defeat their purposes;
5. direct pressure on any member who expresses strong arguments against any of the group's stereotypes, illusions, or commitments, making clear that such dissent is contrary to what is expected of all loyal members;
6. self-censorship of deviations from the apparent group consensus, reflecting each member's inclination to minimize to himself the importance of his doubts and counterarguments;

7. a shared illusion of unanimity, partly resulting from this self-censorship and augmented by the false assumption that silence implies consent;
8. the emergence of self-appointed "mindguards"—members who protect the group from adverse information that might shatter their shared complacency about the effectiveness and morality of their decisions.

Figure 5 presents a schematic analysis showing the main conditions under which a strong concurrence-seeking tendency is likely to become dominant in a policy-making group, giving rise to the symptoms of groupthink and to defective decision making. The antecedent conditions are inferred from comparisons of the fiascoes mentioned above with well-worked-out policy decisions, such as the Truman administration's Marshall Plan and the Kennedy administration's handling of the Cuban missile crisis (see Janis, 1972).

The first two conditions shown in the left-hand box of figure 5 probably have direct effects on the conformity motivation of the members (Cartwright and Zander, 1968). When the cohesiveness of a group increases from a low to a moderate or high level, each member becomes more psychologically dependent on the group and displays greater readiness to adhere to the group's norms. If the group is insulated in such a way that the members have little or no opportunity to discuss certain policy issues outside the group, they can be expected to show an increased tendency to rely upon the judgments of the group on those issues. The third condition, lack of methodical procedures for search and appraisal, affords an unbridled license to conformity tendencies within the group, because of the absence of procedural safeguards against cursory and biased treatment of policy issues. The fourth condition, directive leadership, increases the likelihood that the leader will use his power, subtly or blatantly, to induce the members to conform with his decisions. When a directive leader announces his preference on a policy issue—whether it be to postpone making any decision, to pass the buck to another group in the organization, or to select one particular alternative as the best policy—the members of a cohesive group will tend to accept his choice somewhat uncritically, as though it were equivalent to a group norm. The last pair of conditions (high stress along with a low degree of hope for finding a solution better than the one favored by the leader or other influential members) specifies the prime conditions that foster defensive avoidance. After a leader lets it be known that he favors a particular policy alternative, the members are in the common predicament of having little hope of finding a better solution (because advocating a different alternative will evoke the disapproval of the most esteemed person in the group and of all those who uncritically support him). They will be motivated to reduce the high stress of their decisional conflict by collectively bolstering the choice made by the leader.

We assume that the theoretical model of coping patterns can be applied whether the individual is participating in a group decision with

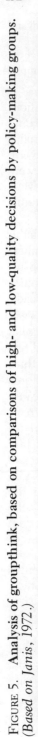

FIGURE 5. Analysis of groupthink, based on comparisons of high- and low-quality decisions by policy-making groups. (*Based on Janis*, 1972.)

fellow members or is making the decision entirely on his own. The main difference is that for each member of a moderately or highly cohesive group, one particular incentive looms very large and exerts considerable influence on his choice when he is participating in a group decision— namely, the social approval or disapproval he anticipates receiving from the leader and from fellow members.

The foregoing analysis is compatible with the assumption that not all cohesive groups suffer from groupthink, though all may display its symptoms from time to time. A group not insulated from outside evaluations, and subject to traditions and norms facilitating critical inquiry and nonauthoritarian leadership practices, is probably capable of making a better decision than any individual in the group working on the problem alone. Yet the potential advantages of having decisions made by groups are often lost because of psychological pressures that arise when the members work closely together, share the same values, and above all face a crisis situation in which everyone realizes at the outset that whatever action the group decides to take will be fraught with serious risks and that there is little hope of obtaining new information that will lead to a satisfactory solution. In these circumstances, the leader and the members of his in-group are subjected to stresses that generate a strong need for affiliation. As conformity pressures begin to dominate, the striving for unanimity fosters the pattern of defensive avoidance, with the characteristic reliance on shared rationalizations that bolster the least objectionable alternative.

CHAPTER **6**

The Decisional Balance Sheet

IN AN EARLIER ANALYSIS of decision-making processes (Janis, 1959), a decisional "balance sheet" of incentives was proposed as a schema comprehending both the cognitive and the motivational aspects of human planning for future action. It is intended to be broadly applicable to all important decisions that are made by a person as a leader of an organization or member of an executive committee, and to those decisions that pertain to his or her own work tasks and personal life. We propose to use the balance sheet as a descriptive schema to supplement the conflict model of coping patterns. We find it especially valuable for analyzing the degree to which a decision maker does a thorough and accurate job of exploring the full range of alternatives open to him and considering the favorable and unfavorable consequences of each alternative.

Whenever we are able to follow up on the fate of an important decision to see how well it has worked out and in what ways it has gone wrong, an analysis of changes in the balance sheet of incentives can be made that enables us retrospectively to specify errors in the forecasts made by the decision maker at the time he committed himself to the decision. The balance sheet schema provides an analytical vocabulary for describing what happens when a decision maker uses a defective coping pattern, such as a crude form of defensive avoidance. The fewest errors in the decisional balance sheet are to be expected when the decision maker meets all seven criteria of vigilant information processing (see chapter 1). Thus, the most incomplete and unrealistic balance sheets are to be expected when vigilance is totally absent—when the entire predecisional period is characterized by the predominance of one or another of the defective coping patterns: unconflicted change, defensive avoidance, or hypervigilance.

In contrast to game-theory schemas that deal with impersonal judgments concerning a choice among alternative payoffs and risks involving a single type of benefit (such as making money in a business deal), the decisional balance sheet schema is intended for analyzing ego-involving decisions among alternative courses of action viewed by the decision maker as entailing a large number of different types of potential benefits, costs, and risks. Accordingly, the many different "reasons" a person has for arriving at a complicated decision are conceptualized in the balance sheet as a large number of entries corresponding to a *multidimensional* set of values. The entries represent all the various anticipated favorable and unfavorable consequences that the decision maker takes into account for each of the alternatives he considers.

Some of the main assumptions of the decisional balance sheet schema are the same as those of various additive gain-loss models suggested by other social scientists (e.g., Blau, 1964; Gergen, 1969; Homans, 1961; Jones, 1964; Thibaut and Kelley, 1959; Vroom, 1969). All these authors assume that a person will not decide, say, to join a group or continue a given course of action unless he expects the gains to exceed the losses. Thibaut and Kelley (1959) emphasize that it is not the *absolute* amount of gain and loss he expects to encounter that determines the value a person will place on a given choice, but the amount relative to a *comparison level*, based on the amount of reward or punishment the person has obtained in the past or has seen other people obtaining. The more the anticipated outcome exceeds the comparison level, the more satisfying it is; the farther it is below the comparison level, the more unsatisfying. Thus, a person will tolerate disagreeable treatment that is far below the standard he or she requires to be satisfied (e.g., an unhappily married person may decide not to seek a divorce), if the comparison level for the alternative (divorce) is so low that it is expected to yield an even worse outcome. In brief, the choice a person makes in deciding, say, whether or not to continue to be affiliated with someone (or with a group) depends upon the relative gains and losses he expects to obtain from the other person or persons. This is one of the elementary assumptions embodied in the decisional balance sheet schema. The schema also includes, however, all the other types of gain and loss that can influence a decision maker's choice—not just social rewards and punishments, the one type on which the analysis by Thibaut and Kelley and the work of most other social psychologists have primarily been focused.

This multivalued schema for analyzing decisional conflicts has been directly influenced by the expectancy theory of Kurt Lewin (1938, 1946, 1948). He postulated that the course of action a person chooses will change as a function of increases or decreases in the relative strength of two psychological forces or vectors arising from the decision maker's expectancies. One is the net vector that motivates him to seek the expected gains, which is the summation of all the positive valences. The other is the net vector that motivates him to avoid the expected losses, which is the summation of all the negative valences. Our formulation also appears to be compatible with Edwards's (1961) concept of subjectively expected utility of alternative courses of action (the SEU model) and with the recent elaborations of Lewin's expectancy theory in relation to achievement motivation (Atkinson, 1964; Atkinson and Birch, 1970) and in relation to management in large organizations (Vroom, 1964; Porter and Lawler, 1968).[1] The main problems to which expectancy theorists have applied their concepts, however, are different from those with which we are primarily concerned, namely, identifying the factors that determine the modes of resolving decisional conflicts.

Four Major Types of Consequence

What are the major kinds of consideration that enter into decisional conflicts? The types of expected consequence of each alternative course of action can be exhaustively classified into the four main categories of the balance sheet schema (see Janis, 1959; Janis and Mann, 1968):

1. utilitarian gains and losses for self;
2. utilitarian gains and losses for significant others;
3. self-approval or -disapproval; and
4. approval or disapproval from significant others.

1. *Utilitarian gains and losses for self.* This category includes all the expected instrumental effects of the decision with regard to personal utilitarian objectives. For example, a graduating senior who is choosing among several medical schools to which he has been accepted typically takes account of such utilitarian considerations as the quality of the instruction he can expect to receive at each (which determines the chances of his attaining his main educational objectives), the prestige of the institution (which affects the prospects of his attaining certain career objectives after he obtains a degree), the living conditions at and in the vicinity of the school, the financial costs, and a variety of other factors that he anticipates will affect his personal welfare while attending the institution and afterward.

2. *Utilitarian gains and losses for significant others.* The instrumental considerations in this category pertain to the goals of persons and groups with which the decision maker is identified or affiliated. When an administrator of a large industrial or governmental organization, for example, is making a policy decision, he is likely to give considerable weight to utilitarian gains and losses pertaining to the productivity and the morale of

TABLE 3. **A schematic balance sheet grid for conceptualizing decisional conflict.** *(Based on Janis, 1959.)*

TYPES OF ANTICIPATION	ALTERNATIVE COURSES OF ACTION					
with examples from research on career conflicts of lawyers	*Alternative 1 (e.g., job with Department of Justice)*		*Alternative 2 (e.g., job with a Wall Street firm)*		*Alternative 3 (e.g., private practice in a small town)*	
	+	−	+	−	+	−

A. Utilitarian gains or losses for self
  1. Personal income
  2. Interest value of daily work
  3. Opportunity to live in a preferred city
  .
  .
  .
  n						

B. Utilitarian gains or losses for significant others
  1. Social status for family
  2. Reducing political corruption in community
  3. Advancing civil rights for nation
  .
  .
  n						

C. Self-approval or -disapproval
  1. Moral considerations pertaining to ethical legal practices
  2. "Ego ideal" of being an independent thinker
  3. Self-image as defender of innocent people
  .
  .
  n						

D. Social approval or disapproval
  1. From wife (or husband)
  2. From close friends
  3. From a national professional organization
  .
  .
  n						

The cells in this schematic grid should be visualized as being filled with positive (+) and negative (−) entries of varying magnitude depicting the strength of the incentives to accept or reject each alternative. The purpose of filling out the grid is to predict vulnerability to subsequent setbacks by identifying the main sources of conflict. Ordinarily the grid is set up with the rows representing the alternative courses of action; the rows and columns are reversed in this table in order to list examples of subcategories within each of the four types of anticipations.

others in the organization; the costs of various alternatives, in terms of financial and other resources the organization has at its disposal; and the prestige value for the organization among its clients or affiliates and among the public at large. When one is making a personal career decision, this category includes all the effects the decision is expected to have for satisfying the needs of people in one's social network, particularly one's family.

3. *Self-approval or -disapproval.* Internalized moral standards, ego ideals, and components of self-image are implicated in every important decision. These considerations, at least in derivative form, involve self-esteem. Among the questions a person might put to himself are "Will I feel proud or ashamed of myself if I make this choice? Will I be living up to my ideals? Will this decision enable me to become the kind of person I want to be?"

4. *Approval or disapproval by significant others.* The potential approval or disapproval of reference groups and reference persons who are expected to evaluate either the decision itself or the individual's competence as a decision maker constitutes another important kind of consideration. Whether he is a prestigious government leader trying to grapple with a military policy decision that could affect the future of millions of people throughout the world or a humble citizen trying to make a choice concerning his own marriage or career, the decision maker is likely to pose to himself the question "Will my friends and other important people in my life feel that I made the right choice?" Anticipated social feedback, which includes being criticized and ridiculed by a group as well as receiving praise and respect, can play a crucial role in determining the decision maker's judgment of the best possible alternative, his willingness or unwillingness to commit himself, and his willingness to stick to a decision or reverse it after he encounters distressing setbacks.

In the most important decisions a person makes throughout his life, all four types of consideration are relevant to some extent, and the outcome is presumably determined by the relative strength of these incentives. Decisional conflicts are conceptualized in our schema in terms of a balance sheet containing positive and negative values corresponding to the potential gains (positive incentives) and potential losses (negative incentives) anticipated by the decision maker with respect to each alternative open to him (see table 3). For most decisions in everyday life, the main considerations in the four categories are likely to be conscious, verbalized anticipations. Occasionally, an important consideration may be temporarily preconscious, but readily accessible to consciousness if someone calls it to the decision maker's attention. By and large, all these considerations are subject to social influence through informational inputs and persuasive arguments presented either in the mass media or in interpersonal discussions. In exceptional instances, the individual remains unaware of an important consideration that is shaping his decision, because of the operation of repression and other psychological defense mechanisms (see the case studies in chapter 4).

Importance of Nonutilitarian Considerations

Utilitarian considerations are sometimes the only ones accounted for in analyses of decision making by social scientists, especially by those concerned with so-called rational choices that maximize an individual's or organization's goals. But such considerations are not necessarily the only ones taken into account by the decision makers themselves. Examples have been cited earlier in which anticipated social disapproval and self-disapproval appear to be major deterrents to choosing an attractive course of action. Sometimes the expected nonutilitarian gains exert so much influence on the decision maker's choice that they counteract the expected utilitarian losses that would otherwise incline him to select a different alternative. According to a *Fortune* magazine survey, conducted in 1969, there was a marked shift during the 1960s among American college students away from choosing a career on the basis of the usual utilitarian goals of money, social status, and good working conditions and toward choosing a form of "meaningful" life work that would enable them to contribute to and feel part of "the community." Physicians who choose to work in public clinics and attorneys who choose to work in legal aid clinics for the poor provide prime examples of career choices governed largely by anticipated social approval from reference groups and anticipated self-approval based on personal ideals.

Social approval from reference groups often seems to reinforce a person's efforts to live up to his ideals and thereby increases his sense of pride and satisfaction with regard to the humanitarian and ethical value of his work. When a physician or lawyer encounters daily signs of approval from the persons and groups that matter most to him (for example, his wife, his friends, his in-group of professional colleagues, and his mentors), he will be inclined to stick with the work he is doing even though elsewhere he encounters serious setbacks in the form of distressing utilitarian losses (such as failure to be promoted, a salary cut, an increased work load, worsening of daily working conditions, or exposure to public vilification by local politicians who oppose his work). Such setbacks, when first encountered by young professional men and women who have chosen low-paying community work on the basis of their strong humanitarian ideals, can generate considerable stress and evoke postdecisional conflict. But the nonutilitarian gains of social and self-approval often enable the harassed professional worker to withstand the accumulated stresses generated by utilitarian losses and to persevere in his difficult line of work even though he may have the opportunity to switch to a much more lucrative and comfortable position. Here again we take note of one of Kurt Lewin's key ideas, related to the "freezing" of opinions, judgments, and decisions: "Only by anchoring his own conduct in something as substantial and superindividual as the culture of the group, can the individual stabilize his new beliefs sufficiently to keep them immune from the day-to-day fluctuations of moods and influences to which he, as an individual, is subject" (Lewin, 1948, p. 59).

Ambivalence in a Dissatisfied Executive

Nonutilitarian gains can also play a major role in the job satisfaction of executives in large industrial organizations, even when they have little interest in humanitarian goals and accept the fact that the main purpose of their work is to help the firm make as much money as possible. A pertinent example was encountered in a study of middle-level executives in a large manufacturing plant.

Sofer and Janis conducted systematic interviews with eighty-one British managers and technical specialists, using questions designed to find out the way these executives perceived their present and future careers, including the place of their work in their personal "identity" and its relationship to other aspects of their lives (see Sofer, 1970). Some of the questions were specifically designed to determine the sources of postdecisional conflict concerning their career choices and the modes of conflict resolution they adopted to cope with unfavorable consequences of their past decisions. The men spoke very freely during these interviews and gave a vivid picture of the pressures to which they felt themselves subjected every day, their worries about being promoted into the upper level of management, the disorganization resulting from "reorganizations" by upper-level managers, and the all-too-few sources of gratification they found in their roles as middle-level executives. Many of the men were thinking about the possibility of trying to find a different job. Each interview was systematically scored according to a content analysis procedure that categorized every relevant favorable (+) or unfavorable (−) statement about their job (or any alternative they were considering) into one or another of the four categories of the decisional balance sheet.

In one interview of a production manager who had said that he was quite satisfied with his present job, we were struck by the extraordinarily large number of minus entries in his decisional balance sheet. These entries were so numerous because he made many complaints about his work—the long hours he had to put in, the constant time pressures from his superiors in the firm, the unpleasant paperwork he was often required to do, and the relatively poor prospects for advancement to a higher-level position, to which he, as a self-styled "ambitious go-getter," keenly aspired. He also criticized the firm for making the life of executives like himself unduly chaotic because of repeated reorganizations. "It's a terrible thing this firm has been doing to us," he said, "and I have spent many a night in a bar trying to convince one or another man [in the firm] to get over his depression."

These entries in the category *utilitarian losses for self* were augmented by several entries in the category *utilitarian losses for significant others*—for example, having little time to spend with his wife and two children. The relatively large number of minus entries in the utilitarian categories placed this man in the upper fifth of the sample of eighty-one executives, so far as complaints were concerned. Most other executives who had that many complaints indicated that they did not plan to stay on with the firm in the future, and would be quite willing to accept an equivalent opening elsewhere. But the production manager, despite all his complaints, said that he was fairly well satisfied with his job. He knew other executives who were disillusioned with the company and wanted to leave; but he was not interested in trying to find another position. Why not?

The answer lay in the nonutilitarian columns of this man's decisional balance sheet. Here we found a large number of plus entries, centered on such considerations as being proud of himself as the leader of a well-organized, competent team with very high morale. He felt that if he were to leave his position, he would be "letting down" the other men on the team; moreover, he would not want to disappoint his immediate superior, with whom he had a warm, friendly relationship. Together they were able to save the team, in his view, from being demoralized by the harassments and oversights of the managers at the top. Thus, he was gratified by having the approval of an in-group of men with whom he worked closely; he anticipated incurring their disapproval if he were to try to leave. These appeared to be the determining considerations in this man's decisional balance sheet, outweighing all the negative utilitarian considerations concerning the long hours, unnecessary paperwork, unreasonable deadlines, and so on.

Nonutilitarian Considerations in Ethical Dilemmas

Internalized moral standards, ego ideals, and other components of a person's self-image tend to be implicated in every important decision, although the decision maker may give them only fleeting attention. This set of considerations can become a major source of postdecisional conflict, especially when the decision maker has been so concerned to be objective that he has completely ignored his own subjective feelings of anticipatory guilt and social anxiety about a "hard-nosed" decision that involves exploiting or harming others. Anticipations of self-approval or -disapproval are often not explicitly formulated, but it is likely that while making a vital decision a decision maker always has some identifiable thoughts that refer, at least in derivative form, to disturbing questions about self-esteem: "Will I feel proud of myself or ashamed? Will I be living up to my ideals or letting myself down?"

Anticipations of self-disapproval, although rarely appraised systematically by a decision maker, are capable of arousing strong feelings of guilt, remorse, and self-reproach. These distressing reactions sometimes incline a person to reject a decision that is seemingly compatible with his utilitarian values and with the norms of the groups and persons with whom he is affiliated. For example, a young man arrested for reckless driving after colliding with another car may feel impelled to plead guilty in order to salve his conscience, even though he would like to hide the truth about his negligence to protect himself and his family from financial loss and social disapproval. Ethical dilemmas of this kind are almost invariably associated with strong anticipations of self-disapproval.

Self-reactions of approval or disapproval may play a crucial role in shaping a fundamental decision that brings in its wake a marked transformation of the individual's personal values or life style. Helen Lynd (1958) has given a detailed account of changes that arise when a person realizes he has made a mistake or reveals a personal weakness that unexpectedly stirs up acute feelings of self-disparagement, even though the precipitating incident may be quite trivial. Lynd speaks of "a wound to one's self-esteem, a painful feeling or sense of degradation excited in the consciousness of having done something unworthy of one's previous idea of one's own excellence" (Lynd, 1958, p. 24). If the person verbalizes his feelings, he speaks in terms of feeling ashamed of himself for failing to live up to his expectations or ideals. While suffering from this traumatic type of shame reaction, the person is burdened with an almost hopeless feeling that the only way he can ever restore the damaged image of himself is to change himself in some fundamental way. As a consequence he may make a fundamental decision to change his entire way of life, as in the case of a dejected businessman who gives up his former career to devote himself to a social cause.

Decisional conflicts involving circumscribed moral or ethical issues frequently arise in the course of carrying out one's assigned duties as an executive or professional. Consider some of the typical ethical dilemmas faced by physicians, psychiatrists, clinical psychologists, nurses, social workers, and other professionals engaged in the delivery of health services. Which of the many patients with incurable heart disease should be selected to be the recipient of a heart transplant? Should an elderly patient be kept alive in a permanently comatose state with the aid of intravenous feedings and drugs? When a mental patient reveals that he has homicidal impulses toward his father, should the endangered parent (and/or the police) be told? A comparatively easy way to resolve such dilemmas, without going through the agony of a crisis of conscience, is to act in accordance with the prevailing norms of a professional organization or some other reference group. When this happens, the incentives that play a determining role in the decisional balance sheet are those in the category of anticipated social approval or disapproval from significant groups or persons. Studies of men and women in "helping professions" suggest that there is a strong tendency among them to adopt just such a solution.

Wiskoff (1960), for example, asked professional psychologists to judge ethical issues of the type that come up from time to time in their professional work, such as whether to inform the threatened person when a client reveals that he is contemplating committing a violent act. He found that clinical and applied psychologists differed in their choices according to reference-group membership. Psychologists who were members of the Counseling and Clinical Division of the American Psychological Association showed a much stronger preference against releasing information about their clients than psychologists who belonged to the Industrial Psychology Division.

A study by Statman and Hershkowitz (1969) reports similar results for advanced trainees in social work and physical therapy. The trainees were presented with realistic case histories of two persons suffering from a deadly kidney disease and were asked to decide which one should be selected to receive treatment with the only available kidney machine. Social work students, in line with the norms of their newly acquired professional reference group, which emphasize the mission of giving aid to persons who are socially disadvantaged, favored the individual or family in greater need of financial aid, whereas the physical therapy students made choices consistent with the prevailing ethics in their profession, which emphasizes reward for individual effort.

It has often been suggested that secondary groups like the national professional organizations to which we have been referring influence their members largely through local face-to-face groups, which select new objectives and set up new standards of behavior. But a professional organization's norms can also shape or reinforce the personal moral standards of many of its members through ethical codes, training, review of performance, and accreditation. In general, anticipated disapproval from either a primary or secondary group, including fellow members of a professional organization that has clear-cut ethical norms, adds one or more negative incentives to the decisional balance sheet when a person is seeking to resolve an ethical dilemma.

Analyzing Modes of Resolution

Quantitative methods for assessing and combining the positive and negative incentive values that enter into decisional conflicts are as yet not very well developed, and until they are the decisional balance sheet cannot be used to predict which choice a person will end up making (e.g., whether he will accept or reject a new policy recommended in a persuasive message). But we expect that the balance sheet will soon prove to be useful for assessing the quality of predecisional planning and for predicting certain aspects of postdecisional behavior, such as the modes of conflict resolution the person will display and the way he will respond to various types of negative feedback after he has committed himself to take action.

Social psychologists point out that when a person is confronted with threatened losses from pursuing a course of action to which he is committed, his mode of resolution depends on the importance of the threat and its imminence (Abelson, 1968; Hardyck and Kardush, 1968; Kelman and Baron, 1968). Specific hypotheses about the influence of the *content* of the threat on modes of resolution can be generated by taking account of the four categories of the decisional balance sheet. We assume that although all decisional conflicts share some of the same basic psychological features with respect to generating stress, there are nevertheless important differences in behavioral consequences, depending upon whether the source of stress is the threat of anticipated loss primarily in the utilitarian, social, or self sphere. More specifically, a different repertoire of conflict resolution comes into operation for conflicts involving utilitarian losses for the self as against conflicts involving utilitarian losses for significant others or conflicts involving social or self-disapproval.[2] One of the main reasons for making distinctions among the four types of anticipation in the balance sheet is to predict these different modes of resolution, which we assume to be in the response repertoire of most people. The following typology is intended to categorize all those instances where (a) the main considerations entering into the decision generally tend to support the decision, but (b) opposing these dominant pluses is a subdominant minus consideration that creates an acute decisional conflict.

Type 1: *Compensating for utilitarian loss to self.* Defensive bolstering is a prevalent mode of alleviating residual conflict after commitment. But when the decision maker encounters clear-cut signs that a prior decision is resulting in an unexpected loss of personal income, unpleasant tasks, physical suffering, or some other form of personal utilitarian loss, defensive bolstering is undermined; the decision maker can no longer succeed in ignoring, minimizing, or denying the salient unfavorable consequences. If he is too committed to reverse the decision, he will display compensatory actions in an effort to belittle these salient minus considerations. For example, a businessman may attempt to make up for anticipated loss of money resulting from a recent decision to finance a new building by plunging into activity oriented toward capitalizing on other positive utilitarian gains, such as increased publicity for his business.

Type 2: *Minimizing utilitarian loss to others.* When a postdecisional conflict arises because of a utilitarian loss to a significant person or a group with whom the decision maker feels identified, he will tend to use the same modes of resolution as when he alone is the loser. However, there are some expected differences when regret or remorse relates to what is happening to someone else rather than to oneself. If he is unable to maintain the belief that in the long run the decision will really turn out to be beneficial to his business or professional organization, the decision maker will attempt to change the ideology of the group in a direction that devalues the given loss. Thus, he may begin to proselytize the other members of his organization or attempt to form a powerful faction with a new ideology that represents a shift in values.[3] If such efforts fail to alleviate his postdecisional conflict, the person may resort to more extreme modes of defensive avoidance, such as losing interest in the organization or shifting his affiliation to a rival organization, so that he no longer feels so concerned about the losses suffered by the organization with which he was originally affiliated. The same type of devaluation is likely to occur when, instead of an organization, the "significant others" are individual members of one's family, a primary group of close friends, or a relatively remote secondary group such as one's political party, church, or nation.

Type 3: *Counteracting self-disapproval.* When a person discovers that a decision requires him to carry out actions that violate his moral code or that have a damaging effect on his self-image, he will exhibit a number of compensatory changes in moral values or ego ideals to belittle the salient minus consideration. For example, if a man has chosen a highly rewarding job that unexpectedly turns out to require dishonest practices, he may begin to devalue the importance of honesty and end up modifying his moral code. But this type of conflict will persist if a major source of stress is intense guilt and loss of self-esteem. The psychological mechanisms used to counteract such affective disturbances tend to be different from those used to resolve any of the other three types of decisional conflict. In attempting to reduce his guilt about engaging in unethical activities entailed by a prior decision, the decision maker may decide to undertake acts of expiation, asceticism, or excessive compliance (Aronson, 1969; Carlsmith and Gross, 1969; Flugel, 1945; Freedman, Wallington, and Bless, 1967; Janis, 1958; McMillen, 1971). For example, a businessman reported in an interview that he felt acutely guilty about having invested a substantial sum of money in merchandise for his store at a time when he should have used it to travel to the "old country" to see his ailing mother. When his mother died, he sold all the misbegotten merchandise at cost in an effort to renounce any gain from the objectionable decision. Other acts of reparation of this kind include an increase in religious observance, a decrease in sexual activity or in pleasurable, leisure-time activities, and changes in many other spheres of daily life that have no logical connection with the guilt-laden decision. A vivid account of the use of this defensive type of moralistic transformation to alleviate guilt and restore self-approval is given in Joseph Conrad's *Lord Jim*—the story of a young naval officer who renounces all his former goals and devotes himself exclusively to self-sacrificing humanitarian acts in a remote part of the world. Conrad's account makes it clear that this fundamental change in the young man's way of life came about as a consequence of self-condemnation following an accident at sea in which he made an impulsive decision to abandon his ship when he should have tried to save the passengers' lives. Similar extreme reactions are suggested by case studies of persons who have undergone a prolonged period of self-blame and depression following a decision that had led to violations of their moral code. In such cases, suicide or other destructive forms of *self-punitive* action, which are probably unique to decisional conflicts of type 3, may predominate.

Type 4: *Counteracting disapproval from others*. After one has made a major decision, the comforting belief that it will be accepted without any serious objections by all the significant persons and groups in one's life is likely to persist until it is rudely shattered by inescapable evidence that the threat of severe disapproval is imminent or has actually materialized. A typical way of dealing with this source of decisional conflict is to try to convince those who disapprove that one's own position is the correct one. If a man has little hope of succeeding at such an attempt, he can at least hope to demonstrate to them that he is a worthwhile person, so that their disapproval should be temperate and not lead to formal censure or informal ostracism. Thus, the person takes on difficult group tasks, makes special sacrifices for the sake of the group, loudly protests his loyalty to the group. and so on—all of which actions are compensatory efforts, although on the surface they seem to be quite irrelevant to the decision in question. If the person fails in these efforts to ward off the sustained disapproval of the group and is unable to secure a satisfying balance of approval from substitute persons or subgroups, he will eventually become psychologically (if not officially) disaffiliated from the disapproving group and will seek other means to satisfy his social needs. Essentially the same process of disaffiliation will occur with respect to a reference person, such as a close friend, a respected leader, or a spouse—the prototype being the child's aggrieved reaction of turning away from one of his parents if that parent subjects him to a prolonged period of painful rejection.[4]

The Defective-Balance-Sheet Hypothesis

The balance sheet provides something more than a useful vocabulary for talking about changes in attitudes and values resulting from events and communications that call attention to the consequences of a decisional choice. There would be little purpose in using this vocabulary if it did not alert us to look into relationships among variables that might otherwise be overlooked and improve our ability to make predictions about the way in which external events and communications will influence a decision maker's behavior.

One major reason for classifying all the pro and con considerations for each alternative into the four categories in the decisional balance sheet is that such a classification enables one to make cogent predictions about the types of negative feedback to which the decision maker will be most vulnerable after he commits himself. The predictions are pertinent to such questions as: How shaken will the decision maker be by a given bit of negative feedback? How much negative feedback will the decision maker be able to take before the decision will be challenged to the point where he begins to consider reversing it?

One of the main conclusions suggested by research with persons who have made stressful decisions such as giving up smoking, going on a diet, or undergoing surgery or painful medical treatments is the following: *the more errors of omission and commission in the decision maker's balance sheet at the time he commits himself to a new course of action, the greater will be his vulnerability to negative feedback when he subsequently implements the decision* (Janis, 1958, 1959, 1971). (Errors of omission include overlooking obvious and knowable losses that will ensue from the chosen course, which makes the balance sheet incomplete; errors of commission include false expectations about improbable gains that are overoptimistically expected, which are tantamount to incorrect entries in the balance sheet). To illustrate the implications of this "defective-balance-sheet" hypothesis, let us consider what is likely to happen to a decision maker who is blithely unaware of the strong objections that his family and a few of his friends will have to his career choice. He will be profoundly shaken by their unanticipated social disapproval during the postdecisional period and also by some of their unfamiliar arguments against his newly adopted plan of action. Being totally unprepared to deal with the challenge, the decision maker is likely to overreact, decide that he made a bad mistake, and set about retrieving a discarded alternative from the decisional scrap heap. But if he is aware beforehand of the negative social feedback he is likely to encounter, he will be more likely to resist being influenced and dismiss the objections as minor drawbacks that he has already contended with. According to the conflict model of coping patterns (figure 3), the probability of ending up with a defective balance sheet is lowest when the decision maker gives positive answers to all four key questions, thus meeting the conditions for vigilant information processing.

The defective-balance-sheet hypothesis asserts that the stability of a decision depends on the completeness and accuracy with which the decision maker has completed his decisional balance sheet *before he begins to implement the decision*. Among the errors of omission in an incomplete balance sheet are the losses to be sustained from foregoing each of the rejected alternatives (the "opportunity costs" of the decision); hence adherence to a decision requires taking note not only of all the negative entries for the chosen course of action but also of all the positive entries for the unchosen alternatives (so that the decision maker will remain relatively uninfluenced by subsequent events and communications that temporarily make one or another of the unchosen ones appear to be more attractive). This is not meant to imply that stability in the face of new, unpredictable information is a virtue; rather, the point is that instability resulting from neglect of information that was readily available at the time of decision is a vice.

A Procedure for Filling In the Gaps

It follows from the defective-balance-sheet hypothesis that if a person is induced to fill in gaps in his balance sheet by being stimulated to recall all that he already knows or can surmise about the alternatives open to him, he will show less postdecisional distress when he subsequently encounters setbacks and losses. To investigate this implication of the hypothesis, a balance sheet procedure was developed by Janis (1968) in a series of pilot studies of young men facing a major career choice.

This procedure takes as its point of departure the tally sheet of pros and cons proposed over two hundred years ago by Benjamin Franklin to deal with multiple-value decisions requiring a tradeoff approach (cited by MacCrimmon, 1973). In a letter dated September 19, 1772, to Joseph Priestly, the great British scientist, Franklin wrote:

> In the affair of so much importance to you, wherein you ask my advice, I cannot, for want of sufficient premises, advise you what to determine, but if you please I will tell you how. When those difficult cases occur, they are difficult, chiefly because while we have them under consideration, all the reasons pro and con are not present to the mind at the same time; but sometimes one set present themselves, and at other times another, the first being out of sight. Hence the various purposes or inclinations that alternatively prevail, and the uncertainty that perplexes us. To get over this, my way is to divide half a sheet of paper by a line into two columns; writing over the one Pro, and over the other Con. Then, during three or four days consideration, I put down under the different heads short hints of the different motives, that at different times occur to me, for or against the measure. When I have thus got them all together in one view, I endeavor to estimate their respective weights; and where I find two, one on each side, that seem equal, I strike them both out. If I find a reason pro equal to some two reasons con, I strike out the three. If I judge some two reasons con, equal to some three reasons pro, I strike out the five; and thus proceeding I find at length where the balance lies; and if, after a day or two of further consideration, nothing new that is of importance occurs on either side, I come to a determination accordingly. And, though the weight of reasons cannot be taken with the precision of algebraic quantities, yet when each is thus considered, separately and comparatively, and the whole lies before me, I think I can judge better, and am less liable to make a rash step, and in fact I have found great advantage from this kind of equation, in what may be called moral or prudential algebra.

In its present incarnation, the balance sheet procedure is intended primarily to prevent errors of omission—especially the tendency to over-look anticipated approval and disapproval from significant others and from oneself. In addition, the procedure stimulates the decision maker to search his memory and to ask others for realistic information bearing on the consequences of the alternative choices, which can lead him to rectify errors of commission.

To pretest the balance sheet procedure, Janis (1968) conducted inter-views with Yale College seniors several months before graduation, when they were trying to decide what they would do during the subsequent year. At the beginning of each interview, the respondent was given a series of questions asking him to state all the alternatives he was considering and to specify the pros and the cons for each alternative. Then the new proce-dure, which consists of showing the person a balance sheet grid with empty cells to be filled in and explaining to him the meaning of each category, was introduced. (Details about the procedure are described in appendix A.) The main steps are as follows: first, the interviewer helps the person fill in the entries he has already mentioned for the most preferred alternatives. Then the interviewer asks the person to examine each cell in the balance sheet again, this time trying to think of considerations that he has not yet talked about. Finally, to encourage the person to explore neglected considerations, he is given a sheet listing all the various types of considerations that might be involved in a career choice like the one he is making (see table 4). The bulk of the time spent on this exercise is usually devoted to those categories with few or no entries, most often those per-taining to self and social approval or disapproval.

During extensive pretesting it was discovered that the explorations and confrontations engendered by this procedure made it into something quite different from the coldly intellectual exercise suggested by the tally sheet format. Some of our pilot subjects appeared to undergo an intense emotional experience as they began to write down potential consequences of their preferred course of action to which they had given little or no thought. One senior who originally was planning to go to a graduate business school for training to become an executive in his father's Wall Street firm was surprised at first when he discovered that the cells in the balance sheet grid pertaining to self-approval or -disapproval were almost completely empty. After looking over the standard list of items to be considered in those categories (table 4), he was stimulated to write down several ways in which his career as a broker would fail to meet his ethical ideals or satisfy his desire to help improve the quality of life for people in his community. As he thought about these neglected considerations, he became worried and depressed. Then, while filling out the cells of the balance sheet grid for his second choice—going to law school—he began to brighten up a bit. Eventually he became glowingly enthusiastic when he

TABLE 4.   **List of considerations that might affect career choice, used in the balance sheet procedure as tested with college seniors facing a decision about what to do after graduation.**

1. Utilitarian considerations: gains and losses for self
   a. income
   b. difficulty of the work
   c. interest level of the work
   d. freedom to select work tasks
   e. chances of advancement
   f. security
   g. time available for personal interests—e.g., recreation
   h. other (e.g., special restrictions or opportunities with respect to social life; effect of the career or job demands on marriage; type of people you will come in contact with)
2. Utilitarian considerations: gains and losses for others
   a. income for family
   b. status for family
   c. time available for family
   d. kind of environment for family—e.g., stimulating, dull; safe, unsafe
   e. being in a position to help an organization or group (e.g., social, political, or religious)
   f. other (e.g., fringe benefits for family)
3. Self-approval or disapproval
   a. self-esteem from contributions to society or to good causes
   b. extent to which work tasks are ethically justifiable
   c. extent to which work will involve compromising oneself
   d. creativeness or originality of work
   e. extent to which job will involve a way of life that meets one's moral or ethical standards
   f. opportunity to fulfill long-range life goals
   g. other (e.g., extent to which work is "more than just a job")
4. Approval or disapproval from others (includes being criticized or being excluded from a group as well as being praised or obtaining prestige, admiration, and respect)
   a. parents
   b. college friends
   c. wife (or husband)
   d. colleagues
   e. community at large
   f. others (e.g., social, political, or religious groups)

Source: I. L. Janis, "Pilot Studies on New Procedures for Improving the Quality of Decision Making," mimeo., Yale Studies in Attitudes and Decisions, 1968.

hit upon the notion that instead of becoming a Wall Street lawyer he might better meet his objectives by being trained for a career in a legal aid clinic or in public-interest law. Finally, his mood became more sober, but with some residual elation, as he conscientiously listed the serious drawbacks (parental disapproval, relatively low income, poor prospects for travel abroad, etc.) of the new career plan he had conceived. Afterward he thanked the interviewer for making him realize he had been on the wrong track and for helping him arrive at his new career plan, which, in fact, he had worked out entirely by himself in response to the open-ended nature of the balance sheet procedure.

A trial run of the balance sheet procedure was made with thirty-six Yale College seniors, half of whom (assigned on a random basis) were given the balance sheet procedure while the other half were given a control interview in which the same amount of time (about half an hour) was spent discussing the decision, using standard interview questions. One of the main findings was that every one of the eighteen subjects given the balance sheet procedure (100 percent) responded by listing risks and drawbacks not previously mentioned during the standard part of the interview, whereas only three of the eighteen subjects in the control group (17 percent) responded in this way to the additional questions in the control interview. Hence the procedure appeared to be a feasible way of stimulating people to explore and fill in major gaps in their decisional balance sheets. That this increased awareness of potential consequences can have profound effects on the decision maker's evaluations of the alternatives under consideration is indicated by the additional finding that more than half the subjects who went through the balance sheet procedure (56 percent) reported at the end of the interview that they were inclined to choose a different alternative than the one they had initially regarded as best, whereas only one of the eighteen subjects given the control interview (6 percent) said so.

Obviously these pilot study results cannot be taken as definitive evidence, since the differences in verbal reports might reflect differential demand characteristics rather than genuine effects of the procedure. The observations merely suggest that college students, after having spent many months deliberating about their career choices, are still likely to overlook many relevant considerations and that they can arrive at more complete balance sheets if they are induced to engage in an intensive memory search by conscientiously carrying out the systematic balance sheet exercise. There are no observations from this pilot study, however, that bear on the crucial question of whether inducing people to work out a more complete balance sheet has the predicted effect of lowering their postdecisional distress. To answer this question, additional follow-up data are required.

Follow-up data were obtained in a field experiment by Mann (1972), who used a similar balance sheet procedure in interviews with high school seniors. In this study, a group of thirty seniors (fifteen males, fifteen females) was randomly selected from the college preparatory program at a large metropolitan high school in Medford, Massachusetts. They were put through a balance sheet procedure three months before making their decision about which college to attend after graduation. A control group of twenty seniors who were not administered the balance sheet procedure was used for comparison on tests made after the decision. Average intellectual ability in the two groups was uniformly high; almost all of the boys and most of the girls applied for and gained admission to reputable four-year colleges in the New England region.

Mann's findings indicate that the balance sheet procedure proved to be effective: approximately six weeks after the students had notified colleges of their decisions, the students given the balance sheet procedure were less likely to express postdecisional distress (as measured by a combined index of regret and concern). The students who filled out the balance sheet were also more open than the students in the control group to communications about potentially unfavorable consequences of their decision, taking advantage of the opportunity to read some derogatory comments about the school of their choice rather than avoiding them and reading only supportive comments. The findings suggest that as a result of going through the balance sheet procedure the students subsequently felt more secure about their choice and had less need to bolster their decision with dissonance-reducing information.

The balance sheet procedure has also been applied with some degree of success in studies of the effectiveness of counseling people at a time when they are making health-related decisions. Colten and Janis (in press), on a random basis, gave eighty women who had come to a diet clinic two separate procedures. First they were given either a low- or a high-self-disclosure interview (with the interviewer in both conditions responding by constantly giving positive, accepting comments). Then they were given either a balance sheet procedure (to explore more fully the pros and cons of going versus not going on a recommended 1,200-calorie diet) or a control procedure that gave the clients essentially the same information without suggesting that they consider the pros or cons of alternative courses of action. The twenty women who were given both the high-self-disclosure interview and the balance sheet procedure showed significantly more adherence to the clinic's recommendations during the following month than the others: they sent in more weekly reports concerning their dieting and, more important, were more successful in losing weight.

Further evidence of positive effects of the balance sheet procedure comes from a field experiment by Hoyt and Janis (1975) with forty women who had signed up for an early-morning exercise class. Twenty of the women, randomly assigned to a relevant-balance-sheet condition, were asked to write down (in the four categories of the balance sheet) all the advantages and disadvantages they could think of that would result from their regular participation in the exercise class. The other twenty, randomly assigned to the irrelevant-balance-sheet condition, were asked to write down (in the same four categories) all the advantages and disadvantages that would result from a different health-oriented decision, abstaining from cigarette smoking. Records of class attendance for a seven-week period were used as unobtrusive behavioral measures of the effects of these treatments.

As predicted, the subsequent attendance of women given the relevant-balance-sheet procedure was much greater than that of those given the irrelevant-balance-sheet procedure, whose rate of attendance did not differ from that of a nontreatment (baseline) control group (see figure 6). For the entire seven-week period, the mean weekly attendance of the women who had filled out the relevant balance sheet was double that of those who had filled out the irrelevant balance sheet.

The accumulated evidence from the various studies just cited indicates that when people are making personal decisions they tend to benefit from the careful consideration of favorable and unfavorable consequences induced by the systematic balance sheet procedure. Of course the procedure may fail to achieve the intended effect if the decision maker is so strongly motivated to persist in the coping pattern of defensive avoidance that he actively resists recognizing and filling in the gaps in his balance sheet. Or, after conscientiously filling out the balance sheet grid for a vital decision, a nondefensive decision maker may be aware of so many complicated ramifications that he suffers from informational overload and becomes confused or inhibited. These and other problems in applying the

FIGURE 6. **Week-by-week attendance for the relevant-balance-sheet group, the irrelevant-balance-sheet group, and the untreated control group.**

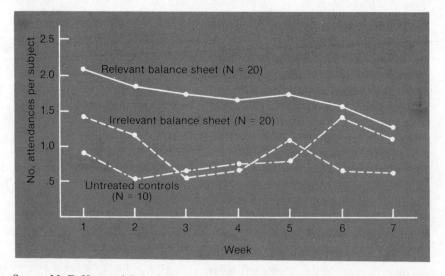

Source: M. F. Hoyt and I. L. Janis, "Increasing Adherence to a Stressful Decision via a Motivational Balance-Sheet Procedure: A Field Experiment," *Journal of Personality and Social Psychology,* 1975, 31, 837. Copyright 1975 by the American Psychological Association. Reprinted by permission.

balance sheet procedure to improve the quality of decision making among large numbers of people are discussed in our final chapter.

Emotional Inoculation for Setbacks

Additional evidence in support of the hypothesized relationship between defective balance sheets and postdecisional regret comes from observations and systematic field experiments on emotional inoculation. An important implication of the defective-balance-sheet hypothesis is the following prescriptive hypothesis: when a counselor intervenes by introducing preparatory information that makes an overlooked risk salient before the decision is implemented, the decision maker will be less vulnerable to postdecisional regret if that risk subsequently materializes. In other words, challenges to the decision will have less psychological impact if the challenging negative consequences have already been anticipated by the decision maker and incorporated into his balance sheet before he acts on the decision. Findings from a number of different types of investigation combine to support this inoculation hypothesis. They indicate that the impact of a postdecisional crisis generated when the decision maker is exposed to the negative consequences of a decision can be dampened by exposure, before the crisis arises, to advance warnings or forecasts about those adverse consequences (Janis, 1971; Meichenbaum, 1975; Meichenbaum, Turk, and Burstein, 1975).

We would expect emotional inoculation procedures to be effective for any decision requiring one to undergo short-term losses before attaining the long-term gains that constitute the main positive incentives for adopting the course of action. Most decisions concerning personal health problems are in this category, since they usually require painful treatments or unpleasant deprivations to improve physical well-being in the long run. Much of the evidence concerning the effectiveness of emotional inoculation comes from studies of such decisions—voluntarily undergoing abdominal surgery, painful medical treatments, tooth extractions, and the like. Janis's (1958) studies of surgical patients indicate that those given preparatory information about what to expect initially showed a moderate degree of preoperative worry and subsequently showed high tolerance for postoperative stress. Some of the main correlational findings from his surgery research, which are pertinent to emotional inoculation, can be readily reformulated in terms of decisional stress: persons given little information tend to remain unaware of the unpleasant consequences of the chosen course of action prior to undertaking it and undergo little or no predecisional stress but subsequently overreact to each setback with intense postdecisional conflict, expressing overt regret, refusing to live up to the commitments entailed by the decision, and displaying resentment against those who try to induce them to do so. The contrasting postdecisional behavior of persons who receive information about the unpleasant consequences and undergo a moderate degree of predecisional stress is in line with predictions from the inoculation hypothesis. Impressive supporting evidence comes from ten controlled field experiments with hospitalized medical or surgical patients (Egbert et al., 1964; Johnson, 1966; Johnson and Leventhal, 1974; Levy and McGee, 1975; Miller and Trieger, 1976; Moran, 1963; Schmidt, 1966; Schmitt and Wooldridge, 1973; Vernon and Bigelow, 1974; Wolfer and Visintainer, 1975).[5]

Evidence that other types of postdecisional stress can also be dampened by preparatory communications comes from studies of job satisfaction and turnover rates in large industrial or commercial organizations (Gomersall and Meyers, 1966; Macedonia, 1969; Weitz, 1956; Youngberg, 1963). In each of these studies, a group of job recruits was given realistic information in advance about the job stresses to be expected, and their subsequent job survival data were compared with those from an equivalent control group. The results consistently show higher job survival rates for those given the realistic preparatory information. They support the hypothesis that being informed in advance about the setbacks to be expected on a new job makes an employee less likely to become disillusioned and to reverse his or her decision when setbacks are subsequently encountered.

In a study by Wanous (1973) a group of women telephone operators was shown a realistic preparatory film at the time they were given a job offer. The film presented both "bad" and "good" features of the job, thus familiarizing the women with many of the more unpleasant aspects of the work. This prepared group was compared with an equivalent control group that was shown a traditional recruiting film, which presented only the "good" aspects of the job. All the women in both groups accepted the job offer after seeing the films, but those who viewed the realistic film had lower initial expectations about job satisfaction. One month later, however, a significantly lower percentage of the women who had seen the realistic film reported that they were thinking of leaving the telephone company.

The evidence from these experiments on job decisions points toward the same conclusion as the ten field experiments we have just cited on health-related decisions: namely, that emotional inoculation applied either just before or just after commitment to a new course of action reduces the impact of subsequent negative feedback. Although the evidence comes from only two types of decision, it seems probable that the inoculation hypothesis applies to all types of consequential decisions. In assuming so, we are also taking account of additional evidence from social psychological experiments suggesting that advance warnings and accurate predictions can have an emotional dampening effect even for relatively impersonal events of an undesirable character, such as the bad news that the Soviet Union had increased its capabilities for producing atomic weapons (Janis, Lumsdaine, and Gladstone, 1951). Similarly, a number of laboratory studies indicate that a person is less likely to display strong emotional reactions or extreme changes in attitude when confronted with a disagreeable experience if he previously has been exposed to a preparatory communication that predicted the unpleasant event (Epstein and Clarke, 1970; Lazarus and Alfert, 1964; Staub and Kellett, 1972). We expect, therefore, that preparatory communications that help to fill gaps in the decision maker's balance sheet by increasing his familiarity with potential threats to economic security, autonomy, social status, self-esteem, or any other important value will likewise prove to have positive effects, enabling the emotionally inoculated person to cope more effectively with whatever predicted setbacks actually do materialize.[6]

Any postdecisional suffering or loss is likely to have a greater negative influence if it was not anticipated beforehand. For example, one of the surgery cases described by Janis (1958) was a young housewife who had been somewhat worried before a lung operation and then, like most moderately fearful people in that situation, showed excellent cooperation and little emotional disturbance throughout the postoperative period—except during one brief crisis she had not expected. She knew in advance about the acute incision pains and other unpleasant aspects of the postoperative recovery treatments, since she had undergone surgery once before and had asked her physician pertinent questions about the present operation. But on the first postoperative day a physician entered her room and told her she would have to swallow a drainage tube, which she had never heard about before. She became extremely upset, could not relax sufficiently to cooperate, and finally begged the physician to take the tube away and leave her alone. In an interview the next day, she said that she began to have extremely derogatory thoughts about the physician when he made the unexpected demand. She suspected that he was withholding information about the seriousness of her condition, that he was unnecessarily imposing a hideous form of treatment on her, and that he was carrying out the treatment "so badly it was practically killing me." At no other time during the long and painful convalescence following the removal of her lung did she have any such doubts about this physician or any other member of the hospital staff; nor did she at any other time display any form of overt resistance.

Perhaps she was right about the ineptness of that particular physician, but there was no evidence that he evoked more than his expected share of such untoward reactions from other patients on the surgical ward. It is highly improbable that the patient's extreme reaction to the drainage-tube procedure could be attributed to unbearable pain or to a physiological defect in her swallowing capabilities, because a short time later another physician was able to talk her into going through the entire procedure successfully, like most other patients do, without her repeating the active resistance she had shown the first time. Evidently that first episode was the one stressful event she had not anticipated and for which she was not psychologically prepared.

The dampening effect of forethought about an unfavorable consequence stems from the fact that the anticipated event comes as no surprise when it materializes and the person has prepared himself to cope with it (see Janis, 1958; Langer, Wolfer, and Janis, 1975). When a person expects beforehand one kind of utilitarian loss (e.g., postoperative incision pain if one undergoes surgery), he may develop reassuring concepts (e.g., "I will gradually feel better, and it is worth going through several bad days of discomfort to be cured of my illness") that enable him to tolerate somewhat better any other form of utilitarian loss he had not specifically anticipated (e.g., boring periods of social isolation during postoperative convalescence). The same functional equivalence may hold for entries in each of the three other main categories of the decisional balance sheet. When a person anticipates that one of his friends will oppose a decision, he may be better able to cope later on and will be less likely to reconsider his decision if he encounters negative social feedback, even if it is not the same person who subsequently expresses disapproval. Expecting beforehand one form of self-disapproval (e.g., shame about loss of bowel control during postoperative recovery) may enable a person to become less upset and regretful about any episode, even if unanticipated, that subsequently evokes self-disapproval (e.g., losing his temper and abusing someone who was trying to help him).

The explanation for these functional equivalences may lie in the fact that whenever a person anticipates a given type of negative feedback, before executing a new decision, he is stimulated to find (through information seeking or memory scanning) an appropriate form of reassurance that will enable him to believe the decision will work out favorably despite the anticipated setback. For example, when the decision maker expects that his friend John will probably disapprove, he may reassure himself that "John will eventually see that I am right" and "most of my other friends will approve of the decision." Then if he unexpectedly encounters negative social feedback from his friends Tom and George, he can apply the same reassuring concepts to mitigate its influence on his own appraisal of the decision. In brief, what we are suggesting is that the realistic reassurances a person develops during the predecisional period to discount the seriousness of any negative entry in a given cell in the decisional balance sheet is likely to be somewhat effective during the postdecisional period in enabling him to discount the seriousness of the actual occurrence of any other entry in that same cell. But we would expect little, if any, of this kind of carry-over effect from entries in one category (e.g., anticipated disapproval from significant others) to those in another category (e.g., anticipated self-disapproval). These hypotheses about restricted carry-over effects have not yet been tested. If confirmatory evidence is obtained, it will bear out our assumption that each of the four main categories in the balance sheet has some degree of functional unity and some degree of functional dissimilarity from the other three.

Illustrative Defects

Since there is no established vocabulary for talking about the micro-processes that mediate the influence of new information on decision-making processes, we propose to conceptualize what happens in terms of changes in the entries on the decision maker's balance sheet in response to each significant communication or event. To illustrate such changes and to show how the defective-balance-sheet hypothesis can be applied to an important personal decision, we examine the case study of a middle-aged man who sought help at our clinic for heavy smokers after he had unsuccessfully tried to cut down on his own.

Our subject, a 40-year-old male whom we shall call Mr. Bingham, became profoundly concerned about the threat of lung cancer after reading newspaper stories about the Surgeon General's report on smoking and health (1964). Bingham subsequently participated in one of our pilot studies on changing smoking attitudes and habits. Some of his reactions to negative feedback were typical of those displayed by many smokers in our field experiments in the smoking clinic.

Bingham's initial decision to cut down on smoking illustrates what might be called a vigilant but partially defective decision—vigilant in that he paid close attention to much of the available information and spent a week thinking about the pros and cons of the viable alternatives, but partially defective in that he overlooked a major set of considerations that left him vulnerable to one particular form of negative feedback, to which he subsequently reacted impulsively by making a new decision that reversed his first one. We shall try to show in some detail how this man's impulsive reversal can be accounted for in terms of the *incompleteness* of his balance sheet during the precommitment stages of decision making. This case study enables us to make some inferences about the micro-processes that may account for the instability of decisions made without full awareness of one or another negative consequence. Table 5 presents our schematic analysis of Mr. Bingham's first decision, which shows the considerations that went into his selection of the alternative of cutting down his daily consumption from thirty cigarettes per day to only about ten per day. Each relevant entry in the positive incentive (+) columns refers to potential gains that Bingham anticipated from adopting one of the alternative policies; each relevant entry in the negative incentive (−) columns refers to his anticipations of potential losses.

Mr. Bingham's complacency about smoking, like that of millions of

TABLE 5. **Illustrative balance sheet at the stage when a decision is being made: Examples of conflicting cognitions verbalized by a smoker challenged by the Surgeon General's report on smoking and health. (Based on Janis and Mann, 1968.)**

Alternative courses of action (policies)	+ or − incentive values	ANTICIPATED UTILITARIAN CONSEQUENCES		ANTICIPATED APPROVAL OR DISAPPROVAL		Final judgment
		For self	For significant others (spouse, friends, family, reference group)	From self	From significant others	
1. Original policy (Continue smoking about one pack per day)	+	Provides daily pleasure; sometimes relieves emotional tension.	By relieving tension, it helps me get along better with my family and friends.	I pride myself on not scaring easily.	My statistician friend will be pleased that I share his skepticism.	Unsatisfactory—wants to change if a satisfactory alternative is available that will yield a net gain (or less net loss).
	−	Possibility of my developing a lung cancer; it will make ordinary respiratory illness more serious; costs money.	Family would also suffer if I were to become a cancer victim.	If I don't live up to my promise, I shall feel like a weak character; if I develop a respiratory illness, I'll feel guilty.	Several friends will lose respect for me, since I promised to try to change my smoking habits; my family doctor will disapprove.	
2. New, recommended policy (Stop smoking)	+	Chances of lung cancer will be greatly reduced; respiratory illness will be less troublesome; money could be put to good use.	Family will be more secure if I reduce chances of contracting lung diseases; my abstinence might exert a good influence on our children.	I shall feel satisfied with myself for living up to my promise; also, responding to new evidence shows maturity and intelligence.	My friends will see that I am living up to my promise; my family doctor and a few anti-smoking friends will strongly approve.	Mixed attitude—prefers a less conflictful alternative if one is available.

−	Unsatisfied craving will be unpleasant; I'll be more irritable and angry; might develop severe anxiety symptoms; might become overweight.	I cause my wife enough trouble without becoming even more irritable; this could be the last straw that breaks up our home.	I might lose my temper more often, which would make me feel like a heel.	My statistician friend will think I am stupid to accept a correlation as proving causation.	Most satisfactory—ready to adopt this policy since no available alternative is more attractive.
3. Alternative, compromise policy (Smoke only one-half pack per day) — +	Same as no. 2 to a milder degree, with less risk of cancer than if I continued unchanged	Same as no. 2 to a milder degree.	Same as no. 2 to a milder degree.	Same as no. 2 to a milder degree.	
−	Same as no. 2 to a milder degree; a slight risk of lung cancer.	Same as no. 2 to a milder degree.	Going only partway may show a lack of self-control.	My family doctor and several friends will not approve of this compromise.	
4. Alternative, nonrecommended policy (Switch to filtered cigarettes, one pack per day) — +	Same as no. 2 to a milder degree, but no money saved and not sure of lung cancer risk.	Same as no. 2 to a milder degree.	Same as no. 2 to a milder degree.	Same as no. 2 to a milder degree.	Satisfactory—but less attractive than an available alternative.
−	Same as no. 1 and no. 2 to a milder degree.	Same as no. 2 to a milder degree.	Same as no. 3 to a stronger degree.	Same as no. 3 to a stronger degree.	

other Americans at the time, had been severely shaken by the Surgeon General's report. Four new negative entries concerning health hazards were consequently added to his decisional balance sheet:

1. concern about the possibility of developing lung cancer;
2. concern about losses to his family if his health became impaired;
3. concern about loss of self-respect if he could not control his smoking habit;
4. concern about loss of respect and approval from friends if he continued to smoke.[7]

Here we have a relatively simple example illustrating how the decisional balance sheet can be used for analyzing the changes induced by an effective message. Each of the added entries constitutes an additional incentive to reject the policy of continuing smoking, thus increasing the likelihood that an alternative policy of cutting down on smoking or stopping completely will be adopted.

Mr. Bingham reported that he began by telling his wife about his decision to cut down to ten cigarettes per day; then he informed his fellow workers in his office and a few friends to whom he had made the promise a week earlier that he would try to change his smoking habit. These new commitments added new incentives to his balance sheet, in the category of *anticipated social approval/disapproval*. (The new entries following commitment are not shown in table 5, which represents Mr. Bingham's balance sheet the week *before* full commitment.) Furthermore, as typically happens following commitment, Mr. Bingham engaged in cognitive bolstering of the new decision by playing up the anticipated gains; thus, he looked forward to less daily fatigue and to other improvements in general health from smoking less. He also played down the anticipated losses, especially the withdrawal symptoms, which he knew about from observing friends who had quit smoking. He reassured himself that since he was going to spread out his allotted ten cigarettes throughout the day, withdrawal symptoms would be mild and would last only a day or two, which turned out to be a grossly overoptimistic expectation.

Mr. Bingham's overoptimism appears to have contributed to his rapid buildup of postdecisional regret: within less than one week after he started implementing his new decision, he became so disillusioned that he gave up the attempt. According to the emotional inoculation hypothesis, if heavy smokers like this man can be made more fully aware of the duration and intensity of withdrawal symptoms and other negative consequences, they will be less vulnerable to negative feedback when they implement a decision to cut down on cigarette smoking.

During the first four days after making the initial decision, with his fresh commitments very salient, Mr. Bingham was apparently able to keep his smoking limited to about ten cigarettes per day despite the unpleasantness of the withdrawal symptoms. He reported in a follow-up interview that during the first two days he was able to fight the strong temptation to smoke more cigarettes, but as his strong craving and nervousness continued into the third and fourth days, he began to feel pessimistic about being able to live up to his resolve. We surmise that the anticipated continuation of withdrawal symptoms constituted a new set of strongly negative entries in the balance sheet.

When someone is successful in carrying out a decision to cut down on smoking, negative feedback is tolerated without producing any important changes in the balance sheet: he regards his suffering from withdrawal symptoms during the first week as temporary and does not alter very much his favorable anticipations about attaining his objectives. But for Mr. Bingham, the temporary suffering had a devastating effect. By the end of the fourth day, the negative feedback had such a powerful impact that he strongly regretted having committed himself to cutting down on his smoking. He became deeply concerned about his unexpectedly severe symptoms of irritability and his loss of mental efficiency at his job, which he attributed to his constant preoccupation with gauging the time before he could allow himself to have his next cigarette.

Whereas Mr. Bingham had arrived at his initial decision to cut down to ten cigarettes a day in a relatively thoughtful way, with much deliberation over a period of more than a week, he made the decision to resume heavy smoking so impetuously, according to his account, that he spent hardly any time thinking about the alternatives. On the morning of the fifth day, instead of feeling full of vim and vigor as he had expected when he started to cut down on smoking, Mr. Bingham felt depressed and annoyed about having to go through another day of miserable tension and constant struggle. While lying in bed in this state of acute postdecisional regret, he suddenly decided "To hell with it!" and told his wife that he could not continue. This impulsive new decision was made, in effect, during a brief interval of only a few minutes of frantic thinking (or perhaps it would be more accurate to say, fantasizing). His recollection about making this second decision was that at one moment he was thinking that he would have to go through the misery of doling out only ten cigarettes to himself that day and the next moment he visualized himself returning to his happy, "normal" life of smoking freely; he then thought to himself "It's worth it," whereupon he announced the to-hell-with-it decision to his wife. He considered only that one alternative to his current course of action and engaged in rapid and highly biased scanning of the two alternatives. His snap judgment that "It's worth it" disregarded the health hazards that had loomed so large in his decisional balance sheet at the time he made the first decision.

Following his return to heavy smoking, Mr. Bingham bolstered the new decision by becoming skeptical about whether the medical findings on lung cancer and emphysema would apply to someone like himself ("Maybe its a matter of heredity; we have not had these diseases in my family"). Nevertheless, he was responsive to communications that dramatized the threat, especially news stories about the death of a movie star who was known to be a heavy smoker before he succumbed to lung cancer. His new-found complacency about the harmlessness of heavy smoking was soon undermined, and he finally reached the point where he began to reconsider alternatives; once again he was in a state of acute decisional conflict. It was at this point that he decided to come back to the Yale antismoking clinic to see if he could get some help that would somehow enable him to cut down without suffering intolerable withdrawal symptoms.

When we look over the criteria for high-quality decision making (chapter 1), we find that most of them were met by Mr. Bingham in making his first decision: he surveyed a fairly wide range of alternatives, sought out relevant information, assimilated new information accurately, and re-evaluated the alternatives after completing his information search. When making his second decision, however, Mr. Bingham failed to do any of these things. Had he done so, he might have found an alternative that would have enabled him to cut down on smoking without continuing to be so completely demoralized by the withdrawal symptoms. For example, he might have decided to experiment with various methods of gradual tapering off (such as reducing his consumption by only one or two cigarettes per day for a week, stabilizing for a week at that level, then cutting down gradually to another, lower level). Instead, as a result of his impulsive second decision, he plunged into what he soon came to regard as an undesirable course of action and tried to consolidate it by bolstering with rather flimsy rationalizations.

Although his first decision (to cut down to ten cigarettes a day) may have met most of the criteria for vigilant information processing, it was nevertheless flawed by his failure to obtain adequate information about the *duration* of the withdrawal symptoms that a heavy smoker like himself should expect to experience. As a result, his balance sheet was incomplete and somewhat distorted with regard to the negative consequences of the decision. This seems to have been a fatal flaw. In terms of the criteria for high-quality decision-making procedures, Mr. Bingham not only failed to obtain information about how to cope with severe withdrawal symptoms, but he also failed to work out contingency plans (such as the alternative of more gradual reduction and leveling off described above) to which he could resort in the event that the suffering became too severe for him to tolerate. Had he been better prepared in this respect, Mr. Bingham might not have succumbed so readily to the accumulated stresses generated by his decision to cut down.

Few people who try to stop smoking show strong resistance to negative feedback after they start cutting down; for every one who succeeds, about ten others try and fail (Mausner and Platt, 1971; Schwartz and Dubitzky, 1968). Many of those who fail, like Mr. Bingham, become rapidly discouraged during the first few days of reduced cigarette consumption when they encounter the full impact of withdrawal symptoms. And, like Mr. Bingham's, their overwhelming reactions of postdecisional regret can often be traced back to errors of omission in their decisional balance sheets before the decision was implemented.

Applications to Personal and Policy Decisions

We expect the defective-balance-sheet hypothesis to be broadly applicable to all types of consequential decision making, mainly because of the research evidence we presented earlier but also because of the large number of case studies we have collected, like that of the heavy smoker just described. Earlier in this chapter we presented an example of the onset of postdecisional regret during a routine but unpleasant postoperative treatment administered unexpectedly to a female surgical patient. She appeared to have made only this one error of omission in an otherwise full and accurate balance sheet that she had vigilantly worked out before deciding to undergo lung surgery. An even more vivid example of the same phenomenon, obtained from a study of persons making decisions about whether or not to seek a divorce, will be described in chapter 14.

In research conducted in our weight-reduction clinic, we have encountered numerous similar instances of impulsive reversal of a decision to adhere to a low-calorie diet that appear to be attributable to defective balance sheets. One woman, for example, knew all about the possible drawbacks of dieting before making a commitment, except that she neglected to explore fully the effect on her husband. He had urged her to go to the weight-reduction clinic but clearly was ambivalent. After she had lost ten pounds, her husband's opposition unexpectedly—for her—began to emerge. On a Sunday outing, he urged her to eat a tabooed chocolate cream pie. "You've been a good girl staying on your diet all these weeks," he told her, "so you deserve a treat." Although she resisted this initial attempt to sabotage her diet, she realized that her husband was displeased about her basking in the attention that her much more attractive figure was eliciting from men in their social circle and that indirectly he was also expressing jealousy of her being influenced by the male psychologist at the Yale dieting clinic. In a state of acute agitation, she announced to the psychologist that she had decided to give up dieting to avoid the risk of ruining her marriage. If she had been aware of her husband's ambivalent attitude before starting on her diet, she might have been able to avoid provoking his reactions of jealousy, and, if those efforts failed, she might have become less agitated about his opposition. (Incidentally, we have run into the ungrateful-husband syndrome sufficiently often among the dieting women in our clinic that we now use an interviewer of the same sex whenever possible and we forewarn wives about the mixed reactions some husbands display when their wives succeed in their goal of attaining a slimmer, more attractive figure.)

We expect that the relationship predicted by the defective-balance-sheet hypothesis will hold for career choices and related personal decisions. A pilot study of twenty-two attorneys (Janis, 1960) suggests a relationship between large gaps in the balance sheet when making a career choice during the final year of law school and discontent with the career choice as expressed in a follow-up interview one year later.

Political leaders who make decisions on behalf of an entire nation are not immune to the types of error that have just been illustrated in case studies of personal decisions. Nor do they appear to be immune to the consequences predicted by the defective-balance-sheet hypothesis. Richard Nixon, for example, expected Congress and the American public to accept the "Saturday night massacre" of October 20, 1973, when he fired Watergate special prosecutor Archibald Cox and Deputy Attorney General William Ruckelshaus for refusing to obey his orders on handling the White House tapes, thus provoking the resignation of Attorney General Elliot Richardson. Nixon's expectation was erroneous, and his effort to avoid releasing any tapes proved futile. Three days later, confronted by a firestorm of protest from supporters as well as opponents, together with impending impeachment hearings by the House Judiciary Committee, Nixon reversed his policy and released some of the tapes, which he could have done earlier with much less damage to himself if he had correctly anticipated congressional and public reaction. Other such instances of gross miscalculation followed by a drastic policy reversal can be culled from the historical records of many other administrations. One of the best-documented examples involves the dramatic sequence of events leading up to America's entry into World War I in 1917.[8]

For more than a year, President Wilson and Count Bernstorff, Germany's ambassador to the United States, had been trying to work out a solution acceptable to the belligerent nations of Europe that would bring an end to the devastating war of attrition that had already cost millions of lives. For somewhat different reasons, the two men in 1916 were pursuing a policy of ending the war between Germany and the Allies and of maintaining U.S. neutrality by applying Wilson's formula of "Peace without Victory." Early in 1917, a twofold crisis arose. First, the German government, ignoring all previous agreements with the United States, opened up unrestricted U-boat warfare against neutral ships. Second, Zimmerman, the recently appointed foreign minister of Germany, sent the notorious telegram to Bernstorff at the German Embassy in Washington, giving instructions to induce Mexico to join with Germany in attacking the United States "to reconquer the lost territory in Texas, New Mexico, and Arizona." This telegram, intercepted by the British Intelligence Service, had such a provocative effect when it was shown to Wilson that, according to his official biographer, "no single more devastating blow was delivered against Wilson's resistance to entering the War" (Baker, 1927–39, vol. 4, p. 474). Completely disillusioned by these events, Wilson abandoned his role as peace negotiator and became a vociferous proponent of war against the "natural foe of liberty." Bernstorff, on the other hand, did not abandon his pro-peace orientation, but ardently kept on trying to convince the German leaders at home that continuing the war would be tantamount to national suicide. He persisted despite the utter defeat of his unpopular policy at home, the loss of all effective support from his former colleagues, and the rebuffs he received from American officials when he became *persona non grata*.

Obviously, the significance of Germany's provocative actions would be quite different for any American leader than for a dissident, but loyal, German official. Nevertheless, by comparing certain characteristic differences in the way the two men approached the tasks of political decision making, we may gain some insight into the psychological factors that contributed to Bernstorff's persistence as against Wilson's drastic reversal of policy following the blow to their joint efforts.

One of Bernstorff's main activities during the preceding year had been preparing detailed political analyses for his home government, which involved collecting information concerning the array of contending political forces in Germany and in the Allied countries as well as in the United States, for the purpose of appraising the chances of attaining one or another form of peace settlement. Bernstorff's continuing efforts to maintain a high level of well-informed objectivity seem to have enabled him to approach each fresh crisis like a medical specialist who assimilates any new unfavorable development into his diagnostic appraisal as he carefully decides on appropriate emergency action. On a number of occasions, Bernstorff took the initiative without waiting for instructions from his home government, but, in so doing, he seems to have steeled himself in advance for possible rebuffs or failures. For example, Bernstorff asserts that, following the formal apology he made after the *Arabic* was torpedoed by U-boats, "I was once more taken to task—a matter that weighed little with me" (Bernstorff, 1920, p. 159). The series of minor crises during 1915–16 induced him to anticipate the undesirable outcomes that might follow from his unpopular decisions, as is implied by his statement that at the time he felt "disposed to give up the diplomatic service as soon as possible, for it can only be of any value when there exists a relation of confidence between the Ambassador and his Chief" (p. 106). It seems probable that this type of contemplation involved a psychological process of emotionally "working through" in advance the heavy blows that might be in store, as well as developing realistic ideas concerning possible ways of minimizing the damage. This process of psychological preparation may have contributed to his capacity to avoid excessive agitation or demoralization when the major crises of 1917 forced him to give up his post.

In contrast, Wilson was shocked by the tremendous setback to his peace plans, and become enraged and bitter. His surprise stemmed partly from his lack of information about the pro-war factions within the German government. Evidently he conceived of Germany as having a relatively homogeneous government and was unaware of the fact that very few of the leading officials shared the German ambassador's views. Wilson's naiveté in this respect was a direct consequence of his deliberate refusal to make use of the channels of information available to him. According to Ambassador Joseph C. Grew's private papers, Wilson had little interest in hearing from American diplomats, habitually treating them like "office boys." Wilson also appears to have avoided the type of contemplation that facilitates psychological preparation for future crises, such as considering what would happen if Germany attempted to use some of its other irons in the fire in an effort to win the war.

Wilson's biographers may find it quite easy to show how the particular features of his decision-making behavior that we have singled out were linked up with his chronic personality predispositions, which were manifested in a variety of ways long before and again after the fateful events of 1916–17. Nevertheless, it seems probable that if Wilson had been exposed to appropriate communications, the influence of these predispositions might have been checked to some extent, so that the severity of his disillusionment and the extreme degree to which he withdrew from his former role of international mediator might have been significantly reduced. For example, during the year preceding the crisis, his spontaneous insulating tendencies might not have been so completely dominant had standard operating procedure required the President, as well as other top government officials, to discuss with well-qualified colleagues the unintended consequences that might ensue from alternative policies and to rehearse mentally a variety of potentially distressing setbacks that might require a shift in perspective.

Present-day diplomats and statesmen in the United States as well as in Europe may resemble Bernstorff much more than Wilson in their approach to international negotiations, perhaps partly because of the object lessons derived from his failures. There still remains, however, a wide range of individual differences in political diagnostic skills, in readiness to anticipate setbacks, and in the capacity to work through potential crises in advance (see Barber, 1972; Elms, 1976; Greenstein, 1969). If special procedures were developed for inducing the appropriate forms of psychological preparation, there might be a considerable improvement in the completeness and accuracy of many policy makers' balance sheets.

Even men like Bernstorff might benefit from the application of special procedures devised to facilitate psychological preparation. For example, Bernstorff might have become more aware of the potential dangers inherent in allowing the Foreign Office in Berlin to transmit anti-U.S. messages, such as the ill-fated Zimmerman telegram, by unethically making secret use of the American cable facility that Wilson had put at his personal disposal with the understanding that it would be used solely for discussions of peace proposals with his home government. In general, many men and women in public life who are hardheaded about taking account of possible utilitarian losses and of the social reactions of others in their organization are likely to neglect the broader social and moral consequences of a given course of action, including foreseeable events that might ultimately generate humiliation, guilt, or remorse. When anticipated self and social rections are fully elaborated in the decisional balance sheet, policy makers are more likely to be deterred from selecting courses of action that violate the principles and standards they consider it desirable to maintain.

CHAPTER 7

Stages of Decision Making

MOST ANALYSES OF personal decision making distinguish between two major phases in the decision-making process—the period preceding the announcement of the decision and the period that follows it (see Festinger, 1964). But when people adopt a new course of action they usually go through more than two distinctive stages. Janis (1968a) has described five stages in arriving at a stable decision, one that people continue to implement indefinitely so long as they do not encounter an extraordinarily powerful threat of intolerable loss from doing so. The stages involve a series of progressive changes in the decision maker's balance sheet of incentives, which also entail changes in his responsiveness to new information about alternative courses of action.

Five Sequential Stages

Janis's five-stage schema was initially based on studies of people who displayed vigilance in reaching a difficult personal decision that they subsequently carried out successfully—such as giving up smoking, losing weight on a low-calorie diet, or undergoing a prescribed medical treatment. We begin this chapter with a descriptive account of the five-stage schema, with illustrations of each stage drawn from the research on men and women who have successfully carried out their decision to give up smoking. Then we shall introduce some systematic evidence and additional case studies from research on career choices, political protest actions, and a number of other types of decision, all of which suggest that the stage-sequence schema may be broadly applicable to stable decisions on a wide variety of personal, organizational, and political issues.

171

The five stages and the major concerns asociated with each are:

STAGE	KEY QUESTIONS
1. Appraising the Challenge	Are the risks serious if I don't change?
2. Surveying Alternatives	Is this (salient) alternative an acceptable means for dealing with the challenge? Have I sufficiently surveyed the available alternatives?
3. Weighing Alternatives[1]	Which alternative is best? Could the best alternative meet the essential requirements?
4. Deliberating about Commitment	Shall I implement the best alternative and allow others to know?
5. Adhering despite Negative Feedback	Are the risks serious if I *don't* change? Are the risks serious if I *do* change?

Some of the above questions, it will be noted, are the same as those in our conflict model (figure 3), but there are also some additional ones. Later on in this chapter we shall indicate where the crucial questions in the conflict model occur in the schema of the five stages (figure 8).

The characteristic features of the stages depend to some extent upon the coping pattern of the decision maker. For example, when the dominant pattern is defensive avoidance, stages 3 and 4 are greatly attenuated. We first give an account of what happens when *vigilance* is the dominant pattern before discussing how the stages differ when nonvigilant patterns are dominant.

Stage 1: *Appraising the Challenge.* Until a person is challenged by some disturbing information or event that calls his attention to a real loss soon to be expected, he will retain an attitude of complacency about whatever course of action (or inaction) he has been pursuing. Being exposed to information about a threat or opportunity that effectively challenges a current course of action marks the beginning of the decision-making process. The challenging information produces a temporary personal crisis if the person begins to doubt the wisdom of continuing in that course. Once the decision maker gives a positive response to the first key question, he proceeds to search for alternatives.

The challenging information can be of two kinds. An *event* may disturb the person's equanimity because a particular threat can no longer be ignored. A cigarette smoker, for example, may notice that he has developed a chronic cough that gets worse each time he smokes. This is a powerful form of negative feedback and is capable of inducing a smoker to reconsider his habitual course of smoking a pack or more of cigarettes each day. Or a challenge may be generated by impressive *communications* that argue in favor of a new course of action. News stories about the Surgeon General's report on smoking and lung cancer (1964), as we pointed out in the preceding chapter, made many smokers begin to take seriously the risks posed by smoking. Cigarette consumption throughout the United States declined by a substantial percentage during the year immediately following publication of that report (Wagner, 1971).

When momentarily challenged by new information that points up the unfavorable consequences of his current course of action, a person is likely to scan it rapidly to see if he can dismiss it as being untrue, irrelevant, or inapplicable to his own particular circumstances. If he ends up accepting the challenge as constituting a genuine threat and as applicable to himself, it is because he now perceives his present course of action as entailing some potential losses that he had not previously taken fully into account. To be effective in initiating the successive steps that lead to the making of a new decision, a challenging event or communication must be powerful enough to induce in the decision maker an image of himself as headed for serious setbacks and as ultimately failing to attain one or more of his main objectives. Such a challenge usually generates at least momentary anticipations of losing the esteem of friends and relatives, as well as losing self-esteem for being a foolish, inflexible die-hard if he were to refuse to acknowledge the need for changing his behavior. This type of image can counteract the person's anticipations of social and self-disapproval for failing to persevere in the course of action he is currently following.

We conceptualize a successful challenge as having the effect of adding new entries to a decision maker's balance sheet, which increase the number or intensity of the incentives making for *rejection* of the course he had been pursuing and consequently result in a net decrease in its overall attractiveness. This change in the decision maker's balance sheet is accompanied by arousal of vigilant interest in finding a more desirable course of action.

Stage 2: *Surveying Alternatives.* After the person's confidence in the desirability of his old policy has been shaken by the information contained in the challenge, he begins to focus attention on one or more alternatives. Having accepted the challenge, he begins to search his memory for alternative courses of action and to seek advice and information from other people about ways of coping with the threat. He typically seeks advice from knowledgeable acquaintances about how to avert the losses made salient by the challenge and becomes more attentive to relevant information in the mass media. He becomes more attentive to recommendations for coping with the challenge, even though the advice may be inconsistent with his present commitments. Most decision makers are inclined, of course, to cling to the policy to which they are currently committed, if possible. But after being exposed to a powerful challenge they are hungry for fresh information about better alternatives.

The initial canvassing of alternatives during this stage may be carried out in either an unbiased or a biased way, depending upon the presence or absence of certain stimulus conditions that make for vigilance as against other modes of coping with the challenge. When vigilance is his dominant coping pattern, the person actively searches for viable alternatives by asking other people for advice.

As he surveys the alternatives during stage 2, the decision maker dismisses or eliminates from further consideration any alternative that appears to be too ineffectual or too costly a means of dealing with the challenge. For example, Leventhal and Watts (1966) found that after viewing a challenging film depicting the threat of lung cancer, many smokers took seriously the film's recommendation to stop smoking, but ignored the recommendation to obtain chest X-rays. Some of their observations indicate that the smokers doubted the efficacy of X-rays for handling the threat of lung cancer. The investigators suggest that this course of action was promptly eliminated as an inadequate solution because the smokers thought that if lung cancer were detected they would have to undergo painful surgery, like that shown in the fear-arousing movie, and would still have little chance of survival.

By the end of stage 2, the decision maker has narrowed down his list of alternatives to those that appear to have a good chance of averting the losses threatened by the challenge without entailing intolerable costs or risks. In terms of the balance sheet schema, this stage is largely devoted to discovering and selecting viable alternatives (like the ones that make up the rows in the balance sheet shown in table 5), with only a cursory, preliminary scanning of the most salient pro and con entries for each one.

Stage 3: *Weighing Alternatives*. The decision maker now proceeds to a more thorough search and evaluation, focusing on the pros and cons of each of the surviving alternatives in an effort to select the best available course of action. Insofar as he is vigilant, he deliberates about the advantages and disadvantages of each alternative until he feels reasonably confident about selecting the one that will best meet his objectives. During this stage the entries in the decision maker's balance sheet become much more fully elaborated. A vigilant decision maker usually becomes aware of certain gains and losses he had not previously taken into consideration. Consequently, the content of the balance sheet may change markedly, with corresponding changes in preference ratings of the alternatives. Any alternative for which the anticipated losses emerge as prohibitive or as incommensurate with the anticipated gains is rejected and precluded from further consideration.

When keenly aware of the possibility of future regret, the decision maker becomes very careful in his appraisal of the alternatives: he searches for more information to confirm the gains and losses to be expected from each alternative. In addition, each of the leading alternatives is "tried on" mentally. For example, a heavy smoker challenged by information about lung cancer may try to imagine himself as a nonsmoker. As he does so, he may think of additional advantages, like feelings of well-being and pride in self-control, that he had not previously thought about.

These new positive entries in his balance sheet may shift the balance in favor of the alternative of stopping smoking entirely. On the other hand, the same imaginative exercise may make salient the disagreeable withdrawal symptoms that the smoker has observed in other heavy smokers who tried to quit, which might incline him to reject that course.

The person's current course of action (e.g., continuing to smoke a pack a day) is subjected to essentially the same mental process. The current course usually serves as a basis of comparison for each of the new alternatives. Sometimes it is so powerfully challenged that the person can no longer dispel an image of its negative consequences (as when a heavy smoker has been informed by a physician that he must stop smoking because the results of his sputum test and X-rays show precancerous cells in his lungs); but challenges are seldom so devastatingly irrefutable. For most smokers who have become concerned about the threat smoking poses to their health, the current policy of smoking a pack or so a day, although somewhat tarnished by the challenging information issued by the Surgeon General and other medical authorities, has not been eliminated from the decisional balance sheet; rather, their long-established, habitual course of action is regarded as an attractive alternative that might still prove to be the most desirable choice.

Sometimes, after deliberating about each alternative in turn, the decision maker becomes dissatisfied with all of them (including his present course of action). At such times, his stress symptoms become especially acute, and, if he is able to avoid becoming demoralized, he will search for a better solution. He will return to stage 2, in an attempt to find a new course that might prove to be better than any of the ones he is currently contemplating. Prolonged frustration during stage 3 can therefore be a goad that induces the decision maker to work out a more complete balance sheet containing more alternatives as well as more specifics concerning the pros and cons of each; and it can lead to the discovery of a creative solution. (See the section "Reversion and Feedback Loops" later in this chapter for further discussion of the conditions that foster creative problem solving.)

In general, stage 3 is characterized by considerable vacillation, as the decision maker is no longer satisfied with his current course of action and is not yet willing to commit himself to any alternative. Even when he reaches the point of feeling certain that he knows the best choice to make, he will usually continue to be responsive to new information indicating that he may be overlooking an important consideration. When vigilance is the dominant pattern, he remains open to new ideas and finds it relatively easy to change his mind, so long as he has not committed himself.

Stage 4: *Deliberating about Commitment*. After having covertly decided by telling himself that he is going to adopt a new plan of action, the decision maker begins to deliberate about implementing it and conveying his intentions to others. Whether he is about to stop smoking, get married, change his job, or start a lawsuit on behalf of his organization against a rival firm, the decision maker realizes that sooner or later the people in his social network who are not directly implicated—family, friends, business associates, and casual acquaintances—will find out about it. As a vigilant decision maker, he becomes concerned about their possible disapproval, which he may not have thought about earlier.

These fresh concerns deter him from taking immediate action without first paving the way by giving his intimates an inkling of the direction in which he is moving. Before letting others know about his choice—particularly if it is a controversial course of action, such as seeking a divorce—he will be inclined to think up ways of avoiding disapproval from family, friends, and other reference groups. This often leads to working out social tactics and auxiliary contingency plans for ensuring the success of a new decision (e.g., preparing strong arguments to give those who might object.)

As the person approaches the point of implementing his decision and revealing it to others, he realizes that once he does so it will become more difficult to reverse it, that he will be "locked into" it. This realization makes for reconsideration of just how serious the risks involved might be. A man ready to try to quit smoking may reassure himself in stage 3 that if the suffering from withdrawal symptoms is more than he can bear he can always start smoking again. But then in stage 4, as he thinks about friends and acquaintances noticing (and perhaps commenting favorably on) his brave new decision, he has to admit to himself that he will not be able to reverse his decision without finding himself in the embarrassing position of revealing his weakness to practically everyone he knows. Such concerns during stage 4 are inhibitory and sometimes lead to a series of cautious, piecemeal commitments over a period of many days or weeks.

Few important decisions can be kept completely secret for very long. The decision maker may start off by letting only a few intimates in on it; then, as others in his social network show that they notice a change in his behavior, he realizes that he had better inform them and perhaps explain the change. The decision maker is likely to announce his choice first to those from whom he expects approval and to withhold the information for a while from anyone whom he suspects will strongly disapprove. Thus, potential critics and scoffers are often reserved for last, except when the decision maker must depend on them for implementing the decision or feels confident that he can quickly convince them that he has made the right choice.

Once he has taken the first steps of committing himself, the person anticipates a loss of self-esteem if he fails to keep his word, as well as the loss of social esteem if he fails to carry out the new course. Each fresh commitment to another person or group becomes an added incentive in the balance sheet for sticking with the decision. As a result, the decision maker is soon left with little hope of finding a better alternative than the course to which he is now committed. Hence, even the most vigilant of decision makers becomes strongly motivated at the end of stage 4 to bolster and consolidate his decision in a way that will enable him to implement it with a minimum of misgivings. (We shall return to this bolstering and consolidating process shortly.)

Stage 5: *Adhering despite Negative Feedback.* Many decisions go through a honeymoon period in which the decision maker is quite happy about his choice and implements it without any qualms. All too often, however, this idyllic postdecisional state is rudely interrupted, sooner or later, by new threats or opportunities. Stage 5 then becomes equivalent to stage 1, in the sense that each unfavorable event or communication that constitutes negative feedback is a potential challenge to the newly adopted policy. However, stage 5 is different from stage 1 in that even when a challenge is powerful enough to evoke a positive response to the first key question, concerning whether the risks are serious if no change is made, the decision maker is only temporarily shaken and soon decides that despite the challenge he prefers to stick with his original decision. In order to feel secure about reaffirming his decision, he is likely to bolster it with fresh rationalizations that help to play up the gains and play down the losses.

In general, postdecisional bolstering raises the threshold for responsiveness to challenges. Minor challenging events and communications, therefore, tend to be promptly discounted in a way that enables the decision maker to give a negative response to the first key question, so that he displays unconflicted adherence and his decisional balance sheet remains essentially unchanged.

Starting with his very first act of commitment, the person may encounger negative social feedback in the form of social disapproval of his new decision. For example, a woman who decides to stop smoking may meet with strong opposition from her husband, who continues to be a heavy smoker and ridicules her for being taken in by "scare propaganda." Negative feedback also arises whenever any of the calculated risks (such as suffering from nicotine withdrawal symptoms) materializes and whenever any of the expected gains falls short of expectation (as when one fails to gain the expected relief from "smoker's cough" after cutting down on cigarettes for a week). Each of these setbacks—and any impressive communication that predicts ultimate failure—is a potential challenge that can create intense postdecisional conflict. Stage 5 persists only so long as all such challenges are ignored, refuted, or somehow counteracted, allowing the decision maker to remain unshaken in his resolve to adhere to the chosen course of action.

The decision maker will remain in stage 5 indefinitely, until he encounters an *effective* challenge that is so powerful as to provoke dissatisfaction with his chosen course of action. Then the decision maker embarks once again on a painful tour through the successive stages, this time seeking a different and hopefully better alternative. Obviously, the stability of a decision depends to a considerable degree upon the amount and intensity of negative feedback that the decision maker encounters when he carries out his chosen course. But stability also depends upon the decision maker's *capacity to tolerate negative feedback*, which depends partly on how completely and accurately he has worked out the decisional balance sheet during the preceding stages of arriving at the decision.

We postulate that the five stages we have just outlined are fully developed only when the decision maker's dominant pattern is vigilance. The stages are greatly attenuated or short-circuited when a minor incremental decision is made on the basis of a pattern of unconflicted change, or when a major decision is made impulsively on the basis of a pattern of defensive avoidance or hypervigilance. If one of these nonvigilant patterns is dominant, stages 2, 3, and 4 are perfunctory and sometimes almost entirely omitted.

Even when vigilance is the dominant pattern, the specific stage reached by a decision maker cannot always be sharply differentiated because earlier key questions keep cropping up if they have not been resolved. In presenting a schematic description of the stages of decision making, we do not intend to imply that a vigilant decision maker always proceeds in a completely orderly way. Some decisions appear to move along in linear fashion from stage 1 to stage 5, but may involve a great deal of fluctuation back and forth. Reverting to stage 2 from stage 3 or 4 is especially likely if the decision involves changing social affiliations, as when a person is contemplating divorce, converting to another religion, or switching membership from one political organization to another. Sometimes reversions result in a prolonged delay in arriving at a decision that can go on for years, as in the case of Louis Fischer's decision to defect from the Communist movement, which is described later in this chapter. The five-stage sequence, therefore, cannot be taken as establishing an ironclad law that specifies the steps every decision must invariably go through. Rather, this conceptualization of the sequence seems to us to provide a useful framework for analyzing how the decision maker's coping pattern is related to responsiveness to new information and to changes in his decisional balance sheet as he moves from one step to the next.

Many different psychological factors affect what happens during each of the stages, and these cannot be specified without taking account of findings from a number of research areas, including cognitive processes, attitude change, and social interaction. For example, in Stage 1, the probability that a person will respond positively or negatively to a given challenge depends partly on various factors that have been investigated in social psychological research on effective persuasion, such as the perceived trustworthiness of the communicator, the explicitness of the message, and the personality predispositions and mood of the person at the time he receives the challenging message (see McGuire, 1968; Triandis,

1971). In stage 2, the number and content of the alternatives generated depend partly on factors determining the intensity of memory search and the efficiency of retrieval, such as the presence of cues that remind the person of previously learned means–end relationships (see Lindsay and Norman, 1972). In stage 3, the cognitive processes involved in evaluating many pieces of information in order to arrive at a final selection of the best alternative are undoubtedly influenced by such factors as the decision maker's prior training in skills that affect his ability to calculate probabilities accurately. Such skills and related factors that influence judgment and choice are discussed in the literature on statistical decision theory, multiple-attribute utility theory, social-judgment theory, and information-integration theory (see Anderson, 1971; Edwards and Tversky, 1967; Kaplan and Schwartz, 1975; Lee, 1971; Tversky and Kahneman, 1974). In stage 4, the decision maker's deliberations about commitment are likely to be influenced by the salience of persons and groups with whom he is affiliated and other such factors investigated in research on interpersonal attraction and group relations (see Argyle, 1969; Huston, 1974; Rubin, 1973). Thus, we expect that fuller understanding of the microprocesses attending each stage of decision making will ultimately come from applying a variety of findings from cognitive and social psychology. For the present, our primary focus—in line with the general approach of this book—is on what happens during the successive stages when the dominant coping pattern is vigilance, as compared with one or another of the other patterns.

Implications for Group Decisions

The five-stage sequence is intended to apply to members of a decision-making group, such as an executive committee of policy makers, as well as to individual decision makers who have sole responsibility for a choice. Of course, all members of a group may not always be at the same stage at the same time. A few members may be considering a problem for the first time (stage 1), even as the discussion is being pushed forward by a few others who have already made a tentative choice (stage 3 or 4). Nevertheless, when we follow the course of decision-making activity in any single member we can see how at each stage he is affected by the group setting.

Compared with individual decision makers, the participants in policy-making groups are probably more vigilant in appraising a challenge (stage 1), provided that the conditions that foster groupthink are not present (see figure 5, page 132). In a nongroupthink type of executive committee, whenever any member perceives a challenge he usually brings it to the attention of the entire group, thus warning otherwise complacent members that a new decision might be necessary. Moreover, many executive groups have standard operating procedures for carrying out a thorough information search and for surveying and weighing alternatives, which foster vigilance during stages 2 and 3 (see Deutsch, 1963). Another feature of group decision making is that if each member searches his memory for new alternatives, a large pool of alternatives can be generated from which to choose. With so many alternatives being suggested by different people having different viewpoints, the likelihood is increased that the most relevant alternative policies will be put before the group during stage 2. Similarly, during stage 3 the pooling of information can make for more complete and accurate balance sheets among the participants. The exchange of ideas during the stage when alternatives are being weighed leads to changes in the aspirations and judgments of individual members as a result of their exposure to fresh information and to the new viewpoints that emerge in the course of the group's debate. This encourages the least vigilant members to reexamine the potential consequences of their original choice. But the potential advantages of group decision making are seldom fully realized, because conformity pressures within the group often foster a pattern of defensive avoidance among the members, rather than vigilance. (See the section "Groupthink" in chapter 5.)

During stage 4, the group setting makes for more intense commitment to the new course of action. The public nature of a group decision and the references to group norms make each member realize that once a consensus has been reached, he is expected to adhere to it. With individual decisions the process of commitment is often piecemeal and fragmentary as the person informs a growing number of people about his choice; in group situations, however, commitment may not be drawn out in this fashion. Pennington, Haravey, and Bass (1958) found that when members participate in a discussion and reach a consensus, they immediately feel committed to carry out the group decision. Recognizing that deviation from the policy will bring about criticism, or perhaps even censure and expulsion, each member finds himself bound to the policy. For these and other reasons, adherence to the decision during stage 5 is facilitated when the decision has to be implemented by the group as a whole, provided that each member has participated in evaluating the choices (Vroom, 1969). To put it another way, commitment to a reference group makes judgments formed in that group more resistant to change (Jones and Gerard, 1967; Kiesler, 1971). The group provides members with social support, enabling each one to withstand criticism during stage 5 better than he might if he alone were responsible.

Implications for Responsiveness to Information

Whether we are considering a decision maker participating as a member of a policy-making group or one acting entirely on his own, the five-stage sequence has some direct implications for the way he will respond to persuasive communications that are capable of changing his evaluations of alternative courses of action. For example, a new bit of antismoking information (such as "Doctors have found that the average person experiences less fatigue if he gives up smoking") will meet with indifference or high resistance before a smoker has been effectively challenged (pre–stage 1), but if the same new bit of information is presented to the person after he has gone through stage 1, it will be more open-mindedly evaluated. If presented at a much later stage, after the smoker has announced that he is going to quit smoking (stage 4), it will be promptly accepted with hardly any critical reflection about it.

The opposite outcomes would be expected with regard to an item of information that argues against the antismoking recommendation (such as "Doctors have found that many people who give up smoking become chronically overweight"). Before stage 1, the complacent smoker would have little interest in such information, although it would be readily accepted if brought to the focus of his attention. After an effective challenge during stages 2 and 3, as he moves toward an antismoking decision, the smoker would display much more interest in the information and would evaluate it in a relatively unbiased way. But then, after commitment following stage 4, if the now ex-smoker has no hope of finding a better alternative than sticking with his decision, he would be highly skeptical of such alleged information and would try to refute it.

To test the generality of the above hypotheses, it will be necessary to investigate many different types of decisions, in addition to the smoking decision that has furnished most of our empirical observations so far. It seems plausible to expect a fairly high degree of generality, in light of observations of similar stages in case studies of ill persons who were faced with the necessity of deciding whether or not to accept their physicians' advice to undergo surgery or painful medical treatments (Janis, 1958), and of normal men and women in the throes of decisional conflict about obtaining a divorce or changing their careers (Janis, 1959). The five-stage schema we have depicted has also been used by Bracken and Kasl (1975) to describe the decision-making process among unmarried women who have to make a decision about what to do about an unwanted pregnancy. During the initial, challenge stage, Bracken and Kasl note that some women use defensive tactics to avoid acknowledging that they are pregnant even after it has become obvious that they have missed their menstrual period; for example, they delay seeking information about their condition from a physician and attribute morning sickness to current emotional tension. During the second stage (surveying alternatives), most women consider three main options—keeping the baby after delivery, letting the baby be adopted after delivery, or having an abortion. The last alternative is most likely to be rapidly eliminated as unacceptable, even though the pregnancy is unwanted, when there are severe legal restrictions or religious prohibitions against that course of action. During the third stage (weighing alternatives), the women who are considering an abortion seek information about it and may then spontaneously "rehearse" the role of having actually made that decision.

> A woman may consider what her life will be like if she goes ahead with the abortion, the reactions of herself and significant others to the abortion, etc. If the role does not feel comfortable, then it may be switched to that of having delivered. If this is even more unpleasant, then the roles may be reversed again [Bracken and Kasl, 1975, p. 1016].

During the fourth stage (deliberating about commitment), the pregnant woman becomes concerned about informing her partner, friends, and relatives. At the beginning of the fifth stage (adhering to the decision), new information may be obtained when the woman tries to implement her decision to have an abortion by making arrangements at an appropriate medical clinic. If the information is negative, she may revert to stage 2 or 3 and end up choosing a different alternative.

Our five-stage schema is consistent with clinical observations reported by Bennis et al. (1968, pp. 338–68) concerning the sequence of change in those memorable instances when a psychotherapist, a counselor, or some other change agent is successful in transforming the values and conduct of a neurotic person or a psychopathic criminal. The schema also corresponds closely to the steps in the decision-making process described by Charles F. Hermann (1969) in his account of how new foreign policies are evolved by government leaders when startling information, such as that which provoked the Cuban missile crisis, challenges their preexisting policies. And it also conforms fairly well to descriptive accounts of the sequence of stages involved in making highly impersonal decisions, such as those made by scientists in response to new evidence. Kuhn (1962), in his account of the recent history of various scientific theories in the natural sciences, calls attention to the resistance of outstanding scientists in physics and chemistry to any fundamental change in their theories until a crisis is generated by impressively challenging data that are completely incompatible with the paradigm to which they are committed. Original experimental data, according to Kuhn, are likely to be belittled and disregarded if they go against a long-established theory that has not yet been seriously challenged (pre–stage 1), but they will be given careful scrutiny if they are presented during the crisis period, before any of the new alternative paradigms has yet been selected (stages 2 or 3). Finally, new experimental findings will meet with least resistance if they are in accord with a new paradigm that has already been accepted by research investigators (after stage 4).

Psychological resistance to realistic information at any stage in the decision-making process results in errors in the decisional balance sheet. In the preceding chapter, we introduced a hypothesis concerning the consequences of defective balance sheets, which emphasized that errors of commission and omission make for exceptionally high vulnerability to negative feedback. The defective-balance-sheet hypothesis can be reformulated as follows in terms of the stage-sequence schema, in a way that makes it easier to spell out more precisely when and how such errors can be prevented. *Incomplete working through of any of the first four stages of the decision-making process results in an incomplete or distorted balance sheet, which leaves the person vulnerable to negative feedback during the final stage* (Janis, 1968).

During stage 1, an initial challenge from an impressive message that conveys the negative consequences of one's preexisting course of action can "get under one's skin," giving rise to a sustained attitude of personal vulnerability to the threat. We surmise that full working through of the challenge injects such a powerful incentive into the person's balance sheet that it tends to counteract any negative incentives that might tempt the person to backslide during stage 5. Just such an effect appears to be produced in emotional role playing experiments (described in chapter 13). In other studies of backsliding, we note that a decision maker seems more likely to develop intense regret during stage 5 when he learns about an attractive alternative if it is one that he had completely overlooked in his survey of alternatives *during stage 2*. Research on postdecisional regret among surgical patients and others who elect to undergo a stressful operation indicates that regret is especially intense during stage 5 when the negative feedback encountered (pain, sleeplessness, etc.) had not been anticipated and assimilated into the balance sheet *during stage 3*, when they were preoccupied with selecting the best alternative, or *during stage 4*, when their reasons for making the decision came under critical scrutiny as they deliberated about committing themselves. The main point is that any weak link in the chain, as the decision maker moves through the successive stages, can result in a distorted balance sheet and thereby contribute to backsliding in response to negative feedback. The more complete the work of stages 1 to 4, the better the chances that stage 5 will persist.

The Stages Prolonged:
Fischer's Break with Communism

In many decisions the person moves rapidly through the various stages, sometimes combining or even skipping stages. But some decisions are played out over an enormous span of time. One of the most striking cases we know of is reported in an autobiographical account by Louis Fischer, a well-known American journalist who broke off his political affiliation with the Soviet Communist movement in 1939. A remarkable feature of Fischer's decision is that it developed so slowly that over a decade elapsed between stage 1 (1928) and stage 4 (1939). This time interval contrasts markedly with the much briefer intervals obtaining in the vast majority of personal decisions.

In *The God That Failed*, six well-known writers, André Gide, Richard Wright, Ignazio Silone, Stephen Spender, Arthur Koestler, and Fischer, discuss how and why, after a period of affiliation with the Communist movement, they decided to reject Communism. Of the six autobiographical accounts, perhaps the most difficult to analyze in terms of the stages sequence is Fischer's. His personal story is noteworthy because it describes in detail the agonizing process of doubt and debate that characteristically precedes defection from a political movement. We interpret his account as illustrating the vicissitudes of conflict generated during successive stages of making a decision to give up something that has both strong positive and strong negative features. As Fischer moved from one stage to the next there were characteristic changes in his responsiveness to new information about the Soviet Union—changes that are consistent with the theoretical expectations derived from the stages schema.

Fischer's work as a free-lance journalist took him to Europe in 1921, where he saw at first hand the wretched aftermath of World War I. In 1922, on a tour of Soviet Russia, he was impressed with the dynamic energy and enthusiasm wrought by the recent revolution. Disillusioned with what seemed to be the failures of Western democracy, Fischer soon became a champion of the Soviet system. He recounts with remarkable candor his tendency, after having become converted to Communism, to discount negative information about the Soviet Union while focusing exclusively on its good points. He says that he regarded all new developments that seemed detrimental to Russia "as ephemeral, dishonestly interpreted, or cancelled out by more significant and countervailing developments" (pp. 183–84). He reports that during the subsequent five years his appraisal of the alternatives to supporting the Communist movement continued to be heavily biased. "Throughout," he writes, "I consciously and subconsciously weighed the Soviet regime in the balance. My reading of the scales, of course, depended on what I put into them" (p. 185). Referring to his attitude in 1924, for example, he felt that there was no question but that "this new society without exploitation outweighed the absence of a free press and the presence of the secret police" (p. 185).

By 1928, however, unmistakable signs that the Bolsheviks had created a police state began to haunt Fischer. He tried to cope with the challenging evidence by minimizing the importance of individual freedom in the overall context of solving basic social and economic problems. Still, there are many indications in Fischer's account that the challenge posed by information about the totalitarian character of the Soviet regime was strong enough at times to jolt him temporarily out of adherence to his old position (stage 5) into the first stage of a decision to quit. He began at times to look for alternatives (stage 2), but apparently had little hope of finding a better course of action than that of maintaining his association with the Communist movement. Throughout the late 1920s and early 1930s, Fischer repeatedly struggled with the issues, but each time he ended up deciding in favor of his initial, pro-Stalinist position (reverting to the old stage 5). But his persistent adherence to the Stalinist cause continued to be punctuated by periods of doubt generated by fresh evidence of the totalitarian character of the Soviet Union. The painful process of trying to find a satisfactory alternative continued on and off for many years; but, Fischer was constantly deterred from renouncing the pro-Soviet position to which he was so deeply committed by virtue of his public writings, his covert political associations, and his personal friendship ties with fellow members of the movement. During this period there was no challenge strong enough to impel him all the way through the successive stages to a new decision. He continued to view the accumulating evidence with biased eyes in an attempt to bolster his reluctance to renounce Communism, but his convictions were slowly being eroded, leaving him more vulnerable than ever to challenge.

> Suddenly in 1935, whispers about a new democratic constitution were heard, and in 1936 it became official. The "Stalin Constitution." I clutched at it. I wanted to believe. I did not want to foreswear a cause in which I had made such a large spiritual investment. . . . While I was assiduously collecting indications to nurture my hopes, they were completely blasted. . . . By the middle of 1936, with the [Moscow Purge] trials to be announced, I sensed the oncoming night and knew that I no longer wished to live in the Soviet Union [pp. 195–96].

Thus, by 1936, the challenge to Fischer's pro-Stalinist position had become so strong that he was constantly in conflict about whether or not to continue to support the movement. Thereafter he appears to have been chronically fixated within a feedback loop between stages 2 and 3 (selecting alternatives, weighing them, feeling unwilling to choose any, returning to the search for a better alternative, then going through the same cycle again). Sometimes he reached the threshold of stage 4 (feeling almost but not quite ready to commit himself to an anti-Communist position). He had long ago arrived at the judgment that the Soviet government was so morally corrupt that the Communist movement did not deserve anyone's support, and yet he could not bring himself to renounce that movement. The main stumbling block appears to have been his extensive social commitments to supporters of the Communist movement.

As Fischer focused on the various losses that would arise as a consequence of breaking with the movement, he continued to be primarily concerned with the inevitable rejection and recrimination he would incur from old friends and colleagues. Following the outbreak of the Spanish Civil War in 1936, he did not want to be cut off from contact with his friends in America who were wholeheartedly supporting the Loyalist cause in Spain. If he wanted to continue these friendships and share in the work for Loyalist Spain, he would have to maintain good relationships with members of the Communist party. He knew that if he defected from the Communist movement he would be mercilessly castigated and ostracized by all party members and by most of their fellow travelers. In addition, Fischer did not want to disrupt his family life, which was centered in the Soviet Union. His wife was Russian and wanted to continue on her job in Moscow, where they were bringing up their two children.[2]

Fischer's reluctance to cut himself off from the social network in which his commitments were anchored might have continued to delay his decision to defect indefinitely were it not for fresh incentives that tipped the balance. As Fischer puts it, "The scales in which I weighed the pros and cons of Sovietism were precariously balanced. A feather would tip them against Russia. Now a ton was dropped on to the anti-Soviet scale" (pp. 199–200). He was referring to the reprisals carried out by the Soviets against Communists who had worked and fought in Spain during the Civil War. When General Franco's forces, aided by Fascist Italy and Nazi Germany, defeated the Spanish Loyalists early in 1939, many Communist party members from all over Europe who had fought in the Loyalist army fled to Russia. But to the surprise and horror of sympathizers with the Loyalist cause, these self-sacrificing Communists were treated as dangerous opponents by the Soviet government. Many were sent to jail; some were sent to Siberia; still others disappeared, never to be heard of again. Despite the personal anguish caused by these new acts of what he now believed to be "Soviet perfidy," Fischer still could not bring himself to act in accordance with his new beliefs. Later in 1939, however, came the "final straw" of the Hitler-Stalin nonaggression pact. Fischer was so appalled that he was no longer reluctant to denounce Communism and to sever his ties with the movement (which many Communist party members and fellow travelers whom he knew were also doing).

Louis Fischer's story illustrates the "slow burn" type of decisional dilemma, in which a person finds himself in a chronically challenged state, overtly adhering to his former commitment but constantly regretting it. On the surface, he appeared to be a loyal adherent of the Communist movement, but psychologically, many years before his public break with the movement, he had already reached stage 3 (a tentative judgment in favor of defecting). In such a situation, the disparity between the decision maker's public and private attitudes can be inferred from the defector's private revelations about current feelings of regret, his appraisals of alternative courses of action, and his subtle efforts to evade full participation in the political movement to which he had previously committed himself. A person in this type of chronic but submerged state of postdecisional conflict is likely, sooner or later, to surprise those friends and acquaintances who are unaware of his private thoughts by suddenly switching his allegiance one day to an entirely different political position.

The marked indecision and repeated backsliding that characterized Fischer's thoughts and feelings during his long period of disillusionment with Communism have been observed in many other defectors from political parties (Almond, 1954). Two-thirds of the respondents in Almond's study of former Communists reported having experienced strong doubts and conflict for more than a year before their final break with the party. In discussing why it was so difficult for a member to decide to leave the Communist party, Almond singles out two main factors: the degree of commitment to the party, and the unavailability of a satisfactory social network outside the party. These two factors appear to have played a crucial role in Fischer's indecision over breaking with Communism, although it should be pointed out that he was never a party functionary, only a close sympathizer. We have seen that his powerful commitment prevented him from making the break even while (from 1937 until 1939) the scales were actually tipped, in his mind, against the Stalinist position. Attachments to close friends within the movement and the prospect of their bitter antagonism and censure functioned as powerful social constraints that kept tipping the balance back in favor of sticking with the movement, even though the Soviet Union's policies and the American Communist party's conformity to each new shift in the Soviet line had become repulsive to him. In addition, Fischer's sense of personal identity was so bound up with his activities as a supporter of communism that he anticipated a loss of self-esteem from defecting, especially since the alternative of using his journalistic skills to denounce the Soviet Union would align him with the anti-Communist reactionaries he had always despised.

For anyone active in politics, the decision to break off affiliation with a political party or movement is heavily influenced by the prospects in store upon leaving. Just as in unhappy marriages, if the alternatives are even less attractive than the current course of action, the person will choose the least undesirable course and avoid making the break. Almond's analysis of the difficulties experienced by defectors from the Communist party emphasizes the emotional needs that were served by party membership; other left-wing or liberal political parties did not represent viable alternatives for the satisfaction of those needs. Thus, a person may be intellectually repelled by the organization with which he is affiliated, but decide to continue membership because he cannot find any alternative group that can meet his needs for social contact and approval. These are conditions that make for prolonged time intervals between the successive stages of decision making.

When a reluctant decision maker enters stage 4 and his transformation finally becomes public, he is likely to explain that he could hold out no longer because "otherwise I would be unable to live with myself." This type of comment, if sincere, suggests that the accumulated challenges gradually build up in the conflicted person a pervading sense of *self-disapproval* for continuing to act in a way he no longer feels is justified.

Thus, as we have already suggested, the decisional balance sheet gradually changes as the challenges mount until a point is reached where the strength of anticipated self-disapproval for continuing the affiliation exceeds that of the anticipated social and self-disapproval for making the break.

Not infrequently the "slow burn" type of chronic reappraisal arises with respect to a person's decision concerning his marriage or career choice. Just as with political defections, people in the decision maker's community are likely to be surprised and perplexed when a long-submerged conflict erupts on the surface. A seemingly contented husband or wife suddenly moves out of the home and takes legal action to obtain a divorce after a marital quarrel that is no different from those the couple has had dozens of times before. A seemingly contented executive submits his resignation after a trivial reprimand from his chief. Those who know the person intimately, however, may not be at all surprised by the sudden and drastic change in behavior, because they realize that the minor provocation preceding the new decision was simply the "last straw" that induced the person to surmount whatever inhibitions had been preventing him for many months or years from doing what he had been wanting to do. Evidently the same sources of inhibition that prevent a man from seeking a divorce or quitting a job can contribute to a political activist's reluctance to defect from a movement to which he has devoted the best years of his life.

Reversions and Feedback Loops

In the case study of Fischer's political defection, we encountered frequent reversions from stages 3 and 4 to earlier stages. We noted that for several years he seemed to be stuck in a feedback loop, going through the same stages over and over again without progressing to the end of stage 4.

Figure 7 indicates the possible reversions and feedback loops that can occur as a person moves from one stage to another. Two main types of reversion, from stage 3 and stage 4, are represented: (1) from weighing to re-searching and (2) from deliberating about commitment to reweighing.[3]

After having reached the point in stage 3 where he has selected the alternative he regards as best (or least objectionable), the vigilant decision maker will revert to an earlier stage if he gives a negative response to the second basic question (which asks whether the chosen alternative meets the essential requirements) and to the supplementary questions that come next ("Can I relax the requirements sufficiently to find the best alternative satisfactory? Might a modification of one of the existing alternatives be better?"). This reversion is depicted in the figure by the broken arrow labeled *no*, which returns from stage 3 to the beginning of stage 2.

An example of the utility of this type of reversion can be cited from one of the most fateful policy decisions of the twentieth century. At a meeting of President Kennedy's Executive Committee on the morning of the first day of the Cuban missile crisis, according to Arthur Schlesinger's account (1965, pp. 803-4), most members temporarily judged that the best possible response was an air strike against Cuba to destroy the missile sites. This military move was attractive because it would eliminate the threat of a nuclear attack against the United States launched from the Cuban missile sites, which were expected to become operative within about ten days. But the group was informed that an air strike would kill many Russian soldiers manning the Cuban missile sites and would run the grave risk of provoking the Soviet Union into drastic retaliation, possibly with nuclear bombs launched from Soviet submarines along the American coast. Realizing that what appeared to be the best course of action failed to meet an essential requirement, Attorney General Robert Kennedy told the others in the group that he thought they needed more alternatives and should search for a less drastic course than bombing. Thereupon the members began considering a number of alternatives they had not previously discussed, including a summit conference, secret negotiations with Castro, and a naval blockade. (The last turned out to be the course finally adopted, three days later, after nine other alternatives the group had generated were debated.) Apparently, many members of the group at that first morning meeting had momentarily reached stage 3, but gave a negative response when they asked themselves if the seemingly best choice would meet the essential requirements (which they were unwilling to relax) and then reverted to the beginning of stage 2—to the search for another alternative.

Before reverting to stage 2, a decision maker will consider whether he is willing to relax the requirements sufficiently to find the best alternative acceptable. If the best alternative still fails to meet the most essential requirements, he will next consider whether it can be modified so as to get rid of its objectionable features. This requires additional search for and evaluation of information about the consequences of the modified alternative. If despite the alterations it is still unsatisfactory, the vigilant decision maker will reexamine one of the other alternatives he had been weighing to see if it, in turn, can be modified to meet the most basic requirements. When all such attempts fail during the third stage, he will revert to stage 2. If his renewed search for alternatives yields an attractive new one that had been overlooked earlier, the decision maker will move on to stage 3. But he will again revert to stage 2 if he judges the new alternative and its modifications to be deficient in meeting essential requirements he is unwilling to violate. Time and again the decision maker may find a new alternative to be better than any of the others but still deficient with regard to meeting one or another of his objectives. Each time his dissatisfaction will impel him to revert to searching for another alternative. This feedback loop will continue until the vigilant decision maker either finds a completely satisfying alternative or modifies his requirements.

FIGURE 7.   Model of the stages of decision making.

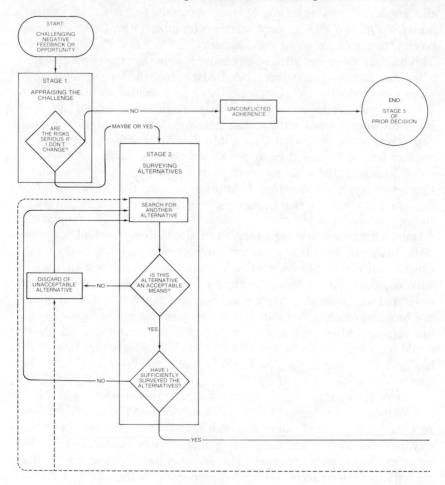

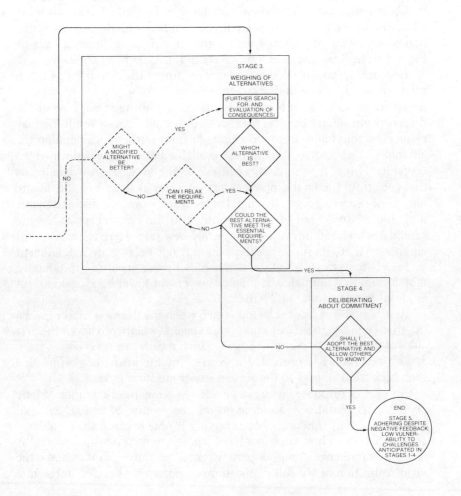

STAGE 3.

WEIGHING OF
ALTERNATIVES

(FURTHER SEARCH
FOR AND
EVALUATION OF
CONSEQUENCES)

MIGHT
A MODIFIED
ALTERNATIVE
BE
BETTER?

WHICH
ALTERNATIVE
IS
BEST?

CAN I RELAX
THE REQUIRE-
MENTS

COULD THE
BEST ALTERNA-
TIVE MEET THE
ESSENTIAL
REQUIRE-
MENTS?

YES

NO

NO

YES

NO

YES

STAGE 4.

DELIBERATING
ABOUT COMMITMENT

SHALL I
ADOPT THE BEST
ALTERNATIVE AND
ALLOW OTHERS
TO KNOW?

NO

YES

END:
STAGE 5.
ADHERING DESPITE
NEGATIVE FEEDBACK.
LOW VULNER-
ABILITY TO
CHALLENGES
ANTICIPATED IN
STAGES 1-4

Sometimes a feedback loop goes on for many years. More often, the decision maker manages to find a solution to the problem after a relatively short time by changing his essential requirements. Having become keenly aware of the shortcomings of all the courses of action he has considered, the decision maker is likely to consider that he is being too unrealistic, too much of a perfectionist, in seeking an ideal solution. He becomes willing to take some calculated risks that he had earlier wanted to avoid, thereby relaxing some of his requirements.

Some forms of vacillation can be conceptualized in terms of the feedback loops within stage 3 and from stage 3 to stage 2. At first the decision maker focuses on one course of action, which he rates as the best available choice. But as he thinks about it, he feels uncomfortable, becomes worried because of its defects, and is induced to go back to search for a better alternative. As first one and then another alternative is considered and reconsidered, the vigilant decision maker will use his ingenuity to modify the alternatives until one is maximally acceptable. Thus, the well-known vacillation that marks decisional conflict may be part of a constructive effort to improve the leading alternatives. (Studies of predecisional vacillation generally fail to capture this "creative modification" process because the researchers ask the decision makers to rate only fixed choices.)

Because the vigilant decision maker continues his search for as much information as he can find about the expected consequences of each alternative, he is likely to learn more and more during stage 3 about the defects of the alternatives he had selected in stage 2. As a result, he may change his mind and decide to eliminate from further consideration the alternative first selected as the best available but no longer deemed acceptable. This is represented in figure 7 by the broken arrow labeled *no* that goes from the final supplementary question in stage 3 to the discard bin. As he repeatedly goes through the feedback loops, the decision maker may discard any or all of the alternatives in the original set of leading candidates and end up with a completely new one. Here again we must emphasize that entering a feedback loop is not necessarily a derailment that leads only to stagnant delay but may be the onset of a productive moratorium that ultimately facilitates movement toward an ingenious solution of the decisional problem.

Another type of feedback loop occurs when the decision maker gives a negative response to the key question in stage 4 (whether to adopt the best alternative and allow others to know), which results in a reversion to stage 3. This reversion is represented in figure 7 by the arrow labeled *no* that goes back from stage 4 to the second major question in stage 3.

A negative response during stage 4 is by no means uncommon. Many people, after tentatively deciding on the best course of action, get cold feet as they start thinking about carrying it out, because they suddenly realize that their choice may not be acceptable to members of their family or to other reference groups or persons. Another source of inhibition is the vivid realization of the full implications of becoming wedded to the new course of action once an irrevocable commitment is made. A decision maker may not realize vividly until stage 4 that if the new course of action fails to work out, he will have great difficulty changing once everyone in his social network gets to know about his choice.

As a result of reversion to stage 3, the decision maker once again reviews his main objectives and worries more than ever about the calculated risks that only a little while earlier he had thought worth taking. If he no longer feels sure that the alternative he has selected will meet all of his essential requirements, he will proceed to the supplementary questions, which can lead to further search and evaluation. At such a time he is especially likely to look for hidden or unknown risks that he had vaguely suspected might be something to worry about but had set aside (see chapter 9).

During stage 4, a vigilant decision maker's balance sheet generally becomes more complete and accurate as a result of the temporary inhibitions aroused by concern about social censure and fear of being "boxed in." For example, as a man visualizes in detail the scene at the dinner table when he announces to his wife that he has decided to invest all their savings in a get-rich-quick scheme, he will experience pangs of doubt and uncertainty and will at least temporarily give a negative response to the key question in stage 4. Reverting to stage 3, he will reconsider whether his choice meets the essential requirements of a satisfactory investment. For the first time he may take account of the undesirable effect the investment might have on his relationship with his wife. This would be tantamount to adding a new essential requirement he had not considered before—a requirement the choice fails to meet. If the outcome of his reconsideration is a negative response to the second key question and also to the two supplementary questions in stage 3, he will revert to stage 2 and perhaps discard completely the course he had been on the brink of adopting.

Thus, when a decision maker retreats from the brink, reverting from stage 4 to stage 3, he is likely to acquire more information and adopt new requirements, which may result in his making a more reality-tested decision. In addition, as he reconsiders the drawbacks of the course he is about to adopt, he is stimulated to work out modifications that include more complete contingency plans. These are potentially constructive effects of entering this feedback loop as a result of the decision maker's wariness about proceeding to implementation during stage 4. But, of course, wariness at the brink of commitment can have deleterious effects if it gives rise to a prolonged delay of necessary action, resulting in loss of the preferred option or a weakening in resolve to execute a well-conceived plan.

Bolstering as the Final Step toward Action

We have already spoken about the possibility that after a long period of search and appraisal, the decision maker's pattern of vigilance may give way to defensive avoidance at the point where he loses hope of finding a better solution than the least objectionable course he has been considering. The result is that after an exhaustive information search accompanied by a relatively unbiased examination of the alternatives, the decision maker starts to bolster, in a highly biased way, the one he regards as best. We postulate that this final step of bolstering occurs very frequently. The reason is that sooner or later a vigilant decision maker will reach the point where he has exhausted all available sources of information and realizes—usually quite correctly—that there is no longer any realistic basis on which to expect to turn up a better solution than the best one that has emerged from his laborious search and appraisal. If the person also realizes that he cannnot shift responsibility and expects that he will sustain serious utilitarian losses or social disapproval if he procrastinates, all the conditions that make for bolstering are present.

During stage 4, as the person thinks about implementing the alternative that seems to be the best he can hope to find, however imperfect he knows it to be, he will move toward commitment by making out the best case for it he can: he will try to play up the anticipated gains and play down the anticipated losses. Hence we regard bolstering as part of the normal process of decisional resolution (see the section "Bolstering before Commitment" in chapter 4).[4]

If the decision maker's attempt to imagine a favorable outcome does not succeed—if he cannot convince himself that the hoped-for gains really will materialize or that the most serious risks really can be averted—he will experience a resurgence of worry and revert to stage 3. But if, after bolstering, the chosen course strikes him as satisfactory, leaving him relatively free from worry, he is ready for action and takes the first step of committing himself by allowing one or more significant persons in his social network to know his choice.

The Combined Conflict and Stage-Sequence Model

Our five-stage sequence was derived mainly from observations of the way people arrive at carefully worked-out decisions they are able to live with. As we have already stated, this origin entails a major limitation: the full sequence, as represesented in figure 7, is to be expected only when a decision maker's dominant coping pattern is vigilance. In terms of our conflict model, we expect the five stages to unfold in the way we have described if the decision maker gives a positive response to each of the four crucial questions that determine his coping pattern. If he gives a negative response to one of the crucial questions, the later stages are attenuated.

The specific forms of attenuation are shown in figure 8, which combines the conflict model (figure 3) with the stage-sequence schema (figure

7).[5] This combined model contains the four key questions that determine the decision maker's coping pattern together with the additional ones that enter into the successive stages of vigilant decision making. It is intended to be applicable to *all* consequential decisions made by *all* decision makers, irrespective of whether vigilance is the dominant coping pattern.

Figure 8 shows graphically the enormous increase in complexity entailed by the vigilance pattern as compared with the other patterns. For the four defective patterns there are only a few key questions, which often can be answered in a relatively short time, sometimes in less than one minute. In contrast, the vigilance pattern encompasses nine key questions (plus two supplementary questions), which generally require prolonged deliberation.

Earlier we pointed out that the conflict model (figure 3) is intended to give a descriptive account of the hot cognitive processes that mediate the decision makers' *current* coping pattern at any given time, and we assume that *fluctuations* from one coping pattern to another will occur during the predecisional period whenever the decision maker obtains new information that induces him to change the answers he gives to any of the basic questions that determine which of the five coping patterns will be the dominant one. The potential fluctuations are represented in the combined model depicted in figure 8. If the decision maker's answer to the first basic question is *yes*, he proceeds to stage 2 and then each time he scans a salient alternative he poses to himself the other three basic questions that determine his coping pattern:

1. Are the risks serious if I change to this alternative?
2. Is it realistic to hope to find a better alternative?
3. Is there sufficient time to search for and evaluate a better alternative?

If his answer to any one of the questions is negative, he gives only perfunctory consideration to the key questions in the next two stages. Without obtaining further information about the pros and cons of the alternatives and with hardly any deliberation about commitment, he proceeds to adopt what seems to him to be a satisfactory course of action and allows others to know. At the time of commitment the decision maker's balance sheet is likely to contain numerous errors of omission and commission; consequently, he will be exceptionally vulnerable to any negative event or communication that challenges his chosen course of action.

When the decision maker's answers to the three basic questions in stage 2 are positive, his dominant coping pattern is vigilance and he proceeds to the final key question of stage 2 ("Have I sufficiently surveyed the alternatives?"). From that point on, the successive stages and feedback loops occur in the manner described above in our discussion of figure 7. However, as a result of the initial feedback loop within stage 2—which we assume occurs in every consequential decision, as the decision maker contemplates first one leading alternative and then another—the sequence

FIGURE 8.   Combined model of coping patterns and stages of decision making.

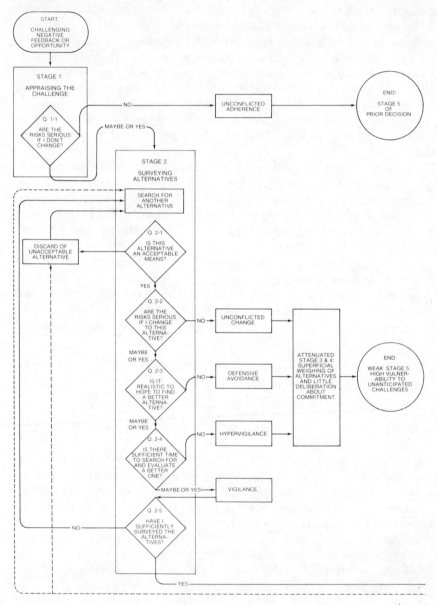

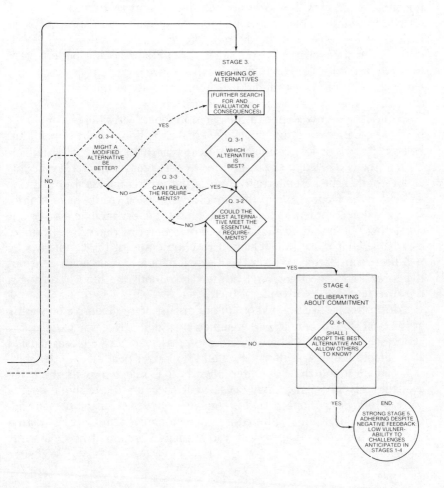

of psychological events becomes much more complicated (see note 3). A decision maker may start off by displaying vigilance as he examines the first two salient alternatives, but several alternatives later, with time and fatigue taking their toll, his vigilance may begin to wane and his dominant coping pattern may change.

A college senior, for example, when urged by his parents to take advantage of the opportunity to go on to graduate school, was keenly aware of the serious risks of following the academic career line his parents wanted him to pursue. Hopeful about finding a better option and with plenty of time to decide, he proceeded in a state of vigilance to survey other alternatives, including volunteering for the Peace Corps and obtaining apprenticeship training in cabinet making. One day, after several weeks of search, appraisal, and distressing indecision, he was offered a job as stock clerk in a record shop where his girlfriend worked, which appealed to him and did not seem to pose any serious drawbacks. At that point, his dominant coping pattern was no longer vigilance but rather unconflicted change: he promptly committed himself to a low-level job after only a perfunctory search and appraisal (much to the despair of his parents, whose objections he did not take seriously).

In order for vigilance to remain the dominant coping pattern, it is necessary that the decision maker *repeatedly* give positive responses to the basic questions for *every* additional alternative he examines during the surveying phase. Otherwise, the feedback loop within stage 2 can terminate in defensive avoidance (if the decision maker loses hope of finding a better alternative) or in hypervigilance (if he continues to be hopeful but believes there is no longer sufficient time to search for a better alternative).

If at the end of stage 3 or stage 4 the decision maker has serious doubts about whether the best alternative meets all the essential requirements, he will enter the feedback loop that involves reversion to the beginning of stage 2. He recommences his search for a satisfactory modification of one or another of the leading alternatives or for a new one that is free from the drawbacks that make him reluctant to choose any of the candidates he had been considering. Within this feedback loop he will again confront the three basic questions, and he may terminate the loop by giving a negative response to any one of them.

Most often, as we pointed out in our discussion of defensive bolstering as the final step toward action, vigilance eventually gives way to defensive avoidance at the point where the decision maker thinks he has exhausted all available sources of information and no longer believes a better solution can be found than the alternative he has selected as the best one available. Hypervigilance may occasionally become the terminal coping pattern following a long period of vigilance, however, if the person suddenly realizes that the deadline for making a choice among risky alternatives is at hand and that he will lose attractive options if he delays any longer.

Complicated as it is, figure 8 fails to depict the full range of complexities resulting from switching from vigilance to one of the other coping patterns after reaching stages 2, 3, or 4. The end results in the lower two circles in the figure can be expected to hold only when the same coping pattern characterizes *most* of the predecisional period. Thus, if vigilance is the dominant pattern for many weeks as the decision maker moves through the successive stages, he acquires considerable information about pros and cons during stages 2 and 3, and makes contingency plans while continuing to fill out and correct his decisional balance sheet as he deliberates about commitment during stage 4. Consequently, it will matter very little if after all that cognitive activity the feedback loop that stems from stage 4 is eventually terminated by defensive avoidance (bolstering the least objectionable alternative after the decision maker loses hope of finding a better one) or by hypervigilance (impulsive commitment to the least objectionable alternative in a state of acute anxiety about a rapidly approaching deadline). The bulk of the essential work of arriving at a high-quality decision will have been completed during the long period when vigilance was dominant. But if vigilance is dominant for only a brief period during stage 2, and is superceded by a shift to one of the other coping patterns before all the available alternatives have been appraised, the decision will be of poor quality, with high vulnerability to negative feedback, as indicated in the middle right-hand circle of figure 8. The more time and effort the decision maker spends in a state of vigilance while deliberating about the key questions during stages 2, 3, and 4, the more likely he is to meet the criteria for high-quality decision making.

The amount of time spent on a decision is not by itself an adequate predictor of quality, because there must also be indications that the decision maker's time was spent going through stages 2, 3, and 4 in a vigilant state, not procrastinating in a state of defensive avoidance or inefficiently flitting from one alternative to another in a state of hypervigilance. This brings us to an essential question that requires empirically testable answers if we are to apply the theoretical model to concrete instances of decision making: what are the indicators that an observer can use to diagnose whether a decision maker is in a state of vigilance while going through a feedback loop stemming from dissatisfaction with the best alternative? One important indicator, which was suggested earlier, is that when a decision maker vacillates between alternatives, he continues to seek information through memory search or by asking other people for advice, which adds new entries to his balance sheet. Another indicator is his modifying an alternative or his discarding one he had initially appraised as an acceptable candidate. Additional signs of vigilant effort are verbal reports of persistently negative responses to the final question in stage 2 (e.g., "I'm still looking for a better option") and to the second one in stage 3 (e.g., "I don't feel confident about that plan because I'm worried about the risks"). The more such signs there are, the greater the chances that the decision maker will be sufficiently vigilant to meet the criteria for a high-quality decision and will subsequently adhere to his commitment.

One of the heuristic values of the combined model in figure 8 is that it calls attention to points at which interventions might improve the quality of a person's decision-making activity. Each of the questions—and especially those in stage 2—can be regarded as a juncture in the decision-making sequence that calls for a specific type of advice and information from a counselor who is trying to help the decision maker arrive at an optimizing decision on a vital issue. Even without supplying any new information, a counselor might aid the decision maker's efforts to meet the criteria for high-quality decision making by raising the questions explicitly in a way that stimulates the decision maker to reconsider what he already knows and to do so in an unbiased way. In stage 1, for example, a counselor could ask the decision maker how likely it is that the challenging threat will materialize and, if it does, what potential losses might arise from continuing his present course of action. Then he might ask a similar set of questions pertinent to each of the other key questions, as the decision maker goes through the successive stages, ending with questions about whether he is reluctant to let any of his relatives, friends, or associates know about the new alternative he has selected and, if so, why.

These and other applications of the combined model for counseling decision makers will be elaborated later when we discuss effective interventions (chapters 13 and 14). In the next five chapters, we shall review major research findings on the psychology of decision making in order to continue our inquiry into how well the available evidence fits the hypotheses derived from the theoretical assumptions that enter into the combined model.

PART 3

Major Research
Findings

CHAPTER 8

Open-minded Exposure to Challenging Information

IN THIS CHAPTER WE EXPLORE some of the implications of the conflict model for analyzing coping patterns. The main focus is on the conditions that promote openness to challenging information, particularly when the decision maker is thinking about committing himself (stage 4 of the decision-making process) or has fully done so (stage 5).

Selective Exposure: The Hypothesis That Deserved to Be True

The selective exposure hypothesis, regarded by an earlier generation of behavioral scientists as a fundamental tenet of social psychology, postulates that people generally censor their intake of messages in a highly biased way so as to protect their current beliefs and decisions from being attacked (see Klapper, 1949). A supplementary postulate is that people generally seek out communications that support their prior attitudes and decisions, especially when they inadvertently encounter negative feedback that makes them less confident. Thus, the selective exposure hypothesis asserts that people generally seek messages with which they agree and avoid those with which they disagree. For many jaundiced observers of the human scene, the notion of selective self-censorship conjured up a plausible image of man as a defensive creature in a world of threatening information; this hypothesis, as McGuire (1968) put it, *deserved* to be true. Whether deserving or not, the selective exposure hypothesis became a linchpin in various consistency theories (e.g., Festinger, 1957). Until the mid-1960s, deviations from the hypothesis were usually regarded as unimportant exceptions to the general rule, rather than as grounds for reconsidering it.

The general tendency toward closed-mindedness postulated by the selective exposure hypothesis was called into question in a review of relevant empirical studies by Freedman and Sears (1965). After that, something of a tradition arose in the field of attitude change research to keep a scoreboard showing the number of published studies that supported or failed to support the selective exposure hypothesis. Freedman and Sears had found that of the seventeen experimental studies published between 1956 and 1965, only five indicated a preference for supportive information; five others showed a preference for *non*supportive information and seven yielded no particular preference at all—hardly encouraging for such a deserving hypothesis. Taking account of additional studies published between 1965 and 1968, Sears and Abeles (1969) updated the scoreboard to read nine "for," 5 "against," and 12 "no preference." The revised scoreboard gave little encouragement to those who would have liked to see the first one discredited. Rather, it indicated once again that there was no general tendency toward selective information exposure. Nonconfirming studies show that a number of specific factors, such as the message's utility (Canon, 1964; Lowe and Steiner, 1968); ease of refutability (Lowin, 1967; Kleinhesselink and Edwards, 1975), topical interest and novelty (Atkin, 1973) can offset, if not swamp, whatever selectivity tendency there might be.

Obviously, the box-score tradition should be quietly put to rest. The challenge that remains is to specify the conditions under which people *do* display selective avoidance, for occasionally people show a remarkable propensity to ignore all but the information that supports their choice.[1]

We believe that the conflict model offers a plausible and parsimonious set of hypotheses that specify and explain the conditions under which decision makers will selectively avoid discrepant information. The same hypotheses specify and explain the conditions under which people will be open to, and will actively search for, challenging information that could very well undermine their prior decisions.

Implications of the Conflict Model for Information Preferences

The conflict model postulates that each pattern for coping with decisional stress is associated with a characteristic mode of information processing, which governs the type and amount of information the decision maker will prefer. Reinforcing the conclusions of many recent investigators, the conflict model indicates that it is futile to search for any single type of information preference that will always be dominant in a wide variety of circumstances. Rather, the model points to a number of markedly different tendencies that can, under certain conditions, become dominant, including open-mindedness, indifference, active evasion of discrepant information, and failure to assimilate new information.

The following hypotheses about information preferences are generated by the conflict model and are briefly summarized in table 6.

1. When the conditions making for *unconflicted adherence* or *unconflicted change* are present (namely, belief that no serious risks are involved from pursuing the current course or from adopting a new course of action), the dominant tendency will be *indifference* toward both supportive and nonsupportive information. Since the decision maker is under no stress, he takes only a casual, low-level interest in messages and information bearing on the inconsequential issue.

2. When the conditions making for *defensive avoidance* are present (namely, awareness of serious losses from any alternative that might be selected, together with loss of hope of finding a satisfactory solution), the individual becomes *closed-minded and biased* in his information preferences. Associated with each of the three defensive avoidance subpatterns is a characteristic type of information preference.

(a) *Procrastination*, the pattern that emerges when there are no deadline pressures, is associated with information *evasion*. There is a slight degree of passive interest in supportive information along with a strong tendency to avoid all challenging information. The decision maker is mainly interested in deferring the decision; information that provokes him to think about the decision is neither sought nor welcomed. The person would prefer to *ignore* the vast majority of relevant messages (a phenomenon rarely, if ever, observed in the laboratory, where subjects are generally *required* to look at or listen to the communications offered by the experimenter, however much they might prefer to ignore them).

(b) When the additional conditions that make for *shifting of responsibility* obtain (namely, strong deadline pressures together with the opportunity to foist the decision onto someone else), the dominant tendency will be to limit information gathering to the activity of *seeking out others*, such as a superior or a so-called expert, who will either take over entirely or instruct the person on what to do, and thereby take responsibility.

(c) When the additional conditions that foster the *bolstering* form of defensive avoidance are present (namely, strong deadline pressures along with little or no opportunity to shift responsibility), the classic pattern of *selective exposure* becomes dominant, marked by active search and preference for supportive information and avoidance of discrepant information.

3. When the conditions making for *hypervigilance* obtain (namely, high conflict and belief that there exists a satisfactory solution, but apparent lack of time to search and deliberate), the decision maker will display *indiscriminate* openness to all information. This pattern of coping is marked by a general failure to differentiate between information that is relevant or irrelevant, reliable or unreliable, supportive or nonsupportive. The person becomes overwhelmed by informational overload as he attempts to absorb the deluge of incoming warnings, biased rumors, advice, and unsubstantiated claims, in addition to objective evidence.

TABLE 6. **The conflict model applied to information preferences.**

Coping Pattern	Dominant Information Mode	Characteristic Information Preferences	Level of Interest in Information
A. Unconflicted adherence	Indifference	Nonselective exposure	Low
B. Unconflicted change	Indifference	Nonselective exposure	Low
C. Defensive avoidance			
C-1 Procrastination	Evasion	Passive interest in supportive information; avoidance of all challenging information	Low
C-2 Shifting responsibility	Evasion	Delegation of search and appraisal to others	Low
C-3 Bolstering	Selectivity	Selective exposure: search for supportive information and avoidance of discrepant information.	Medium
D. Hypervigilance	Indiscriminate search	Active search for both supportive and nonsupportive information, with failure to discriminate between relevant and irrelevant, trustworthy and untrustworthy.	Very high
E. Vigilance	Discriminating search with openmindedness	Active search for supportive and nonsupportive information, with careful evaluation for relevance and trustworthiness; preference for trustworthy nonsupportive information if threats are vague or ambiguous.	High

4. When the conditions making for *vigilance* are present (namely, awareness of serious risks, along with a belief that a satisfactory solution can be found and that there is sufficient time for search and evaluation), a *discriminating and open-minded interest* in both supportive and opposing messages will be displayed, with no tendency toward selective exposure. If there are vague or ambiguous threats that challenge the wisdom of what appears to be the best choice, the vigilant decision maker will actually prefer to obtain warnings and other nonsupportive messages in order to satisfy his need for specific information about the losses he might incur.

Taking account of the conditions that make for vigilance in response to fresh warnings about threatened losses during the final stages of decision making, we extract the following supplemental hypothesis, which elaborates on the fourth proposition: *Whenever a person is confronted with challenging signs that he might sustain losses if he carries out the course to which he is almost ready to commit himself (stage 4) or has fully committed himself (stage 5), he will become motivated to learn more about the threat, provided that he retains the hope of being able to cope with it adequately.* Many people, after partially or fully committing themselves to a new course of action, maintain the belief that improvements can be made in their plans for implementing the decision or for dealing with whatever setbacks may arise. When confronted with an impressive warning of potentially negative consequences that challenges their choice, they are likely to become vigilant. But often their search for an alternative in these circumstances is limited to minor modifications of the recently chosen policy, such as the addition of new contingency plans that are perceived as being compatible with the basic thrust of the policy. Decision makers in this situation consequently remain open to the information contained in warnings and process it as objectively as they can, even though the message is inconsistent with the course to which they are committed.[2]

A Field Study of the Draft Resistance Movement

Evidence consistent with the conflict model was found in a field study of opponents of the Vietnam War by Janis and Rausch (1970). The study was designed to investigate the relationship between the various decisional stands taken by college men on the issue of draft resistance and their preferences for favorable or unfavorable communications concerning the draft resistance movement. The study was carried out in the spring of 1968, at a time of growing civil disobedience throughout the United States among students who were opposed to being drafted to fight in Vietnam. At Yale University, an antidraft declaration known as the We-Won't-Go pledge had been circulating for many months and had been signed by hundreds of students.

During the month when the study was being conducted, the local news media gave daily reports about Senator Eugene McCarthy's campaign, which was devoted mainly to attacking the Johnson administration on moral grounds for its failure to end the war in Vietnam. McCarthy's campaign for the Democratic presidential nomination was receiving strong student support. Moreover, just before the study began, another antiwar campaign was also receiving considerable publicity. The Yale chaplain, Reverend William Sloane Coffin, had been indicted, along with Dr. Benjamin Spock and other leaders of the draft resistance movement. Coffin and the others were repeatedly appealing to Yale students to examine their own consciences on the morality of participating in an immoral war. Thus the draft resistance movement was constantly in the focus of attention of the Yale community.

The antidraft pledge, which was circulated in all the residential colleges, declared:

> We are men of draft age who believe that the United States is waging an unjust war in Vietnam. We cannot, in conscience, participate in this war. We therefore declare our determination to refuse induction as long as the United States is fighting in Vietnam.

The signers realized that they were making a very strong personal commitment to resist being drafted, especially since their names, along with the text of the pledge, were regularly published in local newspapers.

Although there was a great deal of controversy about the legal and moral status of the pledge and about its probable effectiveness as a political tactic, there was general agreement that adhering to it could have serious personal consequences. The students knew that the legal penalty for refusing induction was up to five years imprisonment and a fine of $10,000. Moreover, many draft resisters expected their careers to be seriously disrupted, because being convicted of refusing induction would prohibit them from ever obtaining a U.S. government fellowship, entering the legal profession, or working on any project or in any agency financed by government funds.

Conflict theory leads us to direct our inquiry beyond the question of whether commitment has the effect of increasing or decreasing a man's interest in and acceptance of opposing communications. Rather, the basic problem becomes that of discovering the mediating variables that will allow us to specify when the dominant tendency will be avoidance and when it will be vigilance. With these considerations in mind, Janis and Rausch carried out their field study to learn something about how interest in opposing and supporting communications varies as a function of how the person has responded to the decisional challenge.

On the basis of a standardized interview, sixty-two Yale undergraduates, almost all of whom were against the war in Vietnam, were classified into four groups: (1) signers of the We-Won't-Go pledge, whose names had been published in local newspapers; (2) potential signers who were still undecided (i.e., in stage 3 or 4); (3) those who had been temporarily challenged to sign but had decided after deliberation not to sign; and (4) prompt "refusers," who had never been successfully challenged and hence were never conflicted.[3] The men's answers to a series of interview questions indicated, as expected, that these four categories were highly predictive of the men's expressed intentions to engage in other forms of antiwar protest, such as participating in demonstrations and sit-ins.

First, we shall briefly examine the findings that bear on the men's responsiveness to persuasive communications that argued for or against resisting the draft. Then we shall discuss the evidence bearing on the hypothesis derived from conflict theory concerning the men's interest in being exposed to persuasive messages that supported or went counter to their position.

At the end of the interview, each man was asked to read two articles of about six-hundred words each on the subject of draft resistance, one pro and the other anti. When he had finished reading them, the subject was asked to what extent he agreed with the opinions expressed in each of the two articles. As expected, large and significant differences were found consistent with the subjects' initial stand on the We-Won't-Go pledge. Figure 9 shows that each of the four groups agreed with the pro-pledge article more than with the anti-pledge article, which reflects the fact that at the time this study was made almost everyone in all four groups was opposed to continuing the war in Vietnam (including most of those who were strongly opposed to draft resistance.) However, the two curves in figure 9 show the expected relationships between position on the issue and amount of agreement expressed with the two articles. More specifically, the closer the men were to signing the We-Won't-Go pledge, the more likely they were to express agreement with the pro-pledge article and to express disagreement with the anti-pledge article.[4] As we shall see shortly, the strong disagreement with the anti-pledge article expressed by the draft resisters does not imply that they were any less vigilant than the other students with regard to exposing themselves to opposing arguments.

We turn now to the findings that bear on the "vigilance-despite-commitment" hypothesis, which asserts that vigilance will be the dominant coping pattern even after a person has fully committed himself if he is exposed to realistic warnings that point to serious risks entailed by the chosen course and has not lost hope of finding an improved way of implementing the decision. The men who agreed to act in accordance with the civil disobedience stance of the antiwar movement in 1968 were repeatedly warned by officials in the Department of Justice, by prowar congressmen, and by other influential spokesmen for "law and order" whose views were reported in the mass media; they also

FIGURE 9. **Mean agreement ratings of men with different decisional positions on the We-Won't-Go pledge.** *(Based on Janis and Rausch, 1970.)*

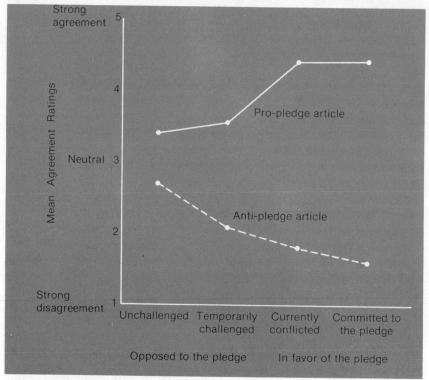

discussed among themselves the risks of civil disobedience and the merits of alternative means for refusing to fight in Vietnam, which continued to be an urgent topic with which they and their companions were preoccupied.

In order to assess open-minded vigilance versus selective exposure tendencies, Janis and Rausch asked the sixty-two men (before they were told to read the pro and con articles used to obtain the data in figure 9) how interested they would be in reading each of eight magazine articles. From the title and a fifty-word summary of each it was apparent that four of the articles were in favor of draft resistance and the other four were opposed. (For example, one pro article was said to be about how sympathetic congressmen will support draft resisters; an anti article was said to be about reprisals threatened against draft resisters by angry congressmen.)

In general, the results support our hypothesis; they are the opposite from what would be predicted by the selective exposure hypothesis, based on the assumption that people invariably try to avoid information that would increase cognitive inconsistency or dissonance. Figure 10 shows preference ratings indicating how much interest the men had in reading the four pro articles and the four anti articles. For the pro articles, there were no significant differences among the four groups. For the anti articles, however, there were large and significant differences in interest scores among the four groups.[5] It will be noted that the linear trend for the anti-pledge articles is in the opposite direction from the acceptance trend shown by the agreement ratings for the anti-pledge article in Figure 9. The men who disagreed most with the anti-pledge articles expressed most interest in reading them.

What can be said about the motives that make people interested in being exposed to messages that oppose their current position? Some clues were obtained from a separate series of intensive interviews of twenty-eight Yale men, carried out as a pilot study to the main investigation. Twelve of the twenty-eight explicitly said that they were definitely planning to refuse induction if drafted. These resisters admitted feeling con-

FIGURE 10. **Mean interest scores of men reading pro-pledge and anti-pledge articles.** *(Based on Janis and Rausch, 1970.)*

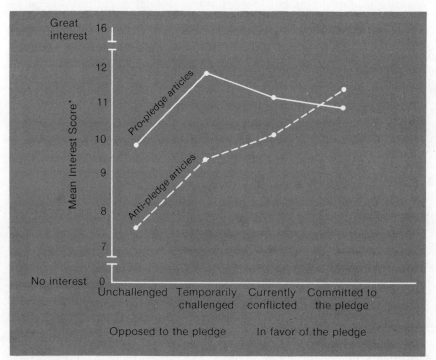

* Ratings were obtained on a five-point scale accompanying the description of each article, ranging from 0 for *No interest* to 4 for *Great interest*. The scores for each set of four articles could therefore range from 0 to a maximum of 16 (4 × 4, for great interest in all four articles).

siderable conflict, anxiety, and uncertainty about the risks entailed by their decision, although all were firmly convinced that their position was morally justified. Their comments indicated two specific sources of vigilance that would incline them to pay attention to counterarguments: (1) vigilant interest in information about the sorts of objection to the draft resistance movement they were likely to encounter, so as to deal effectively with their parents or others in their personal social networks who might attack their views, and (2) vigilant interest in information about the probable unfavorable consequences of adopting one or another specific course of action as a means of implementing the general policy of refusing to fight in Vietnam (for example, applying for conscientious objector status, seeking a teaching or other job carrying an occupational deferment, or escaping the draft by leaving the United States).

The important point is that each resister, no matter how deeply opposed to the war in Vietnam, still faced the question of what he would personally do to avoid being drafted. One reason why each man's decisional conflict about how to implement the pledge was so intense was his realization that every one of the alternatives open to him was very risky. Even those inclined to apply for the Peace Corps or some other means of obtaining a draft deferment knew that the attempt might fail, in which case they might have to resort to a more drastic means of avoiding the draft, which could lead to a jail sentence and possibly permanent damage to their careers. Insofar as the signers in Janis and Rausch's field study were facing this type of implementation conflict, we would expect them to be especially vigilant concerning any of the risks entailed by evading or opposing the draft laws.

Obviously, other motivations might also enter into the decision to expose oneself to a communication that runs counter to one's own stand—for example, a tendency to prefer reading unfamiliar ideas rather than familiar ones, or a desire to be regarded as a fair and judicious person. These and related tendencies have repeatedly been mentioned in the literature on selective exposure (e.g., Brock, Stuart and Becker, 1970; Canon, 1964; Sears, 1968; Wicklund and Brehm, 1976); they could also be operating among the college students who decided to sign the We-Won't-Go pledge and might limit the generality of these findings to college-educated persons who have acquired similar dispositions.

Stages of Decision Making and Information Preferences

A major implication of the conflict position is that it is the pattern of coping rather than the stage of the decision process that is the crucial factor determining receptiveness to information. This formulation affords a rather different picture from the one conveyed in our earlier writings

(Janis, 1968; Janis and Mann, 1968). Earlier we postulated that after decisional commitment, the dominant motivation would always be to avoid exposing oneself to nonsupportive information that would arouse conflict. Our present formulation postulates that this motivation is present but not always dominant: it can be outweighed by vigilance tendencies, which make the individual choose to expose himself to opposing communications and to acquire dissonant information concerning unfavorable consequences. Therefore we do not agree with those predictions from the traditional inconsistency avoidance model based on the assumption that people will generally display a tendency to avoid all communications that oppose the course of action to which they have committed themselves. As we pointed out earlier, the expectation of open-minded vigilance after commitment runs counter to the views of Festinger (1957) and other social psychologists who have assumed that commitment is generally followed by selective avoidance of communications that oppose the chosen course of action. Festinger acknowledges, however, that this general tendency might not necessarily be dominant if the decision maker expects the nonsupportive information to be useful to him or to be easily refuted.

Our position, based on the combined model presented in the preceding chapter, is that irrespective of the specific stage of the decision, the decision maker will be either indifferent, defensively avoidant, hypervigilant, or discriminatingly vigilant with respect to relevant information, depending upon the antecedent conditions determining his mode of coping response. The model can be further elaborated to take account of the typical tasks and challenges associated with specific stages of the decision-making process.

What are the changes that typically occur in selective exposure as a decision maker moves through each of the five successive stages? It follows from our analysis in the preceding chapter that when conflict is high and the decision maker believes that a satisfactory course of action can be found before the deadline is at hand, he will be discriminatingly vigilant and therefore open to all relevant and reliable information throughout the early stages. But as he moves from stage 3 (appraisal of alternatives) to stage 4 (deliberation about commitment), his dominant coping pattern will change from vigilance to the bolstering form of defensive avoidance (once he no longer hopes to find a solution better than the alternative he judges to be least objectionable). This change will be reflected in an increased tendency toward selective exposure. That is to say, the decision maker's equal interest in supporting and opposing communications displayed during the earlier stages should be found to give way, during stage 4, to a selective preference for supporting communications. This will be only a temporary trend, however, if the decision maker continues to be exposed to warnings or reminders of serious risks, which make him realize that he must find the least risky way of implementing his new decision. Under these conditions, vigilance will once again become his dominant coping pattern before the end of stage 4 or early in stage 5. With the return of vigilance, the decision maker will willingly expose himself to opposing messages provided that he believes they contain relevant and fairly reliable information.

Thus, we expect that even when the dominant mode is vigilance, a temporary period of selective interest in supportive information that serves to bolster the chosen course of action will often occur shortly before commitment. This temporary change may have several adaptive functions, including that of increasing the person's feelings of certainty about his choice, a phenomenon described by Mills (1968).[6] It may also be related to the task of "transmission tuning" (Brock and Fromkin, 1968), the process whereby the person looks for information to clarify his decision and to simplify his presentation when he announces it to others. If there are no clear-cut reminders that implementation might be hazardous, selective exposure and other means of bolstering the decision will persist indefinitely until an impressive new threat or opportunity is encountered.

Unfortunately, the research literature does not provide a detailed picture of the changes that occur in information preferences as conditions change during the successive stages of decision making. Most studies, concerned primarily with testing the consistency theory postulate of postdecisional selectivity, have failed to include both pre- and postdecisional assessments in their research designs.[7]

Clearly, the conflict theory analysis of openness to new information and its application to the stages of decision making have not yet been adequately tested. For the present, we conclude that the conflict model has heuristic value in that it calls attention to some neglected aspects of information preferences during decision making and suggests some new types of research problems that should be systematically explored if the field is to advance beyond its current fragmentated state. We believe that the conflict model provides a coherent theoretical framework for organizing the interacting variables that affect preferences for being exposed to supportive or nonsupportive information.

Deciding Which Information to Seek or Avoid

In applying the conflict theory approach to the issues of selective exposure, we find it useful to conceptualize the choice of whether or not to expose oneself to one or another type of communication as a decision in its own right, especially when such exposure entails serious consequences. Like all other decisions, the decision to seek or avoid a communication involves posing and answering all the key questions shown in the combined model in figure 8. When vigilance is the dominant pattern, answers to the key questions in stage 3 ("Which alternative is best?" and "Does it meet all essential requirements?") will be influenced by prior commitments (inclining the person to avoid exposure to opposing communications) in addition to other important factors in the decisional balance sheet (including social pressures to be open-minded, as well as the utilitarian costs of expending time and energy on information search).

In a community plagued by racial conflict, many citizens committed to desegregation may decide to stay away from a political meeting or a propagandistic movie they know will oppose that course, on the basis of a carefully reasoned appraisal of realistic pro and con considerations. After a well-considered choice, a postdecisional resolution to shun opposing communications can be highly adaptive in that it prevents a person from wasting time and suffering unproductive emotional stress that might interfere with his devoting his energies to effectively implementing the policy to which he has just committed himself. On the other hand, if decision makers become uncertain about the best way to combat the arguments of those opposed, they would be inclined to decide to hear what the opposition has to say, like the draft resisters in the Janis and Rausch study.

If we observe an extremely fat person refusing to read a best seller on dieting that plays up the health hazards of being overweight, or refusing to watch a television program on the same subject, can we conclude that he is indulging in defensive avoidance? The answer that follows from our analysis is that such an observation, in itself, is not sufficient evidence from which to draw any conclusion about whether defensive avoidance or vigilance is dominant. There is such a thing as *nondefensive* avoidance of opposing messages based on vigilance. To make a differential diagnosis one first has to make additional observations with respect to the various other behavioral signs that distinguish the two coping patterns, as described in chapter 3 (see tables 1 and 2).

At the beginning of this chapter, we mentioned that many social psychologists, including proponents and opponents of the selective exposure hypothesis, have postulated what are usually called "interfering" or "moderating" factors that may mask and sometimes outweigh selective avoidance tendencies. For example, Lowin (1967) has suggested that a decision maker will choose to expose himself to discrepant communications if he is confident of his position and expects the dissonant message to be easy to refute. Another moderating factor is the degree of commitment. Lowe and Steiner (1968) have reported evidence in support of the assumption that nonsupportive as well as supportive information will be perceived as useful when a decision is reversible. (In their experiment college women who agreed to go on a blind date were asked to choose between two handsome men. After announcing their choice, the women who were told that their decision was reversible showed a high degree of open-minded interest in pro and con information regarding both the chosen and rejected alternatives, significantly more so than those who were told that their decision was irreversible.) In the comprehensive volume on theories of cognitive consistency in social psychology edited by

Abelson et al. (1968), an entire section—containing contributions by Elihu Katz, William McGuire, Judson Mills, and David Sears—is devoted to moderating factors. The factors they discuss are typical of the incentives that might be entered on a balance sheet for a decision about whether to expose oneself to a communication opposing one's chosen course of action; they can be readily classified into the four categories of the balance sheet: utilitarian gains for oneself, utilitarian gains for significant others, anticipated social approval from significant others, and anticipated self-approval for living up to one's own standards of conduct.

Most of the time, a decision to read a given magazine article or view a TV program is a reatively minor one, requiring no costs beyond the time and energy needed to read the article or watch the program. A brief period of mild annoyance or boredom is the only risk. Because such exposure decisions entail only slight risks, we expect that most often the coping pattern of unconflicted adherence or unconflicted change will be dominant and as a result snap judgments will usually be made, with little search or appraisal. Sometimes, however, the decision to expose oneself to a communication or a series of communications takes on much more significance.

Consider, for example, a young Washington bureaucrat interested in all sides of a policy issue who is trying to decide whether to go to hear a potentially informative lecture by a Communist or fringe-group radical when he knows that merely being seen in the audience might have drastically punitive social consequences—such as being spotted by FBI agents, which could get him into trouble regarding his security clearance. Just such considerations often affect the exposure decisions of political appointees and others in sensitive jobs, who may lose considerable sleep worrying about whether to be courageous or expedient.

A comparable example was encountered by the senior author during a visit to Czechoslovakia in 1966. He met a number of scholars in Prague who complained about being unable to satisfy their strong desire to read the latest American books in their field. Their only source of access was the U.S. Information Service Library, located in the American Embassy, which was known to be under constant surveillance by the Czech security police. The scholars debated among themselves whether using the library was worth the political risk of being spotted going in and out of the American Embassy—which could result in their losing their jobs and even ultimately being imprisoned as collaborators of the capitalist enemy. Most of them decided it was too dangerous and resorted instead to the illegal alternative, less risky but also less productive, of getting hold of a few of the American books they wanted from an underground network. This example highlights the dire potential consequences stemming from the *surroundings* in which a communication is accessible—consequences that can loom large in the balance sheet of a decision involving exposure to information. It also calls attention once again to the often overlooked point that a decision to abstain from exposing oneself to relevant communications need not imply defensive avoidance; it may be the result of a careful, unbiased evaluation of deterrents that outweigh the positive incentives.

A conflict analysis of the choice of whether or not to gain access to relevant communications may help us to take a broader view of the factors that can influence selectivity. The hypotheses derived from conflict theory reinforce the position of those psychologists who believe we should abandon the search for any single tendency that will always be dominant in a wide variety of circumstances. We are led to search for the conditions that increase or decrease the probability that a person will decide either to limit his exposure or to be completely open to opposing communications even though he realizes that they could contain potential challenges to his decisional commitments. Similarly, the separate sets of conditions that will increase or decrease the chances of deciding to expose oneself to a *supportive* communication must be analyzed in essentially the same way.[8]

The conflict theory approach may be especially useful in opening up inquiries into the factors that prevent people from exposing themselves to valuable communications under conditions where such exposure is the expected form of behavior. One such problem area has to do with failures in the educational system. Very often, bright high school students from affluent homes, as well as deprived children in ghetto schools, make the decision to pay attention to other students rather than to the teacher. More of their needs are satisfied by focusing on the whispered communications and the antics of their peers than by paying attention to the dominant authority figure. In any classroom, the alternative courses of action open to students and the accompanying incentives lend themselves nicely to an analysis in terms of the decisional balance sheet. Once this kind of analysis is done, it may become clear that there are powerful negative incentives (such as a racial difference between the teacher and the students) that keep students from listening to their teacher.

A similar analysis could be made of the information-exposure preferences of humanistic scholars and scientists. For example, which journal articles and books do they decide to read, and why? Ordinarily these questions are discussed entirely in terms of intellectual trends in the scholar's field of study, such as the scientific interest that attaches to a new discovery or a new theory. But there may be other explanations of why one piece of experimental evidence has been neglected and another not, or why a certain theoretical treatise is widely read while another remains practically unknown. The selective popularity of scholarly works has often been interpreted in terms of inertia in clinging to a dominant theory or paradigm (Kuhn, 1962). But there may be other factors as well—not the least of which may be such unscholarly considerations as entertainment, gossip value, or loyalty to an in-group, which serious scholars seldom talk about (see Merton, 1972; Stephenson, 1967).

Other implications of a conflict analysis would lead us to look at the social contacts of a decision maker to see when he does and does not attend to various competing communicators. For example, a policy maker who has been open to everyone's views in the early stages of decision making may begin to restrict his social contacts to fellow group members after participating in an important *group decision*; he is, in effect, cutting off all opportunities for communication in formal settings from opponents of the decision (see Janis, 1972). Formation of cliques among factions and within political parties after the members have voted a change in policy can often be analyzed from this standpoint. Restricting one's social contacts is sometimes tantamount to making a special type of auxiliary decision to avoid exposure to disquieting messages or to guarantee that one will hear only reassuring information, as exemplified by President Johnson's removal of dissident voices of opposition to the Vietnam War from his team of advisers (see Hoopes, 1969; Reedy, 1970; Thomson, 1968). Decisions to affiliate or disaffiliate are often linked with auxiliary decisions to avoid exposure to dissenting messages. Such decisions have broad ramifications for social psychology in general, because, as in the instance just cited, they determine who are going to be the influential members in a decision maker's social network and whose views will be ignored.

Changes in information selectivity have been found to be a function of anticipated social interaction and related variables that alert a decision maker to the likelihood that he will have to discuss or debate the issue (Clarke and James, 1967). Under the latter circumstances, when he expects to have to defend his decision, a decision maker will remain more vigilant than when he is free to stay away from persons with opposing views. Like the committed draft resisters in the Janis and Rausch (1970) field study, decision makers would have a strong incentive to *increase*, rather than decrease, their exposure to (and mastery of) the opposition's arguments when they are worried about inescapable encounters with powerful opponents who will attack their decision. They may go out of their way to change their social network by cultivating informal contacts with representatives of the opposition to learn how they think, which arguments they take most seriously, and how they can be won over or neutralized—all of which provides valuable information for planning their defense in an impending dispute. Such changes in social contacts, which often occur in the last stages of decision making, might be analyzed in exactly the same way as a decision about whether to read a how-to-do-it book or view a televised political speech, using the decisional balance sheet and the combined conflict and stage-sequence model (figure 8).

CHAPTER 9

Anticipatory Regret

AROUSAL OF ANTICIPATORY REGRET, a major precondition for the coping pattern of vigilance, has the constructive effect of deterring a person from indiscriminately seizing upon a seemingly attractive opportunity without forethought about the consequences. In this chapter we examine case studies and systematic research bearing on anticipatory regret in order to elucidate more fully what we have said earlier about the causes and consequences of vigilance.

An Elusive Phenomenon

During the early 1970s, Elaine Walster and her associates explored the influence of nonobvious threats that generate anticipatory regret when a person is making a choice among desirable sexual partners (Walster, Walster, Piliavin, and Schmidt, 1973). The research started out by testing the old adage that a woman who plays hard to get will be regarded by most men as more desirable than one who is eager for an alliance. After a series of five carefully designed experiments failed to show this predicted differential in desirability, the authors began to refer to the expected but unobtained outcome as an "elusive phenomenon." One of their experiments, for example, was a field study conducted in the context of a computer dating service. Women who signed up for the service were hired as experimenters. When telephoned by computer-matched males, the women responded half the time in an eager manner and half the time in an uneager manner. Questionnaire data obtained from the men showed that this difference in treatment had no effect on the men's liking for their computer-selected dates.

After this failure, the psychologists began to think that the enhanced desirability phenomenon might be restricted to sexual situations involving arousal of the man's erotic interest, which would be increased if he regarded the woman as hard to get. They took their lead from Socrates, who enunciated this principle in the advice he gave his pupil Theodata, a prostitute:

> They will appreciate your favors most highly if you wait till they ask for them. . . . Prompt them by behaving as a model of Propriety, by a show of reluctance to yield, and by holding back until they are as keen as can be; and then the same gifts are much more to the recipient than when they're offered before they are desired.[1]

With Socrates' advice in mind, the investigators took the extraordinary step of shifting their research site to the bedroom, hiring a prostitute to function as the experimenter. On a random basis, the prostitute informed half of her customers as she mixed a drink for them that she would henceforth be working only part time and would be restricting her clientele to the men she liked best. To the other half of her customers, she did not communicate that she would be hard to get. In all cases, the prostitute performed the sex act in her usual professional manner. Follow-up data indicated that, contrary to expectation, those clients who were led to believe that the prostitute would be hard to get were less likely than the controls to call back within the next thirty days for another appointment.

Realizing that in their studies the phenomenon was so elusive as to be nonexistent, Walster and her associates decided that they must have been on the wrong track. Up to this point, they had been assuming that for most men the advantages of becoming intimate with a hard-to-get woman would far outweigh whatever drawbacks and risks there might be. But now they began intensively interviewing male college students to find out how the men viewed the disadvantages as well as the advantages of hard-to-get and easy-to-get women. They soon found that the men expressed considerable uncertainty and conflict about such choices, with each of the two types of woman being regarded as "uniquely desirable and uniquely frightening" (p. 116). The frightening aspects involved different threats from the two types of woman. The easy-to-get woman, although expected to boost one's ego and provide an enjoyable time, was seen as very dangerous because intimacy with her might be regretted if she turned out to be diseased, or hard to get rid of, or a source of embarassment when one's buddies learned about her reputation. The hard-to-get woman, on the other hand, might be more valued, but efforts to become intimate with her might be deeply regretted if she were to behave in an unfriendly, cold, and consistently frustrating manner and humiliate one in front of friends. Thus Socrates might be essentially right after all, provided that the hard-to-get woman behaved toward the man in such a warm, friendly, and interested manner that she conveyed little threat of rejection or humiliation, thereby avoiding the arousal of anticipatory regret.

Having discovered the variety of pros and cons that enter into the choice, Walster and her associates concluded that for the average man the most desirable type of woman would be one who was perceived as *selectively* hard to get—that is, hard for other men to get but comparatively easy for him to get. They designed another experiment to test this hypothesis, again using the computer dating service. When each man arrived at the dating center to choose a date, he was offered five alternatives. The folders for each of five women were prearranged to contain plausible information indicating how she had rated him as compared with several other men after she had read their background questionnaires. In three folders the ratings were contrived to create an impression of three different types of woman: easy for the subject to get but hard for anyone else to get; easy for everyone to get; hard for everyone to get. The other two folders contained no information about how these two women regarded the subject. All descriptive information about the five women—such as their height, religion, class standing, and interests—was held constant by rotating each set of background characteristics among the five folders.

After examining the folders (but before being told the truth and being given the opportunity to make a genuine choice), the majority of men (60 percent) chose to date the selectively hard-to-get woman, whereas less than 10 percent chose the uniformly hard-to-get woman or the uniformly easy-to-get woman. When asked about anticipated difficulties, the men checked fewer "drawbacks" for the selectively hard-to-get woman from a list of potentially regrettable outcomes, which included such items as "might turn out to be sexually promiscuous," "likely to embarass me in public," and "would be too dependent on me." Additional data on the men's ratings of the possible virtues and flaws of each woman support the conclusion that the men preferred the selective type of woman because they "ascribe to her all of the assets of the uniformly hard-to-get and the uniformly easy-to-get women, and none of their liabilities" (p. 120). If the psychological explanation given by Walster and her associates is correct, we should expect to find that it applies not just to desirable sex partners and practitioners of the world's second oldest profession but also to practitioners of all other professions, old or new. A physician, a lawyer, or a computer programmer who announces that he is going to restrict his practice to cases that interest him should be found to decrease or increase the demand for his services depending on whether he presents himself as uniformly hard to get or as selectively so, but with the promise of easy access for the client at hand.

In summary, Walster and her colleagues unexpectedly discovered that decisional choices are strongly influenced by anticipatory regret (although they did not use this term). The threats that evoked anticipatory regret when the men were choosing a sex partner appear to have been distributed among three of the main categories we have described as components of the decisional balance sheet: utilitarian losses for the self (e.g., being damaged by venereal disease), social disapproval (e.g., being humiliated in front of one's friends) and self-disapproval (e.g., losing self-esteem from being rejected by the chosen woman). And it is probable that these considerations governed the men's choice.

Functional Value

Everyone undergoes painful experiences as a result of ill-considered decisions that have turned out badly; everyone receives lifelong social training in the pitfalls of making too hasty a decision. As a result, most of us are likely to be reluctant to commit ourselves to a new course of action, such as starting either a business or a love affair, without first obtaining relevant information and thinking over the desirable and undesirable outcomes that might be in store for us. Having learned from the hard knocks and humiliations that ensued from impulsive decisions in the past, most of us become vigilant when we have to make a choice in the face of uncertainties that could affect our future welfare. For a time, like Hamlet, we allow "the native hue of resolution to be sicklied o'er by the pale cast of thought." Before undertaking any enterprise "of great pith and moment," we usually delay action and think about what might happen that could cause regret.

Anticipatory regret is a convenient generic term to refer to the main psychological effects of the various worries that beset a decision maker before any losses actually materialize, including concerns about each of the four major types of undesirable consequence that enter into the decisional balance sheet—utilitarian losses for self, utilitarian loss for significant others, self-disapproval, and social disapproval. Such worries, which include anticipatory guilt and shame, provoke hesitation and doubt, making salient the realization that even the most attractive of the available choices might turn out badly. Anticipatory regret is conceptualized as a hot cognitive process that has the functional value of motivating the decision maker to mentally construct a comprehensive balance sheet. One of its prerequisites is a *capacity to delay gratification* (see Mischel, 1966). The decision maker puts up with the current stress of worrisome uncertainties and doubts in order to arrive at a larger reward (via better decisions) in the future.[2] To put it another way, we must tolerate the painfulness of predecisional conflict during the various stages of the decision-making process if we are to engage in reality testing rather than wishful thinking.

Although anticipatory regret sometimes leads to excessive procrastination, it often facilitates high-quality decision making. Worrying about what might go wrong motivates the decision maker to search for dependable information and advice throughout the predecisional period, even after he has already made a tentative choice of what appears to be the best available course of action.

Determinants

What circumstances evoke anticipatory regret? We have obtained some clues from interviews of hundreds of persons who have served as subjects in a variety of our studies of decisional conflicts—including middle-level executives in an industrial organization who were discussing choices that might enhance or impede their careers, young lawyers choosing among different legal career lines, husbands and wives contemplating divorce, heavy smokers trying to decide whether or not to quit smoking, overweight people deliberating about whether or not to go on a restrictive diet, and medical patients facing the dilemma of whether or not to undergo a recommended surgical operation. Almost all these decision makers from time to time project themselves into the uncertain future as they worry about whether their preferred choices will really work out well or will turn out to be disappointing.

According to our interviewees' accounts, certain types of message from friends, relatives, or advisers have a marked effect, inducing premonitions about known or unknown risks. Five types of message, which correspond to the conditions making for vigilance, are frequently mentioned as having stimulated worry that a decision might be regretted:

1. The most preferred choice is not necessarily superior to another alternative.
2. The negative consequences that might ensue from the decision could start to materialize almost immediately after the decision is made.
3. Significant persons in the decision maker's social network view the decision as important and will expect him to adhere to it.
4. New information concerning potential gains and losses can be obtained.
5. Significant persons in the decision maker's social network who are interested in this particular decision are *not* impatient about his current state of indecision and expect him to delay action until he has evaluated the alternatives carefully.

The positive effects of these communication themes, if verified by systematic research, might prove to be mediated by positive responses to the four key questions in our conflict model. The first theme makes salient the *relative losses*—the "opportunity costs"—that might be sustained by choosing the old policy (question 1) or the most attractive alternative (question 2). The second theme, which makes the known losses appear to be more *imminent* and hence a more serious threat, also increases the recognition of risks. The third theme calls attention to the importance of social *commitment*; it fosters recognition of the threat of being locked into whatever choice is made, which will prevent one from changing if things happen to work out badly. The fourth theme encourages *optimism* about finding useful information relevant to selecting the best alternative and thereby fosters a realistic hope that a better alternative will be found (question 3). The fifth theme relieves the decision maker from one form of social pressure (to hurry up and make up his mind) and at the same time induces another type of social pressure (to avoid making a hasty, thoughtless decision). Both components of this dual message encourage temporary (but not permanent) *postponement* of the deadline and hence foster the belief that there is sufficient time to search and deliberate (question 4).

We expect, therefore, that exposure to such communication themes will increase the likelihood that the decision maker will examine all the known sources of potential regret, mull over possible hidden risks, and work out a sound resolution of his decisional conflict to the best of his ability. When these themes are emphasized in communications to the decision maker, anticipatory regret is likely to be aroused and to have a constructive effect, resulting in vigilant appraisal of each course of action and inventive solutions that take account of calculated risks. Conversely, the absence of these themes (or their reverse) encourages a person who is making a vital decision to adopt a defective coping pattern (unconflicted adherence or change, defensive avoidance, or hypervigilance), which disposes him to terminate the decisional conflict prematurely, after only superficial search and appraisal.

Five Unfavorable Conditions

We shall now examine the reverse of the five communication themes in more detail in order to elucidate what we think is missing when anticipatory regret is not adequately aroused and sustained. This analysis specifies what happens when anticipatory fear, guilt, and shame—the negative emotions involved in anticipatory regret—are not stimulated.

One Predominant Alternative

When initial scanning of the alternatives turns up what appears to be only one acceptable alternative, without any highly attractive competition, a decision maker is likely to ignore the risks attendant to this alternative and spend little time thinking about the threat of subsequent losses. If there is no information about obvious drawbacks to give him pause, he will move rapidly toward resolution. Evidence of this tendency is provided in a study by Wicklund and Ickes (1972) in which University of Texas coeds were required to choose between courses on sexuality in order to preregister for the following year. When the choice was difficult, by virtue of two equally attractive alternatives, the girls asked for more information and preferred more time in which to consider the alternatives than when the choice was easy.

If all but one course of action seem fraught with serious danger, or too costly to consider, the decision maker perceives himself as having essentially no choice. An *illusion of no real choice*, like the reality of a severely limited choice, makes for rapid termination of decisional conflict. It allows the decision maker to suppress worry and take a passive role in making the decision, since there seems to be nothing else he can do. For example, many middle class Americans see themselves as having no real choice when they have to make a decision about whether or not to undergo medical treatments. A strong recommendation to undergo surgery or some other painful procedure, when it comes from a respected physician, is usually sufficient to make the patient feel that he has no choice but to comply. Hence, without seeking any additional medical opinions or carrying out any other form of information search, the patient rapidly terminates the stress of indecision (generated by the threatening consequences of either doing nothing or going ahead with surgery) by doing exactly what the doctor says. Of course, the perception that one has no real choice is unfortunately not always an illusion. In certain institutions, such as military training camps, old people's homes, prisons, and state psychiatric hospitals, the conscripts or inmates are seldom allowed to exercise significant choice, which can have long-term detrimental effects not only on their decision-making capabilities but also on their mental health (see chapter 10).

Instances of an illusory lack of choice often occur when people consult other professional advisers, such as lawyers, architects, and security analysts. The more respected the counselor, and the more vividly he depicts the disasters that will ensue unless his advice is followed, the more likely the client will have the illusion of no choice. Some professional men exploit the opportunity to issue Jovian pronouncements, presenting their clients with the choice of either doing what is recommended or being damned. These attempts, however, do not always succeed in fostering an illusion of no choice, especially among many recent college graduates who reject experts when they give advice in a hard-sell, authoritarian manner. The conditions that induce an illusion of no choice undoubtedly vary widely among different cultures and subcultures, depending partly on whether the authority of leaders and experts is sacrosanct or under attack. Survey research, along with other systematic investigations, will be required to test the predicted relationship between perceived limitation of choice and quality of decision making.

No Immediate Negative Consequences

Even though a decision maker may be aware of a potential loss that could cause future regret, he will tend to dismiss that loss as trivial, instead of trying to find out how serious it might be, if he believes that it will not materialize in "the foreseeable future." Many young cigarette smokers who know that they might develop lung cancer feel relieved when they learn that the danger is unlikely to materialize in less than twenty years' time. By relegating the danger to the dim, distant future, they avoid the stress of undergoing a here-and-now decisional conflict. When Pervin and Yatko (1965) studied the rationalizations used by smokers to justify the habit, they found a tendency for smokers, in comparison with non-smokers, to give somewhat longer estimates of the minimum number of years required for a smoker predisposed to cancer to get the disease (24.5 versus 22.8 years).

The remoteness of negative consequences is communicated in a more subtle way when a decision maker is informed that the decision will not be *implemented* until others carry out a series of time-consuming steps that might "take forever." People who recruit members to form a new political or civic organization sometimes claim that the act of signing up means very little besides giving moral support, because it will be a long time before the organization will begin to hold meetings or take an active stand on public issues. Getting rid of current stress arising from strong social pressures to join is likely to predominate over qualms about future regret, when no negative consequences are expected to materialize for a long time to come.

Low Social Importance

A decision maker is inclined to terminate predecisional conflict as rapidly as possible when there are signs that the decision is of low social importance or that a poor decision can be easily reversed, with virtually no social disapproval and no damage to his reputation. Any indications that a decision can be kept secret, that few people will be interested in finding out about it, or that reversal can be effected without cost encourages a decision maker to remain relatively unconcerned about potentially negative consequences. Thus, little concern about possible sources of postdecisional regret is shown by some affluent men and women who enter into a whirlwind courtship and marriage believing that if something goes wrong a quick divorce provides an easy way out and will be accepted as a satisfactory solution in their social network.

When a decision maker is led to believe that no one will care whether or not he subsequently reverses his decision, he will become less vigilant about the possible sources of postdecisional regret. Later on (in chapter 11), we shall present evidence from a study by Mann and Taylor (1970) of the predicted differences between decision makers who are told they can easily reverse their decision and those told that their choice will be binding, when all are confronted with the same difficult choice. Those given the low-commitment information made up their minds much more rapidly and exaggerated the positive value of the most attractive alternative before making their final choice.

No Additional Information Available

If a decision maker is led to believe that he will not find any new information bearing on the decision, he will stop searching and seek some other way to reduce the stress of decisional conflict. Knowing this, top-level executives in industrial firms and leaders of other large bureaucratic organizations sometimes deliberately withhold crucial information so as to influence a decision in their favor. They may fail to mention the drawbacks to an offer they wish to be attractive or they may give unwarranted reassurances that induce employees and clients to be relatively unconcerned about personal values that might conflict with the organization's vested interests. For example, in making an offer to employ or promote a junior executive, managerial representatives usually play up the good pay, fine working conditions, fringe benefits, opportunities for advancement, and high prestige of the job but are careful not to mention the disagreeable "dirty work" that will be demanded of him or other defects of the job. Sociologists have documented the conspiracies of silence and the more subtle, nondeliberate collusions that promote managerial ideologies that give paramount importance to the self-serving interests of the organization. Sofer (1971) points out that the managers of industrial and commercial enterprises typically attempt to influence employees' decisions in such a way that they will make choices in line with the organization's interests rather than their own, without being fully aware of it. The more ambiguous the threat, the easier it is for an elite group to manipulate its communications in such a way as to foster unhesitating decisions in favor of the choice they want an individual to make.

There is more to conspiracies of silence than mere control over information. Anyone who raises serious questions about the missing information comes to realize that he is in danger of being judged as an unworthy candidate and may find himself dismissed as a "selection error." Even prospective employees are likely to know that the management of any organization that hires large numbers of people generally expects compliant cooperation and "only fools or knaves disrupt" (Fox, 1971).

Conspiracies of silence that beset consumers may be counteracted to some extent by consumer reports and well-publicized exposés of manufacturers who withhold crucial information about their products, which may help some people make better-informed decisions about what to buy. Comparable exposés are needed from public-spirited institutions or grass-roots organizations to break the information monopoly of powerful organizations that offer training and employment to large numbers of people. At present, the personal cost of seeking information about drawbacks is especially high for students applying to leading universities and for candidates seeking executive positions or other elite jobs. Only those with considerable psychological stamina and ingenuity can hope to break through the institutionally buttressed walls of silence to obtain inside information about the real pros and cons of alternative opportunities.

Impatience of Significant Others

Another condition that prods a decision maker to become almost exclusively concerned with terminating decisional conflict is pressure from others in his social network to arrive at a decision quickly. In administrative decision making, pressures come from superiors and colleagues within the organization who are waiting upon the decision in order to carry out their own tasks or in order to make their own decisions dovetail with it.

With regard to job offers, authority figures in business and political bureaucracies become quite adept at conveying that "if you don't grab our offer without hesitation right now, it will no longer be available to you." In terms of the conflict model, this type of pressure—together with the implicit threat of regarding anyone who delays accepting an offer in order to seek more information as being unenthusiastic, disrespectful, or disloyal and therefore no longer worthy of the offer—fosters the pattern of hypervigilance among employees in a state of acute conflict, which makes for grossly constricted search and appraisal.

In personal dilemmas, pressures most often come from close relatives or friends. Such pressures give the decision maker the impression that, irrespective of a distant official deadline, he has already passed the *informal* deadline so far as the expectations of important others are concerned.

Not wanting to create an impression that he is unresponsive to the needs of others in the organization who are eagerly awaiting his decision, a job applicant or an administrator is likely to forego spending the time necessary to collect all the information he would like to have. Similarly, an undecided college senior who encounters signs that his relatives are impatient about his plans for a career ("Haven't you made up your mind yet?") may terminate his information search prematurely. Sometimes, however, a decision maker attempts to cope with this form of social pressure by silencing or breaking off contact with those who are prodding him to commit himself rapidly. The factors that counteract social pressures making for premature choice have not yet been systematically explored.

The Unknown Rub

From past experience as well as social training, most decision makers realize that in addition to all the well-known uncertainties about the outcome of an important decision, there may also be hidden or as yet unknown drawbacks that would certainly give one pause if only one could find out about them. Knowing what can happen to even the best-laid plans, most people realize, as they contemplate a consequential choice, that their information and forecasts are imperfect, that they might have a distorted image of what the outcome will really prove to be. In terms of the person's balance sheet, the array of pro and con entries based on what he already knows might very clearly favor a given alternative, but he may delay committing himself after selecting what seems to be the best alternative because he realizes there are too many unknowns—blank entries in the balance sheet that, if filled in, might change the picture entirely.

This residual source of conflict involves ill-defined fears about the possibility of unknown risks that might prove to be the "catch" or the "rub." Such fears may arise at the outset of making a decision traditionally categorized as "chancy"—such as investing in a get-rich-quick business venture, undergoing a new form of medical treatment, or getting married after a whirlwind courtship—and may add to the uncertainties faced by a decision maker when surveying and appraising alternatives. But it is during the commitment stage—at the point where the decision maker is about to implement the preferred course of action selected on the basis of the known consequences—that worry over unknown consequences is most likely to play a determining role.

When the social pressures are not so strong as to force him to make an immediate decision, the decision maker's residual fears of an unknown rub incline him to postpone committing himself after he has already selected what he regards as the best course of action. Often the additional delay is very brief. The decision maker limits himself to a quick search and final reappraisal, like a pilot in the cockpit, with his plane already warmed up, making a final check of his instrument panel before taking off. If nothing unusual shows up in the last-minute check, off he goes. But if special cues are present that induce the decision maker to become keenly aware of the possibility of hidden or unknown risks, he may delay his decision for a considerable period, long enough to carry out an extensive new search.

When a person has been under strong pressure to make up his mind, so that he could not postpone the decision without being penalized, he will continue to be preoccupied with the unknown risks he might have let himself in for even after his initial act of commitment. In such instances, instead of showing the usual bolstering tendency following commitment, the hypervigilant decision maker continues to be in a state of conflict and may even show signs of regretting his choice. We shall see in chapter 12 that this type of concern about unknown catches could account for Walster's (1964) finding of a brief period of postdecisional regret among draftees who, upon entering the classic arena of Catch-22, had suddenly been told to choose between two army jobs, neither of which they liked.

Whether cursory or extensive, an information search generated during the commitment stage when the decision maker becomes concerned about unknown risks can occasionally turn up negative consequences he had not previously taken into account and transform his balance sheet of incentives so drastically that he no longer regards the preferred alternative as satisfactory. Thus he may revert to the preceding stage, reconsidering the pros and cons for each alternative, or even beyond that, to searching anew for a more satisfactory alternative.

Maladaptive Responses

Prolongation of the state of indecision resulting from concern about unknown dangers can sometimes be maladaptive. Preoccupation with hidden risks precludes action, and this inhibition can have extremely detrimental consequences at a time when doing nothing is worse than committing oneself to a positive course of action, as in the case of patients in the early stages of cancer who postpone undergoing any kind of medical or surgical treatment (see Blackwell, 1963; Cobb, Clark, Carson, and Howe, 1954; Gold, 1964; Hackett, Cassem, and Raker, 1973; Kasl and Cobb, 1966; Kutner, Makover, and Oppenheim, 1958). Over 30 percent of cancer patients have been found to postpone seeking a diagnosis for three or more months after they first notice growths or other symptoms that they know could be danger signs (Goldsen, Gerhardt, and Handy, 1957). Most of these avoidance reactions cannot be ascribed to ignorance, since it has also been found that cancer patients who decide to postpone going to a hospital or tumor clinic are generally more familiar with the danger signals of cancer than those who decide to be examined promptly (Goldsen et al., 1957; Kutner et al. 1958). Little is known as yet about the differences in the anticipations of those whose anxiety leads to constructive action and those whose anxiety leads to immobilization, but it seems plausible that fear of unknown consequences—such as vague concerns about having to undergo unbearable pain or disfigurement, and anxiety about death—loom large in many cancer patients who decide to postpone seeking medical aid.

Similar concerns may trouble people suffering from other diseases who fail to seek medical care, even when it costs nothing. In England, where the National Health system offers free medical care, a study of a representative sample of families in the London area showed that over one-third of the families had a member who was suffering from pain or discomfort but was not receiving medical treatment (Political and Economic Planning, 1961).

Maladaptive refusal to take preventive action during large-scale disasters also seems to involve fear of unknown dangers that might be worse than the known dangers. In the North Sea floods of 1952, for example, some people in the inundated areas of Holland refused to accept the repeated urgings of rescue personnel to board helicopters for evacuation to a safe area.

For these Dutch farmers and villagers, the rescue operation meant entering an untrusted vehicle which would take them to a strange place, away from others in their family or neighborhood group (Balloch, Braswell, Rayner, and Killian, 1953). Thus . . . hypervigilance among the Dutch flood victims took the form of unwarranted resistance to evacuation. Their refusal to be flown to a safe refuge calls to mind Shakespeare's characterization of the dread of death, which may apply equally to lesser threats: "[We] rather bear those ills we have than fly to others that we know not of" [Janis, 1962].

Fear of a hidden rub may also be an important factor in citizens' decisions to participate in protest actions against public health authorities who attempt to introduce new preventive measures, such as flouridation of the community water supply (Kirscht and Knutson, 1961).

Even when the choice of a course of action does not involve a concern about physical health, as in the case of most career decisions, fear of unknown adverse consequences may lead to prolonged delays in making one's choice or in taking the first steps to implement it. Such delays are dysfunctional when they lead to an extended period of vacillation and preoccupation with the decisional conflict long after a diligent search for information has run its course. When a reluctant decision maker indulges in protracted hesitation, an observer might be inclined to say, with some feeling of exasperation, "What the hell is he waiting for? Doesn't he realize that anything anyone ever does in life has *some* unknown risks?" Compulsive personalities regularly evoke this kind of reaction because they continue to have doubts about the unknown risks inherent in every decision, whether it is a matter of entering into marriage, choosing a career, deciding where to go on a vacation, or selecting a restaurant for dinner (Cameron, 1963). Presumably because of chronic neurotic predispositions, such constricted persons constantly postpone action as they continue to mull over potential dangers that loom exceedingly large for them. But they are certainly not the only ones who fear unknown consequences and procrastinate.

Adaptive Responses

Concern about unknown risks should by no means be relegated to the sphere of neurotic or dysfunctional behavior. On the contrary, it often leads to a postponement of commitment that is highly adaptive. Consider a person who has made a snap judgment and is about to commit himself to participate in a Watergate type of coverup on the basis of incomplete and distorted information that tempts him to think he can gain great rewards with practically no risk of being caught. Or consider the value of a person's action being inhibited at a time when he is feeling so disgusted or dejected that he is ready to take a drastic and irreversible course of self-destructive action, such as committing suicide. In this state of intense emotion, the only possible resolution may appear to be ending it all with an overdose. Yet even a slight twinge of anticipatory regret, arising from the decision maker's vague awareness that "maybe there are serious consequences for my family that I am overlooking," can serve a valuable function if it stimulates him to postpone action long enough to have a discussion with a sensible friend or adviser, which might turn up strong reasons for abandoning the desperate course of action he had selected as the only way out. The emergency telephone service offered by crisis intervention centers, which gives people in acute distress an opportunity to talk with a counselor on the phone before taking irrevocable action, seems to be based on the premise that even a few minutes of discussion with a despondent person to allow him to ventilate his last-minute conflict and to encourage him to rethink his decision may alter the balance sheet sufficiently so that he might change his mind about committing suicide (Lester and Brockopp, 1973; Litman, 1971; McGee, 1974).

Even in the more usual decisions of daily life, we surmise that concern about unknown risks is likely to have adaptive value whenever it leads the person to seek more information to fill in his areas of gross ignorance about negative consequences that he had been assuming to be nonexistent or trivial. A graduating student may feel ready to take the first job offered to him without looking into it carefully because he is mainly concerned about the threat of being unemployed. But a brief twinge of anticipatory regret arising from the sudden thought that there may be drawbacks he does not yet know about can lead him to ask a few questions of a knowledgeable adviser, which might turn up a gross defect that would lead to postdecisional regret if it were ignored.

The classic expression of the inhibitory power of concern about unknown consequences is Hamlet's "To-be-or-not-to-be" speech, the most famous soliloquy in the English language. This passage deserves to be quoted in full in a psychological study of decision making because it captures the sequential form, as well as the content, of an internal debate on this most vital of all human decisions. First come thoughts of the desirability of terminating all the evils that make life seem unbearable; then comes a sharp realization that there could be unknown dangers that might constitute the rub; finally, the decision maker becomes keenly aware of his painful state of conflict and struggles against wanting to procrastinate.

> To be, or not to be, that is the question:
> Whether 'tis nobler in the mind to suffer
> The slings and arrows of outrageous fortune,
> Or to take arms against a sea of troubles,
> And by opposing end them? To die, to sleep—
> No more; and by a sleep to say we end
> The heartache, and the thousand natural shocks
> That flesh is heir to. 'Tis a consummation

Devoutly to be wish'd—to die, to sleep—
To sleep, perchance to dream; ay, there's the rub;
For in that sleep of death what dreams may come
When we have shuffled off this mortal coil
Must give us pause—there's the respect
That makes calamity of so long life.
For who would bear the whips and scorns of time,
Th' oppressor's wrong, the proud man's contumely,
The pangs of dispriz'd love, the law's delay,
The insolence of office, and the spurns
That patient merit of th' unworthy takes,
When he himself might his quietus make
With a bare bodkin? Who would fardels bear,
To grunt and sweat under a weary life,
But that the dread of something after death,
The undiscover'd country from whose bourn
No traveller returns, puzzles the will,
And makes us rather bear those ills we have
Than fly to others that we know not of?
Thus conscience does make cowards of us all,
And thus the native hue of resolution
Is sicklied o'er with the pale cast of thought,
And enterprises of great pith and moment
With this regard their currents turn awry
And lose the name of action.

The inhibition of one's resolution by the "pale cast of thought" is the very core of what we have been describing as the functional value of fear of the unknown. The unknown dangers of life after death, which gave Hamlet pause, could hardly be expected to become illuminated or dissipated by new information, unless one expects to be able to interview a ghost. (Hamlet was able to do so, but it didn't help him very much.) The pause can lead, however, to a more complete assessment of the desirability of going on living by postponing action until the mood of acute despondency subsides.

The images that might constitute the unknown rub for a person contemplating suicide are probably similar to the concerns raised by a substantial percentage of the thirty-thousand readers of the magazine *Psychology Today* who participated in a survey entitled "You and Death" (Shneidman, 1971). In response to the question "What aspect of your own death is the most distasteful to you?" 12 percent gave uncertainty as to what might happen to them if there is a life after death, and 2 percent gave fear of what might happen to their body after death. The most common response, given by 36 percent, was concern about no longer having any experiences. Any source of anticipatory regret that results in at least a brief postponement of action can have a positive value whenever a person is under duress or in an acute state of anger, anxiety, guilt, shame, or despair that inclines him to take violent action, whether against himself or someone else, at a time when the entries in his balance sheet are grossly distorted or incomplete.

Fear of Unknown Risks among Disillusioned Executives

To illustrate how concerns about unknown risks can influence a decision maker's behavior, we shall examine two case studies from the research on middle-level executives in large industrial organizations mentioned earlier[3] Some of the important behavioral consequences of preoccupation with the unknown rub that are generally overlooked in psychological analyses of decision making emerge clearly as we examine the dilemmas experienced by the two executives, both of whom made seemingly irrational decisions against their own best interests. Their conflicts do not match the grand scale of Hamlet's, but reflect rather the everyday misery of people trapped in their jobs and imprisoned by their fears.

Paradoxical Discontent with a "Good" Job

In a number of cases, we have encountered an apparent discrepancy between a man's decisional choice and the array of anticipated gains and losses in his balance sheet. In one such case, from what the man said about the pros and cons, the alternative of remaining on the present job seemed to be clearly more attractive than that of seeking employment in another company. Yet, contrary to expectation, the man decided that his best course of action was to seek employment elsewhere. As soon as he found a satisfactory job in another company, he told the interviewer, he would resign from his present executive position and leave the company.

How did this apparent discrepancy come about? When he spoke of his present position, the executive expressed considerable satisfaction. He liked the work because he found it interesting. It involved him in a wide variety of problems, ranging from production to finance to sales. It also enabled him to have rewarding contacts with other people—to help the men who were working for him, to meet successful people in other firms, to use his skills in conducting negotiations. He felt highly competent in his job and was pleased that the executive position he occupied gave him the freedom to determine how best to carry out the tasks of his unit. The pay was very good; the working conditions and fringe benefits were excellent. He had close friends in the company, including his immediate superior, for whom he had great respect. He also had friendly relations with other superiors in the company's hierarchy. He felt proud of his accomplishments and was confident that he would continue to be a successful executive.

He had some specific complaints about the demands of his job, but said they were all very minor ones. His work took up most of his waking hours, but it would be the same, he asserted, in any other company. He was sometimes burdened with trivial paperwork and with preparing reports that were not essential, which took time away from more important tasks. Occasionally he was distressed by the conflict between the need to be discreet about his company's secret plans to change their models and his desire to be honest with dealers who asked him if the models were about to be changed. Company headquarters, he felt, should have established clear guidelines as to what an executive could tell the dealers about the company's future plans. His main complaint was about the series of reorganizations the company had gone through in recent years, which he believed to have had a disruptive effect on the workers' efficiency and to have lowered morale among many executives. He himself had not suffered from any of the previous reorganizations, but some of his friends had. Now a new merger was in the offing, which would entail yet another drastic reorganization. He was aware of the risk that his unit might be moved to a different building, or possibly even relocated to a distant town.

If we were to draw up a balance sheet embracing these known gains and losses that the executive anticipated if he stayed in his present job, we would conclude that there was a predominance of positive entries (positive incentives for continuing in the present job). There seemed to be only a few, low-level minus entries (minor drawbacks). The alternative, leaving his present job to take a position with a different company, seemed unattractive, characterized by a predominance of strongly negative entries and only a few, minor positive ones. The executive acknowledged that if he were to take a job in another company it would entail many losses, even were it to match his present job with respect to intrinsic interest, pay, and so on. He would miss his friends at his present job, and he would have to start from scratch trying to establish good relations with his superiors and his subordinates in the new company. Similarly, he would have to reestablish, in a new job, his prestige and his prerogatives to do his work in his own way. Why, then, did he show a strong preference for this seemingly unattractive alternative?

The answer has to do with this man's deep-seated uneasiness about the impending reorganization of the company. He knew that the reorganization would most likely have only a slightly adverse effect on his job (adding some minor negative entries to his balance sheet). But over and above the known risks, he had become preoccupied with the *unknown* risks that might be entailed. If we were to represent this unknown danger in his balance sheet as a minus entry of large magnitude with unspecified content, the paradoxical discrepancy between his balance sheet and his tentative decision to leave the firm would disappear.

The executive felt that the top managers of the company had been keeping everyone in the dark. They had made only vague announcements and had refused to give answers to any specific questions about what changes would be made, perhaps because they did not yet know the answers. He had talked it over with his friends in the company, and they all agreed that the impending reorganization was extremely ominous. It could conceivably entail almost all the risks that one would face if one were to take a job in a new company—changes in job function, loss of freedom, finding oneself placed under an unfriendly and disagreeable superior, and so on. Worse yet, the undesirable changes might unfold gradually over months or even years, and he might continue to be left in the dark about what changes to expect. He had lost confidence in the company's ability to handle a reorganization in a way that would enable its executives to feel secure; and now this merger meant an even more drastic reorganization than the earlier ones—there was no way of telling how one would be affected. Rather than go on facing all the unknown threats posed by the merger, he preferred to take his chances in a company whose management could be trusted to tell the truth, where disadvantages were clear-cut and out in the open.

For this man, the known losses entailed by shifting to a new company would be preferable to remaining in a state of uncertainty about the unknown risks of staying in his current job. Anticipatory regret generated by the unknown risks was sufficiently powerful to determine his choice.

It should be mentioned that the decision to leave the company was rare among the forty executives interviewed in the same company, all of whom were also facing the unknown risks posed by the reorganization. The vast majority expressed some concern, but they either minimized the risks or asserted a basic sense of confidence that somehow everything would work out all right for them, just as it had in comparable crises in the past. For these men the known pros and cons clearly determined their decision to remain in their present job, even though most of them had been initially shaken by the first announcement of the reorganization. Thus it should be recognized that the executive who resolved to seek a job elsewhere was an extreme example of preoccupation with the unknown risks of the reorganization. One of the apparent factors disposing him to this extreme reaction was his earlier shock and disappointment when a prior company reorganization had led to the demotion of one of his closest friends, who took it badly, became depressed, and then was stricken with a life-threatening psychosomatic illness. The executive's awareness of what had happened to his friend contributed to his preoccupation with the uncertainties posed by the impending reorganization and his vague fear that "almost anything could happen to any of us."

Paradoxical Refusal of a Promotion

We have encountered other paradoxical cases that are, in a sense, the exact opposite of the case just considered. A person dislikes most aspects of his job but refuses to take steps to obtain a different one because of fears of unknown risks that could make a new work situation even worse. One supervisor felt extremely ambivalent about his job. He was constantly frustrated by deadlines and other pressures imposed by his superiors, which he felt made life in his unit miserable and kept him and his team from doing their work properly. Often they would be pulled off an important assignment and told not to finish it because of a pressing need for a more routine task. As a result, he and others on the team were overworked, did not feel pride in their product, often became irritable with each other, and had little team spirit. On the positive side, the job gave him the opportunity to use his specialized engineering training and to work on certain types of industrial design problems that he took pleasure in being able to solve. He respected the company and was pleased with the quality of the merchandise turned out on their assembly lines.

A month earlier, when sounded out by a superior about his interest in moving up to the position of manager, he had declined. He realized that this was a strange decision, because the gains seemed to outweigh the minor losses. He would have more freedom to choose his assignments, to set his own work schedule, and to avoid many of the harassments that made his present job so unpleasant. There would also be higher pay, more prestige in the company, more esteem from his family and social circle, and a greater sense of success and accomplishment. There were only two specific drawbacks. The manager's job would require a great deal of overtime; but he acknowledged that his present job did too. The new job would also require him to deal with some new types of problem, which might be more difficult than the ones he dealt with on his present job. Still, he realized that once on the job he would undoubtedly find it less difficult than it seemed at a distance.

In terms of the balance sheet, then, the choice of accepting a promotion to become a manager appeared to be clearly favorable, with a predominance of strong positive incentives and only a few minor drawbacks. Again, there is a paradox in that he actually chose what apparently was, from his own standpoint, the less desirable alternative of remaining on a job that he found frustrating and unpleasant most of the time. Why this seemingly irrational choice?

The answer again has to do with anticipatory regret centered on unknown risks far more threatening than the minor drawback of having to solve new and more difficult problems. This man spoke in somewhat vague terms about the possibility that he would turn out to be a failure if he took the job of manager. Except for making a few oblique comments about added responsibilities, he gave no specific reasons for this fear. In response to probing questions, he seemed unable to mention any specific aspects of the job for which he felt unqualified. His main answer was that "if you take a job as manager you never know what will happen, whether you will succeed or fail." His undefined, generalized fear of failure evidently involved concern about unknown risks that somehow might result in failure. Perhaps he intuitively sensed that he might become a victim of the "Peter Principle," which asserts that every man in a hierarchy rises, so long as he is reasonably competent, until he reaches his level of incompetence (Peter and Hull, 1969). Even though he said, "I know that if I took the job of manager I would become more confident," he seemed unable to dismiss the possibility that the higher-level administrative job would somehow, in some unknown way, prove to be beyond his competence. His unwillingness to risk moving out of his unpleasant job into a seemingly more attractive one is another example of Hamlet's point, that we "rather bear those ills we have than fly to others we know not of."

Among women, similar concerns about unknown risks may be tied to vague fears about the appropriateness of female work roles in a man's world. Such concerns apparently lead some bright and energetic women to settle for careers that are well below their capabilities (Horner, 1969).

Being locked into an unhappy job situation because of fear of the unknown risks that might ensue from shifting to a new one is by no means rare among men and women in industrial organizations at all levels, from workers on the assembly line to senior executives on the board of directors. Part of the problem, as we have already suggested, is that few organizations are willing to give job applicants or candidates for promotion an honest picture of what their day-to-day job functions will be like (and what sources of frustration made their predecessors quit).

The person locked into a disagreeable job behaves much like a "sad sack" in the army—lethargic, given to griping and daydreaming, unresponsive to fresh opportunities for job enlargement, seeking his "kicks" elsewhere. Chinoy (1955), in his interviews of men in an automobile factory, found that almost 80 percent thought of getting out of the shop, most to go into a business of their own. But despite their frustrations, feelings of alienation, and uncertainties within the plant, very few could bring themselves to leave. Most of the men, besides having doubts about their abilities, were unwilling to give up the security of familiar routines and established relationships with coworkers for the uncertainties of a new job. Studs Terkel (1972), in his fascinating collection of interviews of blue-collar and white-collar workers in a wide range of occupations, also found that most felt locked into their jobs. The workers used such derogatory terms as *machine, mule, monkey,* and *robot* to describe their condition, but were unable to take the initiative to change their careers.

In terms of the conflict model, the alienated worker or executive satisfies all of the conditions for the procrastination form of defensive avoidance; he is undergoing high conflict (there are losses for both continuing on the job and changing the job) but has lost all hope of finding a satisfactory solution and is under no deadline pressure. The "sad sack" behavior that results from this demoralized state is essentially a manifestation of a marked constriction of career interests and aspirations, relieved only by occasional bursts of petty disruption and disguised negligence on the assembly line or at the conference table.

Constructive Procrastination

In the two examples just presented, fear of unknown risks seems to have played a determining role in the choice of a course of action or inaction. Much more frequently, such concern operates only as a temporary deterrent to making a final commitment, leading to a constructive search for additional information. We have observed this constructive type of temporary procrastination in a number of executives who ended up accepting offers of promotion within their own divisions or making a lateral move to an equivalent position in a division that offered better prospects for promotion. Before committing themselves, they made an effort to find out if there was a hidden catch. Using their informal contacts within the company, some of them turned up unexpected negative features, such as excessive demands to spend most evenings attending meetings. In a few instances, the executive was able to mitigate the newly discovered drawbacks by negotiating with his superiors before accepting the new job.

Postponing a decision because of hestiation to take unspecifiable risks sometimes allows the decision maker to await new events that may change the balance sheet and lead to a more satisfactory solution. Many of the executives who were concerned about the unknown losses they might sustain from the company's impending reorganization postponed making any decision about seeking a different job inside or outside the company until crucial information became available. They waited, for example, until the company announced which divisions would be moved to a remote city. Having done so, they were able to construct a more clear-cut balance sheet of pros and cons. In order to delay the decision, however, each of these executives had to bear the stress of being a "dangling man," like the hero in Saul Bellow's novel of that title.

A person's recollection of exaggerated rumors, crude and irrelevant analogies, and even pure superstitions can stir up unwarranted concern over risks that are unknown in the sense that they are vague or nonspecific. Much more often, however, there is a basis in reality for pausing to consider the possibility of risks that the person cannot specify. Whether realistic or not, such concern can function as an antidote to impetuous action.

As an example, it is instructive to examine the decisional conflict of a government administrator who was urged by local farmers to authorize the use of a poisonous pesticide to kill predatory insects that were destroying their valuable crops.[4] The administrator found that all available scientific evidence on the known effects of the poison and the ecological consequences of eliminating the predators pointed to a favorable outcome, with no known adverse effects. At this point it would seem rational for him to have made a favorable decision. Yet he had strong lingering doubts about the unknown risks involved, based on analogies to unexpected ecological disasters produced by poisons used to kill other predators. The administrator recalled, for example, reading a newspaper account of what happened when federal officials used a toxic chemical called Compound 1080 in special bait that selectively killed predatory coyotes that were harassing livestock and game animals in Arizona. Two unexpected biological chain reactions, with devastating effects, were set off. First, the poison spewed out by the dying coyotes poisoned the grass and soil, which, in turn, poisoned the cattle that ate the affected grass. Second, eliminating the coyotes led to proliferation of rodents, upon which coyotes normally feed; so great were their numbers that they damaged agricultural crops throughout the region.

As a scientifically oriented person, the administrator realized that the findings, bearing on a different chemical and a different predator, could not be given the status of hard evidence offsetting the research supporting the positive effects of the new pesticide. Yet, the analogy functioned as a realistic cautionary tale for the administrator and generated a deep concern about unknown risks, persuading him to carry out an entirely different type of information search from the one he had conducted up to that time (which had been limited to examining published scientific reports on the effectiveness of the new chemical, its side effects, and the ecological consequences of eliminating the predatory insects). The evidence about the effects of the coyote poison reinforced the administrator's readiness to take seriously a simple heuristic rule bearing on unknown risks, which is popular among some people who deal with the problems of changing the ecology of any region: "Avoid introducing any change that could upset the ecological balance."

Now, with the unknown risks in mind, the administrator continued his information search by making a personal field visit to a farming area where the new pesticide had been experimentally tested. In informal chats, he asked the farmers if they had noticed any depredations by new predators or any other unusual changes in the environment, without mentioning that he was looking for side effects that might conceivably be linked with use of the pesticide. The administrator also invested time and energy in contacting a group of competent environmental biologists to see if they would be willing to follow up on whatever leads he picked up from his interviews. He considered initiating some new field studies in the local area whose ecology might be disrupted. He hired a research team to try out the pesticide on a small scale, in a controlled experiment in two different subregions. Their findings indicated that small concentrations of the poisonous chemical, which might not be sufficient to give rise to the overt symptoms investigated in the earlier studies, could be detected in the crops and farm animals in both regions. The administrator then felt justified in initiating more costly research to obtain a more definitive answer. As it turned out, the evidence indicated that the pesticide had some potentially harmful effects, which gave him sound grounds for withholding it and also supplied him with strong arguments to refute his critics in the ensuing political battle.

All of these information-seeking activities involved operations different from those that the administrator had carried out when he was making his original appraisal. But they are costly in time and money. And, if no adverse information is turned up, the responsible executive is threatened with suffering damage to his reputation. If the new experiment produced no evidence that the questionable pesticide had any harmful effects, the administrator who hired the research team would have been blamed by naive insiders in his agency for unnecessarily holding up the decision and for overspending to gather unnecessary information.

There are wide individual differences among decision makers with regard to the type of information search that they carry out to check on unknown risks and the criteria that they use to judge that the search is sufficiently complete to warrant making a final decision. Culture patterns, local traditions, current fashions, and publicity (as in the example of the unknown risks of ecological disaster), as well as the decision makers' emotional responsiveness to whatever threat information they turn up, also affect their motivation to carry out an intensive search. A common form of information seeking when one is faced with an acute decisional conflict consists of repeatedly discussing the pros and cons with many different people in one's social network—with family members, close friends, and esteemed mentors, such as clergymen. This is not always the most efficient way to obtain the hard facts needed, but it sometimes provides opportunities to fill out the balance sheet and sometimes alerts the decision maker to risks he might not otherwise have thought about.

The same can be said of many of the guidance services that cater to the transitory population of isolated, friendless people in large cities and to young people who are unable or unwilling to approach their families. Various free services have sprung up to meet the demand for advice and information about what to do when trouble arises, including telephone counseling centers (Lester and Brockopp, 1973) and talk-back programs (Bryan, 1961), which supplement the long-established advice columns in the newspapers. A striking feature of these services for mass audiences is that professional standards are rarely maintained; counseling is usually offered by nonexperts to anonymous clients on the basis of fleeting, if any, contact, with little or no opportunity for follow-up inquiry to check on the value of the advice given. Yet they may satisfy some of the needs of clients who are in the throes of acute decisional conflict, particularly by providing them with an opportunity to discuss risks they are only vaguely aware of.

From a practical standpoint, there is undoubtedly room for considerable improvement in the information-seeking activities of the average citizen. This is a neglected social problem for which new solutions, in the form of special educational devices and counseling services, might be developed to improve the efficiency of methods used by people facing fundamental life decisions for obtaining and evaluating the most pertinent information bearing on known and unknown risks. Of special importance would be the development of services to help people in low-income families become aware of the hidden consequences of the limited alternatives open to them and work out personal and collective strategies for opening up more choices.

Frequently, decision makers are inclined to deceive themselves into thinking they have conducted a complete information search after brief contact with a so-called expert and perhaps a few informal discussions with friends and acquaintances. This sometimes happens even when the decision is a vital one—such as quitting college, getting married, obtaining a divorce, choosing a career, changing to a different job, or moving to a different city. In such instances—whenever the decision could entail serious, lifelong consequences—any friend or advisor who stimulates concern about unknown risks can serve the valuable function of preventing a premature choice by generating a felt need in the decision maker for prolonging his information search.

Once a threat, no matter how vague, becomes salient, anticipatory regret is aroused, with all the behavioral consequences described earlier in this chapter.

CHAPTER 10

Threats to Freedom of Choice

Decision makers rarely have freedom to choose among all the viable alternative courses of action that might serve their purposes. Authorities constantly impose constraints, and interested parties within one's social network—work colleagues, friends, and relatives—often exert strong social pressures that further limit one's choices. When demands from authorities are accompanied by severe threats of social or physical punishment—like the Mafia godfather's offer that cannot be refused—decision makers sometimes feel they have no choice but to adopt a course abhorrent to them. Under what conditions is a person most likely to resist constraints and pressures? What factors determine whether the effects of a forced choice will be in the direction of inner compliance or inner detachment, resistance, and defiance?

Research workers in psychology and related behavioral sciences, having only recently begun exploring these fundamental questions, can offer at present little more than fragmentary bits of theory and scattered pieces of relevant evidence. In this chapter we shall examine those bits and pieces in relation to the conflict-theory model, with special attention to explanatory hypotheses about why, under different circumstances, people react in different ways to threatened loss of freedom of choice.

Coercive Demands during the Watergate Coverup

We start with extreme examples drawn from governmental investigations of the Watergate coverup conspiracy in the Nixon administration, which illustrate the variety of responses of top-level aides to offers from the White House that *could* be refused—*if* one were willing to have his career in government terminated. Then we shall examine social psychological theory and research dealing with the effects of restrictions on freedom of choice, focusing on several experiments and case studies that point to major determinants of compliance. Finally, we shall return to some of the fundamental issues in the psychology of coercive demands posed by the Watergate coverup conspiracy, giving special attention to the factors that make for resistance, as against malignant obedience, to unscrupulous authorities who make illicit demands that seem to allow no choice but compliance.

Demands from higher authorities to engage in illegal or unethical acts are often made in the name of a "good" cause. Testimony from the congressional inquiries and trials concerning the Watergate coverup directed by Richard Nixon and his confederates on the White House staff during 1972–73 shows that many of the aides and assistants who ended up being sent to jail for obstruction of justice or perjury—Dwight Chapin, John Dean, Herbert Kalmbach, Frederick LaRue, Jeb Stuart Magruder, Herbert Porter, Gordon Strachan, and others—accepted demands for illegal activities from the President's office as orders given for the "legitimate" purpose of preserving the Republican administration. Apparently they regarded perjury and other violations of the law to protect the Nixon administration from scandal as a *duty*—part of the implicit contract of their employment (just as did the majority of subjects in Milgram's social psychological experiments on malignant obedience, discussed later in this chapter). But still there were marked differences among the participants of the coverup in the type of decisional conflict manifested and the way they resolved those conflicts.

John Dean and Jeb Magruder, according to their testimony at the Senate Watergate hearings, willingly acquiesced to various unlawful demands without any apparent conflict. In terms of the conflict model, these men displayed the pattern of unconflicted change. Convinced that the power of the Presidency would in all probability protect them from detection and certainly from any culpability, they saw no serious risk of being punished; nor did they suffer any qualms of anticipatory self-disapproval from violating ethical standards. When asked what reactions he and the other participants in the decision to organize and finance the Watergate burglary had at the time they made their illegal plans, Magruder stated, "We thought there may be some information that could be very helpful to us and because of a certain atmosphere that had developed in my working at the White House, I was not as concerned about its illegality as I should have been at that time." He went on to say, "When these subjects came up, although I was aware they were illegal, we had become somewhat inured to using some activities that would help us in accomplishing what we thought was a cause, a legitimate cause."[1]

Other defendants were highly conflicted about the possibility of being caught and convicted on criminial charges, and sought reassurances. Herbert Kalmbach, Nixon's attorney, became deeply worried when asked by John Dean to collect and disperse "hush money" to the convicted Watergate burglars; he queried John Ehrlichman, one of Nixon's two closest aides, and received a strong assurance that he would be free from any possible culpability.

> I think the primary reason for my concern was the secrecy and the clandestine, covert nature of this activity. . . . I wanted him [John Ehrlichman] to assure me as to the propriety of this assignment. . . . I said, "John, I am looking right into your eyes." I said, . . . "You know that my family and my reputation mean everything to me . . . And it is just absolutely necessary, John, that you tell me, first, that John Dean has the authority to direct me in this assignment, that it is a proper assignment and that I am to go forward on it." . . . He said, "Herb, John Dean does have the authority. It is proper, and you are to go forward."[2]

Subsequently, Kalmbach was shocked to discover how misguided he had allowed himself to become about getting away with such a flagrant obstruction of justice. He accepted the demands transmitted by Dean and Ehrlichman as coming from the President, upon whom he was dependent for his success as an attorney. (He was able to command huge fees for access to Mr. Nixon or other high officials in the Nixon administration.) We surmise that after Kalmbach was definitively informed by Ehrlichman that he was expected to arrange the illegal payments, he had no hope of finding a better solution than compliance with the demands from the White House; thereafter he relinquished feelings of responsibility and bolstered his decision to do what he was asked, thus adopting defensive avoidance as his dominant coping pattern.

Herbert Porter, who had the duty to disburse campaign funds at the Committee for Re-election of the President, was also in state of high conflict when he was asked to commit perjury in order to cover up the illegal payments of hush money to the Watergate burglars, but his coping pattern appears to have been hypervigilance. Porter was told by his superior, Jeb Magruder, that some money had been used for illegitimate "dirty tricks," which could be embarrassing to President Nixon, Attorney General Mitchell, Haldeman, and others if it came to light. To allay Porter's qualms about doing something illegal to help prevent those gentlemen from being embarrassed, Magruder assured him that the dirty tricks were totally unrelated to the Watergate break-in, which he claimed was "something stupid" that Gordon Liddy did entirely on his own. According to Porter's account at the Senate Watergate hearings, Magruder emphasized that there was a grave danger of

> immediate discovery, which means they [government investigators] can come in at any moment and swoop in on our committee and take all of the files and subpoena all of the records and you know what would happen if they did that.
> I conjured up in my mind that scene and became rather excitable and knew I didn't want to see that. So I said, "Well, be specific."[3]

In this excited state, with the threat of immediate discovery vividly in mind, Porter helped Magruder work out a false cover story that could fully account for the illegitimately spent $100,000 and agreed to corroborate it. Subsequently, Porter lived up to the agreement by committing perjury on three separate occasions—when interviewed by agents of the FBI, when questioned by a federal grand jury, and when called as a witness at the trial of the seven Watergate burglars (by which time he certainly must have realized that Magruder had been lying to him when he gave assurances that the need for testifying to the false cover story had nothing to do with the Watergate coverup).

There were also instances of courageous resistance to the same type of pressure. Hugh Sloan, treasurer of the Committee for Re-election of the President, refused to perjure himself before the grand jury when he too was told by his boss, Magruder, that he should lie about how funds were disbursed. In a vigilant way, he immediately consulted a number of colleagues and superiors, expressing his worries about possible illegalities in the way the committee's funds were being handled and the danger that the entire reelection campaign might be compromised. He seems to have received little useful information or advice from the men he consulted, most of whom were themselves secretly involved in the coverup. John Mitchell, who was in charge of the campaign, responded with a cryptic homily; John Ehrlichman told Sloan he did not want to hear any details and offered to help him obtain a lawyer; Fred LaRue discontinued the conversation when he heard that Sloan was not willing to do what Magruder asked; Dwight Chapin told him that "he was only overwrought and needed a vacation."[4] Sloan met with quite a different reception, however, from the two attorneys for the committee when he told them why he was worried and gave them a full accounting of all the cash disbursements he knew about. They evidently confirmed his worst suspicions by telling him angrily, "We have been lied to by the people here." Finally, at a meeting with LaRue, who told him to consider taking the Fifth Amendment if he were called before the grand jury, Sloan remarked that it appeared obvious that "the only way for him to stay in favor with the campaign organization was either to commit perjury or to plead the Fifth Amendment, but that he would do neither." The next morning he did, in fact, hand in his resignation.

Subsequently Sloan went to see Haldeman, Nixon's chief of staff, to tell him that he still felt loyal to the President after explaining "how strongly I felt about certain individuals in terms of what they had done that I thought wrong." Sloan added, "I want you to know that I feel I did not leave the team. As far as I am concerned, the team left me."[5] At that time Sloan did not know that Haldeman was one of the leading conspirators in the Watergate coverup. Later on, when it became apparent that Haldeman was not going to put a stop to the wrongdoings, Sloan decided—after long discussions with his wife—to supply evidence to the

Department of Justice and to investigative reporters, which played a crucial role in helping to expose White House involvement in the Watergate scandal. Sloan's refusal appears to have been the outcome of careful deliberation about the risks of utilitarian losses, social disapproval, and self-disapproval, with vigilance as the dominant coping pattern.

Our brief review of the different reactions of five men invited by the White House to engage in illegal activities suggests that a person's response to an illicit demand, and to the accompanying pressures that restrict his freedom to say no, depends to a large extent on the presence or absence of the crucial conditions that determine the dominant coping pattern, as described by the conflict model. Further implications of the conflict model for reactions to threats and constraints that restrict freedom of choice will be elaborated shortly. But first it is necessary to introduce some closely related issues by examining psychological theories that deal with the problems of freedom of choice from different points of view.

Contrasting Theoretical Approaches

The concept of freedom of choice enters into theoretical analyses of decision making in several different ways. First, according to cognitive dissonance theorists, an important variable in determining the way a person acts after arriving at a decision is the degree of choice he perceives himself as having had prior to and at the time of commitment (Brehm and Cohen, 1962; Festinger, 1964; Linder, Cooper, and Jones, 1967). A necessary condition for dissonance reduction is the decision maker's realization that he has made a choice freely, which makes him feel personally responsible for his judgments and actions. More recent research by dissonance theorists adds two related conditions that also make for dissonance reduction: (a) the person is able to foresee the consequences of his actions at the time he makes his decision (Carlsmith and Freedman, 1968; Cooper, 1971); and (b) the person perceives that he made a voluntary choice among the viable alternatives and is responsible for the decision he made (Wicklund and Brehm, 1976; Zimbardo, 1969).

Freedom of choice is seen by other contemporary theorists, including proponents of attribution theory, as a major determinant of the consistency between a decision maker's attitudes and actions (Bem, 1972; Nisbett and Valins, 1971; Steiner, 1970). When a person is forced by fear of censure to comply to group norms and standards, Kelman (1961) points out, inconsistency between his actions and his personal beliefs is to be expected.

"Reactance," the notion that people are motivated to reestablish their freedom when it is threatened or eliminated, has been used to explain contrariness and opposition to anyone who puts strong pressure on a decision maker to follow his advice. Brehm (1966) and Wicklund (1974) have analyzed reactance to threats stemming from fortuitous events or the pressure of directive agents and have found that, when freedom is threatened, people do whatever they can to reinstate it. A person may protect his freedom of choice by openly refusing to comply when under pressure, by behaving aggressively toward the agent of coercion, or by subtly acting contrarily to what is demanded. The desire to protect one's freedom of action is also reflected in cognitive changes—specifically, the tendency to enhance the value of the restricted act and to depreciate the foisted alternative. Freedom to act may be threatened by social pressures from legitimate authorities and restored by various forms of social protest. In an executive committee, when a threat to freedom is posed by an authoritarian chairman who demands the selection of his preferred policy choice, a member can display reactance by announcing publicly that he reserves the right to make his own choice independently or to file a minority report (see Worchel and Brehm, 1971).

A conceptual antecedent of reactance theory was Allport's (1945) analysis of the psychology of participation. Allport described "reactive" behavior as characteristic of people who have not had a voice in deciding their own destiny: "A person ceases to be reactive and contrary in respect to a desirable course of conduct only when he himself has had a hand in declaring that course of conduct to be desirable" (1945, p. 123). Participation in decision making, according to some organization theorists, can have positive effects on the quality, acceptance, and execution of decisions reached (Vroom, 1969). A study by Coch and French (1948) is a classic illustration of the importance of personal participation as a safeguard against reactive behavior following imposed decisions that affect one's daily work activities. When management at the Harwood Manufacturing Company announced changes in work procedure, telling the workers the reasons at a meeting, production dropped while absenteeism and quitting increased. When workers participated, through their chosen representatives, in planning the changeover, results were better. A third method, that of total worker participation, generated a more rapid increase in production with no resignations.

The Conflict-Theory Position

When a person is confronted with strong demands from his superiors to perform undesirable actions, those new threats induce a high degree of conflict and become major entries in the decisional balance sheet, as in the case of Kalmbach, Porter, Sloan, and numerous other people in the Nixon administration who were urged to participate in the Watergate coverup. The conflict usually centers on threats of social disapproval and utilitarian losses (e.g., "Shall I conform at the risk of being disgraced and sent to jail or shall I refuse at the risk of being despised by my superiors and having my career ruined?"). The threat of self-disapproval is also likely to enter into the decisional balance sheet, especially when the choice confronting an individual is between submitting to intrusive authority figures on the one hand, and defying them in order to assert his independence on the other. Clumsy and excessive social pressure from a boss or any other authority figure who is perceived as misusing his power adds a negative value to whichever alternative he is trying to push. Such pressure threatens not only the person's freedom to select what he wants but also his sense of autonomy, which is a threat to his self-concept as a competent decision maker. These negative effects generally incline the decision maker to resist or defy the restrictive pressures by choosing an opposing course of action. But, according to our analysis of defensive avoidance, in certain circumstances a person becomes so hopeless about finding an adequate solution to a decisional conflict that he is tempted to forego his independence and shift responsibility for the choice onto another agent, particularly if he is trying to reduce feelings of guilt about choosing an unethical or illegal course and wishes to regard himself as having no choice at all. Thus, while threatened loss of freedom of choice may often enter into the decisional balance sheet as a consideration that is negatively valued, it occasionally may be welcomed, depending on whether or not the decision is one for which the person wants to take responsibility.

Conflict theory postulates that whenever a person encounters an attempt to usurp or narrow his freedom of choice, the new threats that become salient affect the answers that the decision maker gives to the four basic questions (see chapter 3). Depending on which threats are most severe, any of the five coping patterns specified by the conflict model—unconflicted adherence, unconflicted change, defensive avoidance, hypervigilance, or vigilance—can be fostered. The pattern followed will play a major role in determining whether the decision maker will relinquish or attempt to retain the alternatives that are being blocked. The implications of this model differ from those of reactance theory, which predicts that the dominant form of response to the threatened removal of an alternative by a restrictive authority figure is ordinarily the vigilant protection of that alternative (Brehm, 1966, p. 9). Conflict theory requires us to specify three additional features of the situation before we predict how the person will respond to such a threat. First, is the decision maker aware of any serious risks attendant to his submitting to the usurpation of choice? If not, he is likely to decide to submit without worrying about it (unconflicted adherence). Second, does he believe it is realistic to hope for a better solution than submission? If not, defensive avoidance (in the form of bolstering the foisted alternative) or buck passing (in the form of conceding to the usurping agent responsibility for the choice) will be the likely outcome. Third, does he believe there is sufficient time for careful search and appraisal? If not, a hypervigilant reaction, consisting of a panicky, impulsive snatching of the threatened alternative (even though it is the weakest one available) may be the response. Unscrupulous salesmen often try to set up the conditions for such an impulsive decision when they hustle a customer into believing that the item under consideration is a "final offer" and that there is a very short deadline after which the price will go up or for some reason the deal will no longer be available. Only when all four basic conditions are present—awareness of the serious risks both of acquiescing and of not acquiescing, hope for a better solution, and time to search for it—do we expect to find a pattern of vigilance, accompanied by judicious appraisal of the gains and losses stemming from attempting to retain or reclaim a threatened or lost alternative.

According to conflict theory, a vigilant decision maker will respond to a threat of elimination of an alternative by examining the entire set of anticipated gains and losses to be expected if he should persist in choosing that alternative. For example, a college senior might find that a vital career alternative, such as obtaining graduate training in one of the sciences, is under threat of elimination when his parents warn him that they will provide no more financial support unless he goes to law school. The threatened alternative should *increase* in attractiveness if the student knows he can easily solve the financial problem (by obtaining a loan or a full fellowship), because he now anticipates an additional positive consequence—he can assert his independence from his family, which outweighs his concern about their disapproval. But when the alternative that is being threatened with elimination will lead to additional negative consequences if chosen (e.g., having to work in order to earn the money needed for graduate training), those negative incentives also enter into the balance sheet and tend to *decrease* its attractiveness. Thus, the reaction of a vigilant decision maker to the threat of elimination of an alternative is a function of concomitant changes in the instrumental value of the threatened alternative.

We do not dispute the fact that people often seek to preserve their full freedom of choice by trying to prevent the loss of threatened alternatives. But if the costs involved in regaining the right to choose a threatened alternative (in time, money, effort, discomfort, and social censure) are seen as outweighing the gains (such as enhanced autonomy and gratifying retaliation against a frustrating authority), then the particular alternative will be devalued rather than magnified in attractiveness. It should be noted that the costs involved in the reinstatement of behavioral alternatives can be incurred in either of two ways: (a) the alternative, if chosen, is no longer worth as much or has more negative features associated with it; and (b) the act of attempting to reinstate it (arguing with the restricting agent, appealing to higher authority, and the like) produces negative reactions. The result in either case is a devaluation of the threatened alternative by a vigilant decision maker, rather than the magnification generally predicted by reactance theory.

Whether the person will elect to regain freedom of choice at the expense of large material and social losses is an empirical question. In recent years, several studies have tested the boundary conditions under which the oppositional effects predicted by reactance theory are limited or attenuated. We shall examine the specific findings shortly. In general, when major social and utilitarian losses are entailed by the effort to assert freedom of choice, avoidance of punitive consequences prevails over reactance and other oppositional tendencies.

Threats and Losses: A Classification

An analysis of the problems investigated under the general rubric of "loss of freedom" reveals four main types of situation in which freedom of choice is threatened or eliminated. Table 7 shows the four types together with some research examples illustrating each. Freedom may be threatened or eliminated as a result of circumstances outside the control of the individual. Such threats stem either from chance events that narrow the range of possible choices (cells 1 and 2 in the table) or from directive agents who attempt to pressure the individual into following a particular path (cells 3 and 4).[6]

TABLE 7. **Four types of situation that limit freedom of choice.**

	SOURCE OF LIMITATION OF FREEDOM	
	Chance occurrences	*Directive agents*
Freedom of choice threatened	1. *Physical barriers* (Brehm and Hammock, 1966) *Psychological barriers* (Wicklund, 1970) *High risk determined by chance* (Mann and Dashiell, 1975)	3. *Coercive or argumentative pressure to comply* (Brehm and Sensenig, 1966) (Milgram, 1974) (Pallak and Heller, 1971)
Freedom of choice eliminated	2. *Lost objects* (Brehm, Stires, Sensenig, and Shaban, 1966) *Damaged objects* (Brehm, McQuown, and Shaban, 1966)	4. *Arbitrary assignment of alternatives* (Hammock and Brehm, 1966) *"No alternative" situations* (Ferrari, 1962)

Major experimental studies on effects of restriction of choice—most of which are discussed elsewhere in this chapter—are indicated in parentheses.

Threat by Chance Occurrence

When a person feels inclined to make a particular choice, such as attending a particular law school, the insertion of a barrier, such as a substantial increase in tuition that makes the cost almost prohibitive, or moving the law building to a remote rural campus of the university, is perceived as threatening his freedom to make that choice. Just as with other constraints, the greater the frustration, the greater the magnitude of aggressive reactance. Of course, if it seems impossible to overcome the barrier, the person may no longer consider the goal (and hence the recovery of his freedom to choose it) worthwhile.

To illustrate the conflict-theory approach to the problems of freedom curtailment, we shall examine in detail a field experiment carried out by Mann and Dashiell (1975) that was designed to test rival predictions about the effects of a chance threat to freedom of choice. A major feature of the study is that it was carried out in a significant field setting, in which extremely important career choices were threatened with restriction and considerable costs were associated with reinstating freedom.

The context of the study was the first Selective Service draft lottery, drawn on December 1, 1969. This event had considerable impact on the career decisions of hundreds of thousands of young American men, the majority of whom were opposed to the Vietnam War and did not want to be drafted. The lottery-by-birthdate was used by the government to determine the draft status of all men aged 19–25 years. Those whose birthdates were drawn first were given low numbers and were scheduled to be the first to be inducted; those whose birthdates were drawn last were given high numbers, which would make them safe from induction for at least a year and perhaps for the rest of their lives. The effect of the lottery in limiting the freedom of the unlucky men to exercise fully their career options made it an ideal occasion for studying the effects of a dramatic impersonal threat based on a random procedure in a natural setting.

The focus of the study, carried out with a group of Harvard students on the days preceding and following the drawing of the national draft lottery, was the change in attraction toward those career choices that were known to carry a draft exemption as against those that were not. There were three draft-exempt choices that would keep a man out of the armed forces: medical school, divinity school, and teaching. Three other alternatives that the majority of men regarded as attractive were nonexempt choices: full-time job, graduate school, and travel. The question under investigation was: what changes in the attractiveness of these two types of career choice occurred among men who received low, medium, and high numbers?

Draft lottery numbers from 1 to 120 were low or "bad" numbers; the men knew that if they received one of these low numbers they would certainly be drafted within a year after graduation and probably much sooner unless they were able to get into a draft-exempt category. Numbers 121–240 were medium numbers; the men who received these numbers were left in the same state of uncertainty as they were in before the lottery, since no one knew when the Selective Service would start calling them up. Numbers 241–365 were high or "safe" numbers; men assigned these numbers knew that it would be at least a year and possibly much longer before all those with medium numbers would be called up, so that they were free to take a job during the coming year, or go to graduate school or travel, without regard to the lack of draft-exempt status of these activities.

Conflict theory makes specific predictions with regard to both the high- and low-number men. What do we expect to happen to a young man's feelings toward various career possibilities when he gets a *low* number in the draft lottery? With respect to nonexempt activities, such as attending graduate school or taking a nonteaching job, the risk of being drafted if one pursues these activities greatly increases; a man knows that if he were to choose one of these options he would probably soon end up as a draftee infantryman in Vietnam. Thus, as a result of receiving a low number in the lottery, the threat of being drafted would become more salient and the tendency to reject or devalue the non-draft-exempt alternatives would increase greatly. But the outcome for draft-exempt choices, such as medicine, teaching, and divinity school, should be the opposite. Men who receive low numbers should perceive these three exempt activities as more attractive because they offer safety with regard to the imminent threat of being drafted.

Turning now to the lucky men who receive *high* numbers, we make exactly the reverse predictions. Non-draft-exempt activities such as graduate school and travel should become more attractive, because the risk previously associated with them is markedly diminished. In contrast, a major positive feature of the draft-exempt activities (namely, safety from the draft) would no longer figure as an important consideration, and hence these alternatives should become less attractive.

In sum, the following predictions were made on the basis of conflict theory: for the unlucky men who received low numbers in the lottery, (a) a significant *decrease* in the attractiveness ratings of the three *vulnerable* alternatives (job, graduate school, travel) and (b) a significant *increase* in the attractiveness ratings of the three *draft-exempt* alternatives (medical school, divinity school, teaching); for the lucky men who received high numbers, (a) a significant *increase* in the attractiveness ratings of the *vulnerable* alternatives and (b) a significant *decrease* in the ratings of the *draft-exempt* activities. Table 8 summarizes these predictions from conflict theory.

Five days before the lottery, eighty-four Harvard seniors were asked what they were planning to do after graduation. The men were also asked to rate on a fifteen-point scale various alternative activities "according to

TABLE 8.   **Summary of predictions from conflict theory on how the draft lottery would affect attitudes toward choice alternatives.**

	PREDICTED CHANGE IN ATTRACTIVENESS RATINGS AMONG MEN WHO RECEIVE:	
ALTERNATIVES	LOW NUMBERS	HIGH NUMBERS
Draft-vulnerable activities (job, graduate school, travel)	Decrease	Increase
Draft-exempt activities (medical school, divinity school, teaching)	Increase	Decrease

Source: L. Mann and T. Dashiell, "Reactions to the Draft Lottery: A Test of Conflict Theory," Human Relations, 1975, 28, 155–73. Reprinted by permission.

their attractiveness to you as ways you would choose to spend the year following graduation." The seven alternatives to be rated were graduate school, medical school, divinity school, teaching, travel, full-time job, and service in the armed forces. On December 2, 1969, the day following the lottery drawing, a posttest questionnaire was distributed to half the men. They were given the same question asking them to rate the seven alternatives; they were then asked to indicate the lottery number they had received. To test for the persistence of the predicted changes in attractiveness ratings over a period of time, each man in the other half of the sample was given an identical posttest questionnaire ten days later.

There was some evidence of reactance motivation immediately after the draft lottery, but the main findings indicate a stronger, more persistent tendency to reduce conflict by derogating the threatened alternatives, as predicted by conflict theory. Figure 11 depicts the pattern of changes in the evaluation of the draft-exempt and draft-vulnerable alternatives for both posttests combined. The results are consistent with three of the four predictions made by conflict theory and with the overall prediction of an interaction effect.[7] By and large, Mann and Dashiell's findings indicate that following an event that threatened to restrict the freedom to choose among a set of career alternatives, the men altered the attractiveness of the various alternatives according to their potential for reducing or increasing the possibility of their being drafted. Thus men with a low lottery number, who perceived their highly vulnerable draft status as a threat not only to their freedom of choice but also to their well-being, became more attracted to low-risk career activities such as teaching, divinity school, and medicine.

The findings are in line with conflict theory, which views the reactance motivation aroused by the threatened or actual loss of freedom of choice as only one of a number of important considerations that enter the deci-

FIGURE 11. **Changes in attractiveness of draft-exempt and draft-vulnerable alternatives.**

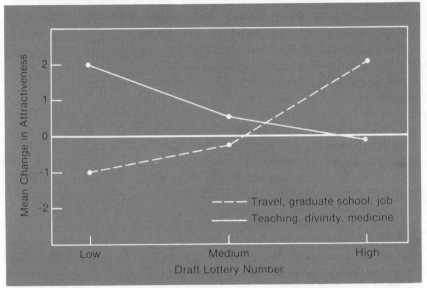

Source: L. Mann and T. Dashiell, "Reactions to the Draft Lottery: A Test of Conflict Theory," *Human Relations*, 1975, 28, 155–73. Reprinted by permission.

sional balance sheet. We assume that the importance of freedom as a consideration when making a vital decision is most pronounced when the person's self-image as an independent free agent is challenged by pressure and coercion; but freedom can be outweighed by other considerations, such as the prospect of censure, financial loss, and severe punishment.

Although many people admire those who are willing to take great risks in defending their freedom, they often do not live up to their ideals when confronted with restrictions. Like Falstaff, they are inclined to decide that "the better part of valour is discretion." In this respect, conflict theory does not present so flattering a view of human nature as does reactance theory.

Loss Due to Chance Occurrence

Reactance may also occur when a choice alternative is actually removed, rather than merely made more difficult, by a chance occurrence. In one social psychological study, for example, a promised phonograph record was accidentally left out of a shipment of records and hence was no longer available for listening (Brehm, Stires, Sensenig, and Shaban, 1966); in another, a movie was damaged in shipment and hence was no longer available for viewing (Brehm, McQuown, and Shaban, 1966). Findings from these studies support the reactance-theory proposition that the chance loss of an alternative results in that alternative being rated as more attractive. Absence of an expected alternative presumably makes the heart grow fonder. If so, it would not be surprising for a decision maker who flips a coin to allow chance to choose for him to turn around and select the "losing" alternative. The realization that choice has been relinquished to chance may induce the person to reestablish his independence by choosing the alternative opposite to the chance-determined one.

We wonder about the psychological function served by magnification of the lost alternative when the person realizes that there is no possibility of reinstating freedom of choice. If an alternative is irretrievably removed—as when one of the choice objects is damaged beyond repair in shipment and there is insufficient time to order a replacement—increasing the attractiveness of the eliminated alternative would only seem to make the loss more keenly felt. It is, of course, possible that immediately following the loss the initial reaction might be magnification and idealization of the unavailable object accompanied by a strong aggressive motivation to regain it (based on earlier experiences in which aggressive protests were effective). But over time, as feelings of loss subside, or as prolonged efforts to regain the object lead only to frustration, reactance would probably give way to devaluation, with a tendency to develop a sour-grapes defense belittling the lost alternative. The notion of a stage sequence in reactions to·loss of an alternative was raised earlier (see note 7); it would seem worthwhile in future studies to include a series of delayed tests to examine whether idealization gives way to devaluation over time.

Threat by Directive Agent

A major concern in social psychology is the effectiveness of techniques used by directive agents for inducing compliance to group norms and values. Threats, rewards, justifications, and social pressures have all been used in order to force a person to act contrary to his own private beliefs and judgments (Asch, 1956; Collins and Raven, 1969; Milgram, 1974). Strategies for trapping the unwary into a sequence of commitments, such as the foot-in-the-door technique (Freedman and Fraser, 1966), represent a more subtle approach to coercive persuasion (see chapter 11). A more direct method is to place the person in a highly controlled social situation designed to make him yield to the overt pressures of an authority figure (Milgram, 1974).

There are times, however, when external pressure backfires, and a person who actually intended to perform a certain action does just the opposite in order to express his resistance to the pressures being put on him by a directive agent. In the attitude-change literature, there is a related phenomenon known as the "boomerang effect," which has been examined mainly in the context of presenting persuasive communications that are extremely discrepant from the recipient's own position (Sherif and Hovland, 1961). In the traditional area of social influence, an analog to the boomerang effect is "contrariness," sometimes called "anticonformity," which occurs when a clumsy attempt to pressure an individual into adopting a particular behavior leads him to choose the opposite course. The influence attempt may not only backfire, producing contrariness, but may also lead to the derogation of the agent who is exerting pressure.

An experiment by Brehm and Sensenig (1966) shows the operation of reactance motivation in the face of social pressure from a directive agent. In this experiment, subjects had a choice of two problems to work on. The problems were essentially identical, but the subjects were told that some people were better at one and some at the other, and therefore the experimenter was giving them a choice. External pressure was introduced by means of a note from another subject who was supposedly making the same choice in another room. In the high-pressure condition, the note read, "I think we should both do problem A." With this note the other subject was not only expressing his preference but also directly trying to influence or usurp the subject's choice. In the second condition, one of minimal pressure, the note simply read, "I prefer problem A." The first condition, in which external pressure was greater, produced less compliance (with only 40 percent choosing the problem suggested on the note) than in the low-pressure condition (where 73 percent of the subjects complied). This study indicates that an attempt to usurp choice by urging a person to select one particular alternative can have the opposite effect of inducing him to avoid choosing that alternative.

When a social influence attempt fails, it is important to ask whether the reason was a reaction against a threat to freedom, resentment at being treated as a "schnook" incapable of making a decision, or annoyance with a poorly conceived, clumsily worded, or insulting influence attempt. (See Abelson and Miller, 1967.) This question is crucial because the literature on social influence shows quite clearly that not all attempts to threaten freedom and control behavior produce a boomerang effect. Some attempts, although much more drastic in their threat to freedom of choice than those used by Brehm and Sensenig, nevertheless succeed in pushing the person into compliance (Asch, 1951; Frank, 1961; Milgram, 1974).

It seems, therefore, that "threats" of the kind used by Brehm and Sensenig create a combination of positive and negative incentives that enter into the decisional balance sheet: positive when the high-pressure agent is a person of competence and credibility, negative when the agent is seen to be acting principally out of self-interest or out of disrespect for the integrity of the individual. The resultant behavior—yielding on the one hand, contrariness or independence on the other—is a function of the strength of these clashing incentives.

That the same form of social pressure can elicit compliance in some people and contrariness in others is shown quite dramatically in a study by Weiner and Brehm (1966). Shoppers in a supermarket were subjected to high pressure by being given monetary and verbal inducements to buy a certain brand of bread. A dominant effect on female shoppers was marked resistance, with only 46 percent accepting the influence attempt. A much stronger effect was observed in males, most of whom (75 percent) were positively influenced when pressured to buy. This study might imply that women are more determined to preserve their freedom of choice than men; a plausible alternative interpretation is that in a domain where a person is not confident of his ability to choose competently (as with the husband in a supermarket), a high-pressure influence attempt is more likely to be productive, than to induce anticonformity based on reactance.

Limits of Reactance

A number of studies, including Mann and Dashiell's (1975) draft-lottery study, bear on the question of specifying the conditions under which reactance or oppositional effects are attenuated. Examples of social conditions that have been found to be associated with weak or nonexistent reactance effects following on a threat to freedom of choice include the following:

1. The restriction of freedom is due to a group norm (Grabitz-Gniech, 1971).
2. The person does not infer that the agent who is restricting his freedom intended to do so (Heller, Pallak, and Picek, 1973; Wicklund, 1974).
3. The person is committed to future interaction with the agent who is restricting his freedom (Pallak and Heller, 1971).
4. The person is offered at least some compensatory choice as to the mode of going along with the agent (Heilman and Garner, 1975), particularly when a choice is offered by the agent rather than obtained by chance (Heilman and Toffler, 1976).
5. The reestablishment of freedom implicates the person in responsibility for an adverse decision (Feldman-Summers, 1975).
6. The agent is powerful and uses the threat of retaliation to pressure the person into going along with his demands (Heilman, 1976).

All of the studies cited reveal that restriction of freedom of choice does not in and of itself automatically produce observable reactance effects. People aparently accept such restriction if it is associated with either mitigating circumstances or intimidating penalties.

Resisting Strong Pressures: A Case Study

Mary McCarthy's autobiographical account of how she became a Trotskyite (McCarthy, 1961, pp. 48–50) represents a particularly good example of contrariness as a reaction to undue pressure by social agents and suggests some of the crucial conditions that make for an anticonformity choice.

At a cocktail party in New York in November 1936, Mary McCarthy was standing in the middle of a circle of people when she was asked a question by a fellow writer who was an active leftist: was Trotsky entitled to a hearing? (At the time, Trotsky had been accused of fostering a counterrevolutionary plot in the Soviet Union.) In McCarthy's words, this is what happened next:

> I blushed, everybody seemed to be looking at me strangely. . . . "What do you want me to say?" I protested, "I don't know anything about it." "Trotsky denies the charges," patiently intoned my friend. "He declares it's a GPU fabrication. Do you think he's entitled to a hearing?" My mind cleared. "Why, of course," I laughed—were there people who would say that Trotsky was *not* entitled to a hearing? But my friend's voice tolled a rebuke to this levity. "She says Trotsky is entitled to his day in court. . . . One thing more, Mary," he continued gravely, "Do you believe that Trotsky should have the right of asylum?" The right of asylum. I looked for someone to share my amusement—were we in ancient Greece or the Middle Ages? I was sure the U.S. Government would be delighted to harbor such a distinguished foreigner. But nobody smiled back. Everybody watched dispassionately as, for form's sake, I assented to the phrasing: yes, Trotsky, in my opinion, was entitled to the right.

A few days later, McCarthy received a letter from the "Committee for the Defense of Leon Trotsky" stating that they demanded for Leon Trotsky the right to a fair hearing and the right of asylum. Wondering who these demanders were, she looked at the letterhead and was surprised to discover her own name.

> I sat down on my unmade studio couch, shaking. How dared they help themselves to my signature? This was the kind of thing the Communists were always being accused of pulling; apparently, Trotsky's admirers had gone to the same school. I had paid so little heed to the incident at the party that a connection was slow to establish itself. Reading over the list of signers, I recognized "names" that had been present there and remembered my novelist-friend going from person to person, methodically polling. . . . In two minutes I had decided to withdraw my name and write a note of protest. Trotsky had a right to a hearing, but I had a right to my signature. For even if there had been a legitimate misunderstanding (it occurred to me that perhaps I had been the only person there not to see the import of my answers), nothing I had said committed me to Trotsky's *defense*.
>
> The "decision" was made, but according to my habit I procrastinated. The severe letter I proposed to write got put off till the next day and then the next. Probably I was not eager to offend somebody who had been a good friend to me. Nevertheless, the letter would undoubtedly have been written, had I been left to myself. But within the next forty-eight hours the phone calls began. People whom I had not seen for months or whom I knew very slightly telephoned to advise me to get off the newly formed Committee. These calls were

not precisely threatening. Indeed, the caller often sounded terribly weak and awkward, as if he did not like the mission he had been assigned. But they were peculiar. For one thing, they always came after nightfall and sometimes quite late, when I was already in bed. Another thing, there was no real effort at persuasion: the caller stated his purpose in standardized phrases, usually plaintive in tone (the Committee was the tool of reaction, and all liberal people should dissociate themselves from its activities, which were an unwarranted intervention in the domestic affairs of the Soviet Union), and then hung up, almost immediately, before I had a proper chance to answer. Odd too—the voices were not those of my Communist friends but of virtual strangers. Those people who admonished me to "think about it" were not people whose individual opinions could have had any weight with me. And when I did think about it, this very fact took on an ominous character: I was not being appealed to personally but impersonally warned.

Gradually, McCarthy learned that all over the city the Communist party was conducting a systematic telephone campaign trying to induce members of the committee to withdraw. Some prominent signers received anonymous threats.

During the first week, name after name fell off the Committee's letterhead. Prominent liberals and literary figures issued statements deploring their mistake. And a number of people protested that their names had been used without permission.

There, but for the grace of God, went I, I whispered, awestruck, to myself, hugging my guilty knowledge. Only Heaven—I plainly saw—by making me dilatory had preserved me from joining this sorry band. Here was the occasion when I should have been wrestling with my conscience or standing, floodlit, at the crossroads of choice. But in fact I was only aware that I had had a providential escape. I had been saved from having to decide about the Committee; I did not decide it—the Communists with their pressure tactics took the matter out of my hands. We all have an instinct that makes us side with the weak, if we do not stop to reason about it, the instinct that makes a householder shield a wounded fugitive without first conducting an inquiry into the rights and wrongs of his case. Such "decisions" are simple reflexes; they do not require courage; if they did there would be fewer of them. When I saw what was happening, I rebounded to the defense of the Committee without a single hesitation—it was nobody's business, I felt, how I happened to be on it, and if anybody had asked me, I should have lied without a scruple. Of course, I did not foresee the far-reaching consequences of my act—how it would change my life. I had no notion that I was now an anti-Communist, where before I had been either indifferent or pro-Communist.

Having made her choice on the basis of a moral principle that constituted her sole decision rule, McCarthy soon recognized that she was in a rather awkward predicament; she knew nothing about the pros and cons of Trotsky's cause, the cause she had decided to "espouse." Since the Stalinists in her circle were being extremely critical and disapproving, she realized that she would have to get together some arguments with which to defend herself. As she began to read the literature on the case—pamphlets, trial reports, the press—it became increasingly clear to her that the trials in which Trotsky had been accused of a counter-revolutionary plot were nothing but a frame-up. Having examined the facts, McCarthy actually began to take Trotsky's side at meetings and social gatherings. She soon acquired the reputation of being a Trotskyite, which meant that she was increasingly shunned by or lost contact with the conventional Stalinists who supported the trials. Her rift with the Communist camp had begun.

McCarthy's break with Stalinism provides an illustration of two interrelated processes;

1. *Extraneous commitment* (the assignment of a position without reference to the person's wishes). First the casual expression of an opinion was either deliberately or unintentionally construed to reflect the person's deeply held policy position. Thus McCarthy was trapped into expressing pro-Trotsky sentiments in front of a group of witnesses at a cocktail party; this then became the basis for attempting to commit her to a committee for Trotsky's defense. Ordinarily the person will reject this kind of manipulation out of hand, as was McCarthy's intention. But sometimes, as in this case, overzealous attacks for apparently siding with a deviant position inadvertently serve to bind the person to it (see chapter 12).

2. *Oppositional motivation* (resistance to pressure exerted by directive agents threatening to eliminate one or more alternatives). The factor that served to preserve McCarthy's alignment with the Trotsky camp was the clumsy, heavy-handed tactics of the Stalinists who attempted to intimidate and implicitly blackmail those people whose names appeared on the Trotsky petition. McCarthy refers to an "instinct" that prompts people to side with the weak against the pressure tactics of the powerful, but she would undoubtedly acknowledge that it is not, alas, an innate, dependable tendency of all homo sapiens. She herself appears to be one of the rare breed who will become more vigilant and make an issue of preserving personal integrity whenever someone seeks to "whip her into shape." The fact that many prominent people knuckled under in the face of the Stalinist pressure tactics did not make her feel hopeless about finding a better solution, which would have led to conformity and bolstering; rather, it increased McCarthy's resolve to chart a course of action that would demonstrate her independence. It is ironic that after being trapped into lending her name to a political position, McCarthy's allegiance to that position was inadvertently affirmed and strengthened because opponents who wished to shake her from it were even more obtrusive in their efforts to violate her jealously guarded autonomy.

Defiance and opposition occur not only when pressure from a directive agent is uninvited, but even when the agent has been sought out for advice. Many people respond to both solicited and unsolicited advice by doing the opposite. In his autobiography (1967), Bertrand Russell recalls that he once received an urgent letter from a young lady asking him whether or not she should marry a persistent suitor. Russell answered her question by citing twelve reasons why she should turn him down. By return post she wrote thanking him for his advice, and announcing her engagement. Apparently Russell's correspondent reestablished her independence to her own satisfaction by choosing the opposite course from the one Russell advised. (Note that she took the trouble to inform Russell of her noncompliant action.)

Loss Due to Directive Agent

Another kind of involuntary elimination of freedom occurs in situations in which a directive agent arbitrarily takes away the possibility of an alternative. The agent might be a deliberately meddlesome person, or a well-intentioned person who interferes with the choice process by arbitrarily assigning a particular alternative to the decision maker without his prior consent or approval. One frequent type of curtailment is known as "Hobson's choice," which refers to a situation where an authority acts in a way that virtually restricts the number of choices to one, or arbitrarily assigns an alternative without reference to the person's wishes in the matter.[8]

Brehm and his associates have shown that when a person expects to have a free choice, an alternative foisted upon him will become extremely unattractive regardless of its intrinsic merits. In an experiment by Hammock and Brehm (1966), 7- to 11-year-old children were led to believe that they would have a choice between candies. However, an experimenter's assistant "arbitrarily" assigned each child one of the candies. Even though the candy foisted onto the subjects had been rated the preferred one, the children showed a strong tendency to re-rate it as less attractive. In a replication with slightly older children (8–12 years old), the experimenters offered toys rather than candy bars. Once again, although the children expected to have a free choice, the experimental assistant "accidently" preempted it by saying, "Here are the toys. Hmmm, well, they both look the same to me. I guess I'm going to give you this one." Here, too, the bestowed object became less attractive. A study by Worchel (1971) showed that restrictions on freedom evoked considerable hostility in college students; the hostility occurred no matter which alternative, the most attractive or the least attractive, was foisted upon the subject.

We know relatively little as yet about which variables affect a person's belief that he is entitled to have an unrestricted choice and his attribution of bad motives to an agent who attempts to narrow down his choice. Resentment and overt hostility are known to depend upon whether the person sees the agent's actions as arbitrary and manipulative or rational and justified (Buss, 1966; Fishman, 1965; Heilman, 1974; Pastore, 1952).

Perception or the agent's intention in limiting freedom is in turn related to the agent's power, attractiveness, and credibility and to the decision maker's predisposition to be self-disparaging and submissive or self-assertive. Grabitz-Gniech (1971) found in a study of individual differences in reactance that subjects with greater feelings of adequacy on the Janis and Field (1959) measure of self-esteem showed the greatest resistance to freedom limitation.

Self-concepts and Freedom

No one would be surprised to find that opposition and defiance become apparent when social pressure takes the form of crude attempts at bribery, blackmail, or demands to perform an illegal act. But what about more subtle dilemmas, wherein yielding to pressure has implications for the person's self-concept as a free and independent agent? Here we must rely on case material, such as Mary McCarthy's autobiographical account of her resistance to Stalinist pressure and Carol Gilligan's (1970) study of draft resisters, to document reactance effects. From intensive interviews of six draft resisters in the Boston area, Gilligan reported that young men who burned their draft cards viewed the draft and the possibility of being sent to Vietnam as constituting a serious threat to their personal freedom in an area intimately related to considerations of self-respect, integrity, and moral values. They saw their act of defiance, however inexpedient it might be, as the only right thing to do. For them, the choice between asserting their freedom to act in accordance with their conscience and succumbing to unjustifiable demands imposed by the government was a moral choice. Similar observations were made by Useem (1973) in a study of over 100 draft resisters, also in the Boston area. According to his report, the first act of resistance, whether it was burning a draft card or returning it in shreds to the draft board, was almost always accompanied by feelings of pride and euphoria and a sense of liberation. Some of the men interviewed by Useem described their immediate reactions to their initial act of resistance in the following terms: "Without question I had a sense of enormous liberation and freedom." "There was a month of uncertainty before the decision was made which caused me great anguish. But once I decided, it was a great high. You're not burdened by this feeling of guilt, the system can no longer morally coerce you, you sing and you cry. It's like an evil that is thrown off a cliff. . . . we had a dance of liberation from the Gods and the powers over us—it was a mystic rite almost." "The sense of liberation was very strong. . . . we felt we were on the offensive and had finally taken control of our lives." "Euphoria and freedom probably describe it."

Relatively few young men defied the government that was blocking their freedom to act in accordance with their conscience. Many more dejectedly yielded to the demands of the Selective Service and allowed themselves to be inducted against their own better judgment, with potentially adverse effects on their self-esteem. What makes one person commit acts of civil disobedience to express his defiance while another submits to a governmental demand even though he considers it illegitimate and immoral? Obviously, one major determinant is a strong personal commitment to an ethical principle, especially when accompanied by affiliation with a social protest movement, which can make the threat of self-disapproval and social disapproval (from violating group norms) more powerful incentives than threat of utilitarian losses (such as fines and imprisonment). But we know relatively little about the more subtle factors that may tip the balance when a young person decides to break with the traditional norms of his family and community by embarking upon a course of action that preserves his freedom of choice at the cost of eliciting strong social disapproval. Personality factors enter the equation, in that a person will exercise freedom of choice only to the extent that he feels competent to assert his independence (De Charms, 1968; White, 1959). An individual may set aside freedom of choice because of feelings of low efficacy, rooted in negative attitudes and concepts about himself.

Human Costs of Losing Choice

We are only now beginning to recognize the exorbitant cost in human suffering of allowing exploitative social conditions to deprive certain groups of people of any meaningful control over their own lives. The most dramatic testimony to the importance of decisional choice for personal well-being is the evidence now emerging of how people react when they discover that all meaningful choice has been systematically stripped away from them. Such is the fate of a number of groups in Western society, particularly prisoners and the elderly. The consequences for the aged of having to endure the hopelessness and humiliation of being deprived of all choice are vividly illustrated in a little-known study by Nelida Ferrari (1962) that provides striking evidence of the significance of freedom of choice for the maintenance of morale and the will to live among the elderly.

Ferrari conducted interviews in a nursing home for the elderly with a sample of fifty-five women having an average age of 82, seventeen of whom perceived that they had no choice but to go to the home, while the remaining thirty-eight women perceived that they had other alternatives. Within four weeks of being admitted to the home, eight of the seventeen women in the no-choice group had died, and within ten weeks all but one were dead. In sharp contrast, only one woman out of the thirty-eight who perceived alternatives died in the ten-week period. Examination of the medical records of the women in the two groups revealed no health differences sufficient to account for this outcome; the deaths were called "unexpected" by the staff.

Obviously, these correlational findings do not establish a cause-and-effect relationship, but they suggest the possibility that withdrawal of freedom of choice might sometimes have lethal effects. The latter implications of the Ferrari study are discussed by Seligman (1974, 1975), who argues that if the perception and exercise of choice is important for the prolonging of life, then the elderly should be provided with some control over their daily activities. Even simple choices involving the selection of food, furnishings, and entertainment could be offered in institutions for the aged to create a genuine sense of having some degree of choice. Since in such a totally dependent environment the elderly cannot regain freedom and control, conditions should be arranged to provide meaningful substitute choices. If adverse effects of helplessness in old people are to be combated, some degree of control over their own lives through decision making must be carefully secured.

Evidence from a carefully controlled field experiment by Langer and Rodin (1976) indicates that expansion of the range of choices available to institutionalized elderly people increases their sense of perceived control over their environment and has positive effects on their mental as well as physical functioning. The investigators arranged for elderly residents in a nursing home to be given greater opportunities to make decisions about their daily activities. As compared with an equivalent control group treated in the usual way, the group of residents given increased freedom of choice was found to be more physically active, more interested in daily events, less dependent, and markedly less dissatisfied with their life situation.

Deprivation of control over one's major decisions emerges as a crucial factor in many other life situations, although none quite matches the stark impact of freedom loss observed in the nursing home. Friedman, Greenspan, and Mittelman (1974) investigated the effect of strong pressure and constricted choice in the decision of women to undergo therapeutic abortions. From a sample of 165 women in a Boston hospital who had just undergone a therapeutic abortion, they estimated that the proportion of women disturbed by the operation was less than 10 percent. However, the link between constricted decision making and postabortion psychiatric illness was striking. Among the women who experienced strong ambivalence, felt that the decision was not their own, or reported having been coerced, the incidence of postabortion illness, ranging from sexual dysfunction to psychotic disorder, was high. Women who were most settled in their decision at the time of the abortion had the smoothest postoperative course.

The investigators present four detailed case reports of postabortion psychiatric illness to illustrate the risks associated with decision making under conditions of intense pressure. A 23-year-old secretary, for example, was living with a boyfriend who was open about his preference for an abortion, although he also stated that he would marry her if she wished. This made her deeply angry, because she felt that if she chose not to have an abortion, he was asking her to shoulder all the responsibilities of the marriage and of having a baby. She strongly desired a baby at that time, but felt forced to decide in favor of an abortion. A year later she contacted the hospital social worker and reported that several months earlier she and her lover had been married but ever since the abortion she had been sexually unresponsive and unable to reach orgasm. In therapy, the patient's anger emerged slowly, first against her parents, then against her husband, as she became more aware of her passive-dependent relationship, especially in giving in to the wishes of others when she made the abortion decision. After an angry discussion with her husband, in which he surprised her by accepting her strivings for more independence, her sexual responsiveness returned. This case study and related observations reported by Friedman et al. suggest that severe restriction on the perceived opportunity to choose freely among alternatives in making a major decision may exact a heavy toll in mental health.

Similar evidence of the benefits of extending freedom of choice beyond the conventional narrow boundaries often imposed by large institutions can be found in a study by Liem (1975). Liem gave half of the students in his introductory psychology class at Rochester the opportunity to choose their recitation section for the course; the other half were assigned to sections in the usual manner by the instructor (although in all cases the section was the one they had indicated they would have preferred). Follow-up data revealed that students given a choice tended to perform better, were more satisfied, and attended more frequently.

Although the evidence from the studies just reviewed is far from conclusive, it suggests that at least among some subgroups, insidious damage can result from restrictions on freedom of choice. Perhaps the worst damage can be prevented if our society can expand the opportunities to make choices by removing some of the constraints on important life decisions affecting one's education, work, health, marriage, family, and home life, all of which are vital for maintaining self-esteem.

Coercive Pressure and Defensive Avoidance

Whenever a person finds himself under coercive pressure from an authority figure to choose an unsavory course of action, he usually resents the demand even if he reluctantly gives in. If the pressure from threats of punishment is so strong that it cannot be resisted, the person's strong reservations about carrying out the decision are likely to result in his doing only the bare minimum, without "putting his heart into it." Attribution theorists emphasize the feelings of indifference and detachment about their actions that people display when they attribute a decision to strong external pressure rather than to their own free choice (Jones et al., 1971). Apsler's (1972) field experiment on the 1970 Selective Service draft lottery showed that the subjects who were assigned by lottery to a "bad" number subsequently became more antagonistic toward U.S. policies in Indochina, although they did not differ significantly from those assigned "good" numbers in their attitude toward military service. A person who attributes his decision to outside pressure feels little responsibility for implementing it and will not spontaneously do so once the pressure is removed. But when social pressures are subtle, according to attribution theorists, a person will attribute his choice of a course of action to himself, spontaneously develop fresh arguments in support of it, and act in a way that shows he feels deeply committed to it.

According to conflict theory, the detachment reaction predicted by attribution theorists as the general consequence of apparent coercion occurs only under certain limited conditions—namely, when *vigilance* is aroused. A vigilant decision maker will carefully examine the course demanded by the coercive authorities and the alternatives that would be tantamount to rejecting their demands. Like the Marrano Jews under the coercive pressure of the Spanish Inquisition, persecuted people may publicly conform but privately maintain and even strengthen their preferred beliefs.

When the conditions fostering the bolstering form of defensive avoidance are present, however—namely, high conflict, lack of hope for finding a better alternative, and a firm deadline in the near future—the decision maker will develop rationalizations in support of the course being forced upon him. He will play up the inherent advantages by inventing new arguments in favor of the imposed course, and play down its obvious drawbacks, including the unfairness and humiliation of having the choice inflicted upon him. Consequently, he will not attribute the decision primarily to external coercive pressure but will regard the pressure as merely incidental. In brief, when defensive avoidance is the dominant coping pattern, the decision maker will display attachment to rather than detachment from the course of action forced upon him by coercive authorities.

The preceding conflict-theory analysis may help account for a number of nonobvious phenomena described in the literature on reactions to extreme coercion in highly stressful situations, such as manifestations of "identification with the aggressor." Bettelheim (1943) describes such anomolous effects among dedicated anti-Nazis who had been arrested and thrown into a Nazi concentration camp. After repeatedly witnessing brutal torture of fellow prisoners who failed to comply with the guards' orders, many of the demoralized, long-term political prisoners began to imitate the Gestapo guard's behavior, wholeheartedly accepting their values, wearing fragments of Gestapo uniforms, and emulating the guards' machismo games.

According to our analysis of defensive avoidance, if a prisoner regards an authority's immediate and drastic coercive threats as implacable, he will have no hope of finding a solution better than yielding and consequently will bolster his decision to comply. Under these conditions, our prediction is opposite to that of attribution theorists, who assume that whenever coercive pressure is explicit and salient the decision maker will generally perceive the pressure as the cause of his compliant behavior and accordingly will exhibit little internalization of the norms imposed upon him.

Insufficient evidence is at hand to test the differential predictions from conflict theory and attribution theory. On this issue one cannot expect to learn very much from social psychologists' laboratory experiments, since it is highly unethical to use strong coercive threats to force anyone to carry out consequential actions against his will. Social psychologists will have to seek data on reactions to coercion from other sources, such as well-documented historical accounts of how people have reacted when demands for specific actions were backed up by strong threats made by powerful political authorities, employers, the police, or armed criminals. Nevertheless, some findings from a few experimental studies are pertinent to specifying the conditions that foster malignant obedience.

The Illusion of No Choice

Malevolent authorities attempt to elicit unswerving obedience by creating an illusion that there is no choice but to follow orders. The problem of obedience to ruthless authority has been dramatically brought to public consciousness during the twentieth century by the genocidal actions of Nazi organizations in Germany during World War II, the gross mistreatment of millions of political prisoners in the Soviet Union before and after that war, and the atrocities in violation of Army rules and the Geneva Convention committed by American soldiers against women and children at My Lai and other villages in Vietnam during the late 1960s. Stanley Milgram's (1974) laboratory studies of obedience have shown that under certain conditions most men and women will yield to the demands and pressures of malevolent authority. When an experimenter gave instructions to administer extreme levels of shock to another person, most subjects in a highly controlled laboratory setting went along with his command. It is instructive to analyze the pressures impinging on a subject in the Milgram experiment, because they give some idea of the conditions that might induce a person to relinquish his independence of action and transfer control over his choices to an authority.

Milgram's experiments deal with the amount of electric shock a subject is willing to give to another person when ordered to administer increasingly severe punishment. The laboratory situation involves three people—the experimenter, a white-coated "square"-looking man in his mid-30s; a naive subject, who is a Yale student or an unemployed man recruited by an advertisement in a New Haven or Bridgeport newspaper; and a stooge or accomplice of the experimenter, who will become the "victim" and receive the shocks. When the subject and the stooge arrive at the Yale laboratory or at a shabby office in Bridgeport, the experimenter gives them a general talk on learning problems and states how little scientists know about the effects of punishment on memory. Subjects are then told that the experiment has to do with punishment and that one member of the pair will serve as teacher and one as learner. Subject and stooge then draw lots, but it is always rigged so that the subject becomes the "teacher" and the stooge becomes the "learner." The learner is then taken to an adjacent room and strapped into an electric chair.

The "teacher" is told that an important part of his task is to administer increasingly higher levels of shock when the learner makes errors. Once the memory test begins, the learner, according to plan, makes many errors, so that before long the subject, in his role as teacher, is required to administer very strong shocks (up to 450 volts). As soon as the shock level approaches 100 volts the learner begins to grunt and moan; this is the point at which many subjects argue vigorously with the experimenter and try to resist. The subject's protests about the treatment being given to the victim are handled by ordering him to continue giving more and more powerful shocks (e.g., "You have no other choice . . . you must go on"). If the subject refuses to obey, the procedure is terminated and the subject is debriefed.

Almost all subjects protested strongly about the victim's suffering at a very early point in the proceedings. Yet, a sizable proportion (65 percent) apparently accepted the experimenter's assertion that they had no choice but to follow orders and continued to administer shocks until the maximum of 450 volts had been reached. Milgram calls this malignant type of obedience the "Eichmann effect," using the name of the notorious Nazi who justified his role in directing the torture and murder of hundreds of thousands of Jews by saying that he was just carrying out orders.

How can one explain the failure of Milgram's obedient subjects to decide to reject the inhuman orders or quit the obnoxious job? First of all, subtle as well as patent pressures are put on the subject to make disobedience difficult. The subject is given the impression that he agreed to comply when he started the task and the experimenter now depends upon him for the success of the research enterprise. The experimenter reinforces the idea that the subject has entered into a form of social contract and that any attempt to break the commitment by way of disobedience constitutes unthinkable behavior. In effect, the subject is trapped in a sequence of commitments that escalate until it is difficult for him to find a way out. Once he has agreed to administer shocks at a low level it is difficult to extricate himself from the momentum of the experiment. In this respect the situation has some of the properties of the "foot-in-the-door technique" (discussed in the next chapter). Having agreed to come to the experiment, to take a sample shock, and to administer low levels of shock to the learner, it becomes difficult for the subject to move from acquiescence to defiance.

Second, the experimenter dehumanizes the situation and emphasises the institutional nature of the role relationship between himself, the subject, and the victim. The experimenter never addresses subject or victim by name, but says things like "Please continue, teacher" and "Whether the learner likes it or not, you must continue." One of Milgram's experiments indicates that when the subjects were given less opportunity to dehumanize the victim, they were more likely to decide not to obey an experimenter's orders. The more they could hear and see the suffering of the victim, the less likely they were to display the "Eichmann effect" (see figure 12). Evidently more direct exposure to negative feedback from the victim increases the subjects' vigilance about the potential damage they might be causing and leads them to reconsider their course of action, rather than continue to be obedient and evade the conflict by defensive avoidance.

FIGURE 12. **Amount of shock a subject inflicts on a "victim" as a function of proximity.** *(Based on Milgram, 1965.)*

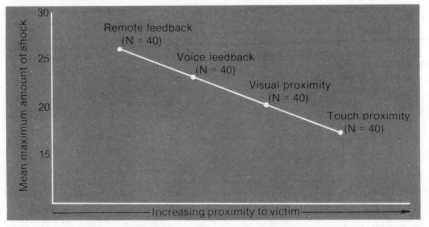

Key: Remote feedback–the victim cannot be heard or seen.
        Voice feedback–the victim's protests can be heard.
        Visual proximity–the victim is in the same room, less than two feet away.
        Touch proximity–same as visual, but the subject is required to put the victim's hand on the shock plate.

Source: I. L. Janis, *Stress and Frustration* (New York: Harcourt Brace Jovanovich, 1971), p. 162. Reprinted by permission.

Third, and most significant for the present discussion, the experimenter manages to create an illusion not only that the subject has no choice in the matter but that he is not responsible for his decisions and actions. Consider the manner in which the experimenter handles the subject's protests and objections. A statement such as "The experiment requires that you go on—please continue" invokes the mystique and authority of scientific rules and procedures. The experimenter also says, "I'm taking full responsibility—please continue," which allows the subject to rationalize that the victim's suffering is not his fault; that whatever the outcome, he will not be held accountable. Finally, the direct command "You have no other choice—you must go on" makes explicit the fact that the subject is regarded as only a cog in a machine.

It is noteworthy that in response to this last command some of the subjects seemed to stiffen in their protests, evidently as a result of reactance provoked by the experimenter's authoritarian stance. A few responded "Of course I have a choice," which seemed to strengthen their resolve to reestablish control over their actions, and they quit. Two examples of this reaction are provided by a replication of the Milgram study carried out by Kilham (1971) with a sample of Australian subjects:

> *Subject* (at 75 volts): "I think that's far enough. Ninety volts is getting a bit dangerous. Do you mind if I don't give it? I rather object to that."
> *Experimenter*: "You have no choice but . . ."
> *Subject* (interrupting him): "I certainly do." (He breaks off.)
>
> *Subject* (at 60 volts): "I can't go on."
> *Experimenter*: "You have no choice, you must."
> *Subject*: "I have *some* choice." (He too quits.)

But most subjects in these studies of obedience behave as if they truly believe that they have no choice in the matter. Only later, in the postexperimental interview, do they come to realize that they have allowed another person to usurp a responsibility that was properly their own. In terms of the conflict model, the subject typically undergoes acute decisional conflict, with no hope of finding a solution that would enable him to obey the experimenter and yet still be compassionate toward the victim—which are the conditions that lead to escaping conflict via defensive avoidance. In Milgram's experiments, the obedient subjects often appeared to display defensive avoidance in the form of giving over responsibility for their actions to the directive agent.

Governmental Power and Restrictions on Personal Freedom

Constraints on individual choice and malignant obedience in the sphere of political action, as well as in everyday life, must be seen within the context of a society, its institutions, and the degree of choice allowed its citizens. In most Western countries, for example, the citizens would be dismayed if only one party were permitted to name candidates in a national election; but in the Soviet Union, the lack of an alternative to the Communist party does not appear to disturb the majority of Russians. During the early 1970s, persistent demands from members of the Soviet Jewish community that they be allowed to leave for Israel puzzled Soviet officials, who felt citizens should not have a choice in the matter of emigration.

A paradox of our times is that in America and Western Europe threats of governmental control over individual choice seem to be on the rise at a time when various oppressed groups, such as blacks, women, adolescents, and prisoners, are demanding, and sometimes achieving, significant gains in their personal freedom. The key to the paradox is that as a society grapples with the problems of overpopulation, unemployment, pollution, crime, and violence, it also moves toward the imposition of greater control and constraint over personal conduct. Numerous highly organized groups like Zero Population Growth and Friends of the Earth have sprung up advocating such measures as strict limitation on the number of children to two per family, tough controls for protection of the environment, and rigid limits on the use of heating fuels and other natural resources.

Robert Heilbroner (1974), in a review of economic and political forces that are shaping human prospects for coming generations, has forecast the rise of "iron" governments, which will resort to severe authoritarian measures and will be "capable of rallying obedience far more effectively than would be possible in a democratic setting." This unwanted loss of individual freedom is seen to be a consequence of the problems of overpopulation, energy shortages, the threat of obliterative weapons, and other dire external challenges of potentially catastrophic proportions.

Within psychology, the debate over freedom of choice and whether it constitutes an essential condition of man's humanity or a menace to his well-being has taken on a new urgency. The publication of B. F. Skinner's *Beyond Freedom and Dignity* (1972), in which the argument was advanced that we can no longer afford freedom, that it must be replaced by control over people, both in their conduct, and their culture, raises the twin specters of Aldous Huxley's *Brave New World* and George Orwell's *1984*. Skinner wrote of a society in which conditioning principles are used to shape individuals into wanting what serves the group interest. The manipulation of men's and women's dispositions in Skinner's blueprint for a psychological utopia would require that freedom of choice take second place to group harmony and absence of intrasocietal tensions. If Heilbroner's forecasts and Skinner's proposals are taken seriously, they lead one to expect severe curtailments on everyone's freedom to choose his or her career and life style, with all such vital decisions limited to a meager set of alternatives that bureaucrats in the "iron" government decide will promote public welfare.

Few psychologists are willing to go gentle into the dying of the light, as envisaged by Heilbroner and Skinner. Erich Fromm, in *Fear of Freedom* (1941), reminds us that to choose, either correctly or incorrectly, is to assert one's basic humanity. Other psychologists, existential psychoanalysts, and theologians have taken a similar view, one that is best summed up in Reinhold Niebuhr's assertion: "The chief source of man's dignity is man's essential freedom and capacity for self-determination." But it is obvious that man's freedom, if not his capacity, can be suppressed in any nation dominated by an antidemocratic government that uses the full coercive power of the police and the military to enforce its demands.

A conflict-theory analysis can shed only a modest bit of illumination relevant to the struggle to maintain the values to which Niebhur refers in the face of increasing bureaucratic pressures that threaten to limit everyone's freedom of choice on fundamental personal, social, and political decisions. We conclude this chapter with a few prescriptive hypotheses that summarize what little can be said about resistance to malignant obedience in the light of our analysis of decisional conflicts. When is a person most likely to consider the alternatives to submitting to the demands of powerful authorities, to find some way of surmounting the restrictions placed on him, and to arrive at a satisfactory decision that enables him to avert the full brunt of punishment for disobedience without violating his fundamental standards of moral conduct? According to our theoretical analysis, it is when the conditions making for *vigilance*, rather than those making for defensive avoidance or any other nonvigilant coping pattern, are present.

Counteracting Malignant Compliance

The same factors that account for the malignant obedience observed by Milgram and other investigators in social psychological experiments probably operate in organizational settings when people are put under pressure to comply with demands to cheat, lie, engage in shady practices, or participate in coverups that violate their personal codes of ethical conduct. But we cannot be sure of this conclusion until dependable evidence is available from studies of resistance to illicit demands within large organizations. So far only a few journalistic and legal studies have been reported that describe cases of individuals in business firms and government agencies who regarded the public interest as overriding the interests of the organization they served and decided to "blow the whistle"—to inform the public or legal authorities that their organization was involved in corrupt, socially harmful, or illegal activity (Nader, Petkas, and

Blackwell, 1972; Peters and Branch, 1972; Weisbond and Franck, 1975). While there were unique features in every case, the whistle blowers seem to have had in common a strong sense of professional standards, a high level of personal self-esteem, and social support from a spouse or close friend, which enabled them to overcome both subtle pressures from their respective organizations to remain "team players" and unsubtle threats of blacklisting, social ostracism, and dismissal. These factors also appeared to be crucial ones in the case of Watergate whistle blower Hugh Sloan.

Evidence from memoirs and interviews concerning private as well as public events leading up to decisions to refuse to comply with illicit demands should ultimately be of great value for answering crucial questions in the psychology of moral courage. What social conditions promote resistance to powerful pressures to participate in illegal or unethical activity when a superior presents a "no-choice" demand in the name of allegiance to some higher authority, and backs up the demand by invoking his power to damage the resister's career? What can educators, legislators, law-enforcement authorities, and concerned citizens do to heighten the resistance of men and women in our society to illicit demands from unscrupulous persons in positions of authority? From the conflict model we can derive several testable hypotheses bearing on these questions, which have practical as well as theoretical significance.

1. The incidence of *unconflicted acceptance* of illicit demands can be decreased by making salient the risks of social and self-disapproval, as well as utilitarian losses, for compliance with such demands. Clearly defining established laws and, where necessary, adding new ones that are reliably enforced can help to eliminate ambiguous "gray areas" of behavior whose existence encourages underlings to assume that they can commit illicit acts without incurring legal or moral responsibility. The contrary assumption—that both the perpetrator of the illicit action and the superior who ordered it bear the responsibility and can get into serious trouble for breaking the law—is facilitated when the law in question is well publicized and reinforced by community norms.

Special educational programs might also increase the chances that the threats of social and self-disapproval will become salient whenever anyone contemplates complying with pressure from a boss, a commanding officer, or a government official to engage in illicit activity. At the very least, the penalties for perjury and other types of felony that white-collar workers and executives are sometimes induced to commit could be taught in such a way that those who are tempted would not make the mistake of assuming that such acts were merely unpunishable misdemeanors. Professional associations and unions with explicit ethical goals might set up special workshops using group discussions of case studies, psychodramas, and other educational devices designed to sensitize people on ethical issues. Courses and workshops might help build a sense of personal responsibility among large numbers of employees and professional men and women in all sorts of enterprises, so that the arousal of anticipatory self-disapproval would become a common reaction whenever there were strong inducements to violate ethical standards.

Internalized standards of ethical conduct, however, probably require constant social reinforcement in order to retain their power to counteract the threat of being fired or penalized, which so often accompanies an unscrupulous superior's demands to lie, cheat, or commit a crime. This is where affiliation with a professional organization or union can play a crucial role, not only in establishing norms that can serve as effective guidelines to ethical conduct but in giving the individual a reassuring conviction that he can rely upon an effective source of power to support him in a struggle against a powerful person. Of course, a professional organization or union may fail to function as a supportive reference group unless it makes provisions for aiding any member who refuses to yield to a superior's orders to carry out an unethical or illegal act. Nevertheless, merely by endorsing the appropriate ethical standards and publicizing the unfavorable consequences of unethical actions, such organizations might increase the likelihood that their members will become aware of the serious risks entailed by uncritically following orders and thereby decrease the incidence of unconflicted acceptance of illicit demands.

2. The incidence of *defensive avoidance* in the form of shifting responsibility or bolstering a decision to yield to a superior's illicit demands can be decreased by making employees aware of available resources of information and advice, so as to maintain their hope of finding a solution better than compliance. Reinforcement of codes specifying that it is an offense to obey illegitimate orders—as in the corrective programs adopted by some U.S. military units, government agencies, hospitals, and nursing homes following the bad publicity they received as a result of congressional hearings—can reduce somewhat the incidence of unconflicted compliance; but salience alone is no guarantee that a person will not end up developing new rationalizations to bolster obedience. Here is where legal aid counselors and local chapters of groups like the American Civil Liberties Union and Nader's Raiders can prove to be crucial, not just in reinforcing ethical norms, but in serving as a realistic source of hope for finding sound advice about how to handle a situation in such a way as to avoid violating ethical norms without creating immense difficulties for oneself within an organization. Perhaps a new institutionalized role for legal counselors—or a new paralegal profession of ethical counselors, protected by the same safeguards of confidentiality that apply to the attorney-client relationship—is needed. Such counselors might provide large numbers of employees in industry, small businesses, and government agencies with a realistic basis for hoping to find a satisfactory solution to ethical dilemmas that arise when they are put under pressure to participate in illegal activity or even just to keep their mouths shut to protect the illegal activities of others. The counselors would require spe-

cial skills to convey good arguments that an employee might use and persuasive ways of putting them across effectively in dealing with an unscrupulous superior. Their goal might be to build up a troubled employee's ability and motivation to induce his superior to become aware of the risks to himself and the organization posed by his illicit demand, so that he will withdraw the demand or at least tolerate noncompliance without retaliating. (If such counselors could be contacted through an emergency telephone service, their ready availability might also prove to be a deterrent to impulsive yielding while in a state of *hypervigilance*, which is likely when a superior makes threatening demands for a highly objectionable action and gives a very short deadline for compliance.)

3. The incidence of *vigilance* among employees confronted with apparent no-choice demands from their superiors can be increased by directing public attention to exemplary models of morally courageous behavior and providing information and commentaries that foster a sense of competence in coping with ethical dilemmas. Here we have in mind the role of mass communications, which might promote the vigilance pattern of coping, to supplement whatever else is being done to undermine tendencies toward unconflicted compliance, defensive avoidance, and hypervigilance. We assume that through exposure to radio and TV commentators, newspaper stories, magazine articles, movies, and a variety of special educational programs designed for a mass audience, people can develop ethical ideals and acquire concepts of themselves as capable of determining their own fate, not as mere pawns in the game plan of their superiors. There are several important messages bearing on self-assurance in the ethical sphere that could also be conveyed by dramatic documentaries presented in the mass media. One important theme involves conveying the latent power that an employee possesses to mobilize the support of others in a struggle against a boss who tries to misuse his power to push underlings into doing something morally wrong. For example, realistic dramas could carry the message that a boss can be influenced to modify or even withdraw his illegal demands if the employee, instead of pretending to agree with his rationalizations, conveys his firm conviction that legal and ethical norms should not be violated, while reminding the boss of the realistic possibility that *all* the violators will be detected and, even if not sent to jail, disgraced. A related theme that might be emphasized is that there is no such thing as a no-choice situation (except perhaps in rare instances of clear and present danger, as when coercion takes place at the point of a gun).[9] Playing up such themes in the mass media might help foster hope and vigilance, encouraging employees who encounter illicit demands to survey all the alternatives, weigh consequences carefully, and engage in constructive deliberation before commitment—all of which activities increase the prospect of finding a viable solution that minimizes the potentially damaging consequences of disobedience without compromising basic ethical values.

Perhaps the most effective way to present these concepts and themes is to familiarize people with authentic examples of men and women who have dealt effectively with strong inducements to illicit obedience, contrasting their admirable behavior with examples of persons who have succumbed. For example, by contrasting Hugh Sloan's firm ethical stance against White House pressures to commit perjury with Gordon Strachan's compliance, it should be possible to highlight some of the important lessons of Watergate. Numerous other historic examples of exemplary behavior by people who courageously acted in accord with ethical values might also be selected for this purpose.

The use of historical models, however, is not without potential risks of miseducating people to believe in oversimplified "lessons of history" that obstruct critical thinking and contribute to overconfidence that the conventional way of doing things is the only right way. Earlier we pointed out that when we describe someone as displaying vigilance we do not expect him to be confident that his preferred choice is the right one; rather, we expect him to be confident about finding a good solution. A vigilant decision maker needs the latter type of confidence precisely because, in his state of vigilance, he *lacks* confidence in any of the alternatives open to him—he is alert to their manifest defects and worried about their hidden risks.

A sound understanding of the lessons of history, in the context of a comparative study of the alternative ways in which men and women have dealt with common dilemmas, should enrich the store of potential solutions to the ethical and practical problems posed by recurrent threats of coercion, whether the decision maker is a statesman dealing with an ultimatum from an enemy or an ordinary citizen dealing with an ultimatum from an unscrupulous superior. In suggesting that Watergate and other historic examples can be used for preparing people to cope more adequately with coercive pressures, we have in mind Santayana's classic adage: "Those who cannot remember the past are condemned to repeat it." But all too often decision makers remember the past and use it in an undifferentiated, unthinking way, as in the case of U.S. policy makers who opposed negotiation with the North Koreans in the early 1950s and with the North Vietnamese in the early 1960s on the grounds that it would be equivalent to giving in to the illicit demands of Hitler and the Nazis in the fruitless attempts at appeasement made during the 1930s (De Rivera, 1968; Janis, 1972; May, 1973; Paige, 1968). In light of the frequent misuses of history, Santayana's formulation requires at least this addendum: Those who can remember only the last war are condemned to be always fighting it.

CHAPTER 11

Effects of Commitment

THE CONCEPT OF COMMITMENT is central to most psychological formulations of the decision-making process. Conflict theorists have linked decisions to actions to which someone is socially committed (Lewin, 1951; Janis, 1959). Consistency theorists, too, have emphasized the essential role of commitment in attitudinal and decisional dynamics (Brehm and Cohen, 1962; Festinger, 1964; Gerard, 1968; Kiesler, 1971; Wilhelmy, 1974). Commitment enters into decisional dynamics before as well as after the making of a choice. The quality of thought processes brought to bear on a problem during the early predecisional stages is markedly influenced by cues that warn the person that he will be bound to his decision. In addition, postdecisional stability is predicated upon commitment insofar as the person makes a "contract," or takes on an obligation in the eyes of other people in his social network, to carry out a chosen course of action.

In this chapter we first analyze factors that anchor a person to his decision—that impel him to maintain a course of action in the face of adverse feedback and criticism. After that we examine some of the commitment-inducing techniques used by social influence agents to trap the unwary decision maker into adopting a course of action against his better judgment. Then we describe some recent studies of the effects of commitment warnings on the arousal of vigilance. The chapter ends with a brief discussion of the development of vigilant decision making in childhood, calling attention to formative experiences that contribute to a person's awareness of the significance of commitment.

Commitment as a Source of Constraint

One of the propositions presented in chapter 3 concerning the functional relationship between decisional conflict and psychological stress

279

dealt with commitment as an antecedent source of stress. The proposition asserts that decisional stress depends partly upon the extent to which the decision maker feels committed to adhere to a course of action at a time when he is exposed to warnings or actual setbacks that motivate him to change. The more committed the decision maker is to the policy under challenge, the greater the degree of stress generated whenever he is tempted to change. The decision maker knows that failure to adhere to a commitment may lead to severe penalties, adverse social criticism, and loss of self-esteem. Anticipations of these various types of loss stemming from commitment constitute major sources of threat, which operate as deterrents to adopting a new policy.[1] We cited as an example of the binding quality of a commitment President Johnson's increased reluctance to reverse his war policy and withdraw U.S. troops from East Asia once he had publicly announced his determination to prevent a Communist victory in Vietnam.

The various types of constraint that function to anchor the person to his decision can be conceptualized as incentives that become new entries in the decisional balance sheet resulting from a social act of commitment (informing one or more other persons of the decision). These entries increase the net incentive value of sticking with the chosen alternative even when new information makes the decision maker reluctant to implement his original decision.

Whenever a decision is solidified in a formal legal contract, the cost of reversal is built in as an additional incentive to stick to the decision. In general, the more binding a formal contract and the more drastic the prescribed penalties for breaching it, the stronger the incentive to avoid reversal. Threats of utilitarian losses resulting from lawsuits are mutually understood when there is an implicit contract, such as a verbal agreement to invest a large sum of money in a new enterprise, or to accept a job offer. Failure to honor any such informal contract can also lead to a tarnished reputation, which adds a threat of social disapproval to the threat of utilitarian losses.

Informal Social Constraints

Among the most pervasive constraints on reversing a decision are the real or potential social pressures that are operative whenever other people in the decision maker's personal network know about his decision. Following a public commitment, the decision maker realizes that others are affected by his decision and expect him to hold to it. The stigma of being known as erratic and unstable is in itself a powerful negative incentive that inhibits even discussing with others the possibility of reversing a decision. In general, the greater the number of those in the decision maker's social network who are aware of a decision, the more powerful the incentive to avoid the social disapproval that might result from reversal.

A political example of how even experienced decision makers can be constrained by social pressures from reversing a decision is reported in Arthur M. Schlesinger Jr.'s account of the Kennedy years, *A Thousand Days*. In the 1960 election, John Kennedy was faced with the difficult problem of chosing a running mate for the vice-presidential nomination. On the one hand, Kennedy was convinced that he needed a midwestern liberal to back his strong civil rights plank and to win the support of liberal and labor leaders. On the other hand, he wanted a man who would help the ticket in the South—and Lyndon Johnson, a Texan who was acceptable to the older generation of party professionals, was suggested as a possible choice.

With only twenty-four hours in which to make up his mind, Kennedy decided to make the first offer to Johnson, confident that Johnson, who was majority leader of the Senate at the time, would not accept the oblivion of the vice-presidency. To Kennedy's astonishment and dismay, Johnson showed great interest in taking the second spot on the ticket. Later on, Kennedy was to say: "I didn't offer the Vice-Presidency to him, I just held it out like this"—holding his hand close to his body—"and he grabbed at it" (Schlesinger, 1965, p. 48). Kennedy, who had made the offer as a gesture intended to appease the older politicians, was now faced with the problem of whether or not to back out. Robert Kennedy was sent to the Johnson suite to test the atmosphere, and if possible to try to cool Johnson's expectations. If Johnson showed any hesitation, the gathering opposition from liberals within the party would be used as an excuse for getting him to "withdraw." By this time, however, Johnson and his principal supporters viewed the offer as a firm commitment. Kennedy, no doubt afraid of earning the enmity of Johnson and his supporters if he backed out at that late stage, decided to go through with the offer.

In an entirely different realm of decision making, Epstein (1962) has observed that some parachutists go through with a parachute jump even though, as the time for the jump gets closer, the desire to avoid the jump may be greater than the motivation that originally entered into making the decision to jump. Epstein postulates that once in the aircraft, the parachutist jumps on the basis of the psychological momentum provided by the difficulty of reversing the decision, particularly as a result of the social commitment, which, if broken, would lead to a loss of face. In effect, the informal social commitment is a powerful new incentive in the decision maker's balance sheet that induces him to stick with his original decision.

Research on social influence illustrates the importance of public or social commitment in either increasing resistance to influence attempts or anchoring the person to a new policy once he is persuaded to engage in it (see Jones and Gerard, 1967; Kiesler, 1971). Hovland, Campbell, and Brock (1957) found that public commitment to a preference makes change to another position difficult. The activity of role playing (e.g., giving a talk in favor of an assigned position) when it occurs in the presence of witnesses, or when a videotape recording is made that will be publicized, may also motivate adherence to the role-played position, functioning somewhat like the public announcement of a decision (Cooper and Worchel, 1970; Collins and Hoyt, 1972; Janis, 1968a).

An impressive field experiment in the Lewinian tradition of action research was conducted by Pallak and Cummings (1975), who tested the effect of public commitment on adherence to a decision to conserve energy. The investigators worked with sixty-five homeowners in the Iowa City area during October–November 1973 (prior to the oil embargo). With the cooperation of the Iowa-Illinois Gas and Electric Company, the homeowners' natural gas meters were read one day before they were contacted by the investigators for an interview. During the interview the homeowners were given information from federal and private sources, heard about a variety of energy conservation strategies, and were told that the investigators were interested in assessing the degree to which personal energy usage could be reduced by individual efforts. Finally, the interviewer explained that the results of the study would be communicated to the public at the conclusion of the research by means of newspaper articles and other media. In the *public commitment* condition, the interviewer explained that the investigators wanted to list the names of homeowners who had agreed to attempt energy conservation. In the *private commitment* condition, the interviewer explicitly stated that participants in the study would not be personally identified. All participants then signed a consent form indicating their agreement to participate, with the explicit provision that they either would be personally identified (public commitment) or would not be personally identified (private commitment). For the *control* condition, homeowners were selected from the same residential area as those in the commitment conditions, but received no interview. At the end of one month, meter readings for natural gas consumption in each home were again taken for everyone in all three groups.

Pallak and Cummings found that while all the homeowners increased their natural gas consumption as a function of seasonal conditions, the increase for those in the public commitment condition was significantly lower than for those in either the private commitment or the control conditions. Specifically, homeowners in the public commitment condition used a total of 422 cubic feet of natural gas less than homeowners in the other conditions during the period under study. In a second experiment conducted as part of the same research project, public commitment produced similar effects during the summer of 1974 with respect to the consumption of electricity for air conditioning.

Commitment plays an important part in generating conformity to social norms in face-to-face situations. Gerard (1965) reexamined data from a study by Deutsch and Gerard (1955) to show that once a subject had yielded or refused to yield to the group consensus in the early trials in an Asch type of group conformity situation, he nearly always continued in the same vein on later trials. This consistency phenomenon was more pronounced when the subject's responses were made in public than when they were made in private. We expect the same outcome when consequential decisions are made by executive committees (see Janis, 1972).

Personal Constraints

A heavy investment of time and energy often leads people to overrate a plan of action. After arriving at a decision that has required a great deal of cognitive work and emotional investment, a person is reluctant to admit to himself that his "baby" is defective, that all his hard work was futile and should be discarded. Furthermore, the weary policy maker fresh from the conference table, like a combat veteran returned from the front, is in no mood to rethink decisions and allow "settled" conflicts to be reactivated. It is not just a matter of intellectual laziness, or of resistance to the idea of working again on the same problem, or of being bored by overfamiliar arguments. All of these factors may enter in; but an entirely different source of cognitive inertia arises after one announces his decision to others—namely, the threat of self-disapproval for violating one's self-image as an effective, reliable person who can be decisive and who can keep his word. Self-esteem is likely to become deeply implicated once a person says to others, "I have made my decision, and that is that; I don't intend to think about it any more." To avoid perceiving himself as weak-minded, vacillating, ineffectual, and undependable, the person turns his back on pressures to reconsider his decision and sticks firmly with his chosen alternative, even after he has started to suspect that it is a defective choice.

A related factor contributing to cognitive inertia is the change in one's self-image as a transformed person, which is sometimes a by-product of going through a difficult decision, especially if it required wrestling with one's conscience. Daniel Ellsberg, for example, after agonizing about the moral dilemma of whether or not to make public the classified "Pentagon Papers," repudiated his own former professional work in support of the Vietnam War. His decision appears to have altered his moral values and ego ideals as well as his political position (Ellsberg, 1972). When such changes occur, the person becomes all the more reluctant to reconsider adopting any of the policies he has recently renounced, because he would despise himself for reverting to his old, "unenlightened" or "immoral" ways.

Personal constraints arising from threats of violating one's self-image—whether as a defender of the old faith or as an ardent convert to the new—constitute a powerful source of dedication to completing a course of action. People sometimes make use of these constraints to counteract their personal weaknesses in carrying out a difficult course of action—such as giving up alcohol, drugs, cigarettes, or rich foods. The overeater who wants to go on a diet but does not trust himself "announces his intention or accepts a wager that he will not break his diet, so that later he will *not* be free to change his mind" (Luce and Raiffa, 1957, p. 75). Schelling (1960) describes this maneuver as making a *side bet* that "worsens" the person's payoff in case he fails to fulfill the commitment. Self-help manuals often recognize this tactic and its power for strengthening the person's resolve. One such manual offers the following advice to prospective nonsmokers: "Tell your friends you have given up smoking. Then, at some point when you are seriously tempted to smoke, the thought of all the derisive laughter you'll get for giving in may well carry you over the crisis" (Brean, 1951). The image of oneself undergoing humiliation probably helps to prevent backsliding because it poses the threat of self-disapproval as well as social disapproval.

Evidence from a field experiment by McFall and Hammen (1971) indicates that commitment followed by reminders and self-monitoring is sufficient to enable a sizable percentage of heavy smokers to carry out their wish to give up smoking. The investigators randomly assigned smokers who came to an antismoking clinic to various therapeutic treatments, which they compared with a simple commitment treatment. The latter consisted of asking each volunteer to deposit twenty-five dollars (to be returned at the end of the treatment), to agree to make an effort to cut way down on his smoking, and to keep a daily record of his smoking behavior. The commitment was made salient not only by the self-monitoring record but also by standard comments made by the interviewer at each contact, which reminded the person that he would have to keep striving in order to succeed in carrying out his intention. The commitment treatment combined with reminders and self-monitoring proved to be as effective as the more elaborate treatments involving special therapeutic procedures.

Degrees of Commitment

Obviously, commitment is not an all-or-nothing affair. We conceptualize the degree of commitment as a function of all the social and self-esteem constraints we have just discussed, each of which contributes to the net increase in the motivation to adhere to the decision because of new incentives added to the decisional balance sheet as a result of announcing the decision. The higher the degree of commitment, the greater the anticipated costs of reversal, and the greater the decision maker's resistance to any challenging event or communication that is capable of making him momentarily regret the decision.

The new incentives added to the balance sheet following each act of commitment are likely to have a profound effect upon the decision maker's coping pattern. When the degree of commitment is such that the decision maker regards it as binding, he perceives the penalties and costs of reversal as too great to bear. At this point, he relinquishes all hope of finding a better solution to the decisional problem than the one to which he has just committed himself. Consequently, although the pattern of vigilance may have been dominant predecisionally, the act of commitment motivates the decision maker to adopt the coping pattern of defensive avoidance. Thereafter, the decision maker's readiness to bolster his decision depends partly upon the salience of the various commitment incentives that have become new entries in his decisional balance sheet.

In terms of the microprocesses represented in the combined model of stages and coping patterns (figure 8), what happens when the decision maker encounters negative feedback that might make him regret his earlier decision? We can specify five different ways in which a high degree of commitment operates as a deterrent to changing to a new course of action.

1. The *higher* the degree of commitment, the *lower* the probability that the challenged decision maker will lightly dismiss the risks associated with changing to another alternative. Here we refer to question 2–2 in figure 8 ("Are the risks serious if I change?"), which determines whether or not unconflicted change will occur. Thus, no matter how attractive an opportunity to adopt a new course of action might be, a highly committed person is likely to be aware of the utilitarian, social, and personal losses that will ensue if he breaks his commitments and therefore will become highly conflicted. At the very least, this prevents him from switching immediately without reconsidering the advantages of sticking with his prior choice.

2. The *higher* the degree of commitment to a prior choice, the *higher* the probability that when alternatives are being considered during stage 2, ~~surveyed alternative~~ the challenged decision maker will be pessimistic about finding a course of action better than the current one. Here we refer to question 2–3 ("Is it realistic to hope to find a better solution?"), which determines whether or not defensive avoidance will be the dominant coping pattern. Once a decision maker becomes strongly committed to his chosen course of action, he will tend thereafter to persist in bolstering that course as he encounters various forms of negative feedback that might challenge the decision.

3. The *higher* the degree of commitment, the *lower* the probability that any alternative to the original course of action will be selected in stage 3 if the challenged decision maker gets to the point of weighing alternatives. Here we refer to question 3–1 ("Which alternative is best?"). The various incentives for sticking with the original course of action that have been added to the decisional balance sheet as a result of his acts of commitment are likely to become salient at the time when he is weighing the alternatives, which will incline him to reject all options to change to a different course of action.

4. The *higher* the degree of commitment, the *higher* the probability

that if a different course of action is temporarily selected as the best one, it will nevertheless be rejected as inadequate at the verge of commitment, when the decision maker poses to himself the final key questions before making his choice (question 3–2: "Could the best alternative meet the essential requirements?"; question 4–1: "Shall I adopt the best alternative and allow others to know?") If the decision maker is strongly committed to his current course of action, he is likely to recall additional commitment incentives as he worries over these questions, prompting him to revert to the original course.

These four types of deterrent can be thought of as hurdles imposed by high commitment that prevent a person from changing in response to challenges that evoke regret: the stronger the threat of loss resulting from breaking the commitment, the more difficult it is to get over all four hurdles, which is necessary in order to arrive at the choice of a new course of action. As with any other type of threat, the strength of each commitment threat depends upon the expected probability that the danger will materialize (if the commitment is broken) and the expected magnitude of the punishment or loss if it does materialize. By definition, a high degree of commitment means that the net incentive value of the various commitment threats is high, which motivates the decision maker to stay with his original decision at each of the four critical junctions during the successive stages of decision making when he might be tempted to move toward adopting a different course of action.

Prior to encountering the four hurdles just described, there is an initial hurdle that operates at the point of challenge to the current policy: the *higher* the degree of commitment, the *less* the likelihood that any given setback or loss entailed by the decision will constitute an effective *challenge*. High commitment makes for an initially high threshold of regret, which is manifested as a tendency to dismiss attacks on the current policy as relatively trivial and unimportant. Each potentially challenging event or communication is evaluated not just in terms of the threats that it makes salient but also on a comparative basis with other known threats pertaining to the same sphere of action. Consequently, when commitment obligations constitute the most pressing consideration, any new threat posed by a setback is likely to be judged as relatively unimportant (compared with what will happen if one tries to avert that new threat by changing) and therefore generates relatively little concern.

The net effect of all five hurdles resulting from high commitment is to decrease the chances that a person will change to a new course of action even if he experiences adverse consequences that give strong reasons for doing so. It is in this sense that a decision is "frozen," to use Kurt Lewin's (1951) term, by social commitments to one's network of family, friends, work groups, and acquaintances in the community, whether or not it is solidified in a legal contract. Even if he is so bitterly disappointed that he wants to undo his decision as soon as possible, the decision maker will continue to answer the key questions in figure 8 in a way that promotes adherence to the regretted decision when he is strongly motivated to avoid suffering the penalties and costs of failing to live up to his commitment.

Commitment Traps for the Unwary

One of our conflict-theory assumptions is that during all stages of decision making preceding the first act of commitment, the more committing and consequential the decision is expected to be, the more vigilant the decision maker will become in trying to make a choice (see chapter 7). An important aspect of vigilance is the capacity to look ahead, to foresee what additional requirements and involvements are entailed in the "fine print" of the decisional contract. Occasionally even the most vigilant decision maker becomes trapped in a network of decisional obligations never imagined, let alone contemplated, when the commitment was made. Less cautious people are much more vulnerable to such commitment "traps." In this section we review some of the ways in which a person may slip unwittingly into a decision, as well as some of the techniques used by manipulative agents to ensnare the gullible into making decisions. These techniques are built upon one or another of the constraints resulting from an act of commitment discussed earlier in the chapter.

Some commitment traps are attributable mainly to sheer carelessness on the part of the decision maker, while others result from clever manipulative efforts by agents who deliberately escalate their demands once the person has made a seemingly innocuous commitment. There is also a third category of commitment trap, typified by the hidden "package deal," that combines both types. Our key assumption is that patterns of nonvigilant decision making—especially unconflicted change and defensive avoidance—are more likely to lead to commitment entrapment than the pattern of vigilance.

Psychologists often talk about commitment as though it were always a standard admission price that everyone knowingly pays each time he starts to carry out a new decision. But commitments sometimes come about involuntarily and in piecemeal fashion, eventually trapping the nonvigilant decision maker into a binding decision against his own better judgment. One typical way in which people find themselves stuck with unwanted decisions is through a gradual, stepwise increase in commitment such that the final action, which would have been rejected if faced head-on, becomes a matter of "Now it's too late to get out of it." A number of well-known social influence techniques have been described that induce a person or group to move through a series of easy steps involving committing actions that culminate in the adoption of a previously resisted decision. Two such techniques, known as the "foot-in-the-door ploy" and "programmed sequences," are used by influence agents to trap unwary people into adopting courses of action that they had previously regarded as undesirable and might even have fiercely resisted at the outset. Before examining these manipulative techniques, however, it will be instructive to consider commitment traps that are self-generated and not deliberately set by manipulative agents.

Slippage and Adaptation

Commitment entrapment is occasionally self-generated, in that the individual imperceptibly slips from one action to another, with subtle changes in self-perception mediating further acts. There need be no deliberate social influence or pressure, although social forces reinforce the escalation of commitments.

Sometimes entrapment (or *slippage*) involves a series of reprehensible acts, terminating in a crime that a person would ordinarily refuse to commit. An extreme example of the potentially antisocial consequences of a stepwise commitment sequence can be found in the pattern of violence among the American soldiers who participated in the massacre at My Lai on March 16, 1968 (Hersh, 1970). After three weeks in the field on futile search-and-destroy missions, the soldiers of Charlie Company were tired, confused, and frustrated. At first, to relieve their frustrations, the soldiers would indulge in vandalizing a village. Then they began to beat up and terrorize Vietcong prisoners and civilian sympathizers. Later, some of them assaulted innocent women and old people. Finally, having fallen into a pattern of violence without any apparent censure from leaders, some of the men who had at first been reluctant to engage in minor acts of violence found themselves under group pressure to "share the guilt" and ended up participating in the atrocities at My Lai. In the eyes of one of the men, My Lai 4 was the culminating step of an escalating sequence that had begun months earlier:

> It was like going from one step to another, worse one. First you'd stop the people, question them, and let them go. Second you'd stop the people, beat up an old man, and let them go. Third, you'd stop the people, beat up an old man, and then shoot him. Fourth, you go in and wipe out a village [Hersh, 1970 p. 43].

The process of *emotional adaptation*, which includes the overcoming of anxiety and guilt about engaging in immoral acts, often accompanies the step-by-step escalation of illegal violence or other crimes. The process of commitment contributes to the escalation insofar as the participants count on each other to cover up their former violations, to share the guilt by agreeing upon rationalizations that justify what they have done, and to continue to be full participants in similar or worse acts each time opportune circumstances arise. In such cases the resulting slippage is partially attributable to social support, in that the first, minor violation is defined by the group as not very serious, setting the stage for the sanction of further such actions.

A stepwise slippage seems to have characterized the sequence of illegal actions by some of the government bureaucrats who became involved in the "White House horrors" and the Watergate coverup. Egil Krogh, for example, first agreed to head up a covert espionage operation, which was not authorized by law, for the White House. Then he gave his approval to at least one illegal break-in (at Daniel Ellsberg's psychiatrist's office), to be carried out by others in his unit. Finally, he was personally under pressure, to which he yielded and for which he ultimately was imprisoned, to cover up the illegal activities by committing perjury at the grand jury inquiry.

A similar self- and group-generated slippage has been observed in presidential decisions that have had vital consequences for entire nations. The policy decisions of the American government escalating the Vietnam War were evidently based on a piecemeal, step-by-step progression of successive commitments. In his book on the Johnson administration and its Vietnam involvement in 1965, Phillip Geyelin quotes "one of the very few high officials who opposed it at almost every step" as follows:

> It was almost imperceptible, the way we got in. There was no one move that you could call decisive or irreversible, not even very many actions that you could argue against in isolation. Yet when you put it all together, there we were in a war on the Asian mainland, with nobody really putting up much of a squawk while we were doing it [Geyelin, 1966, pp. 213–14].

A psychological counterpart to the stepwise escalation sequence is a deescalation technique used by astute arbitrators to produce a satisfactory compromise, namely *fractionating* a larger problem into a set of smaller, minimally acceptable decisions that all parties will find tolerable. Fisher (1969) refers to this approach as the "salami tactic"—cutting up a big issue into smaller slices and chewing on one thin slice after another, concentrating on only one small decision at a time. Henry Kissinger's success as a peace negotiator during the early 1970s was built to a great extent on his ability to divide a large, seemingly insurmountable problem into a set of manageable small issues, subcommitments which would, it was hoped, eventually lead to an overall, "package deal" settlement. "Salami tactics" may have the advantage of preventing the representatives of the contending parties from feeling hopeless about arriving at a solution better than the initial plans proposed by their own groups, which are unacceptable to the other negotiators. The fractionating technique may thus reduce the likelihood that any of the negotiators will bolster an unviable partisan stance or display closed-minded rejection of all compromise proposals. It is easy for a negotiator to justify his intransigence when he is offered a total package of unsliced salami that contains numerous objectionable ingredients; when one slice at a time is served, each discrete proposal is more likely to be dealt with on its merits rather than disputed by bolstering the original belligerent stance with jingoistic slogans and facile rationalizations. Insofar as piecemeal commitment to each circumscribed compromise proposal makes it easier to accept the next specific proposal leading to an overall compromise solution, salami tactics can be viewed as special forms of slippage and adaptation.

The Hidden Package Deal

By a "package deal" is meant a series of small commitments that are difficult to refuse once the first voluntary commitment has been made. It is "hidden" in the sense that if the person were aware of what was at stake and of what was expected of him eventually, he would be inhibited from taking the first, seemingly easy step. A person may readily agree, for example, to donate a little money or to sign a petition to support a good community cause. He may unexpectedly discover afterward that other people who are working for that cause expect him not only to do the same kind of thing again but to do much more, and will be disappointed if he fails to do so. As a result, he begins to anticipate loss of prestige and other socially embarrassing repercussions, such as being labeled "hypocrite," if he fails to take what the others regard as the obvious next steps. Once caught in such a commitment net, a person may strive to preserve his self-esteem as well as his reputation by rationalizing that he knew all along where his first steps were leading and that he now realizes he wants to buy the entire "package."

To secure converts to the revivalist movement, Billy Graham and other evangelist leaders have developed a "package" for committing potential converts (Lang and Lang, 1961). At a revival meeting, the evangelist talks glowingly about redemption and salvation, making a direct appeal to anyone who has long been suffering from depressive feelings of self-disgust or from a sense of being a hopeless sinner. Then, in the midst of visible signs of aroused religious fervor in the mass audience, the evangelist asks for those who are ready to "make an inquiry" or to "bear witness" to stand up and come forward to the platform. Standing on a platform with other witnesses in front of a crowd of thousands of people, the potential convert finds himself, in effect, making a public announcement that he is ready to participate in the religious movement, usually without realizing what will be expected of him.

The next step in the commitment sequence is to ask the convert to sign a pledge card and to promise to meet with representatives of the crusade or attend subsequent religious services. The pledge card involves signing one's name as a witness for Christ, and the format of the card indicates that a vital step has been taken to join the crusade and to abide by its values and goals. In this way the initial decision to come forward to the platform in response to the evangelist's appeal is consolidated.

Anticipating social disapproval from new-found friends and the arousal of powerful guilt feelings for failing to live up to a solemn pledge made to God and his devoted worshipers, the convert is likely to turn up for scheduled meetings with leaders of the religious group. Next, and perhaps of crucial importance, social support is given to the new convert in order to prevent backsliding and to reinforce commitment. Sometimes a mentor or instructor will guide him through the early stages of his religious indoctrination. Occasionally a buddy system is used to make the convert responsible to someone else, and to provide moral support should he begin to waver. It also serves as a constant reminder to both participants of their commitment to the religious group. Usually the commitment process continues by requiring each convert to participate actively in meetings at which he is expected to give personal testimony about his transformation. Such testimonials provide social and informational support for other converts, while strengthening the testifier's commitment to the group.

Often a religious convert becomes involved in the social life of the group in ways that extend far beyond formal meetings. In some religious organizations the requirements for commitment may take an extreme form, with the convert expected to move into living quarters occupied by the group. Father Divine's movement in Harlem and the Black Muslim movement in Chicago required this all-encompassing act of commitment from their members, as did some of the quasi-religious sects that started communes during the 1960s and 1970s. Some extremist political groups parallel to a remarkable degree the religious revivalists in using the technique of stepwise commitment to bind recruits to the movement.

When the package deal is hidden, an essential feature is that the recruit remains unaware of the additional expected requirements at the time he takes his first commitment step. After the initial step is taken, however, the recruit realizes that further steps are expected and it becomes difficult to resist the increased expectations and pressures.

The Foot-in-the-Door Ploy

"Give them an inch, and they'll take a mile" is an old maxim that warns of the tendency of people to take advantage of others who perform a small favor. Our interest in this human foible lies in the converse phenomenon: having given an inch, the donor seems more willing to yield much more ground. The use of a small request to build up pressure to get a person to accede to a large request, known as the foot-in-the-door ploy, is one of the well-known techniques used by manipulative agents to gain the first inch in order to trap the unwary. It involves an escalating commitment sequence that has much in common with the hidden package deal, though it may involve somewhat different psychological processes. The technique, widely practiced by encyclopedia salesmen, relies on the assumption that once the target customer has been induced to comply with a small request (to open the door and let the salesman display his samples), he is "primed" to comply with a larger one. In those social circles wherein a woman is expected to be insulted by a frank invitation to engage in sexual intercourse, a similar, hand-on-the-thigh technique is also widely practiced.

Four plausible explanations, each relating to the commitment constraints described earlier, have been suggested to account for the effectiveness of the foot-in-the-door technique. The *matter of principle* interpretation, based on social and self-approval considerations, invokes the simple idea that once a person agrees to start doing something, he finds it more difficult to offer a satisfactory excuse to himself and others for not continuing to do much the same thing. Because of the precedent he has himself set, he is in no position to appeal to "principles" as an excuse for demurring. Next, there is *engagement with the requester*, an important type of social consideration. Once a person has agreed to a first request, he may believe he has led the other person to expect he will go along with a second request. He is reluctant to disappoint the requester, which might justifiably evoke disapproval, and so feels obligated. The third explanation invokes *issue involvement:* having taken some action, no matter how minor, in connection with an issue, the person becomes more concerned with the problem. He begins to think about it and to consider its personal relevance (invoking a variety of plausible considerations); accordingly, he is more likely to decide to take further action in the same direction if requested. The fourth explanation involves the *change produced in the person's self-image* from "complacent citizen" to "man of action" (another type of self-approval consideration). Freedman and Fraser (1966, p. 201) suggest that there is "a change in the person's feelings about getting involved in action. Once he has agreed to a request, . . . he may become, in his own eyes, the kind of person who does this sort of thing, who agrees to requests made by strangers, who takes action on things he believes in, who cooperates with good causes." The person begins to think of himself as a "doer," and is therefore more prepared to make positive decisions in order to maintain self-approval. If he sees himself as more decisive following an initial decision, he may live up to his new self-image by acting more decisively in response to a new request.

An experiment by Freedman and Fraser (1966) illustrates the foot-in-the-door ploy and provides a test of rival interpretations. The basic procedure in their study was to induce subjects to comply with a small request and then, two weeks later, to present them with a larger demand. The first request was varied across four experimental conditions. California housewives either were asked to put a small sign in their windows (urging people to be safe drivers or to keep California beautiful); or they were asked to sign a petition on behalf of one or the other of these same two causes.

In the second part of the experiment, conducted two weeks later, all the subjects were approached by a different person, who requested permission to install a large sign on their front lawns. The subject was shown a photograph of a very large, poorly lettered sign reading "Drive Carefully," erected in front of an attractive house. The picture was taken so that the sign obscured much of the front of the house and completely concealed the doorway. (The control group was exposed to just one contact—the final, "large" request.)

Freedman and Fraser's findings are shown in table 9. Only 17 percent of the householders in the control condition (with no previous contact) agreed to put up the large sign. But in all four experimental conditions, where the large request had been preceded by a smaller one, a much more substantial percentage of householders acquiesced. When both the task and the issue were similar from the first to the second request, 76 percent of the subjects were prepared to accede. Even when the two requests were dissimilar, almost 50 percent were persuaded to go along. The experimenters allowed their study to terminate at that point; no one from the research team appeared the next day bearing a huge sign and a shovel, so we do not know whether at the "moment of truth"—the implementation

TABLE 9.   **Percentage of subjects agreeing to a large request following a small request.**

Condition		Compliance with the First Request*		Compliance with the Second Request**
I	Similar task Similar issue	Put up a small sign: BE A SAFE DRIVER	79%	76%
II	Similar task Different issue	Put up a small sign: KEEP CALIFORNIA BEAUTIFUL	74%	48%
III	Different task Similar issue	Sign a petition: BE A SAFE DRIVER	96%	48%
IV	Different task Different issue	Sign a petition: KEEP CALIFORNIA BEAUTIFUL	74%	47%
V	Control	No request		17%

* None of the differences between groups on the percentage complying to the *initial* request is statistically significant. Groups initially varied in size from $N = 23$ to $N = 28$. For the second request, groups varied in size from $N = 19$ to $N = 25$.
** The second request was to put up a large sign on the front lawn: "Drive Carefully."

Source: J. L. Freedman and S. C. Fraser, "Compliance without Pressure: The Foot-in-the-Door Technique," *Journal of Personality and Social Psychology*, 1966, 4, 201. Copyright 1966 by the American Psychological Association. Reprinted by permission.

stage—behavioral acquiescence would have dropped sharply. Clearly, however, the results indicate that the probability of a person's making a consequential verbal commitment was increased when he or she had previously been induced to make a minor one.

Freedman and Fraser argue convincingly that change in self-image is the most persuasive explanation for their experimental findings. The remaining three explanations—commitment to a principle, engagement with the requester, and issue involvement—appear less plausible because the percentage of subjects who acquiesced remained high despite variations in task and issue, and despite the fact that two different persons made the first and second requests.[2]

One implication of the self-image explanation is that if subsequent compliance is increased by inducing initial agreement, then it should be *decreased* by inducing noncompliance to the first request. That is, a person who refuses to comply with an initial request will perceive himself as a noncomplier or as someone who does not always perform socially desirable acts and will continue to act accordingly. A test of this subsidiary hypothesis was conducted by Snyder and Cunningham (1975). Subjects were asked to comply first either with a large request, having a low probability of eliciting compliance, or with a small request, having a high probability of eliciting compliance. In line with Freedman and Fraser's findings and with the self-image explanation, subjects who received the small initial request were more likely to agree to a moderate second request than were control subjects who received only the moderate request; while subjects who received the large initial request were *less* likely to comply with the subsequent moderate request than were control subjects. (This latter phenomenon has now been dubbed the "door-in-the-face effect.") As expected, *successful* induction of the initial act of compliance proved to be a necessary condition for producing increased compliance in response to the second request.

The foot-in-the-door technique may be operating in unexpected places—for example, among people who agree to act altruistically after a great deal of hesitation. Schwartz (1970), in an investigation of the psychological correlates of altruistic behavior, reports that 59 percent of a sample of 144 Wisconsin blood donors agreed to put themselves on call as bone marrow donors when so asked by a medical sociologist. The high proportion of people who decided to join the bone marrow pool is surprising, since the decision is an agonizing one, made with great difficulty. Most subjects are concerned about the substantial costs entailed in being a donor (spending a day in the hospital, having marrow drawn under general anesthesia, experiencing discomfort and soreness in the hipbones for several days after the operation, and other drawbacks). Volunteers often debated with themselves for ten or fifteen minutes while the interviewer waited for their decision, and in the weeks that followed many anxiously sought social support and encouragement for what they had done.

A clue to the high rate of agreement may be found in what Schwartz has termed the "momentum of compliance," which leads people to volunteer despite their motivation to refuse. Schwartz points out that even before the potential donors interacted with the interviewer they had started to assume a compliant frame of mind. First of all, before entering the study, they had, of course, agreed to donate blood to the Red Cross. Next, on the request of the interviewer they had agreed to leave their seats in the Red Cross center to go over to his table to talk with him. In the study itself, the interviewer deliberately made three sequential requests designed to test the person's commitment to serve as a bone marrow donor:

1. He asked the subject to agree to have a sample of his blood tested, without making a commitment to donate marrow (95 percent agreed).
2. Next he asked the subject to indicate that there was at least a 50–50 chance that he would donate marrow if his blood turned out to be compatible (83 percent agreed).
3. Finally, he asked the subject to join the general donor pool, to be on call for future bone marrow transplants (it was at this point that 59 percent agreed).

Unfortunately for our purposes, this field study did not include a control group that was given only the third request, so we do not know if Schwartz is correct in surmising that the percentage who conformed was higher as a result of the two easier requests being made first. If Schwartz is correct, the progression of compliance he observed in the Red Cross setting represents another unintended example of the foot-in-the-door ploy. This type of progression may also operate in many experiments in which laboratory subjects are "primed" to go along with the seemingly innocuous requests of an experimenter but then find themselves agreeing to shock a victim or complying with other objectionable requests that they might otherwise have refused (see Milgram, 1974; Orne, 1962).

Commitment, then, in its various forms, is an integral component of several major social influence techniques. The hidden package deal and the foot-in-the-door ploy have an important psychological feature in common—the target person takes one small step which primes him for a larger one. In one technique, the package deal, it is a set of social considerations, such as failure to live up to the expectations of others, that forms the basis of the effect. In the foot-in-the-door ploy, various considerations relating to self-image seem to be the most probable basis for the effect. Both of these stepwise techniques represent commitment "traps" for unwary decision makers. In the hands of unscrupulous influence agents, they can be misused to restrict the effective range of choice (see chapter 10), and to elicit startlingly antisocial decisions whose consequences are unforeseen by the target person when he takes the first step.

Programmed Sequences in Coercive Persuasion

The notorious techniques of coercive persuasion often depend upon an escalating sequence of commitments that combines features of the package deal and the foot-in-the-door ploy. A distinctive feature of coercive control, however, is the use of overt threats of utilitarian and social loss to move the person against his will from one undesirable commitment to another. The coerced victim is forced to move through a programmed sequence of commitments, and when he fails to resist taking the first step it becomes difficult for him to resist taking the next one.

The commitment sequence sometimes depends upon entrapment rather than naked coercion for eliciting the desired momentum toward a decision, with emotional adaptation facilitating the process. The person does not realize he is trapped until he is so far along in the sequence that it is too late for him to back out. This is exemplified by the classic Hollywood plot of the blackmailed pillar of society who gets more and more enmeshed in illegal activity despite futile efforts to struggle free—a plot that turned out to be a true-to-life prototype for some of the Washington bureaucrats caught up in the Watergate scandal. Each of the relatively unimportant initial steps in such a sequence makes it increasingly difficult to instigate a reversal. Nevertheless, a powerful new external threat can result in a prompt reversal—as exemplified by the confessions and plea bargaining of John Dean, Herbert Kalmbach, and a number of other Watergate defendants when they learned that they would be required to give testimony under oath at the Senate Watergate hearings and to the special prosecutor investigators in the Department of Justice, which posed the threat of a very stiff prison sentence for perjury.

Perhaps the most extreme example of a programmed commitment sequence is the so-called brainwashing technique used by the Chinese Communists (Schein, 1956). During the Korean War in the early 1950s, the Chinese leaders followed the policy of requiring overt political compliance from American prisoners of war. Although the demands were so paced that little was required from the prisoner in the early stages, an increasing level of pro-Communist behavior was required. Once the prisoner made some concessions, no matter how trivial, it became difficult for him to resist making further ones. The Communists attempted to move their prisoners toward complete collaboration, including broadcasting anti-American propaganda. Many American prisoners of war resisted these demands, partly because of fear of eventual punishment by U.S. authorities and fear of rejection by buddies. Their motivation to comply, however, was enhanced by special incentives offered by the Communist captors, such as promised rewards of extra food and medicine, and special privileges and status. But the most powerful incentives were negative ones—threats of severe punishment and prolonged imprisonment.

The "brainwashing" procedure involved getting the prisoner first to commit himself to a mildly reprehensible action that would not violate his deep-seated attitudes and values, such as attending a Marxist study group (step 1) and reading *The Communist Manifesto* aloud at one of the sessions (step 2). Having performed these unconventional acts, the prisoner found himself confronted with an additional set of incentives that compelled him to move one step further toward his captors' goal: he was told that unless he carried out the next demand (step 3: to criticize himself in the study group as a product of a bourgeois capitalist culture) he would be deprived of some of the privileges he had recently gained, whereas if he carried out the action he would receive additional rewards. After the prisoner had engaged in self-criticism from a Communist standpoint, the stage was set for his yielding to yet another demand (step 4: to sign a Communist-sponsored peace appeal), an action that would have been quite unacceptable to him earlier. If the prisoner signed the peace appeal, his captors were in a position to threaten to expose him to his cellmates unless he took the remaining step required to induce full collaboration. On the basis of this blackmail threat, the captors succeeded in inducing some of the prisoners to write and broadcast propaganda (step 5), the final act in the programmed sequence. Thus it appears that at the core of the "brainwashing" technique was a graduated series of discrete "forced compliances," carefully controlled by the captors so that although each consecutive step represented an increasingly reprehensible act, the prisoner's motivation to comply could be deliberately manipulated by using additional resources of reward and punishment.

Another incentive that was sometimes deliberately manipulated by the Chinese captors in order to facilitate the entire "brainwashing" program involved social commitment to a group leader. Friendship groups among the prisoners were broken up and new groups of strangers were formed under the leadership of a captor who spoke the prisoners' language. Gradually, the English-speaking captor became a respected authority figure who was seen as protecting the prisoners in his group from the threats of the rest of the captors (Lifton, 1961). Fear of disapproval and rejection by the protective leader in a prison camp environment characterized by fear, isolation, and deprivation may have become a powerful motivation for yielding to the objectionable demands made by the captors.

The effectiveness of all the various forms of commitment traps, ranging from a simple form of slippage, such as volunteering to make a small contribution of time or money to a worthy cause, to the most extreme form of programmed "brainwashing," depends to some extent upon the decision maker's lack of vigilance, which results in his failure to realize what he is letting himself in for when he takes the first step. Even when the crucial information about the additional demands that will be made is deliberately withheld by hidden persuaders, it is often possible for a wary decision maker to obtain some clues that alert him to the possibility of entrapment. There are many old sayings, in addition to the inch-into-mile proverb, and other bits of folklore warning people to be suspicious of the escalating demands that can follow from innocuous beginnings ("Don't let anyone lead you down the garden path"; "Don't fall for sucker bait"; etc.) When the decision maker is in a nonvigilant state, he is not likely to consider the possibility that he is being seduced by sucker bait to move only one little inch down a garden path; nor is he likely to search for and notice cues indicating nasty entanglements just around the bend.

In the language of our conflict model, we expect that a decision maker will be most resistant to commitment entrapment when the conditions making for the coping pattern of vigilance are present, and that he will be most vulnerable when the conditions making for either unconflicted change or the bolstering form of defensive avoidance obtain. These hypotheses concerning the conditions under which any form of commitment entrapment is most likely to occur have not yet been tested; they might provide a fresh, integrating approach to research on the psychology of commitment slippage, the foot-in-the-door ploy, the door-in-the-face reaction, hidden package deals, and programmed sequences in coercive persuasion.

Stabilizing Effect of Commitment

According to our theoretical analysis, as discussed in our presentation of the combined model (chapter 7), an act of commitment tends to stabilize a decision because it adds new incentives to the balance sheet in favor of the chosen course of action. In this sense, an act of commitment can be said to result in increased motivation to adhere to a decision. Charles Kiesler (1971) takes a different approach to the effects of commitment. He argues that an act of commitment in and of itself does not have any motivating effect; rather, when someone takes a stand on an issue or otherwise commits himself publicly, his attitude on the issue as well as its implications for his later behavior become more salient and better defined. Thus, one's commitment provides an anchor by which one's beliefs, attitudes, and behavior are marshaled or organized, which influences the way one evaluates and responds to subsequent appeals or demands. Kiesler maintains that unless the act of commitment is followed by an attack—either by counterpropaganda or by an event that constitutes negative feedback—no observable motivating effects occur. Although we do not wholly agree with Kiesler, our analysis in terms of conflict theory leads us to expect that the changes in motivation resulting from commitment will become most apparent when the decision maker is exposed to negative feedback or some other form of challenge.

An impressive field experiment by Kiesler, Mathog, Pool, and Howenstine (reported in Kiesler, 1971) shows that making a public commitment by signing a petition in favor of an issue renders a person more resistant to attack. The subjects were seventy-three young women living in Yale University apartments for married students, all of whom were known on the basis of pretests to be in favor of birth control. On a random basis, half of this group of women were asked to sign a petition urging that birth control information be disseminated in the local high school (commitment condition). The other half were not asked to sign the petition (noncommitment condition). The next day, half of the women in the committed group and half of those in the noncommitted group found under their apartment doors a printed leaflet that strongly attacked the stand taken by those who signed the petition. (The leaflet is reproduced in figure 13.) The following day, or soon thereafter, all seventy-three women were visited by a young woman purporting to represent a market research survey organization. In the course of the interview, the women's attitudes about birth control and their willingness to sign up for volunteer work for a group that disseminates birth control information were assessed.

The results of the study are shown in figure 14. Signing the petition had a marked effect only when the women were attacked on the issue. Of those whose position was attacked in the leaflet after they had signed the petition, 41 percent agreed to do volunteer work, as compared with only 10.5 percent of those who had not been attacked after signing the petition. The women who had signed the petition showed a boomerang effect in response to attack; that is, unlike the noncommitted women, they became more willing to sign up for volunteer work than if they had not been attacked. A similar pattern of results was obtained when the women were asked a series of seven questions concerning their willingness to volunteer for specific actions in support of the birth control organization, such as contributing money and passing out pamphlets on streetcorners. The majority (68 percent) of the committed-and-attacked group was willing to carry out at least six of the seven acts, in contrast to a much smaller percentage of the other subgroups (e.g., 26 percent of the committed-but-not-attacked group).

Kiesler assumes that the reason public commitment makes the decision maker more resistant to counterattack is that commitment provides information with which the person more clearly formulates his own attitudes. He suggests that a committed person displays a boomerang effect under attack because he tries to justify his previous acts of commitment. Thus, he reacts to strong pressure to change by telling himself that he did the right thing and would do the same thing over again; he demonstrates his perseverance in the face of attack by recommitting himself more fully than before. It follows that a moderate or strong supporter of a social movement or political party can be transformed into an extreme activist if he is first induced to commit himself to an action consistent with his beliefs and then exposed to an attack strong enough to challenge his position but not so strong as to convince him that he is wrong. The same

FIGURE 13. The leaflet used in the birth control information experiment.

---

birth control information
for teenagers ? NO !

> The Board of Education is considering a proposition to make
> birth control information available in New Haven high schools.
> We of the Council of Concerned Citizens feel that this is wrong!
> There are terrible dangers involved which must be made known to
> the voting public. The following are just a few of the many
> reasons why birth control information should not be made avail-
> able in our high schools:

● Information on birth control is TOO PERSONAL to be discussed in
coed classes. Rather it should be discussed in the home.

● STUDENTS will be confused since they WON'T UNDERSTAND how birth
control information should morally affect their own sexual
behavior

● Sexual material presented in a school setting can only lead to
PROMISCUITY. As a further result VENEREAL DISEASE would sharply
increase among high school students.

● The school system has NO RIGHT to determine when children are
mature enough to deal effectively with birth control information.
It is NOT THE RESPONSIBILITY OF THE SCHOOL SYSTEM alone to decide
a question with such complex moral, legal, and ethical considerations.

BIRTH CONTROL INFORMATION SHOULD NOT BE MADE AVAILABLE

IN OUR HIGH SCHOOLS

Source: C. A. Kiesler (Ed.), *The Psychology of Commitment* (New York: Academic Press, 1971), p. 76. Reprinted by permission of the author and the publisher.

---

process may also explain the intensification of attitude found among members of action groups after a public stand they have taken is subjected to attack. Although there is some doubt about the exact mechanism involved, the evidence on boomerang effects points to the freezing of a decision maker's position when an attack or crisis provokes him to take definitive action.[3]

FIGURE 14.   Percentage of women in each condition willing to do volunteer work for an organization advocating the dissemination of birth control information to high school students. *(Based on Kiesler, 1971, p. 80.)*

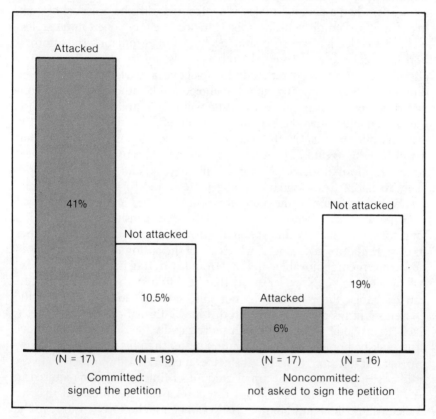

Effects of Commitment Warnings

Conflict theory asserts that the more committing and the more consequential a decision, the more sensitive the decision maker will be to the costs of making a faulty choice, and, accordingly, the higher will be his level of vigilance when he is trying to make a choice. If a decision maker learns—whether from mass media messages, individualized commitment warnings, or other cues—that he will be expected to stick to whichever course he chooses, he is likely to become worried about what he might be letting himself in for. In terms of the conflict model, the increase in stress evoked by a clear-cut commitment warning precludes unconflicted change in response to a challenging event. Commitment warnings also inhibit the tendency to use the bolstering form of defensive avoidance, insofar as they counteract such typical rationalizations as "There's no harm in trying out this choice; I can always shift to another if this one doesn't work out." If there is no urgent deadline pressure, the arousal of worry over the consequences of commitment tends to foster a pattern of vigilance and therefore makes for more conscientious search and apprai-sal. Thus, when a decision maker is confronted with the prospect of mak-ing a binding commitment, he is likely to become more open-minded, less inclined to selective exposure, and less biased in assimilating the informa-tion to which he is exposed. In other words, the tendency to appraise alternatives in a biased rather than objective and vigilant way will be diminished by forewarnings that the choice will be binding. When a con-flicted decision maker believes that he will be committed irrevocably to the chosen alternative, he becomes more careful about evaluating all the available alternatives. On the other hand, if a decision maker believes that it will be easy to undo or reverse his decision—because there is no legal contract, informal social constraints will be weak, and so on—he is more likely to adopt a nonvigilant coping pattern and to make a superficial survey and appraisal of the alternatives.

Suppose a man who is about to buy an expensive color television set is torn between two almost equally attractive models. Each model has its own distinctive advantages, which affect the customer's expectations of how convenient, enjoyable, and free from frustrating malfunctions the set will turn out to be. Now, let us say that he is told by the salesman that he can exchange the purchase "if not fully satisfied" after trying out the chosen set in his own home. With this new information, the customer is likely to arrive at a decision much more rapidly, because he would have little realistic hope of finding a solution better than his first choice, know-ing that if it turns out to be unsatisfactory it can be easily corrected at very little cost (in this case, the small amount of time and effort required to exchange the set). In contrast, if the purchaser were informed that his choice will be final and binding, he would be much more sensitive to the possibilities of postdecisional regret, and would tend to appraise the alter-natives more carefully. He would be much more motivated to guard him-self against making a wrong choice, because under the conditions of an irrevocable purchase he knows that if he becomes discontented with the set he chooses he will face the unpleasant prospect of either putting up with frustration, or else losing a great deal of money by trading in the set for a better one. His anticipation of postdecisional regret induces him to become more cautious before he commits himself.

During the postdecisional period, recalling warnings about the ir-revocability of the commitment tends to stabilize the decision by increas-ing resistance to postdecisional challenges. On the very first day of use the purchaser may find that it is inconvenient to operate the new set, and two weeks later he may discover that one of the ultra-high-frequency channels gives a very fuzzy picture; but, if the purchaser knows that the sale was irrevocable, he will be likely to put up with all such minor frustrations.

Even though a sale may be irrevocable, the decision to continue using a purchased object is always revocable. Consider, for example, a more severe source of frustration—such as suffering the repeated nuisance and expense of having to call in repairmen (who keep on telling him that he should not have bought this notoriously poor model in the first place) because of a series of baffling defects not covered by the guarantee or warranty. This more powerful form of negative feedback might function as a sufficiently strong challenge to induce him to consider a costly, alternative course of action, such as trading in the defective model for a different one, which would entail chagrin as well as financial loss.

An even more powerful challenge, such as being informed by a repairman that the set gives off a dangerous level of radiation, might lead to a rapid decision to abandon it. A new decision to purchase a certifiedly safe color TV set, even though the defective, unsafe model couldn't be traded in, would require the decision maker to sustain a considerable loss; he would have to write off the money he spent on the earlier purchase or else try to obtain some reimbursement by taking costly legal action against the manufacturer or distributor. His losses, of course, would not be confined to the financial sphere. Making a costly new purchase to correct a recent mistake does not pass unnoticed by family members and friends, some of whom will express open disapproval ("You mean to say that after you just spent all that money you are going to buy another new one?"). It also entails loss of self-esteem for having made a stupid mistake that might have been avoided if a little more effort had been made to find out more about the product. For the first time the purchaser may realize (or find out from a more experienced friend) that good advice could have been obtained from a reliable TV repairman, that a consumer publication could have been consulted in the public library, that searching questions could have been asked of the salesman, and so on. Typically, the dissatisfied purchaser is angry at himself as well as at the salesman and the manufacturer for all the unnecessary frustration resulting from the transaction. He thinks to himself—although in more colorful language than the analytical vocabulary we are using—that he should have been more skeptical of what the salesman told him and more vigilant in his information search. When *next* making a purchase he is likely to remind himself, before it is too late, of the painful regret he experienced in the wake of his TV fiasco. It is just such "hard knocks" from direct experience that reinforce throughout a person's adult life his earlier social training in decision making, increasing his sensitivity to the risks of negative consequences along with his repertoire of means for carrying out a vigilant information search before making binding commitments.

Some experimental evidence bearing on the influence of warning signs of commitment is provided in a study by Mann and Taylor (1970). By and large, their findings support the hypothesis that commitment warnings induce an increase in vigilant information processing.

Although working with college students in a social psychology laboratory, Mann and Taylor set up a real-life choice modeled on the type of consumer's choice that enters into shopping for a television set or purchasing an aesthetic household object. In this experiment, the subjects, who were coeds at the University of Melbourne, Australia, participated in a study of art preferences; each subject was told that the study involved examining college students' knowledge about art and their preferences for different styles of painting. After rating a set of twelve art prints, including works by old masters, impressionists, and moderns, the subject was shown a pair of prints and was told that as a reward for her help in the study she could have whichever one she chose. Although the intrinsic utilitarian value of the prints was slight, some degree of ego involvement in the decision was expected because many college women pride themselves on their aesthetic taste; the possibility that friends or members of the family might dislike the reproduction they selected to take home would, it was thought, represent at least a mild threat to their social and self-esteem. Moreover, as in other studies involving this type of payment for participating in a psychological experiment, the decisional conflict is likely to be heightened by the subject's concern that her choice might be evaluated critically by the experimenter.

Three variations were introduced, corresponding to signs of three different degrees of commitment, and were administered to equal numbers of subjects:

1. Information about *revocability*: one group was told that after they made their decision they could change their minds after having the print at home a few days, and return to exchange it if they wished to do so.
2. Warning of *irrevocability*: a second group was told that once they announced their decision they would be asked to sign for the art print and, because the prints were in short supply, would be unable to change their minds.
3. Warning of *irrevocability with an added commitment to justify the choice*: a third group was given the same information about irrevocability as the second group and, in addition, was told that after they made their choice they would be asked to write a 200-word essay justifying it.[4]

All three experimental groups were given a *difficult* choice: that is, the two prints offered to each subject were ones she had initially rated highly and as almost equally preferred. In order to compare the effects of different degrees of difficulty, two additional groups were given an *easy* choice; in these groups, the two prints offered each subject were ones she had initially rated quite discrepantly. One of the groups in the easy-choice condition was given the information about the choice being *revocable*, while the other was given the warning about the choice being *irrevocable*. The experiment also included a control group that was not given the opportunity to choose a print to take home, but was administered the same rating procedure to determine their preferences.

The results obtained for all six experimental groups are shown in table 10. The findings are fairly consistent with predictions from the conflict model of decision making. Subjects given an easy choice (whose preference for one print was markedly stronger than for the other from the outset) should, according to conflict theory, experience little or no conflict; and the rapidity of choice and lack of bolstering among these subjects (groups 2 and 3 in table 10) testify to their lack of conflict. Subjects faced with a difficult choice (i.e., having no marked preference for either alternative) but knowing that they could change their minds after making a decision would be expected to adopt a nonvigilant pattern of coping with the choice; the relatively rapid, bolstering style of decision making shown by subjects in group 4 may be evidence of a defensive avoidance pattern. Group 5, however, shows a mixed pattern, with a longer decision time but a relatively high degree of bolstering.

Subjects in group 6, who were conflicted (because of no marked preference) as well as concerned about finding the best solution (because their decision was irrevocable and they would have to justify their choice publicly), would be expected to adopt a vigilant pattern of information processing. The evidence shows that they took their time, and indulged in relatively little predecisional bolstering of the preferred alternative.

Although this interpretation is fairly consistent with the findings, one cannot rule out alternative interpretations. The important point is that the results of this experiment make it plausible to assume that concern about

TABLE 10.   **Mean scores on decision time and predecisional bolstering among subjects given different types of information about the degree to which they would be committed by their announced choice.**

Experimental Groups	Predicted Coping Pattern	Decision Time in Seconds	Degree of Bolstering
1. Control: no choice	—	—	0.25
Easy choice 2. Revocable decision	Unconflicted choice	2.8	0.50
3. Irrevocable decision	Unconflicted choice	7.8	0.00
Difficult choice 4. Revocable decision	Defensive avoidance	7.0	1.11
5. Irrevocable decision	Minimal level of vigilance	13.1	1.40
6. Irrevocable decision with commitment to justify it	Moderate vigilance	24.9	0.70

* N = 19 ± 1 in each of the six groups.

Source: L. Mann and V. A. Taylor, "The Effects of Commitment and Choice Difficulty on Predecision Processes," *Journal of Social Psychology*, 1970, 82, 225. Copyright © 1970 by The Journal Press. Reprinted by permission.

the consequences of committing oneself to a given choice will act as a deterrent to defensive avoidance and an inducement to vigilance even for minor decisions that entail only mildly threatening consequences.[5]

The Mann and Taylor experiment indicates that the anticipation of having to defend one's future choice, when added to the demand for an irrevocable commitment, markedly increases the amount of time devoted to making a choice, which may reflect an increase in vigilance during the predecision period. If the choice were more ego-involving, we would expect irrevocability alone to induce vigilance. It is debatable whether the essential feature of commitment is the irreversible quality of a choice, the public announcement of a position, or, as Kiesler (1971) maintains, the pledging of the individual to specific behavioral acts. We regard all these as sources of commitment, since they all entail anticipated utilitarian losses, social punishments, or self-disapproval for failure to carry through on a course of action. We do not know at present whether these sources of commitment evoke different psychological processes. Further studies along the lines of the Mann and Taylor experiment, but involving more ego-involving decisions, might supply the missing evidence and illuminate the relationship between various types of commitment warnings and degree of vigilance.

Developmental Aspects of Commitment

We have seen that the powerful effects of commitment on decision makers are a function of personal and social considerations bound up with the self-image of the decision maker as a reliable person who can be trusted to meet his or her social obligations. This sense of commitment is not uniform throughout all sectors of society, nor is it uniform throughout any one person's life history. The very young, for example, are exempt from certain obligations because of their immature understanding of commitment and its implications.

When do young children start responding to acts of commitment in the way that adults do? How do children acquire a sense of the seriousness of acts of commitment? When and how do they learn to make decisions more cautiously following warnings that their choice will be irrevocable? So far, only fragmentary evidence is available bearing on these questions. It remains for the next generation of research workers to combine the methods of developmental psychology with those of social psychology to check and extend the suggestive but limited studies from which we are able to draw a few preliminary conclusions.

A series of experiments by Mann (1971) examined the effects of a commitment warning on the decisional behavior of a sample of American and Australian nursery school children, aged 4 to 5 years. In order to explore the generality of the effects, three groups of preschoolers were included in the experiment: thirty-three white children enrolled in a nursery school in Cambridge, Massachusetts; twenty-six children in a summer school program for black nursery school children in the same city; and forty-five white children at a nursery school attached to Monash University in Melbourne, Australia. A standard procedure was followed for each of the three groups. The experimenter, after spending several days in the nursery school becoming acquainted with the children, invited them to play a game individually in the research room. Five toys were lined up on a table in front of the subject (matchbox toy cars for boys, plastic toy necklaces for girls). The experimenter told each subject that he was trying to find out which toys the children liked best. Preference rankings for the five items were obtained by removing the most preferred one from the table and then asking the subject to judge which of the remaining ones he or she liked best; this procedure was followed until all five toys had been ranked.

Next, the experimenter introduced the decisional problem: "I would like to give you something for helping me. Since I don't have enough of all of them [pointing to the toys], you can choose between these two toys [here the experimenter held up the third- and fourth-ranked items], and you can keep the one you like best." The experimenter then introduced two variations, administered to equal numbers of subjects, which established a condition of irrevocability for one group and revocability for the other. In the *commitment* condition, subjects were cautioned that their decision would be binding; they were told: "Be sure to think about it very carefully, because once you choose one you won't be allowed to change your mind; I'll put it in a paper bag with your name on it and then you can take it home with you." In the *noncommitment* condition, subjects were told: "Be sure to think about it very carefully. Choose one, but if you want to change your mind later and decide that you would like to take the other one, you can bring it back; I'll be happy to change it."

Table 11 shows that for all three groups, decision time for children in the commitment condition was almost twice as long as for those in the noncommitment condition ($p < .05$). This finding is consistent with Mann and Taylor's (1970) findings obtained with college students: even with nursery school children, the warning of a binding commitment induces the individual to pause at least a few moments and reflect on his or her preferences. It is noteworthy that white children in the Cambridge sample took longer to decide in both conditions than Cambridge blacks and Australian whites. This difference might reflect a greater amount of training in decision making obtained by white, middle-class American children.[6]

We still do not know much about how to teach children to develop vigilant forethought and stability combined with flexibility and originality—attributes necessary for sound decision making. When parents caution a child that he will be unable to go back on his word once he

TABLE 11. **Effect of a commitment warning on mean time taken to announce a choice.**

	MEAN TIME (IN SECONDS)	
SUBJECTS	COMMITMENT CONDITION	NONCOMMITMENT CONDITION
1. Cambridge, white children	8.45 (N = 18)	4.27 (N = 15)
2. Cambridge, black children	4.28 (N = 12)	2.43 (N = 14)
3. Melbourne, white children	4.20 (N = 22)	2.57 (N = 23)
TOTAL	5.69 (N = 52)	3.02 (N = 52)

Source: L. Mann, "Effects of a Commitment Warning on Children's Decision Behavior," *Journal of Personality and Social Psychology*, 1971, 17, 76. Copyright 1971 by the American Psychological Association. Reprinted by permission.

agrees to keep a promise, or that he cannot renege once he has accepted an invitation, they are giving direct instruction that may sometimes facilitate the development of a mature concept of commitment. Throughout childhood and adolescence, parents, teachers, peer groups, and other agents of socialization constantly provide training in dependability by threatening disapproval and punishment for failure to implement decisions, and occasionally by trying to act as models of consistency. These socialization experiences undoubtedly impress a child with the social dangers and utilitarian losses that accrue to reversing or vacillating on an important decision after having committed oneself. A key question that remains to be answered by research on child development pertains to *internalization* of these norms. What types of socialization experiences give rise to anticipation of self-disapproval for failing to keep one's word even when there are no objective signs to warrant anticipation of punishment? Until more is known about internalization, psychologists will be unable to explain fully how acts of commitment in adult life come to have the power to alter the array of incentives that enter into a decisional balance sheet, increasing the attractiveness of the chosen course and decreasing the attractiveness of all the unchosen alternatives.

CHAPTER 12

Postdecisional Conflict

THIS CHAPTER SKETCHES in broad outline the main determinants of post-decisional changes, as they emerge from the research done so far. We focus especially on the hot cognitive processes associated with feelings of regret, which come into play when postdecisional conflict is so severe that stage 5 (adherence) gives way to stage 1 (challenge).

When the Honeymoon Is Over

A vivid example of acute postdecisional regret induced by unequivocal negative feedback is to be found in an autobiographical account by James Boswell, who in recent decades has become as famous for his pithy journals about his own life as he used to be for his classic biography of Samuel Johnson. In his *London Journal*, written during 1762–1763, the young Boswell gives the sordid details of an ill-fated liaison with Louisa, a beautiful young actress who suddenly became, in Boswell's eyes, nothing but a "dissembling whore."[1]

During the six months that Louisa was his mistress, Boswell regarded her as a truly "fine" woman, and for her sake he confined his active sexual life to relations with her. Before meeting her, he had had no intention of becoming a monogamist; he was always open to fresh intrigues with actresses and ladies of fashion, usually pursuing several at the same time while continuing to have his customary street affairs with prostitutes. He apparently bolstered his renunciation of affairs with other attractive ladies by idealizing Louisa. In conversations with friends he constantly played up her "many endearing qualities" to the point where they thought she was much too good to be true. They "doubted of her existence, and used to call her my *ideal lady*." As for giving up his habitual pleasures with

309

prostitutes, he now prided himself on being completely safe from the risk of venereal disease.

This honeymoon period came to an abrupt end one rueful day when Boswell discovered that he had unmistakable symptoms of gonorrhea, a disease especially dreaded in those days because of the prolonged and excruciatingly painful treatment inflicted by physicians in their attempts to cure it. Bitterly disappointed and aggrieved, his ecstatic image of the lady rudely shattered, Boswell confronted her with the bad news. Louisa readily admitted having once been infected long before meeting him; but she had felt certain of her full recovery. Fervently and tearfully, she assured Boswell that for the last six months she had had nothing to do with any man besides him. But Boswell refused to believe any of her pleadings or tearful explanations. This lady, who had been so ideal a love object, overnight had become detestable and dangerous—"a most consummate dissembling whore."

Boswell apparently displayed, at least temporarily, a characteristic "never again" reaction that encompassed his entire policy regarding liaisons with women. As soon as he was able to resume his sex life following an agonizing cure and convalescence, he resorted to picking up the "lowest" kind of streetwalker and then "could not but despise myself for being so closely united with such a low wretch."

In Boswell's account of his episode of posthoneymoon disillusionment, there are numerous indications that his idealization of the object of his passion set the stage for what can be described as an extreme overreaction to negative feedback. His disappointment and rage may have been quite commensurate with the magnitude of the bad news; but his fear of being deceived by Louisa's assurances and his plunge into self-abasing promiscuity were clearly excessive.

Sources of Regret

In political life, as well as in love life, evidence that one's current policy has turned out to be a fiasco is likely to lead to a gross reversal. If the bad news is so loud and clear that it cannot be ignored, distorted, or discounted, a chief executive may openly acknowledge the fiasco—as President Kennedy did following the Bay of Pigs debacle. When bolstering and other defensive avoidance tactics no longer succeed in preventing acute postdecisional conflict, the decision maker may become hypervigilant and, like Boswell, impulsively try to undo his error by rushing indiscriminately into the opposite policy. President Kennedy, however, did not handle the Bay of Pigs fiasco in this way. Rather, he cautiously disengaged the United States from further involvement in the attempted invasion of Cuba and set up a board of inquiry within the government to find out how he and his advisers could have been so "stupid" as to let the Central Intelligence Agency go ahead with such an ill-conceived plan. One of

Kennedy's main objectives after the setback was to work out better policy-making procedures that would prevent such stupidity in the future. His coping pattern, after the initial shock, appears to have been much more that of vigilance than of hypervigilance.

The evidence presented earlier in our discussion of the defective-balance-sheet hypothesis (chapter 6) suggests that severe defeats and other extreme forms of negative feedback will be more likely to evoke the vigilance pattern of decision making if the person had contemplated the possibility of those setbacks in advance. When the decision maker is psychologically prepared for a setback that materializes, he presumably can recover more quickly from the initial shock, which evokes hypervigilance. Then he will engage in vigilant search and appraisal before committing himself to a new course of action, proceeding through the successive stages of making a new decision in a way that results in a high-quality decision, with new contingency plans carefully worked out in the event of additional setbacks. But whether the dominant reaction to a severe setback continues to be hypervigilance or changes to vigilance, the decision is so profoundly challenged that stage 5 comes to an end and the person embarks on an urgent quest for a better solution. His *post*decisional regret about the current policy, as we stated earlier, is functionally equivalent to a *pre*decisional conflict about a future policy. The new decision, however, may be to reaffirm the old course of action, despite its defects, rather than to change to a new course.

Postdecisional regret is frequently induced by events or credible communications that call attention to potential financial loss, health impairments, social censure, or other undesirable consequences that might follow from adhering to the course of action to which the person is committed. In addition to these obvious sources of regret, more subtle cues may function as "reminders" of the risks or losses entailed by the decision and may produce the same challenging effect. In a casual conversation, for example, the mere mention of the greater prestige or any other advantage of an attractive job offer that the person has turned down, which reminds him of the gains he has had to forego, may be sufficient to evoke pangs of momentary regret. Sometimes, without any observable prompting, the person's own train of thought leads him to vivid reminders that evoke essentially the same reaction. This type of subjective response, in the absence of any external stimuli that can be identified as instigative, is what we refer to as "spontaneous regret." We assume that the frequency and intensity of spontaneous regret are indicators of the severity of postdecisional conflict. When episodes of intense regret occur frequently following the choice of a marital partner, a job, or a new policy for one's organization they are usually accompanied by profound misgivings, sleeplessness, psychosomatic complaints, and feelings of remorse, all of which are extreme symptoms of postdecisional conflict.

Reactions to Postdecisional Crises

Whenever regret and related symptoms of decisional conflict occur—whether they are elicited by negative feedback, evoked by "reminders," or manifested spontaneously—the decision maker, as a first step toward seeking a better solution, directs his cognitive activity toward *surveying* the damage. This mental activity, as we have repeatedly emphasized, is far from being a matter of cold, logical appraisal of evidence. Initially, the disillusioned decision maker is in a state of high stress and, as with Boswell, his cognitions are red-hot. He feels bitterly disappointed in himself as well as in others, remorseful, and full of self-doubts. Not only does it look like the decision is turning out badly, but the person for the moment sees himself as weak, foolish, and gullible. Why, he asks himself, did he allow himself to be so taken in, to be made a sucker? The blow to his pride as a sound decision maker, as well as the losses he is suffering, is often expressed in the agitated, depressive tone with which he repeatedly says, "My God, what have I done?" Frequently the person feels driven to do something drastic as quickly as possible in order to avert additional losses. In extreme instances the person may follow Othello's impulsive course of quickly terminating his unbearable feelings of remorse, suffering, and self-condemnation by killing himself ("I took by the throat the circumcised dog, and smote him, thus").

According to our conflict model, a state of high postdecisional stress may lead to a behavioral pattern of either defensive avoidance, hypervigilance, or vigilance, depending upon the conditions that hold at the time of the setback. There may be fluctuations and transitions from one pattern to the other, as changes occur with respect to deadline pressures, evidence of the availability of fresh alternatives, or other signs that raise the person's hopes for finding a satisfactory way out of the dilemma.

The coping pattern of defensive avoidance may contribute to the psychological readjustment of a stricken decision maker by facilitating postponement of appraisal and selection of a new course of action until after the acute emotional shock of the disruptive crisis has subsided. The apparently calm emotional state attained through defensive avoidance, however, is superficial in the sense that the person's latent decisional conflict will be reactivated whenever he encounters impressive threat cues that are difficult to ignore or discount.

Defensive avoidance following a setback may take any of its three characteristic forms—procrastination, shifting responsibility, or bolstering. When the disillusioned decision maker is unaware of any deadline pressures and believes that it is not necessary to take precipitate action to avert further damage, procrastination is likely to be the dominant form of defensive avoidance. The person strives to calm down by getting his mind off the crisis, which may require resorting to extreme forms of distraction or to narcotics. Staying drunk or "stoned" is perhaps the most effective way to achieve this goal, but other all-absorbing activities, such as sexual indulgence, exhausting physical labor, and sometimes even intensive creative work in the arts or sciences can function in essentially the same way. Even without exhibiting any change in external activity, however, the person may defensively avoid cues that evoke a high level of emotional stress by purely psychological means, such as selective inattention to reminders of the setback and selective forgetting.

Buck passing in response to a fiasco is a characteristic form of defensive avoidance when circumstances allow the decision maker to deny responsibility, especially if a scapegoat is readily available on whom the blame can be foisted. One simple way of denying personal responsibility is to blame the circumstances of the decision, claiming little or no choice in the matter or undue duress. Sometimes this is done without specifically identifying someone else as the culprit. More often, the decision maker absolves himself of responsibility by pointing to a vulnerable person who is handy to fill the role of scapegoat, such as the superior who set the restricted conditions for a policy decision that has turned out badly.

There is a surprising lack of empirical evidence on postdecisional buck passing, although the phenomenon is popularly regarded as an occupational hazard in many large institutions, such as the military, government agencies, hospitals, and corporate business firms. In our search of the literature we have found one experimental study that illustrates the buckpassing phenomenon in circumstances where individuals discover that a decision they have just made will lead to extremely unpleasant consequences for another person. Harris and Harvey (1975) asked college students to decide which of two laboratory tasks another subject should be required to perform at a later time. The descriptions of the tasks were vague, but the students were offered an opportunity to obtain additional information. For some of them, procuring the information was difficult, involving a hike across campus to consult a senior experimenter. For others, gaining the information was easy, because it could be obtained simply by going down the hall. Almost every subject declined the opportunity to obtain the additional information that would have clarified the alternatives. To their dismay, some subjects then learned that the task they had selected for the other person would involve highly unpleasant consequences—namely, exposure to dangerous and painful electric shocks. When asked to indicate how much choice they had had in selecting the task, those subjects who learned that their decision would lead to unpleasant consequences for another person, and who knew that they could have obtained clarifying information if they had taken the trouble, attributed very little choice in the matter to themselves. On a 21-point scale measuring degree of choice, these subjects rated their own level of choice as just over 3, a rating dramatically lower than any found in the other experimental conditions. The Harris and Harvey study provides evidence on the tendency to absolve oneself of responsibility for a sloppily made, ill-fated decision by denying freedom of choice. The conditions Harris and Harvey created in their experiment, in addition to providing for postdecisional conflict, apparently included sufficient ambiguity with respect to responsibility for the decision to allow the buck-passing mode of defensive avoidance to emerge as the dominant coping pattern. When a decision maker adopts this pattern and denies his own responsibility, he fails to engage in vigilant information processing. Rather, he passively accepts the undesirable situation instead of contemplating a new course of action to correct the error, such as arguing that the earlier decision, made in the absence of crucial information, should not be binding and taking steps to reverse it.

The bolstering form of defensive avoidance has been more extensively investigated than the other two forms. In the initial experiment on post-decisional bolstering, Brehm (1956), using household products as choice alternatives, found postdecisional bolstering, or spreading, only when the subjects (college women) had to make a relatively difficult choice between two moderately attractive articles—and not when they were merely handed one of the articles as a gift. Subsequently, evidence of postdecisional bolstering has also been obtained in field experiments conducted in real-life settings in which people are observed in the course of making a natural decision—including betting at the horse races, casting a vote in an election, and choosing a job, all of which involve a relatively high degree of postdecisional conflict (Brehm and Cohen, 1962; Mann and Abeles, 1970; Knox and Inkster, 1968; Lawler, Kuleck, Rhode, and Sorensen, 1975; Vroom, 1966; Vroom and Deci, 1971). Vroom, for example, studied two classes of graduate students who were nearing completion of a management training program and were in the process of selecting an organization in which to begin their managerial careers. Eight weeks before graduation, when the students already had had a chance to "survey the market" and visit those organizations that looked most promising, each man was asked to list and rate the three in which he was most interested. Approximately a month later, after the students had made their choices and written letters committing themselves to joining a particular organization, they were asked to rerate the attractiveness of the three organizations. Vroom found that the students tended to bolster the attractiveness of the organization they had selected, giving a higher attractiveness rating to the chosen organization and lower ratings to the unchosen ones than in their initial rating. They perceived the organization they had chosen as more instrumental than before to achieving their goals, while the unchosen organizations were now seen as less instrumental to goal attainment. Similar results were obtained by Vroom and Deci in a follow-up study of the same men after they were on the job.

A replication by Lawler, Kuleck, Rhode, and Sorensen (1975) showed essentially the same outcome for trainees in accounting. The trainees' ratings of job alternatives were obtained in the fall of their senior year before they had made a choice and then twice again—in the late spring, shortly after they had chosen the firm they would work for, and about one year after that, when they had had ample opportunity to discover all the ways in which the chosen firm failed to meet their high expectations. The results are shown in figure 15. The ratings by the accountant trainees soon after they had made their job choice showed the characteristics spreading of alternatives, with an increase in attractiveness for the chosen firm and a decrease for the unchosen ones. After one year of employment, the accountants' ratings showed a slight decrease in attractiveness for both the chosen and the unchosen firms, but the chosen firm continued to be much more attractive.[2]

We assume that when undesirable consequences come within the focus of his attention, the decision maker is temporarily challenged but generally remains pessimistic about finding a better way to attain his objectives because the chosen alternative still appears to be superior to

FIGURE 15. **Attractiveness ratings of job alternatives by accountant trainees before and after making their job choice.** (*Based on Lawler, Kuleck, Rhode, and Sorensen, 1975.*)

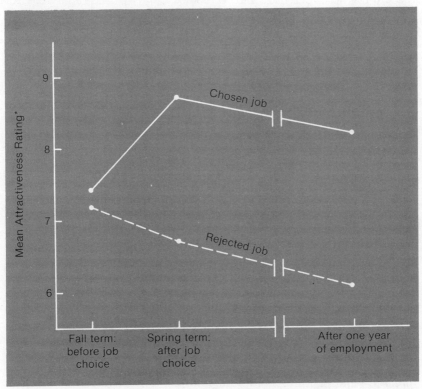

* The original scale has been reversed.

the rejected alternatives; this is especially likely when the act of going back on his commitment would in itself require him to sustain undesirable losses. In these circumstances, the direction of defensive avoidance activity will be toward warding off awareness of the apparent losses that might ensue from continuing to adhere to the chosen course of action. The original decision is bolstered by new rationalizations, whose main theme is "No need to worry, everything will turn out OK." When successful, the rationalizations transform the answer to the first key question ("Are the risks serious if I don't change?") from *yes* or *maybe* to *no*. When this transformation takes place, the acute conflict subsides and the person unambivalently adheres to his original decision. But rationalizations may be such flimsy cognitive defenses that the person is challenged and undergoes a repetition of the same sequence each time he encounters new information about the undesirable consequences of his choosen course. Thus, postdecisional conflict may be reactivated time after time unless robust rationalizations are developed that enable the person to withstand the common, garden-variety challenges to which he is repeatedly exposed. In this way, bolstering can be seen as a gradual process that under ordinary circumstances will result in a shoring up of defenses. But, of course, under extraordinary circumstances the negative feedback may be so persistently irrefutable that the decision maker's defenses are gradually corroded or suddenly shattered. When the decisional conflict becomes acute, a new coping pattern of vigilance or hypervigilance is likely to become dominant.

When, because of extreme time pressures and other factors that make for emotional shock, *hypervigilance* emerges as the dominant postdecisional pattern, the tendency is toward rapid undoing of the decision. Obsessional imaginative activity in a state of hypervigilance may have adaptive value, however—provided it is not carried to excess—insofar as it contributes to preparation for coping with unavoidable setbacks that arise later on. Realizing that the decision could turn out to be a disaster, the person looks for and is likely to detect other signs of weakness in it. For the first time, he may ask himself: What else might go wrong? Who might object to my course of action? Are things as bad as they look, or even worse? How can I anticipate, and prepare for, all the things that might go wrong?

A person is most likely to take impressive threat cues in his stride, and to evaluate them judiciously, if the conditions are present that make for vigilance. Earlier we pointed out that as conditions change during a period of acute postdecisional crisis, an initial reaction of hypervigilance may be followed by a much longer period of defensive avoidance, which, in turn, may be superseded by vigilance. Despite an initial period of high stress, the disillusioned decision maker may end up doing a careful job of appraising and planning before he commits himself to a new course of action. The obsessional "daymares" about what else might go wrong with the battered decision can make for an emphatic *yes* in answer to the prime question, "Do I need to change?" Under certain circumstances, then, a powerful challenge may enable a person to mobilize his resources to reconsider at long last an outworn course of action that is patently defective.

In other instances, the person may end up deciding, after emotional equanimity is restored, that the unexpected disappointment was no so bad as it seemed at first, and that the original decision might still work out all right. In such a case, the initial panic reaction (extreme hypervigilance) leads to awareness of numerous defects in the original plan, which may then be correctable with only slight modifications. Ultimately the person's confidence in himself as a sound decision maker is restored if he discovers that the modifications he makes following the crisis turn out to be successful in keeping losses down to a minimum.

Three Modes of Resolution

One mode of resolving postdecisional conflict is undoing or reversing a decision. Another mode, at the opposite pole from undoing, is reaffirming the decision, with full implementation. A third mode, intermediate between the first two, is that of curtailing implementation, so that partial adherence is combined with partial reversal. To a large extent the mode of resolution is determined by the degree of disillusionment created by the challenging negative feedback and by objective signs indicating whether other alternatives would be better or worse than the tarnished one. In addition, the processing of negative feedback and of all the auxiliary information pertaining to the pros and cons of available alternatives is influenced by the decision maker's coping pattern. Thus, we expect the outcome of a postdecisional crisis to be partly determined by the answers the decision maker gives to the basic questions in the conflict model (figure 8). More specifically, the outcome of a postdecisional crisis will most likely be: (1) undoing of the decision, if the conditions fostering *hypervigilance* are present; (2) a compromise in the form of *partial implementation*, if the conditions fostering *vigilance* are present; or (3) *reaffirmation* of the original decision, if the conditions fostering *defensive avoidance* are present. The following discussion, derived mainly from intensive case studies of personal crises, designates in more detail the antecedents of the complex psychological processes that enter into the three different modes of conflict resolution that follow exposure to a disruptive challenge.

1. *Undoing the decision.* When, as a result of a powerful challenge, the decision maker sees the risks of continuing as much more severe than the risks of changing, his response is to move rapidly toward choosing a new course of action to replace the one that has turned sour. Examples of such behavior are commonly seen by attorneys who specialize in legal problems of marriage. They are consulted by husbands and wives

who have discovered, shortly after getting married, that their spouse has misrepresented or withheld crucial information—for example, that he or she is a bigamist, a chronic alcoholic, a drug addict, a criminal, recurrently psychotic, diseased, sadistic, sexually impotent, or frigid. When such a discovery is made, the red-hot cognitions evoked in the disillusioned person, just as in Boswell's case, move the person to decathect the partner and expunge as thoroughly as possible all signs of prior commitment. The heroine in the musical comedy *South Pacific* epitomizes this tendency when she sings "I want to wash that man right out of my hair," following the discovery that her fiancé neglected to inform her that he already has a wife and children.

The decathexis process, so unmistakably manifested when the disillusioned partner's feelings of love rapidly turn into hate, can also be clearly identified when employees unexpectedly discover that their job requires them to do something that is illegal, dangerous, or damaging to their self-esteem. Again like Boswell, the disillusioned person feels that he has been "had." If in a hypervigilant state, he wants to get out fast, before any more damage ensues. Admiration for the employer turns into bitter contempt and distrust; elation about the new job is transformed into aggrievement. The employee seizes the first opportunity to move to a new firm, or he may resign without even waiting to find another position.

A secondary type of process, which we call *expunging*, enters in after the first steps have been taken to reverse a decision. It involves consolidating and bolstering the reversal by eliminating or obscuring all signs that remind the person of the prior, erroneous decision. External reminders, such as honeymoon photographs, are physically destroyed. Internal reminders are also somehow removed or distorted by means of selective attention and other typical psychological mechanisms of defensive avoidance. Even without a hair-washing ceremony, the disillusioned person's memories of the courtship, wedding, and honeymoon become hazy. The entire episode eventually gets relabeled as a minor little affair that almost didn't happen at all, which promotes feelings of indifference. Expunging the reminders of an earlier commitment when a marital partner has been grossly deceived by a spouse is sometimes facilitated by the way in which the case is handled by the legal system: the law of annulment in most Western countries allows the injured party to think and act as if the marriage never really took place at all. There are equivalent laws for annulling business partnerships and other contracts.

2. *Curtailing implementation.* When a person perceives the risks of not changing to be severe but also perceives the risks of changing to be almost as great or greater, he will examine carefully the possibility of curtailing implementation of the challenged decision. Especially if his dominant coping pattern is vigilance, he will watch for an opportunity to work out a compromise solution that reduces the stress of postdecisional conflict by eliminating the main difficulties while leaving the commitment

essentially unchanged at the verbal level. His solution is to do what is expected of him except that he omits the most distressing acts that are prime sources of regret. A discontented husband or wife who does not want to break up the family until the children are older may adopt a compromise solution of being married "in name only." During an election campaign, a discontented member of a political organization may arrive at a similar compromise, becoming a supporter "in name only" and doing only the bare minimum to avoid having to make an open break.

The two processes of decathecting and expunging that enter into undoing a decision probably also operate, in less extreme form, when a person compromises by curtailing implementation. Positive feelings are transformed into feelings of indifference; reminders of the commitment are avoided. The curtailment course may be subsequently bolstered by rationalizations that justify the decision maker's failure to live up fully to his commitment (e.g., "After all, they lied to me about the work load I would be given, so I have the right to goof off on these extra chores whenever I can get away with it"). The three psychological processes that consolidate a compromise solution—decathecting, expunging, and rationalizing—are likely to create a general attitude of detachment that permits a disenchanted member of any partnership or organization to remain relatively free from guilt about his lack of conscientiousness and also about his cavalier disregard of the norms he is supposedly obligated to follow.

3. *Reaffirming the decision*. When the risks of not changing, though severe, are seen as markedly less damaging than the consequences of changing, cognitive activity is directed toward warding off or minimizing the challenge. Such activity involves developing new defensive attitudes and rationalizations that enable the decision maker to recommit himself by developing the belief that the losses from carrying out his prior commitment can be tolerated and that the chosen course of action is still the best of the available alternatives. In clinical interviews, we have observed clear-cut instances of reaffirmation accompanied by manifestations of defensive bolstering among men and women who have found out that their spouses were having an extramarital love affair. After an initial reaction of angry protest, the disillusioned spouse comes to terms with the episode by adopting new ideological beliefs that transform the apparent loss into an asset. The husband or wife becomes converted to a new position that was formerly anathema, affirming that sexual freedom makes for a better marriage, that an occasional sexual adventure outside the marriage makes for greater sexual responsiveness on the part of both marital partners; that although secret liaisons threaten a marriage, "polite adultery" does not. The forecasts that follow from these new beliefs are often sufficiently ambiguous that they cannot be disproved by the decision maker's subsequent experience and may sometimes actually prove to be confirmed, if only as self-fulfilling prophecies (see Merton, 1957). In either

case, reaffirming and rebolstering a decision can lead to genuine changes in beliefs and values.

Although we have just described undoing, curtailing implementation, and reaffirming as disjunctive modes of resolving postdecisional conflict, we sometimes see disillusioned decision makers mentally try out first one and then another mode before hitting upon a path that leads to a restoration of their emotional equanimity. Shifting from thinking about the extreme modes to the compromise solution of curtailing implementation is particularly likely when vigilance is the dominant coping pattern. This type of shifting is exemplified by a student who returned to college after having taken off a year for traveling through Europe, only to discover that the first week of routine classes and assignments could not compare with the stimulating atmosphere of the Costa Brava, the Alps, or the Norwegian fiords. At first he showed characteristic signs of decathecting and seemed well on his way to completely undoing the decision to continue his education. But he could not set aside his concern about losing the hard-to-replace money he had spent on tuition. There would also be considerable embarrassment if he had to inform people in his hometown, including a prospective employer who had offered him a job after graduation, that he had changed his mind about finishing college that year. The trend toward undoing was confined to his daydreams and was superseded by a plan to curtail implementation: he would skip most of his classes, devote himself to his athletic hobbies, and study only the night before exams, with the expectation that this minimal participation would be sufficient for him to get by with passing grades. But when inescapable signs, such as getting a failing grade on a quiz in one of his required courses, showed him that he could not get away with this attempt to be a student "in name only," decisional conflict was reactivated. At this point, he arranged to see his adviser (the senior author). During the first session, while ventilating his disappointment with college life, he exhibited signs of having given considerable thought to appraising the alternatives, along with other manifestations of vigilance. A week later, he reported that he had spent the entire night after the first session mulling over the problem, unable to fall asleep, until suddenly he "saw the light." Derogatory thoughts about the college environment switched to self-derogation; he now saw himself as a "disgusting, spoiled brat" who was "pampering" himself. He concluded that the major defect was in himself and not in the school, which led him to resolve to do the essential work to which he had committed himself when he registered as a college student. Thus, the earlier undoing and compromise modes of resolution gave way to strong reaffirmation, and he did, in fact, carry out the decision wholeheartedly.

Similar shifts in mode of resolution have been observed in other persons undergoing severe postdecisional conflict. Sometimes the reverse sequence is exhibited: an initial attempt to ignore the damaging negative feedback by reaffirming the decision is followed by an attempt to compromise through curtailing implementation, and then by a more drastic attempt to undo the decision. As suggested in the examples just cited, a decision maker in a state of vigilance, after trying out all three modes of resolving a postdecisional conflict, may end up by selecting any one of them. The main point is that the vigilant decision maker is not likely to overlook any good opportunities for a compromise solution via curtailment of implementation. But, of course, he may end up becoming convinced by the information he has carefully sought and appraised that a more extreme mode of resolution—either complete undoing or complete reaffirmation—is best.

Since our analysis calls attention to the need for gaining more understanding of when, how, and why certain conditions of postdecisional regret promote different modes of conflict resolution, we shall review some evidence bearing on these questions. First we shall look at case material bearing on fundamental changes resulting from an episode of intense regret; then we shall examine research in experimental social psychology bearing on the consequences of spontaneous regret immediately following commitment.

Uses of Regret

Let us examine an act of conscience by an eminent poet who was willing to offend a President of the United States in order to avoid carrying out an impulsive decision that he intensely regretted. In 1965, Robert Lowell, along with twenty other poets and writers, was invited by President Lyndon B. Johnson to participate in a White House Festival of the Arts. Lowell immediately decided to accept the invitation, but a week after notifying the President of his acceptance he had second thoughts and reversed his decision. The President's Vietnam War policy was the major consideration prompting Lowell's postdecisional regret. In a widely published open letter to the President, he wrote:

> I am afraid that I accepted somewhat rapidly and greedily. I thought of such an occasion as a purely artistic flourish, even though every serious artist knows that he cannot enjoy public celebration without making subtle public commitments. But, after a week's wondering, I am conscience-bound to refuse your courteous invitation. . . . Although I am very enthusiastic about most of your domestic legislation and intentions, I nevertheless can only follow our present foreign policy with the greatest dismay and distrust. . . . At this anguished, delicate and perhaps determining moment, I feel I am serving you and our country best by not taking part in the White House Festival of the Arts.[3]

Lowell's letter bears on three facets of postdecisional regret—the sources of regret, the role of commitment, and the subjective emotional state that precedes efforts at resolution. First, incomplete consideration of the consequences of a decision (incomplete balance sheet) leads to a decision made in haste and repented in leisure. ("I accepted somewhat rapidly.") After making an ill-considered decision, the person encounters new information about overlooked losses that induces him to regret and reconsider it. In Lowell's case, reconsideration was probably provoked by negative social feedback from fellow writers and artists, many of whom were strongly opposed to giving any moral support to President Johnson. The nation's press carried reports about a number of well-known persons who refused the President's invitation and their grounds for doing so. Second, a major source of regret is the belated realization that the decision could lead to additional, undesirable commitments. ("Every serious artist knows that he cannot enjoy public celebration without making subtle public commitments.") Third, when the decision maker realizes that his faulty decision is at variance with values that he prizes, he develops feelings of self-disapproval. These feelings act as additional incentives for reversing the decision. ("I accepted . . . greedily. . . . I am conscience-bound to refuse your . . . invitation.")

Remorse over a single decisional choice, as in Lowell's case, motivates the person not only to try to undo the decision but to expiate and compensate for his error. Lowell went out of his way to make a public acknowledgment of his own irresponsibility and a public attack on the President, instead of writing a private note stating his objections or excusing himself on the grounds of unforeseen circumstances. Closely linked with his striving for expiation was an effort to undo the decision in such a way that the same mistake would never happen again. Lowell seems to have undone his decision in two different ways. At the most obvious level, his open attack on the President served as a kind of guarantee that no further honorary invitations would be forthcoming from the White House. But at a more subtle level, the author put himself on record as a serious artist who henceforth would be conscience-bound to refuse being honored in any public ceremony unless he felt certain that he approved of the accompanying subtle public commitments. Lowell appears to have reconceptualized his views of the public role of the artist in a politically polarized society, taking account of certain implications he had not thought about before.

Characteristically, the chastened decision maker who is seeking to atone for his misdeed comes to view the regretted decision not as a minor, all-too-human error but as a massive issue that will be encountered time and again in the future, and he vows that he will *never again* make such a terrible mistake. Postdecisional regret can therefore function as a prod to higher-level conceptual thinking—stimulating the decision maker to move from the concrete level of retrospection about a past mistake to abstract generalizations that can help him avoid making similar mistakes in the future. In a sense, then, such regret can be an important educative experience, leading to insightful intellectual analysis and enriching the person's repertoire of coping capabilities. This seems to be what people vaguely have in mind when they speak of having learned their lessons in the proverbial "school of hard knocks." But the educational potential of decisions that knock one about often fails to be realized. This poses a major problem for innovative psychologists in the field of education. Research on regret not only should help to elucidate the long-term effects of postdecisional crises but, in the practical sphere, should lead to new educational methods that would somehow enable students to make more effective use of their own personal "hard knocks."

Spontaneous Regret

Little is known as yet about the determinants and consequences of those "twinges" of regret that arise spontaneously after a decision is made but before the decision maker encounters any new information that threatens to undermine his decision. As we have seen in chapter 4, most laboratory and field studies of postdecisional reactions do not show any evidence of spontaneous regret; on the contrary, they typically reveal the opposite outcome, a tendency for the subjects to bolster the attractiveness of the choice they have just made. We pointed out that the conflict model of decision making differs from other theories in that it leads us to expect this outcome only when the conditions that make for the *bolstering form of defensive avoidance* are present. For the decision maker to exhibit bolstering he must: (1) be aware of the risks that generate postdecisional conflict; (2) have no hope of finding a better course of action than the one to which he has committed himself; (3) be aware of pressures that require him to take action, so that he is prevented from procrastinating; and (4) not know of anyone to whom he can shift responsibility for making the decision. The differences between conflict theory and other theories will be further highlighted as we examine the implications of the seemingly anomalous findings of a field experiment by Elaine Walster (1964) that dealt with a vital career decision. This experiment first called the attention of social psychologists to spontaneous regret as a tendency that goes counter to bolstering, or dissonance reduction, and resulted in major revisions of cognitive dissonance theory.

Walster's Field Experiment

Walster systematically investigated fluctuations in postdecisional evaluations of alternative job choices. Through the cooperation of the U.S. Army, 277 draftees were made available as research subjects at the Fort Ord reception center, California. Each subject, within a day or two of arriving for military training, was interviewed by Walster in her role as representative of a special army job placement program. The draftee was given to understand that the purpose of the interview was to arrive at a job placement that would be his fixed assignment during his two years in the Army. As part of the interview, the experimenter asked each draftee about his job preferences, examined his vocational test scores, and sought information about his previous job and educational experience. Then the draftee was offered a choice between two jobs that he had previously rated on a pretest as moderately attractive. It was stressed that these two were the only jobs for which he was qualified that were available at the time.

Subjects were randomly assigned to one of four "time interval" conditions. In the *immediate* condition, subjects were required to rerate the attractiveness of the two jobs immediately (less than one minute) after announcing their choice. Subjects in the other conditions rerated the two jobs after an interval of either four, fifteen, or ninety minutes. During these intervals, subjects were left alone in a room with nothing to do. They remained isolated until the experimenter returned and requested them to rerate the job alternatives.

How attractive were the job alternatives after each of the four time periods? Walster found that the men who were required to rerate the jobs immediately after announcing their decision showed a slight but nonsignificant tendency to increase the attractiveness of the chosen alternative. In contrast, the men who rerated the jobs after a four-minute interval showed evidence of a spontaneous convergence of attractiveness ratings, which Walster calls "regret."[4] Although exposed to no new information, the men rated the chosen alternative as less desirable and the rejected alternative as more desirable. But the fifteen-minute group showed the characteristic dissonance-reduction pattern, with the chosen alternative rated as more attractive than it was initially and the rejected alternative as less attractive. The ninety-minute group, like the immediate group, showed no evidence of any significant trend, neither spread of the alternatives nor convergence. (See figure 16.)

When Walster's results were published in 1964, most social psychologists found them surprising. The absence of significant bolstering effects immediately following a decision seemed to be something of an exception in the literature; and the absence of postdecisional bolstering in the ninety-minute condition also appeared to be unusual.

Walster points out that her selection of time intervals was quite arbitrary. There was no way to know, when designing the experiment, which intervals would produce evidence of the onset or termination of dissonance reduction or regret. Of course it is conceivable that if Walster had worked with a different or more inclusive set of intervals, a clearer or more consistent regret-dissonance cycle might have emerged. Nevertheless, Walster's field experiment provides clear-cut evidence of a brief, measurable period of spontaneous regret and suggests that the regret reaction may precede dissonance reduction. Her results challenged the then-current

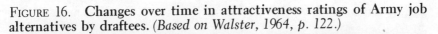

FIGURE 16. **Changes over time in attractiveness ratings of Army job alternatives by draftees.** (*Based on Walster, 1964, p. 122.*)

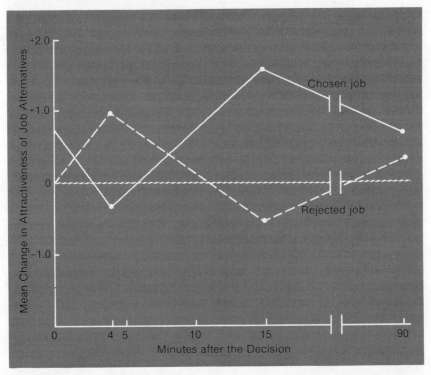

view that the postdecision phase is invariably characterized by bolstering, or dissonance reduction.

The essential parametric studies have not yet been carried out to determine whether there are dependable fluctuations or cycles in a decision maker's ratings of alternatives over successive time intervals following commitment. Consequently, we cannot be sure that Walster's results describe a general phenomenon in decision-making behavior. It is quite conceivable that certain specific features of the particular setting might be responsible for some, if not all, of Walster's findings. The absence of bolstering after ninety minutes, for example, might be attributable to the boredom and resentment created by keeping the men waiting around in isolation for such a long time without giving them anything to do; by the time they were asked for their reratings most of the men may have been too annoyed to bother to give conscientious answers or may have resorted to a perfunctory response based mainly on their spontaneous recall of the ratings they had put down the first time. Still, we must recognize that Walster's experiment dealt with a career decision affecting at least two years of each soldier's life, and it seems unlikely that men would give perfunctory or insincere responses at the outset of their career in the Army.

Because Walster's field experiment was well designed and furnishes the best available data to date on changes in ratings of alternatives following a vital life decision, it has had considerable influence on the views of a number of leading social psychologists. Leon Festinger (1964) and Jack Brehm (1968), for example, have modified their theories of postdecisional behavior on the assumption that Walster's data reveal a genuine phenomenon of spontaneous regret. We shall briefly review their analyses as well as Walster's own interpretation of her findings. Then, tentatively making the same assumption about the genuineness of the phenomenon, we shall indicate a radically different way of interpreting Walster's findings, suggested by our conflict model of decision making.

Alternative Explanations

Festinger (1964) interprets Walster's findings as indicating that a brief period of postdecisional regret regularly occurs prior to dissonance reduction. He postulates that regret is a temporary, transitional stage that is essential for the onset of dissonance reduction. Often the period of regret is so brief, according to Festinger, that it passes unnoticed; but its presence could be detected if measurements were obtained at the right moment shortly after commitment. These would regularly show, asserts Festinger, a tendency toward depreciation of the chosen alternative relative to the rejected alternatives, indicating spontaneous regret, just as in Walster's study; this would always be followed by the reverse outcome (bolstering, or dissonance reduction). Festinger maintains that the reaction of regret is necessary for the work of dissonance reduction to begin. Immediately after a decision is made, the person must focus his attention on any existing dissonance before he can set about dealing with it. Thus, in Festinger's revised theory, spontaneous regret regularly occurs shortly after every decision is made, as a consequence of the salience of dissonant cognitions, and is regularly followed by bolstering of the decision.

A different basis for spontaneous regret is singled out by Brehm (1966, 1972). He attributes spontaneous regret, immediately after making a decision, to a motivational state of *psychological reactance*, which is aroused whenever freedom to select an alternative is usurped, eliminated, or restricted (see chapter 10). Reactance is manifested in the person's attempts to regain lost freedoms and to protect against further loss of choice. Whenever a decision is made, according to Brehm, two freedoms are lost—the freedom to *reject* the chosen alternative, and the freedom to *select* the unchosen alternative. (Wicklund, 1974, suggests that the freedom to remain uncommitted is yet another lost freedom.) Brehm, Linder, Crane, and Brehm (1969) predict that "the selected alternative should tend to become *less attractive* because freedom to reject it has been eliminated, and the rejected alternative should tend to become *more attractive* because freedom to have it has been eliminated." In short, the decision maker will experience displeasure at having reduced his own freedom, and this will be reflected in reratings of the alternatives in the opposite direction from bolstering.[5]

The assumption that spontaneous regret is an invariable but temporary consequence of commitment to a new decision is challenged by Walster and Walster (1970). On the basis of evidence from a later experiment involving a choice between unpleasant tasks, they modified and extended Festinger's dissonance explanation of the spontaneous regret phenomenon. Walster and Walster, like Festinger, emphasize the significance of announcing a decision as a kind of psychological watershed that releases a great deal of concern about the newly chosen course of action.

> Once one is committed to a single choice alternative, the *relative* merits of the alternatives are no longer of primary interest; of primary importance are the consequences that the chosen alternative will have for the individual. . . . In addition, the positive and negative elements of the chosen alternative are bound to have a greater emotional impact after the decision, when they are definite consequences, than they did before the decision [p. 1002].

Thus, immediately following an act of commitment it is not the unchosen alternative but the chosen one that has primary emotional impact, because its consequences move from the realm of the speculative to that of the definite. If there are strongly negative aspects to the chosen alternative, the person will take them more seriously than ever following commitment, and it is this preoccupation that produces spontaneous regret.

The experiment by Walster and Walster that led them to revise Festinger's theory involved asking college students to make a choice between two types of unpleasant stimulation in the laboratory. The experimenter explained that two different experiments were going to be conducted, one requiring the subjects to taste some disagreeable substances that "will be so unpleasant that you will find it intolerable to swallow and difficult to prevent nausea"; the other experiment would require them to undergo "painful and uncomfortable" electric shock. After reading detailed descriptions of both experiments, each student was asked to decide which one he would be willing to subject himself to. (In a control condition, the subjects were asked to read the two descriptions and then, instead of being given a choice, were randomly assigned to one of the two unpleasant experiments.) Ratings of the attractiveness of the two alternatives were obtained before the choice was made and again afterward at varying time intervals, just as in the earlier Walster (1964) experiment. A plausible but irrelevant (visual acuity) task was interpolated between the time of decision and the time of reappraisal.

When they designed the experiment, the investigators had expected that the postdecisional ratings would show dissonance reduction in the form of bolstering the chosen alternative, which might or might not be preceded by momentary manifestations of spontaneous regret. They were surprised to find that there was no evidence at all of bolstering. On the contrary, the longer the time interval after commitment, the *less* attractive the chosen alternative became, as measured by the subjects' ratings.[6] (See figure 17).

Walster and Walster surmise that the unexpected outcome is attributable to the overwhelmingly negative character of the choice alternatives. They point out that the earlier research (e.g., Brehm and Cohen, 1959; Brock, 1963), which showed dissonance reduction following commitment without any preceding manifestations of spontaneous regret, had involved only positive choices. They suggest that after commitment the person realizes he must live with the decision, and that *the more negative the anticipated consequences, the more postdecisional dissatisfaction will be manifested.*

Our conflict theory, which specifies various patterns of coping with

FIGURE 17. **Postdecisional evaluations of alternatives at varying time intervals following commitment.**

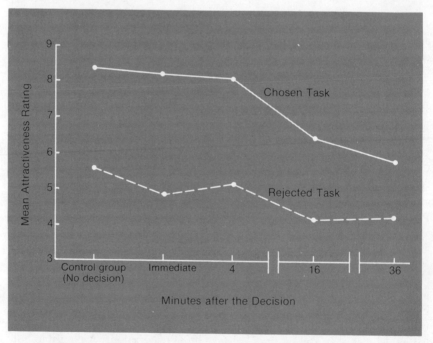

The fifteen-point scale used by Walster and Walster has been reversed so that low numbers mean low attractiveness.

Source: E. Walster and G. W. Walster, "Choice between Negative Alternatives: Dissonance Reduction or Regret?" *Psychological Reports*, 1970, 26, 995–1005. Reprinted by permission of the authors and the publisher.

disruptive feedback, agrees with this conclusion and with the general thrust of Walster and Walster's analysis. Especially compatible with conflict theory is a major implication of their view—namely, that depending upon the nature and magnitude of the losses, spontaneous regret can be either (1) *totally absent*, with bolstering as the only tendency that is manifested; (2) *temporary*, followed by manifestations of bolstering; or (3) *persistently dominant*, with no manifestations at all of bolstering.

Our theory, however, is not the same in all details as the Walsters'. In particular, we disagree on the precise conditions that determine the three different outcomes. Walster and Walster explicitly predict that whenever the choice alternatives are "predominantly negative," as in their experiment on a choice between two forms of unpleasant stimulation, the outcome will be prolonged regret with little or no bolstering (p. 1001). We infer from our theoretical analysis, on the other hand, that although there is a greater likelihood of spontaneous regret when the choice involves predominantly negative alternatives, the outcome is not always the one predicted by Walster and Walster, because other conditions—such as whether or not vigilance is stimulated by signs that *relevant information will be forthcoming* and whether the social milieu fosters the *salience of impending threats or of reassurances that counteract the threats*—can play a determining role.

Walster and Walster's theory implies that any decision entailing clear-cut negative consequences—such as going on a diet or carrying out any costly action for which unpleasant losses are bound to be salient—will generally be followed by spontaneous regret (but will not necessarily be followed by bolstering). In contrast, the conflict model leads us to expect that *neither regret nor bolstering will occur following commitment unless certain conditions are fulfilled that make for persisting decisional conflict*. Thus, our theoretical analysis of postdecisional behavior in terms of conflict dynamics coincides somewhat with Walster and Walster's theory but differs in some crucial ways with regard to the necessary and sufficient conditions for spontaneous regret to occur. We do not question the observations made by adherents of dissonance and reactance theory; we have observed the phenomena to which they call attention, not only in social psychological experiments but also in a variety of clinical settings. But we believe that Festinger, Brehm, and, to a lesser extent, Walster and Walster, have overgeneralized some of the regret phenomena. It seems to us on both theoretical and empirical grounds that there is reason to expect that *spontaneous regret will not occur at all following many vital decisions*, even though the decision maker knows all along that the chosen course of action will have some undesirable consequences.

Before discussing the implications of conflict theory, we shall summarize some clinical evidence that convinces us that a temporary reaction of postdecisional regret is not an invariable phenomenon—that a pattern of unconflicted adherence and implementation, unruffled by any manifestations of regret during the first thirty or forty minutes following commitment, does in fact occur among some decision makers who have just committed themselves to a course of action whose most obvious consequences for the short run are predominantly negative.

Antithesis: The Raring-to-Go Reaction

Our main observations on the absence of postdecisional regret come from intensive interviews with clients at the Yale clinics set up to help people quit smoking or lose weight (Janis, in press). In the clinic, a counselor informs the client that he has no wonderful new gimmick to offer that will make it easy to attain the long-sought goal. Rather, the counselor's recommendations are, in effect, for the client to undergo a painful, "cold turkey" type of cure, or as close to it as he can bear—to stop smoking immediately or to cut down food intake immediately to a rigorous but well-balanced diet of 1000 or 1200 calories. Among the manifestations of predecisional conflict displayed by the clients right after being given these recommendations are their explicit statements of worry about the physical and psychological suffering that may ensue if they accept the recommendations. (Often they strongly emphasize their fear of becoming depressed by yet another failure.) After a discussion with the client of his worries, during which he receives empathic comments intended to strengthen his self-confidence about being able to curb his excessive smoking or eating, the counselor asks the client if he is willing to commit himself to the clinic's recommendations—to start following the rules of the "cold turkey" treatment right now, to send in weekly progress reports, and to return for a follow-up interview a month or so later.

The majority of clients commit themselves to the counselor's set of recommendations. Many are extremely enthusiastic, in a near-elated mood—"raring-to-go." As the interview continues for a half-hour or longer after the act of commitment, these keyed-up clients show no signs of postdecisional regret. Rather, they repeatedly state how pleased they are about having overcome their reluctance to make the difficult decision. They convey this message not only by what they say but by their tone of voice, facial expressions, and gestures, all of which make it appear unlikely that they are merely being polite by telling the counselor what they think he or she expects them to say. Counselors often come out of the interviews utterly convinced of the genuineness of the client's commitment, and impressed with the warm enthusiasm with which their recommendations and assurances were received. Because some clients so fervently express their new-found confidence that "*this* time, nothing is going to stop me from succeeding!" we have felt it necessary to take steps to counteract the potentially detrimental effects of overoptimism by introducing emotional inoculation interventions, including role-playing exercises that require the client to enact typical setbacks, such as suc-cumbing to the temptation to abandon the diet at a social gathering where rich desserts are served or where the hostess would obviously be hurt if her prize offerings were refused.

From these clinical observations, we are led to conclude that during the first half-hour or so after commitment, the presence or absence of spontaneous regret depends upon the conditions that prevail while the decision is being made and after it is announced. Consequently, we expect that the spontaneous regret phenomenon observed by Walster and her collaborators will *not* prove to be a constant effect of commitment (as Festinger and Brehm predict for all decisions, and as Walster and Walster predict for deprivational decisions like going on a strict diet). Rather, we predict an interaction effect that is dependent upon the presence or ab-sence of certain social and situational factors, such as the social stimula-tion or encouragement of a counselor or peer group.[7] To illustrate these factors, however, we must look further into the phenomenology of the decisions under discussion.

Occasionally we have encountered clients who clearly manifest regret immediately after having committed themselves; some of them coun-teract regret by bolstering the decision and some do not. But spontaneous regret appears to be a less frequent reaction than the enthusiastic op-timism expressed by many clients following their explicit commitment to the "cold turkey" regimen. We suspect that a crucial determinant of the latter reaction is the presence of someone who gives the client social support and augments his self-confidence. Most people who come to a clinic are somewhat pessimistic and feel nearly defeated by their previous unsuccessful attempts to conquer their smoking or overeating habits. Jerome Frank (1972) asserts that most persons who seek help at a psycho-logical clinic are in a demoralized state because of their past failures. The clients who come to our clinics do not appear to be exceptions.

At the outset of the interview, the client's level of decisional conflict is generally high. Most clients manifest a pattern of defensive avoidance, giving plausible-sounding rationalizations about why the usual methods others use to change their smoking or overeating habits won't work in their own particular case. The counselor does not accept these ra-tionalizations at face value (though he does not necessarily try to refute them); rather, he offers encouragement by his empathic manner and reas-suring comments, which builds up the client's self-confidence about being able to succeed if he commits himself to the feared "cold turkey" treatment.

In terms of our theoretical model, we interpret the success of the treatment in such cases as being essentially a matter of changing the client's response to the third basic question ("Is it realistic to hope to find a better solution?") from *no* to *yes*, by creating the expectation that the conflict will somehow be resolved or that new information will be available. Presumably the client's responses to the first crucial questions had been positive to begin with, and decisional conflict is still present. The change in response to the third question, should, according to our model, result in a marked decrease in defensive avoidance behavior, with a corresponding increase in vigilant search and appraisal. We think we see evidence of this type of change in many of the clients. As the interview goes on, the clients talk less about excuses for past or future failures and begin to ask realistic questions about specific problems that might cause trouble if they try to follow the recommended "cold turkey" course of action. At the time they commit themselves, some seem to visualize themselves as succeeding rather than failing—a change in self-image that we believe reflects a marked change in outlook and mood, from pessimism to optimism, from low to high morale. This transformation is most apparent in the subgroup of clients who become manifestly elated during the interview. They thank the counselor profusely for giving them the encouragement they need and speak exuberantly of looking forward to conquering their weakness. This is the type of mood that, to varying degrees of intensity, persists throughout the last part of the interview in those clients who show no signs of spontaneous regret after asserting that they will carry out the recommended course of action.

A major contributing factor to postdecisional euphoria as against postdecisional regret is the *continued presence of the supportive counselor*, once he or she is seen as a benign helper. The counselor's confidence about the client's ability to carry out the recommended course of action apparently communicates itself to the client. We gather from comparing follow-up interviews of clients who fail to live up to the commitment during the following months with interviews of those who succeed that a positive image of the counselor not only counteracts spontaneous regret immediately after commitment, but also facilitates adherence to the decision during subsequent weeks. This facilitating effect enables the client to remain unshaken by negative feedback that might otherwise evoke acute regret—provided that the positive image of the helper is reinforced by symbolic contact—for example, by asking the client to make weekly reports or by giving the client an appointment for a face-to-face meeting in the near future. (For the practical implications of the regret-reducing properties of a supportive counselor, see Janis [1975 and in press].)

A Reinterpretation of Walster's Findings

In order to use the conflict model as a source of hypotheses to account for regret phenomena we must elaborate on a number of assumptions mentioned earlier. First of all, we made the assumption that whenever postdecisional regret occurs, the decision maker has encountered a challenging stimulus and has responded to the first crucial question ("Are the risks serious if I don't change to a different course of action?") with *yes* or *maybe*. When regret arises spontaneously, there is no apparent cause for dissatisfaction; the challenging stimulus, therefore, must be either subtle external reminders or internal cues, such as memories and fantasies about the unfavorable consequences of the chosen alternative. These are very weak challenging stimuli that would typically be dismissed with an emphatic negative answer when the decision maker asks himself the first crucial question following commitment to a new course of action. We assume that the higher the quality of decision making, the higher the threshold for a positive response to the first crucial question, because the person is likely already to have "worked through" the unfavorable aspects of the choice and to be well prepared to cope with any source of challenge. It follows that if weak challenging cues evoke even a temporary positive response to the first basic question after a definitive commitment has been made, the choice was most likely *not* based on high-quality, vigilant decision-making procedures.

Let us now examine the various patterns in the conflict model to see if we can find a plausible explanation for the apparent fluctuations in evaluations of job alternatives displayed in Walster's study by Army trainees after committing themselves to a job choice. We surmise that before the decision practically all the draftees would be highly conflicted (two years of their lives and perhaps their physical survival were at stake), and that many expected that a good solution could be found if there were sufficient time; they did *not*, however, have sufficient time to search for and evaluate the alternatives. These three conditions are precisely those that give rise to the hypervigilant reaction, which of all of the conflict patterns is the one most characterized by high rates of vacillation (see table 2).

Many of the draftees probably felt entrapped by the premature deadline because they believed the psychologist to be endowed with the full power of the military establishment to issue binding orders. These men, as a result of being suddenly confronted with the job choice dilemma, would be in a hypervigilant state both before and after they announced their choice.[8]

In a state of hypervigilance, each draftee would frantically search his memory during the few minutes before he was required to announce his choice. He would summon up whatever bits of information he could recall about the alternatives open to him and would try to imagine what the consequences of those alternatives might be. When hypervigilance is aroused, a person uses his imagination to envision the most threatening possibilities that could ensue, such as ending up with a military assignment that is endlessly boring, thoroughly humiliating, or physically dangerous. None of the alternatives open to the draftees would appear to be free from very serious risks, and the aroused decision maker would therefore fluctuate back and forth in his momentary judgment as to which was the lesser evil. After announcing his choice to the psychologist, he would still find himself in a double-avoidance conflict between wanting to avoid the risky job he had just chosen and wanting to avoid the punishment that would result from trying to undo the commitment he had just made.

Hypervigilance, like other states of high emotional arousal, may persist for many minutes and even for hours after the instigating stimuli are no longer present. When hypervigilance is induced by pressure to meet a premature deadline for a vital decision, emotional equanimity is not restored immediately after that deadline is met. The usual closure tendencies do not come into play immediately after commitment; rather, the decision maker continues to display manifestations of anticipatory regret as he obsessionally mulls over the serious risks that he realizes he has let himself in for by making the binding commitment that he wishes he could have evaded or postponed.[9]

The most extreme cases of *persistent hypervigilance* accompanied by acute regret are observed after people in a state of near-panic make uncourageous or foolish emergency decisions, ignoring the plight of others who need their help, during an unexpected disaster (see Erikson, 1977; Grinker and Spiegel, 1945). Earlier we mentioned that this type of reaction is epitomized in Joseph Conrad's *Lord Jim*, which tells the story of a conscientious British merchant marine officer who, during the excitement of a disaster at sea, made a split-second decision to abandon his ship, without attempting to save any of the hundreds of passengers on board. Immediately after entering the lifeboat he was overwhelmed with remorse for having violated the traditional naval code, which formed part of his internalized standards of behavior. The officer's postdecisional regret, which was strongly reinforced by the humiliation of being publicly reprimanded and legally punished for his act of cowardice, led him to devote himself to acts of expiation and persisted for the rest of his life. The *Lord Jim* type of reaction is sometimes observed among combat veterans and civilian disaster victims who blame themselves for having opted for survival during an emergency without having tried to save their companions (see Janis, 1951, 1971; Lifton, 1971).

We assume that the same tendency toward spontaneous postdecisional regret, although much less extreme, will occur whenever a person is required to make a premature commitment—one that he realizes might turn out to be a poor choice because he did not have sufficient time to conduct an adequate information search or to make a proper assessment of costs and risks. Because the crucial condition of being forced to make a premature commitment prevailed in the military-job choice that confronted the draftees in Walster's study, we think it is plausible to reinterpret her findings of temporary postdecisional regret as a manifestation of *hypervigilance* that persisted for at least a short time after the imposed deadline was met.

In summary, our reinterpretation of Walster's experimental evidence highlights the essential differences between our conflict theory of decision making and the alternative theories. Unlike Festinger's theory of cognitive dissonance and Brehm's theory of reactance, our conflict model leads us to expect that the arousal of postdecisional regret and its duration depend upon the conditions under which a decision is made and the conditions that prevail after it is made. In agreement with Walster and Walster, but for different theoretical reasons, we do *not* expect to find an invariable sequence of spontaneous regret followed by bolstering after the act of commitment. We have indicated how our assumptions differ from Walster and Walster's, leading us to predict that spontaneous regret after a binding commitment will predominantly occur under a rather unusual set of circumstances—namely, when the person believes himself to be fully committed but, because of a premature deadline, continues to vacillate because he is still in a hypervigilant state. We are quite prepared to encounter exceptions to this conclusion, however, since research on the conditions that make for regret may turn up other determining factors that we do not yet know about, which may or may not be compatible with our model. Meantime, our model, by rejecting the assumption that postdecisional regret is always present but too subtle or too fleeting to be detected, emphasizes the necessity of searching for situational variables that may determine the intensity and persistence of regret. We expect that the main factors determining *spontaneous* regret following a binding commitment are those that induce hypervigilance. Under conditions where a new challenge *elicits* regret, however, the coping pattern of vigilance can become dominant and give rise to manifestations of vacillation along with the other symptoms of postdecisional conflict.

PART 4

Effective Interventions

CHAPTER 13

Challenging Outworn Decisions

In Nikolai Gogol's best-known story, "The Overcoat," Akaky Akakievich, an impoverished middle-aged clerk, goes through a decisional crisis centered on an economic dilemma that more affluent people are spared. His ragged overcoat is so badly worn that it can no longer protect him from the bitter chill of the St. Petersburg winter. He decides to spend a few rubles, which he can barely spare, to add two or three more patches where they are most needed. At the tailor's shop, Akaky Akakievich goes out of his way to express seemingly great conviction that his decision will work out just fine: "It's like this, Petrovich . . . the overcoat, the cloth . . . you see, everywhere else it is quite strong; it's a little dusty and looks as though it were old, but it is new and it is only in one place just a little . . . on the back, and just a little worn on one shoulder and on this shoulder, too, a little . . . do you see? That's all, and it's not much work . . ."[1] But his confidence is rudely shattered by the tailor's expert appraisal: "No, it can't be repaired; a wretched garment! . . . There is nothing to put a patch on. There is nothing for it to hold on to; there is a great strain on it; it is not worth calling cloth; it would fly away at a breath of wind." The poor clerk is shocked by this confrontation into reconsidering: "So that's it! well, it really is so utterly unexpected . . . who would have thought . . . what a circumstance. . . ." He makes one more feeble attempt to persuade the tailor to do a patching-up job but again is told that it simply cannot be done. "Then Akaky Akakievich saw that there was no escape from a new overcoat and he was utterly depressed."

No longer able to maintain his illusions about the threadbare overcoat, he works out a new plan—to cut down even more on his meager meals, to do without light in his dismal room, and to put up with other privations in order to purchase a new one. As it turns out, this decision has the effect of transforming him for a time into a new person—no longer uncertain,

339

indecisive, and hesitant; "more alive, even more strong-willed, like a man who has set before himself a definite goal."

The poor clerk's long-standing decision, renewed year after year, to keep on using the old overcoat by having it patched had become as outworn as the overcoat itself. And like the threadbare garment, the decision had too little substantive basis left for him to be able to bolster it successfully. There was nothing "to put a patch on," and it could not withstand a "breath of wind," in the form of the tailor's expert appraisal. All outworn decisions are like that. The decision maker, insensitive to the changing realities that make the chosen course of action obsolete, tries right up until the bitter end to maintain illusions based on fanciful rationalizations, invented to bolster the choice. An outworn decision may prove as sorely deficient as Akaky Akakievich's outworn overcoat, yet the decision maker continues with it, until at last an unequivocal confrontation makes him realize that he cannot go on that way, which shocks and depresses him. We have already discussed an authentic example of just such a phenomenon—Louis Fischer's decision to remain in the Communist movement despite his awareness of considerable evidence that this course of action no longer satisfied his goals. In such cases, the bolstering is excessive since it is not merely a patch here and there put in to strengthen weak spots but rather has become the mainstay of support for a worn-out fabric that would otherwise fall apart.

To eliminate the undue influence of unrealistic rationalizations, special forms of intervention seem to be essential. The need for effective confrontations that challenge fantasies and illusions is acute whenever a decision maker continues to ignore or deny negative feedback that should send him scurrying to find a better means for achieving his goals. In this chapter, we describe recent work in the development of intervention techniques that may prove to be effective devices for challenging outworn decisions, and that may even sometimes achieve a fundamental transformation like Akaky Akakievich's. We shall concentrate on two main techniques that were specifically developed for the purpose of aiding people who want to change their behavior but persistently fail to do so. One involves an "awareness of rationalizations" procedure intended to make the decision maker realize his flimsy basis for maintaining a defective course of action. It induces him to formulate, label, and confront the main rationalizations he has been using to ward off decisional conflict. The other, which we refer to as "emotional role playing," consists of requiring the decision maker to participate in a vivid psychodrama. In the assigned role, he imaginatively portrays his reactions to the losses he will sustain if he continues to adhere to his outworn, disadvantageous decision.[2]

These two intervention techniques were evolved during a series of field studies conducted in our clinics for people who want to stop smoking or to lose weight. In the course of investigating the effects of challenging information, we encountered many clinic volunteers who felt that they ought to modify their smoking or eating behavior and yet were extremely reluctant to do so. In these cases we often detected signs of a disguised form of an excessively bolstered decision. We came to realize that little progress would be made unless we could find some way of counteracting the rationalizations that enabled them to keep right on smoking or overeating.

We shall first give a brief summary of the background of clinical observations that led to the development of the two new intervention techniques. Then we shall describe each technique in detail and present evidence from controlled field experiments bearing on their effectiveness. Finally, we shall call attention to the implications of these findings for developing effective intervention techniques that may be applicable to a variety of other types of decisions, including policy decisions made by executives in business firms and government.

Clinical Examples

What can be done to help people who say over and over again that they want to change their behavior, but in practice manage to continue with the same old, unacceptable course of action? In our antismoking and weight-reduction clinics, we have interviewed scores of clients who say quite convincingly that they want to stop smoking or overeating in order to avoid damage to their health; but when the interviewer probes to find out how seriously the client really regards the health hazards, it soon becomes apparent that the client is inordinately complacent about continuing the old course of action because he is bolstering it with numerous rationalizations that prevent full acknowledgment of his vulnerability. Some men and women who smoked two or three packs of cigarettes a day, for example, relied heavily on rationalizations that explicitly minimized the chances of their becoming cancer victims ("It won't happen to me"). Others fully acknowledged the risk of lung disease but adopted a fatalistic attitude or claimed that their habit was so uncontrollable that they could do nothing about it. All such rationalizations by a heavy smoker dampen the impact of information about health hazards, with the result that the smoker is only mildly concerned about the potential costs of his present course of action.

People who cling to outworn decisions react in a characteristic way each time they are confronted with challenging information. They appear to go through the first two or three stages of decision making, but then promptly return to accepting their outworn course of action. When shown a movie or pamphlet about the health hazards of smoking, for example, heavy smokers become momentarily concerned about the potential threat to themselves (stage 1) but still display overt resistance, such as questioning the reliability of the information. Next they start to consider alternative courses of action that might counteract the threat, such as limiting themselves to only one cigarette every three hours (stage 2). They assert that they *ought* to stop smoking entirely but that it is too difficult to do so. At this point their rationalizations about being hopelessly addicted or somehow invulnerable to the threat emerge with full force, and the upshot is that they resume their behavior as heavy smokers (old stage 5). We have come to regard this repeated sequence through stages 1 and 2 and then back to old stage 5 as a *short-circuited decision loop*, which somehow has to be broken if the person is ever to move on to the appraisal and commitment stages required for making a new stable decision.

Of course, there is the possibility that the heavy smoker who asserts that it is too difficult to change may be right. He may be so strongly addicted and may have suffered such severe withdrawal symptoms in the past that the most powerful consideration in his balance sheet is his realistic expectation of *immediate suffering* if he attempts to cut down, which outweighs the lower-probability expectation of *long-term suffering* from lung disease. Consequently, the only new course of action he sees available to him is going to an antismoking clinic where he can repeatedly assert his *wish* to change, while continuing to smoke as usual.

Although this type of balance sheet analysis may be applicable to some of the chronic heavy smokers we have worked with, it certainly is not applicable to all those who exhibit the characteristic short-circuited decision loop. A number of these chronic heavy smokers, after displaying the characteristic loop several times, suddenly encounter a powerful challenge to which they respond by rapidly moving through all five stages of the decision-making process. For example, in a group of very heavy smokers undergoing treatment at the Yale antismoking clinic, one man showed a sudden transformation after seven weekly meetings at which he had consistently described himself as hopelessly addicted to cigarette smoking. At the eighth meeting, he reported a dramatic "conversion" experience. He told the group that a few days earlier he had visited a close friend in the hospital who was dying of lung cancer. After leaving the hospital he had thrown away his cigarettes and hadn't touched one since. He offered to try to arrange for others in the group to visit his dying friend. But just his description of that visit and the effect it had on him was sufficient to break through the short-circuited loop for two other members of the group, both of whom promptly followed his example. One month later, all three of these supposedly hopeless cases were still not smoking. Thus, exposure to a dramatic event or merely hearing a description of it functioned as an effective challenge, terminating the short-circuited decision loop for these heavy smokers. Their earlier assertions that they were too addicted to cigarettes to ever be able to change were obviously not correct descriptions of their capabilities, but rationalizations. In each of these instances, an effective challenge counteracted the person's long-used rationalization and gave rise to a dramatically rapid change in overt action.

In our weight-reduction clinic, overweight persons also use obvious rationalizations to bolster their inertia. They "talk" a good diet but go right on overeating, because they cannot mobilize themselves to resist the temptation to take snacks between meals or indulge in rich desserts. A very fat woman, for example, was unable to carry out her intention to diet until one summer day when she overheard a derogatory comment about her physical appearance as she was walking along a beach wearing a bathing suit. According to her account, this overheard remark by a stranger "shocked" her into realizing that she was wrong in thinking that her gross body proportions went unnoticed by others.

Our working assumption is that many persons who claim that they want to go on a diet, give up smoking, or carry out some other desired form of self-improvement are clinging to excessively bolstered decisions that depend for their continuation upon rather flimsy rationalizations that exaggerate the withdrawal symptoms and other difficulties involved in changing their habits. If these defensive beliefs can somehow be undermined or bypassed, only threadbare support remains for the person's current course of action; he can then move from good intentions to action and wholeheartedly carry out a decision to change instead of merely continuing to say he would like to.

There is some evidence that among people who continue to be heavy smokers and do not go to smoking clinics, a sizable percentage acknowledge that there are strong reasons for changing their smoking habits. An attitude survey conducted by Baer (1966) with 249 male college students who were smokers showed that 70 percent of the heavy smokers as against only 18 percent of the light or moderate smokers said that they smoked too much. Most of the heavy smokers (90 percent) also expressed dissatisfaction with their smoking behavior by asserting that they would not want their children to smoke. Yet, only 40 percent stated that they were trying to limit their smoking behavior, in contrast to 58 percent of the light or moderate smokers. The most impressive finding was that about one out of every three of the heavy smokers claimed that they *could not* stop smoking, whereas only a negligible percentage of the light or moderate smokers made this assertion. This pattern of expressed dissatisfaction with heavy smoking combined with signs of no intention of changing actual smoking behavior suggests that many young smokers are *partly* challenged by information about the undesirable consequences of heavy smoking but nevertheless decide that they cannot change their present course of action. This is the pattern we have observed among many middle-aged smokers in our clinics.

Our case observations of concurrent changes in rationalizations and action—such as those that occurred among some group members when they were told by a fellow member about a dying cancer victim—led us to search for effective forms of intervention that would embody the essential components of those successful challenges that occasionally occur spontaneously. The "awareness-of-rationalizations" treatment involves inducing *cognitive confrontations* designed to counteract the rationalizations that are typically used to bolster outworn decisions. The "emotional role-playing" technique is a form of *emotional confrontation* that we devised for the purpose of undermining and bypassing the cognitive defenses that function as a protective facade for the outworn decision. Both techniques are promising means for transforming mere talk about good intentions into action.

Cognitive Confrontations

Cognitive confrontations that sensitize a person to the inconsistencies between his beliefs and his actions and make him uncomfortable about them have long been recognized as a means for challenging misconceptions, as exemplified by Socrates' method of asking a person to state how he acts, what he believes, and why he believes it. McGuire (1960) points out that the Socratic method of merely asking a person to verbalize his beliefs should be especially effective in inducing changes in the direction of internal consistency when a person has set up two logic-tight compartments based on wishful thinking and has not previously been required to verbalize both of the isolated cognitions within the same conversation. The evidence from McGuire's studies of attitude change indicates that merely inducing college students to assert their beliefs about the truth of various premises and conclusions led them, a week later, to display less wishful thinking and correspondingly more logical consistency.

Another type of cognitive confrontation intended to promote attitude change is the self-insight procedure developed by Katz, Sarnoff, and McClintock (1956). The procedure consists of confronting the subject with a psychological analysis in nontechnical language designed to show the relationship between prejudiced attitudes and certain mechanisms of ego defense. In the first part of the procedure the interviewer describes in general terms the dynamics of scapegoating, projection, and compensation and how they function in the development of prejudice. In the second part, the interviewer presents a case history of a woman college student, similar in age and background to the subjects themselves, to illustrate how these defense mechanisms are used by the student to support her racial prejudice. The authors report evidence that this "insight-inducing" technique is effective in changing prejudiced attitudes.

More recently, a method of cognitive confrontation has been developed by Rokeach (1971) which is designed to make the person "consciously aware of states of inconsistency that exist chronically within his own value-attitude system below the level of his conscious awareness." Rokeach's method consists of four main steps: First, the subject is asked to rank a series of terms in a way that will show how much importance he attaches to values such as "a comfortable life," "freedom," and "equality." Second, the subject is asked to state his position on a controversial issue, such as civil rights demonstrations. Third, the subject is presented with a persuasive communication designed to arouse feelings of self-dissatisfaction by emphasizing the inconsistencies, self-centered values, and implicit hypocrisy displayed by many people. This communication includes tables of data collected in prior research with other college students, which are interpreted as showing that low interest in "equality" is associated with being against civil rights. The final step is to ask the student to examine his own ratings on "equality" and the civil rights movement to see if they show the pattern that has just been criticized.

Rokeach's findings show that this technique is effective in arousing feelings of self-dissatisfaction and in inducing significant changes in verbalized attitudes and values that persist months after the experimental treatment. Impressive behavioral changes were also produced, with subjects responding positively several months later to a promotional letter from the NAACP and in some cases joining the organization. Most of Rokeach's studies, however, deal with purely verbal changes, such as in the rankings of "equality" and "freedom." As expected, he found that these changes, as determined in follow-up questionnaires given from three weeks to over a year later, were most pronounced in those subjects who earlier had expressed the most self-dissatisfaction immediately after being exposed to the cognitive confrontation procedure.

In the same tradition as the foregoing research on cognitive confrontations and self-insight procedures used to modify values and attitudes, Reed and Janis (1974) developed an "awareness-of-rationalizations" technique. Their procedure is designed to modify the decisional balance sheet of heavy smokers by eliminating some of the main rationalizations that serve to bolster the decision to continue smoking. The main purpose is to counteract excessive bolstering so as to make heavy smokers more responsive to challenging information that they typically discount or ignore. The effectiveness of the new technique was tested by Reed and Janis in a controlled field experiment. The main hypothesis investigated was the following: if a person is induced to acknowledge his tendency to make use of certain rationalizations for continuing a potentially dangerous activity (such as heavy cigarette smoking) and is then given information refuting each rationalization, he will be less likely to use those rationalizations as cognitive defenses and will therefore be more responsive to warnings about the risks he is taking. To test this hypothesis, Reed and Janis compared the reactions to fear-arousing communications of a group of heavy smokers who were exposed to an awareness-of-rationalizations treatment with the reactions of an equivalent control group exposed only to information refuting the typical rationalizations used by heavy smokers to defend their smoking behavior.

The study was conducted with seventy-four white middle- or lower-class men and women who had responded to newspaper and radio announcements of the Yale Smokers' Clinic, which offered aid to heavy cigarette smokers who wanted to cut down. Each heavy smoker was seen individually during a single two-hour session. First, the person was asked to fill out a questionnaire concerning his past smoking behavior, feelings of susceptibility to harmful effects of cigarette smoking, and general attitudes toward smoking. Then each subject was randomly assigned to the experimental treatment condition (the awareness-of-rationalizations procedure) or to the control (information only) treatment.

The tape-recorded introduction to the awareness-of-rationalizations procedure stressed the importance of honest exploration and frank acknowledgment of "basic, deep-down thoughts and feelings" about giving up smoking. Following this introduction, the interviewer presented the subject with a list of eight statements (which he referred to as "excuses") and asked the subject whether he was aware of his own tendency to use each "excuse." The eight statements—rationalizations typically used by heavy smokers to bolster their excessive smoking behavior—were selected on the basis of prior studies:

1. "It hasn't really been proven that cigarette smoking is a cause of lung cancer."
2. "The only possible health problem caused by cigarettes that one might face is lung cancer, and you don't really see a lot of that."
3. "I have been smoking for a fairly long time now, so it is probably too late to do anything anyway."
4. "If I stop smoking, I will gain too much weight."
5. "Smoking just seems to be an unbreakable habit for me."
6. "I need cigarettes to relax. I will become edgy, or irritable, without them."
7. "If I prefer to smoke, I am only hurting myself and nobody else."
8. "So smoking may be a risk, big deal! So is most of life! I enjoy smoking too much to give it up."

To facilitate the subject's recognition of his tendency to resort to each rationalization, the interviewer asked as many of the following questions as were necessary to elicit a positive (acknowledgment) response:

1. "Have you ever said this to excuse your smoking?"
2. "Has this excuse ever occurred to you?"
3. "Do you think that, deep down, you might possibly think that this just might be at least a reasonable or valid argument?"
4. "Have you ever heard anyone use this excuse?"

For each "excuse" the interviewer then played a brief, tape-recorded lecture in which he presented factual information designed to refute that "excuse," whether or not the subject had acknowledged using it. This procedure—asking the acknowledgment questions and then presenting the tape-recorded information—was repeated for each rationalization in turn, until all eight were covered.

In the contrasting, "information-only" procedure, the interviewer presented each of the eight excuses in the context of providing information that would be of interest to a smoker. The introduction stressed careful listening to and thinking about each of the excuses. The same tape-recorded lecture used in the awareness-of-rationalizations treatment was played, without any prior discussion about whether or not the subject ever used any of the eight rationalizations. As in the experimental condition, this control procedure was repeated until all eight rationalizations were covered.

When the tape-recorded lecture was completed, everyone in both the experimental and control groups was shown two antismoking films distributed by the American Cancer Society. The first film presented a dramatic case study that played up the threat of lung cancer, while the second depicted the hazards of emphysema and other diseases. Then each subject was asked a series of questions designed to assess his reactions to the antismoking films. Subjects were interviewed again two or three months later to obtain information about changes in their smoking behavior.

The results showed that immediately following the warning messages the subjects who had received the awareness-of-rationalizations treatment expressed (a) greater feelings of personal susceptibility to lung cancer ($p < .03$) and emphysema ($p < .10$); (b) a stronger belief that smoking is generally harmful ($p < .05$); and (c) more complete endorsement of the antismoking communications ($p < .05$). Thus, so far as immediate effects are concerned, the results confirm the prediction that the awareness-of-rationalizations treatment would lead to increased acceptance of antismoking communications containing fear-arousing warnings about health hazards. The results from follow-up interviews on changes in smoking behavior, however, showed that the treatment had a significant effect when given by one psychologist but not when given by another.[3]

In view of the significant effects observed immediately after the treatment, the procedure of inducing an individual to explore and acknowledge his own tendencies to resort to rationalizations just before these rationalizations are refuted appears to be a promising technique for breaking down defensive avoidance tendencies that protect an outworn decision. Insofar as heightened feelings of personal vulnerability increase the chances of a person's accepting the recommendations presented in a warning message, the procedure looks promising as a first step toward increasing a person's willingness to make a new decision. But it remains an open question whether this type of procedure can be made sufficiently effective to induce a person to commit himself to a new decision and live up to it.

From the standpoint of practical educational goals for improving the quality of personal decision making in our society, a number of psychological procedures similar to the Reed and Janis technique might be developed to counteract a decision maker's tendency toward defensive maneuvers that prevent him from seriously considering the alternatives open to him. The evidence at hand suggests that some of the insight-inducing procedures used by psychological counselors could be applied to help people realize the extent to which they are indulging in the kind of wishful or biased thinking that interferes with the task of vigilant decision making.

Perhaps procedures similar to the Reed and Janis technique could also be applied to help legislators and administrators reconsider outworn policies. For example, many congressmen and heads of regulative agencies in the federal government use a variety of rationalizations, according to Jones (1975), to bolster their "do-nothing" stance in the face of the obvious need for regulating industrial wastes that produce air or water pollution. Other national problems, such as energy conservation, are similarly perpetuated in outworn national policies that the responsible leaders do not feel at all proud of but that they rationalize as impossible to change because of alleged inertia elsewhere in the government.

Upon retiring from the United States Senate in 1974, George D. Aiken (R—Vermont) made a refreshingly frank confession in his farewell speech. As reported in the *New York Times* on December 12, 1974, he said: "During the 34 years of my tenure as a United States Senator, I have committed many sins. I have voted for measures which I felt were wrong, comforting myself with the excuse that the House of Representatives, the conference committee, or, if necessary, the chief occupant of the White House would make the proper corrections." No doubt many other governmental decision makers become equally aware of such "sins" long before the day they retire. If so, is it utopian to expect that an appropriate psychological technique might be devised to induce the decision makers to admit to themselves when they are relying on flimsy rationalizations to justify passing the buck? At least a few Aiken-like legislators and government officials might make use of such a technique and might perhaps undergo essentially the same type of psychological change in their readiness to respond to fresh challenges to an outworn decision as we observed when awareness of rationalizations was induced in chronic smokers.

Emotional Confrontations via Role Playing

Many outworn decisions persist because it is difficult to penetrate the defensive facade that makes a person impervious to rational appeals and other cognitive confrontations. Occasionally, however, a dramatic emotion-arousing experience is capable of breaking through the facade, producing a dramatic change from defensive avoidance to vigilant search for and appraisal of fresh alternatives. This type of transformation can be produced by "emotional role playing," an intervention technique designed to challenge decision makers who excessively bolster a potentially harmful course of action. Sufficient research has been done on emotional role playing in antismoking clinics to show that this technique is capable of producing long-term changes in heavy smokers' feelings of personal vulnerability and in their actual smoking behavior. Modifications of the technique are now being explored as potentially effective interventions for a variety of other types of decisions, including policy decisions made by business executives and government officials.

The most dramatic but least understood form of attitude change is the sudden conversion that follows some unusually shocking or painful experience. Research evidence concerning such conversions comes from a field experiment on fear and attitude change conducted by DeWolfe and Governale (1964). Student nurses who were assigned to the tuberculosis wards of a hospital, where they were in constant danger of being infected, showed a remarkable transformation. Thereafter most of them took very seriously and followed scrupulously the safety precautions recommended by their nursing school instructors, whereas a control group of comparable nurses who were given no direct experience on tuberculosis wards did not.

Can people in other situations be challenged in the same sort of way by empathic experiences, without having to be exposed to actual danger or loss? An affirmative answer is suggested by a variety of observations. Some physicians, for example, give up smoking after their first close contacts with lung cancer patients, and the relatives of a cancer victim are sometimes shocked into quitting when they see what is happening to a member of their own family. A striking example of a conversion in smoking habits brought about by direct contact with a relative suffering from cancer is the case of Peggy Talman, widow of actor William Talman. Talman played the perennially losing district attorney in the "Perry Mason" television series. Before he died of lung cancer in August 1968, Talman, who smoked three packs of cigarettes a day, recorded an emotional antismoking message on behalf of the American Cancer Society, in which he said: "You know, I didn't really mind losing those courtroom battles, but I'm in a battle right now I don't want to lose at all, because if I lose it, it means losing my wife and those kids you just met. I've got lung cancer. So take some advice about smoking and losing from someone who's been doing both for years." Mrs. Talman, who herself smoked two packs of cigarettes a day, was unable to quit immediately after the death of her husband. Her conversion came about some months later, when she and her 4-year-old son were watching Talman's message on television. The boy turned to her

and said: "Daddy wants you to stop smoking." Thereafter, according to
the *Palo Alto Times* of August 11, 1969, she quit smoking and devoted
herself to carrying her husband's message to different parts of the country,
appearing on television talk shows, being interviewed in other local media,
and urging the California State Legislature to outlaw cigarette advertising.
In this instance, fear of becoming a victim like her husband may have
contributed to her conversion reaction, but other emotional factors, such
as shame and guilt, may also have been touched off by her child's plea.

We have already mentioned observing several cases of dramatic conversions in smoking attitudes and behavior in our antismoking clinic.
Again, these were cases of heavy smokers who unexpectedly had a personal encounter with a victim of lung cancer. It seems probable that these
conversions are attributable to a kind of empathic reaction that has much
the same emotional impact as personal exposure to danger, involving a
vivid realization of personal vulnerability: "If it can happen to someone I
know, it can also happen to me."

With these empathic conversions in mind, we devised the emotional
role-playing technique for use in antismoking clinics (Janis and Mann,
1965). Our work on the technique, which began before the publication of
the Surgeon General's report *Smoking and Health* and the advent of antismoking commercials, was guided by the assumption that psychodramatic
role playing should be able to provide an emotional-confrontation experience similar to the kind that produces an occasional spectacular conversion to abstinence. In essence, each heavy smoker was required to
play the role of a lung cancer patient who receives bad news from a
physician. We soon found that this disquieting psychodramatic experience
could be so powerful that some heavy smokers would, for the first time,
drop their rationalizations and recognize their personal vulnerability.

A Psychodrama Study with Young Female Smokers

In our first study, the subjects were young women, about 20 years of
age, who were heavy smokers. They volunteered to participate in a research study at Yale without knowing that it had anything to do with their
personal smoking behavior. To understand the impact of the experience,
consider what happens to a young woman in our role-play sessions. On
arriving at the laboratory she is met by the experimenter, who tells her
that the aim of the study is to examine two important problems about the
human side of medical practice: how patients react to bad news and how
they feel about a doctor's advice to quit an enjoyable habit like smoking.
She is then asked to imagine that the experimenter is really a physician
who is treating her for a bad cough that is not getting any better. She is to
assume that this is her third visit to his office, and this time she has come
to learn the results of X-rays and other medical tests that were previously
carried out. The experimenter outlines the scenario of a psychodrama

consisting of five different scenes and asks the subject to act the scenes out, role-playing each one as realistically as possible.

At this point in the procedure, the experimenter dons a white coat, puts a stethoscope around his neck, and begins to take on the manner and tone of a physician. The first scene takes place in the physician's waiting room, where the subject, in the role of patient, waits to be called into his office. Here she expresses her thoughts out loud, verbalizing her worry about the doctor's possible diagnosis and her feelings of conflict about whether or not to smoke a cigarette. In the second scene, the physician ushers the patient into his office—a white-walled room with some conventional props. After the two go through a preliminary exchange of courtesies, the physician proceeds to tell the patient that, on the basis of the X-ray and sputum tests, a small malignant mass has been identified in the patient's right lung. He recommends a lung operation, to be carried out as soon as possible.

In the third scene, the physician leaves his desk and picks up the phone to make arrangements for a hospital bed. The patient is left alone to express out loud her thoughts and feelings; this allows the subject to mull over the information she has learned and reflect on its personal meaning. Here is the soliloquy improvised by one subject, a 20-year-old girl who smoked an average of two packs of cigarettes a day at the time she participated in the experiment:

Cancer . . . Oh, God! I can't believe this . . . This can't be happening to me. Maybe it's nothing . . . maybe. Oh, God, if it's only just benign, that's all I ask for. *One out of three* [survive]! *Holy Smokes*, with my luck I'll be the—one of the fatalities. Why did this have to happen to me . . . cigarettes . . . one out of three. . . . If I ever asked for anything, I asked for this. I've read all those reports and I just wouldn't believe them. Please, just make it be OK. . . . Tomorrow, I'll go in [to the hospital] tomorrow. . . . What will I ever do? How can I ever tell my parents [sob], "Come down and see me in the hospital next week—I might be dead the week afterwards." What a jerk! Nice going! Just deliberately set out and just smoke yourself to death. Why couldn't I have known before this?. . . . Surgery? . . . There must be something else. I don't want him cutting into me and finding things wrong inside me. Why did I ever pick up that stupid habit? I know that it causes cancer. I'm not kidding anybody. I know it does. But I just thought—I was hoping that it would never happen to me. . . . I can't believe it—they're going to operate. I might not ever be able to breathe again. I might be dead. Why did I ever come to him? Why couldn't I die slowly without having to go through this? That cough was not so bad. . . .

In scene four, the experimenter, in his role of physician, informs the subject that surgery will require at least six weeks' hospitalization. Finally, in scene five, the physician raises questions about the patient's smoking history, and after pointing up the connection between smoking and cancer, urges her to quit immediately.

This role-playing procedure, an ordeal lasting just over an hour, produced a great deal of emotional involvement. One subject reported: "I felt after a while that I wasn't acting, it was really true." Another asserted, "It makes it sound so near." A third said, "I started to think, this could be *me—really*." Long after the performance was over, several role players showed signs of having been severely shaken. Their comments included: "You scared me to death!" and "That just shook me up—it *does* scare me—it does!"

One-half of the smokers in this study were assigned at random to a control condition in which they were exposed to the same distressing information about cancer, smoking, hospitalization, and the aftereffects of surgery. These subjects listened to a tape recording of an authentic session that had been conducted with one of the subjects in the experimental group.

The results showed that the emotional-role-playing experience had a marked influence on smoking habits and attitudes. The role players showed a significantly greater increase in (a) their personal belief that smoking leads to lung cancer ($p < .01$); (b) their expectation that "much harm can come to me from my smoking" ($p < .01$); (c) their willingness to try to give up smoking ($p < .01$); and (d) their expressed intention to stop smoking immediately ($p < .05$). Most important from the viewpoint of challenging an outworn decision, practically all of the young women quit smoking or drastically modified their smoking habits within two weeks after the role-play session. (Note the change from July 1963 to August 1963 in figure 18.) There were numerous indications that the high level of fear and vigilance aroused by the realistic quality of the experimental procedure broke through the usual defensive facade erected by the heavy cigarette smoker.

A follow-up study (Mann and Janis, 1968) was carried out eighteen months after the role-play sessions. All but four of the twenty-six subjects who had participated in the original session were successfully contacted by an interviewer from a Connecticut opinion research organization. At the time of the eighteen-month follow-up, subjects who had participated in the psychodramatic role play continued to show significantly less cigarette consumption than subjects in the control group, who only heard the tape recording. (See the results for January 1965 in figure 18.) Many of the women spontaneously volunteered information to the survey interviewer about the impact of the role-playing experiment in which they had participated eighteen months earlier. The following is an example of how the role-play session, according to one subject, brought about her decision to quit smoking:

> The [Surgeon General's] report did not have much effect on me. But I was in this other study [over a year ago]; a professor was doing this psychological thing and I was one of the volunteers. And that was what really affected me. . . . He was the one that scared me, not the report. . . . I got to thinking,

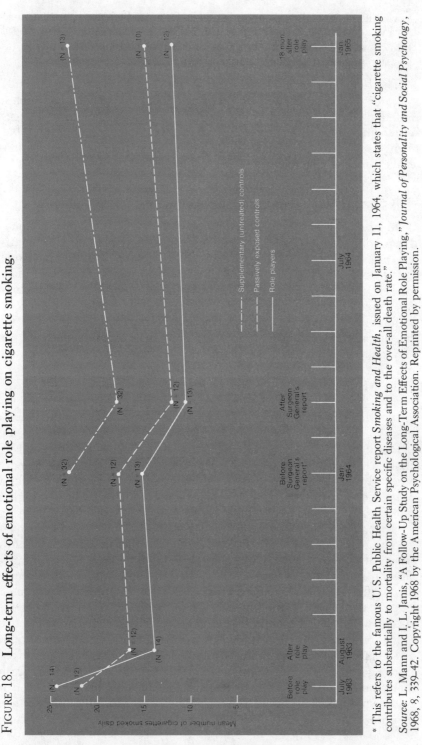

FIGURE 18.   Long-term effects of emotional role playing on cigarette smoking.

* This refers to the famous U.S. Public Health Service report *Smoking and Health*, issued on January 11, 1964, which states that "cigarette smoking contributes substantially to mortality from certain specific diseases and to the over-all death rate."

Source: L. Mann and I. L. Janis, "A Follow-Up Study on the Long-Term Effects of Emotional Role Playing," *Journal of Personality and Social Psychology*, 1968, 8, 339–42. Copyright 1968 by the American Psychological Association. Reprinted by permission.

what if it were really true and I had to go home and tell everyone that I had cancer. And right then I decided I would not go through this again, and if there were any way of preventing it, I would. And I stopped smoking. It was really the professor's study that made me quit.

The long-term outcome found in Mann and Janis's follow-up study indicates that a single brief session of emotional role playing had such a profound effect upon some smokers that it produced significant changes in smoking habits that persisted over a relatively long period of time. But many questions arise regarding the processes of role playing that may account for the effectiveness of the technique.

A Comparison of Fear- and Shame-arousing Psychodramas

In a partial replication and extension of the earlier work on emotional role playing, Mann (1967) focused on some of these problems. One purpose was to compare the effectiveness of *fear arousal* with that of *shame arousal*. Mann reasoned that not all smokers, in particular not all male smokers, will be responsive to the fear-arousing properties of the emotional role-playing situation devised for use in the earlier studies. This assumption was based on the observation of Hammond and Percy (1958) that among the reasons frequently given by male smokers who quit, in addition to health hazards, are moral considerations involving self-control and the challenge posed by the test of one's will power.

In Mann's experiment, the young men and women in the *fear-arousing* condition were asked to role-play a lung cancer patient, following the standard procedure used by Janis and Mann. Those in the *shame-arousing* condition were required to take the role of a patient who is being warned by a doctor that his smoking has made him a "tobacco addict" unable to exercise self-control, whose example adversely influences others. In addition to the two emotional role-playing conditions, Mann introduced a *cognitive* role-playing procedure, in which a third group of subjects was required to take the role of debaters preparing and rehearsing for a debate in which they are to argue that smokers should quit smoking.

The results of this study, like those of the earlier experiment by Janis and Mann, show that the fear-arousing condition resulted in greater modification in attitudes toward smoking than the other role-playing conditions. After the role-playing experience, the fear group reported stronger emotional feelings ("afraid," "shocked," "depressed") on an adjective checklist than did the other two groups, as well as higher retrospective ratings of fear during the role-playing performance ($p < .05$). These findings imply that stronger feelings of personal vulnerability to the hazards of smoking were evoked among those who enacted the role of cancer victim than among those who did not. On an attitude measure of desire to stop or cut down on smoking, the fear group showed significantly more change than the cognitive group ($p < .05$) and somewhat more change (though not statistically significant) than the shame group. When smoking habits were assessed two weeks later, the subjects' reports indicated that the fear group cut down by a larger amount than the other two groups; the difference between the fear and shame groups was statistically significant ($p < .05$).

Another finding of this study was that the amount of attitude change produced in the fear-arousing condition was increased by giving subjects the opportunity for a great deal of verbalization while playing the role. It was also found that females in the fear condition changed their attitudes more than males. When given the opportunity for a great deal of improvised verbalization, males were more affected than females in the shame condition. It is clear, then, that differences in receptivity to various kinds of emotional role-playing techniques are to be expected. Any attempt to modify undesirable habits should accordingly take into account the motivations underlying a person's readiness to change—for example, whether the person is more concerned with the imputation of character weakness than with the threat of lung cancer.

Mann's experiment, carried out shortly after the Surgeon General's report, provides findings that by and large are consistent with the earlier Janis and Mann study. All the observed differences were in the predicted direction, although not all were large enough to be statistically significant. In general, the findings from both studies support the conclusion that emotional role playing can function as a device for impressively "repackaging" information and reducing the usual defensiveness that often prevents people from taking full account of challenging information.

A Psychodrama Study with Middle-aged Chronic Smokers

The studies we have reported so far employed subjects from a population of college students who had not expressed any desire or intention to cut down on their smoking. It is possible that young college students are especially receptive to antismoking communications and to the technique of emotional role playing. In an older group of heavy smokers, with more deeply ingrained habits and greater inhibitions about role playing in a make-believe situation, little change in smoking habits might occur. Replications of the technique among different segments of the population were obviously essential in order to test its scope and limitations.

Nowlis and Janis (1966) attempted to extend the application of the technique to a more heterogeneous population in an antismoking clinic by using subjects who responded to an advertisement in a city newspaper offering aid in giving up smoking. In this field experiment with chronic smokers, most of whom were middle-aged, two role-playing techniques— *emotional* and *cognitive*—were compared. The revised *emotional* role-playing condition was similar to that used by Janis and Mann, with the doctor breaking the news to the patient that his X-ray shows precancerous spots on the lungs. In the *cognitive*-role-playing condition, the task of the subject was to play the role of a journalist interviewing the doctor in connection with the preparation of a pamphlet informing the public of how smokers react to hearing their doctor tell them they have developed lung cancer. In a third condition, the *passive empathy* condition, each subject was passively exposed to all the affect-arousing information that the emotional role players received. The subject listened to the doctor tell in complete detail about a case of lung cancer in someone the same age as the subject. The same informational content, the same dramatic tone of voice, and the same props were used as in the emotional role-playing treatment.

The results of this experiment suggest that the success of the emotional role playing techniques reported earlier is generalizable to chronic smokers who seek aid in giving up smoking after years of unsuccessful attempts. The emotional role-playing condition was found to be more effective than the cognitive in reducing the reported amount of cigarette consumption one month later. Before the experiment, the mean for both groups was thirty cigarettes per day. Cognitive role play led to a reduction of only four cigarettes per day on the average, whereas emotional role playing led to a significantly greater reduction of ten per day.

An important finding was that passive-empathic exposure to a dramatic case report was as effective as the emotional role playing in reducing reported cigarette consumption. This, of course, is consistent with our clinic observations that hearing the details about cancer victims can sometimes produce dramatic effects. Measures of affect indicate that the passive-empathic condition evoked as much affective arousal as the active emotional role playing, which suggests that the crucial factor in breaking down defensive avoidance may be high affective arousal, whether elicited by an empathy-inducing presentation or by a psychodramatic enactment of victimization. This finding implies that being in a spectator role in the presence of such an enactment may be sufficient to undermine the defensive facade of an outworn decision to continue smoking, provided that the person strongly identifies with the events depicted in the psychodrama.

A study by Janis, Kahn, and Higginson (1967) using a psychodramatic procedure in a setting similar to that of Nowlis and Janis, again found that middle-aged persons coming to a smoking clinic could benefit from emotional role playing. This experiment compared three variations of emotional role playing, using similar scenarios with different endings. All three variations (with twenty-one heavy smokers in each group) produced a significant reduction in reported cigarette smoking after five-week and nine-month follow-ups, as compared with an untreated control group. After nine months, the three experimental groups differed significantly from the untreated controls and from a second control group of clinic cases who had been exposed to antismoking communications that included the same basic information presented during the emotional role playing.[4]

The Role of Personality

In the foregoing studies of role playing, we were impressed by the range of individual differences observed in the responses to the psychodramatic procedures. Not every person can be expected to be responsive to emotional role playing. Mindful of the potential importance of empathy in role playing, Elms (1966) investigated the types of personalities most likely to be influenced. Like Nowlis and Janis, Elms worked with a heterogeneous sample of smokers of varying ages. Eighty applicants at the Connecticut State Employment Agency, all of whom were known to be smokers, were hired to participate in the research, without being aware of the purpose of the study. Elms used various psychodramatic situations, all of which resembled the emotional role-playing situation in Janis and Mann's experiment in that the subject was told to imagine that he had developed a serious disease and that his doctor had told him to give up smoking in order to recover. In the role-playing group, each subject was asked to verbalize his feelings about his illness and chances of recovery, his thoughts about resuming smoking, and his advice to a friend based on his own smoking experience. Each role player was paired with a control subject who simply listened to the role player and noted which comments he thought were most effective, without engaging in role playing. Subjects in both the role-playing and control groups were given an immediate post-treatment test of their attitudes and intentions regarding smoking. Follow-up data were obtained three or more weeks later, from a survey ostensibly conducted by a completely different organization asking subjects to report on a variety of health-related practices, including their smoking behavior.

In line with previous studies, changes in attitudes and in reported amount of cigarette smoking were observed to a significantly greater degree in the role-playing group than in the non-role-playing group at the time of the follow-up survey. A strong correlation ($r = +.69$) emerged between pretreatment scores on a scale of empathic fantasy and post-treatment scores on changes in attitudes toward smoking. This finding and others suggest that persons with the capacity to empathize and to imagine a fantasy situation as if it were real are best able to enter fully into the emotional role playing situation, displaying strong affect arousal and subsequent modification in their feelings of personal vulnerability, which could well lead to adherence to a new decision to cut down on smoking. Furthermore, it seems plausible that those persons who can not or will not engage in vivid fantasying of future losses are the ones most likely to adopt a defensive avoidant pattern of denying or blocking out unpleasant information about an outworn decision. Replications in other role-playing situations are obviously needed, however, before any dependable generalizations can be drawn.

Victim versus Authority

The effectiveness of emotional role playing in inducing people to cut down on smoking has been investigated in several additional studies (Himes, Keutzer, and Lichtenstein, 1969; Mausner and Platt, 1971; Platt, Krassen, and Mausner, 1969; Streltzer and Koch, 1968), two of which substantially replicate the Janis and Mann findings. Most similar to the Janis and Mann study was the Streltzer and Koch study, which used essentially the same role-playing script in an investigation of the effects of variations in the status of the experimenter. The results showed that high status of the person playing the role of physician had an effect on the success of the role play in producing attitude change, but no significant effect on subsequent changes in smoking behavior. One experimental group of undergraduate female students had a high-status experimenter (a 32-year-old male who exhibited his credentials showing that he was in fact a physician) while a second group had a relatively low-status experimenter (a 21-year-old female undergraduate student who merely played the role of physician). Three to four weeks after the role-playing sessions, the two groups were found to be about equal in the amount of change in their smoking behavior: both experimental groups showed a significantly greater decrease than the control group in reported amount of cigarette smoking, thus replicating Janis and Mann's findings.

Platt et al. (1969) introduced a new type of role-playing situation in a study of smokers, most of whom were middle aged. Each subject was asked to play the role of physician (after being briefed about what to tell the patient), while the experimenter played the role of the cancer patient. In a contrasting group, each smoker was asked to play the role of a patient who was informed he had lung cancer, while the experimenter, as in the Janis and Mann study, played the role of the physician. These two role-playing conditions were found to be equally effective in producing reported decreases in amount of smoking. All the role players differed significantly from the controls who had not engaged in role playing, again showing the effectiveness of emotional role playing.

An experiment by Mausner and Platt (1971) yielded contradictory results when they compared subjects playing the role of physician with those playing the role of patient. An additional experimental condition was introduced, in which subjects observed the role-playing performance through a one-way screen and listened to the interaction between "patient" and "doctor" through a pair of headphones. There was also a control group that neither observed nor participated in the role playing. All the subjects were male college students. The results (based on analysis of covariance to take account of large initial differences among the four groups in the mean number of cigarettes smoked per day) showed that only the group that played the doctor role differed significantly from the controls in reported changes in the amount of smoking.

In attempting to interpret this failure to confirm the findings from the earlier series of experiments on the effectiveness of playing the patient role, we are struck by the fact that Mausner and Platt made some drastic modifications in the Janis and Mann procedure, which changed the patient in the psychodrama from a victim of lung cancer to a healthy person receiving a general pep talk from his physician. The subject was *not* told that he had lung cancer; instead, he was told that he was in "fundamentally good health," but that the doctor was concerned about his smoking because of "abnormalities" in his "sputum cytology" and "electrocardiogram." The subject was instructed to ask the doctor what he would do if he were faced with the same problem and then to agree to do what he says he would do. The experimenter, in his role as doctor, made it clear that he was himself a smoker (he had an ashtray with butts in front of him) and that he was planning to stop smoking in the near future. He proceeded to give arguments as to why the patient should do likewise, and reinforced his arguments by showing the patient an X-ray of the diseased lung of a former patient who had died from lung cancer.

From Mausner and Platt's description of their experimental procedure, it seems that the subject was required to listen to a proselytizing doctor who was trying to convince him to stop smoking by giving him antismoking arguments along with information about "subclinical changes which were presented as relatively harmless in themselves but as warning signals of possible future trouble" (Mausner and Platt, p. 177); and he was further required to say that he would do whatever the doctor recommended. Mausner and Platt report indirect signs that "many of these subjects, although overtly conforming, were inwardly defiant of the experimenter's influence" (p. 165). The authors attribute the success of the subjects who played the doctor role in cutting down on their smoking to the greater opportunity they had for "review of arguments" as they attempted to persuade the patient to stop smoking. They point out that whereas the "patients were forced to be concerned with the dangers of continuing," the doctor "was given the opportunity to emphasize the gains to be expected from stopping, including the sense of pride, which is especially appealing to healthy young men" (p. 164). If this is so, the main contribution of their study is to show that a cognitive type of role-playing procedure can be effective in challenging an ongoing course of action when it makes use of a psychodramatic setting in which the subject is induced to proselytize a fellow role player.

Thus, Mausner and Platt's negative findings for the patient condition could be set aside as irrelevant on the grounds that their experimental procedure did not induce an emotional role-playing situation comparable to that in their own earlier experiment or the Janis and Mann experiment, in both of which the subject played the role of a cancer victim. Neverthe-less, their findings are consistent with the lack of any significant effect of an emotional role-playing procedure reported by Himes, Keutzer, and Lichtenstein (1969). These negative results require us to acknowledge our ignorance at present concerning limiting conditions. Subsequent investi-gations that vary the conditions of the patient role, including such factors as the degree of victimization and suffering the role player is supposed to portray, might supply some of the information needed for specifying when emotional role-playing procedures will function as an effective challenge to decisions shored up by defensive avoidance. Direct involvement, per-sonalization, and opportunity to verbalize are factors likely to contribute to a successful emotional confrontation with the old decision.

The research just reviewed indicates that emotional role playing is a promising type of intervention for inducing long-term changes in smoking attitudes and behavior. In any practical applications of this form of inter-vention, however, due caution should be exercised in screening suitable subjects, in order to avoid causing unnecessary stress in people who have low tolerance for fear arousal, particularly those with cancer phobia. The technique appears to be especially suitable for individuals with high ability to empathize and to engage in fantasy, "as if" behavior. Further research is obviously essential before firm conclusions can be drawn as to how successful the emotional role playing technique would be in any large-scale program to modify the smoking habits of large seg-ments of the population.

Implications for Policy Making

What are the prospects for using emotional role playing effectively when people seek help on decisions other than cutting down on smoking? We are able to cite some observations from several different sources suggesting that psychodramatic techniques similar to the emotional role-playing procedure used by Janis and Mann for counteracting smokers' outworn decisions might be effective for undermining the defensive avoidant beliefs that bolster other kinds of decisions. A clinical field study by Toomey (1972), conducted with alcoholic patients in a hospital-detoxification unit, was modeled after the Janis and Mann procedures. Her findings suggest that emotional role playing focusing on the destructive effects of chronic alcoholism on marriage and career may be effective in inducing heavy drinkers to "go on the wagon."[5] In an entirely different setting, a social psychological experiment by Clore and McMillan (1971) showed that a role-playing procedure involving enactment of the role of a disabled student in a wheelchair was effective in creating empathy among healthy college students and in evoking support for changes in university policy in the direction of providing more special facilities to meet the needs of disabled students. When compared with a passive control group and an untreated control group, the role players were found to be significantly more favorable toward spending money for improved facilities.

We have observed similar results in our informal use of the emotional role-playing technique in classroom demonstrations with a variety of issues, including some political and economic policy questions that administrators, legislators, and voters might be called upon to decide. In a seminar for advanced students in the social sciences, for example, the senior author presented the issue posed by scientists' warnings about the threat of depleting the ozone level in the earth's upper atmosphere if excessive amounts of exhaust gases are released by supersonic transport planes and by the widespread use of aerosol spray cans. First, the members of the seminar were asked to read articles that appeared in the *New York Times* in the fall of 1974 and the spring of 1975 on the alarming rise in skin cancer to be expected as a result of increased ozone depletion. A secret-ballot questionnaire showed that this warning information had very little effect. As one of the students put it, "There are so damn many other doomsday predictions that are much worse; why bother about this one?" Then, without supplying any additional information, the instructor asked all members of the seminar to project themselves into a disaster situation five years from now, playing the role of a group of skin cancer patients who, as victims of the mounting ozone depletion, have been brought together at a government hospital to receive an experimental form of radiation treatment, as a last resort. During the psychodramatic enactment of a group meeting, the physician in charge informed the group that the new treatment was being discontinued because it was not doing anyone any good. During this role-playing exercise the participants expressed strong emotions. Some gave vent to outrage about the failure of Congress and of the government's regulative agencies to ban aerosol cans and supersonic transport planes. On a secret-ballot questionnaire following the emotional role-playing session, almost all the participants showed a marked increase in feelings of vulnerability to the threat of ozone depletion and greater willingness to support restrictive policies to prevent the threat from materializing.

In management training workshops for executives, similar role-playing procedures are used as training devices for elucidating the pros and cons of policy issues. At one such workshop, for example, the senior author, as a discussion leader, introduced a role-playing procedure to a seminar attended by ten prison wardens. For about a quarter of an hour the wardens had been debating the question of whether or not television sets should be placed in their prisons. Half of the wardens favored the policy on the grounds that it gave the prisoners a window to the outside world and could contribute to rehabilitation; the rest were undecided or opposed. The warden who was most strongly opposed argued that a prison should be a place of punishment, not of entertainment. "Anyhow," he added, "it is out of the question in my prison because there is no free space where we could bring the prisoners together to watch TV, even if we wanted to." The discussion leader proposed that the proponents and opponents try out a role-reversal exercise, and the chief opponent readily volunteered to go first. He was assigned the role of a prisoner making a formal request on behalf of all the prisoners for television sets at a hearing conducted by a prison board that had the power to decide whether to grant the request. Displaying his histrionic abilities with great gusto, the warden made an impassioned opening statement. Then he answered the questions put to him by members of the board by giving vivid examples that embodied the main arguments of his opponents in the earlier debate, along with fresh arguments about the risks of depriving the men of television news, educational programs, dramas, and sports events. While concluding his final plea, he suddenly broke off in mid-sentence with a broad smile. After a brief silence, he announced somewhat sheepishly, "I'll tell you why I'm smiling. I realized that I was selling myself on the idea that we must have TV in my prison, and then all of a sudden I thought of three different places where we can put the goddamn TV sets."

We suspect that in such instances the psychological process is essentially the same as in the emotional role playing studies with chronic smokers—namely, a self-confrontation with hitherto suppressed implications of the challenging information, which undermines the rationalizations that had enabled the decision maker to cling to his old policy without realizing that it had no substantial justification. If this interpretation is correct, psychodramatic techniques might prove to be especially useful for policy planners who wish to overcome their own biases or who want to fully explore the implications of fresh challenges that they suspect are being unjustifiably dismissed by means of rationalizations.

A related type of psychodramatic technique, which has been used in courses and workshops for business executives as a basis for exploring delicate issues of social responsibility, has been described by Scott Armstrong (1974). His scenario, based on a documented case study, involves a crisis faced by the managers of a drug firm. The participants are asked to play the role of top-level managers who have to decide whether to continue distributing a highly profitable drug in the face of repeated warnings about its dangerous side effects. This type of psychodramatic enactment might be effective in sensitizing executives to unfavorable social consequences and to the threat of subsequent self-disapproval with respect to issues that typically are decided predominantly on the basis of the managers' responsibility to the firm's stockholders to increase profits. Obviously, however, controlled field experiments are needed on a variety of policy issues to determine whether emotional role playing within executive settings is generally effective in breaking down feelings of personal invulnerability to threats that would otherwise be ignored.

In earlier chapters we have described some notable instances of large-scale fiascoes resulting from the failure of policy makers to take seriously the warnings they have received about the risks of pursuing their chosen course of action. We have seen, for example, that in the fall of 1941 Admiral Kimmel and his group of high-level naval commanders repeatedly ignored warnings concerning the danger of a surprise Japanese attack on Pearl Harbor (see chapter 5). Another example is the failure of President Truman and his policy advisers in 1950 to take seriously numerous warnings that Communist China would enter the Korean war if U.S. troops were to continue their pursuit of the decimated North Korean army into North Korea. Taking account of these and other case studies of historic fiascoes, Janis (1972) has suggested that psychodramatic exercises, using role-playing procedures similar to those used in war games, might be introduced into policy-planning meetings. The purpose would be to counteract policy makers' illusions of invulnerability and their tendency to arrive at a premature commitment and bolster it by the usual defensive avoidant mechanisms.

> For example, after intelligence experts have given a factual briefing on, say, the Chinese Communists' ambiguous threats during a new international crisis in the Far East, the members of a foreign policy planning group who are most familiar with the beliefs and values of the Chinese leaders might try out a psychodramatic procedure in which they assume the role of their opposite numbers in Peking. The psychodrama might be enacted at a meeting during which the Chinese leaders talk over their options for dealing with the crisis and the countermoves they might make if the United States takes a hard line versus an ameliorative stance. Had this type of role-play exercise been conducted by Truman's advisers in the fall of 1950, they might have taken much more seriously the repeated warnings from Communist China and become reluctant to approve General MacArthur's catastrophic policy of pursuing the North Korean army to the Manchurian border.
>
> The same type of role-playing might be useful in overcoming complacency in a group that collectively judges a series of warnings to be inapplicable and sees no reason to prepare contingency plans for dealing with the potential danger. Suppose that a role-play exercise had been carried out by the group of United States Navy commanders in Hawaii on December 2, 1941, the day that Admiral Kimmel, after being informed by the chief of naval intelligence that no one in the Navy knew where the Japanese aircarft carriers were, jokingly asked if they could be heading straight for Hawaii. If the exercise of playing the role of Japan's supreme military command had been carried out seriously, isn't it likely that at least a few of the high-ranking naval officers responsible for the defense of Hawaii would have argued against the prevailing view that the war warnings they had been receiving during the past week did not warrant the expense of a full alert at Pearl Harbor or a 360-degree air patrol around the Hawaiian Islands? [Janis, 1972, pp. 217–18].

Dosage of Emotional Arousal

In order to develop effective interventions for challenging and counteracting rationalizations that bolster outworn decisions, systematic studies are needed to provide answers to technical and theoretical questions. Some of the most troublesome questions concern the *dosage* of emotional arousal—fear, shame, or guilt—to be used in the emotional confrontation. This is a problem with regard to any type of decision, whether the threat of loss pertains to health, economic security, political power, social status, maintenance of affectionate relations with loved persons, self-actualization, self-esteem, or any other important value. Emotional role playing evokes extremely disturbing thoughts and vivid images of the unfavorable consequences that might be in store for oneself or for one's organization. How can such unwelcome thoughts and images be elicited without running the risk of provoking maladaptive hypervigilance or an increase in defensive avoidance reactions, such as indifference and denial, which are consequences of arousing very high levels of stress?

Although a large number of relevant experiments have been reported, we cannot yet formulate any definitive rule about the intensity of emotional arousal that is most likely to be effective (see Janis, 1967, 1971; McGuire, 1968). On the one hand, some attitude-change experiments show more psychological resistance and less acceptance of precautionary recommendations when strong fear appeals are used in warning messages than when milder ones are used. In the initial experiment on this problem, Janis and Feshbach (1953) gave equivalent groups of high school students three different versions of a dental hygiene communication, all of them containing the same set of recommendations about when and how to brush their teeth. The results showed that there were diminishing returns as the level of fear increased. A number of subsequent studies have supported the conclusion that when fear is strongly aroused by a persuasive communication but is not fully relieved by reassurances, the auditors will be motivated to ignore, minimize, or even deny the importance of the threat (e.g., Janis and Terwilliger, 1962; Rogers and Thistlewaite, 1970).

On the other hand, there have been similar experiments that show a gain in effectiveness when strong threat appeals are used, and these experiments point to the facilitating effects of fear arousal (e.g., Insko et al., 1965; Leventhal, Singer, and Jones, 1965). Evidently, changes in feelings of vulnerability to a threat and in subsequent adoption of a recommended course of action depend upon the relative weight of facilitating and interfering reactions, both of which are likely to be evoked whenever a warning by an adviser arouses fear. Consequently, we cannot expect to discover any broad generalization that will tell us whether a strong fear-arousing presentation that vividly depicts the expected dangers or a milder version that merely alludes to the threats will be more effective in undermining an outworn decision. Rather, we must expect the optimal level of fear arousal to vary for different types of warnings and different types of personalities. *Optimal level of fear arousal* refers to the point on the fear continuum at which the facilitating effects of fear arousal evoked by a warning outweigh the interfering effects. Once the level of fear arousal exceeds the optimal level, interference begins to get the upper hand, and responsiveness to the warning will decrease.

Whenever decision makers are exposed to an adviser's warnings about the undesirable consequences of continuing to adhere to an earlier decision, they are likely to strive to alleviate their unpleasant emotional arousal by scrutinizing the adviser's arguments carefully to discover loopholes that can serve as excuses for dismissing his warnings, which would otherwise require costly or unpleasant protective actions. These reactions make for a relatively low optimal level. By introducing impressive new considerations that arouse vivid images of personal vulnerability, as in emotional role playing, a consultant may be able to prevent the decision maker from denying the personal relevance of what is being said and thus raise the optimal level. The optimal level of stress would also tend to be higher when the adviser's recommended course of action is known to be a feasible, well-tested solution to the threat than when it has all the earmarks of an untested, guesswork solution that might not succeed in averting the danger.

If a warning is given in a way that prevents resistances from becoming dominant, the gain in motivation from strong fear arousal will no longer be outweighed by interfering motivational effects. The results from the experiments on emotional role playing make this implication plausible and indicate that playing the role of a victim of a predicted disaster in a psychodrama induces the person to take account of already available information in a way that increases his feelings of personal vulnerability to hazards that he would otherwise ignore. For many people, enacting the role of victim in a realistic way probably reduces or bypasses psychological resistances, thus enabling them to tolerate a higher level of fear without becoming predominantly defensive (see Janis, 1967).

The findings on cognitive and emotional confrontation techniques described in this chapter encourage us to continue the search for psychological devices that can break through a person's defensive facade. We must study the cognitive and emotional underpinnings of decisions and tailor interventions so that they concentrate on the most vulnerable elements of the outworn decision—like the most threadbare places in Akaky Akakievich's outworn overcoat, where nothing is left to put a patch on. When an intervention is intended to produce a cognitive confrontation, the problem is to select the most cogent evidence together with the most persuasive arguments that will make the person aware of his rationalizations, illusions, and distorted responses to objective information. When an emotional confrontation is intended, the level of stress evoked by the intervention may become a crucial factor. If the optimal level of arousal is not exceeded, psychological techniques like the ones described in this chapter should help to transform a long-standing attitude of defensive complacency into vigilance. This transformation makes for heightened receptivity to relevant information that can function as an effective challenge to outworn decisions.

CHAPTER 14

Improving the Quality of Decision Making

IN THE PRECEDING chapter we examined two kinds of procedure—cognitive and emotional confrontation techniques—that can be used to challenge an outworn decision by counteracting defensive avoidance tendencies responsible for the maintenance of an obsolete course of action or inaction. In this chapter we discuss the main practical implications of our theoretical analysis for developing interventions that help to counteract defective coping patterns after the decision maker has encountered an effective challenge and is trying to arrive at a new course of action. We concentrate on five general types of intervention, based on the key concepts and schemas presented earlier in this book: (1) decision counseling to foster vigilant problem solving; (2) a systematic balance sheet procedure to stimulate more thorough examination of the pros and cons of each alternative course of action; (3) outcome psychodrama to enhance vigilance and induce awareness of preconscious anticipations; (4) emotional inoculation procedures to increase tolerance for the stresses of postdecisional setbacks; and (5) standard operating procedures to prevent a collusive pattern of defensive avoidance among the members of a decision-making group. The research evidence now at hand suggests that these five types of intervention encourage effective search and appraisal, which prevents or corrects distortions in a decision maker's balance sheet. Some of the preliminary studies also provide clues concerning mediating processes that help us to understand how, when, and why the procedures are effective.

The first four types of intervention are discussed mainly in the context of the potential aid that a counselor can give a client who seeks advice in making a vital personal decision about choosing a career, changing jobs, getting married or divorced, undergoing elective surgery, or engaging in any other consequential course of action that could affect his future welfare. Each of the four types of intervention, however, is also applicable, with appropriate changes, when a counselor or adviser is consulted by an executive for advice about a major policy decision affecting the welfare of his organization (or nation). The fifth type of intervention deals specifically with leadership practices in the context of a group of executives working together on developing a policy decision for their organization. All five types of intervention are based primarily on prescriptive hypotheses derived from the conflict-theory model (figures 3 and 8, tables 1 and 2). Confirmatory evidence in support of the prescriptive hypotheses will, of course, provide additional support for the theory, whereas failure to confirm such hypotheses will require revision of the assumptions or rejection of the theory.

Decision Counseling

We use the term *decision counseling* to refer to the joint work of a consultant and client in diagnosing and improving the client's decision-making efforts. This type of counseling can be quite nondirective with respect to the substantive issues involved in the decision: the counselor abstains from giving advice about which course of action the client should choose and even avoids suggesting in any way that he regards certain choices as good or bad. Instead, the decision counselor tries to help his or her clients make the fullest possible use of their own resources for arriving at optimizing decisions in terms of their own value systems. Much of the counselor's work consists of making clients aware of the decision-making procedures they are using and of alternative procedures that they are not using. The counselor may at times be somewhat directive, however, in suggesting where to go for pertinent information, how to take account of knowledge about alternative courses of action, how to find out if deadlines need to be taken at face value or can be negotiated, which risks might require preparing contingency plans, and the like.

Decision counseling is currently used to some extent as a component in the treatments offered by psychotherapists (see the discussion of intentionality in therapy in Rollo May, 1969) and by marital counselors, career counselors, and other clinicians who deal with people at a time when they are making important personal decisions (see Baudry and Wiener, 1974; Broadhurst, 1976). A similar type of counseling is becoming popular as an aid to policy making in large organizations (Schein, 1969). In the latter context, the approach we have in mind overlaps somewhat with the approach called "process counseling," which is oriented toward improving interaction processes within policy-making groups by changing group norms "to help group members discover and implement new, more task-effective ways of working together" (Hackman and Morris, 1975). A process counselor, for example, might call the attention of his executive clients to their tendency to agree upon the most promising choice in their very first discussion of a policy issue and suggest that instead they begin the task of policy making by generating plausible alternatives, postponing their evaluation of any of them until after they have collected and assimilated reports from specialists in their own organization who have information bearing on potential outcomes. Similar suggestions about steps to be taken in arriving at a vital personal decision are made by clinicians who work with individuals seeking guidance in handling problems that arise in private life. Such counselors generally use a completely improvised approach, relying on their personal sensitivity, intuition, and clinical experience to determine what they say to their clients.

In contrast, we propose a more systematic approach, including a set of standard diagnostic procedures and corresponding interventions based on our theoretical analysis of coping patterns. Here we make use of our theoretical model to suggest specific steps to be taken to foster vigilant problem solving rather than defective patterns of coping with decisional stress. Although highly structured, our interview procedures still leave plenty of room for flexibility and improvisation.

The proposed interventions, which require only one or two hours of counseling, obviously cannot be expected to overcome deep-seated neurotic disorders that give rise to chronic procrastination, chronic evasion of responsibility, or chronic denial of unfavorable consequences of vital decisions. Probably some persons are predisposed to one or another of these chronic defensive reactions or to hypervigilance, displaying time and again the same defective coping pattern, irrespective of the issues at stake or the situational opportunities and constraints that uniquely characterize each decision. If so, they require intensive psychotherapy or other psychological treatments far beyond the scope of decision counseling. But for people who occasionally display the more common varieties of defensive avoidance or hypervigilance, which presumably are in everyone's repertoire, a session or two with a skilled counselor might bring about a marked improvement in the quality of their decision-making procedures. It is for such people that the interventions described in this chapter are intended.

The Diagnostic Interview

We begin with prescriptive hypotheses that specify what can be done to enhance the quality of decision making when clients seek advice and guidance from a decision counselor—or from a physician, lawyer, social worker, teacher, clinical psychologist, or any other professional who is qualified to function in that role. In order to apply these prescriptive hypotheses, the counselor must first conduct a structured interview during which he asks the client to express his views about the choice he is facing and to describe what steps he has taken so far in his efforts to select a course of action. A major purpose of the counselor's initial discussion with the client is to enable both participants to arrive at empirically sound answers to the sets of diagnostic questions listed in tables 12 and 13 below. Before considering these questions, however, a few general remarks are necessary about the clinical problems that the decision counselor must be prepared to deal with.

In order to answer the diagnostic questions accurately, it is essential for the client to report truthfully about the search and appraisal activities he has already carried out and about his personal feelings and attitudes. To be effective in the type of diagnostic work required, the counselor must apply a variety of clinical skills that enable him to help the client overcome the usual sources of obfuscation—such as efforts to present oneself in a socially accepted way, to avoid anxiety by relying upon conventional modes of speech and superficial platitudes that cover up emotionally explosive conflicts, and to justify one's past and present actions by rationalizations. Decision counseling, although different from psychotherapy, is probably facilitated by standard features of the clinical stance adopted by many well-trained psychotherapists. One component of this stance consists of making clear that the counselor has no intention of making moral judgments, or of criticizing or admonishing the client. A second component involves conveying a genuine sense of interest in learning the truth for the purpose of helping the client become more fully aware of the truth about himself—but *not* in order to satisfy the counselor's own egoistic needs. A third important component is consistent renunciation of the role of an authority figure who will tell the client what to do. Over and over again, in many different contexts, the counselor communicates the main themes of nondirective counseling and demonstrates them in his behavior—that he sincerely intends to abstain from making any judgment about what would be the best choice for the client to make, that the decision is entirely up to the client, and that what he does to arrive at it is the client's own responsibility.

The counselor's procedural interventions are most likely to be accepted and acted upon if his comments foster a relationship that is socially rewarding to the client. This may require responding to self-disclosures with genuine acceptance statements, which tend to enhance the client's self-esteem, and also conveying to the client that the counselor's demands for careful search and appraisal are limited in scope and that occasional failures to live up to the standards he is advocating will not change his basic attitude of positive regard for the client (see Janis, 1975 and in press).

The first set of diagnostic questions to be answered pertain to the seven criteria for vigilant problem solving (shown in table 12). By observing failures to meet these criteria and discussing them objectively with the client, the counselor may stimulate the client to engage in more effective

TABLE 12.   **Preliminary set of diagnostic questions (based on the seven criteria for effective decision making) to be answered by the decision counselor.**

1. Has the client thoroughly canvassed a wide range of alternative courses of action?
2. Has the client surveyed the full range of objectives to be fulfilled by the choice and the values implicated by it?
3. Has the client carefully weighed whatever he knows about the costs or drawbacks of each alternative and the risks of negative consequences, as well as the positive consequences that could flow from each alternative?
4. Has the client intensively searched for new information relevant to further evaluation of the alternatives?
5. Has the client correctly assimilated and taken account of any new information or expert judgment he has received, even when the information or judgment does not support the course of action he prefers?
6. Has the client reexamined the positive and negative consequences of all known alternatives, including those originally regarded as unacceptable, before making a final choice?
7. Has the client made detailed provisions for implementing or executing the chosen course of action, with special attention to contingency plans that might be required if various known risks were to materialize?

search and appraisal. In effect, these seven diagnostic questions make for *systematic* counseling with regard to various procedures that are *informally* discussed by current practitioners of process counseling.

Hackman and Morris (1975) review a number of experimental studies indicating that when people are asked to engage in problem-solving tasks related to decision making they seldom take time out to plan how to obtain, assimilate, and apply the requisite information available to them, but are inclined to start immediately evaluating whatever solution seems best at the outset. Some suggestive evidence is cited by Hackman and Morris in support of the assumption that task effectiveness and creativity in problem solving might be increased by inducing participants to engage in a preliminary discussion of the strategy of solving the problem before they start to work on it. A few pertinent studies show promising results, but other studies indicate that people resist changing their usual ways of approaching problems and are inclined to ignore suggestions about improving their procedures. In a study by Joyner and Tunstall (1970), for example, groups of advanced students in administrative sciences were trained to use a systematic computer program based on a theory of problem solving developed by Simon (1957) and Cyert and March (1963), which, if followed faithfully, would satisfy all seven criteria of vigilant information processing. But when Joyner and Tunstall tested the groups on two sample problems, the quality of the solutions worked out by those given the opportunity to use the computer program was no better than that of equivalent control groups given no opportunity to use the systematic program. Other studies of the effects of interventions designed to improve problem-solving procedures show only a temporary improvement, with little or no carry-over to subsequent problem-solving activity (Hackman et al., 1974; Maier, 1963; Shure et al., 1962; Varela, 1971).

Counselors working with clients who are making a career choice, contemplating a divorce, or facing other vital personal decisions have made similar efforts to introduce systematic problem-solving procedures, such as those developed by Bross (1953), Gelatt (1962), and Krumboltz (1966). Again, there are serious questions about how often such procedures alone succeed in bringing about any significant change in the way clients carry out search and appraisal tasks before arriving at a final choice. Hansell et al. (1970) describe the anxiety and "fight-flight" tendencies of clients during periods of personal crisis, which interferes with the use of effective problem-solving techniques.

Our theory of alternative patterns of coping with the stresses of decision making (presented in chapter 3) and the observations that support it (presented in chapters 4–12) lead us to expect that people will show strong resistance to any intervention designed to change their approach to the tasks of search and appraisal when making an important decision unless all the conditions are present that foster vigilance. When the decision maker's dominant pattern is defensive avoidance, efforts made by a counselor to improve the quality of search and appraisal procedures are likely to be ignored or subverted unless he can increase the client's hope of finding a solution that will be better than any of the objectionable ones being contemplated. Unconflicted adherence, unconflicted change, and hypervigilance require different types of interventions to change the underlying psychological conditions in a way that will foster vigilance.

This brings us to a set of prescriptive hypotheses that follow from conflict theory which, in order to be applied, require answers to a second set of diagnostic questions (shown in table 13). The questions in the three parts of the table are somewhat overlapping, but the entire set may be needed to determine what specific defects in the client's search and appraisal activities need to be corrected. By examining from different angles how the decision maker is functioning, it should be possible for the decision counselor to select the most appropriate interventions for improving the quality of the client's decision-making procedures.

From a free-style diagnostic interview, using the items in part A of table 13 as guidelines, the counselor should be able to diagnose the client's dominant coping pattern on the basis of his answers to the four key questions. Those counselors who prefer to arrive at a diagnosis by using systematic procedures (and those who want to assess the effectiveness of decision counseling) may find it useful to carry out a systematic content analysis of a tape recording of the diagnostic interview, similar to the analysis Gottschalk and Gleser (1969) have proposed for psychotherapy interviews. Questionnaires may also prove to be useful in gaining diagnos-

TABLE 13. **Diagnostic questions (based on the conflict-theory model) to be answered by the decision counselor in order to determine the most appropriate interventions.**

A. *Reactions to the challenging threat or opportunity*
(Based on the key questions in figure 3)

   1. Does the client believe that the risks are serious if he *does not change* his present course of action?
   2. Does the client believe that the risks are serious if he *does change* his present course of action?
   3. Does the client believe that it is realistic to *hope* to find a satisfactory alternative?
   4. Does the client believe that there is sufficient *time* to search for and evaluate a satisfactory alternative?

B. *The client's decisional balance sheet*
(Based on the schema in chapter 6)

For each of the alternatives he is contemplating, how completely and accurately has the client taken account of the full set of consequences pertaining to:
   1. Utilitarian gains and losses for himself?
   2. Utilitarian gains and losses for significant others?
   3. Self-approval or self-disapproval?
   4. Social approval or disapproval from significant others?

C. *Working through the appraisal and commitment stages*
(Based on the stage-sequence model in chapter 7)

After appraising the challenge to his current course of action (stage 1) and surveying alternatives (stage 2), how much time and effort has the client expended in deliberating with respect to:
   1. Which alternative is best?
   2. Can the best alternative meet all essential requirements?
   3. If the best alternative is unsatisfactory, could one of the existing alternatives be modified to meet all essential requirements?
   4. If the best alternative is satisfactory, what are the drawbacks or obstacles to implementing it and allowing others to know one's choice?

tic information, particularly self-assessment scales that measure variables related to the client's optimism or pessimism about finding an adequate solution to his decisional dilemma—e.g., Luborsky's social assets scale (1973), Phillips's social competence schedule (1968), Quinlan and Janis's state vs. trait of self-esteem scale (Janis, in press).

Counteracting Defective Coping Patterns

Even without using systematic diagnostic procedures, a skilled counselor should be able to ascertain the client's expectations about the risks involved in changing and in not changing, as well as his degree of optimism about finding a satisfactory solution and his expectations concerning deadlines. The counselor would then have to determine whether the dominant coping pattern that has emerged is realistic and adaptive for resolving his decisional conflict.

The following prescriptive hypotheses specify counseling procedures for counteracting defective decision-making patterns:

1. If the counselor ascertains that the client sees no serious risks in persisting in his present course of action and he surmises that this is an unrealistic assessment, he can attempt to prevent *unconflicted adherence* to whatever course of action or inaction the person has been pursuing. He can raise questions about the potential significance of the negative feedback the client has already encountered, induce the client to consider possible unfavorable outcomes in the future, and encourage him to obtain objective information and expert opinion about the costs and risks of not changing.

2. If the counselor ascertains that the client sees no serious risks in adopting an attractive new course of action and he surmises that this is an unrealistic assessment, he can attempt to prevent *unconflicted change*. This requires encouraging the client to obtain objective information and expert opinion about the risks of making the intended change and inducing him to consider the unfavorable outcomes he may be overlooking, including potential losses from failing to live up to prior commitments.

3. If the counselor ascertains that the client is in a state of acute conflict and believes that there is no realistic basis for hoping to resolve the conflict, he can try to counteract this pessimistic expectation in order to prevent *defensive avoidance*. The counselor might encourage the client to discuss his dilemma with respected individuals in his personal network of relatives, friends, or mentors who might give him new perspectives and help him to maintain hope. He can also suggest that more information is available and tell the client where he might find it by mentioning pertinent books, pamphlets, and articles or by recommending professional experts who could be consulted. Above all, the decision counselor can himself convey a sense of optimism about the client's chances of finding a good solution to the problem.

4. If the counselor ascertains that the client is in a state of acute conflict and believes that there is insufficient time to find a good solution, he can try to counteract the panicky vacillation and premature choice that characterizes *hypervigilance*. He might give realistic reassurances about what can be accomplished before the final deadline is at hand. Or he might encourage the client to find out if the deadline is negotiable, to see if he can obtain an extension without serious costs or risks.

All four prescriptive hypotheses are also applicable as "self-help" suggestions for anyone who is striving to attain a vigilant approach, provided that he can somehow take on the role of an objective self-interrogator, which is not easy to do.

Whether applied by a counselor or by the decision maker himself, the four hypotheses are not necessarily mutually exclusive if we consider the entire time span of the predecisional period. For example, in the first session after a counselor has successfully applied the first prescriptive hypothesis, he may soon discover that the second one has become applicable; in later sessions, the other two might in turn become applicable, as the client changes his answers to the key questions in response to new information about probable losses, resources available to him for working out a good solution, and deadlines.

Those counselors who use this approach are likely to become aware of the serious problems of clinical judgment that arise from time to time concerning the proper dosage of fear-arousing communications intended to counteract complacency and the selection of appropriate reassurances to counteract pessimism and demoralization. Considerable clinical skill and ingenuity may be required in order to meet the specific psychological needs of each client. The successful application of the four prescriptive hypotheses, therefore, will depend to a considerable degree on the interpersonal sensitivity, strategic judgments, and communications skills of the counselor who is applying them.[1]

The effectiveness of a decision counselor (as well as of a self-helper) may be enhanced by the use of specific intervention procedures that have been found to facilitate vigilance and to counteract complacency, defensive avoidance, or hypervigilance. Suppose, for example, that a counselor's diagnostic analysis leads him to infer that defensive avoidance is dominant and the client is not taking account of warnings about realistic threats concerning the preferred alternative. The counselor may be able to make effective use of the two special techniques for overcoming excessive bolstering discussed in the preceding chapter—the awareness-of-rationalizations technique and emotional role playing. Other special procedures that may be more widely applicable will be discussed shortly.

Perhaps the four prescriptive hypotheses are already being used to some extent on an intuitive basis by a sizable number of experienced advisers who work on a one-to-one basis or with groups, but it is doubtful that they are being used by very many in a systematic way. If confirmed by evaluative research—including field experiments currently under way—these prescriptive hypotheses should help professional counselors and others in advisory roles to improve their effectiveness.

When people are required to make vital decisions, defensive avoidance is probably the most pervasive defective pattern as well as the most difficult to prevent or correct. Hypervigilance seems to occur much less frequently, except in dire emergencies when oncoming danger is close at hand. The first two patterns—unconflicted adherence and unconflicted change—are manifested most often in response to minor, run-of-the-mill warnings that occur in everyday life. When a person ignores real threats, either unconflicted adherence or unconflicted change can easily be eliminated by giving appropriate information in a manner that makes the person realize the magnitude and imminence of the undesirable consequences that may ensue if he continues to behave in an unwary fashion. When defensive avoidance is the dominant pattern, on the other hand, the person actively resists new information about serious risks in an effort to avoid the psychological stress of decisional conflict, thereby preserving his pseudocalm emotional state.

These considerations lead us to expect that of the four prescriptive hypotheses stated above, the one that will require the most research and development before it can be implemented successfully will be the third one, relating to defensive avoidance. An adviser who does nothing more than give corrective information might often succeed in counteracting the other three defective coping patterns, but he is likely to fail badly most of the time when trying to overcome defensive avoidance. In short, special techniques are likely to be required to counteract defensive avoidance.

Coping Procedures

A field experiment by Langer, Janis, and Wolfer (1975) illustrates the kind of interventions that can be developed to counteract defensive avoidance. This experiment assessed the effectiveness of interventions introduced in brief counseling sessions on the surgical ward of a hospital with patients who had recently decided to accept a physician's recommendation to undergo a major surgical operation and were awaiting the operation. In such a setting, stress is very high and defensive avoidance is a frequent coping pattern. One intervention tried out in this study consisted of a coping procedure that builds up the patient's hopes by encouraging an optimistic reappraisal of anxiety-provoking events and, without encouraging denial of realistic threats, enhances his confidence in being able to deal effectively with whatever setbacks are encountered. The patient is given several examples of the positive or compensatory consequences of his decision to undergo surgery (e.g., improvement in health, extra care and attention in the hospital, temporary vacation from outside pressures). Then he is invited to think up additional examples that pertain to his individual case. Finally he is advised to enumerate these compensatory positive aspects to himself whenever he starts to feel upset about the unpleasant aspects of the surgical experience. Part of the recommendation is to be as realistic as possible about the compensatory features so as to emphasize that what is being recommended is *not* equivalent to trying to deceive oneself. The instructions are designed to promote warranted optimism, with greater awareness of the anticipated gains from the chosen course of action that outweigh the anticipated losses.

Patients about to undergo major surgery were assigned on a random basis to experimental and control groups that respectively were or were not given the reappraisal type of coping procedure. As predicted, the procedure proved to be effective in reducing both pre- and postoperative stress. The data for testing the predictions were obtained from an analysis

FIGURE 19. **Percentage of surgical patients requesting drugs during postoperative convalescence: A comparison between control patients and patients given a cognitive reappraisal type of coping procedure in preoperative counseling.** (*Based on Langer, Janis, and Wolfer, 1975, p. 161.*)

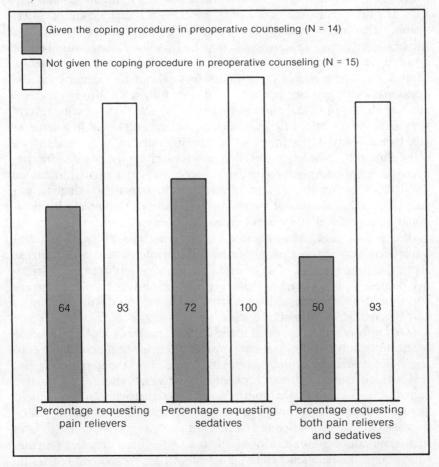

Given the coping procedure in preoperative counseling (N = 14)

Not given the coping procedure in preoperative counseling (N = 15)

| 64 | 93 | 72 | 100 | 50 | 93 |

Percentage requesting pain relievers

Percentage requesting sedatives

Percentage requesting both pain relievers and sedatives

of the nurses' blind ratings of preoperative stress and by an unobtrusive postoperative behavioral measure—the number of times the patients requested pain-relieving drugs and sedatives. The main findings on postoperative coping, shown in figure 19, reveal that the coping procedure had a markedly favorable effect on stress tolerance.

Applying the Balance Sheet Schema

We turn next to the additional diagnostic questions relating to completion of the balance sheet and full working through of the appraisal and commitment stages of decision making (parts B and C of table 13). By using specific probes to supplement the spontaneous comments made by the client during a free-style interview, a counselor may be able to pinpoint some of the major defects in the client's decision-making procedures even if he is unsure of his diagnosis of the client's dominant coping pattern. The answers to these additional questions may suggest special interventions that are needed to fill in apparent gaps in the decision maker's balance sheet. Such interventions may be of value to large numbers of decision makers, because while working on vital decisions that generate conflict most people do not spontaneously fill out all categories in the decisional balance sheet (part B) and do not fully work through stages 3 and 4 of the decision-making sequence (part C). We shall describe several systematic interventions that we have developed and tested in a series of field experiments. These interventions are intended to be applicable by a counselor at the time when the client is approaching the point of making irrevocable commitments to his final choice; they are designed to induce the decision maker to give careful attention to arriving at adequate answers to the key decisional questions so that he can complete his decisional balance sheet and correct erroneous entries.

We assume that some—though certainly not all—of the blocks and inhibitions that prevent people from seeking information and thinking about the consequences of a preferred course of action stem from defensive tendencies to ward off anticipatory fear, shame, and guilt. There are also other psychological sources of inertia having to do with limitations and deficiencies of human information processing. For example, in order to avoid informational overload many decision makers adopt the heuristic of scanning only the most salient considerations to see if acceptable consequences will ensue, without bothering to look into the minor costs and risks (which could, however, collectively outweigh the salient positive incentives). We assume that inertia as well as defensive avoidance might to some extent be overcome by means of exercises that require the decision maker to explore outcomes he had not previously contemplated. One such exploratory exercise involves the use of the balance sheet schema, which helps the decision maker fill out all of the pro and con entries he can think of in each of the four major categories, with special attention to nonutilitarian consequences that typically are overlooked.

According to the defective-balance-sheet hypothesis, (discussed in chapter 6), the more errors of omission and commission in the decision maker's balance sheet at the time he commits himself to a new course of action, the greater will be his vulnerability to negative feedback when he subsequently implements the decision. We described observations from a pilot study (Janis, 1968) dealing with career decisions of college seniors which suggest that a systematic balance sheet procedure can function as a potent inducement for overcoming psychological resistances to thinking about the consequences of alternative courses of action. (The procedure is fully described in appendix A.)

To summarize it briefly, the interviewer starts off by asking the client to describe all the alternatives he is considering and to specify the pros and the cons for each alternative. Next, he shows the client a balance sheet grid with empty cells and explains the meaning of each category. The interviewer helps the client fill in the entries for the alternatives he had just rated as most preferable. Then the interviewer asks the client to examine each cell in the balance sheet again, this time trying to think of considerations that he has not yet mentioned. In order to focus on neglected considerations, the client is given a sheet listing the considerations that might be involved in a choice of the type he is making. The bulk of the time spent on this cognitive exercise is usually devoted to those categories that start off with few or no entries, most often considerations pertaining to approval or disapproval from the self and from significant others.

We reviewed three field experiments on the effects of using this procedure to induce people to fill out their balance sheet as completely as possible, all of which showed a substantial reduction in postdecisional regret and/or increased adherence to the decision. One such study dealt with the choice of a college by high school seniors (Mann, 1972); the second occurred in the setting of a weight-reduction clinic for overweight women who decided to go on a diet (Colten and Janis, in press); and the third was carried out with healthy women who decided to sign up for an exercise class (Hoyt and Janis, 1975).

In light of the evidence accumulated so far, the balance sheet procedure appears to be a promising technique that decision counselors can use to help their clients engage in realistic appraisal of alternatives. But at best it may be of only limited value. Especially when the coping pattern of defensive avoidance is dominant, the balance sheet procedure may often fail to overcome psychological resistances to exploring all the major consequences of the alternative courses of action under consideration. In such instances, more powerful psychological techniques are required.

Outcome Psychodrama

One such procedure—similar to psychodramatic techniques used for diagnostic and educational purposes—was devised as an aid to overcoming resistances that interfere with vigilant examination of consequences during the later stages of decision making. In "outcome psychodrama," the client participates in enacting a scenario that requires him to project himself into the future and to improvise a retrospective account of what has happened as a consequence of his choosing one or another of the most attractive (or least objectionable) alternatives. The procedure is repeated as many times as necessary to explore the potential consequences of each of the main alternatives the client is considering.

Outcome psychodrama resembles emotional role playing, but it differs in one important respect. The purpose of emotional role playing is to overcome defensive avoidance during the first stage of decision making by challenging an outworn decision; the counselor creates a scenario in which the client is confronted with an "as if" experience of being a victim of a specific disaster (e.g., a doctor gives him the bad news that he has lung cancer as a result of his heavy smoking). But since the main purpose of outcome psychodrama is to enhance vigilance during the appraisal and commitment stages of decision making, the counselor *refrains from mentioning any specific consequences*, leaving it up to the client to use his imagination to improvise the specific losses (or gains) that he might sustain. In this respect the procedure resembles cognitive role-playing exercises of the type that require the person to improvise arguments in defense of an assigned position in a debate.[2]

Outcome psychodrama as an intervention for use in decision counseling was developed by Janis in a series of pilot studies. He first used it in interviews with clients having serious marital problems who came to a marital counseling clinic for aid in making a decision about whether or not to seek a divorce. One woman, for example, who in three earlier interviews had consistently described her marriage as nothing but misery and seemed fully convinced that the only solution was to divorce her unfaithful husband, was asked to imagine that one year had gone by since she made her decision. Mrs. Stern, as we shall call her, was told that she would be asked to go through this procedure twice, once as if she had decided to obtain a divorce and a second time as if she had made a genuine effort to keep her marriage going. She was asked to imagine that she had come back to see the counselor for a follow-up interview, and to tell him what had happened during the interim year. Mrs. Stern chose to enact the divorce alternative first. After a brief warm-up period (in which she had to be encouraged to describe her feelings in the present tense instead of using conditional phrases such as "I suppose I would feel . . ."), Mrs. Stern began giving an imaginative account of what her life would be like after the divorce. During the first ten minutes, her statements merely repeated what she had already said in earlier interviews about relief from constant quarreling and other improvements in her daily life that she expected as a result of being rid of her husband. But when asked whether she now felt fairly contented living independently, she blurted out, "No, I feel lonely and miserable, I miss my husband terribly, my life is completely empty now," and she burst into tears. This was the first time in any of the interviews that she displayed any intense emotion and the first time that she alluded to any affectionate feelings toward her husband.

During the second part of the procedure, devoted to enacting a follow-up interview a year after her decision to continue the marriage, Mrs. Stern continued to explore the positive aspects of her relationship with her husband, including (again for the first time) her exclusive sexual attachment to him and her fear of being frigid with any other man. In the final part of the interview, while reviewing what she had said during the psychodramatic enactments, she expressed her surprise at the strong feelings that had momentarily overwhelmed her and said, "I have so much reason to hate him I guess I hadn't been willing to admit to myself that I still love him and will miss him." Thus the psychodramatic enactments enabled Mrs. Stern to gain access to deep-seated emotional attitudes toward her husband that she had defensively avoided acknowledging to herself.

Once these formerly preconscious components became part of her conscious balance sheet, she could make a more thorough assessment of the alternatives and work out more realistic plans for implementation. As it turned out, Mrs. Stern felt convinced that despite her newly acknowledged attachment to her husband, his constant mistreatment of her was so intolerable that she should obtain a divorce. In a final session, one month after the psychodramatic enactments, Mrs. Stern spoke about a definite plan to avoid the loneliness of the separation by moving into an apartment with a girlfriend. It seems probable that this plan was at least partly shaped by the increased awareness she had gained from the psychodramatic enactments of the losses she would sustain from going through with a divorce.

The same outcome psychodrama procedures were used with six other women and two men during the course of marital counseling interviews. In every case, important new considerations came to the surface. None of the other instances was as dramatic as the transformation of Mrs. Stern when she visualized herself as a lovelorn divorcée, but some of the improvised material about potential outcomes did give rise to profound changes in mood and yielded major new entries that the client had not previously included in his or her conscious balance sheet.

Encouraged by the pilot work in the marital counseling clinic, Janis tried out a similar psychodramatic procedure in career counseling. College seniors who were trying to decide what to do after graduation were interviewed about their decisional conflicts and were then asked to go through the outcome psychodrama procedure for each of their main alternatives. In their psychodramatic enactments of follow-up interviews, however, relatively little new material emerged. Better results were obtained when the psychodramatic scenario was revised. Instead of a routine follow-up interview with the counselor, the new scenario called for a heart-to-heart talk with a close friend a year after starting on the job, at a time of crisis, when things were going "very badly, worse than you thought they would."

This scenario, which focuses exclusively on unfavorable consequences, was used first for the career alternative that the student had just rated as his number-one choice and then for the alternative he had rated as his second choice. (For several cases, a supplementary scenario was also used for each alternative to focus on *favorable* consequences, so that four different scenarios were enacted altogether. But the favorable-outcome scenario did not generate any new considerations and, therefore, was dropped from the procedure.)

The postdecisional-crisis scenario was tried out in a pilot study of career decisions with fifteen undergraduate seniors, after each of the students had been interviewed on the pros and cons for the major alternatives and had completed the balance sheet exercise. (For more complete details about the procedures used in this form of outcome psychodrama, see appendix B.) In twelve of the fifteen cases, new entries for the balance sheet emerged during the psychodramatic enactment that had previously not been mentioned during either the initial interview or the balance sheet procedure. About half the students reported feeling surprised at what they dredged up while enacting the crisis scenario. Four of the students were so impressed by the undesirable consequences mentioned for the first time during the psychodrama that they changed their minds, downgrading what had been their first choice and preferring their former second choice instead.

One senior, for example, came up with a number of vivid negative outcomes when he played the role of a lawyer undergoing a postdecisional crisis: the "dull routines," the "stifling of all creativity," and a variety of ethical problems. Afterward, he told the interviewer that he was deeply impressed by these new, "devastating" considerations, in contrast to the "milder" negative considerations that came out during the psychodrama for his second choice, high school teaching. He announced that he was now inclined to shift to a teaching career. Another student became so agitated during the psychodrama about his failures as a would-be city planner that he broke off playing the role before the time was up, announcing that "I would never let things get this bad." In the initial interview he had denied that there were any serious drawbacks to his preferred choice of becoming a city planner. While carrying out the balance sheet procedure he asserted that all the negative entries for that choice were of negligible importance and could even turn out to be advantages. But he became profoundly perturbed by what came out during the psychodrama, and ended up contemplating a new training plan that represented a compromise between his top two alternative career choices—taking a course of graduate study that would equip him for a career in urban research as well as for a career as a programmer in city planning.

In most cases, the new considerations that emerged during the outcome psychodrama did not induce a shift in preference but appeared to make for a less romantic view of both of the leading alternatives. A senior who was debating between two career lines (accepting a job offer to become a junior-college teacher of English literature or going to medical school in order to become a psychiatrist) turned up several new drawbacks during the outcome psychodrama which he subsequently added to his balance sheet for both professions—being required by his dean or chairman to teach courses he did not want to teach, being pressured by professional medical organizations to conform with their self-serving rules, being deprived by both professions of sufficient time to pursue his creative literary interests.

Several other students learned nothing new during the outcome psychodrama for their first choice but arrived at new unfavorable considerations for their second choice, which resulted in a strengthening of their original preference. Even in the case of the three students for whom the outcome psychodrama yielded no new considerations at all for either alternative, subtle changes in the balance sheet may have resulted from the added weight given some of the negative entries. One of these students reported that as a result of the psychodrama the possibility of his being disliked by the students in his high school classes if he did not prove to be a good teacher (his first choice) had become "more real and more frightening."

No controlled field experiments on the effects of outcome psychodrama comparable to those on the effectiveness of the balance sheet procedure in reducing the amount of postdecisional distress have been completed as yet (one is currently being carried out). Until such studies are done, we cannot be sure that the psychodramatic procedure will reliably achieve its purpose of counteracting defensive avoidance during the appraisal and commitment stages of decision making. All that can be said from the observations made during the pilot studies of marital crises and career choices is that outcome psychodrama appears to be a valuable procedure in decision counseling, especially in aiding clients to become aware of emotionally charged considerations that might otherwise remain outside of their conscious deliberations.

Rationale

Outcome psychodrama may be most effective when used in combination with the balance sheet procedure. Why would it be beneficial to go through both the laborious balance sheet procedure and the outcome psychodrama? Why bother to dredge up from the hidden recesses of memory all the favorable and unfavorable consequences one can possibly think of and then write them all down? Our hunch is that a number of functions are served which are essential for preventing gross errors in decision making—so essential, we suspect, that in the not-to-distant future those managers and heads of households who make vital decisions without systematically going through such procedures and recording all the entries they can think of in a balance sheet will be as rare as present-day managers and heads of households who do not record deposits and with-drawals in their bankbooks but try to keep a running balance in their heads.

It seems to us that three different types of function are at least partly fulfilled by systematically going through the balance sheet and psycho-drama procedures.

1. *Stimulating more thorough search for essential information.* When drawing up a balance sheet, the decision maker becomes aware of conse-quences that he had not previously given much thought to, and this can lead him to seek out crucial information that might otherwise not be encountered until it is too late. Combining the balance sheet procedure with outcome psychodrama is especially valuable for overcoming a deci-sion maker's psychological resistances as well as the paucity of his imagi-nation when confronted with a consequential decision. We have seen that while going through these exercises the decision maker dredges up a number of fresh entries in the decisional balance sheet, which can temporarily heighten his decisional conflict and motivate him to engage in a more thorough search for the best course of action.

We do not assume that in all cases the more information seeking the better. Occasionally a decision maker has already completed an adequate search, and more information might make for confusion or generate un-necessary procrastination because information about all sorts of minor unfavorable aspects of the preferred alternative is more salient or more available than information about compensatory positive aspects.[3] But when the decision maker has made little or no attempt to search for pertinent information that might be available to him, increasing his moti-vation to do so could be beneficial.

The decision maker's hunger for new information, stimulated by his awareness of the fresh entries in his decisional balance sheet, can generate intensive memory searches and self-scrutiny as well as requests for advice from experts or acquaintances. If the decision maker discovers that he has an "irrational" feeling of aversion toward the alternative that has emerged as best on the basis of the recorded pros and cons, he soon realizes that something important must be missing from his conscious view of the alternatives. Feelings of strong attraction to a seemingly inferior choice have the same effect of posing the question "Why do I feel that way—what am I leaving out of the picture?"

Earlier we noted that while going through the balance sheet procedure a person is likely to be surprised about some of the entries he thinks up and to experience some degree of emotional arousal as he confronts various considerations he had not thought about before. Emotionality pervades outcome psychodrama to an even greater degree. Much more surprise and more striking changes in affect occur when the decision maker begins to verbalize his vague intuitive feelings about what might happen as a result of his choosing one or another course of action. During the psychodramatic enactment the person may become aware of a feeling of depression or elation, shame or pride, anxiety or relief, sometimes without being able to say anything at all about what is making him feel that way. Vague as they are, the free-floating emotional reactions elicited by the outcome psychodrama appear to provide some access to formerly unverbalized hopes and fears.

After the psychodrama is over, it is useful for the counselor to ask the client to once again examine his decisional balance sheet, to insert into it the new considerations that emerged during the role playing, and to reexamine the altered entries to see if he is now inclined to modify his preferences in any way. When completing the balance sheet, the decision maker may find some way of verbalizing even the vaguest of emotional reactions—such as "I now feel there is something shameful about this alternative, although I don't know why" or "That one would give me a sense of pride." Fleeting twinges of emotion may be experienced while the decision maker is writing down specific entries, as well as while he is enacting an outcome psychodrama. These affective signals can function as goads to an *internal* information search, which may bring into the decision maker's consciousness a concrete image of enjoying a specific gratification or suffering a specific deprivation, which he can then begin to evaluate objectively. Even when the undifferentiated feelings churned up by the exploratory exercises cannot be pinned down by the decision maker in any way, he can at least acknowledge that he has those feelings and take them into account as important items of self-knowledge. For example, if the person's internal search leads him to discover that he has the same "irrational" feeling of uneasiness every time he contemplates switching to a new job that he consciously rates as desirable, safe, and good, he may come to realize that he can expect to suffer subjective discomfort (for some reason he does not know) if he chooses that alternative. Such recurrent feelings of "irrational" uneasiness can be represented in the balance sheet in the category of "anticipated utilitarian losses for self"; if the uneasiness has the emotional tone of guilt feelings, it can also be included in the category of "anticipated self-disapproval." Thus, before making the final choice, the decision maker may be better able to take account of formerly preconscious anticipations and perhaps also of some manifestations of his unconscious motives.

Some of the balance sheet entries arrived at by means of the combined procedures may be ones of which the decision maker had been aware beforehand but to which he had paid little attention because he assumed that they were consequences of dubious importance or unlikely ever to materialize. Seeing these supposedly ephemeral considerations written down along with the other items in the balance sheet gives them a kind of authentic status; they can no longer be dismissed as too vague or trivial to bother about. Sometimes, of course, the new information obtained will correct initial misconceptions about consequences that are by no means trivial and will result in changed judgments about which alternative should be chosen. In general, fuller exploration of the consequences, including those that at first seem to be negligible, can lead the decision maker to modify his choice in a direction that better suits his objectives.

2. *Fostering more comprehensive appraisal of pros and cons.* Behavioral scientists know relatively little as yet about how people arrive at a sound overall judgment to select the "best" alternative in the light of all the pros and cons that enter into a decisional matrix. Nevertheless, it seems safe to assume that as a person becomes increasingly aware of the ramified consequences of a vital choice he becomes less likely to rely upon an oversimplified decision rule for charting his course. A graduating law student who is about to choose among several job offers may feel fairly comfortable at the outset about using a simple heuristic, such as "Select the one that offers the highest initial salary, provided that the chances for promotion are at least as good as with any of the other offers." But he is apt to start using a more complex set of criteria after discovering (let us say with the help of outcome psychodrama) that the available job that clearly meets this simple criterion will probably offer little opportunity to handle the type of cases he wants to work on and will involve him in exploiting loopholes in the law for purposes that he regards as shameful.

An analysis by Herbert Simon and William Chase (1973) of decision making among chess players indicates that chess masters go through essentially the same search processes as novices, but have a much larger repertoire of perceptual patterns to draw upon. As a result of long experience in making strategic decisions and seeing their remote as well as immediate consequences, the grandmasters promptly recognize the attack, defense, and threat potentialities of thousands of chess patterns, which suggest good moves to them. Inexperienced players are severely handicapped by their failure to perceive many of the potential consequences of alternative moves and by the constraints of short-term memory, which can embrace only a limited number of considerations (only about seven chunks of information). A novice will improve, however, as he enlarges his repertoire of perceptual patterns that embody larger chunks of information about the ramified consequences of different moves.

We expect the same type of improvement in the performance of lawyers, physicians, administrators, and other experts who, like good chess players, increase their ability to spot good moves rapidly as a result of practical experience in their specialty. We believe that the novice job seeker, like the novice chess player, will make better choices (from the standpoint of minimizing postdecisional distress) as a result of the special procedures that enable him to see ahead to more of the likely consequences of his alternative moves. In addition, seeing all of those consequences listed in a balance sheet may enable the novice decision maker to compensate for some of the constraints of short-term memory by grouping specific consequences into more general categories and thinking in terms of these larger chunks of information.

Thus, even though no validated method is available for weighting the entries in a balance sheet and adding them all up, the balance sheet procedure and outcome psychodrama can help people make more comprehensive judgments.[4] Writing out entries in a balance sheet may also enable one to notice for the first time that certain alternatives have many equivalent advantages and disadvantages. One can then pinpoint the essential differences between alternatives and define more sharply the tradeoffs entailed by the alternative choices. (See Benjamin Franklin's proposed method of trading off, described in chapter 6.) Above all, when a decision maker is worried about a difficult decision and is inclined to avoid thinking about the most painful aspects, defensive avoidance is counteracted by systematic procedures for exploring the known consequences. Defensive avoidance flourishes when a decision maker relies exclusively on the salient considerations present in short-term memory, without being impelled to search his long-term memory, to ask others for pertinent information, and to record the findings from the information search.

3. *Inducing preparation for dealing with negative feedback when the decision is implemented.* The more conscientiously a decision maker fills out a decisional balance sheet, the better prepared he is to withstand negative feedback once he starts to implement a consequential decision. Psychological preparation is needed not only to cope with inherently unpleasant costs but also to avoid being demoralized by the social humiliation and loss of self-esteem that invariably confronts the decision maker at times when it looks like his chosen course of action is turning out badly. By becoming aware of the potentially negative consequences of the chosen alternative before he starts to implement the decision, the decision maker can make specific contingency plans. When a setback occurs, such as being asked by the boss to commit an illegal act shortly after having accepted his offer of a new job, the beleaguered decision maker is not caught by surprise and left to improvise on the spur of the moment; instead, he can implement a plan he has carefully worked out in advance to counteract just such a threat immediately after it materializes.

Being more fully aware of the *positive* consequences of the chosen course of action as a result of using the proposed exercises can also function to maintain hope and morale in the face of setbacks. Having learned that the genuine positive consequences outweigh the negative consequences, the decision maker may persuade himself that he has made the right choice after all, and be able to maintain confidence that it will work out well in the long run. Otherwise, he might resort to bolstering the decision with flimsy rationalizations that can easily be refuted by the people around him, making him all the more vulnerable to fresh onslaughts of negative feedback.

New entries added to other categories within the balance sheet can also function in the same way: the self-persuasion effect is enhanced by increased awareness of the *negative* consequences of each *unchosen* alternative. One is less likely to regret the choice of a new job when trouble arises if one knows about even worse things that could have gone wrong with the other jobs available.

New entries pertaining to *positive* consequences of the *unchosen* alternatives might also function in a way that helps to stabilize a decision in the face of temptations to switch to another choice. An ex-bachelor who is aware of and has come to terms in advance with the opportunity costs of being married will be less responsive after the honeymoon is over to fresh challenges posed by encounters with attractive women.

Along with contingency planning and the heightening of confidence about having made the correct choice, there is a related effect resulting from exploring as many of the anticipated consequences as possible before they occur—an emotional inoculation effect, which is stimulated by becoming aware beforehand of the most threatening challenges to be encountered. When a decision counselor induces a client to go through the exploratory work required by the procedures we have been discussing, he may to some extent be facilitating the emotional inoculation of his client. But he may find it worthwhile to do much more than that—to present the client with various types of preparatory information specifically designed to accomplish the goals of emotional inoculation, to which we now turn.

Emotional Inoculation for Postdecisional Setbacks

Another major type of intervention, then, that can make for greater stability of decisions involves exposing the decision maker to preparatory information that is specifically designed to provide emotional inoculation for postdecisional setbacks. The crucial information pertains to expected negative consequences of the chosen course of action. Preparatory information functions as a form of emotional inoculation if it enables a person to increase his tolerance for postdecisional stress by developing effective reassurances and coping mechanisms. The process is called emotional inoculation because it may be analogous to what happens when antibodies are induced by injections of mildly virulent toxins.

Objectives

Studies of people facing major surgical operations, debilitating illnesses, and community disasters point to the need for emotional inoculation (Caplan, 1961; Egbert et al., 1964; Janis, 1958; Janis and Leventhal, 1965). The evidence reviewed in chapter 6 included findings from seven studies of surgical patients, all of which indicated that preparatory information designed to produce emotional inoculation before an operation increased the patients' tolerance for setbacks and suffering during the postoperative period (Egbert et al., 1964; Johnson, 1966, Moran, 1963; Schmidt, 1966; Schmitt and Wooldridge, 1973; Vernon and Bigelow, 1974;

Wolfer and Visintainer, 1975). Reduction of postdecisional stress as a result of emotional inoculation was also found in studies of women undergoing childbirth (Breen, 1975; Levy and McGee, 1975), patients undergoing tooth extraction (Miller and Trieger, 1976), and hospitalized patients undergoing a disagreeable medical examination (Johnson and Leventhal, 1974). We also reviewed five studies of job satisfaction showing favorable effects on postdecisional attitudes and behavior of giving preparatory information about undesirable features of a job to employees before they decide to accept a job offer (Gomersall and Meyers, 1966; Macedonia, 1969; Wanous, 1973; Weitz, 1956; Youngberg, 1963). All of these findings support the conclusion that many people will display higher stress tolerance in response to undesirable consequences if they have been given warnings in advance about what to expect, together with sufficient reassurances, so that fear does not mount to an intolerably high level.

We know that there are exceptions, of course, such as neurotic personalities who are hypersensitive to any threat cues. Emotional inoculation may also be inappropriate for some types of unmitigated personal disaster—incurable cancer and severe burns, for example, requiring painful treatments that leave their victims only "withered remnants of their former selves" (Hamburg, Hamburg, and De Groza, 1953). Among those victims, blanket denial may be the only effective means of avoiding overwhelming anxiety and depression. But these considerations do not preclude the possibility that techniques of emotional inoculation might be developed for a wide range of anticipated postdecisional setbacks, especially those encountered by people who agree to a course of action that almost always requires undergoing temporary suffering in order to prevent serious disability or achieve some other long-term goal.

Unlike the balance sheet procedure, which is administered before the decision maker has made up his mind, emotional inoculation procedures are typicaly introduced shortly after the choice has been made, before the new decision is fully implemented. Emotional inoculation is probably worthwhile at any time prior to the onset of negative feedback. As we have just suggested, however, the more completely the balance sheet is worked out at the time of commitment, the less the need for emotional inoculation after commitment.

> The goal of emotional inoculation is to make the person aware of an impending crisis or disaster well in advance of the full confrontation. That way he has an opportunity to anticipate the loss, to start working through his anxiety and grief, and to make plans that might enable him to cope more effectively with the subsequent crisis. . . .
>
> Conceivably, the amount of time and effort required for effective emotional inoculation might be reduced by the judicious use of films, recorded lectures, and pamphlets that are specially prepared to convey the essential preparatory information. The United States Peace Corps, for example, has developed a set of such communications for use in conjunction with group

discussions. They are intended to provide emotional inoculation for volunteers who are about to leave for an arduous assignment overseas, where they will be separated from family and friends, subjected to cultural shock in an under-developed country, and probably exposed to a series of failures and other stresses that could make them feel depressed or demoralized. Unfortunately, we do not as yet have any systematic data from evaluation studies to indicate whether this program of emotional inoculation has achieved its objectives. In fact, there are only a few careful evaluative studies . . . that can be cited as a basis for extending the use of these preparatory techniques to large numbers of persons. . . [Janis, 1971].

Successful emotional inoculation probably requires exposure to in-formation that pinpoints the main sources of acute postdecisional conflict. For example, when a heavy smoker decides to stop smoking, the pre-paratory information he is given before he starts to implement the deci-sion might include a detailed description of each of the typical withdrawal symptoms (intense craving for cigarettes, nausea, irritability, etc.) as well as warnings about situations that make the temptation to smoke difficult to resist (social gatherings where companions are smoking, work conferences where one is under pressure to put in long hours without adequate periods of relief from tension, and the like).

Obviously, we cannot expect all preparatory communications to be effective. Very brief preparatory messages that take only a few minutes to convey information about impending threats may be too weak to stimu-late the development of effective reassurances and therefore have no ef-fect at all (see Langer, Janis, and Wolfer, 1975; Meichenbaum, 1975). At the opposite extreme, when a preparatory communication is too strong it can unintentionally stimulate expectations in the receiver of being help-less to avert intolerable losses. Like an overdose of antigens, an overen-thusiastic inoculation attempt can produce the very condition it is in-tended to prevent.

Inasmuch as emotional inoculation requires breaking down unwar-ranted feelings of invulnerability and preventing excessive bolstering ten-dencies that lead one to disregard realistic warnings, a number of special problems arise concerning the proper dosage of fear-evoking stimulation. The problem of working out appropriate dosages to avoid exceeding the optimal level of emotional arousal is discussed at length by Janis (1967, 1971) and McGuire (1969). Suffice it to say, in the light of findings on sensitization reactions to warnings (Janis, 1971), that preparatory com-munications can be expected to be effective only if they arouse vigilance and, at the same time, help to build up the person's confidence that he can cope with the anticipated threat. But this generalization is not very helpful when one faces the practical task of preparing people to cope with set-backs. Until a preparatory communication is tested systematically with different types of personalities and evaluated under actual stress condi-tions, one cannot be sure that it will successfully induce emotional inoculation.

The need to take account of personality differences is highlighted by the findings from two field experiments conducted on surgery wards by Andrew (1970) and DeLong (1971), which show that not all personalities react the same way to preparatory information. These studies suggest, for example, that those persons whose characteristic coping style is defensive avoidance do not respond well to emotional inoculation procedures. They probably require special forms of confidence-enhancing interventions by a counselor—along the lines we have suggested earlier—in order to build up their hopes of finding a satisfactory solution to their decisional conflict before being given preparatory communications that call attention to all the various impending threats.[5]

Psychological Processes

A number of interrelated cognitive and motivational processes that may mediate the effects of emotional inoculation are suggested by case studies of how hospitalized men and women react to severe postdecisional setbacks after having decided to permit surgeons to operate (Janis, 1958, pp. 352–94; 1971, pp. 95–102). Some of the case studies deal with surgical patients who for one reason or another were *not* emotionally inoculated. These patients were so overwhelmed by the usual pains, discomforts, and deprivations of the postoperative convalescence period that they manifestly regretted their decision and on some occasions actually refused to permit the hospital staff to administer routine postoperative treatments. Before the disturbing setbacks occurred, these patients typically received relatively little preparatory information and retained an unrealistic conception of how nicely everything was going to work out, which functioned as a blanket type of reassurance, enabling them for a time to set their worries aside. They sincerely believed that they would not have bad pains or undergo any other disagreeable experiences. But then, when they unexpectedly experienced incision pains and suffered from all sorts of other unpleasant deprivations that are characteristic of postoperative convalescence, their blanket type of reassurance was undermined. They thought something had gone horribly wrong, and could neither reassure themselves nor accept truthful reassurances from doctors or nurses.

Like someone traumatized by an overwhelming accident or disaster, uninoculated patients experience acute feelings of helplessness and overreact with symptoms of acute fright. After the frightening episode is over, they are likely to become angry and resentful toward members of the hospital staff, believing that what they have just gone through was exceptionally bad and somehow could have been prevented if only the caretakers were more concerned about them. At this point the patients' uncooperative actions and bitter words convey regret about their decision to undergo surgery.

In contrast, emotionally inoculated patients show an entirely different sequence of changes in beliefs and images about the operation, and of accompanying emotional states. Before the operation, upon receiving preparatory information about what specifically is in store for them, these patients start to worry about the postoperative period and wonder how bad it is really going to be. As they mentally rehearse undergoing the predicted pains and deprivations, they are much less calm than those who are uninoculated. The inoculated patients work hard at regaining some degree of equanimity by developing reassuring conceptions of each of the different types of threat they are worried about (e.g., "Most of the pains from the incision will last only a short time"; "If any pains get to be unbearable I will be given a pain-killing drug"). Insofar as the patients have realistic information about the threat, the reassurances they develop continue to function effectively, without being undermined when the threat materializes. Consequently, throughout the convalescent period these patients are able to maintain a basically optimistic outlook about surviving each ordeal intact and can feel a sense of pride about being able to "take it," without ever becoming severely frightened, angry, or regretful about their decision.

The process of mentally rehearsing anticipated losses while in a somewhat agitated state and developing reassuring conceptions that can at least partially alleviate fear is referred to as the "work of worrying" and is assumed to be stimulated by preparatory information concerning any type of impending threat to one's physical, material, social, or moral well-being (Janis, 1958). Essentially the same cognitive and emotional changes that were discerned in the case studies of surgical patients have been noted in comparable case studies of people who have encountered setbacks following other types of decisions, including choosing a career, going to an out-of-town college, getting married, and taking legal action to obtain a divorce (Janis, 1971).

Setbacks Involving Loss of Self-esteem: A Case Study

We turn next to an illustrative case study showing how emotional inoculation can influence a person's reactions to setbacks arising from marital discord. This case study is based on the senior author's interview notes of five sessions with a 35-year-old woman who came for counseling at a time when she was in an acute state of indecision about how to deal with her estranged husband, with whom she was still in love.

About one month after her husband had moved out of the house, Mrs. Roberts (as we shall call her) decided to try to win him back by resuming sexual relations with him. He had left home after a big fight and had said he wanted a divorce. During the period of separation, he had acquired a mistress, with whom he was seen around town. He visited his wife only one evening a week, ostensibly to see their three children. Mrs. Roberts said that she treated him coldly and rejected his sexual advances. But she felt that this might not be the best way to deal with him, since she wanted to have him back. Before making the decision to resume sexual relations with her husband, she discussed with the counselor in considerable detail the potentially unpleasant consequences of this course of action. She focused on her concern about becoming deeply disappointed and enraged if, after resuming sexual relations with her husband, she were to find out that he was still seeing his mistress. That would be a terrible blow to her pride, she felt, because she was convinced that her husband had no interest in his mistress except as a source of sexual gratification.

After the first week of implementing the decision, all seemed to be going well: she had enjoyed the lovemaking and felt that her husband's basic affection for her was still there. But the next day, her aunt (a chronic snooper) told her that she had seen the husband double-parked in front of the business office where his mistress was employed, obviously to pick her up after work. Mrs. Roberts was very disappointed to hear that the outcome she feared had materialized, but she did not become enraged or depressed. She reassured herself with a plausible explanation she had worked out beforehand—that her husband might continue seeing his mistress for a while because he might break off that relationship gradually. This idea, Mrs. Roberts reported, enabled her to respond affectionately without recriminations when he came to sleep with her again, two nights later.

The following night her husband again returned and unexpectedly proposed that he move back some of his clothes and live part-time at home with her. He made it absolutely clear, however, that he wanted to do this only if he could have complete freedom to come home or stay away at night whenever he felt like it, without being required to give any advance notice or offer any excuses. This offer was very gratifying to Mrs. Roberts, because she saw it as a big step toward achieving her goal of attracting her husband back home permanently. Elated by her husband's renewed interest in returning to her, she promptly accepted his offer, without thinking over its potentially unfavorable consequences.

By the time Mrs. Roberts came to the counselor for her next session, she had already encountered a severe setback that made her regret the impulsive way in which she had made the second decision. In a highly agitated and depressed mood, she explained that after she had agreed to the new arrangement her husband came home on four successive nights and gave her intimate gifts. He told her that he was still hooked on her and that he might want to move back home on a full-time basis. But then came the weekend, and he did not show up at all until the following Monday night. With her hopes raised so high and her affectionate and sexual needs once again strongly aroused, she was bitterly disappointed and felt acutely depressed throughout the entire weekend. When he finally did appear and offered no explanation, she could not control her agitation and "spoiled her whole plan" by an angry outburst that provoked a bitter fight. Once again he stormed out, bellowing that the marriage was finished—she had broken their agreement, she could not respect a man's freedom, divorce was the only solution. He never returned.

Thus, following her first decision, when a setback occurred that Mrs. Roberts had anticipated beforehand, she was already prepared with a reassuring way of interpreting the cruel facts and was able to cope well. But when an unanticipated setback followed her second (impulsive) decision, as a result of her husband's using the freedom she had granted him, she was bitterly disappointed. Unprepared emotionally, she overreacted with extreme resentment and thus spoiled whatever prospects there were of reconciliation. If Mrs. Roberts had acknowledged to herself before making her second decision that there might be just such a setback she would have been better prepared to accept it as just another bump on the rocky road toward her goal of regaining her husband. Whether or not that road would have been a "good" choice in the long run is a separate question that the counselor had just started to take up with her when the whole issue was abruptly settled by her husband's decision to obtain a divorce.

Like the case studies of surgical patients, this case study of a marital decision suggests that one of the main functions of emotional inoculation is to tone down the decision maker's optimism about how beautifully everything is going to work out now that he or she has hit upon the best course of action. Preparatory information given shortly after a choice is made can prevent excessive bolstering of a new decision, so that instead of elatedly believing that "nothing bad will happen as a result of this choice," the decision maker becomes resigned to accepting a somewhat more pessimistic view of human enterprises, believing that "some bad things will probably happen but everything will still work out all right—and it's worth it." This differentiated view, unlike an oversimplified, Panglossian reassurance, moves the decision maker to worry about the bad consequences he is likely to encounter, which stimulates the work of worrying. As a result, the decision maker develops supportive beliefs that are both realistic and reassuring, which help to mitigate the emotional impact of subsequent setbacks. In order for the work of worrying to be complete, it seems that *each source of stress* must be anticipated and "worked through" in advance.

Three Essential Steps

The theoretical analysis of the cognitive and emotional changes that enter into successful emotional inoculation points to three steps that a decision counselor can initiate to induce psychological preparation for setbacks at the point where the client has made up his mind about which course of action to pursue:

Step 1: *Call the client's attention to information about impending losses and risks* that the client is selectively forgetting or unrealistically discounting in his efforts to bolster the new decision. The counselor can gently but firmly challenge the client's unrealistic blanket reassurances by frankly presenting his own views of the rough road ahead or by quoting from authoritative warning communications. It might also be helpful to ask the client to engage in psychodramatic enactments of the main setbacks that can be anticipated. In one way or another, the counselor can make the client keenly aware of specific points of vulnerability for which he needs to be prepared and stimulate him to begin the work of worrying (see Breznitz, 1971).

Step 2: *Encourage the person to work out ways of reassuring himself* about the ultimate success of the course of action he is pursuing each time a major setback is encountered. The counselor can remind the client of his personal assets and of the resources available from his family, his social network, and his community, all of which can prevent feelings of helplessness in a future crisis. He can also go over the positive entries in the balance sheet to enable the client to work out realistic answers that he can give himself at moments of grave doubt as to whether the new course of action is worth the costs. By discussing the client's imaginings of the future, asking pertinent questions, and emphasizing well-known reassuring facts, a skilled counselor can help the client develop a balanced outlook that will enable him to continue to be reasonably confident about the success of his chosen course of action in the long run while at the same time maintaining realistic expectations about the numerous ways in which it could be temporarily troublesome and unsatisfying.

Step 3: *Supplement the client's spontaneous efforts to arrive at effective reassuring beliefs* by supplying him with accurate new information about how potential setbacks can be handled or their effects mitigated (e.g., with surgical patients, reassuring medical facts about pain-killing drugs; with clients facing marital or career crises, reassuring information about the availability of the counselor for emergency sessions if they should subsequently feel the need to consult him again).

In general, the learning process whereby unrealistic reassurances are gradually replaced by a more effective set of reassuring beliefs tends to be facilitated when the person is given concrete information concerning the nature of the potential losses or setbacks, the ways in which the setbacks can be surmounted, and the mitigating or protective aspects of his environment. By presenting the decision maker with an accurate blueprint of the stresses that are in store for him and the coping resources at his disposal, a preparatory message can help him to build a basic attitude of self-confidence and develop specific beliefs that will have a reassuring effect during and after each crisis.

Counteracting Defensive Avoidance in Policy-making Groups

So far we have limited our discussion to techniques for the improvement of individual decision making. But what about group decision making, and the common tendency of cohesive groups to slip into a group-think syndrome—to mutually reinforce a shared pattern of defensive avoidance in their policy decisions? We assume that the emotional inoculation hypothesis is applicable to all consequential decisions, which would include those made by executives and policy-planning committees as well as the personal types of health, marital, and work-related decisions discussed in the preceding sections. The three steps whereby counselors induce psychological preparation in their clients can be modified for use with policy makers before they announce a new decision; similarly, the balance sheet procedure and other cognitive- and emotional-confrontation techniques described earlier might also be of considerable value to policy-making groups, for counteracting tendencies toward defensive avoidance. But who would serve as a decision counselor? Anyone in that role from outside the inner circle, no matter how much expertise and prestige he possesses, will generally meet insurmountable resistance if he tries to get the powerful personages he is counseling to dwell upon painful matters that they feel require no further discussion.

Of course, the leader of a policy-making group can himself take on the role of decision counselor and introduce all the various interventions we have been discussing. But again, only limited success can be expected. The chief decision maker certainly cannot be expected to raise issues with his group in a dispassionate and nondirective manner, since it is his responsibility to participate in choosing the best policy, to work out ways of implementing it, and to encourage everyone in the organization to express appropriate supportive attitudes about its desirable features (see Campbell, 1969). As an active participant in selecting and promoting a policy, he cannot be expected to be motivated to take the painful steps necessary to counteract defensive avoidance and to initiate emotional inoculation at a time when the members of the group—himself included—share the belief that there is no hope of finding a solution better than the one they have just agreed upon.

Rather than counting on a deeply involved leader or an uninvolved but ineffectual outsider to take on the role of decision counselor in a policy-making group, the policy makers might find it feasible to prevent their group from making avoidable errors by themselves adopting a set of standard operating procedures designed to counteract the psychological conditions that foster defensive avoidance. If the anti–defensive-avoidance procedures are not institutionalized but are rather left to the discretion of the leader or the members, they will be more honored in the breach than in the observance. Hackman and Morris (1975) point out that members of decision-making groups in large organizations are not willing to spend time working out their problem-solving methods. They generally assume that everyone in the group already knows how to go about the task and that discussion about how to tackle the problem is a waste of time. Hence it is unlikely that new procedures will be used unless a group is specifically required by institutionalized norms of the organization to use them.

Such standard operating procedures would obviously have to be carefully assessed to find out if they are, in fact, worth the time and effort. It is also essential to make sure that they will not have serious side effects that make the remedy worse than the disease. Unfortunately, operations research on effective procedures for policy-planning groups is still in its infancy (see Campbell, 1969; Crow and Janis, 1975; Hackman and Morris, 1975). We cannot cite even preliminary findings that warrant recommending any specific intervention for improving the quality of group policy making. As yet, there are none comparable to the findings on the effectiveness of the balance sheet procedure for improving the quality of personal decision making.

We believe that the balance sheet procedure and other techniques found to be useful in individual counseling of clients who seek help in making personal decisions should be regarded as prime candidates for research on new procedures that might be applicable to policy-making groups. For example, it might turn out to be worthwhile for many organizations to institute the balance sheet procedure as standard operating procedure for their policy-planning committees. The new norm might be reinforced and monitored by asking committee members to append to their final report on policy recommendations a balance sheet grid in which they list the major alternatives examined and summarize in the appropriate categories all the pro and con considerations that went into their appraisals. The technique of outcome psychodrama might also prove effective if it could be institutionalized. A comparable technique has reputedly been successfully used by some planners in the federal government who play "political games" in which the players are given realistic feedback by a computer or by human referees after each decision (Bloomfield, 1973; Crow and Noel, 1965; Wilson, 1968).[6]

Promoting Multiple Advocacy

A number of experts on the psychology of large organizations have called attention to some of the procedural implications of management studies showing that conflicts and disagreements among the members of a decision-making group, including those stemming from clashing interests among rival subunits within a bureaucracy, can have a constructive effect on the quality of the group's search for and analysis of alternatives (Bower, 1965; George, 1974; Hoffman, 1961; Maier, 1963 and 1970; Vroom, 1969). George (1974) proposes a set of new organizational norms to change the problem-solving culture of small groups of policy advisers. The purpose is to make constructive use of the ubiquitous "game of bureaucratic politics" (Allison and Halperin, 1972; Halperin, 1974). In order to promote a system of "multiple advocacy," George proposes that a norm should be adopted regulating the way participants are selected for each policy-planning group: they should represent the divergent positions within an organization, so as to cover the full range of policy options available on each important issue. George points out, however, that merely appointing proponents of diverse points of view and allowing them to speak their piece is not sufficient; those whose position deviates from the dominant majority must be given full opportunity and encouragement to develop their case. This means that insofar as possible the advocates of diverse positions should have roughly the same degree of power, influence and competence, with sufficient staff and intelligence resources for them to function as effective advocates.

Even so, other malfunctions in the policy-making process may still need to be prevented or corrected. No advocate may be available for an unpopular policy option; some information may be available from only one channel; or the advisers may thrash out their disagreements privately and confront the chief executive with a unanimous recommendation. One type of safeguard suggested by George is an institutionalized role of "custodian" whose sole responsibility would be to monitor and manage the workings of the policy-making process within the organization.

Institutionalizing the selection of policy planners and monitoring their procedures in the manner proposed by George would probably go a long way toward preventing planning groups from making some of the grosser errors that arise in unmonitored, homogeneous groups whose members share the same outlook from the outset. If we assume that conflict *between* members fosters conflict *within* each member, the multiple advocacy system can be regarded as an aid to fulfilling one of the essential conditions for fostering the coping pattern of vigilance. An absence of conflict within each of the policy planners would preclude a vigilant problem-solving approach. But our theoretical analysis indicates that conflict alone is not sufficient. When conflict is high, defensive avoidance or hypervigilance can prevail unless other conditions are also met that are required in order for the pattern of vigilance to predominate.

Preventing Groupthink among Executives

We turn next to standard operating procedures designed to counteract the symptoms of groupthink among members of cohesive groups of executives—which, as we pointed out earlier (in chapter 5), often appear to result from a collusive pattern of defensive avoidance. In our earlier discussion we described a set of antecedent conditions that give rise to the symptoms of groupthink, which, in turn, leads to defective policy-making procedures (see figure 5). These unfavorable conditions include directive leadership, insulation of the group, and lack of methodical procedures for search and appraisal. We assume that when these conditions are present in a cohesive group at a time when decisional stress is high, the striving for concurrence fosters the pattern of defensive avoidance, with characteristic lack of vigilance, unwarranted optimism, sloganistic thinking, suppression of worrisome defects, and reliance on shared rationalizations that bolster the least objectionable alternative. The bolstered alternative is often the one urged by the leader. When the other conditions that foster a collusive pattern of defensive avoidance are also present, the leader's initial bias in favor of the preferred alternative remains uncorrected even when his advisers have access to impressive evidence showing his preference to be inferior to other feasible courses of action.

In *Victims of Groupthink*, Janis (1972) presents nine prescriptive hypotheses suggesting standard operating procedures to counteract the conditions that make for this shared pattern of defensive avoidance. Six of the prescriptive hypotheses relate directly to procedures that can be carried out within a policy-making group if the role of the leader is institutionalized in such a way that he and everyone else in the group accept that it is part of his job to put them into operation:

1. The leader, when assigning a policy-planning mission to a group, "should be impartial instead of stating his preferences and expectations at the outset. This practice requires each leader to limit his briefings to unbiased statements about the scope of the problem and the limitations of available resources, without advocating specific proposals he would like to see adopted. This allows the conferees the opportunity to develop an atmosphere of open inquiry and to explore impartially a wide range of policy alternatives."

2. The leader of a policy-forming group should at the outset "assign the role of critical evaluator to each member, encouraging the group to give high priority to airing objections and doubts. This practice needs to be reinforced by the leader's acceptance of criticism of his own judgments in order to discourage the members from soft-pedaling their disagreements."

3. At every meeting devoted to evaluating policy alternatives, one or more members "should be assigned the role of devil's advocate." In order to avoid neutralizing the devil's advocates, the group leader will have to give each of them "an unambiguous assignment to present his arguments as cleverly and convincingly as he can, like a good lawyer, challenging the testimony of those advocating the majority position."

4. "Throughout the period when the feasibility and effectiveness of policy alternatives are being surveyed, the policy-planning group should from time to time divide into two or more subgroups to meet separately, under different chairmen, and then come together to hammer out their differences."

5. Whenever the policy involves relations with a rival organization or outgroup, "a sizable bloc of time (perhaps an entire session) should be spent surveying all warning signals from the rivals and constructing alternative scenarios of the rivals' intentions."

6. Immediately following a preliminary consensus about what seems to be the best course of action, the policy-planning group "should hold a 'second chance' meeting at which every member is expected to express as vividly as he can all his residual doubts and to rethink the entire issue before making a definitive choice."

Three additional hypotheses describe standard operating procedures that require the cooperation of other units and of persons in the organization outside the policy-planning group.

7. One or more experts or qualified colleagues within the organization who are not core members of the policy-planning group "should be invited to each meeting on a staggered basis and should be encouraged to challenge the views of the core members."
8. Each member of the policy-planning group should periodically "discuss . . . the group's deliberations with trusted associates in his own unit of the organization and report back their reactions."
9. "The organization should routinely follow the administrative practice of setting up several independent policy-planning and evaluation groups to work on the same policy question, each carrying out its deliberations under a different chairman."[7]

These proposed remedies, like the ones suggested by George (1974) to create and maintain a multiple advocacy system, have not yet been validated. Each of them must ultimately be carefully tested to make sure that it achieves the predicted improvements without undue strain on the participants. After pretesting these procedures, a collaborative team made up of research experts on policy-making procedures and specialists who know how their organization works from the inside ought to be able to find a feasible way to carry out field studies to assess their long-range effectiveness. Objective evaluations made by a team of behavioral scientists and administrators could weed out ineffective or harmful procedures and provide solid evidence to support adopting the good ones as standard operating procedure.

Although undesirable costs and unintentional side effects cannot yet be precluded, the prescriptive hypotheses appear sufficiently promising to warrant the trouble and expense of their being tested as potentially useful for counteracting groupthink in policy-planning groups. Some of the antigroupthink procedures might not only prevent the collusive form of defensive avoidance but also help counteract initial biases of the members, prevent pluralistic ignorance, and eliminate other sources of error that can arise independently of defensive avoidance (see Elms, 1976).

Implications for Professional Training and General Education

Standard operating procedures like the ones we have been discussing can be easily sabotaged or subverted if the leader or the majority of the members in a policy-making group regards them as useless or objectionable. Consequently, before any changes in standard operating procedure are put into operation, they need to be fully explained in a way that will motivate the participants to give them a fair trial. In-service training courses and management workshops might be useful contexts for conveying the rationale behind such changes.

Janis and Crow (1975) have proposed a brief training program for executives to provide a desirable educational background for introducing various antigroupthink procedures in policy-planning committees. On the assumption that appropriate information about the causes and consequences of groupthink can have a beneficial deterring effect, their curriculum includes impressive case studies illustrating the symptoms and harmful effects of groupthink together with recommendations for prevention. Janis and Crow suggest that such an in-service training program precede application of any of the nine prescriptive hypotheses to any policy-making or planning group on the verge of changing its operating procedures. A consultant or instructor starts by presenting to the members the twenty-minute film *Groupthink* (in the Psychology Today training films series, 1974), which depicts a typical policy-planning group in action and describes the symptoms of groupthink and their detrimental consequences. This is followed by a group discussion of the film, with special reference to its application to the group's own purposes and procedures. In a second session, the specific recommendations contained in the prescriptive hypotheses are explained to the group in terms of the conditions that make for groupthink (as shown in figure 5). This briefing is again followed by a group discussion, during which the instructor gives special attention to the members' objections and qualms about adopting the new procedures. The instructor may also provide additional information and suggestions in an attempt to counteract whatever sources of resistance become manifest. But he will not deny that there are potential costs in terms of time, effort, and frustration. In fact, it would be part of his role to make the participants aware of the possible disadvantages that might arise, so that they could watch out for them and try to mitigate their effects.

A similar in-service educational program might be an essential prerequisite for attempting to improve policy-making procedures in other ways, such as by introducing the selection and monitoring procedures designed to create a multiple advocacy system. A much broader program that deals with all the concepts and procedures discussed in this chapter could be envisaged as part of a more comprehensive educational program for executives. Their training might include a variety of modules specifically designed to increase an executive's ability to meet the seven criteria of vigilant search and appraisal as a participant in all of the various types of decision for which he has some degree of responsibility. For example, some time might be devoted to discussing what can be accomplished at each stage of decision making (chapter 8), the values and limitations of alternative decision-making strategies (chapters 2 and 12), ways of coping with threats to freedom of choice (chapter 10), and the dangers of commitment traps (chapter 11). Other topics could also be included that do not deal directly with procedures for improving the quality of decision making but that might help executives to be more alert to common sources of error—such as illusions of probability that can affect predictions of future outcomes (Tversky and Kahneman, 1974); biases in attributing motives, abilities, and other dispositions to persons whose cooperation is required to implement one's decisions (Jones and Nisbett, 1971); self-deception with regard to one's long-term values (Rokeach, 1973); misleading "rules of the game" governing bureaucratic politics (Halperin, 1974); and the misuses of historical analogies or so-called lessons of the past (May, 1973). Trainees could also be given instructive examples of the detrimental effects of an overidealized image of executives as paragons of decisiveness, which inclines some of them to overreact to challenges, to plunge themselves into making decisions when none are required, and to deal with genuine challenges by committing themselves forcefully to new policies without going through constructive phases of doubt and hesitation for fear that indecision would be a sign of weakness.

A central feature of an executive training program based on the framework presented in this book would be to present the main concepts and diagnostic approach represented in tables 12 and 13, along with realistic exercises in applying the balance sheet procedure, emotional inoculation, and other techniques devised to promote vigilant problem solving. If successful, the type of executive training program we have sketched out would result in a marked improvement in the quality of decision-making procedures among trained executives. In effect, each executive would learn to function as a decision counselor, which should help him to curtail defensive avoidance tendencies and to function more often as a vigilant decision maker in his role either as chairman or as regular member of the various policy-planning groups to which he is assigned. We would also expect some carry-over effects that would improve the quality of the more routine work-task decisions he makes entirely on his own with respect to such matters as who should be hired in his subunit, who should be recommended for promotion, how the flexible items in his budget should be allocated, and how his own time should be allocated among the various assignments for which he is given responsibility. His training as a decision counselor might also be expected to have occasional positive effects on the quality of his personal decisions concerning his own career—and perhaps also those pertaining to his marriage, health problems, and the like.

Of course, it is only within very circumscribed limits that a person can be expected to be successful as his own decision counselor. Self-analysis cannot be counted on to enable one to correctly answer the diagnostic questions in table 13 concerning defective coping patterns, particularly when one's dominant pattern is defensive avoidance. But executives who have been trained to use the appropriate diagnostic and remedial procedures ought to be able to function effectively as decision counselors for each other on policy decisions, work-task decisions, and even personal career decisions.

If the training proves to be valuable for executives in the ways we have just suggested, comparable training programs might be made available to people in other professions. Physicians, dentists, lawyers, architects, city planners, university administrators, scientists, teachers, social workers—all could benefit from improving the procedures they employ in making the day-to-day decisions required by their work roles, as well as more fundamental policy decisions. And professional workers who are prepared to function as effective decision counselors for each other would probably improve the quality of their personal decision making and also function more effectively on those occasions, whether rare or frequent, when they are asked by their professional association or some other organization to serve on a policy-planning committee.

If training in decision making does work for executives and professionals, why not institute it for people in every occupation, as part of everyone's general education? It seems reasonable to expect that a curriculum could be developed to help many students become more adept at carrying out sound decision-making procedures. Such educational developments are already under way. Daniel Wheeler (1975) has designed a course on decision making and problem solving for undergraduate college students, which presents a systematic framework derived from the conflict-theory analysis presented in an early draft of this book. Wheeler's course includes practical exercises to familiarize students with the balance sheet procedure and other techniques for improving the quality of their own decision making. A more simplified curriculum that makes extensive use of role-playing exercises, also based on an earlier draft of this book, has been worked out by Gregory Landis (1973) for use in high school courses. High school and college courses like those developed by Landis and Wheeler could be incorporated into a curriculum designed to prepare students both to deal more competently with their personal and work-task decisions as breadwinners and to function more effectively in their future roles as parents, voters, and members of juries, neighborhood improvement organizations, school boards, and other decision-making groups in their communities. Such courses on decision making, if they present realistic examples to illustrate key concepts along with practical exercises designed to improve the quality of each student's decision making, might go a long way toward satisfying the demand for "relevance" in education. What students could learn in a sound course on decision making would help them become more effective persons while they are in school and for the rest of their lives.

Earlier in this chapter, we discussed two essential tasks for the next generation of researchers: namely, to test and improve the effectiveness of (a) intervention procedures to be used by decision counselors (including outcome psychodrama and other new types of exercise based on the balance sheet schema) and (b) standard operating procedures designed to counteract defensive avoidance in policy-making groups. Just as with these proposed procedures, each of the proposed training programs on effective decision making requires systematic assessment to see if it achieves its objectives before it can be recommended for widespread adoption.[8]

All three types of applied research that we have been discussing will be facilitated, we believe, if a more basic type of research is carried on concurrently, pertaining to the theoretical underpinnings of the proposed training programs. The basic research that is needed, as we have repeatedly pointed out, consists of investigating the effects of varying the conditions postulated as antecedent to each of the five patterns of coping with decisional stress—including such variables as the presence or absence of warnings that increase the magnitude of decisional conflict, messages that promote optimism versus pessimism about finding a satisfactory solution, and high versus low deadline pressures. A few field experiments on the effects of such variables have been described; more such experiments are essential to test the full range of implications of the conflict-theory model presented in this book. If the results continue to be consistent with predictions from the model, conceptual replications will be needed involving a variety of different decisions (including several types that we have not looked into at all, such as investment decisions by financiers and brokers, medical decisions by surgeons and physicians, and legal decisions by judges in state and federal courts). Replications are essential in order to test the generality of the key propositions and to specify their limiting conditions. In any case, we expect that the analysis of coping patterns presented in this book will provide some new directions for basic as well as applied research on decisional conflict, choice, and commitment.

The Balance Sheet Procedure

THE BALANCE SHEET PROCEDURE was designed to aid people making vital decisions, to help them survey all the viable alternatives and explore the consequences of each. (Chapter 6 presents a brief description of the procedure and summarizes the results of systematic research on its effectiveness.) Although evidence of the value of the procedure comes so far from only two types of decision (career choices and health-related decisions, such as going on a diet), decision counselors may find it useful for a variety of other types of decision.

The following are the detailed steps of the procedure, as it was used with college seniors who were making a career choice. Only slight changes in wording are necessary to apply the procedure to other types of decision.

Step 1: *Open-ended interview.* The counselor begins the session with an open-ended interview concerning the most salient alternatives and their consequences. There are five main questions:

1. How are your plans for next year shaping up? How does the whole issue of your future career look to you at present?
2. You have already mentioned one (or some) of the alternatives you have considered. Please list all the various alternatives you have seriously considered at one time or another in recent months.
3. How do you rank these plans in terms of what now seems best for you? List your first choice, your second choice, and so on.
4. Now I'd like to ask you to focus on the top two alternatives: _____ and _____. What are the various positive and negative points—that is, the pros and cons—of each of these two alternatives?

    Let's start with your *first* choice, _____. Try to think of all the possible arguments or considerations in favor of and against this plan. What are the various pros and cons? Can you think of anything else? Anything else?

405

Now let's go on to your second choice, _____. What are the various pros and cons for this choice? Can you think of anything else? Anything else?

5. Now, suppose you had to make up your mind to act on some final decision today—to commit yourself to a final decision right now. What would you think about? What I want now is for you to talk about all your thoughts that would go into making this final decision at the point where you had to act on it and commit yourself to it.

Step 2: *Introducing the balance sheet grid.* To stimulate the client to think about nonsalient considerations, he is given a balance sheet grid (shown in figure 20) whose cells are to be filled in. A separate grid sheet is used for each alternative. The grid is introduced with the following statement: "You've talked about some of your alternatives and their pros and cons. What I'd like you to do now is to go through the possible considerations in a more systematic way."

The counselor uses his notes from the preceding interview to aid the client in filling in the grid for the first two choices. This initial step serves the function of helping to define the four main categories in the balance sheet schema by means of examples (e.g., "You mentioned that for alternative no. 1, the job would pay well but would require long hours; write "good pay" in this upper-left-hand box and "long hours" in this upper-right-hand box").

After the salient considerations mentioned in the interview for the two main alternatives are entered, the client is asked to fill out grid sheets for each additional alternative he is seriously considering. Then all the grid sheets are put in front of the client and he is asked, "Can you think of any other considerations that should be put into any of the boxes on any of these sheets?"

Step 3: *Using a List of Pertinent Considerations.* Next, the client is encouraged to explore neglected pros and cons for the main alternatives by being shown a list of pertinent considerations. (The list of considerations involved in a career choice is shown in table 4.) The client is given the following instructions:

We have constructed a list of some of the expectations that people have about their career (or course of action after graduation). I want you to go through this list and see how these considerations might apply to your two main alternatives: _____ and _____. Here is the list. The considerations are grouped under the four headings: utilitarian (or tangible) gains and losses for self; utilitarian (or tangible) gains and losses for others; self-approval or -disapproval; approval or disapproval by others. Why don't you take a look at the list for a few moments.

Let's start with the tangible gains and losses for self that might be expected for _____ [first alternative]. Then we'll go through this same category for each of the other alternatives. Look over all the considerations in the first category. Try to see how they bear on your choice. Some you've already

FIGURE 20. **The balance sheet grid.**

Alternative #_____

	Positive Anticipations +	Negative Anticipations –
1. Tangible gains + and losses – for SELF		
2. Tangible gains + and losses – for OTHERS		
3. Self-approval + or self-disapproval –		
4. Social approval + or disapproval –		

mentioned and written on the grid. But there will be others you haven't mentioned. I'd like you to concentrate on these. First tell me what bearing the consideration would have on your choice. Be as specific as possible and say whether this would be an advantage or disadvantage. I'll ask some questions to try to make sure that we've touched on all the considerations that might be relevant to you.

The same procedure is repeated for each of the other three categories. Whenever the client mentions a new pro or con consideration, he is asked to write it down in the appropriate box in the balance sheet grid for each alternative. If a given consideration cannot readily be classified in one of the four categories, the counselor discusses it with the client and, if necessary, explains that the important thing is to get the item listed in the appropriate plus or minus *column*, that the row does not particularly matter.

Step 4: *Identifying the Most Important Considerations*. To increase the client's awareness of differences in the *importance* of the various considerations he has listed in the balance sheet grids, he is told:

All of these are items you might consider in deciding on a career (or what to do next year). But when it comes down to making a choice some considerations are more important than others. What I'd like you to do is go back over the list and tell me which are the considerations that are most important to you. I'd like you to give, let's say, the four considerations about _____ [first alternative] that are most attractive, its four greatest advantages. They can be ones you just discussed or ones you mentioned earlier. . . . Now I'd like you to give the four considerations about _____ [first alternative] that are most unattractive, its biggest disadvantages. . . . Let's do the same for _____ [second alternative] and for each of the other alternatives.

Note: Instead of using this crude selection procedure the client can be asked to give ratings for every item in the balance sheet grid on a standard scale (e.g., a 7-point scale ranging from "hardly important at all" to "extremely important").

Step 5: *Exploring Alternatives*. After the balance sheet grids have been filled out for the leading alternatives, the final step is to fill out a balance sheet grid for any new alternatives mentioned by the client after the initial interview. The procedure for the additional alternatives is the same as described in steps 1–4 above. When the grids for all previously mentioned alternatives have been filled out, the client is asked, "Has any other alternative occurred to you?" If he mentions a new one, a substantial modification of any alternative already examined, or a combination of two such alternatives, another balance sheet grid is filled out.

Step 6: *Ranking the Alternatives*. To stimulate the client to think over in a comprehensive way all the entries in his balance sheet, he is asked to study all the grid sheets and then asked once again to rank all the alternatives. For this purpose, the third question from the initial open-ended interview is repeated. After completing the final ranking, the client is advised to regard this ranking as tentative, i.e., as subject to change later on because he may learn more about the consequences of some of the alternatives or have second thoughts about them. This advice is given to avoid creating in the client a premature sense of commitment to his first choice.

Procedures for Outcome Psychodrama

THE OUTCOME PSYCHODRAMA technique was devised to help overcome the decision maker's psychological resistances to exploring the potentially negative consequences of the two main alternatives—the course of action that he is most inclined to choose and his second choice (see chapter 14). Before introducing the technique in a decision counseling session, it is essential to carry out an *open-ended interview* about the main alternatives being considered and their salient consequences (using questions along the lines of those in step 1 of appendix A). In our work on decision counseling, the outcome psychodrama typically comes immediately after the main steps in the balance sheet procedure have been completed (steps 1–5 in appendix A).

1. *Instructions.* The counselor begins by explaining that it is usually helpful to project oneself into the future when one is making an important decision, especially in order to take account of all the various things that could go wrong. By doing this, the client is told, a person can sometimes become more fully aware of how he would feel if certain of the risks or losses, including the less obvious ones, were to materialize.

The client is given the following instructions when making a career decision (only slight changes in wording are necessary for other types of decision):

> We are going to do something now that is very different from what we've done so far. What I'd like you to do is something called role playing or psychodrama. This technique seems to be an effective way of getting people to experience some of their attitudes and feelings very directly. What I'll ask you to do is play the role of yourself *after* you have made the decision as to which type of work (or training) you want. I'll ask you to put yourself first in the place of a working _____ [first choice] and then later on in the place of a working _____ [second choice].

But before we do the role playing let's establish the situation more clearly. Let's get a few details down before we start. First, if you become a _____, what's the most probable job you'd have, after getting into the field?

OK, now let's imagine that you haven't been wildly lucky but you've gotten the kind of job you wanted. Where would you be living?

Now we're about ready to do the role playing. The role you will play is yourself one year from the time you started on the job of a _____. For the role play to work you'll have to try hard to put yourself in the situation of being a _____. I'll give you some directions, but you'll be free to create the details of the situation or to go into specifics. Be as realistic as possible, and please talk in the present tense. Try to experience the emotions you will have, and express them freely as if you are having them.

Once the role play starts, you will assume the new role and I will also assume a new role. Keep this role until the role playing is finished. If you have any questions, ask them *before* we start role playing. Any interruptions for questions and answers during the role play would break the mood and reduce the value of the role playing. Do you have any questions right now?

Here is the first situation. You decided to go into _____. You got a position one year ago. Things have gone badly, very badly, worse than you thought they would. Everything that could have gone wrong *has* gone wrong. You've just about had it. You want to talk it out with someone. You call up a very close friend. I'm playing the role of that friend. You haven't seen me for some time, but I've always been someone you can be completely frank with. You call me up and say you want to talk to me. I invite you over to my house. You come over and we begin talking. That is the situation. Do you have any questions before we start?

Remember, try to be as open and spontaneous as possible. Try not to break the dramatic role-playing situation by making any side comments or by raising procedural questions. Please ask me right now, before we begin, any questions that you have.

Once we begin, try to answer my questions in your role and fit your answers into the dramatic situation we are enacting. Add any details that are appropriate. Remember, the situation is that you now feel discouraged about your work, everything that could have gone wrong *has* gone wrong.

Let's begin.

2. *The Interviewer's Role.* The interviewer begins the psychodrama with the following statements (which he has memorized): "It's good to see you again, _____. You sounded pretty unhappy over the phone. You said it had something to do with your job [or profession, or work]. You said that it's been bothering you for a while. You called so late at night that I figure it must be pretty serious. What's the matter?"

Some subjects give detailed descriptions of what has gone wrong. Others may not say much, or may describe misfortunes that are really peripheral to their career. Whenever necessary, *the interviewer redirects the psychodrama.* He asks questions containing suggestions about what might have gone wrong, using the list the subject has given of important disadvantages. For example, if the subject has said that the uncertainty of being successful in the area is a great disadvantage, the interviewer can incorporate this consideration into a pointed question: "I remember you weren't sure you could make it big being a _____; I guess you haven't really made it. Is that right? . . . How do you feel about it? . . . Does this bother you a lot?" If the subject had listed parental disapproval as an important disadvantage, the interviewer might say: "As I remember, your parents weren't too keen on your being a _____. I suppose their reaction hasn't been too good? How have they taken it?"

After about ten minutes, or earlier if the client seems to have exhausted his imagination as to what could have gone wrong, the interviewer says: "I guess you're really fed up with being a _____. Remember you had to choose between _____ and _____. I bet you pretty much regret the choice you made. How does _____ look now to you? . . . What do you miss most about not being a _____?"

The psychodramatic scene is terminated by the interviewer with the closing remark, "I sure hope things turn out OK."

Next, *the interviewer*, in a different tone of voice, *introduces the second enactment:* "OK, that's it for that scene. Now let's do a different scene, assuming you have chosen to be a _____ [second choice]. I'd like us to do pretty much the same thing, except now you are a _____." The interviewer repeats the last two paragraphs of the instructions and starts the new psychodramatic scene with the same opening statement.

Counselors should be prepared in advance with a repertoire of remarks and questions that will be responsive to what the client says during the psychodramatic enactments. Examples of remarks that might be useful are:

I know what you mean!
Whew! (or Wow!)
I know how you feel.
God, I didn't realize what you were up against.
Mmmm, that sounds bad.

Questions that might draw out specific details are:

How did that happen?
What happened then?
How do you account for that?

Counselors who plan to use outcome psychodrama are encouraged to obtain coaching from someone with experience in drama; they should act concernedly, like a close friend, and express their emotions openly, providing a good model for the subject. By plunging wholeheartedly into his role, the counselor encourages the client to do likewise.

3. *The Final Interview*. After completing the outcome psychodrama for the two main alternatives, the counselor conducts a *free-style interview* to help the client formulate whatever new considerations he may have

become aware of and put them into perspective. For this purpose, the balance sheet procedure may again be useful.

Among the *final questions* designed to aid the client in assimilating any new inputs from the outcome psychodrama are the following:

1. Now that we have explored your decision in detail, what considerations do you think are the most important?
2. We have talked a lot about the future; has the image of your future changed in any way?
3. Has anything come up today that, maybe, you hadn't considered before?
4. Have you thought of any new ways to work on your decision to make sure everything will turn out as well as possible?
5. Can you think of any new information you would like to have that might affect your choice?

In our use of outcome psychodrama, the final step is to ask the client to make the appropriate entries into the balance sheet grids, so that he writes down every new consideration that emerges from the procedure in the context of all the other considerations he had previously listed while going through the balance sheet procedure. The client is then asked to reexamine the entire set of considerations for each alternative before making up his mind. In this way, the counselor can prevent the client from being unduly influenced by the emotional impact of any of the new considerations and can help the client evaluate them from the broader perspective of the entire matrix of pros and cons for the leading alternatives.

Notes

Chapter 2. Decision-making Strategies

1. In applying the term *strategy* for basic types of search and choice procedures—optimizing, satisficing, mixed scanning, etc.—we are following the terminology of George (1974), Etzioni (1968), and other social scientists who have made recent contributions to the analysis of decision-making processes. We do not use the term *strategy* in the technical meaning it has in game theory.

2. There are, of course, obvious weaknesses in questionnaire research on corporate decision making. Reliance on reports from a self-selected sample of vice-presidents can be a risky venture, since industrial executives are likely to be untrained observers with a strong inclination to bias their responses.

To test the inter-observer reliability of his data, Stagner computed correlation coefficients for the responses provided by pairs of executives responding from the same firm. The level of correlation for pairs of executives describing the decision-making process for their firm was statistically significant ($r = +.46$, $N = 52$). While this level of agreement is encouraging, the amount of disagreement it implies suggests that, within firms, executives are not uniform in their observations of decision making. Moreover, no estimate can be made of the extent to which the correlation is inflated by the shared goals of so-called good public relations among the pairs of executives who decided to return the questionnaires. Nevertheless, some of the specific findings are not in accord with the usual myths and ideologies promoted by large corporations, which suggests that the executives in his sample were at least somewhat candid.

3. We are indebted to Robert Sternberg (private communication) for suggesting that the two main types of strategy described in the administrative sciences literature, optimizing and satisficing, are conglomerates of a number of different variables that should be specified.

4. Incrementalism, as described by Lindblom, is treated by most social scientists as a separate strategy, coordinate with the satisficing strategy. But it is apparent that it is a variant of the satisficing strategy once one recognizes that the

content of the minimal requirements or the minimal cutoff points may change from one incremental decision to the next.

5. Dror's critique of the "science of muddling through" emphasizes that giving priority to the value of minimizing risks by continuing in the same direction may be appropriate in an unchanging social environment, but becomes inappropriate when conditions arise that require a fundamental change.

> Unless three closely interrelated conditions are concurrently met, incremental change by "successive limited comparison" is not an adequate method for policy making. *These three essential conditions are: (1) the results of present policies must be in the main satisfactory (to the policy makers and the social strata on which they depend), so that marginal changes are sufficient for achieving an acceptable rate of improvement in policy-results; (2) there must be a high degree of continuity in the nature of the problems; (3) there must be a high degree of continuity in the available means for dealing with problems.*
>
> When the results of past policies are undesirable, it is often preferable to take the risks involved in radical new departures. For instance, in newly developing states aspiring to accelerated socio-economic development, the policies followed by the former colonial policy makers clearly do not constitute an acceptable basis to be followed with only incremental change [Dror, 1969, pp. 167–168].

6. We expect that if we were to examine all the important decisions that any person makes in the course of his or her life, we would find considerable variation in the decision strategies that the person uses and corresponding variation in the degree to which the criteria for vigilant information processing are met. Some of that variation is undoubtedly attributable to cognitive limitations, some to bureaucratic politics (or its equivalent in the person's family and social network), and some to other familiar factors—objective features of the environment that facilitate or interfere with search and appraisal, the person's belief system about how to exercise good judgment, changes in the person's interests, willingness to take risks, level of aspiration, or other personality predispositions, etc. (see Barber, 1972; Elms, 1972, 1976). But if the influence of all of these variables could be assessed, a large amount of the variance would probably still remain unexplained. We believe that a big chunk of that remaining variance will be accounted for by the variables that emerge from our analysis in chapter 3 of the conditions under which one or another coping pattern is used to deal with the psychological stress generated by decisional conflict.

Chapter 3. A Conflict Model of Decision Making

1. The psychology of pleasant emotions is hardly developed at all, whereas the psychology of unpleasant emotions has been so extensively studied that a great deal is known that can be applied to decision making. Subsequent theoretical analyses will undoubtedly work out some implications of the psychology of pleasant emotions, as research and theory in that area develop, and will perhaps integrate the hypotheses that emerge with those we arrive at in the present analysis. It should be apparent, then, that we regard the enterprise we are undertaking in this chapter and in those that follow as still belonging to the early stages of developing a comprehensive conflict theory of decision making.

2. Gerard (1967) offered college students an opportunity to choose between two prints of paintings, one of which they could take home with them as payment for their services. On the surface this type of choice would be classified as an approach-approach choice, which, according to the typology developed by Kurt Lewin (1951) and elaborated by Neal Miller (1944), would generate little or no conflict. But when students are offered such a choice in a psychology laboratory it is likely to create a double approach-avoidance conflict. Some degree of stress is generated because the students are likely to become worried about being evaluated by the psychologist and may anticipate a loss of social and self-esteem if their choice betrays a lack of ability to make good judgments (Rosenberg, 1965).

In Gerard's experiment, continuous records were obtained of the subjects' finger pulse amplitude, which reflects the amount of constriction in the arterioles and is a psychophysiological indicator of stress. The data show that as subjects moved toward a decision there was a systematic decrease in finger pulse amplitude, indicating an increase in stress. After the decision there was a further brief decrease in amplitude, followed by an increase. Within several minutes, finger pulse amplitude was almost back to its predecision level, suggesting that the person's conflict may have been resolved, leaving him free from emotional tension.

The findings on physiological arousal in Gerard's study were borne out by similar experiments by Fleischer (1968), in which subjects were required to choose between two disliked foods, and by Jones and Johnson (1973), in which subjects were given a choice of drug doses with different risks of unpleasant side effects. (Gerard's and Fleischer's studies both show the indicators of stress rising even further immediately after the decision, just before decreasing to the initial level, which suggests either physiological inertia or a momentary twinge of regret.)

All of these physiological studies bearing on decisional stress must be regarded as providing evidence that is merely suggestive and not conclusive. The various physiological measures of stress, including the heart rate measure used in the experiment by Mann, Janis, and Chaplin (1969), have also been found to be associated with the arousal of attention. The status of these measures as valid indicators of stress is still being debated by specialists in psychophysiology.

3. Studies on forced compliance by Cooper (1971), Collins and Hoyt (1972), and Nel, Helmreich, and Aronson (1969) indicate that dissonance effects occur only when a person is committed to carrying out an action that could have important consequences for which he would be responsible. This line of research suggests that some of the conclusions derived from studies of personal beliefs or attitudes involving the expression of judgments that do not entail any ego-involving consequences for the person are not applicable to consequential decision making.

Responsiveness to even slight degrees of consequentiality is indicated by the results of experiments by Singer and Kornfield (1973), O'Neal (1974), Deutsch, Krauss, and Rosenau (1962), and Gerard, Blevans, and Malcolm (1964). Using Piaget's conservation tasks, which require subjects to judge equivalent quantities of candy or juice in differently shaped containers, Singer and Kornfield found that older children and adults gave correct answers that surmounted perceptual illusions when the problems were presented as intellectual exercises but not when they were told that they could eat the candy or drink the juice. O'Neal found that halo effects occur when the choice of teammates is consequential and not when the choice is nonconsequential. In a food-tasting experiment, Deutsch et al. observed that postdecisional reevaluation of the alternatives in the direction of bolstering the chosen one occurred when subjects were told that their choice reflected on them personally but not when they were given to understand that their expressed preference had no personal implications. Similar findings were reported by Gerard et al. when the choices were paintings. Postdecisional bolstering occurred after the subjects were told that they could choose which one of two prints they wanted to take home as a gift, but not after they were told merely to indicate which one they liked better.

An experiment by Taylor (1975) provides a dramatic illustration of the importance of the consequentiality variable in person perception. Her experiment was originally designed to test the implications of recent theory and research on self-attributions (Bem, 1972; Jones and Davis, 1965; Jones and Nisbett, 1971), which indicate that cognitions about one's own desires and preferences can be modified by external information that gives specific cues of the kind used to draw inferences about other people's desires and preferences. For example, a man will judge himself to be sexually attracted to a woman if he notices that in her presence his body manifests unmistakable signs of sexual arousal. Presumably everyone is capable of drawing correct inferences about his own motivations, not only in sexual situations but in a variety of other social settings involving a wide variety of different goals, on the basis of the information available to him about his own behavior. When a person is more or less indifferent on an issue and has not given it much thought, his awareness of how he acted on that issue the last time it came up might sometimes be a determining factor in forming a judgment. Richard Nixon was uninterested in party politics at the outset of his career as a lawyer in California, until one day when a local banker with whom he had become friendly asked him if he was a Republican. Nixon's answer was "I guess so. I voted for Dewey" (Wills, 1971). Our analysis of decisional conflict, incidentally, does not contradict the assumption that everyone is capable of assimilating information about the self and making appropriate changes in self-attributions; but it leads us to expect that under certain specified conditions of decisional stress, such changes will be inhibited or suppressed by defensive avoidance tendencies.

Taylor's (1975) experiment was conducted with female students in a Catholic college for women. Invited to participate in a study on what women find attractive about men, the subjects were shown photographs of ten unfamiliar men and asked to rate their attractiveness. One week later, subjects were invited to participate in a physiological experiment in which their galvanic skin response (GSR)—a measure of autonomic arousal—to photographs of the men was measured. Subjects overheard that their physiological response to the photograph of "David" had been especially strong and noticeable. The key variable, that of choice consequentiality, was then introduced. In the *"future consequences"* condition, each woman was told that in a few weeks she and other subjects would meet informally at a social gathering with some of the men whose photographs were used in the study, and since not all of the men could be invited to the gathering she could choose which one she wanted to have invited. Other subjects, in the *"no future consequences"* condition, were merely told that at the end of the experiment they would be asked to complete a questionnaire assessing their attitudes toward psychology experiments. Finally, each woman was asked again to rate the attractiveness of the men while viewing the photographs one more time, and then to state her preferences.

The results show that for the women making a consequential decision about "David"—i.e., whether to meet with him at a social gathering—the information about his arousing effects led to a *decrease* in attraction ratings; whereas among the women for whom the entire exercise was merely hypothetical, with no consequences hinging upon their judgments, the same information led to an increase in attraction toward him.

Taylor's findings are in line with our general expectation that the psychological laws governing real-life decisions are not always identical with those governing judgments and opinions elicited on nonconsequential issues presented in the laboratory. The evidence suggests the following conclusions: new information about the self will be readily assimilated when the person is making a cold cognitive judgment that has no ego-involving consequences. But the very same piece of information may be discounted or may even produce a countereffect when the decision may have important consequences for the person. It is highly likely that the young women who were told that they could choose to meet a male whose photograph had apparently "turned them on" were thinking not only about the possible positive consequences of such a meeting but also about possible sources of anxiety, such as embarrassment and sexual conflicts, which would tend to heighten the decisional conflict. In any case, the women reacted by rejecting and going against the implications of the information they were given about their positive reactions.

Taylor argues that her results indicate that social psychologists should shift to studying how people think and act when making decisions that have personal consequences instead of obtaining trivial or misleading results from laboratory studies of hypothetical choices that have no implications for people's lives. We regard research on hypothetical decisions as valuable for elucidating basic cognitive processes but as having only limited applicability to real-life decisions. We share the view that conclusions drawn from laboratory studies of inconsequential choices can be grossly misleading when applied to consequential choices. This view is reflected throughout the book: on every topic, we give priority to evidence from those laboratory and field studies that deal with real-life decisions. In view of the findings from the various experiments just cited, we are inclined to be wary of drawing any inferences about actual decision-making behavior from the large number of experiments that rely on purely hypothetical issues or that revolve around relatively trivial, inconsequential games that are played in the laboratory. Fortunately, there are systematic studies on consequential choices that we can draw on, although not all of them are labeled "decision-making" studies.

4. None of the studies carried out so far was intended to be a "crucial" experiment that would definitively test the model or enable one to decide whether conflict theory is "better" than cognitive dissonance theory, attribution theory, or any other rival theory that has something to say about decision making. Efforts to design so-called crucial experiments at the present early stage of research on decision making are, in our opinion, premature, and such experiments would undoubtedly turn out to be as ambiguous and fruitless as the misdirected efforts on this score in other areas of social psychology (see Bem, 1972; Greenwald, 1975; Smith, 1974). We draw upon the conflict model for its heuristic value in suggesting novel hypotheses about determinants of defective decision making and about new types of interventions that might improve the quality of decision making.

Chapter 4. Defective Search and Appraisal under High Conflict

1. Neodissonance theorists have revised dissonance theory to include the type of motivation emphasized by conflict theory. They stress the importance of involvement of the self in unacceptable action. Bramel (1968) typifies this new wave in dissonance theory: "I am arguing that dissonance is a feeling of personal unworthiness (a type of anxiety) traceable to rejection of oneself by other people either in the present or in the past. Any information which implies that one is incompetent or immoral arouses dissonance" (p. 365). Other neodissonance theorists also emphasize that bolstering is not to be expected unless the decision maker is concerned about engaging in consequential actions that could get him into trouble (e.g., Cooper and Worchel, 1970; Collins, Ashmore, Hornbeck, and Whitney, 1970). Aronson (1968, 1969) also suggests that bolstering occurs primarily when there is dissonance between a cognition about the self as being adequate, reliable, and trustworthy and a cognition about acting or having acted in a way that violates this self-concept. Wicklund and Brehm (1976, p. 70) take the position that "dissonance arousal requires the perceptions of a strong causal link between oneself and the potentially dissonance-arousing event." They specify that dissonance effects occur only if one perceives a connection between an action for which he or she feels *responsible* and a negative consequence of that action.

These recent revisions of dissonance theory, which move away from the concept of the person as invariably attempting to reduce cognitive dissonance whenever he becomes aware of holding contradictory beliefs, are compatible with the conflict-theory approach. The somewhat different motivations emphasized by the neodissonance theorists that we have just cited might turn out to be specific instances of the more general motivation, postulated by conflict theory, of avoiding the stress of decisional conflict.

2. Of the 88 subjects in the Mann, Janis, and Chaplin (1969) experiment, 25 reversed the rank order of the alternatives from the first rating to the second rating. It is impossible to interpret the data on the bolstering effect for the reversers. (Which alternative should be considered as C_1 and which as N_1?) Consequently, data from these 25 subjects were excluded from the main analysis. Approximately equal numbers of these excluded subjects came from each of the experimental conditions and the subjects in each of the conditions gave essentially the same reasons for reversing their preferences. Moreover, there were no significant differences between the nonreversers and the reversers on initial ratings of the alternatives. Hence, no obvious source of bias seems to have been introduced by eliminating the subjects who made unstable ratings.

3. The question of whether predecisional bolstering occurs seems to be one that cannot be answered by empirical evidence at present if the onset of the postdecisional phase is taken to be the point at which the person makes a subjective or implicit decision without socially committing himself. As yet there is no dependable method for ascertaining the implicit decisions a decision maker makes before he publicly announces his choice, which may not only be unstable but also distorted when an experimenter requires an overt expression of preference during the predecisional period. Thus, in order to identify the point at which a person makes a final implicit decision, the investigator must rely upon indirect evidence of dubious validity.

Our interviews of persons who have not yet committed themselves to a major decision concerning career, marriage, or health-related choices such as optional surgery indicate that implicit decisions often can be detected but are so unstable that an observer cannot tell which one is the final decision until after commitment. For example, it is not at all unusual for a client to report something like this to a marital counselor: last night he (or she) had definitely decided to obtain a divorce and felt firmly resolved to go through with it; but today, when about to phone for an appointment with a lawyer, all the old qualms had reappeared, undermining last night's resolution and making it seem more desirable right now to seek a reconciliation.

At the time the Mann, Janis, and Chaplin (1969) study was carried out, one of the main controversial issues in the psychology of decision making involved the extent to which people are objective and open-minded about alternative courses of action during the period preceding the making of a decision (Festinger, 1964; Janis and Mann, 1968; Jones and Gerard, 1967; Miller, 1968; Zajonc, 1968). After Leon Festinger and his coworkers carried out the first systematic investigations of decisional bolstering, they concluded that the reduction of cognitive dissonance by spreading of the alternatives occurs only after the decision maker has announced his decision: "Reevaluation of alternatives in the direction of favoring the chosen or disfavoring the rejected alternative, or both, is a post-decision phenomenon" (1964, pp. 30–31). Prior to commitment, according to their findings, there is no tendency to distort the value of the alternatives.

Festinger (1964) cites evidence from three experiments that support his view, but they involve either hypothetical issues or minor approach-approach conflicts and provide only indirect evidence that can be readily interpreted in other ways. One study, by Davidson and Kiesler (1964), required teenage girls to play the role of someone "responsible for hiring a man to become a first vice-president" in a firm they "own and control." The predecisional ratings were obtained at a time when the subjects were led to believe that more information would be forthcoming. Not surprisingly, those ratings showed no tendency toward predecisional bolstering.

An experiment by Jecker (1964) set up a more realistic minor conflict by offering high school girls a choice between two desirable phonograph records. From postdecisional ratings of the records, Jecker inferred that there probably had been no bolstering at all before the decision was made. But the study provides no direct evidence concerning predecisional ratings and cannot preclude the possibility that there had been temporary bolstering before commitment followed by subsequent changes. The same criticism applies to the third experiment, by Allen (1964), which is similar to Jecker's experiment. (For a detailed summary and critique of the experiments see Janis and Mann, 1968, and for a resumé of the predecisional versus postdecisional bolstering issue see Insko and Schopler, 1972). All three experiments are open to plausible alternative explanations, and the indirect evidence they provide does not appear to outweigh the direct evidence of precommitment bolstering from the study by Mann, Janis, and Chaplin (1969).

In a more recent experiment on predecisional choices, Linder and Crane (1970) claimed to have obtained an outcome opposite to that of Mann, Janis, and Chaplin (1969). In their experiment female undergraduates who had agreed to undergo an interview about their sexual attitudes and behavior were asked to choose between two male psychology interviewers. The amount of time prior to the decision was varied by telling the subjects that before making their choice they would have an opportunity to chat with both interviewers for three, eight, or fifteen minutes. The findings showed that ratings of the alternatives converged as the time for decision approached. Since the longer time intervals would presumably give the subjects greater opportunity to obtain more information about the two alternatives, the authors assert that the findings can be interpreted as indicating that the *more* information a decision maker expects, the *more* spreading (or less convergence) was observed, which is exactly the opposite of what was found by Mann, Janis, and Chaplin (1969). But this interpretation was subsequently withdrawn by Linder, after he carried out a near-replication experiment (Linder, Wortman, and Brehm, 1971) in which the amount of time remaining was not confounded with the amount of information to be expected (by holding the latter variable constant). The results of the second experiment again showed that the shorter the time interval remaining until the decision had to be announced, the more nearly equal the alternatives were rated in attractiveness. The authors conclude that the amount of information expected in this situation is irrelevant and that "in both experiments . . . the difference in attractiveness of the two alternatives was a direct function of the amount of time remaining until the decision," which they regard as "a manifestation of reactance aroused by the loss of freedom implied by any felt preference for one of the alternatives over the other" (p. 284).

Indirect correlational evidence in support of the assumption that bolstering can occur prior to commitment is provided by three studies (Mills and O'Neal, 1971; O'Neal, 1971; O'Neal and Mills, 1969), which are based on Mills's concept of avoidance of uncertainty. According to Mills (1965), people become biased prior to commitment in order to feel certain that the chosen alternative will not lead to worse or less favorable consequence than one of the other alternatives. (This conception of avoidance of uncertainty seems to be roughly equivalent to our conception of reducing conflict by means of the pattern of defensive avoidance.) All three studies showed that subjects' ratings of alternatives on diverse attributes prior to commitment were more highly intercorrelated when a choice had to be made among them than when no choice was required. These findings can be interpreted as indicating that when people are about to make a choice they enhance the most preferred alternative by playing up its desirable features and/or by playing down the desirable features of the alternatives they are about to reject, thus reducing residual uncertainty (or conflict). Additional research by Mills (1965) and by Mills and Jellison (1968) provides experimental evidence of selective exposure to information well before decision makers have to announce their decisions, indicating bias in favor of the most perferred alternative prior to commitment. All these studies by Mills and his associates, like the Mann, Janis, and Chaplin (1969) study, support the assumption that bolstering or other manifestations of defensive avoidance of conflict can occur during the precommitment period, before a decision maker announces his or her choice to anyone.

Chapter 5. Defensive Avoidance among Policy Makers

1. Although the bureaucrats in the school system set up a new position of Director of Desegregation, the man appointed to it was not relieved of other pressing duties and practically all his operating budget was earmarked to defray the expenses of the augmented computer facility and to pay the salary of a new

computer specialist. As another token gesture, the bureaucrats set up two staff committees to work on the desegregation problem; but, again, they failed to relieve the members of any of their other duties and gave them insufficient funds to do anything more than have a few ceremonial meetings devoted mainly to listening to lectures by the computer specialists. Neither of the two staff committees, according to Weiner, had any discernible impact on the outcome of the desegregation planning process.

2. Weiner's (1974) personal communication on the way the professionals in the San Francisco school system approached the task of developing a desegregation plan is drawn upon here to supplement his published report.

3. We think the garbage can is an unfortunate analogy for community decision making, because it has the connotation that all the objectives and solutions thrown into the hopper are worthless rubbish. A more apt analogy would be a family storage closet, which may contain many valuable objects that are temporarily shelved together with some mementos of sentimental value, along with essentially worthless items that are merely gathering dust, any of which may be discarded when moving day approaches because no one in the family is willing to fight to retain them.

4. For details see Wohlstetter (1962), Janis (1972), and *Hearings before the Joint Committees on the Investigation of the Pearl Harbor Attack* (1946).

5. The quotation is from Wohlstetter, p. 66.

6. All quotations about Kimmel's reactions on December 6, 1941, are from Brownlow, 1968, p. 127.

7. Raven (1974) reports evidence of symptoms of groupthink in the Nixon group responsible for the Watergate coverup. A similar analysis has been made by other psychologists (e.g., Green and Conolley, 1974). These analyses indicate that many of the symptoms of groupthink were manifested, but the evidence bearing on the background conditions is not wholly consistent, particularly with regard to the cohesiveness of the Nixon group.

Some of the phenomena of groupthink are similar to those observed in studies of group polarization effects. An article by Myers and Lamm (1975) discusses the dozens of laboratory experiments carried out during the 1960s that purported to demonstrate that the average individual was more prone to take risks after participating in a group discussion than when making a decision on his own (e.g., Kogan and Wallach, 1967; Stoner, 1961). They also take account of more recent findings and analyses that call into question the generality of the so-called risky-shift tendency (e.g., Cartwright, 1971; Pruitt, 1971). Their analysis of the accumulated evidence points to the operation of a group polarization tendency such that the group decision enhances whichever point of view, risky or conservative, is initially dominant within the group.

Chapter 6. The Decisional Balance Sheet

1. The balance sheet schema also appears to be compatible with Estes's (1970) analysis of choice behavior in terms of information processing and Fishbein's (1967) concept of behavioral intention as a function of the decision maker's beliefs about the consequences of a course of action and about what other people think he should do. (Our category of anticipated self-approval or disapproval enters Fish-

bein's formula as another type of consequence, namely, how the person thinks he will subsequently react on the basis of his own internalized standards.)

2. It must be recognized, of course, that the four types of anticipation are not necessarily mutually exclusive. For example, anticipation of a major utilitarian loss (e.g., money) or of social disapproval from a normative reference group may result in simultaneous anticipations of losing self-esteem. Some powerful incentives—such as the threat of being sent to jail for an illegal act—involve losses in all four categories. Nevertheless, it may often be possible to analyze decisional conflicts according to the predominating consideration that runs counter to the decision. Certain decisional conflicts can be singled out as "primary" types in that they contain only one major type of incentive to reject the decision. After the behavioral consequences of these primary types have been systematically investigated, it should be possible to use many of the findings to analyze the more complex decisional conflicts that involve two or more types of anticipated loss.

3. An extreme example is presented by Festinger, Riecken, and Schachter (1956) in their classic study *When Prophecy Fails*, which deals with a small religious sect headed by a Mrs. Keech, who prophesied that a flood would swamp most of the earth on December 21, 1955. In preparation for their rescue to another planet, the believers decided to quit their jobs, give away their belongings, and publicly declare their faith in Mrs. Keech's prophecy. When the flood did not materialize and the sect was ridiculed in the news media, Mrs. Keech rationalized that the people in her group had saved the world from destruction because of the light and goodness emanating from them. She and her followers promptly set about proselytizing for converts to this new quasi-religious ideology.

4. In all four types of conflict, the modes of resolution are assumed to represent the product of common socialization experiences in family, school, and peer-group settings. The various modes can be regarded as a repertoire of alternative adjustive tendencies that are called forth by the four different types of decisional conflict. A great deal of research will be needed, however, to determine the effects of cultural differences and variations in child-rearing practices on the acquisition of the modes of conflict resolution that enter into a person's repertoire. Research on individual differences in conflict behavior may also require careful investigation of life-history data in order to understand the conditions under which different types of personality display one or another mode of resolution (see Barber, 1972; Elms, 1976).

5. Egbert, Battit, Welch, and Bartlett (1964) designed a field experiment specifically to test the implications of Janis's (1958) correlational findings on the inverse relationship between amount of preoperative information and degree of postoperative distress. Ninety-seven patients hospitalized for elective abdominal operations were assigned at random to the experimental and control groups, which proved to be well equated with respect to age, sex, and type of operation. The patients in both groups had a visit from the anesthetist on the night before the operation and were given routine information about the time and duration of the operation, the nature of the anesthesia, and the fact that they would awaken in the recovery room. The patients in the control group were told nothing more, whereas those in the experimental group were given four additional types of information: (a) a description of postoperative pain—where they would feel it, how intense it would be, how long it was likely to last; (b) explicit reassurance that postoperative

pain is a normal consequence of an abdominal operation; (c) advice to relax their abdominal muscles to reduce the pain, along with special instructions about how to shift from one side to the other by the use of their arms and legs without tensing muscles in the sensitive area; and (d) assurance that they would be given pain-killing medication if they could not achieve a tolerable level of comfort. Neither the surgeons nor the ward nurses were told about this experiment, so as to ensure that the patients in both groups would not receive any other differential treatment.

On the day of the operation both groups required about the same amount of pain-reducing narcotics, but on each of the next five days the experimental group required significantly less. In fact, requests for medication to relieve their pain were so infrequent from the well-informed patients that their postoperative narcotic requirements were reduced by about one-half, as compared with the uninformed control group ($p < .01$). Blind ratings by a physician showed that the patients in the experimental group were more comfortable and in better emotional and physical condition than the controls. Further evidence of the more rapid improvement of the well-informed patients is provided by data on the duration of hospitalization. Completely unaware of the experimental or control treatments received by the patients, the surgeons sent the well-informed patients home an average of 2.7 days earlier than the uninformed patients ($p < .01$).

The Egbert et al. study provides systematic evidence in support of the conclusion, derived from the earlier studies, concerning the positive value of advance information about postoperative pain and other negative consequences of undergoing surgery. In this study, the preoperative information and reassurances were reiterated during the first few postoperative days, which may have contributed to the effectiveness of the preparatory communication. Conceivably, the postoperative reassurances or the coping advice alone might have been responsible for the outcome. There are also other possible interpretations that will have to be checked in subsequent research. It should be noted, however, that the results of this field study are substantiated by a number of subsequent field experiments on the effects of preparatory communications in which reassurances and advice were not repeated during the postoperative period.

Four other studies of adult surgical patients (Johnson, 1966; Schmidt, 1966; Schmitt and Wooldridge, 1973; Vernon and Bigelow, 1974) used preoperative procedures similar to those used by Egbert et al. but did not reinforce them by postoperative follow-up. All four of these studies report findings supporting the conclusion that when nurses or other members of the hospital staff have given preoperative information about the stresses of surgery and ways of coping with those stresses, patients show less postoperative distress and/or better recovery from surgery.

Positive results on the value of psychological preparation have also been found in studies of childbirth (Levy and McGee, 1975), tooth extraction (Miller and Treiger, 1976), and obnoxious medical examinations requiring patients to swallow stomach tubes (Johnson and Leventhal, 1974). Field experiments by Moran (1963) and by Wolfer and Visintainer (1975) with children on pediatric surgery wards have yielded similar findings.

6. Another corollary of the defective-balance-sheet hypothesis is that if a person confines himself to considering positive and negative entries in only one category of the balance sheet (e.g., utilitarian gains for self), the decision will tend to be much less stable than if there are entries in all four categories. This corollary

should not be taken to imply, however, that having a very large number of considerations in the balance sheet is always necessarily better than having a moderate number. In fact, when a person tries to scan a very large number of entries it is difficult for him to focus on the most important consequences; he may then resort to satisficing or other inefficient decision strategies as a result of informational overload. For each alternative, the most significant considerations, of course, are those that pertain to the major gains and the major risks that the person will in all probability encounter if he carries out that course of action.

7. The four considerations generated by the Surgeon General's report constituted a strong challenge to Mr. Bingham's complacent attitude ("I like to smoke, I've been doing it for twenty years, and there is no good reason why I shouldn't keep on"). The four new entries in the balance sheet, it will be noted, occur within a complex matrix of other positive and negative incentives. All the remaining entries in the decisional balance sheet are based on inferences from an intensive interview with Bingham dealing with the various considerations he raised when agonizing over the alternatives available to him. At that time he was still smoking heavily, but was dissatisfied about it and kept promising himself that "one day soon" he was going to change. It is apparent from his balance sheet that the third alternative, that of cutting down his smoking to about half a pack per day, appeared to him to be the most satisfactory one. This was, in fact, the choice to which he subsequently committed himself, about a week after the interview.

8. The account of the contrasting reactions of Count Bernstorff and President Wilson was derived from Baker (1927–39), Bernstorff (1920), Lansing (1935), Seymour (1926–28), and Tuchman (1958). An earlier version of this case study was presented by Janis (1959b).

Chapter 7. Stages of Decision Making

1. If the answer to the second key question in stage 3 is negative, the following supplementary question comes next: "Can I relax the requirements sufficiently to find the best alternative satisfactory?"

If the answer to this question is also negative, an additional supplementary question is raised, which leads either to further weighing of the existing alternatives or to search for a new alternative: "Might a modification of one of the existing alternatives be better?"

Both these supplementary questions are shown along with the major ones in figure 7.

2. Alex Inkeles, personal communication, November 1975.

3. The stages schema represented in figure 7—including the main questions shown in each of the stages and the reversions from one stage back to an earlier one—was developed by Janis (1968, 1974) on the basis of detailed protocols of major personal decisions, starting first with diary records of several of his own decisions. The assumptions were modified on the basis of additional protocols obtained from (a) five intensive interviews of friends (concerning major personal decisions from the time of challenge through commitment and implementation); (b) nine students in a seminar on decision making who were asked at the beginning of the course (before they became familiar with the concepts presented in this book) to keep a diary of their thoughts and actions concerning their ongoing career

decision; and (c) thirty interviews of men and women in pilot studies of health-related decisions in an antismoking clinic, a weight-reduction clinic, and a medical clinic. Janis and Mann collaboratively revised the stages schema shown in figure 7 (and the combined model shown in figure 8) so as to conform as closely as possible to the sequences and reversions that could be inferred from all of the additional case studies available to them.

Besides the feedback loops described in the text, two others are represented in figure 7, both of which occur *within stage 2:*

(a) After the decision maker appraises the risks as serious if he does not change his current course of action (stage 1), his search for an alternative may yield at the outset of stage 2 a salient one that he judges to be unacceptable, because it does not adequately meet the challenge or because it will be too costly or entail too many risks. As depicted by the sequence starting with the arrow labeled *no* stemming from the initial question in stage 2, the decision maker discards the unacceptable alternative and returns to the search for another alternative. As he contemplates other alternatives, made salient either from his deliberate memory search or from seeking the advice of others, the decision maker may go through the same loop again and again until he finds an alternative that appears to be an acceptable candidate. During this phase of searching for acceptable alternatives, the original course of action may be discarded as unacceptable; thereafter, the decision maker searches for an entirely different course of action. But the original course of action is rarely discarded completely; it is usually retained as a possible candidate, although regarded as much less attractive than before the challenge.

(b) After locating an alternative he judges to be acceptable, a vigilant decision maker will ask whether he has sufficiently surveyed the available alternatives, which is the second key question of stage 2. If he realizes that he has not yet carried out an exhaustive search (within his own memory and among knowledgeable acquaintances who might offer good suggestions), his answer will be *no*. As indicated by the arrow leading from the second question in stage 2, the decision maker will then return to the search for another alternative and repeat the cycle once again. This feedback loop will continue until he believes that he has surveyed the alternatives sufficiently.

4. The experimental evidence reported by Mann, Janis, and Chaplin (1969) bears directly on the assumption concerning the tendency to engage in precommitment bolstering when no further information can be expected. See also Jones and Gerard's (1967) concept of "unequivocal behavioral orientation" and their account of the function of predecisional bolstering in facilitating unconflicted action.

5. The combined schema represented in Figure 8 was developed on the basis of the same detailed protocols of major decisions that were used to develop the stages schema represented in figure 7. (See note 3 above.)

Chapter 8. Open-minded Exposure to Challenging Information

1. The evidence that has accumulated since the mid-1960s has continued to run counter to the hypothesis that discrepant information will be avoided merely because it is unpleasant, or that supportive information invariably is sought after for the comfort it affords. The problem at present is to identify the variables that

determine whether selective exposure, rather than open-mindedness or indifference, will be manifested. When the appropriate conditions are present, the effects may extend beyond selective exposure; supportive and nonsupportive information may be *processed* differently by the decision maker, with more careful attention given to supportive messages (see Brock and Balloun, 1967).

Preference for supportive messages has been reported in some field studies and in some carefully controlled laboratory experiments (e.g., Adams, 1961; Ehrlich et al., 1957; Mills, Aronson, and Robinson, 1959; Mills, 1968, p. 774). When selective exposure is observed, it is usually relative rather than absolute. Typically, decision makers in the laboratory choose a relatively greater number of supportive messages, express somewhat greater preference for them, or pay relatively closer attention to them, but with rare exceptions they still willingly expose themselves to inconsistent information (see Mills, 1968). Because college instructors frequently endorse social norms and strictures against closed-mindedness, it is not surprising that active avoidance of discrepant information is rarely observed when students serve as subjects in college laboratories. In clinical case studies, however, some examples of strenuous avoidance of discrepant information have been documented (see Janis, Mahl, Kagan, and Holt, 1969).

2. So far, very little research on the question of information preferences has been conducted directly within a conflict framework. Most studies designed as tests of the selective exposure hypothesis do not lend themselves readily to a conflict analysis. Often the experiments deal with trivial or hypothetical decisions and are therefore relevant at best only to the two nonconflict patterns of coping. Furthermore, the measures commonly used to test for selective exposure do not discriminate finely between the various patterns identified in table 6. Such coarse measures as ranked preferences for reading supportive over nonsupportive material, or amount of time spent on various messages, provide an inadequate picture of information gathering and processing activities. For example, several studies have reported that cigarette smokers show a preference for reading information linking smoking and lung cancer (Feather, 1962), or are equally interested in supportive and nonsupportive information about the smoking-cancer link (Feather, 1963). A decision maker's lack of preference for supportive over discrepant information could reflect the indifference that accompanies unconflicted adherence or unconflicted change if his level of interest is low, but his lack of preference could indicate vigilance if his level of interest in both types of information is high. Accordingly, the absolute level of interest and not just a preference or lack of preference for one kind of information over another is crucial for identifying and testing the various patterns. An important implication of the conflict model, then, is the need for more refined and sensitive measures of information preference. (See Brock and Balloun, 1967, for an additional critique of the methodology of selective exposure research.)

3. Because the vast majority of Yale students had not, in fact, signed the We-Won't-Go pledge, special steps were taken in order to obtain a sizable sample of men who had overtly committed themselves by signing it. The investigators started by working from the published lists of signers, whose names had appeared in local newspapers as part of their act of overt commitment. After a sample of these names was selected on a random basis, the men were sought out in their residential colleges. A total of twenty-three signers were interviewed; a sample of thirty-nine nonsigners was obtained in the same residential colleges by knocking

on doors, in the same way that the signers were approached. The small percentage of men who did not agree to be interviewed was approximately the same for signers as for nonsigners.

4. The correlational findings shown in figure 9 bear out the familiar generalization that people who strongly favor a given position on a controversial issue are less likely than others to express agreement with persuasive communications that argue against that position (see Festinger, 1964; Jones and Gerard, 1967; McGuire, 1968). What is suggested by the comparisons among the four groups investigated in this study is that instead of merely classifying people as for or against a given position, we might be able to use a more refined set of categories for differentiating among people with varying positions on an issue by taking account of their decisional position.

It should be noted that in the Janis and Rausch study, men in the unchallenged group ($N = 12$) and in the temporarily challenged group ($N = 16$) showed significantly less agreement with the pro-pledge article than those in the currently conflicted ($N = 11$) and committed ($N = 23$) groups. The last two groups did not differ significantly, however, probably because of a ceiling effect: the currently conflicted men agreed almost completely with the article, and so there was practically no possibility of the committed men showing even higher agreement.

5. For the pro articles, $F = 1.06$, $p > .25$; for the anti articles, $F = 3.18$, $p < .05$. A detailed examination of the findings in figure 10 indicates four distinct patterns of information preference.

(a) Among the unchallenged men, who were unconflicted in their decision not to sign, there was somewhat more interest in pro-pledge than in anti-pledge information, but comparatively little interest in either, which is indicative of unconflicted adherence (hypothesis 1). The selective exposure hypothesis would have predicted that these nonsigners would seek out supportive, anti-pledge material and avoid discrepant, pro-pledge articles. As can be seen, the reverse outcome was obtained.

(b) Among the men who had been challenged but had decided after some deliberation not to sign, there was open-minded preference for information in favor of the pledge, consistent with the vigilance pattern (hypothesis 4). Again, according to the selective exposure hypothesis, men opposed to signing the pledge should have expressed greater interest in reading anti-pledge material than pro-pledge material, which clearly was not the case.

(c) Among the men in favor of signing the pledge but still highly conflicted and undecided, there was a relatively high level of interest in information, with a slight (not statistically significant) preference for supportive (pro-pledge) over nonsupportive (anti-pledge) material. These findings suggest that while the men in this group were predominantly vigilant, exhibiting high interest in anti-pledge articles as well as pro-pledge articles, there may have been a subdominant tendency among some of the men toward defensive avoidance (see hypothesis 2c). The men who were currently conflicted (who said they might sign the pledge) constituted the only group to show a trend toward the classic selective exposure pattern of greater interest in supportive than in discrepant information. But according to Festinger's (1964) analysis of decision making in terms of cognitive dissonance theory, this should have been the only group to show open-minded interest in information, since the men in this group were the only ones still in a state of predecisional conflict at the time of the interview and none had committed himself.

(d) Among the men who had decided to sign the pledge and had publicly committed themselves by having their names appear in local newspapers, there was a high level of interest in information, not just supportive but also nonsupportive (anti-pledge) information, a pattern indicative of vigilance (hypothesis 4). Again, this outcome contradicts the selective exposure hypothesis, with its prediction of postdecisional bias in favor of being exposed to supportive communications.

The vigilant coping pattern was probably adaptive for the situation confronting committed draft resisters in the spring of 1968. In the face of severe threats from the government and pressure from relatives to avoid ruining their careers, group support may have enabled the draft resisters to maintain a high degree of vigilance and open-mindedness. The draft resisters appear to have been a close-knit group, who gave each other moral and social support, exchanged information, and encouraged open-mindedness in selecting the best possible means of resisting the draft. (An entirely opposite effect of group support on information preferences is discussed in chapter 5 in the final section, "Groupthink.")

With regard to the conclusions to be drawn from the results shown in figure 10 (as well as figure 9), Janis and Rausch point out that since these data are correlational, one must consider the possibility that some predispositional differences among the four groups—perhaps involving a personality, subcultural, or ideological variable—might account for the outcome. (see Clark and James, 1967; Feather, 1967). To test the hypotheses based on the assumption that decisional coping patterns determine preference for supportive or discrepant communications, a different type of experimental investigation will have to be carried out, in which subjects are exposed to experimental conditions affecting level of conflict, beliefs about prospects of finding a satisfactory solution, and perceptions of deadline pressures. Such experiments are needed to determine whether receptiveness to information is a function of the presumed antecedent conditions of the various decisional coping patterns.

6. Mills's (1965) analysis of selective exposure makes the assumption that "people want to feel certain when they take an action that it is better than the alternatives, that it will lead to the most favorable consequences for motive satisfaction." This is equivalent to our assumption that people attempt to reduce conflict about choosing a course of action. It is not surprising, therefore, that the predictions Mills has formulated and tested would also be made by our theoretical model of conflict. For example, Mills has predicted that when people are not committed, the more uncertain (i.e., conflicted) they are about which course of action is the best, the more interested they will be in information favoring one of the alternatives. This corresponds to our assertions about the role of conflict in producing vigilance that, under appropriate conditions of hope for an adequate solution and absence of an imminent deadline, will lead to vigilant information search and appraisal. Mills (1965) tested his prediction with college men who were given the opportunity to chose between two fairly valuable products, such as a portable tape recorder and an electric shoeshine kit. An experimental group of men who were given a choice between two products that they had ranked as almost equal in desirability spent significantly more time reading advertisements about one of the products than an equivalent group who were given a choice between the same product and another one that they had ranked much higher. Thus, those confronted with a low-certainty choice (i.e., one that evoked relatively high conflict) were more likely to show vigilant attention to

pertinent information about one of the alternatives than those who faced a choice involving high certainty (i.e., one that evoked little or no conflict).

7. Pre- and postdecisional assessments of information preferences were obtained in three laboratory studies.

In an experiment by Jecker (1964) college students were asked to make a rather trivial choice of a partner for a competitive laboratory game. Consistent with our assumption that when no major risks are involved the coping pattern will produce indifference, Jecker's subjects were nonselective before and after the choice, showing little interest in reading information about the choice alternatives.

An experiment by Behling (1971) involved high school students in a "market research survey" in which they could choose to keep a product, such as an alarm clock, camera, fan, or lamp. Behling found that uncommitted subjects spent more time reading supportive as opposed to nonsupportive information, while committed subjects showed no preference for supportive over nonsupportive information. As so often happens when a study is conceived within a different theoretical framework, one cannot tell if the antecedent conditions specified by conflict theory that might account for Behling's findings were or were not present in his experiment.

A third experiment, by Brock, Stuart, and Becker (1970), involved a more consequential decision. College students were required to swallow a capsule containing a "drug" that they had previously chosen. When offered the opportunity to listen to taped communications concerning the side effects of the drug, the uncommitted subjects showed no preference for supportive over nonsupportive information. But subjects who were committed (after having already ingested the drug) revealed a complicated pattern of preferences. There was a very low level of interest in both supportive and nonsupportive communications if the information offered was familiar. However, if the information offered was new or unfamiliar, there was substantial interest in obtaining the nonsupportive information, although there was even more interest in obtaining the supportive information. The latter finding, which suggests some degree of vigilance combined with a slight tendency to bolster the decision, is not surprising when one considers that the decision was irreversible after the drug had been ingested.

8. The ready availability of supportive information in the environment is a major reason for *de facto* selective exposure (Freedman and Sears, 1965; Sears, 1968): regardless of the individual's interests or needs, he is sometimes surrounded almost entirely by supportive, nonchallenging information.

Chapter 9. Anticipatory Regret

1. The quotation is from Xenophon's *Memorabilia* (London: Heinemann, 1923), p. 48.

2. Undoubtedly there are wide individual differences, having to do with personality and cognitive style, in the capacity to tolerate the stresses of prolonged decisional conflict. Reflective people who characteristically approach problems with caution will almost always be inclined to look for and think about potential losses. They move slowly through the stages of decision making and attempt to postpone decisions as long as possible, even for relatively unimportant issues. At

the other extreme are people who are generally intolerant of uncertainty, frustration, and delay. They often commit themselves impulsively, without first carrying
out a careful search for relevant information and sound advice. A reflection-
impulsiveness dimension, which describes the degree to which the person reflects
on the validity of his solutions to difficult problems, has been reliably identified in
both children (Kagan, 1965) and adults (Yando and Kagan, 1968). This dimension
is related to the amount of time spent on making a choice in various decisional
situations (see Mann, 1973).

Autonomy-dependence is another personality dimension that is related to
tolerance for delay and other aspects of decision-making style. Brim et al. (1962)
found that more dependent subjects tended to be more optimistic about the outcomes of their actions, considered fewer outcomes while evaluating alternatives,
and were less consistent in their preferences.

3. Intensive interviews of the two executives were conducted in 1967 by I. L.
Janis.

4. The case study of the government administrator is based on an interview
conducted in 1971 by I. L. Janis.

Chapter 10. Threats to Freedom of Choice

1. Testimony given before the Senate Select Committee on Watergate,
quoted in the *New York Times*, June 15, 1973, pp. 18–19.

2. Testimony given before the Senate Select Committee on Watergate,
quoted in the *New York Times*, July 17, 1973, p. 29.

3. The quotation is from the Senate Watergate Hearings, 1973, p. 224.

4. The quotation is from *The Senate Watergate Report* (New York: Dell, 1974),
p. 100.

5. Testimony given before the Senate Select Committee on Watergate,
quoted in the *Washington Post*, June 17, 1973, pp. C2–C3.

6. Reactance theorists postulate that reactance behavior also occurs in the
usual decision-making situation, whenever the person himself relinquishes alternatives on a voluntary basis, albeit reluctantly, as a result of making a choice
(Wicklund, 1974). In this chapter we confine ourselves to an examination of involuntary eliminations; elsewhere we examine the effects of voluntary removal of
freedom, which is usually accompanied by pre- and postdecisional regret (see
chapters 4, 9, and 12).

7. Like all naturalistic field studies, the draft lottery study by Mann and Dashiell
(1975) has its methodological limitations. There were sampling problems, with
small numbers of cases in some of the cells; and the possibility remains that
following the lottery the most reactance-prone young men may have selected
themselves out of the study. Before any definitive generalizations can be drawn
about the conditions that determine the relative strengths of the reactance aroused
by threats to freedom of choice versus the anxiety aroused by threats of other types
of losses, additional studies dealing with men and women in various age groups
who are facing different types of choice-narrowing threats will obviously be
needed.

The question arises whether the results obtained could have been equally well predicted or explained by any of the current major social psychological theories dealing with choice behavior. Most social psychological theories (attribution theory, dissonance theory, cognitive balance theory) would not have made any specific predictions in this experiment, although any of these theories could provide a plausible *ad hoc* explanation for whatever outcome was obtained. Reactance theory could have made specific predictions about attitude changes following the draft lottery, but they would have been opposite to the ones made by conflict theory. Brehm (1966) asserts that reactance is aroused by threatened as well as actual restrictions of choice alternatives. According to Brehm, restriction of a behavior should lead to an increase in the value of that behavior. Thus, reactance theory would predict that after the lottery, men who obtained low numbers would show an *increase* in their attractiveness ratings of draft-vulnerable alternatives (job, graduate school, travel), since the lottery outcome had the effect of threatening their freedom to choose those alternatives. A low-number man might feel implicitly pressured to choose from among the draft-exempt alternatives; reactance motivation would then be reflected in *derogation* of these "foisted" alternatives. Reactance theory would make no specific prediction for the high-number men, since these men would not lose any freedom of choice.

For the reactance hypothesis to be supported by the results, a linear trend would be required, such that enhancement of vulnerable alternatives is associated with low lottery numbers. As figure 11 shows, the trend for vulnerable alternatives is inconsistent with a reactance explanation.

It should be noted that the proponents of reactance theory recognize that there may be "positive" forces operating in a direction opposite to reactance motivation that would outweigh considerations of freedom, especially in the case of social-influence threats to freedom (Brehm and Sensenig, 1966; Worchel and Brehm, 1971). Thus the question of the applicability of conflict theory or reactance theory may very well boil down to the question of which is the more powerful motive in a situation in which considerations of regaining freedom and avoiding material losses clash. For the young men confronted by the threat of the draft following the drawing of a low number in the lottery, it would appear that conflict reduction (implying lowered attraction toward alternatives that involved the threat of negative consequences) prevailed over reactance motivation.

A possible point of reconciliation between the two theories is the time aspect, here represented by the period elapsed after the draft lottery. The study found a significant main effect for time of post-lottery test, with a general tendency for threatened alternatives to be magnified on the day following the lottery and depreciated ten days later. This finding provides some encouragement for the thesis that a sequence of stages obtains in reactions to threats to behavioral freedom. When important career decisions are at stake, reactance and the idealization of lost and threatened alternatives may be an immediate response. But in the long run, the decision maker must adjust to a changed reality, in which the threatened alternatives play a reduced part. Depreciation of the threatened, draft-vulnerable alternatives may function, like sour-grapes rationalization, to refocus interest in the surviving, safe alternatives. Thus it is conceivable that both reactance motivation and conflict motivation exist side by side, with the reactance motive at its strongest in the period immediately following a threat and conflict motivation at its most intense at a later stage, as the individual takes up the task of making the best of the altered state of affairs.

8. The essayist Richard Steele (1712) has described the historical origin of the term *Hobson's choice*. "Tobias Hobson was the first in this island [England] to let out hackney horses. . . . When a man came for a horse, he was led into the stable, where there was a great choice, but he was obliged to take the horse which stood next to the stable door . . . from whence it became a proverb when what ought to be your election was forced upon you, to say 'Hobson's Choice.' " We are not told how Hobson's customers reacted to this curtailment of their freedom (they could, of course, have chosen to walk, but if they wanted to ride they had no choice). Presumably their understanding of Hobson's motives for limiting their choice would determine their feelings. One would expect the amount of resentment and reactance to depend on whether or not Hobson took the trouble to explain that rather than being an arbitrary authoritarian, he had the welfare of his horses in mind, and was determined to let them out in rotation so as to prevent the more popular ones from becoming overworked or lame.

9. In *The Gulag Archipelago*, Solzhenitsyn argues that despite the enormous coercive power of the secret police in the Soviet Union throughout the 1930s and 1940s, Soviet citizens could have resisted more effectively when millions of innocent people were being arrested and sent off to slave labor camps. Everyone, according to Solzhenitsyn, was much too docile—the victim, his family, and neighbors who saw the secret police agents making the arrest. If they had argued, protested, attracted large crowds, and physically threatened the agents conducting the arrests, the number of victims would have been far fewer. Solzhenitsyn asserts that the police organization would not have had the manpower to cope with widespread resistance and would therefore have been forced to reduce drastically their weekly quotas of arrests. Because the victims went quietly and everyone else remained silent and looked away, the secret police found it very easy to meet the huge quotas that were set for them.

From Solzhenitsyn's account, we surmise that the majority of ordinary citizens displayed a pattern of defensive avoidance in response to the challenge posed by witnessing innocent neighbors being arrested. From what he says, it also seems plausible to assume that the vast majority of people had no hope of any alternative other than silent acquiescence to the secret police, and that they bolstered their decision to be utterly passive about the arrests of their neighbors by developing rationalizations (e.g., "Maybe most of those arrested really are guilty of doing something against the state; but I am completely innocent, so they will leave me alone").

Chapter 11. Effects of Commitment

1. Our position on commitment effects is similar to Gerard's (1968) analysis, which emphasizes the implications for the decsion maker in terms of future rewards and costs. Gerard discusses irrevocability in terms of the "costs involved in reversing the decision" (p. 457).

2. According to Jonathan Freedman (personal communication, 1969), the overall rate of terminal compliance also depends on the amount of sacrifice required by the first request. If a large sacrifice is requested to begin with, one that

few people will agree to, compliance to the second request will tend to be relatively low; making a smaller request at the outset, one that almost everyone would agree to, will elicit more compliance. Of course, if the initial request is *too* simple and routine (e.g., a request to give someone a glass of cold water on a warm day), so little resistance is overcome that it will fail to prime the person for the second request. Presumably there is an optimal level of difficulty of the initial request—a level at which most people overcome their initial reluctance, agree to the request, and thereafter are strongly influenced by the psychological significance of their act.

3. The main finding of a boomerang effect resulting from an attack on the position held by the committed women in the field experiment was replicated in a laboratory experiment (involving the use of different strategies in playing a card game) reported by Kiesler (1971, pp. 66–74), which he carried out in collaboration with Roberta Mathog.

Kiesler's findings show that making a small commitment does *not* invariably incline a person to make a larger one. In the birth control field study, the women who signed the petition but were not attacked did not become more interested in doing volunteer work for the birth control organization than those who were not asked to sign the petition. This outcome appears to be inconsistent with research on the foot-in-the-door ploy, which leads one to expect that compliance with a small request (signing a petition) should prime a person to agree to perform a larger one (doing volunteer work). If Kiesler's findings are confirmed in a variety of field settings, a modification of the scope and limitations of the foot-in-the-door effect would be called for.

There are some intriguing suppositions that might reconcile Kiesler's findings with Freedman and Fraser's (1966). For example, the California housewives who agreed to Freedman and Fraser's first committing request (to put up a sign or sign a petition) might have been verbally attacked by their husbands or neighbors, and this attack might have motivated them to defend their decision and even go one step further. Another possibility is that a small commitment may prime a decision maker to make a greater commitment when he perceives the cause he is supporting to be noncontroversial (as in the case of Freedman and Fraser's request to help promote safe driving), but not when he knows that the cause is a controversial issue in the community (as in the case of the request by Kiesler and his collaborators to promote birth control instruction in the local high school).

4. The third group of subjects was not included in the original design of the experiment and hence was not drawn from the initial pool of 115 volunteers who were randomly assigned to the five other conditions listed in table 10. When it became apparent from the preliminary results of this study that it would be valuable to have a condition embodying stronger degree of commitment than was represented by the "irrevocability" condition, twenty more volunteers were recruited from the same residential colleges. These volunteers were comparable in all important respects to the subjects who had already participated in the other conditions.

5. Like the earlier experiment by Mann, Janis, and Chaplin (1969) discussed in chapter 4, this experiment contradicts the assumption that bolstering or spreading of alternatives never occurs during the period preceding commitment. The experimental evidence points to specific conditions that determine whether or not

predecisional bolstering will occur. Practically no change in evaluation occurred among the subjects given an easy choice (neither group differed significantly from the control group), whereas a substantial amount of predecisional bolstering occurred among the subjects who faced a difficult choice ($p < .05$). Among the three difficult-choice groups there were differences forming a somewhat complicated pattern. The most highly committed group (irrevocable decision with commitment to justify the choice) showed less bolstering than the other two ($p < .10$), which did not differ significantly from each other. Consistent with this pattern of differences, only 30 percent of the subjects in the most highly committed group displayed predecisional bolstering behavior, while in each of the other two groups about twice as many subjects did ($p < .05$).

6. A related question was also investigated in Mann's (1971) study: namely, did the experimenter's admonition that the decision would be irrevocable influence the kind and quality of responses made to later, unrelated decisional problems? That is, did the commitment warning make the children vigilant beyond the immediate decision? In order to obtain some relevant data, two unrelated problems were presented in the final part of the session to test whether the earlier admonition of commitment with respect to the toy decision would carry over and affect responses to an issue for which a warning had not been given. A "party dilemma" was presented that required the children to weigh the problem of whether to renege on an already accepted alternative in order to obtain something much more attractive. Specifically, they were given the following hypothetical problem: "Pretend you are invited to a party given by someone you don't like very much and you say you will go. Then someone you like a whole lot invites you to his party on the same day. What would you do?" Responses to the dilemma, many of them extremely sophisticated, fell into several categories, which reveal the nursery school childrens' conceptions of commitment:

a. *Break the commitment:* "I'd cancel the first one and go to the nice boy's party."
b. *Honor the commitment:* "If I promised someone I didn't like, I'd still go"; or, "I would have to say that I will have to go to the don't-like party."
c. *Devise a compromise solution;* "I'd spend half the time at one party, the rest at the other party"; or "Go to the first, then go to the other one"; or, "Ask first person to give his party on another day."
d. *Escape:* "I couldn't go to either one—it would be unfair"; or, "I'd go where my mother would take me"; or, "I'd have to stay home because I can't go to two parties on the one day" [Mann, 1971, p. 77].

Did prior exposure to a commitment warning influence responses to the hypothetical decision about going to a party? The commitment subjects in the first experiment made fewer *"don't know"* or *nonsense* responses to the party dilemma ($p < .05$), fewer *break commitment* responses ($p < .10$), and more responses in the other three categories—*honor commitment*, *devise a compromise*, and *escape* ($p < .01$). These findings indicate that the prior experience of receiving a commitment warning on the toy decision carried over to influence responses to the later, party problem. It appears that the commitment warning induced some of the children to think over their subsequent choice more carefully.

What is the psychological significance of a commitment warning for a four- or five-year-old? Such warnings are frequently conveyed in the form of instruction from parents, who urge the child to bear in mind the ego-involving consequences of choosing a particular course of action. For a young child, exposure to such warnings, in conjunction with punishment for failure to heed them, may represent a significant learning experience; for an older child, such warnings often represent a cue that the decision is important and therefore must be taken seriously. Of course, the study just described does not show that children learned to become more cautious in their decision making during the course of the session; they may have learned cautious behavior in response to commitment warnings earlier and merely had this type of response activated by the experimenter's warnings regarding the first task. But the study does reveal that a commitment warning is capable of eliciting more mature responses on an unrelated problem as well as an increase in vigilance on an immediate decision, suggesting that a tendency to approach choices more carefully was induced.

Chapter 12. Postdecisional Conflict

1. See Boswell's *London Journal* (New York: McGraw-Hill, 1950), pp. 153–60 and p. 256.

2. The results reported by Vroom (1966), Vroom and Deci (1971), and Lawler et al. (1975), although suggestive, cannot be taken as definitive evidence of postdecisional bolstering, because field studies of this type cannot control various inputs that might affect the outcome and that can usually be controlled only in laboratory settings. For example, it is conceivable that between the initial (predecisional) measure and the first postdecisional measure the trainees vigilantly sought for new information and discovered that the to-be-chosen firm had certain objective advantages over the other firms, which could account for the observed spreading of the alternatives.

3. Quoted from *Time* magazine, June 11, 1965.

4. In Walster's (1964) study, the men did not at any time show a *reversal* of their preferences. The crossover of the two curves at the four-minute time interval in figure 16 pertains only to change scores; the actual attractiveness ratings do not show a crossover. In other words, although there was a significant amount of convergence in the ratings of the two alternatives, the chosen job continued to receive higher attractiveness ratings than the unchosen alternative. (On a 31-point scale of attractiveness with 1 as the highest rating, the chosen alternative was rated about 15 on the average before the decision, which was more than 5 points higher than the rejected alternative; it was still rated about 4 points higher four-minutes after the decision.) This significant but slight convergence trend would not be considered a manifestation of "regret" by those behavioral scientists who use the term to refer to a postdecisional reversal such that the alternative "not chosen seems [to the decision maker] to be the more attractive one" (Lewin, 1938, pp. 206–7). Both Festinger and Walster (in Festinger, 1964, pp. 99–128) use the term *post-decision regret* to refer to any *tendency* toward reversing the decision after commitment, as manifested by a decrease in the *relative* preference for the chosen alternative. According to this usage, any significant convergence of the preference ratings following an act of commitment is labeled *regret*, even if the attractiveness rating of the unchosen alternative has not increased to the point where it is higher than the (lowered) attractiveness rating for the chosen alternative. In discussing the studies by Festinger and Walster, we follow their usage of the term *regret*.

5. Like Festinger, but for a different reason, Brehm conceives of spontaneous regret as virtually inevitable following every consequential decision. Brehm's theory of reactance pertains mainly to the immediate postdecisional period and acknowledges the possibility of subsequent dissonance reduction or bolstering. It has more recently been generalized to apply to the predecisional period by assuming that self-generated threats to freedom are implicated when a person starts moving toward a decision (see Linder, Wortman, and Brehm, 1971).

6. Walster and Walster (1970) point out that although the attractiveness of the chosen task appears to decrease somewhat more than the attractiveness of the rejected task, the slopes of the two curves are not significantly different. Consequently, they do not conclude that their data show an increase in "regret" over time, because their operational definition of regret requires a significant convergence in the ratings of the two choice alternatives. They assert, however, that their best estimate is that the subjects were less satisfied with their choice at thirty-six minutes than at four minutes after commitment, and that convergence was not detected because subjects "tended to become increasingly regretful that they had ever made the decision to 'get themselves in this mess' instead of focusing entirely on the specific choice alternatives" (p. 1001). This statement suggests that if the investigators had obtained measures of the third, *unmentioned* alternative—that of leaving the laboratory without participating in either of the unpleasant experiments—they might have detected the convergence of alternatives that is expected when spontaneous regret becomes the dominant reaction.

7. In both experiments revealing evidence of postdecisional regret (Walster, 1964; Walster and Walster, 1970) the subject was left alone during the period following the decision while waiting for the postdecisional test. Leaving the person to contemplate his choice in isolation might make for maximal regret. The mere presence of others, because of the distraction or social support they provide, might inhibit this tendency to some extent.

Wicklund and Brehm (1976, pp., 108–123) review a number of laboratory studies dealing with the sequence of regret and dissonance reduction following commitment to relatively nonconsequential choices. They conclude that "most of the evidence shows that dissonance reduction increases as time after the decision elapses" (p. 123). The changes, however, do not occur at the same time intervals as were found in Walster's (1964) field experiment. For example, Crano and Messé (1970) observed dissonance reduction immediately following commitment (which consisted of writing a counterattitudinal essay) but found no dissonance reduction at fifteen to twenty minutes, the point at which Walster found the most dissonance reduction. Wicklund and Brehm point out that in many instances the dissonance effects observed in the laboratory studies are "extremely short-lived" (p. 123). The lack of consistency in the findings from the various studies on postdecisional ratings of the alternatives suggests that one should expect to find interaction effects rather than any main effects.

8. The premature deadline with which the draftees in Walster's study were confronted is not a condition likely to prevail in all situations where difficult choices are made and communicated to others. For example, in our dieting and antismoking clinics the clients know that the counselor has no power to punish them for postponing the deadline or for undoing their commitment. They realize that his professional role would preclude the counselor from saying anything

abusive, and that he would undoubtedly continue to be friendly and helpful if a client revealed that he or she did not feel ready to do the expected thing. Hence, the deadline posed during a counseling session, unlike that imposed in the job interviews in Walster's study, would not be perceived as precluding the option of finding out the essential facts before making a decision.

Perhaps some of the draftees in Walster's study, when asked to announce their choice to the psychologist, felt that they were only partly committing themselves. Included in this category would be both the most naive and the most sophisticated of the draftees. The very naive ones would believe that a soldier would have a good chance of getting his job assignment changed if he were to offer sensible arguments to the appropriate officer. The very sophisticated ones would know that in the military hierarchy it is very difficult to change arbitrary orders once issued, but they would nevertheless assume that there is always some way to get around regulations, to finagle a change if it is really important to do so. For different reasons, both types of men would hope to find a better solution later on than the seemingly least objectionable one. They would anticipate having time to search for it during subsequent days by obtaining information and advice from noncommissioned officers or other old timers, despite being required to express a preference to the psychologist. Consequently, for these men the conditions were conducive to vigilance. The essential point is that they would still be in the *predecisional* phase at the end of the session, since they would be thinking in terms of postponing their final decision until they could obtain more information so as to know which choice they really wanted to make. Shortly after making a *partial* commitment by telling the psychologist which of the two jobs they preferred, they would be inclined to deliberate about the drawbacks of the chosen alternative, and to consider that perhaps it was not so preferable as they had just thought, that maybe it would be worse than the other one. That *partial* commitment is likely to be followed by momentary regret and vacillation is shown in an experiment by Festinger and Walster (1964), in which the subjects, after being offered a gift in exchange for their services, were asked to give their preference rankings—tantamount to conveying a *tentative* decision—and then later on were asked to make their final choice.

In Walster's Army experiment, any draftees who assumed that they could later reverse their choice were in effect making tentative decisions. Any subsequent changes in preference could be interpreted as involving essentially the same type of *predecisional* vacillation as was observed in the Festinger and Walster experiment.

If individual cases in Walster's Army field study could have been followed in detail during the hours immediately after the premature deadline was imposed, we expect that several different types of shift in dominant coping patterns would have emerged. Several minutes after making their choice, all those in a state of hypervigilance would be expected to vacillate and would therefore show momentary reactions of regret, which was the dominant trend revealed in Walster's finding for the four-minute interval. (This same immediate reaction is also to be expected of anyone who believed the commitment to be nonbinding and who remained in a predecisional state of vigilance.) Thereafter, however, we would expect marked individual differences in the rate and amount of vacillation. For example, some of the men, rapidly recovering from the hypervigilant state, might after a short time arrive at and bolster a fairly stable judgment as to which alternative was least objectionable; many others might continue to be very worried and vacillate for hours, but at different rates. If so, the ratings obtained ninety minutes after the announced choice would be an averaged product of so many different individual sequences that they would not be meaningful.

9. The carryover effect we have alluded to in reinterpreting Walster's (1964) findings on regret in terms of hypervigilance can be subsumed under a general principle of *residual coping patterns*. Throughout the book we have postulated the essential continuity between pre- and postdecisional processes. Consistent with this postulate is our assumption that when a decisional conflict has not been resolved at the time of full commitment, residues of the predecisional coping pattern are likely to be observed in postdecisional attempts to resolve the conflict. Thus, defensive avoidance before the decision is likely to be followed by defensive avoidance modes of response after. The same essential continuity between the dominant pre- and postdecisional coping patterns should hold for all five patterns, provided that there are no new major inputs that drastically change the balance sheet.

Chapter 13. Challenging Outworn Decisions

1. The quotations from "The Overcoat" are from the translation by Constance Garnett in the collection edited by Leonard Kent (1964), pp. 570–73.

2. Although primarily designed to challenge excessively bolstered decisions, these same procedures might also prove useful in challenging more moderately bolstered decisions, whenever the person is ignoring negative feedback by relying on unrealistic cognitive defenses.

3. Follow-up interviews on smoking behavior showed that clients given the awareness-of-rationalizations treatment by one psychologist, who happened to be a white male, reported greater success in cutting down on cigarette smoking than did those given the control treatment. But no such difference was found in the results obtained with the second psychologist, who happened to be a black male. Since the two psychologists were at the same stage of training and were equally skilled as interviewers, these serendipitous results suggest a latent bias against the black psychologist among the all-white sample of clients in this study. But with only two experimenters in the study no definitive conclusion can be drawn as to whether skin color was the effective stimulus variable that gave rise to the observed discrepancy. The authors conclude from the lack of consistent significant differences in their follow-up data on reported changes in smoking behavior that the brief form of awareness-of-rationalizations treatment was not sufficiently powerful to be considered a "cure" for heavy smokers. The evidence clearly shows, however that the treatment reduces cognitive resistance to fear-arousing warnings. Perhaps a more intensive counseling session, focusing on each smoker's personal rationalizations, would have a stronger effect, and induce a substantial proportion of the clients who come to a smoker's clinic to stop smoking.

4. In the Janis, Kahn, and Higginson study, there were some weak indications that one of the emotional role-playing variations was somewhat more effective than the other two. Five weeks after the session, the net proportion of change in smoking behavior was found to be highest ($p < .05$) for the group given a role-playing scenario involving both (a) enactment of the decision to quit smoking and (b) final relief (doctor informing the patient that his precan-

cerous lung condition has cleared up). (One of the comparison groups had been given the same scenario without the final relief, and the other the same scenario without enactment of the decision to quit smoking.) But the subsequent finding that all three versions of emotional role playing were almost equally effective after nine months implies that in the long run, effectiveness does not depend in a crucial way either upon enactment of the decision or upon the presence or absence of emotional relief at the end of the psychodrama. Rather, the crucial component seems to be playing the role of a victim confronted with unambiguous information that is difficult to block out, distort, deny, or rationalize in a defensive avoidant manner.

5. In Toomey's (1972) study, one experimental group of alcoholic patients was given a role-playing treatment that focused on the negative consequences of drinking. In the first session, subjects were asked to list all the unfavorable consequences for themselves and their families of continuing to drink heavily and were then given the emotional role-playing procedure, which induced them to enact the experience of undergoing some of the worst consequences. In a second session, held the next day, the alcoholic patients heard and discussed tape recordings of their own role-playing performances, again focusing on the threatening consequences of continuing to drink heavily. This role-playing-with-discussion treatment was found to be effective when the patients were subsequently compared with a control group of equivalent patients given only the standard hospital treatment. It was also found to be just as effective as an elaborate package of treatments given to another experimental group of alcoholic patients, consisting of emotional role playing, an informative communication designed to induce emotional inoculation, and a balance sheet procedure involving exploration of the pros and cons of the alternative courses of action. One month after discharge from the hospital, the two experimental groups differed significantly from the control group with respect to amount of alcoholic consumption, but they did not differ from each other. This pattern of results suggests that the emotional role-playing procedure was the major component responsible for the effectiveness of the treatments given to the experimental groups.

Chapter 14. Improving the Quality of Decision Making

1. The four hypotheses require systematic investigation in a variety of field settings to see whether and to what extent they prescribe effective procedures for counteracting defective coping patterns. At present they are untested implications of the conflict-theory model.

2. Numerous social psychological experiments show that when people are induced to engage in the debate type of improvised role playing they think up and take seriously new arguments they had not considered before, sometimes to the point of persuading themselves that their initial position on the issue was wrong, which leads to marked changes in attitude (Elms, 1969; Girado and Strickland, 1974; Greenwald, 1969; Janis, 1968; McGuire, 1969). The type of role playing that requires improvisation of arguments must be distinguished from the nonimprovisational type investigated in many experiments on forced compliance, which require the subjects to express an assigned opinion to someone else but provide little or no opportunity for improvising new arguments. For example, in the best known of all forced compliance experiments, Festinger and Carlsmith (1959) hired each

subject, after completing a dull task, to tell a fellow student that he liked the task. This nonimprovisational type of role playing can also produce attitude change, but probably in a different way. An illusion of commitment may be created when the role player is led to believe that he must take personal responsibility for the new position he was induced to advocate and for its effects on other people, which can lead him to reduce cognitive dissonance between his initial position on the issue and the opposing position to which he has just committed himself (Collins and Hoyt, 1972; Cooper and Worchel, 1970; Janis, 1968).

The role-playing activity in outcome psychodrama requires a considerable amount of improvisation because it is intended to produce open-minded exploration of the consequences of alternative courses of action. For the same reason, the procedures are constructed in such a way as to avoid creating any sense of commitment at all. Therefore whatever attitude changes occur when a decision maker engages in improvised psychodramatic enactment of imagined outcomes of the decision are most likely caused by self-persuasion resulting from his taking account of important new considerations or arguments that he had not previously taken into account.

3. In the absence of any valid formula for integrating all the pluses and minuses in the decisional balance sheet into a single quantitative rating for each alternative, any procedure that increases the amount of information the decision maker has to process could have some undesirable side effects, which might make the decision maker worse off than he was before. For example, Hendrick, Mills, and Kiesler (1968) found that when there were six rather than two choice alternatives there was a significant tendency to make a rapid decision, with little scrutiny of the alternatives. An executive or a homeowner might become demoralized by the overwhelmingly large number of diverse consequences to be taken into account in making a hugely expensive purchase or investment and become more inclined than ever to put on blinders by resorting to a simplistic decision rule, perhaps reverting from a coping pattern of vigilance to one of defensive avoidance. Adding more information to the balance sheet also requires more time for search and deliberation, which can cause a fatal delay if the success of a crucial decision depends upon acting at a propitious moment. Part of the role of the decision counselor is to detect incipient symptoms of these unintended effects before they emerge full-blown, to discuss them with the client, and to try to counteract them so that the positive values of the exercises can be achieved.

4. Perhaps additional aids to decision making can be developed that enable decision makers to rate the importance of each consequence listed in the balance sheet grid, and the estimated probability of occurrence of each, in order to obtain quantitative scores for each alternative. In Mann's (1972) study of high school seniors who were deciding on the choice of a college, a simple quantitative rating procedure was introduced by asking the students to score each entry in the balance sheet on a 5-point scale according to its importance. More complex weighting methods, such as those used in subjective utility analysis, have also been tried out, mainly with hypothetical decisions (Edwards and Tversky, 1967). The validity for consequential decisions of these quantitative methods for combining entries so as to select the "best" choice will continue to remain open to question until data are available showing observable advantages over the nonquantitative approaches spontaneously used by most decision makers.

5. When opportunities for emotional inoculation are made available, personality factors may play an important role in determining who will choose to take advantage of those opportunities and who will not. A study by Lapidus (1968) of pregnant women indicates that when preparatory information about the stresses of childbirth is offered free of charge, passive-submissive women who are most in need of emotional inoculation are unlikely to obtain it if it is left up to them to take the initiative. In order to reach those persons who prefer not to learn anything about the unpleasant aspects of stressful experiences that are in store for them, it may be necessary to set up a preparation program as a standard part of admission procedures in clinics and hospitals. The clients should probably be screened in advance for their knowledge about the consequences of the treatment they have agreed to undergo as well as for their capacity to assimilate unpleasant information. The same considerations apply to any other large organization, such as an industrial plant, where an emotional inoculation program might be introduced to prevent overreactions to job stress and high turnover rates among new employees.

There are, however, serious limitations to mass media presentations of preparatory messages. Janis and Leventhal (1965) point out that one of the implications of experimental studies on the effectiveness of fear-arousing communications is that in order to attain a positive motivating effect, the preparatory communications given to certain types of personalities, such as those who are chronically anxious, have to be different from those given to other types of persons. Any large-scale program of emotional inoculation for patients receiving medical or surgical treatment would probably risk failure if it did not make use of nurses or paramedical personnel who were trained to function as professional counselors.

> Pamphlets, magazine articles, lectures, and films might be able to fulfill some limited role in preparing people to face the stresses of illness and hospitalization, but they have obvious disadvantages since they are essentially fixed, prepackaged messages. When there is direct verbal interchange with the recipient in a personal interview, a psychologically skilled communicator can make use of the opportunity to observe the effects his statements are having and can change his message accordingly. For example, he can temporarily curtail his intended description of the impending threat if he notes that the client is becoming exceptionally upset; he can "handtailor" his reassuring remarks to help alleviate specific sources of fear after hearing the client express his personal fantasies and expectations; and above all, he can take account of obvious misunderstandings and more subtle manifestations of resistance that prevent the client from absorbing the full significance of the message.
>
> Many of the same interpersonal skills and strategic judgments that are essential for successful work in individual and group psychotherapy are undoubtedly required for successful work in emotional inoculation [Janis and Leventhal, 1965].

6. For group decisions whose consequences are highly dependent upon the reactions and countermoves of other people, gaming procedures along the lines of outcome psychodrama, in which several decision makers on each team play out a game to learn something about the outcome of one alternative and then replay the game for a different alternative or a different way of implementing the policy, might be useful. The psychodramatic game might be enacted several times, first

assuming the *most likely* outcome, then assuming the *best possible* outcome for each of the dominant alternatives, and finally assuming the *worst possible* out- come. The first and second enactments might enable the decision makers to discover new entries for the balance sheet and to become aware of overoptimistic assumptions. A realistic enactment of the third scenario could be especially valu- able as emotional inoculation.

7. The quotations are from Janis (1972), pp. 209–18.

8. In principle, the success of a training program could be evaluated by observa- tions of subsequent changes in the quality of the participants' actual decision making (as assessed by ratings of the seven procedural criteria summarized in table 12, which would be compared with those obtained with an equivalent group of controls). Although it might be difficult to score reliably each of the seven criteria on an absolute basis, *changes* in the degree to which each criterion is met—e.g., *more* information search, *less* bias in assimilating relevant information, and *fewer* instances of mindguarding—may be fairly easy to score reliably, on the basis of systematic records. These ratings could be used as relative scores on the various criteria. In practice, however, it is often difficult to obtain full records showing how each participant makes real-life decisions after a training program is over. More feasible means of assessing the effectiveness of a training program may have to be devised. For example, sample decision-making exercises that could be scored in terms of the seven criteria might be developed, which could be given at the beginning and again at the end of the training period.

References

Abelson, R. P. Computer simulation of 'hot' cognition. In S. Tomkins and S. Messick (Eds.), *Computer simulation of personality*. New York: Wiley, 1963.

Abelson, R. P. A summary of hypotheses on modes of resolution. In R. P. Abelson et al. (Eds.), *Theories of cognitive consistency: A sourcebook*. Chicago: Rand McNally, 1968.

Abelson, R. P. Script processing in attitude formation and decision making. In J. S. Carroll and J. W. Payne (Eds.), *Cognition and social behavior*. New York: Lawrence Erlbaum Associates, 1976.

Abelson, R. P., E. Aronson, W. J. McGuire, T. M. Newcomb, M. J. Rosenberg, and P. H. Tannenbaum (Eds.). *Theories of cognitive consistency: A sourcebook*. Chicago: Rand McNally, 1968.

Abelson, R. P., and J. C. Miller. Negative persuasion via personal insult. *Journal of Experimental and Social Psychology*, 1967, 3, 221–333.

Adams, J. S. Reduction of cognitive dissonance by seeking consonant information. *Journal of Abnormal and Social Psychology*, 1961, 62, 74–78.

Allen, V. Uncertainty of outcome and post-decision dissonance reduction. In L. Festinger (Ed.), *Conflict, decision, and dissonance*. Stanford, Calif.: Stanford University Press, 1964.

Allison, G. T. *Essence of decision: Explaining the Cuban missile crisis*. Boston: Little, Brown, and Co., 1971.

Allison, G. T., and M. H. Halperin. Bureaucratic politics: A paradigm and some policy implications. *World Politics*, 1972, 24 (Supplement—entire issue).

Allport, G. W. The psychology of participation. *Psychological Review*, 1945, 53, 117–32.

Almond, G. A. *The appeals of Communism*. Princeton, N.J.: Princeton University Press, 1954.

Anderson, N. H. Integration theory and attitude change. *Psychological Review*, 1971, 78, 171–206.

Andrew, J. M. Recovery from surgery, with and without preparatory instructions, for three coping styles, *Journal of Personality and Social Psychology*, 1970, 15, 223–26.

Appley, M., and I. Trumbull (Eds.). *Psychological stress: Issues in research*. New York: Appleton-Century-Crofts, 1967.

Apsler, R. Effects of the draft lottery and a laboratory analogue on attitudes. *Journal of Personality and Social Psychology*, 1972, 24, 262–72.

Argyle, M. *Social interaction*. New York: Atherton Press, 1969.

Armstrong, J. S. Social irresponsibility in management. Mimeo working paper presented at the Third Annual Workshop in Marketing at Brussels, April, 1974.

Arnold, M. *Emotions and personality*. 2 vols. New York: Columbia University Press, 1960.

Arnold, M. Perennial problems in the field of emotion. In M. Arnold (Ed.), *The Loyola symposium: Feelings and emotion*. New York: Academic Press, 1970.

Aronson, E. Dissonance theory: Progress and problems. In R. P. Abelson et al. (Eds.), *Theories of cognitive consistency: A sourcebook*. Chicago: Rand Mc-Nally, 1968.

Aronson, E. The theory of cognitive dissonance: A current perspective. In L. Berkowitz (Ed.), *Advances in experimental and social psychology*. Vol. 4. New York: Academic Press, 1969.

Asch, S. E. Effects of group pressure on the modification and distortion of judgments. In H. Geutzkow (Ed.), *Groups, leadership and men*. Pittsburgh: Carnegie Institute of Technology Press, 1951.

Asch, S. E. Studies of independence and conformity: A minority of one against a unanimous majority. *Psychological Monographs*, 1956, 70.

Atkin, C. Instrumental utilities and information seeking. In P. Clarke (Ed.), *New models for mass communication research*. Beverly Hills, Calif.: Sage, 1973.

Atkinson, J. W. *An introduction to motivation*. Princeton, N.J.: Van Nostrand, 1964.

Atkinson, J. W., and D. Birch. *The dynamics of action*. New York: Wiley, 1970.

Baer, D. J. Smoking attitude, behavior, and beliefs of college males. *Journal of Social Psychology*, 1966, 68, 65–78.

Baker, G. W., and D. W. Chapman (Eds.). *Man and society in disaster*. New York: Basic Books, 1962.

Baker, R. *Woodrow Wilson: Life and letters*. 8 vols. New York: Doubleday Doran, 1927–39.

Bales, R. F. The equilibrium problem in small groups. In T. Parsons, R. F. Bales, and E. A. Shils (Eds.). *Working papers in the theory of action*. New York: Free Press, 1953.

Balloch, J., L. R. Braswell, J. R. Rayner, and L. M. Killian. Studies of military assistance in civilian disaster; England and the United States. Unpublished report, Committee on Disaster Studies, National Academy of Sciences–National Research Council, August 20, 1953.

Barber, J. D. *The presidential character: Predicting performance in the White House*. Englewood Cliffs, N.J.: Prentice-Hall, 1972.

Barton, A. H. *Social organization under stress: A sociological review of disaster studies.* Washington, D.C.: Committee on Disaster Studies, National Academy of Sciences–National Research Council, 1963.

Barton, A. H. *Communities in disaster: A social analysis of collective stress situations.* Garden City, N.Y.: Doubleday, Anchor Books, 1970.

Baudry, F., and A. Weiner. The pregnant patient in conflict about abortion: A challenge for the obstetrician. *American Journal of Obstetrics and Gynecology,* 1974, *119,* 705–11.

Behling, C. F. Effects of commitment and certainty upon exposure to supportive and nonsupportive information. *Journal of Personality and Social Psychology,* 1971, *19,* 152–59.

Beier, E. G. The effect of induced anxiety on flexibility of intellectual functioning. *Psychological Monographs,* 1951, *65,* No. 9.

Bem, D. J. Self-perception theory. In L. Berkowitz (Ed.), *Advances in experimental social psychology.* New York: Academic Press, 1972.

Bem, D., M. Wallach, and N. Kogan. Group decision making under risk of aversive consequences. *Journal of Personality and Social Psychology,* 1965, *1,* 453–60.

Bennis, W., E. Schein, D. Berlow, and F. Steele (Eds.). *Interpersonal dynamics.* Homewood, Ill.: Dorsey, 1968.

Berkowitz, L., and D. R. Cottingham. The interest value and relevance of fear-arousing communications. *Journal of Abnormal and Social Psychology,* 1960, *60,* 37–43.

Berkun, M. M., H. M. Bialek, R. P. Kern, and I. Yogi. Experimental studies of psychological stress in man. *Psychological Monographs,* 1962, *76,* 1–39.

Bernstein, D. A. Modification of smoking behavior: An evaluative review. *Psychological Bulletin,* 1969, *71,* 418–40.

Bernstorff, J. *My three years in America.* London: Skeffington and Son, 1920.

Bettelheim, B. Individual and mass behavior in extreme situations. *Journal of Abnormal and Social Psychology,* 1943, *38,* 417–52.

Bickman, L. The effect of another bystander's ability to help on bystander intervention in an emergency. *Journal of Experimental Social Psychology,* 1971, *7,* 367–79.

Bickman, L. Social influence and diffusion of responsibility in an emergency. *Journal of Experimental Social Psychology,* 1972, *8,* 438–45.

Blackwell, B. The literature of delay in seeking medical care for chronic illnesses. *Health Education Monograph,* 1963, No. 16, 3–31.

Blau, P. M. *Exchange and power in social life.* New York: Wiley, 1964.

Bloomfield, L. P., and C. J. Gearin. Games foreign policy experts play: The political exercise comes of age. *Orbis,* 1973, *16,* 1008–31.

Boswell, J. *London Journal, 1762–1763.* New York: McGraw-Hill, 1950.

Boulding, K. Review of *A strategy of decision. American Sociological Review,* 1964, *29,* 931.

Bower, J. L. The role of conflict in economic decision-making groups: Some empirical results. *Quarterly Journal of Economics,* 1965, *79,* 263–77.

Bracken, M. B., and S. V. Kasl. Delay in seeking induced abortion: A review and theoretical analysis. *American Journal of Obstetrics and Gynecology*, 1975, *121*, 1008–19.

Bramel, D. Dissonance, expectation, and the self. In R. P. Abelson et al. (Eds.), *Theories of cognitive consistency: A sourcebook*. Chicago: Rand McNally, 1968.

Braybrooke, D., and C. E. Lindblom. *A strategy of decision*. New York: Free Press, 1963.

Brean, H. *How to stop smoking*. New York: Vanguard, 1951 (1963).

Breen, D. *The birth of a first child: Towards an understanding of femininity*. London: Tavistock, 1975.

Brehm, J. W. Post decisional changes in the desirability of alternatives. *Journal of Abnormal and Social Psychology*, 1956, *52*, 384–89.

Brehm, J. W. *A theory of psychological reactance*. New York: Academic Press, 1966.

Brehm, J. W. Attitude change from threat to attitudinal freedom. In A. G. Greenwalk et al. (Eds.), *Psychological foundations of attitudes*. New York: Academic Press, 1968.

Brehm, J. W. *Responses to loss of freedom: A theory of psychological reactance*. Morristown, N.J.: General Learning Press, 1972.

Brehm, J. W., and A. R. Cohen. Re-evaluation of choice alternatives as a function of their number and qualitative similarity. *Journal of Abnormal and Social Psychology*, 1959, *58*, 373–78.

Brehm, J. W., and A. R. Cohen. *Explorations in cognitive dissonance*. New York: Wiley, 1962.

Brehm, J. W., and T. Hammock. Unpublished study. Cited in J. Brehm, *A theory of psychological reactance*. New York: Academic Press, 1966.

Brehm, J. W., D. Linder, C. Crane, and S. S. Brehm. The effect of predecision reactance on post-decisional dissonance reduction. Unpublished manuscript, 1969.

Brehm, J. W., D. McQuown, and J. Shaban. The desire to have an eliminated alternative as a function of total number of alternatives. In J. Brehm, *A theory of psychological reactance*. New York: Academic Press, 1966.

Brehm, J. W., and J. Sensenig. Social influence as a function of attempted usurpation of choice. *Journal of Personality and Social Psychology*, 1966, *4*, 703–7.

Brehm, J. W., L. K. Stires, J. Sensenig, and J. Shaban. The attractiveness of an eliminated choice alternative. *Journal of Experimental Social Psychology*, 1966, *2*, 301–13.

Breznitz, S. A study of worrying. *British Journal of Social and Clinical Psychology*, 1971, *10*, 217–79.

Brim, O. G., D. C. Glass, D. E. Lavin, and N. Goodman. *Personality and decision processes*. Stanford; Calif.: Stanford University Press, 1962.

Broadhurst, A. Applications of the psychology of decisions. In M. P. Feldman and A. Broadhurst (Eds.). *Theoretical and experimental bases of the behavior therapies*. London: Wiley, 1976.

Brock, T. C. Effects of prior dishonesty on post-decisional dissonance. *Journal of Abnormal and Social Psychology*, 1963, *66*, 325–31.

Brock, T. C., and J. L. Balloun. Behavioral receptivity to dissonant information. *Journal of Personality and Social Psychology*, 1967, *6*, 413–28.

Brock, T. C., and H. L. Fromkin. Cognitive tuning set and behavioral receptivity to discrepant information. *Journal of Personality*, 1968, *36*, 108–25.

Brock, T. C., M. Stuart, and L. Becker. Familiarity, utility and supportiveness as determinants of information receptivity. *Journal of Personality and Social Psychology*. 1970, *14*, 292–301.

Bross, I. D. *Design for decision*. New York: Macmillan, 1953.

Brown, R. *Social psychology*. New York: Free Press, 1965.

Brown, R. Further comment on the risky shift. *American Psychologist*, 1974, *29*, 468–70.

Brownlow, D. G. *The accused*. New York: Vantage, 1968.

Bruner, J. S., J. J. Goodnow, and G. A. Austin. A *study of thinking*. New York: Wiley, 1956.

Buss, A. Instrumentality of aggression feedback, and frustration as determinants of physical aggression. *Journal of Personality and Social Psychology*, 1966, *3*, 153–62.

Cameron, N. A. *Personality development and psychopathology*. Boston: Houghton Mifflin, 1963.

Campbell, D. T. Reforms as experiments. *American Psychologist*, 1969, *24*, 409–29.

Cannell, C. F., and R. L. Kahn. Interviewing. In G. Lindzey and E. Aronson (Eds.), *Handbook of social psychology*. Vol. 2. Reading, Mass.: Addison-Wesley, 1968.

Cannell, C. F., and J. MacDonald. The impact of health news on attitudes and behavior. *Journalism Quarterly*, 1956, *33*, 315–23.

Canon, L. K. Self-confidence and selective exposure to information. In L. Festinger (Ed.), *Conflict, decision and dissonance*. Stanford, Calif.: Stanford University Press, 1964.

Caplan, G. *An approach to community mental health*. London: Tavistock Publication, 1961.

Carlsmith, J. M., and J. L. Freedman. Bad decisions and dissonance: Nobody's perfect. In R. P. Abelson et al. (Eds.), *Theories of cognitive consistency: A sourcebook*. Chicago: Rand McNally, 1968.

Carlsmith, J. M., and A. E. Gross. Some effects of guilt on compliance. *Journal of Personality and Social Psychology*, 1969, *11*, 240–44

Carroll, J. S., and J. W. Payne (Eds.). *Cognition and social behavior*. Washington, D.C.: Lawrence Erlbaum Associates, 1976.

Cartwright, D. Risk taking by individuals and groups: An assessment of research employing choice dilemmas. *Journal of Personality and Social Psychology*, 1971, *20*, 361–78.

Cartwright, D., and A. Zander (Eds.). *Group dynamics: Research and theory* (3rd ed.). New York: Harper and Row, 1968.

Chinoy, E. *Automobile workers and the American dream*. Garden City, N.Y.: Doubleday, 1955.

Clarke, G. What went wrong: Time essay. *Time*, December 10, 1973, pp. 39–40.

Clarke, P., and J. James. The effects of situation, intensity and personality on information seeking. *Sociometry*, 1967, *30*, 235–45.

Clore, G. L., and K. L. McMillan. Role playing, attitude change, and attraction toward a disabled other. Unpublished paper, University of Illinois, 1970. Cited in J. S. Wiggins and others, *The psychology of personality*. Reading, Mass.: Addison-Wesley, 1971.

Cobb, B., R. Clark, M. Carson, and C. D. Howe. Patient-responsible delay of treatment in cancer. *Cancer*, 1954, *7*, 920–26.

Coch, L., and J. R. P. French, Jr. Overcoming resistance to change. *Human Relations*, 1948, *1*, 512–32.

Coelho, G. V., D. A. Hamburg, and J. E. Adams. *Coping and adaptation*. New York: Basic Books, 1974.

Cohen, M. D., J. G. March, and J. P. Olsen. A garbage can model of organizational choice. *Administrative Science Quarterly*, 1972, *17*, 1–25.

Collins, B. E., R. D. Ashmore, F. W. Hornbeck, and R. E. Whitney. Studies in forced compliance: XIII and XV. In search of a dissonance-producing forced compliance paradigm. *Representative Research in Social Psychology*, 1970, *1*, 11–23.

Collins, B. E., and M. F. Hoyt. Personal responsibility for consequences: An integration and extension of the "forced compliance" literature. *Journal of Experimental Social Psychology*, 1972, *8*, 558–93.

Collins, B. E., and B. H. Raven. Group structure: Attraction, coalitions, communication and power. In G. Lindzey and E. Aronson (Eds.), *Handbook of social psychology* (2nd ed.). Vol. 4. Reading, Mass.: Addison-Wesley, 1969.

Colten, M. E., and I. L. Janis. Effects of self disclosure and the decisional balance-sheet procedure in a weight reduction clinic. In I. Janis (Ed.), *Counseling on personal decisions Theory and field research on helping relationships*. New Haven, Conn.: Yale University Press, in press.

Committee on Disaster Studies (I. L. Janis, D. W. Chapman, J. P. Gillin, J. Spiegel). *The problem of panic*. Civil Defense Technical Bulletin T.B.-19-2. Washington, D.C.: U.S. Government Printing Office, 1955.

Conrad, J. *Lord Jim*. London: The Albatross Ltd., 1947.

Cooper, J. Personal responsibility and dissonance: The role of foreseen consequences. *Journal of Personality and Social Psychology*, 1971, *18*, 354–63.

Cooper, J., and S. Worchel. Role of undesired consequences in arousing cognitive dissonance. *Journal of Personality and Social Psychology*, 1970, *16*, 199–206.

Crano, W. D., and L. A. Messé. When does dissonance fail? The time dimension in attitude measurement. *Journal of Personality*, 1970, *38*, 493–508.

Crow, W. J., and I. L. Janis. Effectiveness of procedures for improving the quality of decision making by policy-planning groups (Preliminary research concept paper). La Jolla, Calif.: Western Behavioral Sciences Institute, 1975.

Crow, W. J., and R. C. Noel. *The valid use of simulation results*. La Jolla, Calif.: Western Behavioral Sciences Institute, 1965.

Cyert, R. M., W. R. Dill, and J. G. March. The role of expectations in business decision-making. *Administrative Science Quarterly*, 1958, *3*, 307–40.

Cyert, R. M., and J. G. March. A *behavioral theory of the firm*. Englewood Cliffs, N.J.: Prentice-Hall, 1963.

Cyert, R. M., H. A. Simon, and D. B. Trow. Observation of a business decision. *Journal of Business*, 1956, 29, 237–48.

Darley, J. M., and B. Latané. Bystander intervention in emergencies: Diffusion of responsibility. *Journal of Personality and Social Psychology*, 1968, 8, 377–83.

De Charms, R. *Personal causation*. New York: Academic Press, 1968.

DeLong, D. R. Individual differences in patterns of anxiety arousal, stress-relevant information and recovery from surgery. Unpublished doctoral dissertation, University of California, Los Angeles, 1971.

De Rivera, J. *The psychological dimension of foreign policy*. Columbus, Ohio: Merrill Publishing Co., 1968.

Deutsch, K. W. *The nerves of government*. New York: Free Press, 1963.

Deutsch, M., and H. B. Gerard. A study of normative and informational social influence upon individual judgment. *Journal of Abnormal and Social Psychology*, 1955, 51, 629–36.

Deutsch, M., R. M. Krauss, and N. Rosenau. Dissonance or defensiveness. *Journal of Personality*, 1962, 30, 16–28.

DeWolfe, A. S., and C. N. Governale. Fear and attitude change. *Journal of Abnormal and Social Psychology*, 1964, 69, 119–23.

Doar, J. M. "Summary of information" presented to House Judiciary Committee. Reported in *New York Times*, July 23, 1974, p. 24.

Dror, Y. Muddling through—science or inertia? In A. Etzioni (Ed.), *Readings on modern organization*. Englewood Cliffs, N.J.: Prentice-Hall, 1969.

Easterbrook, J. A. The effect of emotion on cue utilization and the organization of behavior. *Psychological Review*, 1959, 66, 183–201.

Edwards, W. Behavioral decision theory. *Annual Review of Psychology*, 1961, 12, 473–98.

Edwards, W., and A. Tversky, (Eds.). *Decision making: Selected readings*. Baltimore: Penguin Books, 1967.

Egbert, L., G. Battit, C. Welch, and M. Bartlett. Reduction of postoperative pain by encouragement and instruction of patients. *New England Journal of Medicine*, 1964, 270, 825–27.

Ellsberg, D. *Papers on the war*. New York: Simon and Schuster, 1972.

Elms, A. C. The influence of fantasy ability on attitude change through role-playing. *Journal of Personality and Social Psychology*, 1966, 4, 36–43.

Elms, A. C. (Ed.). *Role playing, reward, and attitude change*. New York: Van Nostrand-Reinhold, 1969.

Elms, A. C. *Social psychology and social relevance*. Boston: Little, Brown, 1972.

Elms, A. C. *Personality and politics*. New York: Harcourt Brace Jovanovich, 1976.

Engel, J. F., D. J. Kollat, and R. D. Blackwell. *Consumer behavior*. New York: Holt, Rinehart and Winston, 1968.

Epstein, S. The measurement of drive and conflict in humans: Theory and experiment. In M. R. Jones (Ed.), *Nebraska Symposium on Motivation*. Lincoln: University of Nebraska Press, 1962.

Epstein, S., and S. Clarke. Heart rate and skin conductance during experimentally induced anxiety: Effects of anticipated intensity of noxious stimulation and experience. *Journal of Experimental Psychology*, 1970, 84, 105–12.

Epstein, S., and N. P. Fenz. Steepness of approach and avoidance gradients in humans as a function of experience: Theory and experiment. *Journal of Experimental Psychology*, 1965, 70, 1–12.

Erikson, K. *Report on Buffalo Creek*. New York: Simon and Schuster, 1977.

Erlich, D., J. Guttman, P. Schonbach, and J. Mills. Postdecision exposure to relevant information. *Journal of Abnormal and Social Psychology*, 1957, 54, 98–102.

Estes, W. K. Of models and men. *American Psychologist*, 1957, 12, 609–17.

Estes, W. K. *Learning theory and mental development*. New York: Academic Press, 1970.

Etzioni, A. Mixed scanning: A third approach to decision making. *Public Administration Review*, 1967, 27, 385–92.

Etzioni, A. *The active society*. New York: Free Press, 1968.

Farber, M. *A theory of suicide*. New York: Funk and Wagnalls, 1968.

Feather, N. T. Cigarette smoking and lung cancer: A study of cognitive dissonance. *Australian Journal of Psychology*, 1962, 14, 55–64.

Feather, N. T. Cognitive dissonance, sensitivity, and evaluation. *Journal of Abnormal and Social Psychology*, 1963, 66, 157–63.

Feather, N. T. A structural balance approach to the analysis of communication effects. In L. Berkowitz (Ed.), *Advances in experimental social psychology*. Vol. 3. New York: Academic Press, 1967.

Feldman-Summers, S. Implications of the buck-passing phenomenon for reactance theory. Unpublished manuscript, University of Washington, 1975.

Fellner, C. H., and J. R. Marshall. Kidney donors. In J. Macauley and L. Berkowitz (Eds.), *Altruism and helping behavior*. New York: Academic Press, 1970.

Fenno, R. F. *The President's cabinet*. Cambridge, Mass.: Harvard University Press, 1959.

Fenno, R. F. *The power of the purse: Appropriations politics in Congress*. Boston: Little, Brown, 1966.

Ferrari, N. A. Institutionalization and attitude change in an aged population: A field study in dissonance theory. Unpublished doctoral dissertation, Case Western Reserve University, 1962.

Festinger, L. A theory of social comparison processes. *Human Relations*, 1954, 7, 117–40.

Festinger, L. *A theory of cognitive dissonance*. Evanston, Ill.: Row Peterson, 1957.

Festinger, L. (Ed.). *Conflict, decision and dissonance*. Stanford, Calif.: Stanford University Press, 1964.

Festinger, L., and J. M. Carlsmith. Cognitive consequences of forced compliance. *Journal of Abnormal and Social Psychology*, 1959, 58, 203–10.

Festinger, L., H. Riecken, and S. Schachter. *When prophecy fails*. Minneapolis: University of Minnesota Press, 1956.

Festinger, L., and E. Walster. Post-decision regret and decision reversal. In L. Festinger (Ed.). *Conflict, decision, and dissonance*. Stanford, Calif.: Stanford University Press, 1964.

Fischer, L. Worshippers from afar. In R. H. Grossman (Ed.), *The God that failed*. New York: Harper and Row, 1949.

Fishbein, M. Attitude and the prediction of behavior. In M. Fishbein (Ed.), *Readings in attitude theory and measurement*. New York: Wiley, 1967.

Fisher, R. *Basic negotiating strategy: International conflict for beginners*. London: Allen Lane, 1969.

Fishman, C. Need for approval and the expression of aggression under varying conditions of frustration. *Journal of Personality and Social Psychology*, 1965, 2, 809–16.

Fleischer, L. Conflict, dissonance, and the decision sequence. *Dissertation Abstracts International*, 1969, 30 (A-13), 1921. Ph.D. dissertation, 1968, University of California, Riverside.

Flugel, J. C. *Man, morals and society*. London: Whitefriars Press, 1945.

Foreman, P. Panic theory. In D. Schultz (Ed.), *Panic behavior*. New York: Random House, 1964.

Forman, R. E. Resignation as a collective behavior response. *American Journal of Sociology*, 1963, 69, 285–90.

Fox, A. *A sociology of work in industry*. London: Collier Macmillan, 1971.

Frank, J. *Persuasion and healing*. Baltimore: Johns Hopkins Press, 1961.

Frank, J. The role of hope in psychotherapy. *International Journal of Psychiatry*, 1968, 5, 383–95.

Frank, J. The bewildering world of psychotherapy. *Journal of Social Issues*, 1972, 28, 27–44.

Freedman, J. L. Personal communication. 1969.

Freedman, J. L., and S. C. Fraser. Compliance without pressure: The foot-in-the-door technique. *Journal of Personality and Social Psychology*, 1966, 4, 195–202.

Freedman, J. L., and D. O. Sears. Selective exposure. In L. Berkowitz, (Ed.), *Advances in experimental social psychology*. Vol. 2. New York: Academic Press, 1965 (a).

Freedman, J. L., and D. O. Sears. Warning, distraction, and resistance to influence. *Journal of Personality and Social Psychology*, 1965 (b), 1, 262–66.

Freedman, J. L., S. A. Wallington, and E. Bless. Compliance without pressure: The effect of guilt. *Journal of Personality and Social Psychology*, 1967, 7, 117–24.

Freud, A. *The ego and mechanisms of defense*. New York: International University Press, 1946 (written in 1936).

Freud, S. Fragment of an analysis of a case of hysteria. In *The Standard Edition* (Vol. 7). London: Hogarth Press, 1971 (written in 1901).

Friedman, C., R. Greenspan, and F. Mittelman. The decision making process and the outcome of therapeutic abortion. *American Journal of Psychiatry*, 1974, 131, 1332–37.

Fritz, C., and E. Marks. The NORC studies of human behavior in disaster. *Journal of Social Issues*, 1954, *10*, 26–41.

Fromm, E. *Fear of freedom*. New York: Holt, Rinehart, and Winston, 1941.

Garner, W. R. Information integration and form of encoding. In A. W. Melton and E. Martin (Eds.). *Coding processes in human memory*. Washington, D.C.: V. H. Winston, 1972.

Gelatt, H. Decision making: A conceptual frame of reference for counseling. *Journal of Counseling Psychology*, 1962, *9*, 240–45.

George, A. The Chinese Communist intervention in the Korean War. In A. George and R. Smoke, *Deterrence in American foreign policy: Theory and practice*. New York: Columbia University Press, 1974.

George, A. Adaptation to stress in political decision making: The individual, small group, and organizational contexts. In G. V. Coelho, D. A. Hamburg, and J. E. Adams (Eds.), *Coping and adaptation*. New York: Basic Books, 1974.

Gerard, H. B. Deviation, conformity, and commitment. In I. D. Steiner and M. Fishbein (Eds.), *Current studies in social psychology*. New York: Holt, Rinehart, and Winston, 1965.

Gerard, H. B. Choice difficulty, dissonance, and the decision sequence. *Journal of Personality*, 1967, *35*, 91–108.

Gerard, H. B. Basic features of commitment. In R. P. Abelson et al. (Eds.), *Theories of cognitive consistency: A sourcebook*. Chicago: Rand McNally, 1968.

Gerard, H. B., S. A. Blevans, and T. Malcolm. Self-evaluation and the evaluation of choice alternatives. *Journal of Personality*, 1964, *32*, 395–410.

Gergen, K. J. *The psychology of behavior exchange*. Reading, Mass.: Addison-Wesley, 1969.

Geyelin, P. *Lyndon B. Johnson and the world*. New York: Praeger, 1966.

Gilligan, C. Unpublished study, Harvard University, 1970.

Ginzberg, E., S. W. Ginsburg, S. Axelrad, and J. L. Herma. *Occupational choice*. New York: Columbia University Press, 1951.

Girodo, M., and L. H. Strickland. A conflict-theory interpretation of attitude change in forced compliance situations. *Canadian Journal of Behavioral Science*, 1974, *6*, 385–97.

Gogol, N. *The collected tales and plays of Nikolai Gogol*. Leonard J. Kent (Ed.) and Constance Garnett (Trans.). New York: Pantheon Books, 1964.

Gold, M. A. Causes of patients' delay in diseases of the breast. *Cancer*, 1964, *17*, 564–77.

Goldsen, R. K., P. T. Gerhardt, and V. H. Handy. Some factors related to patient delay in seeking diagnosis for cancer symptoms, *Cancer*, 1957, *10*, 1–7.

Gomersall, E. R., and M. S. Meyers. Breakthrough in on-the-job training. *Harvard Business Review*, 1966, *44*, 62–72.

Gottschalk, L., and G. C. Gleser. *The measurement of psychological states through content analysis*. Berkeley: University of California Press, 1969.

Grabitz-Gniech, G. Some restrictive conditions for the occurrence of psychological reactance. *Journal of Personality and Social Psychology*, 1971, *19*, 188–96.

Green, D., and E. Conolley. *Groupthink and Watergate*. Paper presented at the annual meeting of the American Psychological Association, 1974.

Greenstein, F. I. *Personality and politics*. Chicago: Markham, 1969.

Greenwald, A. G. The open-mindedness of the counterattitudinal role player. *Journal of Experimental Social Psychology*, 1969, 5, 375–88.

Greenwald, A. G. On the inconclusiveness of "crucial" tests of dissonance versus self-perception theories. *Journal of Experimental Social Psychology*, 1975, 11, 490–99.

Greenwald, A. G., T. C. Brock, and T. M. Ostrom (Eds.). *Psychological foundations of attitudes*. New York: Academic Press, 1968.

Grinker, R. R., and J. P. Speigel. *Men under stress*. Philadelphia: Blakiston, 1945.

Hackett, P. T., N. H. Cassem, and J. W. Raker. Patient delay in cancer. *New England Journal of Medicine*, 1973, 289, 14–20.

Hackman, J. R., J. A. Weiss, and K. Brousseau. *Effects of task performance strategies on group performance effectiveness*. Tech. Rep. No. 5, Dept. of Administrative Sciences, Yale University, 1974.

Hackman, J. R., and C. G. Morris. Group tasks, group interaction process, and group performance effectiveness: A review and proposed integration. In L. Berkowitz (Ed.), *Advances in experimental social psychology*. Vol. 8. New York: Academic Press, 1975.

Halperin, M. H. *Bureaucratic politics and foreign policy*. Washington, D.C.: Brookings Institution, 1974.

Hamburg, D. A., G. V. Coelho, and J. E. Adams. Coping and adaptation: Steps toward a synthesis of biological and social perspectives. In G. V. Coelho et al. (Eds.), *Coping and adaptation*. New York: Basic Books, 1974.

Hamburg, D., B. Hamburg, and S. de Groza. Adaptive problems and mechanisms in severely burned patients. *Psychiatry*, 1953, 16, 1–20.

Hamilton, D. Cognitive biases in the perception of social groups. In J. S. Carroll and J. W. Payne (Eds.), *Cognition and social behavior*. New York: Lawrence Erlbaum Associates, 1976.

Hamilton, V. Socialization, anxiety and information processing: A capacity model of anxiety-induced performance. In I. G. Sarason and C. D. Spielberger (Eds.), *Stress and anxiety*. Vol. 2. New York: Wiley, 1975.

Hammock, T., and J. W. Brehm. The attractiveness of choice alternatives when freedom to choose is eliminated by a social agent. *Journal of Personality*, 1966, 34, 546–55.

Hammond, E. C., and C. Percy. Ex-smokers. *New York State Journal of Medicine*, 1958, 58, 2956–59.

Hansell, N., M. Wodarczyk, and B. Handlon-Lathrop. Decision counseling method: Expanding coping at crisis-in-transit. *Archives of General Psychiatry*, 1970, 22, 462–67.

Hansen, F. *Consumer choice behavior*. New York: Free Press, 1972.

Hardyck, J. A., and M. Kardush. A modest modish model for dissonance reduction. In R. P. Abelson et al. (Eds.), *Theories of cognitive consistency: A sourcebook*. Chicago: Rand McNally, 1968.

Harris, B., and J. H. Harvey. Self attributed choices as a function of the consequence of a decision. *Journal of Personality and Social Psychology*, 1975, 31, 1013–19.

Hearings before the Joint Committee on the Investigation of the Pearl Harbor Attack, 79th Congress. (39 vols). Washington, D.C.: U.S. Government Printing Office, 1946.

Hebb, D. O. *The organization of behavior*. New York: Wiley, 1949.

Heilbroner, R. L. *An inquiry into the human prospect*. New York: Norton, 1974.

Heilman, M. E. Threats and promises: Reputational consequences and transfer of credibility. *Journal of Experimental Social Psychology*, 1974, 10, 310–24.

Heilman, M. E. Oppositional behavior as a function of influence attempt intensity and retaliation threat. *Journal of Personality and Social Psychology*, 1976, 33, 574–78.

Heilman, M. E., and K. A. Garner. Counteracting the boomerang: The effects of choice on compliance to threats and promises. *Journal of Personality and Social Psychology*, 1975, 31, 911–17.

Heilman, M. E., and B. Toffler. Reacting to reactance: An interpersonal interpretation of the need for freedom. *Journal of Experimental Social Psychology*, 1976, 12, 519–29.

Heller, J. F., M. Pallak, and J. M. Picek. The interactive effects of intent and threat on boomerang attitude change. *Journal of Personality and Social Psychology*, 1973, 26, 273–79.

Hendrick, C., J. Mills, and C. A. Kiesler. Decision time as a function of the number and complexity of equally attractive alternatives. *Journal of Personality and Social Psychology*, 1968, 8, 313–18.

Hermann, C. F. *Crises in foreign policy*. New York: Bobbs-Merrill, 1969.

Herodotus. *The histories*. Aubrey de Selincourt (Trans.). Baltimore: Penguin Books, 1954.

Hersch, S. *My Lai 4: A report on the massacre and its aftermath*. New York: Random House, 1970.

Hilton, T. L. *Cognitive processes in decision making*. Coop. research project number 1046. Carnegie Institute of Technology, 1962.

Himes, K. H., C. S. Keutzer, and E. Lichtenstein. Emotional role-playing and smoking: Some procedural refinements. Unpublished paper, University of Oregon (Cited in Mausner and Platt, 1971, pp. 162 and 185).

Hirschman, A. O., and C. E. Lindblom. Economic development, research and development, policy making: Some converging views. *Behavioral Sciences*, 1962, 7, 211–22.

Hoffman, L. R. Conditions for creative problem solving. *Journal of Psychology*, 1961, 52, 429–44.

Hoffman, L. R. Group problem solving. In L. Berkowitz (Ed.), *Advances in experimental social psychology*. Vol. 2. New York: Academic Press, 1965.

Holsti, O. R. Time, alternatives, and communications: The 1914 and Cuban missile crises. In C. F. Hermann (Ed.), *International crisis: Insights from behavioral research*. New York: Free Press, 1972.

Homans, G. C. *Social behavior: Its elementary forms*. New York: Harcourt, Brace, and World, 1961.

Hoopes, T. *The limits of intervention: An inside account of how the Johnson policy of escalation in Vietnam was reversed.* New York: McKay, 1971.

Horner, M. Fail: Bright women. *Psychology Today*, 1969, 3, 36–38.

Horowitz, M. J. *Stress response syndromes.* New York: Jason Aronson, 1976.

Hovland, C. I., H. Campbell, and T. Brock. The effects of 'commitment' on opinion change following communication. In C. I. Hovland (Ed.), *The order of presentation in persuasion.* New Haven, Conn.: Yale University Press, 1957.

Hovland, C. I., I. L. Janis, and H. H. Kelley. *Communication and persuasion.* New Haven: Yale University Press, 1953.

Hoyt, M. F., and I. L. Janis. Increasing adherence to a stressful decision via a motivational balance-sheet procedure: A field experiment. *Journal of Personality and Social Psychology*, 1975, 31, 833–39.

Huston, T. (Ed.). *Foundations of interpersonal attraction.* New York: Academic Press, 1974.

Huxley, A. *Brave new world.* London: Chatto and Windus, 1964.

Inkeles, A. Personal communication. November, 1975.

Insko, C. A., A. Arkoff, and V. M. Insko. Effects of high and low fear arousing communications upon opinions toward smoking. *Journal of Experimental Social Psychology*, 1965, 1, 256–66.

Insko, C. A., and J. Schopler. *Experimental social psychology.* New York: Academic Press, 1972.

Janis, I. L. *Air war and emotional stress: Psychological studies of bombing and civilian defense.* New York: McGraw-Hill, 1951.

Janis, I. L. *Psychological Stress: Psychoanalytic and behavioral studies of surgical patients.* New York: Wiley, 1958.

Janis, I. L. Motivational factors in the resolution of decisional conflicts. In M. R. Jones (Ed.), *Nebraska symposium on motivation.* Vol. 7. Lincoln: University of Nebraska Press, 1959 (a).

Janis, I. L. Decisional conflicts: A theoretical analysis. *Journal of Conflict Resolution*, 1959 (b), 3, 6–27.

Janis, I. L. A pilot study of postdecisional conflict among young attorneys. Mimeo. research report. Yale Studies in Communication and Attitudes, 1960.

Janis, I. L. Psychological effects of warnings. In G. W. Baker and D. W. Chapman (Eds.), *Man and society in disaster.* New York: Basic Books, 1962.

Janis, I. L. Effects of fear arousal on attitude change: Recent developments in theory and experimental research. In L. Berkowitz (Ed.), *Advances in experimental social psychology.* Vol. 3. New York: Academic Press, 1967.

Janis, I. L. Attitude change via role playing. In R. P. Abelson et al. (Eds.), *Theories of cognitive consistency: A sourcebook.* Chicago: Rand McNally, 1968 (a).

Janis, I. L. Group identification under conditions of external danger. In D. Cartwright and A. Zander (Eds.), *Group dynamics: Research and theory.* New York: Harper and Row, 1968 (b).

Janis, I. L. Stages in the decision-making process. In R. P. Abelson et al. (Eds.), *Theories of cognitive consistency: A sourcebook.* Chicago: Rand McNally, 1968 (c).

Janis, I. L. Pilot studies on new procedures for improving the quality of decision making. Mimeo. research report. Yale Studies in Attitudes and Decisions, 1968 (d).

Janis, I. L. *Stress and frustration*. New York: Harcourt Brace Jovanovich, 1971.

Janis, I. L. *Victims of groupthink*. Boston: Houghton Mifflin, 1972.

Janis, I. L. Diaries and interview notes on major personal decisions, 1971–74. Unpublished manuscript, 1974 (a).

Janis, I. L. Vigilance and decision-making in personal crises. In D. A. Hamburg and C. V. Coelho (Eds.), *Coping and adaptation*. New York: Academic Press, 1974 (b).

Janis, I. L. Effectiveness of social support for stressful decisions. In M. Deutsch and H. Hornstein (Eds.), *Applying social psychology: Implications for research, practice, and training*. Hillsdale, N.J.: Lawrence Erlbaum Associates, 1975.

Janis, I. L. (Ed.). *Counseling on personal decisions: Theory and field research on helping relationships*. New Haven: Yale University Press (in press).

Janis, I. L., and W. J. Crow. Improving the quality of decisions in planning groups. Unpublished grant application submitted to Department of Health, Education, and Welfare. 1975.

Janis, I. L., and S. Feshbach. Effects of fear-arousing communications. *Journal of Abnormal and Social Psychology*, 1953, 48, 78–92.

Janis, I. L., and P. B. Field. Sex differences and personality factors related to persuasibility. In C. I. Hovland and I. L. Janis (Eds.), *Personality and persuasibility*. New Haven, Conn.: Yale University Press, 1959.

Janis, I. L., M. Kahn, and W. Higginson. Changes in smoking behavior induced by emotional role-playing: Effects of variations in enactment of the decision to quit smoking and of being cured of a precancerous lung condition. Mimeo. research report. Yale Studies in Attitudes and Decisions, 1967.

Janis, I. L., and H. Leventhal. Psychological aspects of physical illness and hospital care. In B. Wolman (Ed.), *Handbook of clinical psychology*. New York: McGraw-Hill, 1965.

Janis, I. L., and H. Leventhal. Human reactions to stress. In E. Borgatta and W. Lambert (Eds.), *Handbook of personality theory and research*. Chicago: Rand McNally, 1968.

Janis, I. L., A. A. Lumsdaine, and A. I. Gladstone. Effects of preparatory communication on reactions to a subsequent news event. *Public Opinion Quarterly*, 1951, 15, 488–518.

Janis, I. L., G. Mahl, J. Kagan, and R. Holt. *Personality: Dynamics, development, and assessment*. New York: Harcourt, Brace, and World, 1969.

Janis, I. L., and L. Mann. Effectiveness of emotional role-playing in modifying smoking habits and attitudes. *Journal of Experimental Research in Personality*, 1965, 1, 84–90.

Janis, I. L., and L. Mann. A conflict-theory approach to attitude change and decision making. In A. Greenwald, T. Brock, and T. Ostrom (Eds.), *Psychological foundations of attitudes*. New York: Academic Press, 1968.

Janis, I. L., and C. N. Rausch. Selective interest in communications that could arouse decisional conflict: A field study of participants in the draft-resistance movement. *Journal of Personality and Social Psychology*, 1970, *14*, 46–54.

Janis, I. L., and R. Terwilliger. An experimental study of psychological resistance to fear-arousing communications. *Journal of Abnormal and Social Psychology*, 1962, *65*, 403–10.

Jecker, J. D. The cognitive effects of conflict and dissonance. In L. Festinger (Ed.), *Conflict, decision and dissonance*. Stanford, Calif.: Stanford University Press, 1964 (a).

Jecker, J. D. Selective exposure to new information. In L. Festinger (Ed.), *Conflict, decision and dissonance*. Stanford, Calif.: Stanford University Press, 1964 (b).

Jervis, R. *Perception and misperception in international relations*. Princeton, N.J.: Princeton University Press, 1975.

Johnson, J. E. The influence of purposeful nurse-patient interaction on the patient's postoperative course. *A.N.A. Monograph Series #2. Exploring Medical-Surgical Nursing Practice*. New York: American Nurses' Association, 1966.

Johnson, J. E., and H. Leventhal. Effects of accurate expectations and behavioral instructions on reactions during a noxious medical examination. *Journal of Personality and Social Psychology*, 1974, *29*, 710–18.

Johnson, R. J. Conflict avoidance though acceptable decisions. *Human Relations*, 1974, *27*, 71–82.

Jones, C. O. *Clean air: The policies and politics of polution control*. Pittsburgh: University of Pittsburgh Press, 1975.

Jones, E. E. *Ingratiation: A social psychological analysis*. New York: Appleton-Century-Crofts, 1964.

Jones, E. E., and K. E. Davis. From acts to dispositions: The attribution process in person perception. In L. Berkowitz (Ed.), *Advances in experimental social psychology*. Vol. 2. New York: Academic Press, 1965.

Jones, E. E., and H. B. Gerard. *Foundations of social psychology*. New York: Wiley, 1967.

Jones, E. E., and C. A. Johnson. Delay of consequences and the riskiness of decisions. *Journal of Personality*, 1973, *42*, 613–37.

Jones, E. E., and R. E. Nisbett. The actor and the observer: Divergent perceptions of the causes of behavior. In E. E. Jones et al., *Attribution: Perceiving the causes of behavior*. Morristown, N.J.: General Learning Press, 1971.

Jones, R. A., D. E. Linder, C. A. Kiesler, M. Zana, and J. W. Brehm. Internal states or external stimuli: Observers' attitude judgments and the dissonance-theory–self-persuasion controversy. *Journal of Experimental Social Psychology*, 1968, *4*, 247–69.

Joyner, R., and K. Tunstall. Computer augmented organization problem solving. *Management Science*, 1970, *17*, B-212–B-225.

Kagan, J. Reflection-impulsivity and reading ability in primary grade children. *Child Development*, 1965, *36*, 609–28.

Kaplan, M. F., and S. Schwartz (Eds.). *Human judgment and decision processes*. New York: Academic Press, 1975.

Kasl, S. V., and S. Cobb. Health behavior, illness behavior, and sick role behavior. *Archives of Environmental Health*, 1966, *12*, 246–66 and 531–41.

Katona, G. Rational behavior and economic behavior. *Psychological Review*, 1953, *60*, 307–18.

Katz, D., and R. L. Kahn. *The social psychology of organizations*. New York: Wiley, 1966.

Katz, D., I. Sarnoff, and C. G. McClintock. Ego-defense and attitude change. *Human Relations*, 1956, *9*, 27–46.

Kelley, H. H., J. C. Condry, Jr., A. E. Dahlke, and A. H. Hill. Collective behavior in a simulated panic situation. *Journal of Experimental Social Psychology*, 1965, *1*, 20–54.

Kelley, H. H., and J. W. Thibaut. Experimental studies of group problem solving and process. In G. Lindzey (Ed.), *Handbook of social psychology*. Vol. 2. Cambridge, Mass.: Addison-Wesley, 1954.

Kelman, H. C. The induction of action and attitude change. In S. Coopersmith (Ed.), *Personality research*. Copenhagen: Munksgaard, 1961.

Kelman, H. C., and R. M. Baron. Determinants of modes of resolving inconsistency dilemmas: A functional analysis. In R. P. Abelson et al. (Eds.), *Theories of cognitive consistency: A sourcebook*. Chicago: Rand McNally, 1968.

Keutzer, C. S. Behavior modification of smoking: The experimental investigation of diverse techniques. *Behavior Research and Therapy*, 1969, *7*, 275–82.

Kiesler, C. A. Conflict and the number of choice alternatives. *Psychological Reports*, 1966, *18*, 603–10.

Kiesler, C. A. (Ed.). *The psychology of commitment*. New York: Academic Press, 1971.

Kiesler, C., F. Mathog, P. Pool, and R. Howenstine. Commitment and the boomerang effect: A field study. In C. Kiesler (Ed.), *The psychology of commitment*. New York: Academic Press, 1971.

Kiesler, C. A., T. S. Roth, and M. S. Pallak. Avoidance and reinterpretation of commitment and its implications. *Journal of Personality and Social Psychology*, 1974, *30*, 705–15.

Kilham, W. J. Level of destructive obedience as a function of transmittor and executant role in the Milgram situation. Unpublished honors thesis, University of Sydney, 1971.

Killian, L. The significance of multiple-group membership in disaster. *American Journal of Sociology*, 1952, *57*, 309–14.

Kirscht, J. P., and A. L. Knutson. Science and flouridation: An attitude study. *Journal of Social Issues*, 1961, *17*, 37–44.

Klapper, J. T. *The effects of the mass media*. New York: Columbia University Bureau of Applied Social Research, 1949.

Kleinhesselink, R. R., and R. E. Edwards. Seeking and avoiding belief discrepant information as a function of its perceived refutability. *Journal of Personality and Social Psychology*, 1975, *31*, 787–90.

Knox, R. E., and J. A. Inkster. Post-decision dissonance at post time. *Journal of Personality and Social Psychology*, 1968, *8*, 319–23.

Kogan, N., and M. Wallach. Risk taking as a function of the situation, the person, and the group. In G. Mandler et al., *New directions in psychology*. Vol. 3. New York: Holt, Rinehart, and Winston, 1967.

Korner, I. N. Hope as a method of coping. *Journal of Consulting and Clinical Psychology*, 1970, 34, 134–39.

Krisher, H. P., S. A. Darley, and J. M. Darley. Fear provoking recommendations, intentions to take preventive actions, and actual preventive action. *Journal of Personality and Social Psychology*, 1973, 26, 301–8.

Krumboltz, J. Behavior goals for counseling. *Journal of Counseling Psychology*, 1966, 13, 153–59.

Kuhn, T. S. *The structure of scientific revolutions*. Chicago: University of Chicago Press, 1962.

Kutner, B., H. B. Makover, and A. Oppenheim. Delay in the diagnosis and treatment of cancer: A critical analysis of the literature. *Journal of Chronic Diseases*, 1958, 7, 95–120.

Lamm, H. Will an observer advise high risk taking after hearing a discussion of the decision problem? *Journal of Personality and Social Psychology*, 1967, 6, 467–71.

Landis, G. Teaching personal decision making in high school: A proposed curriculum. Unpublished senior project essay, Yale University (prepared under supervision of I. L. Janis), 1973.

Lang, K., and G. E. Lang. *Collective dynamics*. New York: Crowell, 1961.

Langer, E. J. The illusion of control. *Journal of Personality and Social Psychology*, 1975, 32, 311–28.

Langer, E. J., I. L. Janis, and J. A. Wolfer. Reduction of psychological stress in surgical patients. *Journal of Experimental Social Psychology*, 1975, 11, 155–65.

Langer, E. J., and J. Rodin. The effects of choice and enhanced personal responsibility for the aged: A field experiment in an institutional setting. *Journal of Personality and Social Psychology*, 1976, 34, 191–98.

Lansing, R. *War memoirs of Robert Lansing: Secretary of State*. Westport, Conn.: Greenwood Press, 1970 (reprint of 1935 edition).

Lapidus, L. B. Cognitive control and reaction to stress: Conditions for mastery in the anticipatory phase. *Proceedings, 77th annual convention*, APA (American Psychiatric Association), 1969.

Latane, B., and J. M. Darley. Social determinants of bystander intervention in emergencies. In J. Macauley and L. Berkowitz (Eds.), *Altruism and helping behavior*. New York: Academic Press, 1970.

Lawler, E. E., W. J. Kuleck, J. S. Rhode, and S. E. Sorensen. Job choice and post decision dissonance. *Organizational Behavior and Human Performance*, 1975, 13, 133–45.

Lazarus, R. S. *Psychological stress and the coping process*. New York: McGraw-Hill, 1966.

Lazarus, R. S., and E. Alfert. The short circuiting of threat by experimentally altering cognitive appraisal. *Journal of Abnormal and Social Psychology*, 1964, 69, 195–205.

Lee, W. *Decision theory and human behavior*. New York: Wiley, 1971.

Leites, N. A *study of Bolshevism*. New York: Free Press, 1953.

Lester, E., and G. W. Brockopp. *Crisis intervention and counseling by telephone.* Springfield, Ill.: C. C. Thomas, 1973.

Leventhal, H. Experimental studies of anti-smoking communication. In E. Borgotta and R. Evans (Eds.), *Smoking and health behavior.* Chicago: Aldine, 1968.

Leventhal, H. Changing attitudes and habits to reduce chronic risk factors. *American Journal of Cardiology,* 1973, *31,* 571–80.

Leventhal, H. The consequences of depersonalization during illness and treatment: An information-processing model. In J. Howard and A. Strauss (Eds.), *Humanizing health care.* New York: Wiley, 1975.

Leventhal, H., and P. Niles. A field experiment on fear arousal with data on the validity of questionnaire measures. *Journal of Personality,* 1964, *32,* 459–79.

Leventhal, H., R. P. Singer, and S. Jones. Effects of fear and specificity of recommendation upon attitudes and behavior. *Journal of Personality and Social Psychology,* 1965, *2,* 20–29.

Leventhal, H., and J. C. Watts. Sources of resistance to fear-arousing communications on smoking and lung cancer. *Journal of Personality,* 1966, *34,* 155–75.

Levy, J. M., and R. K. McGee. Childbirth as crisis: A test of Janis' theory of communication and stress resolution. *Journal of Personality and Social Psychology,* 1975, *31,* 171–79.

Lewin, K. *Dynamic theory of personality.* New York: McGraw-Hill, 1935.

Lewin, K. *The conceptual representation and the measurement of psychological forces.* Durham, N.C.: Duke University Press, 1938.

Lewin, K. Action research and minority problems. *Journal of Social Issues,* 1946, *2,* 34–46.

Lewin, K. Group decision and social change. In T. Newcomb and E. Hartley (Eds.), *Readings in social psychology.* New York: Holt, 1947.

Lewin, K. *Resolving social conflicts: Selected papers on group dynamics.* Gertrude W. Lewin (Ed.). New York: Harper, 1948.

Lewin, K. (Collected writings). In D. Cartwright (Ed.), *Field theory in social science: Selected theoretical papers.* New York: Harper, 1951.

Lidz, T. *The person: His and her development throughout the life cycle.* New York: Basic Books, 1976.

Liem, G. R. Performance and satisfaction as affected by personal control over salient decisions. *Journal of Personality and Social Psychology,* 1975, *31,* 232–40.

Lifton, R. J. *Thought reform and the psychology of totalism: A study of "brainwashing" in China.* New York: W. W. Norton, 1961.

Lifton, R. J. Existential evil. In N. Sanford and C. Comstock (Eds.), *Sanctions for evil.* San Francisco: Jossey-Bass, 1971.

Lindblom, C. E. The science of muddling through. *Public Administration Review,* 1959, *19,* 79–99.

Lindblom, C. E. *The intelligence of democracy.* New York: Free Press, 1965.

Linder, D. E., J. Cooper, and E. E. Jones. Decision freedom as a determinant of the role of incentive magnitude in attitude change. *Journal of Personality and Social Psychology,* 1967, *6,* 245–54.

Linder, D. E., and K. A. Crane. Reactance theory analysis of predecisional cognitive processes. *Journal of Personality and Social Psychology*, 1970, *15*, 258–64.

Linder, D. E., C. B. Wortman, and J. W. Brehm. Temporal changes in predecision preferences among choice alternatives. *Journal of Personality and Social Psychology*, 1971, *19*, 282–84.

Lindsay, P., and D. Norman. *Human information processing*. New York: Academic Press, 1972.

Litman, R. E. Suicide prevention: Evaluating effectiveness. *Life Threatening Behavior*, 1971, *1*, 155–62.

Lowe, R. H., and I. D. Steiner. Some effects of the reversibility and consequences of decisions on postdecision information preferences. *Journal of Personality and Social Psychology*, 1968, *8*, 172–79.

Lowell, R. Letter to President, 1965. Cited in *Time Magazine*, June 11, 1965.

Lowin, A. Approach and avoidance: Alternative modes of selective exposure to information. *Journal of Personality and Social Psychology*, 1967, *6*, 1–9.

Luborsky, L., T. C. Todd, and A. H. Katcher. A self-administered social assets scale for predicting physical and psychological illness and health. *Journal of Psychosomatic Research*, 1973, *17*, 109–20.

Luce, R. D., and H. Raiffa. *Games and decisions: Introduction and cricial survey*. New York: Wiley, 1957.

Lynd, H. *On shame and the search for identity*. New York: Harcourt, Brace and World, 1958.

MacCrimmon, K. R. An overview of multiple objective decision making. In J. L. Cochrane and M. Zeleny (Eds.), *Multiple criteria decision making*. Columbia: University of South Carolina Press, 1973.

Macedonia, R. M. Expectations-press and survival. Unpublished doctoral dissertation, New York University, 1969.

Maier, N. R. F. *Problem solving discussions and conferences: Leadership methods and skills*. New York: McGraw-Hill, 1963.

Maier, N. R. F. Group problem solving. *Psychological Review*, 1967, *74*, 239–49.

Maier, N. R. F. *Problem-solving and creativity in individuals and groups*. Belmont, Calif.: Brooks/Cole, 1970.

Mann, L. The effects of emotional role playing on smoking attitudes and behavior. *Journal of Experimental Social Psychology*, 1967, *3*, 334–48.

Mann, L. Effects of a commitment warning on children's decision behavior. *Journal of Personality and Social Psychology*, 1971, *17*, 74–80.

Mann, L. Use of a 'balance-sheet' procedure to improve the quality of personal decision making: A field experiment with college applicants. *Journal of Vocational Behavior*, 1972, *2*, 291–300.

Mann, L. Differences between reflective and impulsive children in tempo and quality of decision making. *Child Development*, 1973, *44*, 274–79.

Mann, L., and R. P. Abeles. Evaluation of presidential candidates as a function of time and stage of voting decision. *Journal of Psychology*, 1970, *74*, 167–73.

Mann, L., and T. Dashiell. Reactions to the draft lottery: A test of conflict theory. *Human Relations*, 1975, *28*, 155–73.

Mann, L., and I. L. Janis. A follow-up study on the long-term effects of emotional role playing. *Journal of Personality and Social Psychology*, 1968, *8*, 339–42.

Mann, L., I. L. Janis, and R. Chaplin. The effects of anticipation of forthcoming information on predecisional processes. *Journal of Personality and Social Psychology*, 1969, *11*, 10–16.

Mann, L., and V. Taylor. The effects of commitment and choice difficulty on predecision processes. *Journal of Social Psychology*, 1970, *82*, 221–30.

March, J. G. Power of power. In D. Easton (Ed.), *Varieties of political theory*. Englewood Cliffs, N.J.: Prentice-Hall, 1966.

Matza, D. *Delinquency and drift*. New York: Wiley, 1964.

Mausner, B. Report on a smoking clinic. *American Psychologist*, 1966, *21*, 251–55.

Mausner, B., and E. S. Platt. *Smoking: A behavioral analysis*. New York: Pergamon Press, 1971.

May, E. R. *Lessons of the past*. New York: Oxford University Press, 1973.

May, R. *Love and Will*. New York: W. W. Norton, 1969.

McCarthy, M. My confession. In *On the contrary*. New York: Farrar, Straus, and Cudahy, 1961.

McFall, R. M., and L. Hammen. Motivation, structure and self-monitoring: Role of nonspecific factors in smoking reduction. *Journal of Consulting and Clinical Psychology*, 1971, *37*, 80–86.

McGee, R. K. *Crisis intervention in the community*. Baltimore: University Park Press, 1974.

McGuire, W. J. Cognitive consistency and attitude change. *Journal of Abnormal and Social Psychology*, 1960, *60*, 345–53.

McGuire, W. J. The current status of cognitive consistency theories. In S. Feldman (Ed.), *Cognitive consistency: Motivational antecedents and behavioral consequents*. New York: Academic Press, 1966.

McGuire, W. J. Selective exposure: A summing up. In R. P. Abelson et al. (Eds.), *Theories of cognitive consistency: A sourcebook*. Chicago: Rand McNally, 1968.

McGuire, W. J. The nature of attitudes and attitude change. In G. Lindzey and E. Aronson (Eds.), *The handbook of social psychology*. Vol. 3. Reading, Mass.: Addison-Wesley, 1969.

McGuire, W. J. The yin and yang of progress in social psychology. *Journal of Personality and Social Psychology*, 1973, *26*, 446–56.

McMillen, D. L. Transgression, self-image, and compliant behavior. *Journal of Personality and Social Psychology*, 1971, *20*, 176–79.

Meehl, P. E. *Clinical versus statistical prediction*. Minneapolis: University of Minnesota Press, 1954.

Meichenbaum, D. A self-instructional approach to stress management: A proposal for stress inoculation training. In C. D. Spielberger and I. G. Sarason (Eds.), *Stress and anxiety*. Vol. 1. New York: Wiley, 1975.

Meichenbaum, D., D. Turk, and S. Burstein. The nature of coping with stress. In I. G. Sarason and C. D. Spielberger (Eds.), *Stress and anxiety*. Vol. 2. New York: Wiley, 1975.

Merton, R. K. The unanticipated consequences of purposive social action. *American Sociological Review*, 1936, *1*, 894–904.

Merton, R. K. Insiders and outsiders: An essay in the sociology of knowledge. In R. K. Merton et al., *Varieties of political expression in sociology*. Chicago: University of Chicago Press, 1972.

Merton, R. K., G. G. Reader, and P. L. Kendall (Eds.). *The student-physician: Introductory studies in the sociology of medical education*. Cambridge, Mass.: Harvard University Press, 1957.

Milgram, S. Behavioral study of obedience. *Journal of Abnormal and Social Psychology*, 1963, *67*, 371–78.

Milgram, S. Some conditions of obedience and disobedience to authority. *Human Relations*, 1965, *18*, 57–76.

Milgram, S. *Obedience to authority*. New York: Harper and Row, 1974.

Miller, D. W., and M. K. Starr. *The structure of human decisions*. Englewood Cliffs, N.J.: Prentice-Hall, 1967.

Miller, G. A. The magical number seven, plus or minus two. *Psychological Review*, 1956, *63*, 81–97.

Miller, J. C., and N. Treiger. Personal and situational determinants of presurgical stress. Unpublished manuscript (submitted for publication), 1976.

Miller, N. E. Experimental studies of conflict. In J. McV. Hunt (Ed.), *Personality and the behavioral disorders*. Vol. 1. New York: Ronald Press, 1944.

Mills, J. The effect of certainty on exposure to information prior to commitment. *Journal of Experimental Social Psychology*, 1965, *1*, 348–55.

Mills, J. Interest in supporting and discrepant information. In R. P. Abelson et al. (Eds.), *Theories of cognitive consistency: A sourcebook*. Chicago: Rand McNally, 1968.

Mills, J., E. Aronson, and H. Robinson. Selectivity in exposure to information. *Journal of Abnormal and Social Psychology*, 1959, *59*, 250–53.

Mills, J., and J. M. Jellison. Avoidance of discrepant information prior to commitment. *Journal of Personality and Social Psychology*, 1968, *8*, 59–62.

Mills, J., and E. O'Neal. Anticipated choice, attention, and the halo effect. *Psychonomic Science*, 1971, *22*, 231–33.

Mischel, W. Theory and research on the antecedents of self-imposed delay of reward. In B. A. Maher (Ed.), *Progress in experimental personality research*. Vol. 3. New York: Academic Press, 1966.

Monat, A., J. R. Averill, and R. S. Lazarus. Anticipatory stress and coping reactions under various conditions of uncertainty. *Journal of Personality and Social Psychology*, 1972, *24*, 237–53.

Moran, P. A. An experimental study of pediatric admission. Unpublished master's thesis, Yale University School of Nursing, 1963.

Morison, S. E. The rising sun in the Pacific: 1931–April, 1942. *History of United States naval operations in World War II*. Vol. 3. Boston: Little, Brown, 1950.

Myers, D. G., and H. Lamm. The polarizing effect of group discussion. *American Scientist*, 1975, *63*, 297–303.

Nader, R., P. J. Petkas, and K. Blackwell. *Whistle blowing*. New York: Grossman Publishers, 1972.

Neisser, U. The imitation of man by machine. *Science*, 1963, *139*, 193–97.

Neisser, U. *Cognitive psychology*. New York: Appleton-Century-Crofts, 1967.

Nel, E., R. Helmreich, and E. Aronson. Opinion change in the advocate as a function of the persuasibility of his audience: A clarification of the meaning of dissonance. *Journal of Personality and Social Psychology*, 1969, *12*, 117–24.

New York Times June 15, 1973, pp. 18–19. Excerpts from testimony given before Senate Select Committee on Watergate.

New York Times July 17, 1973, p. 29. Excerpts from testimony given before Senate Select Committee on Watergate.

Nisbett, R. E., and S. Valins. Perceiving the causes of one's own behavior. In E. E. Jones et al. *Attribution: Perceiving the causes of behavior*. Morristown, N.J.: General Learning Press, 1971.

Nixon, R. M. *Six Crises*. Garden City, N.Y.: Doubleday, 1962.

Nowlis, G., and I. L. Janis. Factors influencing the effectiveness of emotional role playing in modifying attitudes and actions. Yale Studies in Attitudes and Decisions, 1966.

O'Neal, E. Influence of future choice importance and arousal upon the halo effect. In H. London and R. E. Nisbett (Eds.), *Thought and feeling: Cognitive alteration of feeling states*. Chicago: Aldine, 1971.

O'Neal, E., and J. Mills. The influence of anticipated choice on the halo effect. *Journal of Experimental Social Psychology*, 1969, *5*, 347–51.

Orne, M. T. On the social psychology of the psychological experiment: With particular references to demand characteristics and their implications. *American Psychologist*, 1962, *17*, 776–83.

Osgood, C. S., G. J. Suci, and P. H. Tannenbaum. *The measurement of meaning*. Urbana: University of Illinois Press, 1957.

Osler, S. F. Intellectual performance as a function of two types of psychological stress. *Journal of Experimental Psychology*, 1954, *47*, 115–21.

Paige, G. D. *The Korean decision*. New York: Free Press, 1968.

Pallak, M. S., and W. Cummings. Commitment and voluntary energy conservation. Paper presented at the annual meeting of the American Psychological Association. Chicago, 1975.

Pallak, M. S., and J. F. Heller. Interactive effects of commitment to future interaction and threat to attitudinal freedom. *Journal of Personality and Social Psychology*, 1971, *17*, 325–31.

Palo Alto Times. Story about Peggy Talman. August 11, 1969.

Pastore, N. The role of arbitrariness in the frustration–aggression hypothesis. *Journal of Abnormal and Social Psychology*, 1952, *47*, 728–31.

Pennington, D. F., Jr., F. Haravey, and B. M. Bass. Some effects of decision and discussion on coalescence, change, and effectiveness. *Journal of Applied Psychology*, 1958, *42*, 404–8.

Pervin, L., and R. Yatko. Cigarette smoking and alternative methods of reducing dissonance. *Journal of Personality and Social Psychology*, 1965, *2*, 30–36.

Peter, J. J., and R. Hull. *The Peter principle*. New York: W. Morrow, 1969.

Peters, C., and T. Branch. *Blowing the whistle*. New York: Praeger, 1972.

Phillips, L. *Human adaptation and its failures*. New York: Academic Press, 1968.

Piliavin, I. M., J. A. Piliavin, and J. Rodin. Costs, diffusion, and the stigmatized victim. *Journal of Personality and Social Psychology*, 1975, *32*, 429–38.

Piliavin, I. M., J. Rodin, and J. A. Piliavin. Good Samaritanism: An underground phenomenon? *Journal of Personality and Social Psychology*, 1969, *12*, 289–99.

Platt, E. S., E. Krassen, and B. Mausner. Individual variation in behavioral change following role playing. *Psychological Reports*, 1969, *24*, 155–70.

Political and Economic Planning. *Family needs and the social services*. London: G. Allen and Unwin, 1961.

Pollack, I. Action selection and the Yntema-Torgerson 'Worth' function. Paper read at the 1962 meetings of the Eastern Psychological Association, April 27, 1962.

Popper, K. R. *The open society and its enemies*. Vol. 1. Princeton, N.J.: Princeton University Press, 1963.

Porter, L. W., and E. E. Lawler. *Managerial attitudes and performance*. Homewood, Ill.: Irwin-Dorsey, 1968.

Powell, J. W. A poison liquor episode in Atlanta, Georgia. In *Conference on field studies on reactions to disasters*. Chicago: National Opinion Research Center, 1953.

Pressman, J., and A. Wildavsky. *Implementation*. Berkeley: University of California Press, 1973.

Pruitt, D. G. Conclusion: Toward an understanding of choice shifts in group discussion. *Journal of Personality and Social Psychology*, 1971, *20*, 495–510.

Psychology Today training films series. *Groupthink*. 1974 (20-minute film).

Quarantelli, E. L. The nature and conditions of panic. *American Journal of Sociology*, 1954, *60*, 267–75.

Quarantelli, E. L., and R. R. Dynes. When disaster strikes. *Psychology Today*, 1972, *5*, 66–70.

Radloff, R., and R. Helmreich. *Groups under stress: Psychological research in Sealab II*. New York: Appleton-Century-Crofts, 1968.

Raven, B. The Nixon group. *Journal of Social Issues*, 1974, *30*, 297–320.

Reed, H. D., and I. L. Janis. Effects of a new type of psychological treatment on smokers' resistance to warnings about health hazards. *Journal of Consulting and Clinical Psychology*, 1974, *42*, 748.

Reedy, G. E. *The twilight of the presidency*. New York: World, 1970.

Rogers, R. W., and D. L. Thistlethwaite. Effects of fear arousal and reassurance on attitude change. *Journal of Personality and Social Psychology*, 1969, *11*, 301–8.

Rokeach, M. Long-range experimental modification of values, attitudes and behavior. *American Psychologist*, 1971, *26*, 453–59.

Rokeach, M. *The nature of human values*. New York: Free Press, 1973.

Rosenbaum, M. E., and D. E. Franc. Opinion change as a function of external commitment and amount of discrepancy from the opinion of another. *Journal of Abnormal and Social Psychology*, 1960, *61*, 15–20.

Rosenberg, M. When dissonance fails: On eliminating evaluation apprehension from attitude measurement. *Journal of Personality and Social Psychology*, 1965, *1*, 28–42.

Rubin, Z. *Liking and loving*. New York: Holt, Rinehart, and Winston, 1973.

Russell, B. *The autobiography of Bertrand Russell, 1914–1944*. Boston: Little Brown, 1967.

Sarason, I. G. Anxiety and self preoccupation. In I. G. Sarason and C. D. Spielberger (Eds.), *Stress and anxiety*. Vol. 2. New York: Wiley, 1975.

Sartre, J. P. *"No Exit"–a play in one act—and "The Flies"—a play in three acts*. (English versions by Stuart Gilbert.) New York: Knopf, 1954.

Schachter, S. *The psychology of affiliation*. Stanford, Calif.: Stanford University Press, 1959.

Schein, E. H. The Chinese indoctrination program for prisoners of war. *Psychiatry*, 1956, *19*, 149–72.

Schein, E. H. *Process consultation*. Reading, Mass.: Addison-Wesley, 1969.

Schelling, T. C. *The strategy of conflict*. Cambridge, Mass.: Harvard University Press, 1960.

Schlesinger, A. M. Jr. *A thousand days: John F. Kennedy in the White House*. Boston: Houghton Mifflin, 1965.

Schmidt, R. L. An exploratory study of nursing and patient readiness for surgery. Unpublished master's thesis, Yale University School of Nursing, 1966.

Schmitt, F. E. and P. J. Woolridge. Psychological preparation of surgical patients. *Nursing Research*, 1973, *22*, 108–16.

Shneidman, E. S. You and death. *Psychology Today*, 1971, *5*, 43–45 and 74–80.

Schwartz, J. L., and M. Dubitzky. One-year follow-up results of a smoking cessation program. *Canadian Journal of Public Health*, 1968, *59*, 161–65.

Schwartz, S. Elicitation of moral obligation and self-sacrificing behavior: An experimental study of volunteering to be a bone marrow donor. *Journal of Personality and Social Psychology*, 1970(a), *15*, 283–93.

Schwartz, S. Moral decision making and behavior. In J. Macauley and L. Berkowitz (Eds.), *Altruism and helping behavior*. New York: Academic Press, 1970(b).

Sears, D. O. The paradox of de facto selective exposure without preference for supportive information. In R. P. Abelson et al. (Eds.), *Theories of cognitive consistency: A sourcebook*. Chicago: Rand McNally, 1968.

Sears, D. O., and R. P. Abeles. Attitudes and opinions. *Annual Review of Psychology*, 1969, *20*, 253–88.

Sears, D. O., and J. L. Freedman. Effects of expected familiarity of arguments upon opinion change and selective exposure. *Journal of Personality and Social Psychology*, 1965, *2*, 420–25.

Sears, D. O., and J. L. Freedman. Selective exposure to information: A critical review. *Public Opinion Quarterly*, 1967, *31*, 194–213.

Seligman, D. A special kind of rebellion—what they believe: A Fortune survey. *Fortune*, January, 1969, *79*, 66.

Seligman, M. P. Giving up on life. *Psychology Today*, 1974, *7*, 80–85.

Seligman, M. P. *Helplessness*. San Francisco: Freeman, 1975.

Senate Select Committee on Presidential Campaign Activities. *The Watergate hearings: Break-in and cover-up*. Edited by staff of the *New York Times*. New York: Viking Press, 1973.

Senate Select Committee on Presidential Campaign Activities. *The Senate Watergate Report*. New York: Dell, 1974.

Seymour, C. (Ed.). *The intimate papers of Colonel House*. 4 vols. Boston: Houghton Mifflin, 1926–28.

Shepard, R. N. On subjectively optimum selections among multi-attribute alternatives. In M. W. Shelley and G. L. Bryan (Eds.), *Human judgments and optimality*. New York: Wiley, 1964.

Shepard, R. N., C. I. Hovland, and H. M. Jenkins. Learning and memorization of classifications. *Psychological Monographs*, 1961, 75 (13, Whole No. 517).

Sherif, M., and C. Hovland. *Social judgment: Assimilation and contrast effects in communication and attitude change*. New Haven, Conn.: Yale University Press, 1961.

Shure, G. H., M. S. Rogers, I. M. Larsen, and J. Tassone. Group planning and task effectiveness. *Sociometry*, 1962, 25, 263–82.

Simmons, R. G., S. D. Klein, and K. Thornton. The family member's decision to be a kidney transplant donor. *Journal of Comparative Family Studies*, 1973, 4, 88–115.

Simon, H. A. *Models of man: Social and rational*. New York: Wiley, 1957.

Simon, H. A. *Administrative behavior: A study of decision-making processes in administrative organization*. 2nd ed., New York: Macmillan, 1957; 3rd Ed., New York: Free Press, 1976.

Simon, H. A. Political research: The decision making framework. Paper delivered at the annual meeting of the American Political Science Association, New York, September 1963.

Simon, H. A. Motivational and emotional controls of cognition. *Psychological Review*, 1967, 74, 29–39.

Simon, H. A., and W. Chase. Skill in chess. *American Scientist*, 1973, 61, 394–403.

Singer, D. G., and B. Kornfield. Conserving and consuming: A developmental study of abstract and action choices. *Developmental Psychology*, 1973, 8, 314.

Skinner, B. F. *Beyond freedom and dignity*. London: J. Cape, 1972.

Slovic, P. Limitations of the mind of man: Implications for decision making in the nuclear age. *Oregon Research Institute Bulletin*, 1971, 11, 41–49.

Slovic, P., B. Fischloff, and S. Lichtenstein. Cognitive processes and societal risk taking. In J. S. Carroll and J. W. Payne (Eds.), *Cognition and social behavior*. New York: Lawrence Erlbaum Associates, 1976.

Smith, M. B. Criticism of a social science: Review of *The context of social psychology*, J. Israel and H. Tajfel (Eds.). *Science*, 1973, 180, 610–12.

Smith, M. B. *Humanizing social psychology*. San Francisco: Jossey-Bass, 1974.

Snyder, M., and M. R. Cunningham. To comply or not comply: Testing the self-perception explanation of the "foot-in-the-door" phenomenon. *Journal of Personality and Social Psychology*, 1975, 31, 64–67.

Sofer, C. *Men in mid-career*. Cambridge: Cambridge University Press, 1970.

Sofer, C. *Social control in organizations with special reference to appraisal schemes*. Cambridge University, Department of Engineering Management studies Tr. 2., 1971.

Solzhenitsyn, A. I. *The Gulag archipelago, 1918–1956*. New York: Harper and Row, 1974.

Sorenson, T. C. *Kennedy*. New York: Bantam edition, 1966. Reprinted by permission of Harper and Row, Publishers.

Spielberger, C. D., and I. G. Sarason (Eds.). *Stress and anxiety*. Vols. 1 and 2. New York: Wiley, 1975.

Stagner, R. Corporate decision making: An empirical study. *Journal of Applied Psychology*, 1969, *53*, 1–13.

Statmen, J., and A. Hershkowitz. The role of value-orientation in the resolution of a moral dilemma. Paper presented at Eastern Psychological Association, 1969.

Staub, E., and D. Kellett. Increasing pain tolerance by information about aversive stimuli. *Journal of Personality and Social Psychology*, 1972, *21*, 198–208.

Steele, R. *The spectator*. No. 409, 1712.

Steinbruner, J. D. *The cybernetic theory of decision*. Princeton, N.J.: Princeton University Press, 1974.

Steiner, I. D. Perceived freedom. In L. Berkowitz (Ed.), *Advances in experimental social psychology*. New York: Academic Press, 1970.

Stephenson, W. *The play theory of mass communication*. Chicago: University of Chicago Press, 1967.

Stoner, J. A. F. A comparison of individual and group decisions involving risk. Unpublished master's thesis, Massachusetts Institute of Technology, School of Industrial Management, 1961.

Stotland, E. *The psychology of hope*. San Francisco: Jossey-Bass, 1969.

Streltzer, N. E., and G. V. Koch. Influence of emotional role playing on smoking habits and attitudes. *Psychological Reports*, 1968, *22*, 817–20.

Swigar, M. E., D. M. Quinlan, and S. Wexler. Abortion applicants: Characteristics distinguishing dropouts remaining pregnant and those having abortion. *American Journal of Public Health*, in press.

Taylor, D. W. Toward an information processing theory of motivation. In M. R. Jones (Ed.), *Nebraska Symposium on Motivation: 1960*. Lincoln: University of Nebraska Press, 1960.

Taylor, D. W. Decision making and problem solving. In J. March (Ed.), *Handbook of organizations*. Chicago: Rand McNally, 1965.

Taylor, S. E. On inferring one's attitudes from one's behavior: Some delimiting conditions. *Journal of Personality and Social Psychology*, 1975, *31*, 1126–33.

Terkel, S. *Working*. New York: Pantheon, 1972.

Thibaut, J. W., and H. H. Kelley. *The social psychology of groups*. New York: Wiley, 1959.

Thomson, J. G., Jr. How could Vietnam happen? An autopsy. *The Atlantic Monthly*, April, 1968, *221*, 47–53.

Toomey, M. Conflict theory approach to decision making applied to alcoholics. *Journal of Personality and Social Psychology*, 1972, *24*, 199–206.

Townsend, R. *Up the organization: How to stop the corporation from stifling people and strangling profits*. New York: Knopf, 1970.

Triandis, H. *Attitude and attitude change*. New York: Wiley, 1971.

Tuchman, B. *The Zimmerman telegram*. New York: Viking Press, 1958.

Tversky, A. Elimination by aspects: A theory of choice. *Psychological Review*, 1972, 79, 281–99.

Tversky, A., and D. Kahneman. Judgment under uncertainty. *Science*, 1974, 185, 1124–30.

United States National Advisory Commission on Civil Disorders. *Report*. New York: Bantam Books, 1968.

United States Surgeon General. *Smoking and health: Report of the Advisory Committee to the Surgeon General of the Public Health Service*. Washington, D.C.: United States Government Printing Office, 1964.

Useem, M. *Conscription, protest, and social conflict: The life and death of a draft resistance movement*. New York: Wiley, 1973.

Varela, J. A. *Psychological solutions to social problems*. New York: Academic Press, 1971.

Vernon, D. T. A., and D. A. Bigelow. Effect of information about a potentially stressful situation on responses to stress impact. *Journal of Personality and Social Psychology*, 1974, 29, 50–59.

Vroom, V. H. *Work and motivation*. New York: Wiley, 1964.

Vroom, V. H. Organizational choice: A study of pre- and post-decision processes. *Organizational Behavior and Human Performance*, 1966, 1, 212–25.

Vroom, V. H. Industrial social psychology. In G. Lindzey and E. Aronson (Eds.), *Handbook of social psychology*. Vol. 5. Reading, Mass.: Addison-Wesley, 1969.

Vroom, V. H., and E. L. Deci. The stability of post-decision dissonance: A follow-up study of the job attitudes of business-school graduates. *Organizational Behavior and Human Performance*, 1971, 6, 36–49.

Vroom, V. H., and P. W. Yetton. *Leadership and decision making*. Pittsburgh: University of Pittsburgh Press, 1973.

Wagner, S. *Cigarette country: Tobacco in American history and politics*. New York: Praeger, 1971.

Waller, W. W. *The family: A dynamic interpretation*. New York: Cordon Co., 1938.

Walster, E. The temporal sequence of post-decision processes. In L. Festinger (Ed.), *Conflict, decision, and dissonance*. Stanford, Calif.: Stanford University Press, 1964.

Walster, E., and G. W. Walster. Choice between negative alternatives: Dissonance reduction or regret? *Psychological Reports*, 1970, 26, 995–1005.

Walster, E., G. W. Walster, E. Piliavin, and L. Schmidt. Playing hard to get: Understanding an elusive phenomenon. *Journal of Personality and Social Psychology*, 1973, 26, 113–21.

Wanous, J. P. Effects of a realistic job preview on job acceptance, job attitudes, and job survival. *Journal of Applied Psychology*, 1973, 58, 327–32.

Washington Post. Senate hearings (on Watergate). June 17, 1973, pp. C2–C3.

Weick, K. E. When prophecy pales: The fate of dissonance theory. *Psychological Reports*, 1965, *16*, 1261–75.

Weick, K. E. Systematic observational methods. In G. Lindzey and E. Aronson, (Eds.), *Handbook of social psychology*. Vol. 2. Reading, Mass.: Addison-Wesley, 1968.

Weiner, J., and J. W. Brehm. Buying behavior as a function of verbal and monetary inducements. In J. W. Brehm, *A theory of psychological reactance*. New York: Academic Press, 1966.

Weiner, S. S. Personal communication about how the professionals in the San Francisco school system arrived at their desegregation plan. April 22, 1974.

Weiner, S. S. Participation, deadlines and choice. In J. A. March and J. P. Olsen (Eds.), *Ambiguity and choice in organizations*. Bergen, Norway: Bergen University Press, 1975.

Weinstein, E., and R. Kahn. *Denial of illness*. Springfield, Ill.: Thomas, 1955.

Weisbond, E., and T. Franck. *Resignation in protest*. New York: Grossman, 1975.

Weitz, J. Job expectancy and survival. *Journal of Applied Psychology*, 1956, *40*, 245–47.

Wheeler, D. A practicum in thinking. *Improving Thinking*, 1975, *1*, 9–10.

White, R. W. Motivation reconsidered: The concept of competence. *Psychological Review*, 1959, *66*, 297–333.

Wicklund, R. A. Prechoice preference reversal as a result of threat to decision freedom. *Journal of Personality and Social Psychology*, 1970, *14*, 8–17.

Wicklund, R. A. *Freedom and reactance*. Potomac, Md.: Lawrence Erlbaum Associates, 1974.

Wicklund, R. A., and J. W. Brehm. *Perspectives on cognitive dissonance*. Hillsdale, N.J.: Erlbaum Associates, 1976.

Wilensky, H. L. *Organizational intelligence*. New York: Basic Books, 1967.

Wilhelmy, R. A. The role of commitment in cognitive reversibility. *Journal of Personality and Social Psychology*, 1974, *30*, 695–98.

Wills, G. *Nixon Agonistes*. New York: Signet Books, 1971.

Wilson, A. *The bomb and the computer*. New York: Dell, 1968.

Wiskoff, M. Ethical standards and divided loyalties. *The American Psychologist*, 1960, *15*, 656–60.

Withey, S. Reaction to uncertain threat. In G. W. Barker and D. Chapman (Eds.), *Man and society in disaster*. New York: Basic Books, 1962.

Wohlstetter, R. *Pearl Harbor: Warning and decision*. Stanford, Calif.: Stanford University Press, 1962.

Wolfer, J. A., and M. A. Visintainer. Pediatric surgical patients' and parents' stress responses and adjustment as a function of psychologic preparation and stress-point nursing care. *Nursing Research*, 1975, *24*, 244–55.

Worchel, S. The effect of simple frustration, violated expectancy, and reactance on the instigation to aggression. Unpublished doctoral dissertation, Duke University, 1971.

Worchel, S., and J. W. Brehm. Direct and implied social restoration of freedom. *Journal of Personality and Social Psychology*, 1971, *18*, 294–304.

Xenophon. *Memorabilia*. London: Heinemann, 1923. (Written in the 4th century B.C.)

Yando, R., and J. Kagan. The effect of teacher tempo on the child. *Child Development*, 1968, 39, 27–34.

Young, S. *Management: A systems analysis*. Glenview, Ill.: Scott, Foresman, 1966.

Youngberg, C. F. An experimental study of job satisfaction and turnover in relation to job expectations and self-expectations. Unpublished doctoral dissertation, New York University, 1963.

Zajonc, R. Attitudinal effects of mere exposure. *Journal of Personality and Social Psychology*, 1968, 8, 1–29.

Zimbardo, P. G. The human choice: Individuation, reason and order versus deindividuation, impulse and chaos. In W. J. Arnold and D. Levine (Eds.), *Nebraska Symposium on Motivation*. Lincoln: University of Nebraska Press, 1969.

Errata

The following references were inadvertently omitted from the alphabetical order of the preceding list:

Davidson, L. R., and S. B. Kiesler. Cognitive behavior before and after decisions. In L. Festinger (Ed.), *Conflict, decision, and dissonance*. Stanford, Calif.: Stanford University Press, 1964.

Katz, E. On reopening the question of selectivity in exposure to mass communications. In R. P. Abelson et al. (Eds.), *Theories of cognitive consistency: A sourcebook*. Chicago: Rand McNally, 1968.

Miller, N. As time goes by. In R. P. Abelson et al. (Eds.), *Theories of cognitive consistency: A sourcebook*. Chicago: Rand McNally, 1968.

Name Index

Subject Index

IRVING L. JANIS, Professor of Psychology at Yale University, has long been a leading contributor to research on psychological stress and attitude change. More recently he has turned to research on decision making, including social psychological studies of foreign-policy decisions and fiascoes reported in *Victims of Groupthink* (1972), as well as studies of personal decisions. Dr. Janis's work on conflict theory was facilitated by a year as a Fellow at the Center for Advanced Study in the Behavioral Sciences (1973–1974) with the concurrent award of a Guggenheim Foundation Fellowship. Earlier, Dr. Janis was awarded the Hofheimer Prize by the American Psychiatric Association for his studies of surgical patients reported in *Psychological Stress* and the Socio-Psychological Prize by the American Association for the Advancement of Science for a paper on fear arousal and attitude change. In 1974 he was elected a Fellow of the American Academy of Arts and Sciences. He is on the editorial board of the *Journal of Conflict Resolution* and *American Scientist*. His current research on decision making is supported by a research grant from the National Science Foundation.

LEON MANN is Professor of Psychology in the School of Social Sciences, Flinders University of South Australia. An Australian, he attended the University of Melbourne, receiving his B.A. (1961) and M.A. (1962) in the field of social psychology. His doctoral work at Yale was carried out as a member of the Communication and Attitude Change project. After receiving his Ph.D. (1965) he returned to Australia to teach at his alma mater. During 1968–1970 he taught in the Department of Social Relations at Harvard University and during 1971–1972 at the University of Sydney. He took up his present position at Flinders University in 1972. Dr. Mann, who is a Fellow of the Australian Academy of the Social Sciences, has held visiting professorships at Stanford University and the Hebrew University of Jerusalem. His research interests include studies of crowd behavior, social influence, and decision making. He is the author of *Social Psychology* (1969) and *Collective Behavior* (forthcoming).